Pro ASP.NET 2.0 Website Programming

Damon Armstrong

Apress®

Pro ASP.NET 2.0 Website Programming

ISBN (pbk): 1-59059-546-7

Printed and bound in the United States of America 9 8 7 6 5 4 3 2 1

Lead Editor: Tony Davis
Technical Reviewer: Damien Foggon
Editorial Board: Steve Anglin, Dan Appleman, Ewan Buckingham, Gary Cornell, Tony Davis, Jason Gilmore, Jonathan Hassell, Chris Mills, Dominic Shakeshaft, Jim Sumser
Project Manager: Denise Santoro Lincoln
Copy Edit Manager: Nicole LeClerc
Copy Editor: Julie McNamee
Assistant Production Director: Kari Brooks-Copony
Production Editor: Kelly Winquist
Composition, proofreading, and indexing: Argosy Publishing
Artist: Kinetic Publishing Services, LLC
Cover Designer: Kurt Krames
Manufacturing Director: Tom Debolski

Distributed to the book trade worldwide by Springer-Verlag New York, Inc., 233 Spring Street, 6th Floor, New York, NY 10013. Phone 1-800-SPRINGER, fax 201-348-4505, e-mail `orders-ny@springer-sbm.com`, or visit `http://www.springeronline.com`.

For information on translations, please contact Apress directly at 2560 Ninth Street, Suite 219, Berkeley, CA 94710. Phone 510-549-5930, fax 510-549-5939, e-mail `info@apress.com`, or visit `http://www.apress.com`.

The source code for this book is available to readers at `http://www.apress.com` in the Source Code section. You will need to answer questions pertaining to this book to successfully download the code.

for Teresa

Contents at a Glance

Contents

Foreword

As I write this foreword, we are days away from Visual Studio 2005 becoming official. The software has been "complete" for several months now and the last weeks of the project involve scouring the code to ensure no rogue bug appears. As the multiple development teams move their code from their team branches into escrow, the level of anticipation is reaching a crescendo within the developer community. And rightfully so because for many developers, ASP.NET 2.0 will revolutionize the way they build software by simplifying many of the common tasks, in much the same way as ASP.NET 1.0 did for Active Server Page developers.

I recall a similar event when .NET 1.0 was released. Microsoft web developers had to bide their time with Active Server Pages, which was a great technology at the time, but it was mostly script based or interpreted. ASP.NET 1.0 changed the way developers thought about writing their applications. For example, the new Cache API allowed developers to skip the often used hack of storing commonly accessed data in application state memory; server controls allowed us to take concepts of reuse found at the component layer and "componentize" the UI. Of course, there was much, much more, but the biggest improvement by far was that ASP.NET was built on top of the Common Language Runtime (CLR), providing ASP.NET with a host of benefits ranging from garbage collection to multiple language support. Here is an interesting piece of .NET trivia: Did you know that ASP.NET was the first product group within Microsoft to agree to build their new platform, later to be known as .NET? How far we've come…

The planning for .NET 2.0, codenamed *Whidbey*, began before version 1.0 even shipped, just as the planning and development for the next version, codenamed *Orcas*, is already underway. An interesting aside: If you drive north from Redmond towards Canada, home of Whistler-Blackcomb—one of the best snowboarding (skiing too) destinations in North America—there is a restaurant at the base of these mountains called *Longhorn* (the Windows Vista codename). On the way to Longhorn, as the crow flies, you'll pass the city of Everett (codename of .NET 1.1) and the islands of Whidbey and Orcas.

Every adventure needs a trusted guide. In this exploration of ASP.NET 2.0, whether you are new to technology or intimately familiar with it, Damon's book will be a trustworthy companion. Damon shares his experience as a professional ASP.NET 2.0 software developer who has not only been studying ASP.NET 2.0 but has used it extensively.

The opening chapters of the book examine defensive programming concepts new to ASP.NET 2.0, in particular those related to managing the configuration system. The ASP.NET XML driven configuration system, aka `Web.config`, not only receives many new settings but also a programmatic API for managing the system. Although the XML can still be edited directly, the APIs now allow those settings to be managed through tools as well.

Starting in Chapter 3, Damon begins to explore some of the new user interface features of ASP.NET 2.0. Master Pages and themes provide us with many more options for customizing the look-and-feel of our web applications. Damon also examines page skinning, a feature that originated in ASP.NET Forums (now Community Server) and enables developers to build modular controls whereby their UI is decoupled from their implementation.

Chapter 6 deals with the new Personalization features of ASP.NET 2.0. The Personalization, Membership, Role Management, Provider Design Pattern, and Caching features are ones I'm particularly passionate about, as I had the opportunity, while working at Microsoft, to design these features. ASP.NET's new Profile system is unique. Not since the days of Site Server 3.0 have developers had a robust personalization API available for their use, and this one provides developers with an easy-to-use API, along with innovative capabilities such as load on demand, profile property delegation through providers and, of course, strongly typed properties on the `Profile` object. In short, `Profile` is now the API of choice for storing user data.

In the later chapters, Damon assesses the new Web Parts Framework, which enables anyone to build web portals, against the option to download or buy one. He shows how to use the new wizard control to better control the workflow of data entry. Finally, he investigates topics such as file uploads, security, and dynamic image creation using HTTP Handlers.

As you immerse yourself in the following pages, you'll find this book to contain practical examples written by an experienced software developer. And thus I present to you *Pro ASP.NET 2.0 Website Programming*.

Rob Howard
Telligent Systems

About the Author

Damon Armstrong has been developing business applications for almost 10 years and has a passion for just about every web-based technology on the planet. Currently, he is a technology consultant with Telligent Systems in Dallas, Texas, where he works with some of the most active and knowledgeable people in the .NET community, specializes in ASP.NET, and has recently been focusing on client development projects for early adopters of ASP.NET 2.0. He is certified in VB .NET and ASP.NET, and holds a Bachelors of Business Administration in Management of Information Systems from the University of Texas at Dallas.

Damon lives in Carrollton, Texas, with his wife Teresa Kae and their black-lab mix Cloe. When he's not in front of a computer, he's usually out playing softball, disc golf, or procrastinating on some home-improvement project. He's also a leader, along with his wife and a bunch of other absolutely awesome people, with Carrollton Young Life. He can be contacted at `damon.armstrong@gmail.com` or online at `http://www.damonarmstrong.com`.

About the Technical Reviewer

Damien Foggon is a freelance programmer and technical author based in Newcastle, England. He's technical director of Thing-E Ltd., a company specializing in the development of dynamic web solutions for the education sector, and founder of Littlepond Ltd. He started out working for BT in the UK before moving on to progressively smaller companies until finally founding his own company so that he can work with all the cool new technologies and not the massive monolithic developments that still exist out there.

Damien has coauthored books for Microsoft Press and Apress and acted as a technical reviewer for both Wrox and Apress. His first solo outing as an author, *Beginning ASP.NET 2.0 Databases* (also from Apress), will be arriving soon. He can be contacted at `damien@littlepond.co.uk` or online at `http://www.littlepond.co.uk`.

Acknowledgments

Writing a book is one of the most arduous tasks I have ever endured, and it would have been unendurable without the help and support of a great number of people. Although words are not enough, I would like to thank the following…

My wife, Teresa. Your unceasing kindness, patience, support, understanding, and love helped me get through the long nights of coding and writing. I look forward to getting away with you now that this is all over.

Tony Davis helped take an idea and turn it into a book. Thank you for your encouragement and guidance in shaping this work.

Damien Foggon had the insurmountable job of ensuring the technical accuracy of the entire book. Thank you for all your time, research, insight, and well-placed humor, and for keeping the quality of the code and explanations up to such a high standard.

Julie McNamee, grammatical master, went through the entire book in about three weeks and ensured the tone, style, spelling, and formatting of the text was consistent and did an absolutely amazing job.

Denise Santoro Lincoln, the book's project manager, helped keep everything on track, which is hard to do when working with someone as prone to procrastination as I am. Thank you for keeping on top of things even through all the chapter splitting, content rearranging, and out-of-order submissions.

Ty Anderson, who got me into this whole ordeal in the first place. You're not any good at keeping a dog in your yard while I'm out of town, but your insight into publishing has been invaluable, and your friendship even more so. Keep keeping it real.

Rob Howard, for taking the time to write the foreword for this book and for building an awesome company where people matter and shoes are, in fact, optional.

Tony Frey and Kirk Nativi. Anywhere in the book where I mention working on a project with someone, chances are it was one of these two. Tony helped set up the HTML formatting for the sample application and made otherwise stagnant meetings a lot of fun with his insightfully sarcastic witticism. Keep the attitude. And Kirk has saved me, in one way or another, on many a project.

Jonathon Wimberley, Nick Reed, and Matt Maloney. Why I waited two years to finish remodeling parts of house, I do not know. And why I decided to finish when I was writing a book, I don't know either. But your help was invaluable on those home-improvement projects I decided to undertake when I should have been writing.

Matt, Schall, Scott, Ted, Dave, and the rest of the Carrollton Crew. Fox rules. We'll get together soon and I'll re-educate you as to why that is. Assuming Schall doesn't get eaten by a puma.

And finally, my parents, James and Mary Armstrong. You have always been, and continue to be, there for me. Your dedication as parents is unparalleled. And after 500 some odd pages and almost 200,000 written words, I know that you will never let me live down the fact I came home in fifth grade after a keyboarding class grumbling about how I would never learn how to type.

Introduction

Microsoft revolutionized web-application development with the original release of ASP.NET, increasing developer productivity to a level unmatched with any other technology. I have worked with Java, Perl, PHP, Cold Fusion, and ASP 3.0, and in my experiences, projects in ASP.NET took less time to build, were easier to maintain, simplified code reuse, and had a better return on investment. And that was just the first release. ASP.NET 2.0 includes a number of much needed additions that continue to set it apart as the leader in web-based development technologies. But functionality is meaningless unless applied correctly, and so the aim of this book is to discuss how to apply ASP.NET to solve real-world business issues.

As a consultant, I've had the opportunity to see a range of different applications implemented to varying degrees of success, and, more importantly, a chance to reflect on what made them succeed and fail. After looking at a number of projects, I came to realize that successful projects tend to excel in a few common areas:

- *Configuration Management:* Configuration settings allow administrators to change the behavior of an application without recompiling the source code. Applications move from server to server. Domain names change. IP addresses get shifted around. Configurable applications make it easy to adapt to these changes and reduce maintenance costs.

- *Exception Management:* Exceptions are an inevitable part of the development process, and applications should handle exceptions gracefully to avoid damaging your application's credibility with users. You can even log exceptions and use that information to your advantage to help identify problem areas and manage user perception by responding to issues before customers have a chance to contact you to complain.

- *Visual Appearance:* You can control user perception by paying attention to graphical detail and ensuring your site has a consistent look and feel. Consistency exudes professionalism and makes for a crisper, cleaner-looking site. Because users often judge an application on its appearance long before they judge it on its functionality, you can use this to your advantage to build user confidence in your application. You can also allow users to personalize the appearance of a site to ensure it fits their particular needs and preferences.

- *Page Messaging:* Displaying status information to users about actions that occur on the page is imperative if you want them to remain informed. If an action fails, users should be notified to ensure they don't navigate away from the page and lose their data. If an action succeeds, users should be notified so they don't attempt to resubmit the information and make a duplicate entry. Informed users make more logical decisions, which helps keep them from breaking your applications in ways that you never imagined possible.

- *Reusable Controls:* Taking time at the start of a project to identify and build components you can use throughout the rest of the development process can save you an enormous amount of time. You also gain a higher degree of maintainability because you can update the component from a single location.
- *User Management and Security:* Business applications often manage vital business information, and it's imperative to protect that information from falling into the wrong hands. Applications should take full advantage of the various security mechanisms in Windows, IIS, and ASP.NET to ensure users are properly authenticated and authorized to avoid letting sensitive information slip through the cracks.
- *Searching and Reporting:* As the amount of data in an application grows, so does the need to effectively search and display that information. Applications with well-built searching and reporting tools make it easier to locate and view information, increasing the effectiveness of the application as a whole.

Another realization I've had while analyzing projects is that excellence is not the result of chaotic effort, but rather of design and planning followed by focused action. This is by no means a stunning revelation because everyone knows that planning something out before you tackle it helps you accomplish what you set out to do. But for some reason, when burdened by budgetary restrictions and tight deadlines, developers often forgo design in the hope that frenzied coding will somehow bring them out in front when the dust settles. I have yet to see this approach work.

Although the aforementioned list is far from exhaustive, focusing design efforts on these areas, before a project begins, helps create a solid infrastructure on which to build the rest of your application. When you have a good configuration strategy in place, then your applications tend to be configurable. When you have an exception-management strategy defined, then your application is more likely to handle exceptions gracefully. When you have a well-designed visual interface, your applications are bound to look more professional. When you have page messaging in place, your applications are more inclined to communicate effectively. In other words, a well-built infrastructure drives you to build better applications. And building a solid infrastructure for your applications is what this book is all about.

All the chapters in this book contain practical examples for building different portions of an application using ASP.NET 2.0. They are drawn directly from my experience with client engagements, so you know they are applicable in real-world scenarios. I also introduce each chapter by outlining business benefits to the approach suggested so you know not only the "how," but also the "why" behind a specific design and implementation.

Who Should Read This Book?

If you are a .NET developer who wants to know how to build a solid web-based business application using ASP.NET 2.0, then this book is for you. Inside you'll find practical examples drawn from real-world situations that cover configuration management, exception handling, themes, control skins, building server controls, user management, profiles, developing against the Web Parts Framework, keyword and phonetic searching, sorting and paging reports, building web-based wizards, uploading files, storing binary information in a database, security, thumbnail generation, and content management. Although this book is geared toward beginner- and intermediate-level developers who have some experience with ASP.NET and VB .NET, even the most experienced professionals should find something new and interesting.

System Requirements

To follow along and run the examples in this text, you should have access to the following:

- Microsoft .NET 2.0 Framework
- Visual Studio .NET 2005
- Internet Information Server (IIS) 5.0 or 6.0
- SQL Server Express Edition (2005)
- Microsoft's `Northwind` Sample Database

When you install Visual Studio .NET 2005, it automatically installs the Microsoft .NET 2.0 Framework and gives you the option of installing SQL Server Express. You can install IIS via the **Windows Components** tab in the **Add or Remove Programs** section of the **Control Panel**. You can find the `Northwind` sample database on the Microsoft website. Unfortunately, the link to the page consists mostly of random characters and is far from intelligible. The easiest way to locate the `Northwind` database is to search Google for "Northwind and Pubs Sample Databases." You can also find a link to the sample database in the Links section of the sample application in the Source Code area of the Apress website.

All the examples in the book come preconfigured for the default installation folder. If you deploy the sample files to another folder, then you'll need to change configuration settings in the `Web.config` file to match your deployment location. SQL Server Express can connect directly to database files, but the connection string requires a physical path to that file. So, you'll need to change the connection string to point to the appropriate location. Following is an example connection string showing how to set up a connection to a database file (`.mdb`) on the file system:

```
Data Source=.\SQLEXPRESS;
AttachDbFilename="C:\PRO ASP.NET 2.0\Chapter 8\NORTHWIND.MDF";
Integrated Security=True;User Instance=True
```

Also know that when you specify the connection string in `Web.config`, you have to use proper XML formatting, so the quotes become `"` as shown in the following example:

```
<add name="Northwind"
    connectionString="Data Source=.\SQLEXPRESS;
      AttachDbFilename=&quot;C:\PRO ASP.NET 2.0\Chapter 8\NORTHWIND.MDF&quot;;
      Integrated Security=True;User Instance=True"/>
```

Of course, the easiest thing to do is to deploy the sample code to its default directory.

Downloading the Source Code

For your convenience, the full source code for the examples in this book is available in the Source Code area on the Apress website at `http://www.apress.com`. Click the Downloads link on the home page and follow the directions to download the code. Please review the `Readme.html` file in the sample download for deployment instructions.

CHAPTER 1

Configuration Strategy

When a project lands on your desk, resist the temptation to start coding without giving some serious thought to how you will handle configuration. Developers who have not adopted a configuration strategy are more likely to use hard-coded references to resources such as web servers, databases, IP addresses, and file locations, all of which tend to change given enough time. This usually makes your application extremely difficult and costly to maintain.

Not too long ago, I was able to see exactly how costly poor configuration practices can be when I was assigned to a project for a major delivery company. Over the years, our client had built a dozen or so different ASP (Active Server Pages) 3.0 applications to help manage the business. These applications were hosted on three different web servers and two different database servers, none of which were very powerful. To reduce maintenance costs, the client purchased two high-end servers: one to host web applications and the other to host all the client's databases. A colleague and I were tasked with moving all the applications and databases over to these new machines.

As we surveyed the code for the applications, one thing became readily apparent. Every single resource the applications referenced was hard-coded: file locations, network shares, servers, passwords, IP addresses, and FTP sites. The application lacked the capability to easily change program settings without recompiling the application. In other words, it lacked configurability. We were only able to successfully move the applications through tedious line-by-line searching, replacement, recompilation, and full regression testing. Financially, this translated into almost $15,000 of unnecessary work that could have been avoided had the original developers used a better configuration strategy.

Proper configuration practices are essential to making a project cost effective over the entire software development lifecycle. Unfortunately, budgetary and time constraints often convince developers to forgo those practices and rush into other areas of development without giving much thought to the long-term consequences. If you plan and budget time at the beginning of a project to properly deal with configuration issues, then you will likely reduce the overall time required to develop the project.

In this chapter's sections, I cover a variety of topics and techniques to help you implement a high-quality configuration strategy:

- *New Configuration Tools in .NET 2.0:* Demonstrates the new tools available for creating and maintaining configuration settings in your web application. Using these tools greatly simplifies the task of configuring an application and keeps you from manually editing the `Web.config` file.

- *Configuration Basics:* Outlines how to avoid hard-coded references to application settings and connection strings using the `<appSettings>` and `<connectionStrings>` sections of the `Web.config` and the configuration management objects in the .NET Framework.
- *Strongly Typed Configuration Classes:* Illustrates how to consolidate your configuration settings into a single class so those settings can be easily maintained from one location.
- *Custom Configuration Sections:* Discusses how to build configurable custom components by implementing a configuration section specially designed for the component.
- *Storing Configuration Settings in a Database:* Explains how to store simple configuration settings and entire objects in the database.

New Configuration Tools in ASP.NET 2.0

Microsoft took a leap in the right direction with the two new configuration tools shipping with the ASP.NET 2.0 release. The most notable addition is a web-based application administration tool—Web Site Administration Tool—that can help you set up security and application variables, and even helps you manage users and roles using a database. In fact, it can create the database tables necessary to house that data as well. The second addition is a property page available in IIS (Internet Information Server) that assists you with common settings in the `Web.config` and `Machine.config` files.

■ **Note** This is only an introduction to the new tools in ASP.NET 2.0, not an in-depth guide to their use. I highly recommend that you use the online help features of the tools to familiarize yourself with them as thoroughly as possible.

Web Site Administration Tool

The Web Site Administration Tool offers a number of site-maintenance options that you will access throughout the lifecycle of your application. It offers some configuration options, although they are not as extensive as the configuration options available via the ASP.NET IIS Property Page discussed next. You can open the Web Site Administration Tool from the Visual Studio IDE (Integrated Development Environment) by selecting **Website ➤ ASP.NET Configuration** from the menu. When you click on the menu option, your default browser opens and a screen similar to the one shown in Figure 1-1 displays. The links and descriptions in the middle of the page correspond to the navigational tabs running across the top.

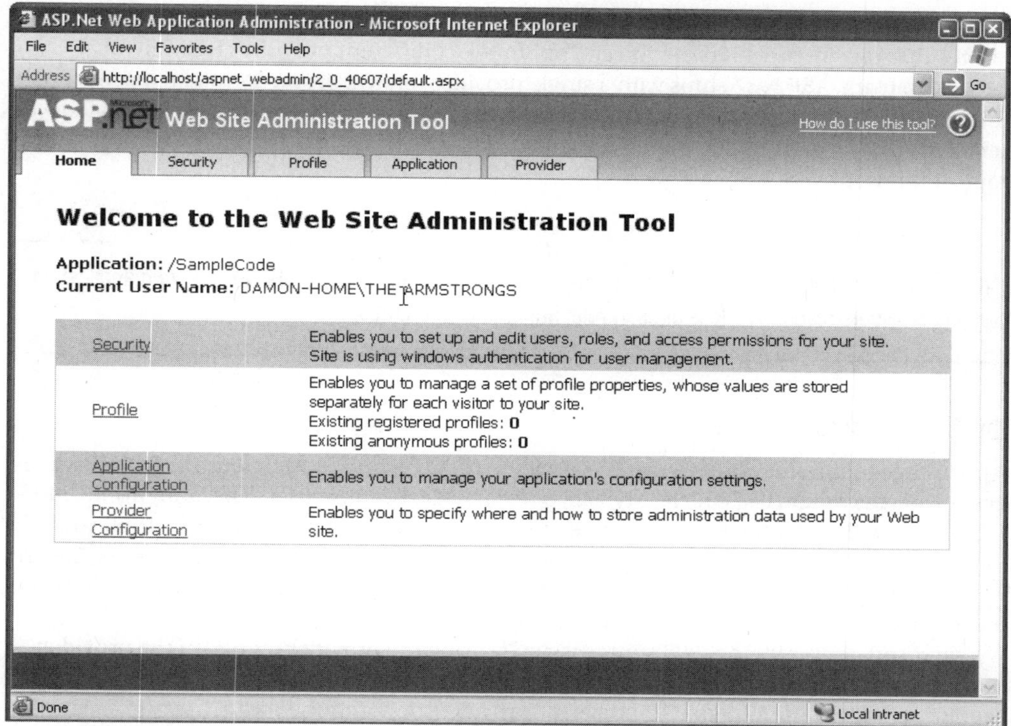

Figure 1-1. *Web Administration Tool start page*

The Provider Tab

You have two options when it comes to configuring providers for your application. You could try to remember all the XML (Extensible Markup Language) syntax, assemblies, types, and properties associated with providers and then manually enter all that information into the `Web.config` file. Or, you can open the **Provider** tab, which walks you through setting up providers in a step-by-step format, which I've found to be much more productive.

A number of different features in ASP.NET rely on providers:

- *Membership:* The membership provider tells ASP.NET how to handle usernames, email addresses, login information, and password recovery. The `Login` control is one of the many controls that uses membership features to access user and login information.
- *Roles:* The role provider helps maintains a list of roles for your web application and a list of which users are in what roles.
- *Profiles:* The profile provider tells ASP.NET how to store and retrieve profile information about users who access your web application. The `Profile` object uses the profile provider extensively.
- *Personalization:* When you work with Web Parts later on in Chapter 7, the Web Part personalization settings for each page are stored using a provider.

The initial page of the **Provider** tab allows you select a single provider for the ASP.NET features that rely on providers, or you can opt to select different providers for individual features. In truth, ASP.NET ships with a single provider for SQL Server so you are pretty much limited to the SQL Server provider until third-party vendors start coming out with providers of their own. You can also build your own provider implementations, but that is well beyond the scope of this book.

■ **Note** You should set up your provider information before adding users or roles to your web application. Changing providers results in a loss of user, role, and profile information.

Why Are Providers Necessary?

Data-storage requirements of websites are widely varied. Some applications use SQL Server or Access whereas others use Oracle, MySQL, or even XML. Because user, role, and profile information is stored in a database, it makes sense to use whatever database the web application is already using to store that information. ASP.NET 2.0 has a number of new components that are dependent on users, roles, and profiles, so the concern is how to design these components to be compatible with any existing and future data source.

Microsoft addresses the data source issue by using the provider model. In the provider model you define functionality for a component in an interface and then build data source–specific implementations of that interface to "provide" the component with a way to access the data source. Figure 1-2 depicts this concept.

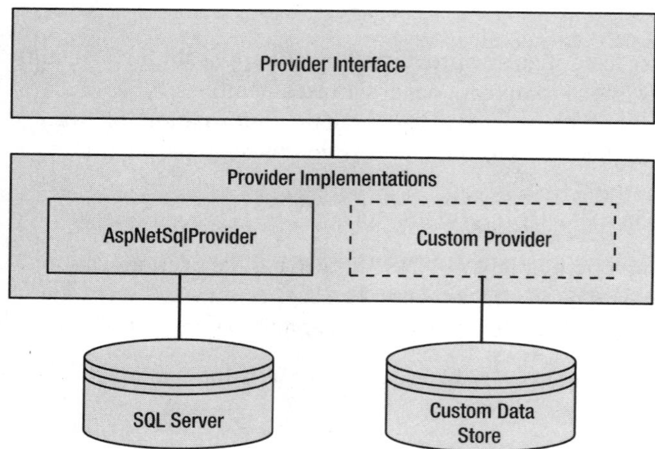

Figure 1-2. *In the provider model, functionality is defined in an interface and then implemented by specific "Provider" classes.*

As a hypothetical example, assume you have defined a `Person` object and one of the methods it exposes is the `GetToWork()` method. Because people can get to work in a number of different ways, and new ways are being invented on an ongoing basis, you can use the provider model to "provide" the `Person` object with various implementations of the `GetToWork()` method as shown in Listing 1-1.

Listing 1-1. *Hypothetical Provider Example*

```
Dim Person1 as New Person
Person1.GetToWorkProvider = CarProvider
Person1.GetToWork()

Dim Person2 as New Person
Person2.GetToWorkProvider = BusProvider
Person2.GetToWork()
```

In this example, `Person1` gets into his car and drives to work. `Person2` stands at a bus stop, waits for the bus, gets on, hops off at her stop, and walks the rest of the way to work. But, even though they had different ways of arriving at their destination, both `Person1` and `Person2` will be at work after the `GetToWork` function executes. Similarly, if you call `Profile.Save()` from a web form, regardless of whether you are using a provider for SQL Server, Oracle, XML, or some other custom store, the profile is saved. Understand, however, that the providers in ASP.NET are normally configured in `Web.config` and not explicitly set in code as in the hypothetical example.

The Security Tab

Most of the functionality in the Web Site Administration Tool is located under the Security tab, so you will likely be spending a great deal of time here. When you first access the tab, you'll see some descriptive text and three boxes at the bottom of the screen containing links allowing you to manage users, roles, and access rules. You can jump to these sections individually, or you can opt to use the Security Wizard to walk you through the security configuration process. Following is a description of each subsection of the Security tab:

- *Users*: This section allows you to set the type of authentication the application uses. If Forms Authentication is enabled, then you can search for, add, edit, and delete users. From the Add/Edit User page, you can also select the roles to which a user belongs. If Windows Authentication is enabled, then you will not be able to manage users because they are managed inherently by Windows.

- *Roles*: You can enable and disable roles regardless of the type of authentication you use, but it is mainly used for Forms Authentication. Once enabled, you can add and delete roles and use the Manage Roles page to see listings of which users are in what roles. You can also add and remove users from roles on the Manage Roles page.

- *Access Rules*: Access rules, also known as authorization settings, are used to set up authorization for a directory based on username or role. Access rules are greatly simplified by using the Access Rule builder. The Access Rule builder is a web-based tool that gives you a point-and-click interface for easily adding new `<authorization>` entries to `Web.config` files in your application. Previously, creating access rules required you to manually edit `<authorization>` entries for the directories in your application, similar to the one shown here:

```
<configuration>
    ...
    <system.web>
      ...
      <authorization>
        <deny users="?" />
        <allow roles="admin_user" />
        <deny roles="normal_user" />
      </authorization>
      ...
    </system.web>
  </configuration>
```

- Using the Access Rule builder, you can select a directory from the application's directory tree and set up the appropriate access restrictions using the graphical interface. As you create new rules, the appropriate `<authorization>` entries are placed in a `Web.config` file that resides in the directory you selected from the directory tree.
- *The Security Wizard*: The Security Wizard does not introduce any new functionality. It just walks you through the three sections that were already mentioned and is smart enough to skip any unnecessary sections based on your configuration choices. For instance, if you choose Windows Authentication mode, the wizard will not take you to the user-management screen because you have no need to manage users.

Although the Security tab's purpose is to help you manage users and roles, you are not required to use it. You can manage users and assign roles programmatically and even allow users to register for their own accounts using the new Login tools. Chapter 5 contains more information on the new login controls and programmatic support for users and roles.

The Application Tab

The most notable feature of the Application tab is the Application Settings section. This section allows you to add, edit, and delete values from the `<appSettings>` section of the `Web.config` file. You can also configure SMTP settings, set debugging and tracing options, and define a default error page from the Application tab.

ASP.NET Property Page in IIS

Microsoft has said from the beginning that .NET would support side-by-side execution. In other words, you can have 20 different versions of the .NET Framework installed on your computer and your application can use whatever Framework it needs. However, configuring your web applications to use different version of the framework was not very intuitive because it required the use of the `aspnet_regiis.exe` command-line utility. This has been simplified with the release of the .NET 2.0 Framework. You can now configure individual virtual directories within IIS to use different versions of the .NET Framework using the ASP.NET property page. The property page also gives you access to a number of application configuration options.

After you install the .NET Framework 2.0 or greater, you will notice the new ASP.NET property page in the properties window for sites and virtual directories. See Figure 1-3 for an example of how this property page appears.

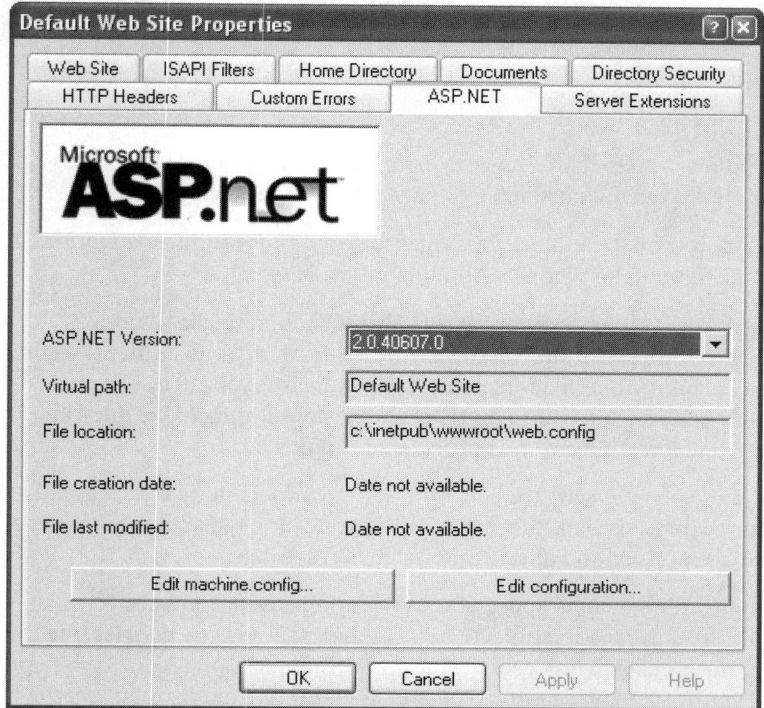

Figure 1-3. *ASP.NET property page in IIS*

A drop-down list on the page displays the individual versions of the .NET Framework installed on your system. Configuring a virtual directory to use a specific version of the .NET Framework is as easy as selecting it from this list.

■ **Note** If you are trying to debug an older web application project in Visual Studio 2003, you might get an error telling you that the debugger cannot attach to the process. To remedy this, open the ASP.NET property page for your application's virtual directory and select a different ASP.NET version from the drop-down list. You need to choose version 1.0 if you used Visual Studio 2002 to build the application, or version 1.1 if you used Visual Studio 2003.

If you are viewing the properties of a virtual directory configured to use the 2.0 Framework, then you will notice near the bottom of the ASP.NET property page an **Edit configuration** button. This button launches the **ASP.NET Configuration Settings** utility for the `Web.config` file located in the root directory of your web application. This utility has far more configuration options than the Web Site Administration Tool (Web Tool), but it does not allow you to maintain users or roles, and creating access rules is much less intuitive. It is designed more for configuration than maintenance, so use the Web Tool to maintain your site and use the Configuration Settings tool to configure more advanced settings. Following is a brief description of the configuration settings you can change from each tab in the utility:

- *General tab:* Allows you to define application settings and connection strings for your application.
- *Custom Errors tab:* Allows you to define custom error pages for specific HTTP status codes, or you can define a default custom error page for all HTTP status codes.
- *Authorization tab:* Allows you to define access rules for your application. As mentioned before, it is less intuitive than the Web Site Administration Tool.
- *Authentication tab:* Allows you to configure your web application to use Windows Authentication, Forms Authentication, Password Authentication, or no authentication at all. If you choose Forms Authentication, you can also specify a number of Forms Authentication parameters such as the login URL, cookie name, and cookie duration. Also, you can specify membership and role providers from this tab.
- *Application tab:* Allows you to specify the user you want to impersonate if your application needs to use impersonation. Aside from that, the Application tab allows you to set a number of default page options and obscure globalization settings.
- *State Management tab:* Allows you to specify how your application stores session state information (for example, the session object) and whether or not to use cookies, the URI, or some other mechanism to link users to the appropriate session object. If you opt to use the `StateServer` or `SQLServer` options for your session state mode, then you are given an area to enter connection string information.
- *Advanced tab:* Allows access to seven tabs in one. A drop-down list at the top of the Advanced tab allows you to select which advanced set of configuration options you want to view. Those options include Pages & Tracing, Compilation, HTTP Handlers, HTTP Runtime, Locations, HTTP Modules, and Trust.

■ **Note** If you see an italicized item in the ASP.NET Configuration Utility, it means that the item is defined in the `Machine.config` file and has been inherited by your `Web.config` file. Placing items in the `Machine.config` file allows you to create settings in a single location that can be reused from all your applications. If you change an italicized item, the new setting is written to your application's `Web.config file` and overrides the value from the `Machine.config`.

If you are viewing the ASP.NET property page of the site, then you will notice a second button on the property page: Edit `Machine.config`. This launches the same ASP.NET Configuration Utility, but instead of editing the `Web.config` file in your root directory, it brings up the `Machine.config` for your system.

Configuration Basics

Building configurable settings into your application is a relatively painless process because Microsoft has done most of the difficult work for you. The Web.config file has two sections entirely devoted to storing ad-hoc configuration data: the <appSettings> and the <connectionStrings> sections. Microsoft has also created out-of-the-box components that retrieve the data from these sections so you can use the information in your web application.

Application Settings

Since its inception, the .NET Framework has supported the <appSettings> section of the Web.config file. The section should appear between the opening <configuration> and closing </configuration> tags and allows you to define configuration settings as name-value pairs. An example <appSettings> section is shown here:

```
<?xml version="1.0" encoding="utf-8"?>
<configuration>
    <appSettings>
        <add key="UploadPath" value="C:\Uploads\"/>
        <add key="FTPSite" value="127.0.0.1"/>
        <add key="FileExtension" value=".CSV"/>
        <add key="BirthDate" value="6/3/1980"/>
        <add key="SomeNumber" value="4"/>
    </appSettings>
</configuration>
```

■ **Caution** The XML in the Web.config file is case sensitive. If you accidentally capitalize or fail to capitalize a character, your application will experience runtime errors.

You can access any of the application settings you have defined in Web.config via the ConfigurationManager class located in the System.Configuration namespace. This class exposes a shared object named AppSettings, which contains a key-based listing of all the name-value pairs defined in the <appSettings> section of the Web.config file. You can access configuration settings using the setting name as the key, just like you would do when retrieving values using the Request.QueryString or Request.Form objects. Following is an example that retrieves the UploadPath setting from your Web.config file:

```
Imports System.Configuration.ConfigurationManager
...
Dim UploadPath As String = AppSettings("UploadPath")
```

Before we continue, let me point out something very important. You may have noticed that a date and a number are defined in the <appSettings> section. And, you may expect the AppSettings object to return those settings as a date and an integer, respectively, but that is not the case. The AppSettings object only returns strings. If you want to convert something from a string to a different data type, then you must do it manually:

```
Imports System.Configuration.ConfigurationManager
...
Dim BirthDate as Date = CDate(AppSettings("UploadPath"))
```

Also, if you are going to be working with the AppSettings object repeatedly, you should use the Import System.Configuraation.ConfigurationManager statement. It makes for a lot less typing.

Connection Strings

Most web applications rely on databases to store information, and connection strings are required to connect to database. So, you will most certainly be interacting with connection strings as a developer. Database servers also have a tendency to be relocated, renamed, or have their users or passwords updated. This means that connection strings should not be hard-coded into your application.

Fortunately, ASP.NET 2.0 has a brilliant new mechanism for managing connection strings that promotes proper configuration principles. Instead of intermingling the connection string settings with the other application settings, as was done in .NET 1.x, you have a specific configuration section entirely devoted to connection strings. You define all your connection strings in the <connectionString> section of the Web.config file and assign each a friendly name. The friendly name becomes, in essence, a way to refer to the connection string. You can refer to the static friendly name from your web application and feel free to change the connection string associated with that friendly name whenever the need arises. Let's look at an example. Following is a <connectionString> section that you might find in Web.config:

```
<?xml version="1.0"?>
<configuration>
  <connectionStrings>
    <add name="VendorDB" connectionString=
      "Server=localhost;User ID=user;Password=password;Database=Vendors;"/>
    <add name="ProductsDB" connectionString=
      "Server=localhost;User ID=user;Password=password;Database=Products;"/>
  </connectionStrings>
</configuration>
```

Two connection strings are defined in this section. One is named VendorsDB and has a connection string that points to the Vendor database; the other is named ProductsDB and has a connection string that points to the Products database. If you want to use the connection string as the value for a property in an ASP.NET control located on your web form, then you use the following syntax:

```
<asp:SqlDataSource id="SqlDataSource1" runat="server"
     ConnectionString="<%$ ConnectionStrings:VendorDB %>" />
```

Note that the <%$ ConnectionStrings:FriendlyName %> tag is only valid when assigning a value to a property of an ASP.NET web control. If you try to use it anywhere else—that is, directly on the page—then your page will not compile.

■ **Note** You can also use `<%$ AppSettings:Key %>` to reference a value from the `<appSettings>` section of your `Web.config` file. Like the connection string tag, this declaration can only be used when assigning a value to a property of an ASP.NET web control.

You also have the option of accessing connection strings directly in your code, and the syntax is very similar to working with items in the `<appSettings>` section. An example of how to do so is shown next:

```
Imports System.Configuration.ConfigurationManager
...
Dim MyConnectStr as String = ConnectionStrings("FriendlyName").ConnectionString
```

In the preceding example, `ConnectionStrings("FriendlyName")` actually returns a `ConnectionStringSettings` object, not a string. You can access the actual connection string via the `ConnectionString` property, as we have done in the preceding example.

Also, if you do not want to use the `<%$ ConnectionStrings:FriendlyName %>` tag in your web forms, you can opt to use `<%= ConnectionStrings("FriendlyName").ConnectionString %>` instead, assuming that you have imported `System.Configuration.ConfigurationManager` at the top of your page. This is entirely a matter of preference.

Configuration Guidelines

Now that you know about the `<appSettings>` and `<connectionStrings>` sections, it is time to discuss some guidelines for determining whether or not a setting should be stored in one of these locations. The guidelines for connection strings are relatively concrete.

- Do not hard-code any connection strings in your application. There is no compelling reason to do so, especially considering the tools available to help you avoid it.
- All connection strings should be placed in the `<connectionStrings>` section of the `Web.config` file. Do not place any part of your connection string in the `<appSettings>` section.
- Use meaningful, friendly names for your connection strings. The Visual Studio 2005 IDE actually uses these names to help you select connection strings from a drop-down list in some tools, so using meaningful names can only help you out.

Application settings can encompass just about anything in your web application that you may need to change. Here are some general guidelines for locating them in your application:

- If it can change, then it's a candidate for being an application setting. It's a painful experience to recompile your application just to change a mundane setting.
- If it can change, but you are 100% sure that it won't change, then it's still a candidate for becoming an application setting. You may think that your database server is never going to move or that the `R:` drive you mapped will always be around, but time has the power to change such absolutes.

- File locations, directories, server names, and IP addresses should normally be configuration settings. Also, look for numbers in your application that have an effect on the user interface (UI). One example is the number assigned to the `PageSize` property of `GridView` objects in your application. The `PageSize` property determines how many items are displayed on each page of a `GridView`, and users have a tendency to think that they are seeing too few or too many items at a time. Making properties such as this configurable will save you the hassle of recompiling the application every time someone thinks they should be changed.

- Always ask yourself how often a setting is going to change. Application settings are usually items that will change over the course of months or years, not days or hours. If you have an item that will be changing constantly, think about storing it in a database instead of the `<appSettings>` section. Making changes to your `Web.config` file may have some undesirable effects on the web application. We will discuss these adverse effects and how to store configuration settings in a database later in this chapter.

- Avoid placing settings in the `<appSettings>` section that could be placed in a cascading style sheet. For example, if you want the font, font-size, and colors in your web application to be configurable, your time will be much better spent setting up a style sheet than making a bunch of application settings.

- Redirection URLs to sites or documents outside your web application can usually be made into application settings. However, URLs to web forms in your web application more than likely do *not* need to be application settings. If the workflow of your application is changing to the extent where you will be redirecting to a new or alternate web form, then it probably means that you need to recompile the application anyway.

- The `<appSettings>` section is not a surrogate content-management system, so avoid using it to store reams of text to display on your web form. Use code-behind files to separate your HTML and your server-side code so you can easily manage content with an HTML editor.

- Try not to use too many application settings. An average site may have anywhere from 5 to 10 application settings. If you have 50 or 100 settings, then you may have gone a little overboard and managing your application settings may be much more difficult.

Remember, these are just guidelines and not absolutes to be rigidly enforced. Use your intuition, and over time, you will develop a more acute sense for which items need to be turned into application settings.

Strongly Typed Configuration Classes

Now that you know the necessary code to access configuration data using the .NET Framework, let's discuss a best practice for encapsulating your configuration data. It involves creating a strongly typed configuration class that exposes a shared property for each configuration item in the `<appSettings>` section of the `Web.config` file.

This approach allows you to speed up your development time because you no longer have to worry about casting a string into the appropriate data type each time you need to use an application setting. The casting code is only written once, and then the appropriately cast value can be used throughout the entire application. Additionally, if you are using the Visual Studio IDE, you can get a comprehensive list of all configuration settings via IntelliSense. This helps you avoid spelling errors that won't be caught by the compiler, and keeps you from having to dig into `Web.config` every time you want to see what's there.

The Strongly Typed Configuration Sample Application

The best way to become familiar with strongly typed configuration classes is to start building them. For this example, you need to create a new Visual Basic ASP.NET website. Choose **File ➤ New Website**, and the **New Website** dialog box appears. Make sure to select **Visual Basic** as the **Project Type**, and **ASP.NET Website** as the template. In the **Location** field, enter the folder in which you want your website files to reside. When you are done, click the **OK** button.

Adding the Web.config File

By default, the `Web.config` file is not created when you create a project, so you have to create one yourself. You can accomplish this by right-clicking the project icon in the Solution Explorer and selecting **Add New Item**. The **Add New Item** dialog box appears listing a number of different file templates. Choose the **Web Configuration File** template, and accept the default name `Web.config`. After you click the **Add** button, Visual Studio adds the `Web.config` file to your project in the root folder.

Now you need to create the `<appSettings>` and `<connectionStrings>` sections to use in the example. Open the `Web.config` file and locate the line that reads `<appSettings/>`. Replace that line with the following text:

```
<appSettings>
    <add key="MyString" value="www.Credera.com"/>
    <add key="MyInteger" value="5" />
    <add key="MyDateTime" value="8/20/1980" />
    <add key="MyBoolean" value="True" />
    <add key="MyPrimeNumberArrayList" value="1;2;3;5;7;11;13;17"/>
</appSettings>
```

Now locate the line that reads `<connectionStrings/>` and replace it with the following text:

```
<connectionStrings>
    <add name="MyConnectionString"
         connectionString="Server=Localhost;User id=usr;Password=pwd;"/>
</connectionStrings>
```

The `<appSettings>` section has six items defined that are all, conveniently, of differing data types. This will help our discussion of casting from strings to other data types and casting to more complex objects.

The Config Class

Now you need to add a new class to your application by right-clicking the project icon in the Solution Explorer and selecting **Add New Item**. Choose the **Class** template from the template list, and enter `Config.vb` as the name. Also, make sure to select Visual Basic in the **Language** drop-down list. Click the **Add** button. Visual Studio tells you that class files should be placed in the App_Code folder and asks if you want the class file to be placed there. Click **Yes**. Visual Studio automatically creates the App_Code folder and places the Config.vb class in the App_Code folder.

The first thing that you need in the Config.vb file is an imports statement so you do not have to fully qualify the AppSettings or ConnectionStrings objects. Also shown here is the declaration for the Config class:

```
Imports System.Configuration.ConfigurationManager

Public Class Config
```

Next, you define a series of private shared variables that cache the values from the AppSettings and ConnectionStrings objects.

```
    '***************************************************************************
    'Private Shared Variables used for Caching Settings
    Private Shared _MyString As String
    Private Shared _MyInteger As Integer
    Private Shared _MyDateTime As DateTime
    Private Shared _MyBoolean As Boolean
    Private Shared _MyPrimeList As ArrayList
    Private Shared _MyConnectionString As String
```

Then, you can move on to the actual properties that expose the items from the <appSettings> section. Six of these items are exposed as shared, read-only properties with varying return types. The first, MyString, is a fairly straightforward example because it returns a string, thus no casting is involved:

```
    '***************************************************************************
    Public Shared ReadOnly Property MyString() As String
        Get
            If _MyString = Nothing Then _MyString = AppSettings("MyString")
            Return _MyString
        End Get
    End Property
```

This property first checks to see if _MyString, the private class-level variable that caches the AppSettings value, has been initialized. If it isn't initialized, then it will be equal to Nothing and you initialize it by pulling the value from AppSettings("MyString") and storing it in the _MyString variable. Finally, you return _MyString.

The next property, MyInteger, follows the same basic structure as the previous example, but the value returned by the AppSettings object is a string, not an integer. Thus, you have to cast the string into an integer before storing it in the _MyInteger caching variable:

```
    '**********************************************************************
    Public Shared ReadOnly Property MyInteger() As Integer
        Get
            If _MyInteger = Nothing Then _
                _MyInteger = CInt(AppSettings("MyInteger"))
            Return _MyInteger
```

```
        End Get
    End Property
```

Assuming that the string returned from AppSettings("MyInteger") is a valid number, CInt(AppSettings("MyInteger")) casts the string into an integer before storing it to the _MyInteger variable. So, what happens if AppSettings("MyInteger") does not return a valid number? The call to CInt() throws an error. We will discuss error handling in the Config class a bit later in this chapter, so for now assume that the strings returned from the AppSettings object are in the appropriate format for casting.

Next, the MyDateTime and MyBoolean properties show two more examples of casting properties to their appropriate types:

```
    '***************************************************************
    Public Shared ReadOnly Property MyDateTime() As Date
        Get
            If _MyDateTime = Nothing Then _
                _MyDateTime = CDate(AppSettings("MyDateTime"))
            Return _MyDateTime
        End Get
    End Property

    '***************************************************************
    Public Shared ReadOnly Property MyBoolean() As Boolean
        Get
            If _MyBoolean = Nothing Then _
             _MyBoolean = CBool(AppSettings("MyBoolean"))
            Return _MyBoolean
        End Get
    End Property
```

You are not limited to just casting your application setting directly to a native data type, you can also use the setting to build a more complex object. This next property, called MyPrimeNumberArray, actually returns an ArrayList.

```
    '***************************************************************
    Public Shared ReadOnly Property MyPrimeList() As ArrayList
        Get
            If _MyPrimeList Is Nothing Then
                _MyPrimeList = New ArrayList
                Dim TempPrimeList As String() = _
                  Split(AppSettings("MyPrimeList"), ";")

                For index As Integer = 0 To TempPrimeList.Length - 1
                    _MyPrimeList.Add(CInt(TempPrimeList(index)))
                Next

            End If
```

```
            Return _MyPrimeList
        End Get
    End Property
```

The MyPrimeList property first checks to see if the _MyPrimeList variable is initialized. If it isn't, then a new ArrayList is created and assigned to _MyPrimeList. Then you get the string value from the AppSetting object and split it using ";" as the delimiter. The Split function returns an array containing each number as an individual string. You then iterate through each number in this list, cast each one into an integer, and add each one to _MyPrimeList using the Add method. Finally, you return _MyPrimeList.

Some complex objects have so many properties that creating them from a single string stored in the <appSettings> section is not be the best option. We will discuss custom configuration sections later in this chapter to address that issue.

Building a property to expose a connection string is very similar to returning a string from the AppSettings object:

```
'**************************************************************************
Public Shared ReadOnly Property MyConnectionString() As String
    Get
        If _MyConnectionString = Nothing Then _MyConnectionString = _
            ConnectionStrings("MyConnectionString").ConnectionString
        Return _MyConnectionString
    End Get
End Property

End Class
```

Remember that the call to ConnectionStrings("MyConnectionString") returns a ConnectionStringSettings object, not a string, so you need to use the ConnectionString property of the returned object to access the actual connection string. Also notice the End Class statement as this is the last property in the example class.

Using the Config Class in Your Code

Now that you have the Config class built, let's discuss how to use it. Each property in the class is a shared, read-only property. With shared properties, you do not have to instantiate an object to call the property. So you can access the properties directly from the Config class in the following manner:

```
Dim StringSetting as String = Config.MyString
Dim IntegerSetting as Integer = Config.MyInteger
Dim SomeArrayList as ArrayList = Config.MyPrimeList
```

Remember that each property is strongly typed, so MyString returns a String, MyInteger returns an Integer, and MyPrimeList returns an ArrayList. Casting is handled inside of each property, so you do not need to worry about casting every time you access a setting.

You cannot assign values to the properties in the Config class because they are all read-only. Although it is possible to change a setting in the <appSettings> and <connectionStrings> section of the Web.config file using the XML objects available in the .NET Framework, I do not recommend placing the code to do so directly in the property. Remember, settings in Web.config should be fairly static so changes to them should be few and far between. If the setting needs to change often, then seriously consider storing it in a database. If you need remote configuration or setup capabilities, then place the code to make changes to the Web.config in an administrative page so it's isolated from the rest of the system.

Error Handling in the Config Class

There is no error handling code for any of the properties in the Config class, even though a casting error could throw an exception. The reason for this is because it's not a good return on your time to include error-handling code in your configuration properties for a couple of reasons.

When an application is first deployed, the Web.config file should contain valid configuration settings. This helps the individual who needs to edit the configuration because the syntax for the new setting should follow the syntax of the existing setting. For instance, if the MyInteger setting is 5, and needs to be changed to 10, then the person editing Web.config will probably not enter "ten" as the new setting. Also, if a setting is complicated, then XML comments can be included to help guide the user to an appropriate entry.

Another issue is how to let someone know that a configuration setting is invalid if you never throw the exception. Allowing the exception to be thrown produces a visual sign that something is wrong. A quick look into the error message will reveal which property of the Config class threw the exception, and a system administrator can look into the issue.

Finally, exception handling is an expensive operation that is inherently slow. If you put an invalid setting into Web.config, you don't want an exception-handling operation running each time you access the property. For simple data types, you can implement error checking to avoid an exception instead of handling it when it occurs. In the following example, the application checks to see if the MyInteger setting is a numeric value before returning it. If it isn't, then it returns a default value of 5:

```
'***************************************************************************
Public Shared ReadOnly Property MyIntegerWithErrorChecking() As Integer
    Get
        If IsNumeric(AppSettings("MyInteger")) Then
             _MyInteger = CInt(AppSettings("MyInteger"))
        Else
            'Setting in the Web.config is invalid so set a default value
            _MyInteger = 5
        End If
        Return _MyInteger
    End Get
End Property
```

Error checking only works when you determine if a settings is valid before casting it into the target data type, so it's harder to implement for complex data types. For example, if your application requires a valid GUID (Globally Unique Identifier) for some operation, then you would have to implement error handling instead of error checking to ensure it returns a valid GUID:

```
'*********************************************************************
Public Shared ReadOnly Property MyGuidWithErrorHandling() As Guid
    Get
        Try
            If _MyGuid = Nothing Then _MyGuid = _
                New Guid(AppSettings("MyGuid"))
        Catch ex As Exception
            'Error occured so set a default value
            _MyGuid = New Guid("{05F8B079-5367-42a8-B97F-6C72BAC4915C}")
        End Try
        Return _MyGuid
    End Get
End Property
```

When you implement exception handling in your configuration properties, you should use a variable to cache the property value because it keeps the exception handling to a minimum. Notice that an exception only occurs the first time you access the property. On subsequent calls, the MyGuid variable contains a value so the property does not attempt to reload the value from Web.config.

Now, my views on error handling come from my experiences, and so far I have had no issues with leaving error handling and error checking out of my strongly typed configuration classes. It is a matter of preference, so you will have to see what works best for your situation.

Caching Application Settings and Connection Strings

In your Config class, many lines are devoted to caching values from the AppSettings and ConnectionStrings objects. This may leave you wondering if you have to cache those settings or if you can just skip the caching code. If you do not want to use caching in your application, then you can strip the properties of their caching code and reduce them to the following:

```
'*********************************************************************
Public Shared ReadOnly Property MyIntegerWithNoCaching() As Integer
    Get
        Return CInt(AppSettings("MyInteger"))
    End Get
End Property
```

This property returns the MyInteger setting, but does not cache the value. As you can see, the code for this is much simpler than the code involving caching. Also, you do not have to define a set of private shared variables in which to cache the values. But all things come at a cost, and the penalty for not caching your settings is a minor performance hit.

How bad is the performance hit? I created a benchmarking test that is included in the Chapter 2 sample code in the Source Code area of the Apress website (http://www.apress.com).

The page is called CacheBenchmark.aspx, and it allows you to enter the number of iterations you want to test and then executes two loops. The first loop uses a noncached property to assign a value to a variable, and the next loop uses a cached property to assign a value to a variable. On my computer, the noncached property runs about 375,000 iterations per second and the cached property runs at about 115 million iterations per second. That's a significant difference numerically, but when you get right down to it, you are probably not going to be accessing a property that many times in your application.

So, the decision to cache or not to cache is up to you. If you are building a smaller application that will not be accessed by many people, then you can get away with not caching your configuration settings. If, however, you are building an enterprise application with a massive user base, you will definitely want to consider it.

Custom Configuration Sections

We've covered how to store simple name-value configuration settings in the <appSettings> section of Web.config, but what about more complex configuration scenarios? What happens when you need to configure objects with a lot of parameters or even lists? The <appSettings> section is not well suited for such tasks. Instead, you may need to create a custom configuration section to handle more complex configuration data.

Configuration Section Architecture

Each configuration section in Web.config has a configuration section handler specifically designed to read data from the configuration section and return an object that exposes that data. These configuration sections and their handlers must be defined in the <configSection> element. Here is an example of how the <appSettings> section is defined in Machine.config:

```
<configuration>
    <configSections>
        ...
        <section name="appSettings"
            type="System.Configuration.AppSettingsSection, System.Configuration,
            Version=2.0.0.0, Culture=neutral, PublicKeyToken=b03f5f7f11d50a3a"
            restartOnExternalChanges="false" />
        ...
    </configSections>
</configuration>
```

The name parameter of the <section> element defines the name of the configuration section as it appears in the configuration file; the type parameter defines the configuration section handler that reads data from the configuration section and returns an object containing that data. In the preceding example, "appSettings" is the name of the section, which is why you can use the <appSettings> section in your Web.config file. The <appSetting> section hander is the System.Configuration.NameValueFileSectionHandler type located in the System assembly.

■ **Note** All the commonly used configuration sections are defined in `Machine.config` because `Web.config` inherits those settings. This is why you can use the `<appSettings>` section in your `Web.config` file without always having to set up the `configSection` entry to define it.

You can create your own custom configuration section by doing the following:

1. Create a data structure that can hold your configuration data. These data structures, and the `IConfigurationSectionHandler` discussed in step 2, must be defined in a separate project from your web application.
2. Create a class that implements the `IConfigurationSectionHandler` interface. This class reads the data from your configuration section and stores it in the data structure defined in step 1.
3. Add a new configuration section definition to the `<configSections>` element in your `Web.config` file. This requires giving your configuration section a name, and appropriately referencing the class you created in the second step.
4. Add the configuration section and configuration data to your `Web.config` file using the section name defined in step 2.
5. Launch your configuration section handler by calling the `GetSection` method of the `ConfigurationManager` class. This method executes your configuration section handler and returns the data structure containing your configuration data.
6. Store the configuration data returned by your configuration section handler for use in your application.

Let's take a detailed look at how this process works.

The Custom Configuration Section Sample Application

Here's the scenario. You have a client who wants to display a list of files that have been uploaded to a website. Each file should be displayed with an icon representing the document type. For instance, Word documents, rich text document, and text files should have an icon that looks like a little word pad, whereas Excel documents and comma-separated value files should have an icon that depicts a spreadsheet. The document type is determined by the file extension.

Your client wants a configurable solution so they can define icons and which extensions should be associated with those icons. They also want to be able to define an icon to represent unknown extensions. Lastly, each icon should have a description that will be used as the alternate text (the `alt` parameter of the `<img>` tag in HTML) for the icon image.

Following is an example of how the client wants to define the configuration:

```
<unknownIcon imageUrl="Icons/unknown.gif" description="Unknown File Type"/>
<icon imageUrl="Icons/word.gif" description="Word Processing Document">
    <ext>.DOC</ext>
    <ext>.RTF</ext>
    <ext>.TXT</ext>
</icon>
<icon imageUrl="Icons/excel.gif" description="Excel Document">
    <ext>.XLS</ext>
    <ext>.CSV</ext>
</icon>
<icon imageUrl="Icons/image.gif" description="Picture/Image">
    <ext>.GIF</ext>
    <ext>.TIFF</ext>
    <ext>.JPG</ext>
    <ext>.BMP</ext>
    <ext>.PNG</ext>
</icon>
```

Your objective is to implement a custom configuration section that can handle this type of configuration data.

Creating the Configuration Data Structures

Custom configuration handlers may be defined directly in your project, or in an external assembly so it can be reused. In this example, you'll use an external assembly, so you need to add a new project to your solution. You can do this by right-clicking on the solution file and then selecting **Add ➤ New Project**. The **Add New Project** dialog box appears. Select **Visual Basic** for the **Project Type** and **Class Library** as the **Template**. Name the new project `IconConfiguration`. After you click the **OK** button, a new project appears in the Solution Explorer window.

Take a look at the XML configuration for the icons. You should notice a collection of icons, and each icon has a collection of extensions—a list of lists. If you were to build a data structure to hold this data in the exact same hierarchical structure, searching for an appropriate icon using the extension as the starting point would be too cumbersome. Instead, you'll create a data object that can store the `ImageUrl`, `Description`, and `Extension` properties together, allowing you to maintain a single list that can be searched with relative ease.

By default, the new project will include a class file named `Class1.vb`. Change the name of this file to `IconConfigurationItem.vb`. The `IconConfigurationItem` class holds all the icon information:

```
Public Class IconConfigurationItem

    '**********************************************************************
    Private _IconImageUrl As String
    Private _Description As String
    Private _Extension As String
```

```
    '*********************************************************************
    Public Property IconImageUrl As String
        Get
            Return _IconImageUrl
        End Get
        Set(ByVal value As String)
            _IconImageUrl = value
        End Set
    End Property

    '*********************************************************************
    Public Property Description As String
        Get
            Return _Description
        End Get
        Set(ByVal value As String)
            _Description = value
        End Set
    End Property

    '*********************************************************************
    Public Property Extension As String
        Get
            Return _Extension
        End Get
        Set(ByVal value As String)
            _Extension = value
        End Set
    End Property

    '*********************************************************************
    Public Sub New(ByVal IconImageUrlParam As String, _
      ByVal DescriptionParam As String, _
      ByVal ExtensionParam As String)
        IconImageUrl = IconImageUrlParam
        Description = DescriptionParam
        Extension = ExtensionParam
    End Sub

End Class
```

IconConfigurationItem is a relatively simple class. It contains three public properties and their related fields to store the location of the image to display as the icon, the description, and the extension. It also includes a constructor to help initialize these properties.

Next, you need to create an object capable of storing a list of IconConfigurationItem objects. This is accomplished through a strongly typed collection class. Add a new class file to your project named IconConfigurationCollection.vb. Then, add the following code to the file:

```
Public Class IconConfigurationCollection
    Inherits CollectionBase

    '*****************************************************************
    Public UnknownIconInfo As IconConfigurationItem
```

The IconConfigurationCollection class inherits its list-storage functionality from the CollectionBase class. You should notice that the List property, which is an inherited property, is used throughout the class. Under the class declaration, you will see a public field capable of storing a reference to the unknown icon information. Remember that one of the requirements for this exercise was to have a catchall icon that can be displayed in the event of an unknown extension.

The GetExtensionIndex function, which is responsible for searching through the List property, looks for an IconConfigurationItem with a particular extension. It then returns the index of that item or -1 if the item is not found.

```
    '*****************************************************************
    Private Function GetExtensionIndex(ByVal Extension As String) As Integer

        Dim IconConfigItem As IconConfigurationItem
        Extension = Extension.ToUpper

        For index As Integer = 0 To List.Count - 1
            IconConfigItem = DirectCast(List.Item(index), IconConfigurationItem)
            If IconConfigItem.Extension.ToUpper = Extension Then
                Return index
            End If
        Next

        Return -1

    End Function
```

In terms of speed, this search algorithm is nothing spectacular, but it gets the job done. First, it converts Extension into an uppercase value to ensure proper string matching later on in the function. Then, the function loops through each IconConfigurationItem in the List property and checks to see if the Extension value passed into the function matches any of the Extension values of the items in the list. If so, the index of the matched item is returned. If not, the loop exits and the function returns -1, indicating that the icon associated with the extension was not located.

With the GetExtensionIndex function out of the way, you can move right into the GetIconInfo property:

```
'*******************************************************************
Default ReadOnly Property GetIconInfo(ByVal Extension As String) _
   As IconConfigurationItem
    Get
        Dim Index As Integer = GetExtensionIndex(Extension)
        If Index = -1 Then Return UnknownIconInfo
        Return DirectCast(List.Item(Index), IconConfigurationItem)
    End Get
End Property
```

This property has one parameter, Extension, which contains a string representing the extension of a file type. The objective of this property is to return the IconConfigurationItem associated with the given extension. If one does not exist, then the property returns the IconConfigurationItem associated with the unknown icon. This is accomplished by using the GetExtensionIndex function to return the index of the appropriate item. If the function returns -1, then you just return UnknownIconInfo. Otherwise, you return the IconConfigurationItem at the appropriate index in the list.

Last, the Add function allows you to add IconConfigurationItem objects to the list:

```
    '*******************************************************************
    Public Function Add(ByRef obj As IconConfigurationItem) As Integer
        Return List.Add(obj)
    End Function

End Class
```

With the data structures complete, you can now turn your attention to the actual configuration section handler.

Implementing an IConfigurationSectionHandler

You will create a class named IconConfigurationHandler that implements the IConfigurationSectionHandler interface. The IConfigurationSectionHandler interface only exposes a single function, the Create function, which is responsible for returning an object that stores your configuration data. In the example, you will be returning an IconConfigurationCollection object. Because there is only a single function in the class, the entire class is displayed here:

```
Imports System.Configuration
Imports System.Xml

Public Class IconConfigurationHandler
    Implements IConfigurationSectionHandler

    '**********************************************************************
    Public Function Create(ByVal parent As Object, _
                           ByVal configContext As Object, _
                           ByVal section As System.Xml.XmlNode) As Object _
                           Implements IConfigurationSectionHandler.Create
```

```
        Dim ReturnObj As New IconConfigurationCollection
        Dim IconItem As IconConfigurationItem

        Dim IconNodes As XmlNodeList = section.SelectNodes("icon")
        Dim ExtensionNodes As XmlNodeList
        Dim IconNode As XmlNode
        Dim ExtensionNode As XmlNode

        'Acquire and Process the Icon Nodes
        For Each IconNode In IconNodes
            ExtensionNodes = IconNode.SelectNodes("ext")
            For Each ExtensionNode In ExtensionNodes

                IconItem = New IconConfigurationItem( _
                  IconNode.Attributes.GetNamedItem("imageUrl").Value, _
                  IconNode.Attributes.GetNamedItem("description").Value, _
                  ExtensionNode.InnerText)
                ReturnObj.Add(IconItem)

            Next
        Next

        'Acquire and Process the Unknown Icon Node
        IconNode = section.SelectSingleNode("unknownIcon")
        If Not IconNode Is Nothing Then
            ReturnObj.UnknownIconInfo = New IconConfigurationItem( _
            IconNode.Attributes.GetNamedItem("imageUrl").Value, _
            IconNode.Attributes.GetNamedItem("description").Value, _
            String.Empty)
        End If

        Return ReturnObj

    End Function

End Class
```

The `Create` function has three parameters: `parent`, `configContext`, and `section`. In theory, the `parent` parameter contains configuration settings from a parent configuration section, and the `configContext` contains contextual information about the configuration. In practice, however, they are usually `NULL` and almost never useful. Disregard them unless you have a compelling reason to do otherwise. The `section` parameter, on the other hand, contains all the XML data located inside your configuration section, so it plays a key role in this function. After the function declaration, you define a set of variables as shown in Table 1-1.

Table 1-1. *Variables Used in the* `Create` *Function*

Variable Name	Type	Description
`ReturnObj`	`IconConfigurationCollection`	This is the object returned by the function. It contains a collection of `IconConfiguration➥Item` objects that represent the data from the configuration section.
`IconItem`	`IconConfigurationItem`	Used as a placeholder for the creation of `IconConfigurationItem` objects before they are added to the `ReturnObj`.
`IconNode`	`XmlNodeList`	Holds a collection of `XmlNode` objects. This is used to build a collection of all the icon elements in the configuration section.
`IconNode`	`XmlNode`	Used to reference a single image element, or `XmlNode` in the `IconNode` collection.
`ExtensionNodes`	`XmlNodeList`	Holds a collection of `XmlNode` objects. This is used to build a collection of `ext` elements located inside an image element.
`ExtensionNode`	`XmlNode`	Used to reference a single `ext` element, or `XmlNode`, in the `ExtensionNodes` collection.

In those variable declarations, you will notice the following line:

```
Dim IconNodes As XmlNodeList = section.SelectNodes("icon")
```

The `SelectNodes` function of the `XmlNode` object accepts an XPath query, and returns a `XmlNodeList` containing all the nodes that match the XPath query. The XPath query is just a string that, in this case, represents the element name of the elements that you want returned.

■ **Note** XPath is a powerful XML query language that is capable of much more than just searching for elements by name. For a more in-depth look at the XPath syntax and capabilities, visit the following Web site for an online tutorial: `http://www.w3schools.com/xpath/xpath_intro.asp`.

After the variable declarations, you begin looping through all the image elements in the `IconNodes` variable. Inside the first loop, you acquire all the `ext` elements in the current `image` element and store them in the `ExtensionNodes` variable. Then, you begin iterating through each of those `ext` elements in the second loop.

Inside the second loop, you call the `IconConfigurationItem` constructor and pass in values for the image URL, description, and extension. Both the image URL and the description are parameters of the `image` element, so their values can be accessed in the following manner:

```
IconNode.Attributes.GetNamedItem("imageUrl").Value
IconNode.Attributes.GetNamedItem("description").Value
```

The extension, however, is stored as the inner text of an `ext` element, not as a parameter. To access the extension value you need to use the following:

```
ExtensionNode.InnerText
```

After the `IconConfigurationItem` is created (and assigned to the `IconItem` variable), it is added to the `ReturnObj`. The `IconItem` variable exists for the sake of clarity; it is not an integral part of the solution. By the time these loops exit, the `ReturnObj` is populated with a list of extensions and each extension's corresponding image URL and description.

Next, you need to acquire the unknown icon information. There should only be one `unknownIcon` element in the configuration section, so use the `SelectSingleNode` function to find it:

```
IconNode = section.SelectSingleNode("unknownIcon")
```

If the specified element is not found, `IconNode` is set to `Nothing`. If it is found, then you create a new `IconConfigurationItem` and assign it to `ReturnObj.UnknownIconInfo`. An empty string is passed in as the extension for this new object because the extension information is unnecessary for the unknown icon. For reference, if you have multiple `<unknownIcon>` sections in the configuration section, then the `SelectSingleNode` function returns the first one it locates.

Reference the Class Library from Your Web Application

After you have created the class library containing your configuration data structures and configuration section handler, you need to add a reference to the class library from your web application. Right-click the web application project in the Solution Explorer and then choose **Add Reference**. The **Add Reference** dialog box appears. Select the **Projects** tab. You will see a listing of projects in your solution (aside from the web application). In the sample application, there is only a single project called **IconConfiguration**, so select it from the list. Click the **OK** button.

If you do not receive any error messages, then your reference has been set up correctly. You can confirm this by expanding the `Bin` folder of your web application and checking to see if `IconConfiguration.dll` is present in the folder.

Defining the Custom Configuration Section

Before you can put a custom configuration section in `Web.config`, you have to let the `Web.config` file know of its existence. This is accomplished by adding a new section entry to the `configSections` element. Open the `Web.config` file for your web application and add the following XML at the very top of the `<configuration>` section:

```
<configSections>
  <section name="iconConfig"
           type="IconConfiguration.IconConfigurationHandler, IconConfiguration"/>
</configSections>
```

■ **Note** The `<configSections>` element must be the first item defined in the `<configuration>` section. If you place any other elements in the `<configuration>` section before the `<configSections>` element, you will receive a compilation error.

The `name` parameter defines the name of your new configuration section as it appears in the `Web.config` file. It is case sensitive, so you need to make sure that this name and the name used in the opening and closing tags of your configuration section are identical. Using the preceding example, the configuration section would have to read:

```
<iconConfig>
    <!-- configuration data here -->
</iconConfig>
```

The `type` parameter defines the configuration section handler that can be used to parse the data inside of the configuration section. For the most part, you will use the following syntax for the type parameter:

```
type="NameSpace.Type, Assembly"
```

If you are using a configuration section defined in your web application, then you do not need to specify the assembly name. You only need to specify the assembly name for external assemblies and, when you do, the assembly name should not include the `.dll` extension of the assembly. You can also specify `version`, `culture`, and `publicKeyToken` parameters for the type if you need to point to a very specific instance of the type.

■ **Caution** Assemblies may have a root namespace that mimics the assembly name. In our example, for instance, `IconConfiguration` is both the assembly name and the root namespace. It appears redundant, but avoid the temptation to remove the initial namespace. For example, the following will work:

```
type=" IconConfigurationHandler, IconConfigurationHandler.IconConfiguration"
```

But this will not:

```
type=" IconConfigurationHandler, IconConfiguration"
```

In addition to being able to define new custom configuration sections, you can also define new section groups. A *section group* is an XML element that surrounds one or more configuration sections. Our example does not use a section group, but here is an example of how one may be defined in `Web.config`:

```
<!- - Define the Sections -->
<configSections>
  <sectionGroup name="myConfigurationGroup">
    <section name="SectionA" type="MySections.SectionA, MySections"/>
    <section name="SectionB" type="MySections.SectionB, MySections"/>
  </sectionGroup>
</configSections>

<!-- Use the Sections -->
<myConfigurationGroup>
  <SectionA>
    ...
  </SectionA>
  <SectionB>
    ...
  </SectionB>
</myConfigurationGroup>
```

Section groups are useful for grouping similar items together. For example, if you have a set of components that are logically related, you could group their configuration sections together to reinforce the point. Or, if your company develops a set of components that need to be configured, then you can use the company name as a grouping section to compartmentalize those configuration sections.

Adding the Custom Configuration Section

A few rules govern the placement of your custom configuration section in the `Web.config` file. First, it must reside directly in the `<configuration>` section. Do not add it outside of the `<configuration>` section and do not add it to a section inside the `<configuration>` section.

Second, it should appear after the `<configSections>` section. You defined your custom configuration section in `<configSections>`, so placing it before this section will cause an exception to be thrown.

Lastly, the name of your configuration section must match the name defined in `<configSections>`. Remember, it is case sensitive. If either the opening tag or the closing tag of your configuration section is incorrect, an exception will be thrown.

Next, you will see how your `Web.config` file should appear with your custom configuration section included:

```
<configuration>

  <configSections>
      <section name="iconConfig"
        type="IconConfiguration.IconConfigurationHandler, IconConfiguration"/>
  </configSections>

  <iconConfig>
      <unknownIcon imageUrl="Icons/unknown.gif" description="Unknown File Type"/>
      <icon imageUrl="Icons/word.gif" description="Word Processing Document">
```

```
            <ext>DOC</ext>
            <ext>RTF</ext>
            <ext>TXT</ext>
        </icon>
        <icon imageUrl="Icons/excel.gif" description="Excel Document">
            <ext>XLS</ext>
            <ext>CSV</ext>
        </icon>
        <icon imageUrl="Icons/image.gif" description="Picture/Image">
            <ext>GIF</ext>
            <ext>TIFF</ext>
            <ext>JPG</ext>
            <ext>BMP</ext>
            <ext>PNG</ext>
       </icon>
  </iconConfig>

  <!-- Remaining Configuration Settings -->

<configuration>
```

Accessing Custom Configuration Data in Your Application

In an attempt to keep all the configuration settings in a single location, you'll create an `IconData` property in the `Config` class to expose the icon configuration data. This property uses classes in the `IconConfiguration` namespace, so include the following line at the top of the `Config.vb` file so you don't have to fully qualify those class names:

```
Imports IconConfiguration
```

In the `Config` class, locate the section containing the private shared variables used for caching configuration settings. You'll cache the `IconData` property, so you need to add a private variable to the class to hold the cached value:

```
'***************************************************************************
'Private Shared Variables used for Caching Settings
Private Shared _MyString As String
Private Shared _MyInteger As Integer
Private Shared _MyDateTime As DateTime
Private Shared _MyBoolean As Boolean
Private Shared _MyPrimeList As ArrayList
Private Shared _MyConnectionString As String
Private Shared _IconData As IconConfigurationCollection
```

Remember that your configuration section handler returns an `IconConfiguration➥ Collection` object, so that type of object ultimately needs to be stored. Next, you have the code for the actual `IconData` property:

```
'*****************************************************************
Public Shared ReadOnly Property IconData() As IconConfigurationCollection
    Get
        If _IconData Is Nothing Then _IconData = _
             DirectCast(ConfigurationManager.GetSection("iconConfig"), _
               IconConfigurationCollection)
        Return _IconData
    End Get
End Property
```

The IconData property follows the same structure as the configuration properties discussed earlier. It first checks to see if IconData is initialized, and if not, it calls ConfigurationManager.GetSection("iconConfig"). The GetSection function accepts one parameter, a string representing the name of the configuration section to acquire, and accomplishes all the following when it executes:

- Determines which configuration handler is associated with the configuration section specified. Remember, this information was set in the <configSections> section of the Web.config file.
- Creates an instance of that configuration handler.
- Reads the data from the configuration section and places it into an XmlNode object.
- Calls the Create function of the configuration handler and passes in the XmlNode object containing the configuration data as the section parameter.
- Returns the object returned by the Create function.

The end result of all this is that the IconData variable is assigned the IconConfiguration➥Collection object returned by the configuration section handler you implemented earlier. Then, on the last line of the property, you return the cached value stored in IconData.

Creating the Icon Display Page

Now that you can access the custom configuration section from a strongly typed property in the Config class, you can build the icon display page with relative ease. Add a new web form to your web application and name it IconDisplayPage.aspx. Open the web form in the designer and place a new literal on the page named myLiteral. Then, open the code-behind file, and add the following code to it:

```
Imports IconConfiguration
Imports System.IO

Partial Class IconDisplayPage_aspx
    Inherits Page
```

```
    '*****************************************************************************
    Private Sub OutputFile(ByVal Filename As String)

        Dim IconInfo As IconConfigurationItem
        IconInfo = Config.IconData.GetIconInfo(Path.GetExtension(Filename))

        'Add HTML to the literal control to display file and associated icon
        myLiteral.Text &= "<img src='" & IconInfo.IconImageUrl & "'"
        myLiteral.Text &= "alt='" & IconInfo.Description & "'> "
        myLiteral.Text &= Filename & "<BR>"

    End Sub

    '*****************************************************************************
    Private Sub Page_Load(ByVal sender As Object, ByVal e As System.EventArgs) _
      Handles Me.Load

        'Print out documents
        OutputFile("WordDocument.doc")
        OutputFile("ExcelDocument.xls")
        OutputFile("ImageFile.bmp")
        OutputFile("SourceFile.vb")

    End Sub

End Class
```

The `OutputFile` procedure encapsulates the code necessary to display a file and its associated icon. First, you use the `Path.GetExtension` function to determine the extension of the file name contained in the `Filename` parameter. That value is then passed into the `Config.➥IconData.GetIconInfo` function, which returns the icon information associated with the extension. Finally, HTML is added to the `myLiteral` control to display the icon image and the file name.

The `Page_Load` method executes whenever the page's `Load` event fires and is responsible for calling `OutputFile` for a series of file names. The file names are hard-coded in the sample code for the sake of simplicity. When you view the page, you should see a list of file names and icon images representing each different file type.

Remember, all the code we have been discussing is available for download from the Source Code area on the Apress website (`http://www.apress.com`). See the introduction of this book for instructions. The sample code for this chapter includes the icon files used in this example as well as some additional icons you can use to see how easy it is to configure icon extensions using this sample application.

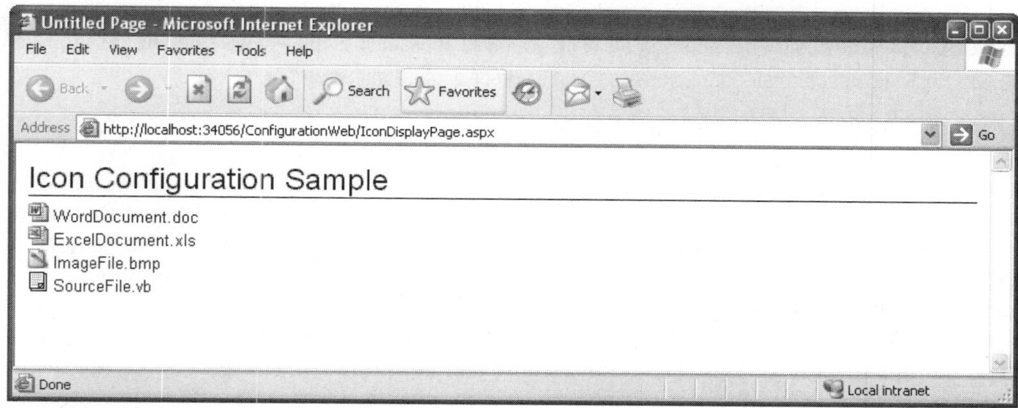

Figure 1-4. `IconDisplayPage.aspx` *displaying file list with associated icons*

Storing Configuration Settings in a Database

Although `Web.config` is a convenient place to store configuration data, it is not always the best place. It has some downsides that you will want to know about before you encounter them. Fortunately, you can opt to store configuration settings in other locations, like a database. In this section, you'll learn how to create a database table capable of storing configuration settings as name-value pairs, and how to write the code required to read and write those settings. Additionally, you'll learn how to store entire objects into the database using XML serialization.

The examples in this section assume that you have some form of SQL Server installed on your computer and that the database you are using is named `SampleCode`. See the introduction of this book for more information on how to obtain a copy of SQL Server Express, which Microsoft provides free for personal and developmental use.

When to Avoid the Web.config File

In a few scenarios, the `Web.config` file is not an ideal location for storing configuration settings. One of those scenarios is when you will be updating the configuration settings on a regular basis while users are accessing your application.

ASP.NET constantly monitors the `Web.config` file for changes. When the file is modified, ASP.NET reloads your application so the changes to `Web.config` can take effect. By default, ASP.NET uses in-process state management, meaning that the `Application` and `Session` objects are stored in the same memory space as your application. When your application reloads, that memory space is wiped out, so you will lose any data you have stored in `Session` objects or the `Application` object. Unless you account for this scenario, you could have scores of users complaining each time you change a setting in `Web.config`.

Caution Modifying the `Web.config` file while your web application is running will clear the `Session` and `Application` object of their data if you are using in-process state management.

Another scenario where `Web.config` is troublesome is when you want to save modified configuration settings back to `Web.config`. There is no built-in support for writing settings back to the `Web.config` file, so you must build your own tools to accomplish this task. If you developed your own tools, you would then have to modify the security permissions on the `Web.config` file because the default account that ASP.NET runs under does not have permission to write to the `Web.config` file. And, if you set up the permissions correctly, you would still have a problem with your application resetting every time you wrote to `Web.config` anyway. Configuration settings stored in a database avoid all these issues.

Lastly, you may want to avoid `Web.config` if you have an exorbitant number of configuration settings. XML is not the most readable of formats. Looking through 5 or 6 configuration settings in `Web.config` is relatively easy, but sifting through 50 or 100 becomes a bit more irksome. If you have a large number of configuration items, think about putting them in a database and building a configuration settings page.

Caution Database connection strings should be stored in the `<connectionStrings>` section of `Web.config`. You cannot access a database without a connection string so it would make little sense to store connection strings in a database. If you are worried about connection string security, read Chapter 12 to learn how to encrypt configuration sections.

Creating a Database Table to Store Configuration Settings

Before you can store data in a database, you need to create an appropriate table to store that data. Configuration settings are usually stored as name-value pairs, so your table needs to mimic this structure as shown in Table 1-2.

Table 1-2. *Configuration Settings Table Structure*

Column Name	Column Type	Description
`SettingName`	`varchar(50)`	Unique name of the configuration setting
`Value`	`text`	String representation of the setting's value

Open up a query window in SQL Express Manager and paste the following SQL statement into that window:

```
CREATE TABLE [dbo].[Settings] (
    [SettingName] [varchar] (50) NOT NULL ,
    [Value] [text] NOT NULL,
    CONSTRAINT [PK_Settings] PRIMARY KEY  CLUSTERED
    (
        [SettingName]
    )  ON [PRIMARY]
) ON [PRIMARY] TEXTIMAGE_ON [PRIMARY]

INSERT INTO [Settings](SettingName,Value)VALUES('MyString'    ,'Hello World');
INSERT INTO [Settings](SettingName,Value)VALUES('MyInteger'   ,'5');
INSERT INTO [Settings](SettingName,Value)VALUES('MyDateTime'  ,'8/20/1980');
INSERT INTO [Settings](SettingName,Value)VALUES('MyBoolean'   ,'True');
INSERT INTO [Settings](SettingName,Value)VALUES('MyPrimeList','');
```

This query adds a new table named `Settings` with two columns: `SettingName` and `Value`. `SettingName` stores a string value up to 50 characters. It is also the primary key for the table, so values in this column must be unique. `Value` is a text column capable of storing an obscenely long string, which will come in handy when we discuss serializing objects into XML.

The last part of the SQL statement has a series of inserts that adds a couple of setting names and values to your newly created table.

■ **Tip** If you have a large number of configuration settings in your database, it's always a good idea to add a description column to your settings table. It allows you to comment your configuration settings so you know what each one does, which can be exceptionally helpful if you haven't dealt with the application in a long time.

Avoiding SQL Injection Attacks

Before you get knee deep in SQL, let's discuss a common issue that many people accidentally overlook, usually with frustrating or devastating consequences, depending on the situation. Strings in SQL are represented as text surrounded by single quotes. So, you may see a SQL statement like this:

```
UPDATE [Customer] SET [LastName]='Smith' WHERE [ID]=50;
```

An issue arises when you want to use a string in SQL that contains a single quote, because it terminates your string prematurely. For example, say you are dealing with a last name like O'Reilly:

```
UPDATE [Customer] SET [LastName]='O'Reilly' WHERE [ID]=50;
--THIS IS AN INVALID SQL STATEMENT
```

This SQL statement never runs because the SQL parser sees the string `'O'` and fails because no keyword name `Reilly` exists. Furthermore, there is an unterminated string `' WHERE [ID]=50` at the end of the statement, adding insult to injury.

Unfortunately, grief is not the only thing you have to worry about it when it comes to single quotes. Malicious users can actually use single quotes to gain access to poorly designed login systems or even destroy data. It's known as a SQL injection attack, and it involves using single quotes and the comment character (--) to inject malicious SQL code into a statement.

Assume you use the following SQL statement to check a user's name and login before granting them access to your application:

```
SELECT * FROM [Users] WHERE [UserName]='user' AND PASSWORD='Pwd';
```

Now, let's see what happens if a malicious enters a valid username with a single quote and a comment character behind it (for example, `user'--`):

```
SELECT * FROM [Users] WHERE [UserName]='user'--' AND PASSWORD='Pwd';
```

Notice that the username string is terminated "prematurely," but the rest of the line is commented out (avoiding syntax errors with the nonterminated string), so the SQL statement remains valid but lacks the password validation. And, it gets worse. If a really malicious user wants to attack your system, he could use a login name like `user'; DELETE FROM [Users]; --`. This turns your seemingly innocuous login statement into this:

```
SELECT * FROM [Users] WHERE [UserName]='user';
DELETE FROM [Users];
--' AND PASSWORD='Pwd';
```

Now you have a real problem because your entire user table is erased and an evil user is logged in to your application. Luckily, there is an easy way to avoid these issues: use parameterized queries instead of building SQL statements manually. Parameterized queries use parameters as placeholders for values you want to use in the SQL Statement. Before you execute the SQL statement, you add parameters to the command object so the SQL statement knows which values you want to use for the parameters. Following is an example of how to use a parameterized query:

```
Dim SQL As String = "SELECT * FROM [Table] " & _
    "WHERE [SomeParam]=@MyParam1 AND [SomeOtherParam]=@MyParam2;"
Dim dbConn As New SqlConnection(Config.MyConnectionString)
Dim dbCmd As New SqlCommand(SQL, dbConn)

'Setup the SettingName Parameters
dbCmd.Parameters.Add("@MyParam1", Data.SqlDbType.VarChar).Value = "Value1"
dbCmd.Parameters.Add("@MyParam2", Data.SqlDbType.Int).Value = 5
```

You need to be aware of a couple of things when using parameterized queries. First off, you do not need to put quotes around the parameter in the SQL statement. Notice that `@SettingName` is not surrounded by quotes even though it is a string (varchar) value. The command object automatically determines the appropriate quotation marks required for the SQL statement based on the type of the parameter, which you specify when you create the parameter. The command object also escapes any single quotes contained in the parameter value, which is why parameterized queries are not as prone to SQL injection attacks.

Note To escape a single quote in SQL, you prefix it with another single quote. For example, 'O''Reily' is a valid string value in SQL.

Second, each parameter you define in the SQL statement must have a corresponding SqlParameter object in the Parameters collection of the SqlCommand object. You use the Add function to add parameters to the Parameters collection. The Add function allows you to add a parameter either by passing in a parameter object that you have already created and initialized, or by specifying the values for the parameter name and parameter type. In the example, I use the latter option because it is more succinct. Although it would make things even more succinct, you cannot pass the parameter's value into the Add method. Instead, you must set the parameter's value after the parameter is added to the Parameters collection. Fortunately, the Add method returns a reference to the parameter object it adds, so you can set the value on the same line. In the example, the bolded lines show the calls to the Add method, which returns the added parameter object. The nonbolded part sets the value property of the returned parameter. It is like having two calls on the same line. You should familiarize yourself with this technique because it is used fairly often with parameterized queries.

Finally, parameter names and the order in which they are added to the Parameters collection must match the parameter names and order in which they appear in the SQL statement. Failure to do so results in a runtime error.

Creating the DataConfig Class

All the shared properties that expose your configuration settings and the functions to help read and write those settings to the database are in a class named DataConfig. Right-click on the App_Code folder of the ConfigurationWeb sample project, and select **Add New Item**. Select **Class** as the template, and name the new class DataConfig.vb. Click the **Add** button, and Visual Studio adds the file to the App_Code folder. After creating the file, make sure to add the following Imports statement so you can access the SQL Server data objects without having to fully qualify them:

```
Imports System.Data.SqlClient
```

Reading Configuration Values from the Database

The following function accepts a string representing the name of a name-value pair and returns the value associated with that name from the database:

```
'***************************************************************************
Private Shared Function ReadValueFromDatabase(ByVal Name As String) As String

    Try
        Dim SQL As String = "SELECT [Value] FROM [Settings] " & _
                            "WHERE [SettingName]=@SettingName;"
        Dim dbConn As New SqlConnection(Config.MyConnectionString)
        Dim dbCmd As New SqlCommand(SQL, dbConn)
```

```
        'Set up the SettingName Parameters
        dbCmd.Parameters.Add("@SettingName", _
          Data.SqlDbType.VarChar).Value = SettingName

        dbConn.Open()
        ReadValueFromDatabase = CStr(dbCmd.ExecuteScalar())
        dbConn.Close()

    Catch ex As Exception
        Return String.Empty
    End Try

End Function
```

First, let's discuss the objects used in this function. SQL is a string variable representing the parameterized SQL statement that retrieves the value associated with the name passed into the function. The dbConn variable is a SqlConnection object used to connect to the database where your Settings table is located. Notice that the connection string used to initialize dbConn comes right from the Config class you implemented earlier, so make sure the connection string in your Web.config file has the appropriate connection information. Finally, the dbCmd is a SqlCommand object that you use to set up parameters and execute the SQL statement you defined earlier.

After the variables are defined, the code in the function is straightforward. First, the code sets up the @SettingsName parameter name, type, and value for the dbCmd object using the tactics described earlier. Then it opens the database and executes the statement using the ExecuteScalar function of the dbCmd object. ExecuteScalar returns a single value from the database as an Object that must be cast into its target type. In this case, it is a string containing the value of the setting name passed into the function. The result of ExecuteScalar is assigned to the name of the function, indicating that it is to be returned when the function exits. After that, the code closes the database, the function terminates, and the value is returned. If an error occurs at all during this process, an empty string is returned as a default value. With this function, reading a setting from the database can be accomplished using the following statement:

```
Dim MyString as String = ReadValueFromDatabase("MyString")
Dim MyInteger as Integer CInt(ReadValueFromDatabase("MyInteger")
```

Note that if ReadValueFromDatabase("MyInteger") returns an empty or nonnumerical string, then an exception will be thrown.

Writing Configuration Values to the Database

The write function is very similar to the read function, but you are updating a value instead of retrieving it:

```
'***************************************************************************
Public Shared Function WriteValueToDatabase(ByVal Name As String, _
  ByVal Value As String) As Boolean

    Try
        Dim SQL As String = "UPDATE [Settings] SET [Value]=@Value " & _
```

```
                        "WHERE [SettingName]=@SettingName;"
        Dim dbConn As New SqlConnection(Config.MyConnectionString)
        Dim dbCmd As New SqlCommand(SQL, dbConn)

        'Setup the Value and SettingName parameters
        dbCmd.Parameters.Add("@Value", Data.SqlDbType.VarChar).Value = Value
        dbCmd.Parameters.Add("@SettingName", _
          Data.SqlDbType.VarChar).Value = SettingName

        dbConn.Open()
        WriteValueToDatabase = (dbCmd.ExecuteNonQuery() > 0)
        dbConn.Close()

    Catch ex As Exception
        Return False
    End Try

End Function
```

The WriteValueToDatabase function takes two parameters: the Name of the setting and the Value. It uses the function parameters to set the parameter values for the SQL statement, similarly to what was done in the ReadValueFromDatabase function. Notice that the SQL only contains an UPDATE statement. This method assumes that the configuration setting already exists in the database. It then opens a connection to the database, and executes the SQL statement using the ExecuteNonQuery function of the dbCmd object. ExecuteNonQuery returns an Integer indicating the number of items that were updated, so (dbCmd.ExecuteNonQuery() > 0) evaluates to True if an item was updated or False if nothing was updated. This value is then assigned to the name of the function so it will be returned when the function exists. The database is then closed. If an error occurs at all during this process, False is returned.

With this function, writing a setting to the database can be accomplished using the following statement:

```
WriteValueToDatabase("MyString","Hello World")
WriteValueToDatabase("MyInteger",CStr(MyInteger))
```

Properties of the DataConfig Class

Now that you're armed with functions to read and write configuration settings to a database, you can create strongly typed properties for the DataConfig class with relative ease. Remember that caching is still extremely important because database calls can be just as expensive in terms of processing time as reading a file. Following is the list of private shared variables that you need in the DataConfig class to cache the settings:

```
'***************************************************************************
'Private Shared Variables used for Caching Settings
Private Shared _MyString As String
Private Shared _MyInteger As Integer
Private Shared _MyDateTime As DateTime
Private Shared _MyBoolean As Boolean
Private Shared _MyPrimeList As ArrayList
```

Now you can write the code for the MyString property:

```
'***************************************************************************
Public Shared Property MyString() As String
    Get
        If _MyString = Nothing Then _MyString = ReadValueFromDatabase("MyString")
        Return _MyString
    End Get
    Set(ByVal value As String)
        WriteValueToDatabase("MyString", value)
    End Set
End Property
```

Notice that it follows almost the exact same structure as the MyString property defined in the Config class, but instead of getting data from the AppSetting object, it is using the ReadValueFromDatabase function. Another notable difference is that you can change this configuration setting and save the changes back to the database, whereas the MyString property in the Config class is read-only.

Following are examples of properties involving casting values from strings into other data types. Note that if your configuration setting's value in the database is NULL or improperly formatted, then these functions will throw an exception. See the section titled "Error Handling in the Config Class" earlier in this chapter for suggestions regarding error handling.

```
'***************************************************************************
    Public Shared Property MyInteger() As Integer
        Get
            If _MyInteger = Nothing Then _
                _MyInteger = _
                  CInt(ReadValueFromDatabase("MyInteger"))
            Return _MyInteger
        End Get
        Set(ByVal value As Integer)
            WriteValueToDatabase("MyString", CStr(value))
        End Set
    End Property
    '***************************************************************************
    Public Shared Property MyDateTime() As Date
        Get
            If _MyDateTime = Nothing Then _
                _MyDateTime = _
                  CDate(ReadValueFromDatabase("MyDateTime"))
            Return _MyDateTime
        End Get
        Set(ByVal value As Date)
            WriteValueToDatabase("MyString", CStr(value))
        End Set
    End Property
```

```
'***************************************************************************
Public Shared Property MyBoolean() As Boolean
    Get
        If _MyBoolean = Nothing Then _
            _MyBoolean = _
              CBool(ReadValueFromDatabase("MyBoolean"))
        Return _MyBoolean
    End Get
    Set(ByVal value As Boolean)
        WriteValueToDatabase("MyString", CStr(value))
    End Set
End Property
```

Serializing and Deserializing Objects in the Database

Serialization is the process of taking an object that exists in-memory and converting that object into a format (usually binary data or XML) that can be stored out-of-memory in a file or a database. Deserialization is the process of taking that stored data and recreating the object in-memory.

Interestingly enough, the `Value` column in the table you created to store configuration settings can store large amounts of textual data, and the .NET Framework has tools that help serialize in-memory objects into XML. This means that you can serialize entire objects and store them as configuration settings in a database.

First, you need to create a generic function that can serialize an object into an XML representation. In this example, you will use the Simple Object Access Protocol (SOAP) XML formatter to handle the serialization details. Right-click on your web application icon in the Solution Explorer and select **Add Reference**. In the **.NET** tab, locate and select **System.Runtime.Serialization.Formatters.Soap.dll** from the list of components. Click the **OK** button and a reference to the assembly is added to your project. Then make sure you import the following namespaces at the top of the class file:

```
Imports System.IO
Imports System.Runtime.Serialization.Formatters.Soap
```

After you have the imported the SOAP formatter assembly and added the appropriate `Imports` statements, then add this function to the `DataConfig` class:

```
'***************************************************************************
Private Shared Function SerializeToXML(ByVal Obj As Object) As String
    Try
        Dim sf As New SoapFormatter()
        Dim ms As New MemoryStream
        sf.Serialize(ms, Obj)
        Dim ascEncoding As New System.Text.ASCIIEncoding()
        Return ascEncoding.GetString(ms.GetBuffer)
    Catch
        Return String.Empty
    End Try
End Function
```

The SerializeToXML function accepts a single object as a parameter. It then creates a SoapFormatter object, which is responsible for converting an object into an XML representation. The Serialize function of the SoapFormatter object accepts two parameters: the object that is to be converted and the stream to which the XML data is written. In this case, the stream is stored in memory and not in a file. The memory stream holds the XML as a giant byte array, so the ASCII encoding object converts that byte array into a string, which is then returned from the function. If any error occurs during this function, an empty string is returned.

Now that you can convert an object into XML, you need a way to convert it back. The Deserialize function takes care of this task:

```
'***************************************************************************
Private Shared Function DeserializeFromXML(ByVal XML As String) As Object
    Try
        Dim ascEncoding As New System.Text.ASCIIEncoding()
        Dim ms As New MemoryStream(ascEncoding.GetBytes(XML))
        Dim sf As New SoapFormatter
        Return sf.Deserialize(ms)
    Catch
        Return Nothing
    End Try
End Function
```

The Deserialize function accepts a string containing the XML representation of an object. It then converts that string into a byte array using the ASCIIEncoding object and creates a new memory stream from it. That memory stream is then passed into the Deserialize function of the SoapFormatter and the object represented by the XML is reconstructed and returned as an Object. You need to cast it to the appropriate type when you use this function, as shown in the following example. If an error occurs during processing, then Nothing is returned.

Armed with the ability to serialize and deserialize objects, you can now implement the MyPrimeList property, which serializes and deserializes an entire ArrayList to and from the database:

```
'***************************************************************************
Public Shared Property MyPrimeList() As ArrayList
    Get
        If _MyPrimeList Is Nothing Then
            Dim XML As String = ReadValueFromDatabase("MyPrimeList")
            If Not XML = String.Empty Then
                _MyPrimeList = CType(DeserializeFromXML(XML), ArrayList)
            End If
        End If
        If _MyPrimeList Is Nothing Then _MyPrimeList = New ArrayList()
        Return _MyPrimeList    End Get
    Set(ByVal value As ArrayList)
        _MyPrimeList = value
        SaveMyPrimeList()
    End Set
End Property
```

```
'***************************************************************************
Public Shared Sub SaveMyPrimeList()
    WriteValueToDatabase("MyPrimeList", SerializeToXML(_MyPrimeList))
End Sub
```

A bit more code is involved with serialization and deserialization because it is a bit more complicated. In this property, you first check to see if the value has already been cached. If not, the XML associated with the "MyPrimeList" setting is acquired from the database. If the XML is an empty string, then the property returns Nothing. Otherwise, the XML is deserialized, and the resulting object is cached. At this point, if the cached variable is still nothing, a new ArrayList is created and assigned to the cache. This ensures that you will have an object with which to work, even if your database does not contain any XML to create the object. Finally, the property returns the cache variable.

The Set portion of the property sets the MyPrimeList cache variable equal to the incoming value. It then calls SaveMyPrimeList, which is responsible for serializing the object to XML and then writing that XML back out to the database.

You may be wondering why there is a special function to save the MyPrimeList value to the database. Any time you change a property that is a native type (String, Integer, Date, and so on), then the code in the Set portion of the property executes. When you are working with objects, such as an ArrayList, the Set code only executes when an actual object assignment is made. Other changes to ArrayList objects occur at the object level, so the Set code is never called. Here's an example:

```
MyPrimeList = new ArrayList()  'This causes the Set code to fire.
MyPrimeList.Add(11)            'This causes the Get code to fire
```

In the first line, you are making an assignment and setting the property equal to a new ArrayList, so the Set portion of the property fires and MyPrimeList is saved. In the second line, however, you are actually using the Get portion of the property to acquire the ArrayList and, after you have it, calling the Add function on the object itself. It's a subtle distinction, but it means that changes made to the MyPrimeList itself will not save the object automatically. Thus, you need the auxiliary function to explicitly save the object after an update:

```
MyPrimeList.Add(11)          'Update the object
Config.SaveMyPrimeList()     'Explicitly Save MyPrimeList
```

This ensures that any values you update are immediately saved for future retrieval.

Summary

Configuration is an often-overlooked aspect of web application development. Many times, budgetary or time constraints force developers to sidestep proper configuration practices in the hope that it will somehow speed up the development time table. In reality, proper configuration practices such as using custom configuration sections and strongly typed configuration files may take a bit more time in the beginning, but you quickly make that time back up over the course of the development process.

In this chapter, you have learned about the new configuration tools available in ASP.NET 2.0 and how to use them to manage application settings, connection strings, users, roles, and the profile object. You have looked at guidelines to help you determine the best location to store configuration data and built a strongly typed configuration class. You have also seen how to create custom configuration settings for advanced configuration scenarios and how to read and write configuration settings to a database. In fact, you can even serialize and deserialize objects to and from XML for storage in that database. So, you should be well equipped for just about any configuration scenario that's thrown at you.

CHAPTER 2

Exception Management

Applications have errors. It's an inevitable consequence of the development process arising from our inability to account for every possible scenario in which something may go awry; the workflow application I recently helped develop for a large government organization was no exception. The application helped to coordinate proposals, bids, and sign-offs for projects occurring all across the country, with a user base consisting largely of upper-level management—not the type of people who enjoy dealing with errors that stop them from getting their jobs done.

One of the requirements for the project was to use a third-party, Java-based workflow management engine, which was slow, cumbersome, and prone to timeouts while waiting for database transactions to occur. This led to workflow documents being placed in invalid states, and users getting a nasty message when they tried to access their documents. To make matters worse, after an item was in an invalid state, it had to be reset by a system administrator, meaning that the user had to contact us to fix a problem.

Luckily, we had great exception management. Whenever a timeout occurred, our customer support rep was notified concerning which user experienced the error, and then the rep contacted the user immediately to head off any frustrations. On multiple occasions, people who experienced a problem were contacted in less than 30 seconds and were amazed with our responsiveness. Our clients never got a chance to complain about errors because they were dazzled by our ability to serve them. We also analyzed our error log to help pinpoint the cause of the problem, which turned out to be a database-locking issue.

Everyone's applications will have unexpected errors, but how you handle those unexpected errors and what you learn from them is what will ultimately set you apart.

This chapter covers techniques for managing exceptions that will allow you to see where they occur, when they occur, and which users are experiencing them. You'll learn how to analyze those errors so you can make your application less error prone, how to incorporate global error handling, and even how to leverage errors to manage customer perception and satisfaction.

Here is a breakdown of the chapter content:

- *Exception Basics:* A quick refresher on exceptions, exception handling, error propagation, and the nuances of the `Try Catch Finally` block.

- *Global Error Handling:* Discusses how to use custom error pages and global error pages as a catchall for exceptions that may arise.

- *Logging Exceptions for Analysis:* Demonstrates how to log application exceptions as they occur in your application.

Exception Management Basics

Before we get into a more advanced discussion about exception management, you need to have a solid understanding of exception-management basics. What are exceptions? What are their benefits and drawbacks? How can they be handled accordingly? After you have a grasp of these concepts, it will be easier to see how you can use proper exception-management techniques to manage customer perception and fortify your code.

■ **Note** Many of the examples shown in the "Exception Management Basics" section are located in the `ExceptionBasics.vb` file in the sample project for Chapter 2 in the Source Code area of the Apress website (http://www.apress.com). You can find the more advanced examples by running the application and selecting the appropriate sample from the menu on the left side of the page.

What Are Exceptions?

In the .NET Framework, an *exception* is both a concept and an object. Conceptually, an exception arises when your application attempts to complete an operation, but the operation fails for one reason or another. Or more simply put, an error occurs. Instead of continuing as though the error never occurred, the .NET Framework stops the execution of the current code block and reports the error by throwing an exception.

When an exception is thrown, an exception object is created and populated with information about the exception and why it occurred. This object is useful for taking corrective actions, informing the user of a problem, or for debugging purposes.

All exceptions derive from the same base class, `System.Exception`, so they share a number of common properties. The three most important are the `Message` property, which describes the exception and may point you to a resolution, the `StackTrace`, which pinpoints the exact execution point where the exception occurred, and the `InnerException` property, which helps chain multiple exceptions together. Most exception objects have additional properties that can help pinpoint specifics about why an error occurred. For instance, the `FileNotFound➥Exception` has a `FileName` property to identify the file that could not be found, and the `SqlException` has properties to help identify the line number on which a T-SQL statement failed and the database server on which the error occurred.

To see a listing of all the exceptions in the .NET Framework, you can select **Debug ➤ Exceptions**. This displays the Exceptions window. Expand the **Common Language Runtime Exceptions** node to see a list of namespaces in the .NET Framework. You can then expand a namespace to see which exceptions reside in the namespace. This window also allows you to tell the debugger to break when a specific type of exception occurs, or when it is unhandled, by checking the appropriate check box next to the exception name.

Handling Exceptions with the Try Catch Statement

When your application throws an exception, your code can handle the exception in a `Try Catch Finally` block. The `Try` section surrounds a block of code that could produce an exception and, if that code produces an exception, the runtime jumps down into the `Catch` section to handle the exception accordingly. Look at the following function in Listing 2-1 to see an example of using a `Try Catch` block (line numbers are for reference only).

Listing 2-1. `Try Catch` *Statement Example #1*

```
01: '**************************************************************************
02: Public Function IntegerDivide(ByVal N As Long, ByVal D As Long) As Long
03:     Try
04:         Dim ReturnValue As Long
05:         ReturnValue = (N \ D)
06:         Return ReturnValue
07:     Catch ex As Exception
08:         Return 0
09:     End Try
10: End Function
```

This function takes a numerator (`N`) and a denominator (`D`), and returns the result of an integer division operation. Normally, the code creates a temporary variable, stores the result of the `(N \ D)` operation in that temporary variable, and returns the temporary variable as the result of the function. However, it's possible that someone could errantly pass the value 0 in for `D`, which results in a `System.DivideByZeroException` being thrown from line 5. If this exception is thrown, execution flow skips the rest of the code in the `Try` block and immediately jumps down into the `Catch` block on line 7. The `Catch` block is where you can remedy the exception, if possible. The remedy used in this function is to return `0` if an exception occurs.

■ **Caution** Code in your `Catch` statements can throw errors as well, and these are not automatically caught. So, if you are running code in your `Catch` statement that could throw an error, remember to surround it in a `Try Catch` statement as well.

You should place `Try Catch` statements around code that has a decent chance of failing, but not around code that will normally be safe. For instance, you would not want to write code that looks like Listing 2-2.

Listing 2-2. *Code That Will Not Break*

```
'**************************************************************************
Public Shared Function AddTwoNumbers(ByVal x As Long, ByVal y As Long) As Long
    Try
        Return x + y
    Catch ex As Exception
        Return 0
    End Try
End Function
```

The chances of an add operation failing are virtually nonexistent, so placing a `Try Catch` block in this function is a waste of your time. Save the `Try Catch` block for situations where you are accessing external resources or other scenarios where an exception is more likely.

Another area where you need to devote some thought when creating a `Try Catch` block is exception resolution. There are really two types of exception resolution, namely *substitution* and *notification*.

Resolution via substitution involves implementing a fall-back that can be used when an error occurs. For instance, if you have a function that generates a custom greeting for your customers by acquiring their name from the dataset, you could always default to "Dear Customer" if an error occurs. The major thing you need to watch out for when implementing a default value is that your default value makes sense and is not misleading. For instance, if you are building a function that returns the total number of users in your database, you do not want to default to 4 or 73 when an error occurs. Even a default of 0 could be misleading, so you may want to use -1 to denote that an error occurred.

Exception resolution via notification is used when an exception cannot be resolved by a default value. For instance, if you are in the middle of a purchase transaction and something fails, what are you going to do? Naturally, you can attempt the transaction again to see if it works the second time around, but at some point you must admit defeat and just let the user know that an error occurred. The objective of notification is to keep the user from seeing a confusing or intimidating error. Usually it involves redirecting the user to an error page or returning them to the page from which they originated and displaying a message describing the issue. Do not allow the user to continue to the next page because they may just cause more errors and become more frustrated with your application.

You should also know that letting an exception occur is a valid option, especially when you are building reusable components. This allows the error to propagate up the call stack so that you have the flexibility to make a decision about how to handle the exception appropriately in different circumstances.

■ **Note** Handling an exception is an expensive operation, so avoid exceptions where possible. Understand, however, that you only incur an expensive performance hit when your application actually handles an exception, not simply because a `Try Catch Finally` block appears in your code. As such, you can feel free to use the `Try Catch Finally` block where appropriate without fear that the block itself is causing any performance problems.

Using Multiple Catch Statements

In a `Try Catch` statement, you can actually have multiple `Catch` statements to help catch specific errors. For instance, take a look at the function in Listing 2-3.

Listing 2-3. *Multiple Catch Statements*

```
'*************************************************************************
Public Shared Function ReadFile(ByVal FileAndPath As String, _
                                ByRef ErrorInfo As String) As String

        Try
            Dim SR As New System.IO.StreamReader(FileAndPath)
            Dim FileContent As String = SR.ReadToEnd()
            SR.Close()
            Return FileContent

        Catch dirEx As System.IO.DirectoryNotFoundException
            ErrorInfo = "The directory was not found"
            Return String.Empty

        Catch fileEx As System.IO.FileNotFoundException
            ErrorInfo = "The file was not found"
            Return String.Empty

        Catch ioEx As System.IO.IOException
            ErrorInfo = "There was an IO Exception: " & ioEx.Message
            Return String.Empty

        Catch ex As Exception
            ErrorInfo = "There was an Exception: " & ex.Message
            Return String.Empty

        End Try
End Function
```

ReadFile accepts two parameters. The first is a path to a text file, and the second is a by reference variable used to return error information in the event an exception occurs. Normally, ReadFile creates a StreamReader object using the FileAndPath parameter, reads the file into a temporary variable, closes the stream, and returns the temporary variable as the result of the function. However, if the FileAndPath parameter does not point to a valid file name, an exception occurs when creating the StreamReader.

The exact exception that occurs depends on what was wrong with the file name. If the .NET Framework cannot find the directory specified in the FileAndPath parameter, then a System.IO.DirectoryNotFoundException occurs. If the path is found, but the file is not, then a System.IO.FileNotFoundException occurs. And if the length of the FileAndPath parameter is too long, then a System.IO.PathTooLongException occurs.

Notice that multiple Catch statements are used in the Try Catch block. The first catches the DirectoryNotFoundException and the next catches the FileNotFoundException, but the third one catches an IOException. So, what happens when the PathTooLongException is thrown? Well, it all comes down to inheritance. When an exception is thrown, the .NET runtime looks through each Catch statement looking for a match. A match obviously occurs when the exception type specified in the Catch statement is an exact match with the thrown exception type, but a match also occurs when the exception type specified in the Catch statement is a parent type of the thrown exception. See Figure 2-1 to see the inheritance chain for the System.IO.PathTooLongException.

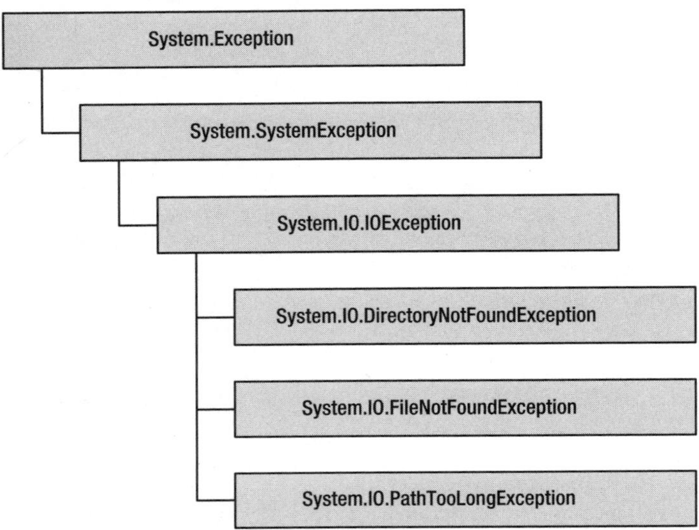

Figure 2-1. *Exception inheritance*

Notice that the PathTooLongException derives from System.IO.IOException. As such, when the runtime hits the Catch statement for System.IO.IOException, it catches the PathTooLongException. Because the runtime checks for exact types as well as parent types when catching exceptions, you must be careful in your ordering of Catch statements. Listing 2-4 shows a bad example of how to set up multiple Catch statements.

Listing 2-4. *Bad* Catch *Statements Ordering*

```
'***************************************************************************
Public Shared Sub BadCatchExample()
    Try
        Throw New System.IO.IOException()
    Catch ex As Exception
        'Run Exception Handling
    Catch ioEx As System.IO.IOException
        'Run IOException Handling
    End Try
End Sub
```

In the Try block, a System.IO.IOException is purposely thrown. If you refer to Figure 2-1, you'll see that the System.IO.IOException class derives from the System.Exception class, so the first Catch statement always handles the exception. The second Catch statement is never reached.

■ Caution When you specify multiple `Catch` statements in a `Try Catch` block, you have to place exceptions that are deeper in the inheritance hierarchy first, or else the parent exceptions will be picked up first. For instance, don't place `System.Exception` before other exception types because all exceptions derive from `System.Exception`.

Catching Specific Errors Using the When Clause

Another tactic for catching specific errors is to use the `When` clause. This is especially useful when an exception type does not clarify the actual error. For example, the `PathTooLong➥ Exception` is fairly specific about what the problem is; however, the only exception type in the `System.Data.SqlClient` namespace is `SqlException`. So, if the username or password in your connection string is wrong, you get a `SqlException`; if you attempt to access a table that does not exist, then you get a `SqlException`; and if your SQL syntax is invalid, you get a `SqlException`. Not overly helpful if you are trying to resolve a specific issue.

That's where the `When` clause of the `Catch` statement comes in handy. You can use the `When` clause to qualify a `Catch` statement so it only executes if the type specified in the `Catch` is a match, and the `When` clause is satisfied. Let's look at an example in Listing 2-5 to better understand this concept.

Listing 2-5. *Catching Exceptions with the* `When` *Clause*

```
'***************************************************************************
Public Shared Sub WhenExample(ByRef ErrorMsg As String)
    Try
        Dim dbConn As New SqlConnection(Config.MyConnectionString)
        Dim SQL As String = "SELECT * FROM [settings]"
        Dim dbCmd As New System.Data.SqlClient.SqlCommand(SQL, dbConn)
        Dim dbDr As SqlDataReader

        dbConn.Open()
        dbDr = dbCmd.ExecuteReader()
        dbConn.Close()

    Catch ex As SqlException When InStr(ex.Message, "The ConnectionString ") > 0
        ErrorMsg = "You did not initialize the connection string."

    Catch ex As SqlException When InStr(ex.Message, "Login failed") > 0
        ErrorMsg = "Your login information was invalid."
```

```
    Catch ex As SqlException When InStr(ex.Message, "Invalid object") > 0
        ErrorMsg = "You referenced a non-existant table, view,  etc."

    Catch ex As SqlException When InStr(ex.Message, "Invalid column") > 0
        ErrorMsg = "You referenced a non-existant column."

    Catch ex As Exception
        ErrorMsg = "An exception occurred: " & ex.Message

    End Try

End Sub
```

This is an example of a fairly routine data access procedure that opens a database connection and executes a SQL statement. The interesting part occurs when an exception is thrown. Look at the end of the procedure and you'll notice five `Catch` statements in the `f` block. The first four use the `When` clause to check for specific text within the `Message` property of the `SqlException` object. If the text is found, then the `Catch` statement catches the error and should execute the appropriate code to either identify the error accordingly or attempt to correct it. In this case, the code is just identifying the error in plain English. If the text is not found, the .NET runtime moves on to the next `Catch` statement and tries to make another match. If no match can be made using the `When` statements, then the final `Catch` statement catches any other exception that was thrown.

Also know that you are not limited to just using the `Message` property in a `When` clause; you can use any valid `Boolean` statement and any property that appears in the object type you are catching.

■ **Note** You will most likely not use the `When` clause of the `Catch` statement very often, but it can be very useful in certain situations, so it helps to know it exists.

Using the Finally Keyword

The last aspect of the `Try Catch` block is the `Finally` keyword. You can place code in the `Finally` section that needs to be executed regardless of whether an error occurred, making it a perfect place to close connections, close files, and perform cleanup operations. Code placed in the `Finally` section always executes, even if you try to exit the function using the `Return` or `Exit` statement inside the `Try` section. Listing 2-6 shows the `Finally` keyword and how it can be used to close down a database connection after a `Return` statement has been issued:

Listing 2-6. *Finally Example*

```
'***************************************************************************
Public Shared Function FinallyExample() As Object

    Dim dbConn As SqlConnection = Nothing

    Try
        Dim SQL As String = "SELECT Count(*) FROM [settings];"
        Dim dbCmd As SqlCommand = Nothing
        dbConn = New SqlConnection(Config.MyConnectionString)
        dbCmd = New System.Data.SqlClient.SqlCommand(SQL, dbConn)
        dbConn.Open()
        Return dbCmd.ExecuteScalar()
    Catch ex As Exception
        Return 0
    Finally
        'The following line will ALWAYS be executed.
        If Not dbConn Is Nothing Then dbConn.Close()
    End Try

End Function
```

When the `ExecuteScalar` function returns its value, execution immediately jumps down to the `Finally` section and ensures that the database is closed. This is helpful when you want to use the `Return` statement directly instead of returning a temporary variable or the function name to store the result of the database action.

One nuisance with the `Try Catch Finally` block is scoping. Variables declared inside the `Try` section are only accessible from within the `Try` section, so any variables that you need to access in more than one section of the `Try Catch Finally` block need to be declared outside of the `Try Catch Finally` block, like the `dbConn` variable in Listing 2-6. The other variable declarations appear inside the `Try` section and therefore limit the scope of those variables to the `Try` section because they are not used in any other sections.

Throwing Exceptions

Sometimes, you need to throw an exception from your code to indicate that something is wrong. This can be accomplished using the `Throw` keyword. Listing 2-7 is an example of a function that will return the object type name. If the `obj` parameter is `Nothing`, however, the function throws an `ArgumentNullException`.

Listing 2-7. *Throwing an Exception*

```
'***************************************************************************
Public Shared Function GetObjectName(ByVal obj As Object) As String
    If obj Is Nothing Then _
        Throw New ArgumentNullException("The obj parameter cannot be null.")
    Return obj.GetType.ToString()
End Function
```

Exception objects should have a constructor that allows you to specify a message to describe the problem in some detail. Helpful messages usually identify the problem in such a way that a resolution for the issues is inherently suggested. In Listing 2-7, for instance, the message `"The obj parameter cannot be null."` both identifies the issue and implicitly presents a solution for remedying it—make sure the `obj` parameter is not `Nothing`.

■Tip Your exception messages should include as much detail as possible to help you track down a problem when it occurs. Debugging becomes much simpler when you have helpful messages to identify the reason and location an error occurred.

At times, you might want to catch an exception and then rethrow it. The most common situation where this occurs is when you are logging errors (see Listing 2-8).

Listing 2-8. *Logging and Rethrowing*

```
'***************************************************************************
Public Shared Sub ThrowLogAndReThrow()
    Try
        Throw New Exception("Force an exception")
    Catch ex As Exception
        'Place logging code here...
        Throw
    End Try
End Sub
```

In the `Catch` statement, you place your logging code first, and then you call the `Throw` statement without any parameters to rethrow the exception that was caught. You can also rethrow the exception by using `Throw ex`, but doing so changes the stack trace location to point at the line where you rethrew the exception instead of the line where the exception originally occurred. As such, you should use the `Throw` keyword by itself to maintain the original exception location unless you have a compelling reason to do otherwise.

Creating Custom Exception Classes

You may find that the exceptions built in to the .NET Framework to not adequately describe a particular exception in your application or do not expose certain custom properties that may be required to handle an exception accordingly. If that is the case, then you can create your own custom exception classes. You just need to create a class that inherits from the `System.Exception` class or another exception class that you want to extend. A quick implementation of a custom exception class is shown in Listing 2-9.

Listing 2-9. *Custom Exception Class*

```
'***************************************************************************
Public Class NegativeNumberException
    Inherits System.Exception

        Sub New(ByVal message As String)
            MyBase.New(message)
        End Sub

        Sub New(ByVal message As String, ByVal innerException As Exception)
            MyBase.New(message, innerException)
        End Sub

End Class
```

The NegativeNumberException class inherits its base functionality from the System.Exception class and exposes two different constructors. The first constructor allows you to create a new NegativeNumberException object without an inner exception, and the second constructor allows you to create one with an inner exception. Both of these constructors simply rely on the base constructor to actually populate the object with message and inner exception information. You can use this class in your code just like any other exception (see Listing 2-10).

Listing 2-10. *Using a Custom Exception*

```
'***************************************************************************
Public Shared Function CalculateSalary(ByVal Rate As Double, _
                                       ByVal Hours As Double) As Double

    If Rate < 0 Then Throw New NegativeNumberException("Rate is negative")
    If Hours < 0 Then Throw New NegativeNumberException("Hours is negative")
    Return Rate * Hours

End Function
```

NegativeNumberException is a bit more descriptive than a generic exception class such as System.ArithmeticException. Aside from a more descriptive name, your exception class can also have properties to help you better communicate information about the error. Listing 2-11 provides a more advanced example of the NegativeNumberException.

Listing 2-11. *Custom Exception Class with Properties*

```
'*************************************************************************
Public Class NegativeNumberException
    Inherits System.Exception

    Public NegativeNumber As Double
    Public Parameter As String

    Public Sub New(ByVal Parameter As String, ByVal NegativeNumber As Double)
        Me.NegativeNumber = NegativeNumber
        Me.Parameter = Parameter
    End Sub

    Public Overrides ReadOnly Property Message() As String
        Get
            Return String.Format("Negative Number ({0} specified for {1}", _
                                 NegativeNumber, Parameter)
        End Get
    End Property

End Class

'*************************************************************************
Public Shared Function CalculateSalary(ByVal Rate As Double, _
                                       ByVal Hours As Double) As Double

    If Rate < 0 Then Throw New NegativeNumberException("Rate", Rate)
    If Hours < 0 Then Throw New NegativeNumberException("Hours", Hours)
    Return Rate * Hours

End Function
```

This exception class has two fields that allow you to specify the parameter name and the actual value of the negative number. This information can then be used in the `Catch` statement that ultimately handles the exception to perform different tasks as shown in Listing 2-12.

Listing 2-12. *Using Custom Exception Properties in the Catch*

```
'*************************************************************************
    Public Function GetSalary() As String
        Try
            Return "Your salary is " & CalculateSalary(-100, 10).ToString()
        Catch ex As NegativeNumberException
            Select Case ex.Parameter
                Case "Rate"
                    Return "You may want to check your rates!"
                Case "Hours"
```

```
                Return "You may want to check your hours!"
            End Select
        End Try
End Sub
```

Inner Exceptions and Exception Wrapping

Each exception object has an `InnerException` property that can reference another exception object. This is useful for chaining related exceptions together or for wrapping a nondescript or confusing exception object in another more descriptive exception object. The `System.Web.Mail.SmtpMail.SendMail` function, although marked obsolete in ASP.NET 2.0, provides a great example of both exception chaining and exception wrapping when used improperly. When calling the function, you're supposed to pass in a `from` address, a `to` address, a `subject`, and a `message`. If you fail to pass in a `to` or `from` address, then the function will throw an exception:

```
'This is invalid, so an exception is thrown.
System.Web.Mail.SmtpMail.Send("", "", "", "")
```

■Note `System.Web.Mail` has been marked as obsolete in ASP.NET 2.0 and is used here only for demonstration purposes. You should use the objects in the `System.Net.Mail` namespace to send email.

Figure 2-2 shows the exception chain generated when the previous line of code is executed. Take note of the exception types and messages for each exception.

The `Send` function uses a COM (Component Object Model) object to send the mail message, so a `System.Runtime.InteropServices.COMException` is thrown if the operation fails. The `COMException` actually has useful information about the problem that can be helpful in resolving the issue, but it then causes a `System.Reflection.TargetInvocationException` to be thrown. This exception is more generic and less helpful than the information in the `COMException`, so if it was all you had to go by then you would be completely in the dark. Fortunately, ASP.NET places the `COMException` in the `InnerException` property of the `TargetInvocationException`, so you can still access it and its useful information. Lastly, `TargetInvocationException` is wrapped by a `System.Web.HttpException`, and the helpful message from the `COMException` is restored so you don't have to dig into the `InnerException` properties to find out the real cause of the problem.

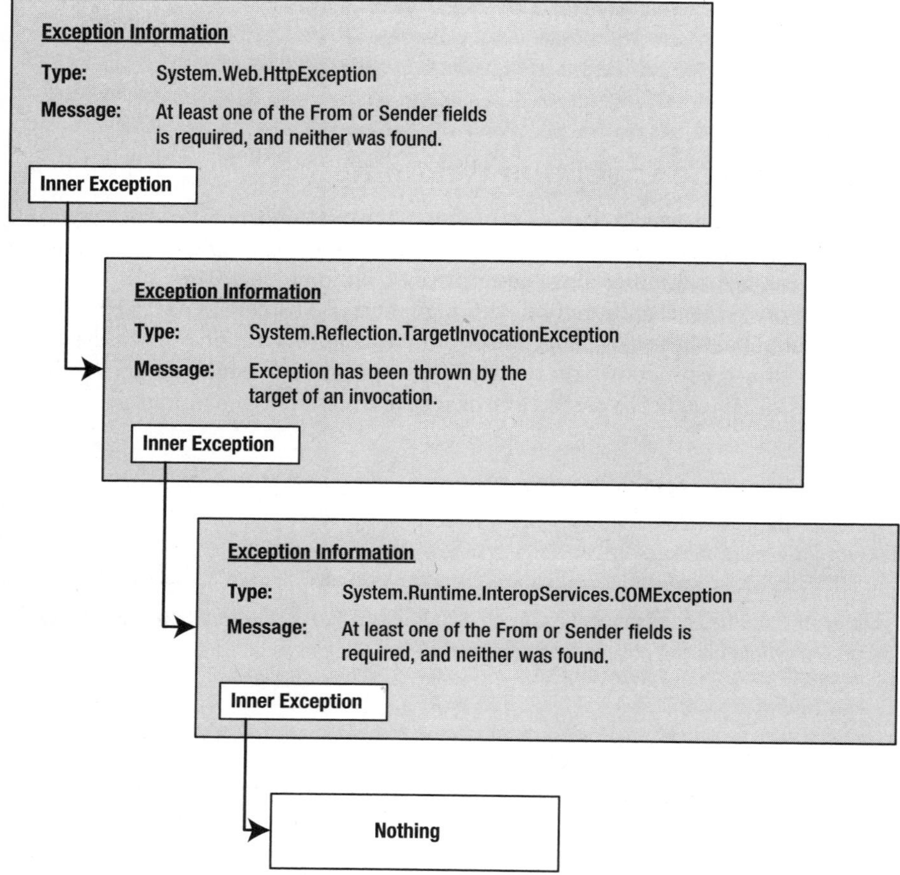

Figure 2-2. *Resulting exception chain for an SMTP mailing error*

You can implement the same type of functionality in your applications. Listing 2-13 is a function that demonstrates how to wrap an exception in a more detailed and informative exception.

Listing 2-13. *Wrapping an Exception*

```
'**************************************************************************
Public Function AddNumbersInStringArray(ByVal Numbers() As String) As Long
    Try

        Dim Total As Long = 0
        For Each s As String In Numbers
            Dim l As Long = CLng(s)
            Total += l
        Next
```

```
    Catch ex As Exception

        Dim Message As String = "There was an invliad number in the " & _
                                "Numbers array.  All of the values " & _
                                "in the Numbers array must be string " & _
                                "representations of numerical values."

        'Wrap orig. message in a new exception with a detailed message
        'ex (the original exception) will become the inner exception of
        'the ArgumentException.
        Throw New ArgumentException(Message, ex)

    End Try

End Function
```

This function accepts a string array that it expects to contain string representations of numeric values ("1", "2", "3", and so on). If a nonnumeric string is present in the array, for instance the value "five" instead of a "5", then an exception is thrown. Specifically, it causes a System.InvalidCastException to be thrown with a message stating Conversion from string "five" to type 'Long' is not valid.

The System.InvalidCastException is caught by the Catch statement in the example. A message is then constructed that better describes the situation and why it is occurring. The message and the original exception object are passed into the constructor for a new ArgumentException object, which is then thrown. The exception then propagates up the call stack until it is handled.

If you diligently use wrapping to identify where and why an exception occurred, the exception chain you end up with when you are debugging will be helpful in quickly and accurately addressing problems.

Error Propagation

When an exception is thrown, the current code block stops executing and the appropriate exception object is instantiated. If the code that produced the exception is contained directly in a Try Catch block, then the .NET runtime checks to see if a Catch block matches the error being thrown. If there is no Try Catch block or a Catch statement does not match, then the exception is passed up the call stack to the calling method. Then the process of checking for the existence of a Try Catch block and an appropriate Catch statement is played out again.

Listing 2-14 is a demonstration of error propagation and how an exception is passed up the execution chain until it is handled.

Listing 2-14. *Error Propogation Example*

```
'***************************************************************************
    Public Function A() As String
        Try
            Return "Diamonds" & B()
        Catch ex As Exception
            Return ex.Message & " (and handled in the A Function)"
        End Try
    End Function

    '***************************************************************************
    Public Function B() As String
        Return "are " & C()
    End Function

    '***************************************************************************
    Public Function C() As String
        Throw New Exception("Exception Thrown from the C Function")
        Return "forever."
    End Function
```

When function A is called, it begins to execute. Before it's done processing, it needs to call function B. When this occurs, execution of function A is put on hold while function B executes. Function B, in turn, needs to call function C, so function B is put on hold while function C executes. During the execution of function C, however, an error is thrown.

Because function C contains no Try Catch block, the exception is propagated back to function B. Function B does not have a Try Catch block either, so the exception is passed back to function A. Luckily, function A has a Try Catch block and can handle the exception. Function A will then use the Exception object from function C to return a message defining the exception.

So, you might ask, what happens if an error continues to propagate and never encounters a Try Catch block that can handle it? Well, the exception continues to make its way up the call stack until it reaches the ASP.NET runtime, at which point the runtime generates an exception page similar to the one shown in Figure 2-3 to display the exception name, message, and stack trace information.

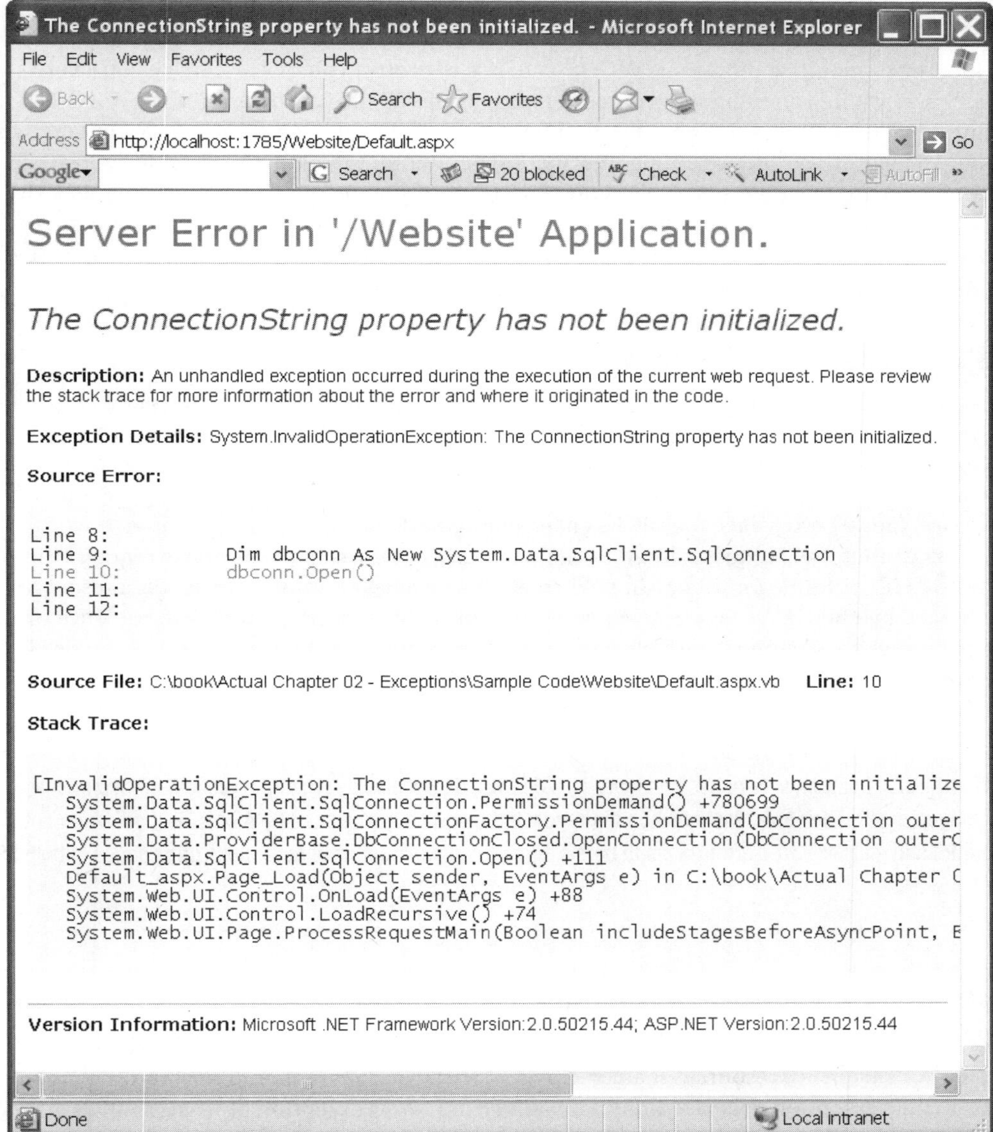

Figure 2-3. *Unhandled exception detail page generated by the ASP.NET runtime*

Of course, you want to keep your users from experiencing such an unpleasant dump of exception information when using your application. We'll discuss how to avoid all this in the next section.

Global Error Handling

Global error handling represents your last chance to protect your users from seeing a very nasty error. When an unhandled exception propagates all the way back up to the ASP.NET runtime, ASP.NET uses settings in the configuration file to either generate a page containing a dump of stack trace and exception information or attempt to redirect the user to a more user-friendly error page. In terms of client perception management, you *don't* want your users to see the ASP.NET exception page because they will have no doubt that your application failed to handle the error appropriately. If you redirect them to a user-friendly page, you can at least maintain that your application gracefully handled the exception.

IIS versus ASP.NET Errors

IIS is responsible for fulfilling requests for resources. Some resource requests it can fulfill on its own, such as request for images, HTML pages, and static files (Word documents or Excel spreadsheets). When an error occurs attempting to access a resource managed by IIS, then IIS generates the error response. For example, if you request a nonexistent HTML page, then IIS displays the 404 error page that IIS has been configured to display.

IIS cannot fulfill requests for ASP.NET pages on its own, so it passes those requests off to the ASP.NET runtime for processing. When an error occurs attempting to access a resource managed by ASP.NET, then ASP.NET generates the error response, not IIS. So, you have two locations where you must configure your error pages if you want to maintain consistency for resources managed by IIS and resources managed by ASP.NET.

■ **Caution** Custom error pages configured in ASP.NET do *not* display when the requested resource is managed by IIS. They only display when the requested resource is managed by ASP.NET. If you want both your IIS and your ASP.NET error pages to be the same, then you must configure those error pages in both IIS and ASP.NET.

Defining a Default Error Page for ASP.NET

You can create a default error page that ASP.NET displays as a last-resort when an unhandled exception occurs for resources managed by ASP.NET. This guarantees that your users never see an ugly exception page. Defining a default error page is exceptionally easy, so there's no excuse for not implementing one. All you need to do is point the `defaultRedirect` parameter of the `<customErrrors>` element to a valid page in your application and set the mode parameter to `On` or `RemoteOnly` as shown in Listing 2-15.

Listing 2-15. *Defining a Defult Error Page in* `Web.config`

```
<config>
  ...
  <system.web>
    ...
    <customErrors mode="On" defaultRedirect="~/ErrorPages/GenericError.html"/>
  </system.web>
</config>
```

When you add a `Web.config` file to your project using the **Add New Item** dialog box, ASP.NET creates a commented out `<customErrors>` section with the mode parameter set to `RemoteOnly`. After you uncomment this section, you should probably leave the mode setting alone because the `RemoteOnly` setting is the most versatile of the three mode options. Table 2-1 displays all the values that the mode parameter can have and a description of each.

Table 2-1. *Possible Values for the Mode Parameter of the* `<customErrors>` *Element*

Value	Description
`Off`	ASP.NET always generates a page containing detailed information about the exception and a stack trace. Users are never redirected to an error page.
`On`	ASP.NET always redirects the user to an error page.
`RemoteOnly`	Users on the machine running the application (developers) see a page containing detailed information about the exception and a stack trace. Remote users (clients) are redirected to an error page. This setting is very useful if you need to view exception details on a live application without end users seeing a nasty message as well.

■ **Note** The mode parameter of the sample application is set to `On`, not `RemoteOnly`, because you are likely accessing the sample application from your local machine. Take a look at the Custom Error Page demo with mode set to `On`, and then look at it with mode set to `RemoteOnly` to see the behavioral differences.

Using an ASPX Page as the Default Error Page

You can specify any valid page in your application as the `defaultRedirect` parameter, even an ASP.NET web form. Of course, ASP.NET web forms have the potential to throw unhandled exceptions, so you could be setting yourself up for a bit of trouble unless you make very sure that your default error page does not throw any unhandled exceptions. Fortunately, ASP.NET is smart enough not to go into a recursive loop of throwing errors and then redirecting back to the page that threw the error. Instead, it generates an exception page like the one shown earlier in Figure 2-3 with a less than intuitive message about how the `<customErrors>` settings in your `Web.config` file is improperly configured.

Defining Custom Error Pages in ASP.NET

The default error page is a catchall for any type of error that may occur for resources managed by ASP.NET, so it has to be relatively generic. Unfortunately, in some situations, generic error pages may not tell the whole story or may leave the user at a dead end. For example, if a user attempts to access a nonexistent resource managed by ASP.NET, then the user receives a 404 error. If, however, you have only specified a default error page, then ASP.NET displays that error page without ever mentioning that the resource was not found. This makes it appear as though the resource exists and is having errors.

You can avoid this problem by using custom error pages. ASP.NET allows you to create custom error pages tailored for specific error types so you can give your users more information about a problem and a possible resolution. In our preceding 404 example, you could create a 404 error page that informs the user that the page they are trying to access does not exist so they know they entered the wrong URL. You could even go as far as displaying a site map, links, or a search box to allow the user to more easily locate their desired content.

Defining custom error pages requires adding an `<error>` inner element to the `<customErrors>` element in `Web.config`. Listing 2-16 is an example that defines a custom error page for the 404 error.

Listing 2-16. *Defining a Custom Error Page in* `Web.config`

```
<config>
  ...
  <system.web>
    ...
    <customErrors mode="On" defaultRedirect="~/ErrorPages/GenericError.html">
      <error statusCode="404" redirect="~/ErrorPages/Error404.html"/>
    </customErrors>
  </system.web>
</config>
```

The `statusCode` parameter of the `<error>` element defines the server status code for which the error page should be returned. The `redirect` parameter defines the actual error page location. In this example, if a 404 error occurs, ASP.NET redirects the user to the `Error404.html` page. Because the 404 error is the only custom error defined, any other error will cause the user to be redirected to the `GenericError.html` page.

Defining Custom Error Pages in IIS

You can also define custom error pages for specific types of HTTP errors in IIS, although the process is a bit different. Furthermore, you can configure IIS to display the exact same custom error pages that ASP.NET uses. This allows you to display the same error regardless of whether ASP.NET or IIS manages the requested resource.

To configure custom error pages in IIS, open IIS and locate your virtual directory. Right-click on the virtual directory and select **Properties** from the context menu. The **Properties** dialog box appears displaying a series of tabs. Select the **Custom Errors** tab. You'll see the dialog box display a tab similar to the one shown in Figure 2-4.

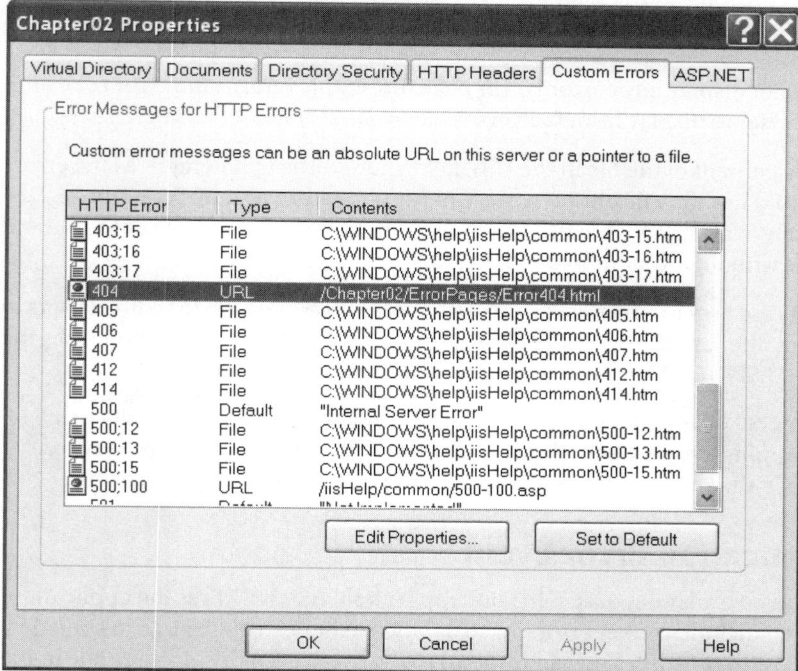

Figure 2-4. *Custom Errors tab in the IIS virtual directory Properties dialog box*

The **Custom Errors** tab displays HTTP error numbers in a list format. Locate and select the error for which you want to define a custom error page. With the item selected, click on the **Edit Properties** button. The **Error Mapping Properties** dialog box similar to the one shown in Figure 2-5 displays.

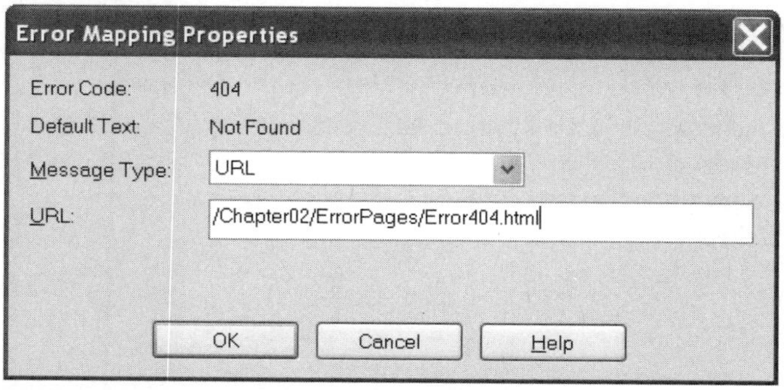

Figure 2-5. *Error Mapping Properties dialog box*

The **Error Mapping Properties** dialog box allows you to define what IIS displays when the selected error occurs. Notice that it displays the current **Error Code** you are editing and the **Default Text** for that error. You cannot change either of these because they are HTTP standards. You can, however, change the **Message Type** and the **File/URL**. There are three options in the **Message Type** drop-down list, and the option you select determines whether you need to enter a file name, URL, or nothing at all:

- *Default:* Does not display any custom error page. IIS simply returns the error code and allows the browser to display its default error message.
- *File:* Reads the content of the file in the URL field and returns that content as the error page. You should use the **File** option when you want to return a static HTML page. *Do not* point the file at an ASP.NET page because IIS simply reads the content of the file and returns it as-is without any additional processing.
- *URL:* Redirects the user to a relative or absolute URL. This allows you to redirect users to ASP.NET pages after an IIS error. Because the user is redirected, ASP.NET processes the request for the ASP.NET error page normally.

If you want both ASP.NET and IIS to use the same error pages, just point the file name or URL in the **Error Mapping Properties** dialog box to the location you defined for the corresponding error code in the `<error>` entries in the `<customErrors>` section of `Web.config`.

Using the Application Error Event

Whenever an unhandled exception occurs in your application, ASP.NET fires the application `Error` event. This even includes server errors, such as when a requested resource managed by ASP.NET does not exist (404 Error). You can respond to the `Error` event by placing code in the `Application_Error` procedure in `global.asax`.

For the most part, the `Application_Error` method should only be used to log error information. Some people like to use it to redirect the user to a custom error page when an exception occurs, but that task is better accomplished using the default and custom error page definitions in the `Web.config` file. Oddly enough, no exception information is directly passed into the `Application_Error` procedure. You have to acquire the exception information using the `Server` object, as shown in Listing 2-17.

Listing 2-17. `Application_Error` *Event Handler Example*

```
'**************************************************************************
Sub Application_Error(ByVal sender As Object, ByVal e As EventArgs)
    Try
        Dim ex As Exception = Server.GetLastError()
        ExceptionManager.Publish(ex)
    Catch ex As Exception
    End Try
End Sub
```

You should encapsulate any code you have in the `Application_Error` procedure in a `Try Catch` statement to ensure that it doesn't throw an error, but know that the consequences of allowing an exception to slip through are not overly problematic. The default exception page displays regardless, assuming it is defined.

Logging Exceptions for Analysis

Applications with appropriate exception handling and custom error pages shield users from experiencing alarming, confusing, or just ugly error messages. By gracefully handling an exception, the application appears to be dealing with the situation normally even though, technically, something went wrong. In terms of user experience, this is exactly what you want because the error appears to be part of the application and either provides an informative error message and/or suggestions for resolution. Most people have the confidence to continue using the application after the error and simply try again. Sometimes the very act of trying again solves the issue. As such, the user simply continues along and does not report the problem. Other times, trying again does not solve the issue, and users call you to report the issue. Unfortunately, users are notorious for vague descriptions of errors and what they were doing when the error occurred, so user reporting may not be overly helpful in your quest to track down bugs.

Exception logging is an extremely helpful way to identify, log, and analyze all the exceptions that occur in your application. Any time an exception occurs, the exception information (type, message, stack trace) as well as environmental conditions (date/time, machine name, user ID, form data, query string values, and so on) present when the exception occurred are stored in the database. This helps resolve both of the issues mentioned previously. All exceptions are logged, so you can rely on the exception log to report errors instead of users. And the exception log contains detailed information about the exception and the environmental situation in which the exception occurred, so you do not have to rely solely on a user's personal recollection to determine what happened. Exception logging ensures that you are aware of exceptions and gives you enough information to start tracking down bugs. Additionally, storing exception data in a database allows you to analyze the exceptions to look for recurrent patterns. How often is an exception occurring? To whom? When? On which server? A database of exception information makes these types of determinations much easier to make and is invaluable for determining which bugs should be classified as high-, medium-, and low priority, and it is especially useful when an application is first deployed.

Choosing an Exception Logging Tool

One of the decisions you must make when implementing exception logging in your application is whether to use a prebuilt tool to help speed up development or to build your own from scratch. I highly recommend that you use an existing tool because there are a number of freely available, amply configurable, highly extensible tools at your disposal. Microsoft, for example, recently released the Enterprise Library, which, among other things, includes an Enterprise-grade exception-management module with myriad features and configuration options.

■ **Note** At the time of this book's writing, the Enterprise Library was not ready for use with the .NET 2.0 Framework, but a .NET 2.0-compliant version should be out shortly after Visual Studio 2005 ships.

Microsoft also offers the Exception Management Application Block, which is the predecessor of the exception-management module in the Enterprise Library. It offers a slightly scaled back and simpler solution that is still very powerful, but does not have all the advanced configuration options or complexities of the Enterprise Library. Log4Net is also a popular logging solution, as are many other solutions found on mainstream development sites and blogs on the Internet. Links to these products are provided under the Links section of the example application (in the Source Code area of the Apress website), or you can opt to search for the product using a search engine.

Ultimately, you must decide which tool to use based on your personal preference and project environment. In some situations, the Enterprise Library may be overkill or present too much of a learning curve. For other situations, the Exception Management Application Block may not provide enough configuration options. And there could always be a spectacular feature in another tool that is so well suited for your particular need that it compels you to use that tool over another one.

Regardless of which tool you opt to use, each is likely to have its own proprietary configuration options and extensibility framework. You'll have to consult the documentation for specific implementation guidelines because I cannot cover all of them in this text. In the example that follows, you'll look at a custom exception logging implementation that demonstrates the basics of exception logging. You can then apply what you learn to whichever tool you decide to use. Also know that the exception logging classes presented in the upcoming example can be reused inside of another logging solution if you so desire, or they can act as a starting point for your own implementation.

Architecture Overview

In the following example, you are creating a series of classes to help save exception logging information to a database and building a web-based interface for reviewing those exceptions. Table 2-2 provides a breakdown of the items in the example and their purposes.

Table 2-2. *Exception Logging Example Items*

Item	Type	Project	Description
`ExceptionLog`	`Class`	`SqlExceptionLogging`	Object representation of the exception information stored in the database. Also includes loading and saving routines for exception data.
`ExceptionLog➥ Collection`	`Class`	`SqlExceptionLogging`	Maintains a list of `ExceptionLog` objects. Also includes loading routines for list-oriented operations.
`ExceptionLogger`	`Class`	`SqlExceptionLogging`	Contains the `Log` function, which can be used to save exception information to the database. This class is responsible for populating `ExceptionLog` objects and saving them to the database.
`ShowException➥ List.aspx`	`WebForm`	`WebSite`	Displays a brief listing of all the exceptions currently in the database.
`ShowException. aspx`	`WebForm`	`WebSite`	Displays details about a specific exception.

In a full-fledged exception logging solution, there would be many more classes to help manage configuration and extensibility. This example, however, strives for simplicity so there are not many auxiliary classes or functionality. We'll begin by looking at the database structure required to store exception log information. After that, we'll move on to the exception logging actual classes, starting with the `ExceptionLog` class.

Creating the ExceptionLog Table to Store Data

Before you can store information in a database, you need to build out an appropriate data structure to hold the data. In the example application for Chapter 2 (in the Source Code area of the Apress website), you'll find a SQL Server database named `Chapter02.mdf`. This database contains a table named `ExceptionLog`, which stores all the exception information for the sample application. Table 2-3 provides a rundown of the fields in the table and their purposes.

Table 2-3. `ExceptionLog` *Table Fields*

Field	Type	Description
`ExceptionID`	`int (identity)`	Unique identifier for the record.
`ParentID`	`int`	Links an inner exception to its parent exception and defines the hierarchy of exception in an exception chain. When nonzero, this field indicates that the record is an inner exception and references the `ExceptionID` of the parent. A value of zero for this field indicates that the record is a top-level exception that has no parent.
`MachineName`	`varchar(50)`	Network name of the machine on which the exception occurred.
`UserID`	`varchar(50)`	User ID identifying the web-based user who experienced the exception.
`UserAgent`	`varchar(255)`	Identifies the type of browser used.
`ExceptionDate`	`datetime`	Date and time when the exception occurred.
`ExceptionType`	`varchar(50)`	Type name of the exception.
`Exception➥ Message`	`varchar(255)`	Message of the exception.
`Page`	`varchar(255)`	Application relative path of the page on which the error occurred (for example, `~/Default.aspx`).
`StackTrace`	`text`	Stack trace at the time the exception occurred. This contains information that helps identify what chain of methods were executing at the time of the exception.
`QueryStringData`	`text`	Listing of all the query string variable names and values.
`FormData`	`text`	Listing of all the form variable names and values.
`ChainID`	`uniqueidentifier`	`GUID` value that helps group all the exceptions in an exception chain together. All exceptions in the chain (the original exception and its chain of inner exceptions) have the same `ChainID`. This allows you to select all the exceptions in an exception chain from the database using the `ChainID` instead of resorting to a more complicated stored procedure or series of recursive database calls.

You are free to add and remove fields from the database as you see fit. If you only have one server, for example, it may not be worth your time to save the machine name. Or if you think it would be helpful to store the referring page along with the exception data so you know where the user came from originally, you may do so. Also notice that the query string and form data are stored in a single field. You could break the name-value pairs out into their own table structure for advanced analysis. For the time being, however, we'll keep it simple.

ExceptionLog Class

You use the `ExceptionLog` class to store, retrieve, and delete exception log information from the database. Because this is a standalone class that is not tied to any specific tool, you can either use it as-is or as a starting point for whichever exception logging tool you decide to use. As you look through the class (see Listing 2-18), understand that you can capture as much or as little exception logging information as you want or need. This is by no means an extensive listing of the information available, but it does represent some of the most useful items when it comes to debugging an issue.

Listing 2-18. `ExceptionLog` *Class*

```
Imports System.Data.SqlClient

Public Class ExceptionLog

#Region "Fields"

    '***************************************************************************
    Private _ExceptionID As Integer = 0
    Private _ParentID As Integer = 0
    Private _MachineName As String = String.Empty
    Private _UserID As String = String.Empty
    Private _UserAgent As String = String.Empty
    Private _ExceptionDate As Date = Now
    Private _ExceptionType As String = String.Empty
    Private _ExceptionMessage As String = String.Empty
    Private _Page As String = String.Empty
    Private _StackTrace As String = String.Empty
    Private _QueryStringData As String = String.Empty
    Private _FormData As String = String.Empty
    Private _ChainID As Guid = Guid.Empty

#End Region

#Region "Properties"

    '***************************************************************************
    Public Property ExceptionID() As Integer
        Get
            Return _ExceptionID
```

```
        End Get
        Set(ByVal value As Integer)
            _ExceptionID = value
        End Set
    End Property

    '*************************************************************************
    Public Property ParentID() As Integer
        Get
            Return _ParentID
        End Get
        Set(ByVal value As Integer)
            _ParentID = value
        End Set
    End Property

    '*************************************************************************
    Public Property MachineName() As String
        Get
            Return _MachineName
        End Get
        Set(ByVal value As String)
            _MachineName = value
        End Set
    End Property

    '*************************************************************************
    Public Property UserID() As String
        Get
            Return _UserID
        End Get
        Set(ByVal value As String)
            _UserID = value
        End Set
    End Property

    '*************************************************************************
    Public Property UserAgent() As String
        Get
            Return _UserAgent
        End Get
        Set(ByVal value As String)
            _UserAgent = value
        End Set
    End Property
```

```
'****************************************************************************
Public Property ExceptionDate() As Date
    Get
        Return _ExceptionDate
    End Get
    Set(ByVal value As Date)
        _ExceptionDate = value
    End Set
End Property

'****************************************************************************
Public Property ExceptionType() As String
    Get
        Return _ExceptionType
    End Get
    Set(ByVal value As String)
        _ExceptionType = value
    End Set
End Property
'****************************************************************************
Public Property ExceptionMessage() As String
    Get
        Return _ExceptionMessage
    End Get
    Set(ByVal value As String)
        _ExceptionMessage = value
    End Set
End Property
'****************************************************************************
Public Property Page() As String
    Get
        Return _Page
    End Get
    Set(ByVal value As String)
        _Page = value
    End Set
End Property
'****************************************************************************
Public Property StackTrace() As String
    Get
        Return _StackTrace
    End Get
    Set(ByVal value As String)
        _StackTrace = value
    End Set
End Property
```

```
    '***************************************************************************
    Public Property QueryStringData() As String
        Get
            Return _QueryStringData
        End Get
        Set(ByVal value As String)
            _QueryStringData = value
        End Set
    End Property

    '***************************************************************************
    Public Property FormData() As String
        Get
            Return _FormData
        End Get
        Set(ByVal value As String)
            _FormData = value
        End Set
    End Property

    '***************************************************************************
    Public Property ChainID() As Guid
        Get
            Return _ChainID
        End Get
        Set(ByVal value As Guid)
            _ChainID = value
        End Set
    End Property

#End Region

    '***************************************************************************
    Public Function Save(ByVal dbConn As SqlConnection) As Boolean

        Dim SQL As String = _
          "INSERT INTO [ExceptionLog] (ParentID, MachineName, UserID, " & _
            "UserAgent, ExceptionDate, ExceptionType, ExceptionMessage, " & _
            "Page, StackTrace, QueryStringData, FormData, ChainID)" & _
          "VALUES (@ParentID, @MachineName, @UserID, @UserAgent, " & _
            "@ExceptionDate, @ExceptionType, @ExceptionMessage, @Page, " & _
            "@StackTrace, @QueryStringData, @FormData, @ChainID);"

        Dim cmd As New SqlCommand(SQL, dbConn)
        cmd.Parameters.Add("@ParentID", SqlDbType.Int).Value = ParentID
        cmd.Parameters.Add("@MachineName", SqlDbType.VarChar).Value
            = CheckEmpty(MachineName)
        cmd.Parameters.Add("@UserID", SqlDbType.VarChar).Value = CheckEmpty(UserID)
```

```
        cmd.Parameters.Add("@UserAgent", SqlDbType.VarChar).Value _
            = CheckEmpty(UserAgent)
        cmd.Parameters.Add("@ExceptionDate", SqlDbType.VarChar).Value _
            = CheckEmpty(ExceptionDate)
        cmd.Parameters.Add("@ExceptionType", SqlDbType.VarChar).Value _
            = CheckEmpty(ExceptionType)
        cmd.Parameters.Add("@ExceptionMessage", SqlDbType.VarChar).Value _
            = CheckEmpty(ExceptionMessage)
        cmd.Parameters.Add("@Page", SqlDbType.VarChar).Value = CheckEmpty(Page)
        cmd.Parameters.Add("@StackTrace", SqlDbType.NText).Value _
            = CheckEmpty(StackTrace)
        cmd.Parameters.Add("@QueryStringData", SqlDbType.Text).Value _
            = CheckEmpty(QueryStringData)
        cmd.Parameters.Add("@FormData", SqlDbType.Text).Value = CheckEmpty(FormData)
        cmd.Parameters.Add("@ChainID", SqlDbType.UniqueIdentifier).Value = ChainID

        If cmd.ExecuteNonQuery() > 0 Then
            cmd.CommandText = "SELECT @@IDENTITY;"
            ExceptionID = CInt(cmd.ExecuteScalar())
            Return True
        Else
            Return False
        End If

    End Function

    '****************************************************************************
    Private Function CheckEmpty(ByVal s As String) As String
        If s = Nothing Then Return "" Else Return s
    End Function

    '****************************************************************************
    Public Function LoadByID(ByVal ExceptionID As Integer, _
      ByVal DBConn As SqlConnection) As Boolean

        Dim ReturnVal As Boolean = False
        Dim SQL As String = _
          "SELECT * FROM [ExceptionLog] WHERE [ExceptionID]=@ExceptionID"

        Dim cmd As New SqlCommand(SQL, DBConn)
        cmd.Parameters.Add("@ExceptionID", SqlDbType.Int).Value = ExceptionID

        Dim dr As SqlDataReader = cmd.ExecuteReader()
        If dr.Read Then
            MapData(dr)
            ReturnVal = True
        End If
```

```
        dr.Close()
        Return ReturnVal

    End Function

    '******************************************************************************
    Public Sub MapData(ByVal dr As SqlDataReader)
        ExceptionID = CInt(dr("ExceptionID"))
        ParentID = CInt(dr("ParentID"))
        MachineName = CStr(dr("MachineName"))
        UserID = CStr(dr("UserID"))
        UserAgent = CStr(dr("UserAgent"))
        ExceptionDate = CStr(dr("ExceptionDate"))
        ExceptionType = CStr(dr("ExceptionType"))
        ExceptionMessage = CStr(dr("ExceptionMessage"))
        Page = CStr(dr("Page"))
        StackTrace = CStr(dr("StackTrace"))
        QueryStringData = CStr(dr("QueryStringData"))
        FormData = CStr(dr("FormData"))
        ChainID = DirectCast(dr("ChainID"), Guid)
    End Sub
```

■ **Note** The `DirectCast` method casts one type to another type without any intermediary conversion. So, `DirectCast("1",Integer)` fails because `"1"` is a `String`, not an `Integer`. `CType` has the capability to convert an item from one type to another during the cast. Thus, `CType("1", Integer)` succeeds because `CType` can successfully convert the `String "1"` into an `Integer`. In this example, `dr("ChainID")` actually returns a `Guid` object that does not need to be converted. Thus, you use `DirectCast` instead of `CType` because it has a slight performance advantage.

```
    '***************************************************************************
    Public Function DeleteChain(ByVal DBConn As SqlConnection) As Boolean

        Dim SQL As String = "DELETE FROM [ExceptionLog] WHERE [ChainID]=@ChainID;"
        Dim cmd As New SqlCommand(SQL, DBConn)
        cmd.Parameters.Add("@ChainID", SqlDbType.UniqueIdentifier).Value = ChainID
        cmd.ExecuteNonQuery()
        Return True

    End Function

End Class
```

Fields and Properties

All the properties in the class are fairly standard, so they don't require too much explanation. Each property has a corresponding private field in which to store its value and has a matching field in the database. Refer to Table 2-3 for a more detailed description of each property.

Save Function

As its name implies, the Save function saves exception log information to the database using the SqlConnection passed in as a parameter. The function begins by defining a parameterized SQL insert statement, and then uses that statement and the SqlConnection to create a new SqlCommand object. Because the command object contains a parameterized SQL statement, it needs parameter values for all those parameters. You can see directly under the SqlCommand definition that the function creates a parameter for each field in the statement and passes in the value of the corresponding class property. It uses the CheckEmpty function to ensure string values are set to an empty string "" and not to Nothing. If a parameter value is Nothing, then the SqlCommand object throws an execution when the command executes because it thinks you never supplied a value. The ExceptionID field is not included in this list because the database auto-generates its value during the insert.

After populating the command object with parameters and values, the Save function executes the command using the ExecuteNonQuery method, which returns the number of records affected by the query. If no records were affected, then the Save failed and the function returns false. If at least one record was affected, then the Save succeeded and the function goes on to acquire the new ExceptionID value.

Because SQL Server automatically generates the ExceptionID during the insert, you have to select it out of the database. The @@IDENTITY variable stores the value of the last auto-generated number for the current connection. Inside the affected record check, you can see that the Save function updates the SqlCommand object's CommandText to acquire the auto-generated number and assigns it to the ExceptionID property using the ExecuteScalar method. ExecuteScalar returns a single value from the database without the need for a data reader. Finally, the function returns true indicating that the Save was successful.

CheckEmpty Function

This function checks an incoming string to determine whether it is set to Nothing. If so, it returns an empty string "". If not, the function returns the actual string's value.

LoadByID Function

LoadByID accepts an ExceptionID and a SqlConnection as parameters and loads the requested exception information from the database into the ExceptionLog object. It begins by creating a Boolean variable named ReturnVal and setting it to false. This variable keeps track of whether or not the ExceptionID requested is actually found and loaded.

The command-building process for LoadByID is similar to that of the Save function. It starts by defining a parameterized query, builds a SqlCommand object that uses the query and the SqlConnection, and then creates the ExceptionID parameter value. LoadByID then runs the ExecuteReader method on the SqlCommand object and stores the resulting data reader in the dr variable. After getting a reference to the data reader, the function checks to see if the data reader is pointing to any information by calling the Read method. If Read returns True, the function knows that the exception information was successfully located. It then copies the data from the data reader to the object using the MapData function and sets the ReturnVal to True indicating that the information was successfully located. Finally, the function closes the data reader and returns ReturnVal as the result of the function. If the exception information was not located, then ReturnVal will still be False.

MapData

MapData simply copies database field values from the data reader into the appropriate properties on the object. You'll notice that methods in both the ExceptionLog and ExceptionLogCollection classes use this function when they need to pull data from a data reader.

DeleteChain

This function executes a SQL statement that deletes a chain of exceptions based on the ChainID. It makes little sense to delete a single exception within a chain, so the entire chain is deleted all at once.

ExceptionLogCollection Class

As with any logging tool, your end goal is to review the log for analysis. Many times you can analyze data directly in a database tool such as Enterprise Manager. In this example, however, you are reviewing data directly in the browser. So, you need a way to organize and obtain lists of ExceptionLog objects, and the ExceptionLogCollection class exists to do just that. Listing 2-19 shows the code for the ExceptionLogCollection class, followed by a brief description of the functions and their purposes.

Listing 2-19. ExceptionLogCollection *Class*

```
Imports System.Data.SqlClient

Public Class ExceptionLogCollection
    Inherits CollectionBase

    '**************************************************************************
    Public Function Add(ByVal obj As ExceptionLog) As Integer
        Return InnerList.Add(obj)
    End Function

    '**************************************************************************
    Default Public Property Item(ByVal index As Integer) As ExceptionLog
        Get
            Return InnerList.Item(index)
```

```
        End Get
        Set(ByVal value As ExceptionLog)
            InnerList.Item(index) = value
        End Set
    End Property

    '*************************************************************************
    Public Sub LoadAll(ByVal DBConn As SqlConnection)

        Dim SQL As String = "SELECT * FROM [ExceptionLog] " & _
          "WHERE [ParentID]=0 ORDER BY [ExceptionID] DESC;"

        Dim cmd As New SqlCommand(SQL, DBConn)
        Dim dr As SqlDataReader = cmd.ExecuteReader()
        Dim obj As ExceptionLog

        Me.Clear()
        While dr.Read
            obj = New ExceptionLog()
            obj.MapData(dr)
            Add(obj)
        End While

    End Sub

    '*************************************************************************
    Public Sub LoadChain(ByVal ChainID As Guid, _
      ByVal DBConn As SqlConnection)

        Dim SQL As String = "SELECT * FROM [ExceptionLog] " & _
          "WHERE [ChainID]=@ChainID ORDER BY [ExceptionID];"

        Dim cmd As New SqlCommand(SQL, DBConn)
        cmd.Parameters.Add("@ChainID", SqlDbType.UniqueIdentifier).Value = ChainID

        Dim dr As SqlDataReader = cmd.ExecuteReader()
        Dim obj As ExceptionLog

        Me.Clear()
        While dr.Read
            obj = New ExceptionLog
            obj.MapData(dr)
            Add(obj)
        End While

    End Sub

End Class
```

Class Definition

The ExceptionLogCollection class is a strongly typed collection designed solely to work with ExceptionLog objects. It inherits its core collection functionality from the CollectionBase class, which provides access to an internal ArrayList used to store and manage objects in the collection. The class also inherits common, nontype-specific properties and methods such as the Count property, the Clear method, and the RemoveAt method. Nontype-specific members don't need to know the type of object stored in the collection in order to function. For example, it doesn't matter whether you're storing ExceptionLog objects or Employee objects, the Count is always going to return an Integer specifying the number of items in the collection.

You are expected to implement your own type-specific properties and methods. This class, for example, contains a strongly typed Item property and Add function so they specifically deal with ExceptionLog objects. Optionally, you can create your own Contains, IndexOf, Insert, and Remove functions if necessary.

Add Function

This function allows you to add ExceptionLog objects to the collection. All this function does is accept an ExceptionLog object as a parameter, pass that ExceptionLog object to the Add function of the InnerList, and then return the index in the collection where the ExceptionLog object was added. Basically, the Add function acts as a filter so you can ensure that only ExceptionLog objects make it into the InnerList because, technically, the InnerList can hold any type of object.

Item Default Property

You access individual items in the collection (by index) using the Item property. Like the Add function, the Item property simply reuses the InnerList for most of its functionality. The get portion of the property returns a strongly typed ExceptionLog from the specified index in the collection, whereas the set portion of the property assigns the ExceptionLog objects to the specified index.

Also notice that the Item property is the default property for the class. This means that you can reference this property using an array notation on the object. For example, if you have an ExceptionLogCollection named MyExceptions, then you can access an exception in the collection using MyExceptions(5) instead of MyException.Items(5).

LoadChain Method

Sometimes you need to know about all the exceptions in the exception chain to fully understand what an error is or how it occurred. The LoadChain method accepts a ChainID and populates the ExceptionLogCollections with all the exceptions for that particular exception chain.

LoadChain accepts an open database connection named DBConn and the ChainID of the requested desired chain as parameters. The function begins by defining a parameterized SQL query and a SqlCommand that uses the open database connection and that query. Then it adds the @ChainID parameter value to the command using the ChainID value passed into the function. Next, the command executes the query using the ExecuteReader method and stores the resulting data reader in the dr variable. Before reading through all the values, the function calls the Clear method to remove any existing data from the collection. It then iterates over each row of data returned by the query. For each row, LoadChain creates a new ExceptionLog object and populates the object's properties from the data reader using the object's MapData method. It then adds the newly created object to the collection using the Add function.

LoadAll Method

When you review exceptions in the browser, you'll need a list of the exceptions that have occurred on the system. LoadAll populates the ExceptionLogCollection object with all the top-level exceptions currently listed in the database, that is, exceptions that have no parents and therefore their ParentID = 0. This function works like the LoadChain method, but it does not have any parameters for the SQL query.

ExceptionLogger Class

Most exception-logging tools contain a class with a shared method used to log exceptions as they occur. Using the Exception Management Application Block, for example, you call ExceptionManager.Publish(exception) to log an exception. In the Enterprise Library, exception policies govern how to handle exceptions so the call looks something like ExceptionPolicy.HandleException(ex, "PolicyName"). Every other tool you encounter has its own way of doing things, but this tends to be the "norm" for exception logging.

For this example, you'll use ExceptionLogger.Log(ex) to log an exception. In Listing 2-20, you'll see how the Log function uses the ExceptionLog object to log exception information to the database. This will be helpful when you implement exception logging in your own application.

Listing 2-20. ExceptionLogger *Class Code*

```
Imports Microsoft.VisualBasic.ControlChars
Imports System.Collections.Specialized
Imports System.Configuration.ConfigurationManager
Imports System.Data.SqlClient
Imports System.Web.HttpContext

Public Class ExceptionLogger

    '***************************************************************************
    Private Shared _connectionString As String = ""

    '***************************************************************************
    Public Shared Property ConnectionString() As String
        Get
            Return _connectionString
        End Get
        Set(ByVal value As String)
            _connectionString = value
        End Set
    End Property
```

```
'****************************************************************************
Public Shared Sub Log(ByVal ex As Exception)

    Dim exLog As New ExceptionLog
    Dim parentID As Integer = 0
    Dim chainID As Guid = Guid.NewGuid()
    Dim dbConn As SqlConnection = New SqlConnection(ConnectionString)

    dbConn.Open()

    'Iterate through all of the exceptions in the exception chain
    While Not ex Is Nothing
        'Create a new Exception Log object for the exception
        exLog = New ExceptionLog()

        'Acquire the username
        If Current.User.Identity.IsAuthenticated Then
            exLog.UserID = Current.User.Identity.Name
        Else
            exLog.UserID = "<Anonymous User>"
        End If

        exLog.ParentID = parentID
        exLog.MachineName = Current.Server.MachineName
        exLog.UserAgent = Current.Request.UserAgent
        exLog.ExceptionDate = Now
        exLog.ExceptionType = ex.GetType.ToString
        exLog.ExceptionMessage = ex.Message
        exLog.Page = Current.Request.AppRelativeCurrentExecutionFilePath()
        exLog.StackTrace = ex.StackTrace
        exLog.QueryStringData = GetQueryStringData()
        exLog.FormData = GetFormData()
        exLog.ChainID = chainID

        'Save Exception Log, Get New ParentID, Get Next Inner Exception
        If exLog.Save(dbConn) Then
            parentID = exLog.ExceptionID
            ex = ex.InnerException
        Else
            'Set ex to nothing so While loop ends
            ex = Nothing
        End If
    End While

    dbConn.Close()

End Sub
```

```
    '***************************************************************************
    Private Shared Function GetQueryStringData() As String
        Dim Data As New System.Text.StringBuilder(256)
        For Each key As String In Current.Request.QueryString.Keys
            Data.Append(key)
            Data.Append("=")
            Data.Append(Current.Request.QueryString(key))
            Data.Append(CrLf)
        Next
        Return Data.ToString
    End Function

    '***************************************************************************
    Private Shared Function GetFormData() As String
        Dim Data As New System.Text.StringBuilder(256)
        For Each key As String In Current.Request.Form.Keys
            Data.Append(key)
            Data.Append("=")
            Data.Append(Current.Request.Form(key))
            Data.Append(CrLf)
        Next
        Return Data.ToString
    End Function

End Class
```

Static ConnectionString Property

You use the ConnectionString property to specify the connection string that ExceptionLogger should use to connect to a database. You could acquire the connection string directly from Web.config, but that approach unnecessarily ties the ExceptionLogger to a particular application configuration. Because the component is designed for reuse, it makes more sense to make it as flexible as possible by simply exposing a property that accepts a connection string without any specific configuration requirements. The only caveat to this approach is that you have to set the ConnectionString property on the ExceptionLogger before you log an exception. A good place to do this is in the Application_Start method in the Global.asax file as shown in Listing 2-21.

Listing 2-21. *Setting Up the* ConnectionString *in the* Global.asax

```
<%@ Application Language="VB" %>
<%@ Import Namespace="System.Configuration.ConfigurationManager" %>
<script runat="server">
```

```
    '************************************************************************
    Sub Application_Start(ByVal sender As Object, ByVal e As EventArgs)
        SqlExceptionLogging.ExceptionLogger.ConnectionString = _
         ConnectionStrings("Chapter02").ConnectionString
    End Sub

</script>
```

Static Log Method

When you log an exception, you have to account for the chance that the exception exists as an exception chain and has a series of inner exceptions. As such, each exception needs to know its ParentID and ChainID so it knows which exception chain it belongs to and which exception in that chain is its parent. The Log method accepts a single exception named ex as a parameter and is responsible for iterating through each exception in the chain and saving it with the appropriate exception information, ParentID, and ChainID.

At the beginning of the Log method, you can see the declarations for all the variables used throughout the code. There are a few things you need to be aware of in the declarations. First, the method sets ParentID to 0 because the first exception in the chain has no parent. Also notice that it assigns the ChainID a new Guid value using the Guid.NewGuid() function. This value links all the exceptions in the chain together and does not change from one exception to the next. And, finally, the code creates a new database connection string defined in the ConnectionString property.

After defining variables, the code opens the database connection and jumps into a While loop that continues until the ex variable no longer points to an exception. Inside the While loop, the Log method creates a new ExceptionLog object and then populates that object with exception and environmental data that can help track down the cause of the exception. Table 2-3 contains a detailed listing of the properties and what they represent if you need to refresh your memory as to what a properties stores.

After the ExceptionLog properties have been set, the Log function saves the ExceptionLog object using the object's Save method and the open database connection. If the save was successful, the method assigns the parentID variable the value just given to the saved ExceptionLog object. This ensures that the next exception will have an appropriate ParentID. It then sets ex to ex.InnerException, which causes the While loop to continue until all the inner exceptions have been saved. After exiting the While loop, the method closes the database connection and all the exceptions in the exception chain are in the database.

GetQueryStringData and GetFormData Functions

Knowing what the user entered into a web form is invaluable knowledge when it comes to debugging an exception. Because most user input arrives at the server in the form of query string or form variables, you'll find it very helpful to save query string and form variable data in the exception log.

The GetQueryString and GetFormData functions help format that information into a more human-readable format by outputting each name-value pair on its own line. Because a significant amount of string concatenation is going on, both functions also use the StringBuilder object to build the string as it's well suited for building strings quickly and efficiently.

Using the ExceptionLogger Class in Your Code

You normally find exception loggers in the `Catch` portion of a `Try Catch` statement because that's normally where you end up with an exception you need to log. So, normal-looking exception logging code looks like Listing 2-22.

Listing 2-22. *Example Exception Logging*

```
Try
    'Code that may cause an exception
Catch ex As Exception
    ExceptionLogger.Log(ex)
    'You can rethrow the exception if you want or your exception-logging utility
    'may have configuration settings to specify rethrows for certain exceptions
End Try
```

That's all there is to it. Just make sure you include the exception logging in your `Try Catch` blocks so you can keep a record of what's going on.

Reviewing Exceptions Online

After you start logging exceptions in your application, you need a way to review those exceptions so you can start prioritizing and fixing them. The question is, what do you use to do that. One simple solution is to use the database directly because it provides a powerful set of analysis and query tools. It also has the added benefit of not requiring any additional time, money, or effort to build.

The problem with using direct database access is that it becomes increasingly more difficult to manage as you work on larger and larger projects. Larger projects normally have teams of developers, project managers, quality assurance testers, and help desk personnel, all of whom need access to exception information. Although developers normally have experience navigating a database, other people on a project may not. So, it may be beneficial to expose exception information as an administrative screen in your application.

In the sections that follow, you will see a brief example demonstrating how to list exception information in your application.

Listing Exceptions with ShowExceptionList.aspx

Before you can see the details of a specific exception, you need some way of looking through all the exceptions stored in your database. In a production environment, this may mean that you need a search page to narrow down results based on the page name, user ID, exception type, or message. In this example, you'll simply display a list of all the exceptions in the database.

■ **Tip** Chapter 9 describes some great techniques for building effective search pages that are very applicable when it comes to searching through exception information.

The first thing you need is a GridView capable of displaying exception information. The GridView definition in Listing 2-23 displays five different columns: a **View** link in the left column allowing the user to get more detail regarding a specific exception, the date when the exception occurred, the exception type, the page on which the exception occurred, and the user for whom the exception occurred.

Listing 2-23. GridView *Capable of Displaying Exception Information*

```
<asp:GridView ID="gridExceptions" runat="server" AutoGenerateColumns="False">
  <Columns>
    <asp:TemplateField HeaderText="">
      <ItemTemplate>
        <a href='ShowException.aspx?ExceptionID=<%#Eval("ExceptionID")%>'>View</a>
      </ItemTemplate>
    </asp:TemplateField>
    <asp:TemplateField HeaderText="Date">
      <ItemTemplate>
        <%#Eval("ExceptionDate")%>
      </ItemTemplate>
    </asp:TemplateField>
    <asp:TemplateField HeaderText="Type">
      <ItemTemplate>
        <%#Eval("ExceptionType")%>
      </ItemTemplate>
    </asp:TemplateField>
    <asp:TemplateField HeaderText="Page">
      <ItemTemplate>
        <%#Eval("Page")%>
      </ItemTemplate>
    </asp:TemplateField>
    <asp:TemplateField HeaderText="User ID">
      <ItemTemplate>
        <%#Eval("UserID")%>
      </ItemTemplate>
    </asp:TemplateField>
  </Columns>
</asp:GridView>
```

Notice that the template references properties found in the ExceptionLog class. The grid is bound to an ExceptionLogCollection, so the data item for each row is an ExceptionLog object. Also notice that the first column contains a link that redirects users to the ShowException.aspx page and specifies a query string parameter identifying which exception details to display. Next in Listing 2-24, you'll see the code-behind file that populates a grid named gridExceptions.

Listing 2-24. *Displaying Exceptions in a* `GridView` *Control*

```
Imports SqlExceptionLogging
Imports System.Configuration.ConfigurationManager
Imports System.Data.SqlClient

Partial Class ShowExceptionList
    Inherits System.Web.UI.Page

    '***************************************************************************
    Protected Sub Page_Load(ByVal sender As Object, _
      ByVal e As System.EventArgs) Handles Me.Load

        Dim dbConn As New _
          SqlConnection(ConnectionStrings("Chapter02").ConnectionString)
        Dim ExceptionCol As New ExceptionLogCollection
        dbConn.Open()
        ExceptionCol.LoadAll(dbConn)
        dbConn.Close()
        gridExceptions.DataSource = ExceptionCol
        gridExceptions.DataBind()

    End Sub

End Class
```

This code-behind page is fairly simple because most of the logic is contained in the `ExceptionLogCollection` class. The page begins by creating a database connection using the "Chapter02" connection string from `Web.config`. It then instantiates a new `ExceptionLog➥Collection` object, opens the database, loads all the exceptions from the database into the `ExceptionLogCollection` using the `LoadAll` method, and closes the database connection. Next, it assigns the `gridException` control's `DataSource` property to the populated `ExceptionLog➥Collection` and then data binds the grid. This causes the grid to pull in all the exception information from the collection and display it as shown in Figure 2-6.

Users who visit the `ShowExceptionList.aspx` page can browse through the listing of exceptions until they find the one they want to view. Then, they click on the **View** link to see a more detailing listing of the exception.

	Date	Type	Page	User ID
View	8/30/2005 4:45:55 AM	System.OverflowException	~/Employee/Edit.aspx	HOME\damon
View	8/30/2005 3:24:39 AM	System.NullReferenceException	~/Employee/Edit.aspx	HOME\damon
View	8/30/2005 3:24:37 AM	System.InvalidCastException	~/Customers/Search.aspx	HOME\damon
View	8/30/2005 3:24:35 AM	System.IndexOutOfRangeException	~/App/ExamplePage.aspx	HOME\damon
View	8/30/2005 3:24:32 AM	System.FormatException	~/App/ExamplePage.aspx	HOME\damon
View	8/30/2005 3:10:59 AM	System.DivideByZeroException	~/App/ExamplePage.aspx	HOME\damon
View	8/30/2005 12:32:28 AM	System.ArgumentException	~/Default.aspx	HOME\damon

Figure 2-6. *List of exceptions from* `ShowExceptionList.aspx`

Reviewing Exception Details with ShowException.aspx

Listing the exceptions gives a good general glimpse of the exceptions in the application, but the detailed exception page is where you can really dig into an exception and get useful information about what was going on when it occurred. As mentioned before, users can access the `ShowException.aspx` page by clicking on the **View** link next to an exception in the `ShowExceptionList.aspx` page.

`ShowException.aspx` has a lot of visual layout markup that is not pertinent to the functional portion of the page. Listing 2-25 simplifies things a bit by showing the ASP.NET controls on the page with the layout markup stripped out.

Listing 2-25. *Web Controls on the* `ShowException.aspx` *Page*

```
<asp:GridView ID="gridExceptionChain" runat="server" AutoGenerateColumns="False">
  <Columns>
    <asp:TemplateField HeaderText="">
      <ItemTemplate>
        <a href='ShowException.aspx?ExceptionID=<%#Eval("ExceptionID")%>'>View</a>
      </ItemTemplate>
      </asp:TemplateField>
      <asp:TemplateField HeaderText="Date">
        <ItemTemplate>
          <%#Eval("ExceptionDate")%>
        </ItemTemplate>
      </asp:TemplateField>
      <asp:TemplateField HeaderText="Type">
        <ItemTemplate>
          <%#Eval("ExceptionType")%>
        </ItemTemplate>
      </asp:TemplateField>
      <asp:TemplateField HeaderText="Message">
        <ItemTemplate>
          <%#Eval("ExceptionMessage")%>
        </ItemTemplate>
      </asp:TemplateField>
    </Columns>
</asp:GridView><br />
<asp:Button runat=server ID=btnDelete Text="Delete Exception Chain" /><br />
<asp:Label  runat=server ID=lblExceptionID /><br />
<asp:Label  runat=server ID=lblPage /><br />
<asp:Label  runat=server ID=lblExceptionDate /><br />
<asp:Label  runat=server ID=lblExceptionType /><br />
<asp:Label  runat=server ID=lblMessage /><br />
<asp:Label  runat=server ID=lblMachineName /><br />
<asp:Label  runat=server ID=lblUserID /><br />
<asp:Label  runat=server ID=lblUserAgent /><br />
<asp:Label  runat=server ID=lblQueryStringData /><br />
<asp:Label  runat=server ID=lblFormData /><br />
<asp:Label  runat=server ID=lblStackTrace />
```

Most of the page consists of `Label` controls that display detailed exception information. At the top of the page, however, there is a `GridView` control named `gridExceptionChain` that is very similar to one displayed on the `ShowExceptionList.aspx` page. It displays all the exceptions in the exception chain, highlights the position of the current exception in the chain (the highlighting is done in the code-behind file), and allows you to jump to another exception in the chain from a **View** link. A button is also on the form named `btnDelete` that allows you to delete all the exceptions in a chain. Figure 2-7 shows the `ShowException.aspx` page as it appears in the browser.

Exception Chain

	Date	Type	Message
View	8/30/2005 3:24:32 AM	System.FormatException	Test
View	8/30/2005 3:24:32 AM	System.Exception	Test (Inner Exception #1)
View	8/30/2005 3:24:32 AM	System.Exception	Test (Inner Exception #2)
View	8/30/2005 3:24:32 AM	System.Exception	Test (Inner Exception #3)
View	8/30/2005 3:24:32 AM	System.Exception	Test (Inner Exception #4)
View	8/30/2005 3:24:32 AM	System.Exception	Test (Inner Exception #5)

Delete Exception Chain

Exception ID	119
Page	~/GenerateExceptions.aspx
Exception Date	08/30/2005
Exception Type	System.Exception
Message	Test (Inner Exception #2)
Machine Name	HOME
User ID	HOME\damon
User Agent	Mozilla/4.0 (compatible; MSIE 6.0; Windows NT 5.1; SV1; .NET CLR 1.1.4322; .NET CLR 2.0.50215)
Query String Data	
Form Data	__VIEWSTATE=/wEPDwULLTEyODEyNjA4MzdkZL4e9h+B4XFcNegLHmC8mGZDVgVr ctl00$ContentMain$ddlCount=6 ctl00$ContentMain$txtMessage=Test ctl00$ContentMain$btnGenerate=Generate Exception(s) __EVENTTARGET= __EVENTARGUMENT=
Stack Trace	

Figure 2-7. *Exception details from* `ShowException.aspx`

Following is the code-behind file for the markup that determines which exception to show based on the query string value, acquires that data from the database, and displays it on the page:

```
Imports SqlExceptionLogging
Imports System.Data.SqlClient
Imports System.Configuration.ConfigurationManager

Partial Class ShowException
    Inherits System.Web.UI.Page

    '***************************************************************************
    Private ExLog As ExceptionLog
```

```
'***************************************************************************
Private ReadOnly Property ExceptionID() As Integer
    Get
        If IsNumeric(Request.QueryString("ExceptionID")) Then
            Return CInt(Request.QueryString("ExceptionID"))
        Else
            Return 0
        End If
    End Get
End Property

'***************************************************************************
Protected Sub Page_Load(ByVal sender As Object, _
  ByVal e As System.EventArgs) Handles Me.Load

    Dim ExChain As ExceptionLogCollection
    Dim dbConn As New SqlConnection( _
      ConnectionStrings("Chapter02").ConnectionString)

    dbConn.Open()

    'Acquire Exception
    ExLog = New ExceptionLog
    ExLog.LoadByID(ExceptionID, dbConn)

    'Acquire Exception Chain
    ExChain = New ExceptionLogCollection
    ExChain.LoadChain(ExLog.ChainID, dbConn)

    dbConn.Close()

    'Populate Form Data
    Me.lblExceptionDate.Text = Format(ExLog.ExceptionDate, "MM/dd/yyyy")
    Me.lblExceptionID.Text = ExLog.ExceptionID.ToString
    Me.lblExceptionType.Text = ExLog.ExceptionType
    Me.lblFormData.Text = ExLog.FormData.Replace(ControlChars.CrLf, "<BR>")
    Me.lblMachineName.Text = ExLog.MachineName
    Me.lblMessage.Text = ExLog.ExceptionMessage
    Me.lblPage.Text = ExLog.Page
    Me.lblQueryStringData.Text =
      ExLog.QueryStringData.Replace(ControlChars.CrLf, "<BR>")
    Me.lblStackTrace.Text = ExLog.StackTrace.Replace(ControlChars.CrLf, "<BR>")
    Me.lblUserAgent.Text = ExLog.UserAgent
    Me.lblUserID.Text = ExLog.UserID
```

```
        'Bind Chain Information
        Me.gridExceptionChain.DataSource = ExChain
        Me.gridExceptionChain.DataBind()

    End Sub

    '***************************************************************************
    Protected Sub gridExceptionChain_RowDataBound(ByVal sender As Object, _
      ByVal e As System.Web.UI.WebControls.GridViewRowEventArgs) _
      Handles gridExceptionChain.RowDataBound

        If e.Row.RowType = DataControlRowType.DataRow Then
            Dim rowData As ExceptionLog = DirectCast(e.Row.DataItem, ExceptionLog)
            If rowData.ExceptionID = ExLog.ExceptionID Then
                e.Row.Style.Add("background-color", "#FFFF99")
            End If
        End If

    End Sub

    '***************************************************************************
    Protected Sub btnDelete_Click(ByVal sender As Object, _
      ByVal e As System.EventArgs) Handles btnDelete.Click

        Dim dbConn As New SqlConnection( _
          ConnectionStrings("Chapter02").ConnectionString)

        dbConn.Open()
        ExLog.DeleteChain(dbConn)
        dbConn.Close()
        Response.Redirect("ShowExceptionList.aspx")

    End Sub

End Class
```

Page Variables

When the page loads, it acquires an ExceptionLog object for the requested ExceptionID so it can populate the form with data. The btnDelete_Click event handler also requires an ExceptionLog object for the requested ExceptionID. Instead of reloading the data, you simply store the reference in a page-level variable, ExLog, so the same object can be referenced in both methods.

ExceptionID Property

Both the ExceptionLog and ExceptionLogCollection classes expect the ExceptionID to be passed in as an integer value, but the value passed in along the query string is a string representation of an integer. The read-only ExceptionID property parses the integer out of the string and returns the expected Integer value. It also does some checking to make sure that an exception does not occur if someone places gibberish in the query string.

Page_Load Method

The Page_Load method is responsible for connecting to a database, retrieving exception information, and populating the web form with that exception information. It begins by declaring a new ExceptionLogCollection named ExChain, and then creates and opens a database using the "Chapter02" connection string defined in Web.config.

After connecting to the database, Page_Load assigns the ExLog a new ExceptionLog object, and then populates the object using the LoadByID method. Notice that it passes in the open database connection and the value integer value from the ExceptionID property into the LoadByID method. After loading the exception object from the database, the page has access to ChainID of the exception. So, the page loads the exception chain information into the ExChain variable by passing the open database connection and ChainID to the LoadChain method.

After the Page_Load method has the exception and exception chain information, it closes the database connection and populates the form with the appropriate exception information values. Notice that it replaces the line breaks in the QueryStringData, FormData, and StackTrace properties with <BR/> tags so they display appropriately on the page. Also notice that it data binds the gridExceptionChain GridView to the ExceptionLogCollection stored in ExChain. This causes the grid to display all the exception chain information on the form.

gridExceptionChain_RowDataBound

Earlier you read that the ShowException.aspx page highlights the current exception in the exception chain so the user can easily determine its position. That highlighting occurs in the gridExceptionChain_RowDataBound method, which fires each time a row of data is added to the grid.

This method starts by checking to see if the current row being data bound is a data row. If not, the method does nothing because it only needs to look at rows that contain data. If it is a data row, then the method acquires a reference to the row's data item. It then compares the ExceptionID from the row's data item to the ExceptionID of the ExLog variable, which contains a reference to the currently selected exception. If the two numbers match, then the row is highlighted.

btnDelete_Click

This method opens up a database connection, deletes the exception chain, closes the database, and then redirects the user back to the ShowExceptionList.aspx page. This effectively deletes the current exception as well as all other related exceptions in the exception chain.

Summary

Exception management should be a high priority on your project checklist because it has the potential to impact a variety of different areas. When your application handles routine exceptions without missing a step, it builds user confidence in the application and in you as the developer of the application. It can also save time and money because you end up getting fewer calls from users with system issues that need to be addressed. Exception management can also help smooth out the development, testing, and maintenance phases by continually capturing and logging exceptions as they occur.

In this chapter, you reviewed basic exception-handling techniques, built custom exception classes, created custom error pages, and implemented global error handling. You also got a general overview of logging exceptions and storing them in a database, which you can apply to other technologies, such as third-party exception-handling and logging tools. As your next step, consider downloading and learning a specific exception-management tool so you can use it in your next project.

CHAPTER 3

Master Pages, Themes, and Control Skins

Appearance matters. Whether you like it or not, people make decisions about how well they like your application and how well they think it works based on its visual appearance. Web applications exhibiting a consistent look and feel exude professionalism and instill confidence in users that the application is well built and reliable. People naturally conclude that the attention to the visual design is on par with that of the functional capabilities of the application. First glances aside, consistency also enhances the user experience because people feel most comfortable when they are in a familiar environment. By creating a consistent location for certain page elements, users will inherently know how to get around in your application even when accessing pages to which they are not normally accustomed. My favorite news site, for example, always lists the news categories and stories in a menu structure on the left hand side of every page. No matter where I am on their site, I have the comfort of knowing that I can navigate to a different news category or story using that menu.

Aside from the CSS (Cascading Style Sheet) support inherent in HTML, ASP.NET 1.x did not have any features to help you maintain a consistent look and feel throughout your application. ASP.NET 2.0 remedies that shortcoming with the introduction of Master Pages, themes, and control skins. Master Pages, a much needed and highly anticipated feature, allow you to define and maintain page layouts and common page content from a single file. Themes enable you to apply different CSS and control skins to your application. Control skins allow you to apply properties to specific ASP.NET controls throughout the entire application.

This chapter briefly covers each technology and how to use it in your applications. Here is an outline of what you'll find inside:

- *Master Page:* Demonstrates how you can use Master Pages to create page templates to control the look, feel, and layout of pages in your application.
- *Themes and Control Skins:* Discusses how to create and apply different visual styles to your application using CSS and control skins.

Master Pages are, by far, the most popular of these new additions to ASP.NET 2.0, so we'll begin by taking a look at them and how they can really simplify development.

Master Pages

One of my current projects truly exemplifies the need for Master Pages. We are building an article-management system for an online publisher whose existing site is managed entirely in static HTML. All the pages on the static site look very professional because the layouts, fonts, colors, and other visual styles are consistent across all the pages. The problem is that they achieved that consistency by copying the base HTML layout into each and every page. As a result, any changes to the site layout have to be made on hundreds of individual pages to maintain consistency.

Master Pages allow you to control the look, feel, and behavior of multiple pages in your application from a single location. In a Master Page, you define the basic page layout using HTML and ASP.NET controls and the behavior using server-side code. Building a Master Page is, for the most part, just like working with any standard ASP.NET web form. The most notable difference is that you can add `ContentPlaceHolder` controls to a Master Page. A `ContentPlaceHolder` control defines a region where you can inject content into the Master Page. All other content on the Master Page is locked, so the `ContentPlaceHolder` controls represent the only locations where content differs from page to page. Pages that employ Master Pages define `Content` controls that contain the page content. ASP.NET processes requests for these pages by injecting the `Content` controls on the page into the appropriate `ContentPlaceHolder` controls on the Master Page at runtime. Figure 3-1 depicts the process.

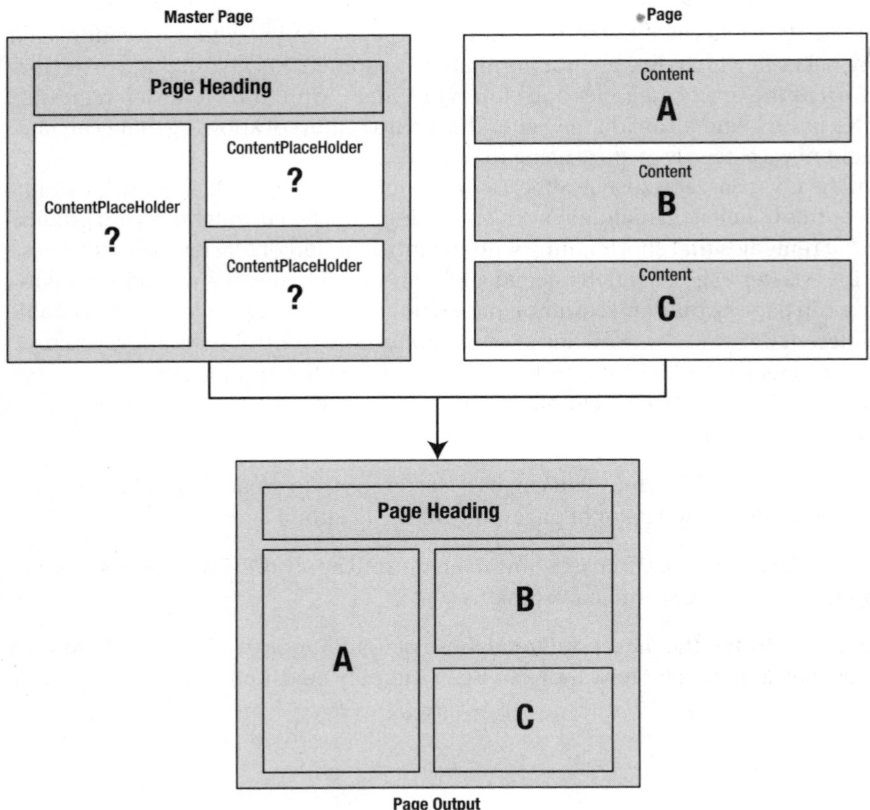

Figure 3-1. *Injecting page content into a Master Page*

Creating a Master Page

You add new Master Pages to your application by right-clicking on the web project in the Solution Explorer and selecting the **Add New Item** option from the context menu. Alternatively, you can select **Website ➤ Add New Item** in the Visual Studio IDE. Either way, Visual Studio displays the **Add New Item** dialog box (Figure 3-2), which allows you to select the type of item you want to add to your project. Select the **Master Page** item from the list and enter a name for the new Master Page in the **Name** text box. Like a normal ASP.NET page, you can put the server-side code for the Master Page directly in the markup file or in a code-behind file. If you want to use a code-behind file, make sure you check the **Place code in separate file** option. Click the **Add** button and Visual Studio adds the appropriate files to your web application.

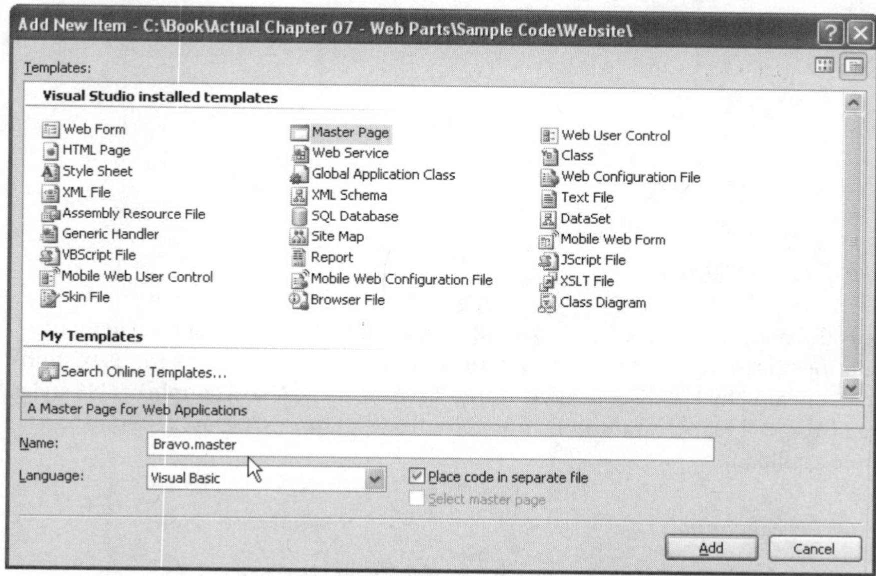

Figure 3-2. *Visual Studio's Add New Item dialog box*

After Visual Studio adds the Master Page to your application, you can interact with it in the editor as though it was a normal page. You can add HTML, styles, JavaScript, and web controls to the page and even create server-side code to respond to page and control events. As you design the Master Page, you'll run across sections that should contain page-specific content. When you do, drop in a `ContentPlaceHolder` control so you can inject page content into the Master Page at that location.

As an example, let's say you are creating an intranet application for the Bravo Corporation, a fictitious organization that makes things and then sells them to people. All the pages in the application need to have the same header and layout, but the content for each page is different. A Quick Links section in the subheader displays important links that are relevant to the current page. In other words, the page content and the quick links change from page to page, but the heading and overall page layout should be consistent across all pages. Figure 3-3 shows an example of the page layout.

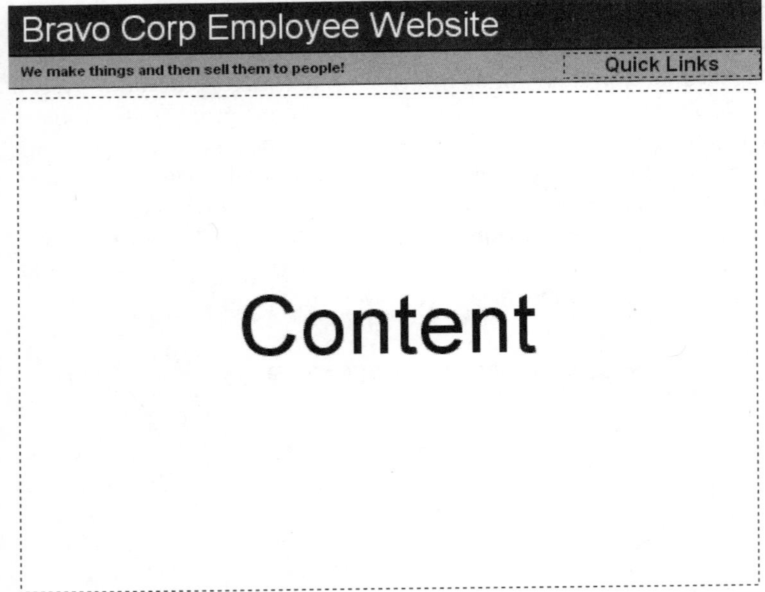

Figure 3-3. *Bravo Corp page layout*

Following is the markup required to make a Master Page for the layout shown in Figure 3-3. All the code specific to the Master Page content is shown in bold, and the various sections of the page are delineated by HTML comments (`<!-- Comment -->`). Also a couple of CSS styles are used in the Listing 3-1 HTML that can be found in the `/App_Themes/Default/Default.css` file in the sample application.

Listing 3-1. *Master Page Example*

```
<%@ Master Language="VB" CodeFile="Bravo.master.vb" Inherits="Bravo" %>
<html xmlns="http://www.w3.org/1999/xhtml" >
<head id="PageHeading" runat="server">
    <title>Bravo Company</title>
</head>
<body topmargin=0 bottommargin=0 leftmargin=0 rightmargin=0>
  <form id="formMain" runat="server">
    <table style="width:100%;" border=0 cellpadding=0 cellspacing=0>

      <!--Header Section -->
      <tr>
        <td class="PageHeading">Bravo Corp Employee Website</td>
      </tr>
```

```
        <!--Sub-Header Section -->
        <tr>
          <td class="PageSubHeading">
            <table style="width:100%;" cellpadding=0 cellspacing=0>
              <tr>
                <td align=left class="TagLine">
                  We make things and then sell them to people!
                </td>
                <td align=right class="TagLine">
                  <asp:contentplaceholder id="QuickLinks" runat="server">
                  </asp:contentplaceholder>
                </td>
              </tr>
            </table>
          </td>
        </tr>

        <!-- Main Body Section -->
        <tr>
          <td>
            <table cellpadding=5>
              <tr>
                <td>
                  <asp:contentplaceholder id="MainContent" runat="server">
                  </asp:contentplaceholder>
                </td>
              </tr>
            </table>
          </td>
        </tr>
      </table>
    </form>
  </body>
</html>
```

At the top of the Master Page, the `<%@ Master %>` directive tells ASP.NET how to handle the page. Visual Studio generates this section for you automatically. Know, however, that it is almost identical to the `<%@ Page %>` directive.

Inside the page markup, you'll find two `ContentPlaceHolder` controls: one in the subheader section and one in the main body section. The one in the subheader is named `QuickLinks` and allows you to inject links into the subheader area; the second one in the main body section is named `MainContent` and allows you to create the body of the page. Next, you'll see how to create a content page that uses a Master Page.

Creating Content Pages

Any page that uses a Master Page is known as a *content page*. You add new content pages to your application using the **Add New Item** dialog box as described earlier with Master Pages. But, instead of selecting Master Page from the list of items, you select the **Web Form** item (see Figure 3-4). After you select Web Form, follow these steps to create a content page:

1. Specify the page name in the **Name** text box.
2. Check the **Place code in a separate file option** if you want to use a code-behind file.
3. Make sure you check the **Select Master Page** option. This tells the Add New Item dialog box that the new page is a content page that requires the uses a Master Page.
4. Click the **Add** button.

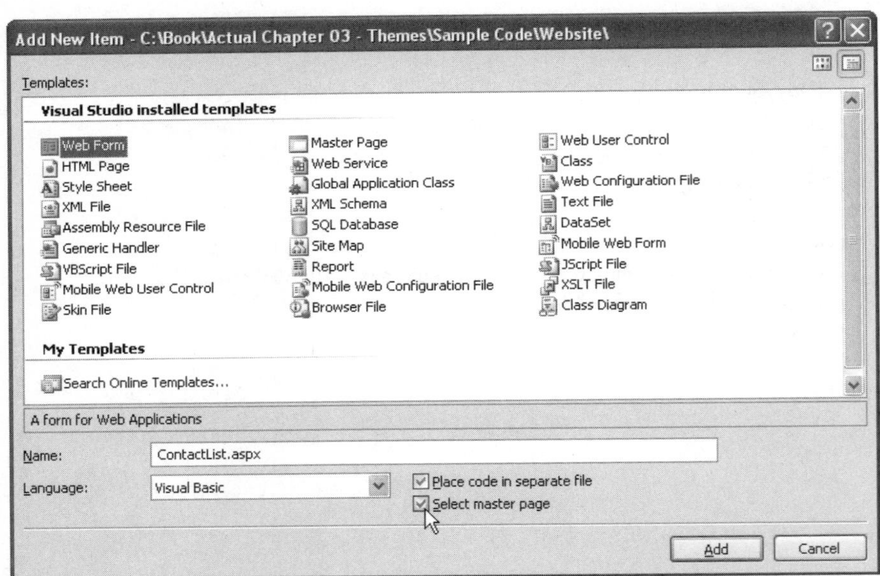

Figure 3-4. *Add New Item dialog box showing the Select master page check box*

After you click on the **Add** button, Visual Studio displays the **Select a Master Page** dialog box as shown in Figure 3-5. This dialog box displays your application folder structure and allows you to select which Master Page you want to use for the new page. As you select directories on the left side of the dialog box, Master Pages in that folder appear on the right-hand side. When you locate the one you want to use, click to select it and then click the **OK** button.

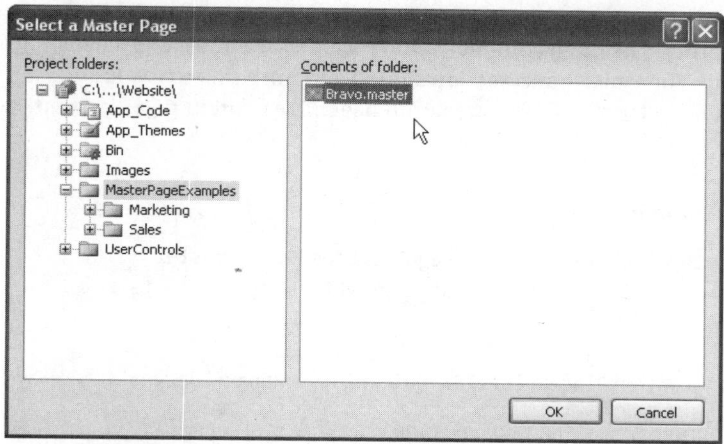

Figure 3-5. *The Select a Master Page dialog box*

After you click the **OK** button, Visual Studio creates a new content page with the appropriate `<@% Page %>` directive parameters that define which Master Page the content page uses. It also automatically creates `Content` controls that match up with the `ContentPlaceHolders` in the Master Page. `Content` controls have a property named `ContentPlaceHolderID`, which identifies the `ContentPlaceHolder` control on the Master Page where the content should be injected. Listing 3-2 shows the content page generated by Visual Studio for use with the Master Page shown earlier.

Listing 3-2. *Content Page*

```
<%@ Page Language="VB" MasterPageFile="~/MasterPageExamples/Bravo.master"
    AutoEventWireup="false" CodeFile="ContactList.aspx.vb" Inherits="ContactList"
    title="Untitled Page" %>

<asp:Content ID="Content1" ContentPlaceHolderID="QuickLinks" Runat="Server">
</asp:Content>

<asp:Content ID="Content2" ContentPlaceHolderID="MainContent" Runat="Server">
</asp:Content>
```

Notice the `MasterPageFile` property in the `<@% Page %>` directive at the top of the code listing. This property points to the Master Page file that the page should use in conjunction with its content. Also note that the page does not contain any standard `<HTML>` or `<BODY>` tags normally found in a page. Instead, it has two `Content` controls. You cannot specify any HTML or web controls for a content page outside of a `Content` control, although you do have free reign inside the `Content` control. Finally, observe that the `ContentPlaceHolderID` values in the `Content` controls match up with the `ID` values for the `ContentPlaceHolder` controls from the Master Page. If you accidentally specify a nonexistent `ContentPlaceHolderID` value, then you should receive an error in the task list. Your project will still build successfully, but if you run the page, it will throw an exception.

Returning to the example, let's say that you wanted to create a company contact list using the Master Page discussed earlier. The main content should include the names and extensions of the people in the company. The Quick Links section should contain a link to the Phone System Help page and a link to an Update My Contact Info page. The content page markup would look like Listing 3-3.

Listing 3-3. *ContactList.aspx Example Content Page*

```
<%@ Page Language="VB" MasterPageFile="~/MasterPageExamples/Bravo.master"
    AutoEventWireup="false" CodeFile="ContactList.aspx.vb" Inherits="ContactList"
    title="Company Contact List" %>

<asp:Content ID="Content1" ContentPlaceHolderID="QuickLinks" Runat="Server">
    <a href="">Phone System Help</a> |
    <a href="">Update My Contact Info</a>
</asp:Content>

<asp:Content ID="Content2" ContentPlaceHolderID="MainContent" Runat="Server">
    <div style="width:400px;">
        Welcome to the employee directory page.  You can find a list of
        phone numbers in the table below.  Have fun calling people!<br /><br />
    </div>
    <table cellpadding=5 style="border:1px solid black;">
        <tr style="font-weight:bold; color:White; background-color:DarkBlue;">
            <td>Name</td><td>Extension</td>
        </tr>
        <tr><td>Anderson, Ty</td><td>x 5891</td></tr>
        <tr><td>Armstrong, Teresa</td><td>x 1212</td></tr>
        <tr><td>Haynes, Tim</td><td>x 2911</td></tr>
        <-- etc -->
    </table>
</asp:Content>
```

As you can see, only content is specified in the `ContactList.aspx` content page. No layout, no header, and no subheading are defined in the content page. When ASP.NET renders the page, it injects the content into the Master Page, and the final result looks like Figure 3-6.

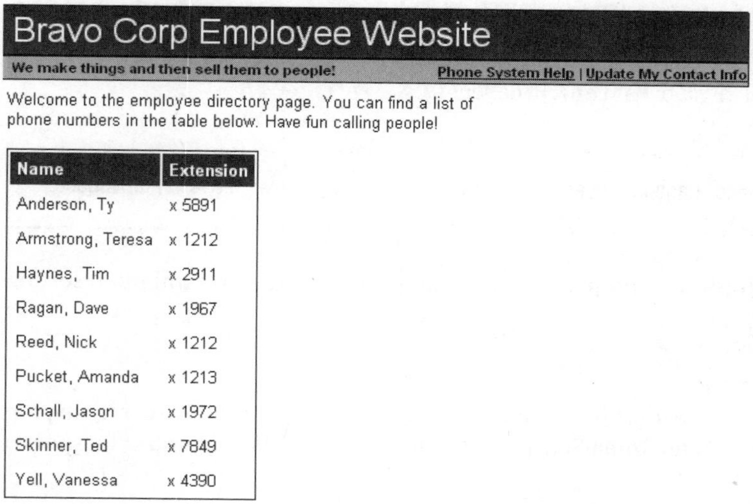

Bravo Corp Employee Website

We make things and then sell them to people! Phone System Help | Update My Contact Info

Welcome to the employee directory page. You can find a list of phone numbers in the table below. Have fun calling people!

Name	Extension
Anderson, Ty	x 5891
Armstrong, Teresa	x 1212
Haynes, Tim	x 2911
Ragan, Dave	x 1967
Reed, Nick	x 1212
Pucket, Amanda	x 1213
Schall, Jason	x 1972
Skinner, Ted	x 7849
Yell, Vanessa	x 4390

Figure 3-6. *ContactList.aspx displayed in the browser*

Accessing Master Pages from Content Pages

Many scenarios occur in which a content page may need access to controls or functionality in the Master Page. You can do this via the Master property of the Page object. Every ASP.NET page stores a reference to its Master Page in the Master property. If the page does not use a Master Page, then the reference is set to Nothing. By default, the Master property is a MasterPage type. This allows you to access any method or property normally found in the MasterPage base class from which all Master Pages ultimately inherit.

One of the most useful methods on the Master property is the FindControl method, which reaches up into the Master Page to look for controls. For example, if you have a Label control defined on your Master Page named lblTitle, then you can acquire a reference to that Label control by using Master.FindControl("lblTitle") and then casting the control returned to a Label control. This allows you to set controls in the Master Page based on logic from the content page.

Another useful tactic for interacting with the Master Page is to strongly type the Master property using the <@% MasterType %> directive. To do this, just add the <@MasterType> directive below the <%@ Page %> directive and point the VirtualPath at the Master Page file:

```
<%@ Page Language="VB" MasterPageFile="~/MasterPageExamples/Bravo.master"
    AutoEventWireup="false" CodeFile="ContactList.aspx.vb" Inherits="ContactList"
    title="Company Contact List" %>
<%@ MasterType VirtualPath="~/MasterPageExamples/Bravo.master" %>
```

Strongly typing the Master property gives you direct access to public methods and properties defined in that Master Page without having to cast it from a MasterPage into the target type. For example, let's say that you have a Master Page with a menu on the left-hand side. All pages use the exact same menu, so you define it directly in the Master Page. Some pages, however, do not use the menu at all, so you want to hide it on those pages. As such, you create a public function named HideMenu on the Master Page. The method simply sets the visible property on the menu section to `false` to hide it from view. If you do NOT strongly type the `Master` property, then you end up having to cast the `Master` property before you can use the public method you defined:

```
DirectCast(Master, ASP.Bravo_Master).HideMenu()
```

Note You can access Master Page and user control resources for the page via the ASP namespace.

When you strongly type the `Master` property, you can simply call the method without resorting to any casting:

```
Master.HideMenu()
```

This makes working with and reading the code a bit easier. As an added benefit, strongly typing the `Master` property gives you full IntelliSense support for the methods and properties specified in the Master Page.

Defining a Default Master Page for Your Application

All content pages usually specify which Master Page they use via the `MasterPageFile` property in the `<%@ Page %>` directive. If you leave it off, ASP.NET throws an error when you access the page and informs you that `Content` controls can only be used in conjunction with a Master Page. There is one exception to that rule. You can define a default Master Page in `web.config` in the `<pages>` element as shown in Listing 3-4.

Listing 3-4. *Default Master Page Defined in* `Web.config`

```
<configuration>
  ...
  <system.web>
    ...
    <pages theme="Default" masterPageFile="~/MasterPageExamples/Bravo.master" />
    ...
  </system.web>
</configuration>
```

When you specify a default Master Page in `Web.config`, all the content pages without a `masterPageFile` value defined in the `<%@ Page %>` directive default to the Master Page in `Web.config`. You can use this feature to help manage which Master Pages your application uses from a single location.

Note ASP.NET only applies the default Master Page to content pages that do not have a Master Page explicitly defined in the `<%@ Page %>` directive. ASP.NET is also smart enough to check that the page is a content page (that is, it contains `Content` controls) before applying the default Master Page setting. You can still have normal pages in your application that do not use Master Pages even if you set a default Master Page.

Changing Master Pages in Code

You can programmatically change the Master Page in code using the `MasterPageFile` property on the `Page` object; however, there are a few limitations when using this approach. First, you can only set the `MasterPageFile` property during the `PreInit` event. Attempting to change the Master Page past this point results in a runtime exception. Second, the Master Page that you specify in code must have `ContentPlaceHolder` controls whose `ID` properties match up with the `ContentPlaceHolderID` properties for the `Content` controls defined in the content page. If they don't, an exception is thrown.

Remember, this is how a content page determines where to inject content into the Master Page. Listing 3-5 demonstrates how to set the Master Page in code.

Listing 3-5. *Setting the Master Page in Code*

```
'***************************************************************************
Protected Sub Page_PreInit(ByVal sender As Object, _
  ByVal e As System.EventArgs) Handles Me.PreInit
    Page.MasterPageFile = "Delta.master"
End Sub
```

Nested Master Pages

ASP.NET allows you to create nested Master Pages. In other words, you can specify a Master Page for a Master Page. One scenario in which this may be useful is creating a corporate intranet for a company with multiple departments or divisions. You can control the overall look and feel for the company using one Master Page, and you can control the overall look and feel for a department using a nested Master Page.

Listing 3-6 is the markup for the `BravoSales.master` file, an example nested Master Page that defines the look and feel for pages in the Bravo Corporation's Sales Department. It uses the `Bravo.master` file for the overall corporate look and feel. Figure 3-7 demonstrates how nested Master Pages allow you to inherit the look and feel of one Master Page into another.

Listing 3-6. `BravoSales.master` *Example*

```
<%@ Master MasterPageFile="~/MasterPageExamples/Bravo.master" Language="VB"
    CodeFile="BravoSales.master.vb" Inherits="BravoSales" %>
<%@ MasterType VirtualPath="~/MasterPageExamples/Bravo.master" %>

<asp:Content ID="Content1" ContentPlaceHolderID="QuickLinks" Runat="Server">
    <a href="SalesHome.aspx">Sales Dept. Home</a>
    <asp:ContentPlaceHolder runat=server ID="SalesQuickLinks" />
</asp:Content>

<asp:Content ID="Content2" ContentPlaceHolderID="MainContent" Runat="Server">
    <span style="font-size:20pt;">The Sales Department!</span><hr />
    <asp:ContentPlaceHolder runat=server ID="SalesMainContent" />
</asp:Content>
```

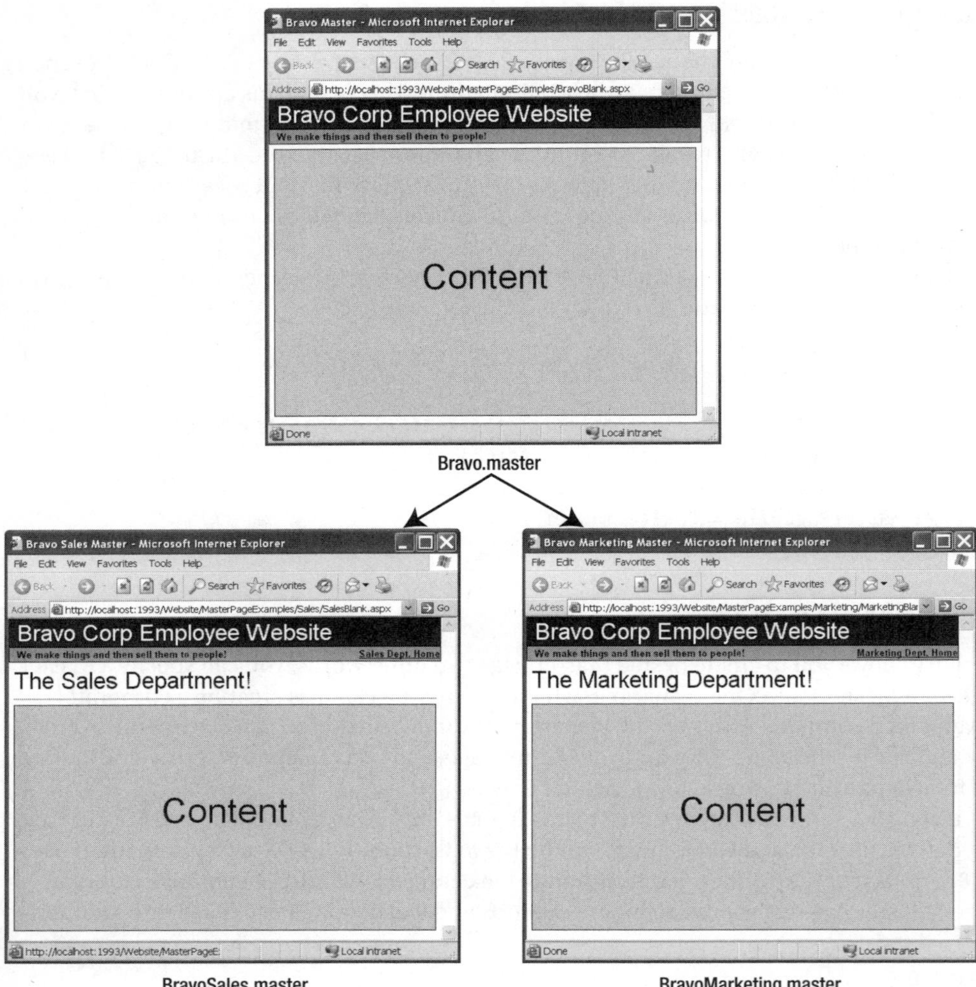

Figure 3-7. *Nested Master Pages*

Creating a nested Master Page is virtually identical to creating a content page, but instead of using a `<%@ Page %>` directive, you use a `<%@ Master %>` directive. You still specify the Master Page using the `MasterPageFile` property, you can still strongly type the Mater Page using the `<%@ MasterType %>` directive, and the `Content` controls still have to specify the appropriate `ContentPlaceHolderID` so ASP.NET knows where to inject the content into the Master Page. The main difference is that you can define any number of new `ContentPlaceHolders` in the nested Master Page, which you can then use in subsequent content pages.

Caution Visual Studio.NET 2005 (Beta 2) does not support visual editing of content pages that uses nested Master Pages. If you strongly prefer the graphical editor, then you may want to avoid using nested Master Pages.

Themes and Control Skins

Themes allow you to control the look and feel of your entire web application using CSS and control skins. If you have worked with web applications in the past, then you know that CSS styles control the way HTML elements appear in the browser by defining visual and behavioral properties. Control skins are, in many respects, style sheets for ASP.NET controls. Instead of hard-coding visual information into each ASP.NET control in your application, now you can create a control skin that defines how you want that control to appear throughout your entire application. When that type of control is rendered by the ASP.NET runtime, the control skin dictates property settings on that control that govern its visual appearance.

Creating a Theme

To add a theme to your web application, right-click on your web project and select **Theme Folder** from the **Add Folder** context menu. This adds an `App_Themes` folder to your application as well as a subfolder called `Theme1`, although you should change this name to something more meaningful to your application.

Each theme in your application requires a new subfolder under the `App_Themes` folder, and you can add a new theme by selecting **Theme Folder** from the **Add Folder** context menu. If you want a theme called Bluish Haze, then you would add a new subfolder named "Bluish Haze" to the `Themes` folder. If you wanted a theme called GreenTheme, then you would name the folder "GreenTheme." You get the idea. After you create the folder, you then need to create any control skin files for your theme and, optionally, the theme's CSS. Figure 3-8 shows an example of a Themes file structure with CSS and control skin files.

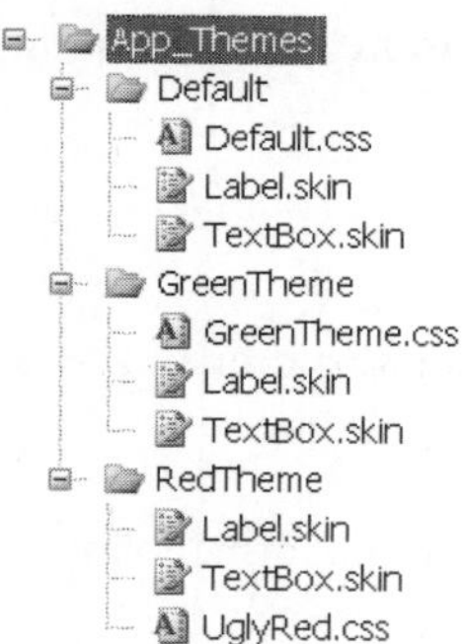

Figure 3-8. `Themes` *folder showing control skins and CSS.Note that the* `.css` *file names match the folder names.*

Adding a Cascading Style Sheet to Your Theme

After you have created your theme's folder, you can create a CSS for your theme. To do so, right-click on your theme's folder and select **Add New Item** from the context menu. Select the **Style Sheet** template from the template list and name your style sheet using the same name as your theme. If you are creating a style sheet for the GreenTheme, then name your style sheet **GreenTheme.css**. You can then edit the style sheet and add any necessary style definitions and classes that you may need.

Note You are not required to create a CSS for your theme. In fact, you can have a completely blank theme that does not have a style sheet or any control skins if you want your page to render without any CSS styles or ASP.NET properties to be applied to the page.

When you specify a theme for a page, the page is required to have a `<head RunAt=server>` tag. ASP.NET automatically places a `<link>` tag in the head section that points to the CSS for your theme, assuming that you have one specified. If the page does not have a `<head➥ RunAt=server>` tag, then an exception is thrown.

Creating Control Skins for Your Theme

As mentioned before, control skins are like style sheets for ASP.NET. You define control skins inside `.skin` files that reside in the various themes folders in your application. You can lump all your control skins into a single file, or you can create a series of `.skin` files to hold different control skins. It is mostly a matter of organizational preference. If you decide to use multiple `.skin` files, then the naming convention is normally

```
[ControlName].skin
```

Thus, the control skin file for `Textbox` controls should be named `TextBox.skin`, and the skin file for `Label` controls should be called `Label.skin`. The sample application uses the individual file-naming method.

To create a skin file for a `TextBox` control, follow these steps:

1. Right-click on your theme's folder, and then select the **Add New Item** button from the context menu.

2. When the **Add New Item** dialog box appears, select **Skin File** from the list of templates, and name it **TextBox.skin**.

3. Click the **Add** button. The `TextBox.skin` file appears in the Solution Explorer and opens in the Visual Studio IDE.

Creating the content for a skin file is as easy as defining a control on a web form. Following is an example of a `TextBox` control skin:

```
<asp:TextBox Runat="Server" BackColor="Gainsboro" Font-Bold="True"
             BorderStyle="Solid" BorderColor="Green" BorderWidth="1px"
             ForeColor="DarkGreen" Font-Italic="False" />
```

The control skin content is similar to any `TextBox` definition you would see on a web form, but notice there is no `ID` or `Text` property specified. You don't specify the `Text` property because the `Text` value changes from one control the next so you do not want to specify a global value. If you specify an `ID` property in the `.skin` file, the application will not compile. When ASP.NET encounters a server control while rendering a page with themes, it determines whether there is a control skin for that control type in the appropriate theme folder. If one is found, it reads the skin information and automatically maps any of the properties specified in the skin file onto the control it is rendering. So, if you have a TextBox control defined in your application that looks like this:

```
<asp:Textbox Runat="Server" ID="MyTextbox" Text="My Text Value" />
```

It will be rendered as though it was defined like this:

```
<asp:TextBox Runat="Server" ID="MyTextbox" Text="My Text Value"
             BackColor="Gainsboro" Font-Bold="True" BorderStyle="Solid"
             BorderColor="Green" BorderWidth="1px" ForeColor="DarkGreen"
             Font-Italic="False" />
```

Notice that the only properties from the actual definition are the ID and the Text properties, all the other properties come from the skin file.

■ Caution If you have a property defined in both a control and in the skin file, the skin file property overwrites the property on the control. This is in stark contrast to the way CSS files work, so you need to be conscious of it, especially if you are used to working with CSS files.

Disabling Control Skins

Whenever ASP.NET encounters a control, it tries to apply the applicable control skin. Sometimes, however, you'll have a control you do not want the skin to apply to. In these instances, you just have to set the EnableTheming property to False on the control. When ASP.NET encounters a control with the EnableTheming property set to False, it does not attempt to apply any skin to the control. For example, ASP.NET does not attempt to skin the following control:

```
<asp:TextBox Runat="Server" ID="MyNonSkinnedTextBox" EnableThemeing="False"/>
```

Creating Named Control Skins for Your Theme

At times, you'll also want to apply a skin to a control, but you want it to be different than the skin you already have defined. That's when named control skins come into play. Named control skins are defined in the same file as control skins, so you can have one control skin and multiple named control skins in a single .skin file. Following is an example of a TextBox skin file that contains both a control skin and a named control skin:

```
<asp:TextBox Runat="Server" BackColor="Gainsboro" Font-Bold="True"
   BorderStyle="Solid" BorderColor="Green" BorderWidth="1px"
   ForeColor="DarkGreen" Font-Italic="False" />
```

```
<asp:TextBox Runat="Server" SkinID="MultiLine" Height="75px" Width="300px"
   BackColor="Gainsboro" Font-Bold="True" BorderStyle="Solid"
   BorderColor="Green" BorderWidth="1px" ForeColor="DarkGreen"
   Font-Italic="False" />
```

The first section of the code contains the control skin for a TextBox. The second section contains a named control skin. You can tell the second item is a named control skin because it contains a SkinID property to "name" it. Also notice that it specifies a height and width to properly display multiline text boxes (hence the name MultiLine). If you have a multiline text box that needs to use this skin, it would be defined as follows:

```
<asp:TextBox Runat="Server" ID="MyMultiLineTextBox" SkinID="MultiLine"
          TextMode="MultiLine" />
```

When ASP.NET encounters this control, it looks for a TextBox control skin specifically named MultiLine in the appropriate theme folder. If it cannot find the MultiLine named skin in the folder, then no skin is applied. Not even the unnamed control skin for the control type.

Applying Themes to Specific Pages or the Entire Application

You can apply a specific theme to a page using the Theme parameter of the Page directive. In the following example, the GreenTheme theme is applied to the page:

```
<%@ Page Language="VB" CompileWith="ThemeDemo.aspx.vb" ClassName="ThemeDemo_aspx"
title="Theme Demo" EnableViewState="False" Theme="GreenTheme" %>
```

If you want to apply a theme to every page in your entire application, then you can use Web.config to specify a theme. This is accomplished via the theme property of the <pages> element:

```
<configuration>
    ...
    <system.web>
        ...
        <pages theme="GreenTheme" />
        ...
    </system.web>
</configuration>
```

On the off chance that one of the pages in your application needs a different theme than the one specified in the Web.config file, you can override Web.config by specifying a theme in the Page directive, as described earlier. It has precedence over Web.config.

Programming with Themes

Another option for setting the theme for a page is to do it programmatically. The Page class exposes a property called Theme you can use to set the page's theme in code. Like the Master➥PageFile property, you can only set the Theme property during the PreInit event. If you attempt to change it after the PreInit event, an exception is thrown.

Following is an example of how to programmatically set a page's theme. It assumes the appropriate theme name is passed in as a parameter in the query string.

```
Private Sub Page_PreInit(ByVal sender As Object, ByVal e As System.EventArgs) _
    Handles Me.PreInit
        Page.Theme = Request.QueryString("Theme")
End Sub
```

Summary

Using a consistent look and feel throughout your application helps build the perception that it is well built, well thought out, and reliable. Before ASP.NET 2.0, however, maintaining a consistent look and feel was difficult because there was no formal structure for making global layout, behavior, and visual changes aside from the inherent support for CSS in HTML. The introduction of Master Pages, themes, and control skins gives you a distinct advantage in terms of global site maintenance. As you use them on projects, you'll find they are major time-savers.

CHAPTER 4

Developing Reusable Components: The Skinned Page-Message Control

Building an application is a far easier task when you have the appropriate reusable components at your disposal. Reusable components allow you to implement functionality more easily, more accurately, and faster than you could by copying and pasting code from one place to another or re-implementing it each time you need it. Plus, you have the added benefit of updating a reusable component from a single location instead of having to rummage through each page in your project to apply a fix. Before you begin a project, you should always take time out with your project team to brainstorm a list of features in your application that can be consolidated into reusable components, and you should budget time to implement those components. You will find that although custom components take a big chunk out of your initial development time, they save a lot more time in the long run.

Page messaging is a great example of functionality that you can easily consolidate into a reusable component. All your applications should display informative messages back to the user in response to successful or failed actions. Otherwise, you risk making your users confused or frustrated, neither of which is very helpful. Confused users tend to break your application. Frustrated users tend to hate your application. I had to deal with both when working on a project in which page messaging was an afterthought instead of a priority. My experience came while developing a worker's compensation claims system for a governmental institution. We were replacing an older application designed for single office use with a newer application designed for the entire enterprise. Time was short and the budget was tight. Not an ideal environment for developing a relatively ambitious workflow application. One of the features that suffered most under this time constraint was page messaging.

Conceptually, outputting a message on the page is a fairly simple task. In fact, each message should only take a single line of code to output. It becomes significantly more painstaking, however, if you do not have the right tools. Such was the case in this application. Instead of taking the time to build a proper page-messaging control in the first place, we decided to "save time" by slapping a label control into the application whenever we needed to output a message. Thus, there was no standard location for messages, no consistent look and feel for messages, no easy way to format messages, and no easy way to concatenate multiple messages. Multiply those problems by the number of pages that required messaging, and you can see why we spent more time battling with our "time-saving" method than we would have had we taken the time to build a full-featured control capable of gracefully handling all the messaging tasks.

Obviously, lost development time was a result of the decision to forgo creating a page-messaging control, but it was not the only one. Because the label-based messaging approach was difficult for developers to code, messaging throughout the system was not implemented as thoroughly as it should have been. Many times, confirmation messages were not displayed after successful add or update operations. This confused some people and they figured the update never occurred. As such, they simply reentered the information. In turn, this led to a data duplication issue that hurt system usability. Another issue that we encountered was that error messages were displayed when an error occurred, but the page did not automatically scroll up to the error message. Because it was not visible on the page, users did not see the error message and were left thinking the update succeeded when in fact it had failed. Users were extremely frustrated when they attempted to access the data they entered only to find it was not available.

After analyzing the situation, we went back and created a much more sophisticated page-messaging control that automatically handled formatting, concatenation, and page scrolling. Because it was well designed, we made it part of our standard project toolset, and it has been saving us time and effort on every project since. This chapter contains information about building reusable components for your application and discusses the new features ASP.NET 2.0 has for creating and using those controls. Here's what you will find inside:

- *New Control Features in ASP.NET 2.0*: Describes the new design time rendering of `UserControls` and global tag registration.

- *Developing Server Controls Using the Control State*: Demonstrates how to use the new control state mechanism in your custom server controls by implementing a very simple custom server control. This also acts as basic server control primer before you start building the page-message control.

- *Building a Skinned Page-Message Control*: covers the design and implementation of a page-message control you can reuse in projects to communicate messages with users. This control uses a technique known as *skinning* so you can change the visual display of the control from project to project without ever having to modify the actual control code. You'll also learn the difference between skinning and the ASP.NET 2.0 control skins discussed in the previous chapter as they are two separate and distinct concepts.

Let's start by taking a look at some of the control-oriented features you'll find in ASP.NET 2.0. We'll then work our way into the more advanced topics.

New Control Features in ASP.NET 2.0

Visual Studio 2005 and ASP.NET 2.0 introduced a couple of new features that make it easier to work with controls: the design-time rendering of user controls feature and the global tag registration feature. Design-time rendering of user controls, a much anticipated addition to Visual Studio, allows page creators to actually see how a user control will be displayed in a page. The new global tag registration feature means that you can create a single tag registration entry in `Web.config` instead of having to add them over and over again to each page of your application.

Design-Time Rendering of User Controls

User controls, which are like miniature web forms, have been around since the inception of ASP.NET. You can create content for them, drop server controls in them, and even write code to respond to page and control events. They are useful when you need to make a reusable component specifically for a single application because they are simpler to create and use than a full-blown server control.

User controls are stored in `.ascx` files along with all the other files in your application. Adding one to a page simply requires dragging the `.ascx` file from the Solution Explorer onto the form designer and dropping it wherever you want it to end up—equivalent to adding a control from the toolbox. Visual Studio automatically creates the appropriate `Register` directive and control tag for you.

In Visual Studio 2002 and 2003, the design-time rendering of a user control was, to be nice, rather meek. Instead of seeing the HTML from your user control, you would see a gray box with text inside identifying it as a user control and displaying the control's ID (see Figure 4-1). Considering the entire web form designer revolves around displaying HTML, this display method seemed a bit strange.

MyUserControl - VS 2003
This shows the design time rendering of the
MyUserControl in Visual Studio 2003
UserControl - MyUserControl1

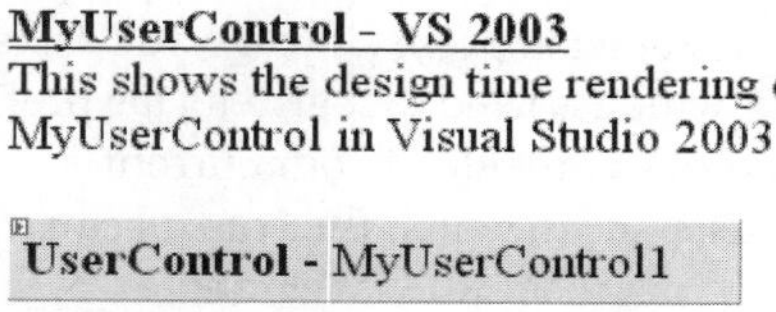

Figure 4-1. *User control displayed as gray box in Visual Studio 2003*

Fortunately the issue has been rectified in Visual Studio 2005. Now when you create a user control and add it to the page, the control appears in all its visual glory. This makes it much easier to see how the final page will look when displayed in the browser. Figure 4-2 shows a user control displayed in Visual Studio 2005.

MyUserControl - VS 2005
This shows the design time rendering of the
MyUserControl in Visual Studio 2005

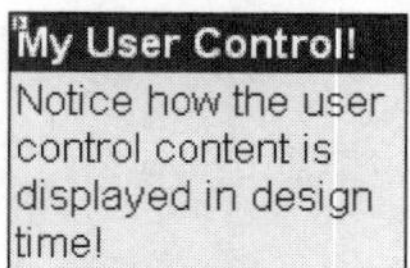
My User Control!
Notice how the user control content is displayed in design time!

Figure 4-2. *User control displayed in Visual Studio 2005*

Global Tag Registration

Whenever you drop a custom server control or a user control on one of your web forms, a tag is added to your `.aspx` page that looks similar to the following:

```
<!-- Custom Server Control -->
<msgControls:ControlStateExample ID="ExampleControl1" Runat="server" />

<!-- User Control -->
<uc1:MyUserControl ID="MyUserControl1" Runat="server" />
```

The TagPrefix and TagName for each control appear in bold in the code snippet. The TagPrefix appears before the colon and helps identify the library in which the control resides. The TagName appears after the colon and specifies which type of control the tag represents. For the tag prefix to function, however, it needs to be defined. Before ASP.NET 2.0, the tag prefix had to be registered on each page that wanted to use a custom server control or a user control. The following is an example of these registrations:

```
<-- Custom Server Control -->
<%@ Register TagPrefix="msgControls" Namespace="Messaging" Assembly="Messaging" %>

<-- User Control -->
<%@ Register TagPrefix="uc1" TagName="MyUserControl"
    Src="UserControls/MyUserControl.ascx" %>
```

You can still use this syntax on the top of a page to register a tag prefix, if you want. Take a look at the first Register directive listed in the preceding, which is used to register a tag prefix for a custom server control. Server controls reside in assemblies outside of your current project, so ASP.NET needs to know the assembly and namespace in which the control can be located. Thus, when ASP.NET runs into the tag <msgControls:ControlStateExample />, it looks in the MessageControls assembly in the MessageControls namespace for the ControlStateExample control.

The second Registers directive is used to register the tag prefix and the tag name for a user control. User controls reside in your current application, so instead of specifying an assembly and namespace to point to the control, you need to specify the control's source location. You also need to specify a tag name for the control so ASP.NET can parse the tag appropriately. Thus, when ASP.NET encounters the tag <uc1:MyUserControl/>, it knows to load the user control located in UserControls/MyUserControl.ascx.

Now that you know how the Register directive at the top of a page works, you can use that same knowledge to create global tag registrations in Web.config. The syntax for doing so is virtually identical to creating a tag prefix at the top of a web form:

```
<configuration>
  ...
  <system.web>
    ...
    <pages>
      <controls>
        <add tagPrefix="msgControls" namespace="Messaging" assembly="Messaging" />
        <add tagPrefix="uc1" tagName="Menu" src="~/UserControls/Menu.ascx"/>
      </controls>
    </pages>
    ...
  </system.web>
</configuration>
```

After you declare these tags in `Web.config`, you no longer need to register them on the pages where you want to use the controls they reference.

Developing Server Controls with the ControlState

Most developers who have worked with ASP.NET 1.x are familiar with the concept of the `ViewState`, the mechanism by which ASP.NET stores control and web form data between page requests. The `ViewState` has been both a blessing and a curse for developers the world over because although it can greatly simplify the development process, it has a tendency, when left unchecked, to bloat the size of a web page immensely.

In an effort to counter this tendency, many developers simply disable the `ViewState` on troublesome controls or on the entire page. Unfortunately, this can have unintended consequences because the `ViewState` contains two different types of data. One type is the "nice-to-have" data that helps avoid requerying a database by storing lists or values in the `ViewState`. This type of data is usually responsible for bloating the `ViewState`. The other is the "critical-for-proper-control-functionality" data, which is necessary for making the control work appropriately. Before ASP.NET 2.0, there was no way to tell the difference between critical and nice-to-have data, so disabling the `ViewState` could easily render a control useless.

Enter the `ControlState`, ASP.NET 2.0's storage mechanism for critical data. Any information you store in the `ControlState` is always available to the control, even when the `ViewState` is disabled. In the upcoming example, you'll see how to use the `ControlState` as you implement a very simple server control named `ControlStateExample`. All this control does is count the number of times the page has been displayed. This allows you to explore the behavioral differences between the `ControlState` and `ViewState` when you see the control in action.

As with any server control, you place the code for the `ControlStateExample` in a web control library project so you can reference it from your web application. The source code for this control is also available in the Chapter 4 sample code, under the MessageControls web control library project in the Source Code area of the Apress website (`http://www.apress.com`).

Building the ControlState Example Control

Because the source code for the `ControlStateExample` is fairly brief, it's shown here in its entirety followed by a discussion of the relevant sections.

```
Imports System.Web.UI
Imports System.Web.UI.WebControls

< _
ToolboxData("<{0}:ControlStateExample runat=server></{0}:ControlStateExample>") _
> Public Class ControlStateExample
    Inherits WebControl
```

```
'***************************************************************************
Public Property ViewStateCounter() As Integer
    Get
        If ViewState("ViewStateCounter") Is Nothing Then Return 0
        Return CInt(ViewState("ViewStateCounter"))
    End Get
    Set(ByVal value As Integer)
        ViewState("ViewStateCounter") = value
    End Set
End Property

'***************************************************************************
Private ControlStateCounter As Integer = 0

'***************************************************************************
Protected Overrides Sub OnInit(ByVal e As System.EventArgs)
    MyBase.OnInit(e)
    Page.RegisterRequiresControlState(Me)
End Sub

'***************************************************************************
Protected Overrides Function SaveControlState() As Object
    Return New Object() { _
        MyBase.SaveControlState(), _
        ControlStateCounter}
End Function

'***************************************************************************
Protected Overrides Sub LoadControlState(ByVal savedState As Object)
    Dim StateArray() As Object = CType(savedState, Object())
    MyBase.LoadControlState(StateArray(0))
    ControlStateCounter = CInt(StateArray(1))
End Sub

'***************************************************************************
Protected Overrides Sub Render(ByVal writer As System.Web.UI.HtmlTextWriter)
    writer.WriteLine("<div>")
    writer.WriteLine("ViewState Counter: ")
    writer.WriteLine(ViewStateCounter)
    writer.WriteLine("<br />ControlState Counter:")
    writer.WriteLine(ControlStateCounter)
    writer.WriteLine("</div>")
End Sub
```

```
    '***************************************************************************
    Private Sub ControlStateExample_Load(ByVal sender As Object, _
                                    ByVal e As System.EventArgs) Handles Me.Load
        ViewStateCounter += 1
        ControlStateCounter += 1
    End Sub

    '***************************************************************************
    Public Sub ClearCounters()
        ViewStateCounter = 1
        ControlStateCounter = 1
    End Sub


End Class
```

Class Definition

Like most other server controls, the ControlStateExample class inherits most of its functionality from the WebControl class. This gives your control access to the ViewState, ControlState, Server, Request, Response, and Page objects that you'll need when writing your control. Another notable piece of code is the ToolboxData class attribute:

```
< _
ToolboxData("<{0}:ControlStateExample runat=server></{0}:ControlStateExample>") _
> Public Class ControlStateExample
```

When you drop a control from the toolbox onto the web form designer, Visual Studio automatically adds the necessary HTML to your .aspx file. The ToolboxData attribute helps Visual Studio know how to format that HTML. The {0} is a placeholder for the tag prefix for your web control library.

ViewStateCounter Property

ViewStateCounter is a classic ViewState-based property. Its Get section determines if the value exists in the ViewState and, if not, returns a default value of 0. If the value is in the ViewState, then it is converted to an Integer and returned. The Set section simply places the new property value directly in the ViewState for future use. If the ViewState is disabled, then the value that is left in the ViewState when the page is finished processing is not saved. Thus, when the page is posted back, the ViewStateCounter reverts back to the default setting of 0.

ControlState Property Storage Variables

Unlike the ViewState, the ControlState does not have a property bag in which you can store ad-hoc values. You have to create your own variables in which to store control state data. The ControlStateCounter variable is used for this purpose:

```
Private ControlStateCounter As Integer = 0
```

You will likely want to initialize the variable with a default value because the ControlState mechanism will not load values into the variable until a postback occurs.

Registering the ControlState

If your control requires the ControlState mechanism, then the page your control is on needs to be notified. You can accomplish this by overriding the OnInit method and calling Page.➥ RegisterRequiresControlState(Me). This notifies the page that your control needs to use the ControlState, and the page makes the ControlState mechanism available. Also, remember to call the OnInit method of the base class, so it can run any necessary tasks.

Saving and Loading the ControlState

The ControlState is a bit more cumbersome than the ViewState partly because you have to manually save and load ControlState data via the SaveControlState and LoadControlState methods.

Just before the page renders, it runs through all the controls that use the ControlState and executes each one's SaveControlState function. The objective of the SaveControlState function is to produce a serializable object containing data that can be used to initialize the control back to its former state when the page posts back. The page gathers all these objects and serializes them as encoded text in a hidden field on the page.

■ Note The page actually stores the serialized ControlState data inside the __VIEWSTATE hidden field. Although you can disable the ViewState, you cannot entirely eliminate the mechanism from the page. As such, the designers of ASP.NET 2.0 apparently decided to embed the ContolState data in the page using the existing ViewState functionality.

When the page posts back, it deserializes the encoded text in the hidden field and recreates the objects. It then passes each one of these objects back into its respective control's LoadControlState method. The objective of the LoadControlState method is to use the object originally created by the SaveControlState function to initialize the appropriate control values.

Creating the SaveControlState function consists entirely of returning an array containing all your ControlState data. It is also a good habit to save the object created by the Save➥ ControlState in the base class:

```
'***************************************************************************
Protected Overrides Function SaveControlState() As Object
        Return New Object() { _
            MyBase.SaveControlState(), _
            ControlStateCounter}
End Function
```

This function simply returns an Object array containing two items. The first item is the object returned by the call to MyBase.SaveControlState, which stores any ControlState data required by the base class. This is necessary if you are inheriting from a control that uses the

ControlState. If you're sure that your base class does not require any ControlState data, then you don't have to worry about retrieving and storing this information. In this example, for instance, the call to the base class always returns Nothing, but it's used here to demonstrate the technique. The second item is the ContolStateCounter variable value. Storing this value allows you to reinitialize the ControlStateCounter variable after the page posts back. If your control had more variables, you would need to add more items to the array to account for those variables.

When the page posts back, it deserializes the information from the ControlState and reproduces the object originally returned by the SaveControlState function. It then passes that object to the LoadControlState method so you can initialize your control:

```
'***************************************************************************
Protected Overrides Sub LoadControlState(ByVal savedState As Object)
        Dim StateArray() As Object = CType(savedState, Object())
        MyBase.LoadControlState(StateArray(0))
        ControlStateCounter = CInt(StateArray(1))
End Sub
```

Because the SaveControlState function returns an Object array, the LoadControlState method assumes the incoming data is an object array and casts it accordingly. It then sends the first object in the array to the base class via the MyBase.LoadControlState call, which allows the base class to initialize itself. It then casts the second item into an Integer and uses it to initialize the ControlStateCounter variable. At that point, the control has been initialized and is ready for use.

Rendering, Loading, and Clearing the Control

The ControlStateExample control overrides the Render method of the WebControl base class and uses an HtmlTextWriter to output the necessary HTML to the page. Once again, this is a very simple control that outputs simple HTML to display the values stored in the ControlStateCounter variable and the ViewStateCounter property.

When the ControlStateExample control is loaded, both the ViewStateCounter and the ControlStateCounter properties are incremented. This allows the control to count the number of times it has been displayed. Resetting these values can be achieved by calling the ClearCounters method.

Creating the ControlState Demo Page

Now that you have a ControlStateExample control, you need to put one on a web form to see how it behaves. This requires your web project to reference the assembly that contains the ControlStateExample control before you try to run the application. To do this, right-click your web project, select **Add Reference** from the context menu, and browse for the appropriate assembly.

Create a new page in your web application and name it ControlStateDemo.aspx. Add the following Register directive to the top of the page:

```
<%@ Register TagPrefix="msgControls" Namespace="MessageControls"
    Assembly="MessageControls" %>
```

In the sample code for Chapter 4 (in the Source Code area of the Apress website), you'll find the ControlStateExample control in the MessageControls assembly, which is why the Namespace and Assembly parameters are set to "MessageControls" in the preceding code. If you placed the control in a different assembly or used a different root namespace for your assembly, then you'll need to adjust these settings accordingly. Also take note of the TagPrefix parameter as you'll use this later.

Add the following controls between the server form tags on the page:

```
<asp:RadioButton ID="rbViewStateOn" Runat="server" Checked=True
     GroupName="ToggleViewState" Text="Enable View State" AutoPostBack="True"/>
<asp:RadioButton ID="rbViewStateOff" Runat="server" Checked=False
     GroupName="ToggleViewState" Text="Disable View State" AutoPostBack="True"/>
<br />
<msgControls:ControlStateExample ID="ExampleControl1" Runat="server" /><br />
<br />
<asp:Button ID="btnClearCounters" Runat="Server" Text="Clear Counters" />
<asp:Button ID="btnPostBack" Runat="server" Text="Post-Back" />
```

Notice how the tag prefix for the ControlStateExample control corresponds to the TagPrefix defined in the Register directive at the top of the page. ASP.NET reads the tag prefix, or the part before the colon, and searches for the appropriate Register directive to determine the assembly in which to look for the specified control, which appears after the colon.

Now that you have defined all the controls you'll need on the page, add the following code to the code-behind file:

```
'*****************************************************************************
Sub Page_Load(ByVal sender As Object, ByVal e As System.EventArgs)
    If Me.rbViewStateOn.Checked Then
        Me.EnableViewState = True
    Else
        Me.EnableViewState = False
    End If
End Sub

'*****************************************************************************
Sub btnClearCounters_Click(ByVal sender As Object, ByVal e As System.EventArgs) _
  Handles btnClearCounters.Click
    Me.ExampleControl1.ClearCounters()
End Sub
```

The Page_Load procedure turns the ViewState mechanism on or off based on whether or not the radio button rbViewStateOn is selected. The btnClearCounters_Click simply resets the counters.

Viewing the ControlState Behavior in the Demo Page

Set ControlStateDemo.aspx as the startup page for your web application and run the project. When the page first displays, the ControlStateExample control shows 1 for both counters. Make sure the **Enable View State** radio button is selected and then click on the **Post-Back** button a couple of times. Each time the page posts back, both counters increment. Because `ViewState` is enabled, the counter information for the `ViewState` successfully saves during each postback.

Next, disable the `ViewState` by selecting the **Disable View State** radio button. Click on the **Post-Back** button a few times. Notice that the `ViewState` counter remains set to `1` and never increments. Each time the page posts back, the `ViewState` is empty so the counter is effectively reset to 1 each time. Figure 4-3 shows the `ControlStateExample` control when the `ViewState` is enabled and when it is disabled.

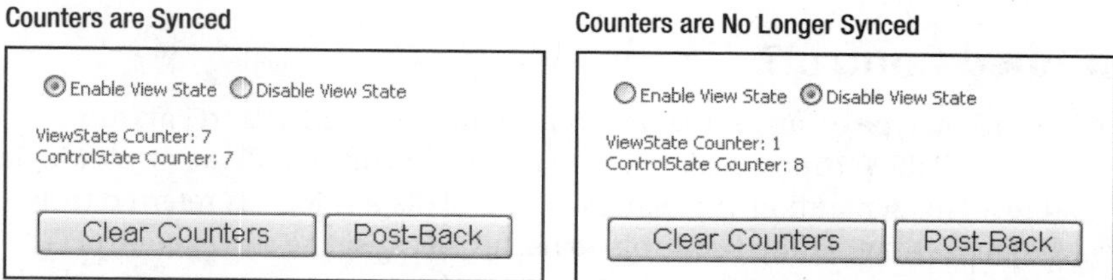

Figure 4-3. *The* `ControlStateExample` *control when the* `ViewState` *is enabled versus disabled. Notice that the* `ControlState` *maintains its counter even when the* `ViewState` *is disabled.*

Now that you have built a simple control, let's take a look at the more advanced skinned page-message control.

Building a Skinned Page-Message Control

Communicating information to the individuals who use your application is an extremely important task that is often slapped together on a page-by-page basis with nothing more than a label and a bit of concatenation code. As was explained in the opening of this chapter, the label-on-each-page approach may seem like a time-saver, but it may eat away at your timeline in the long run. Because page-messaging is an element that continually comes up from project to project, this chapter focuses on building a reusable page-message control that you can deploy in just about any project scenario.

The page-message control is responsible for displaying three different types of messages: page messages, error messages, and system messages. Page messages include action confirmations or perhaps helpful tips that you want to display on the page. Error messages include action failure messages or any other message indicating that something is wrong on the page. For instance, I use error messages to display information about business rule violations. Lastly, system messages may contain important systemwide information such as a message informing the user of an impending shutdown or scheduled maintenance. System messages are not page-specific. Instead, they appear on every page in the system that has a page-message control, thus allowing you to easily communicate ad-hoc information to everyone using your application. In terms of storage, you just need a couple of collections to store the various types of messages, and a few methods to add messages to the control. It is really not overly complicated.

Visual flexibility, however, is an entirely different story. You could use the page-message control in a variety of different projects, each of which will have its own visual requirements for messages. Some projects may need messages displayed as a bulleted list, or a dashed list, as series of rows in a table, as a JavaScript popup box, or even with icons to visually depict which type of message is being displayed. When you start throwing color combinations, font sizes, and other formatting options into the mix, you can see that things can get complicated very quickly. One option is to account for every conceivable scenario and expose an inordinate number of properties so you can configure the control accordingly. Of course, you'll eventually run into a scenario you did not account for, and it would take a lot of work building all the properties and rendering code for the control to draw itself in so many different ways. Instead, I'll show you how to build a skinned control that avoids the complexities but keeps all the flexibility.

What Is a Skinned Control?

A skinned control is a special type of custom server control that relies on a `UserControl` to define its visual interface. All the business logic exists in the server control. All the display logic exists in the `UserControl`. This separation of business logic and display logic is referred to as *decoupling* and is what makes the skinned controls so useful. Because the server control is completely decoupled from its visual interface, it must load an interface before it can render to the page. So, the skinned control loads up a `UserControl`, manipulates the visual interface in that `UserControl` based on the business logic, and then renders the `UserControl` thus providing the interface.

Of course, you are not bound to a single `UserControl`. You can load up any `UserControl` you want as long as it's designed to work with the skinned control that loads it. This allows you to create an unlimited number of visual displays (that is, skins) for your skinned control. If you want a bulleted list of items for the page-message control, then you build a `UserControl` capable of displaying a bulleted list. If you want a dashed list, then you can build a `UserControl` capable of displaying a dashed list. Because the `UserControl` consists of HTML markup, you can adjust the layout and style to fit whatever situation you need in ways that would be impossible to achieve through properties on a normal custom control. And, you only have to write the business logic once because it remains constant regardless of which `UserControl` you load.

■ **Note** Do not confuse the term *skinned control* with the *control skins* discussed in Chapter 3. The terminology is very similar so it can be confusing at first, but understand that control skins are confined to Chapter 3 and are not used in this chapter.

How Does the Server Control Manipulate the UserControl?

As mentioned before, a skinned control consists of two decoupled components: a server control containing the business logic for the control and a series of `UserControls` containing the different visual interfaces. The question is, if they are decoupled, how can they work together? The answer lies in coupling (or binding) them back together. Before we continue, understand that ASP.NET 2.0 includes no built-in support for skinned controls. You are responsible for implementing all the loading and binding functionality that is about to be discussed. You will, however, be implementing most of the functionality in a reusable base class that will make building skinned controls a much simpler task.

When you build a skinned control, the server control expects the `UserControl` skin to contain a specific set of ASP.NET server controls with specific ID values. When the server control loads the `UserControl` skin, it uses the `FindControl` method to reach into the `UserControl` skin and acquire references to the controls it needs based on the expected ID values. After those references have been acquired, the business logic in the server control can manipulate the controls and even handle their events on a postback. You can think of the expected ID values as a pseudocontract that exists between the `UserControl` skin and the server control. The server control does not care what is in the `UserControl` skin as long as it can find the controls necessary to run its business logic. If the server control cannot find those controls, it throws an exception. Figure 4-4 illustrates the concepts of expected ID values and coupling.

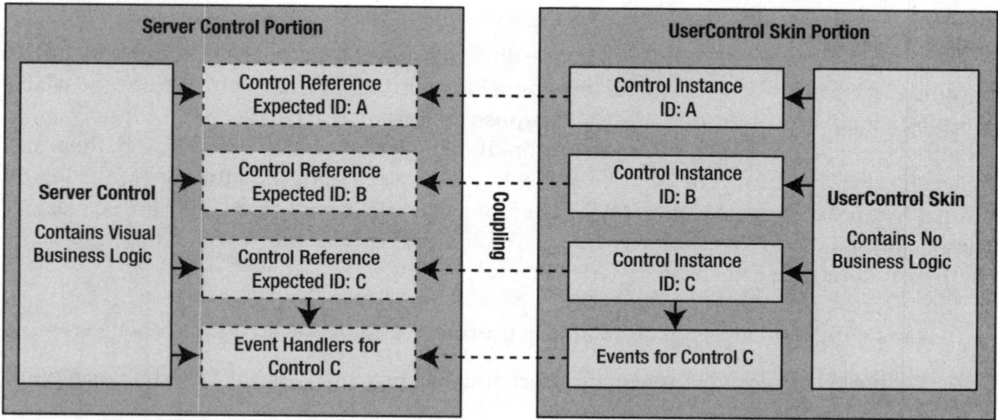

Figure 4-4. *Shows the two portions of a skinned web control: the web control portion that defines the busines logic, and the skin file portion that defines the user interface*

How Are Skinned Controls Implemented?

For the sake of discussion, let's say you want to create a login control that could be used in different areas of your website. It has two different visual styles. One style is meant to be the central focus of a page, such as on a login page. The other style is a more compact design meant to be displayed on a left- or right menu bar for quick login access. An example of how these styles, or `UserControl` skins, look is shown in Figure 4-5.

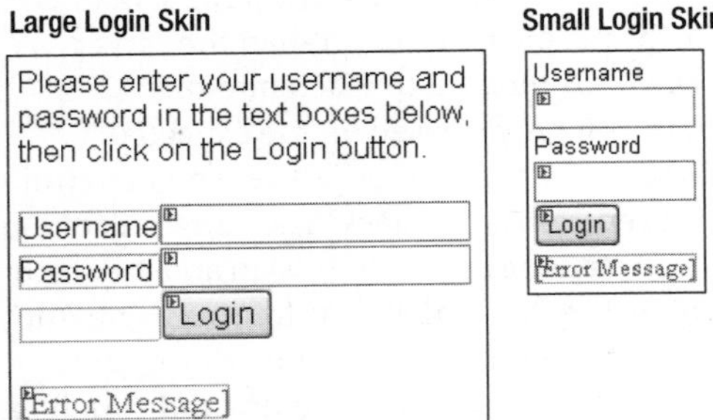

Figure 4-5. *Large and small login skins for a skinned login control*

Although the two `UserControl` skins have different layouts and verbiage, they both contain the same server controls: a Username text box, a Password text box, a Login button, and a label to display a login error message. They also expose the same functionality. Users enter their credentials and then click on the **Login** button. If the credentials are authenticated, then the login succeeds. Otherwise, the error label displays a message informing the user of the login failure. The only difference is the way the user interface (UI) is presented. This is a scenario where a skinned control will definitely work. Implementing this control as a skinned server control would require the following steps:

1. Create the business logic to validate a username and password against a data store.
2. Define variables to reference the Username text box, the Password text box, and the error message label.
3. Develop the code to search through a `UserControl` skin file and set up references to the Username and Password text boxes, as well as the Error Message label. The code also needs to add a handler to the skin's Login button to execute the login business logic when a user clicks on the Login button
4. Create `UserControl` skins for the two different login styles.

The references to the Username and Password text boxes are used by the business logic to acquire the username and password that the user entered into the control. These credentials are then authenticated against the user list. If authentication fails, the label reference should be used to output a message to the user regarding the issue.

As for the login skins, both must contain a text box control for the username, a text box control for the password, a label to display error messages, and a button to submit the login information. You can include additional markup in the `UserControl` skin as long as the skin contains the four previously mentioned elements. Each skin must also adhere to the expected ID values for those controls. For example, the skinned control may expect the Username text box to be named `txtUserName`, so the `UserControl` skins are expected to identify the Username text box accordingly.

Architecture of the Skinned Page-Message Server Control

Before delving into making all the parts of the skinned page-message control, I want you to get a quick high-level overview of all the pieces that make up the component so you know exactly where you are in the process. As implemented in this example, the skinned page-message server control includes five classes and three skins. Figure 4-6 should help you see how those items fit into the overall picture, followed by Table 4-1, which further describes the point and purpose of each item.

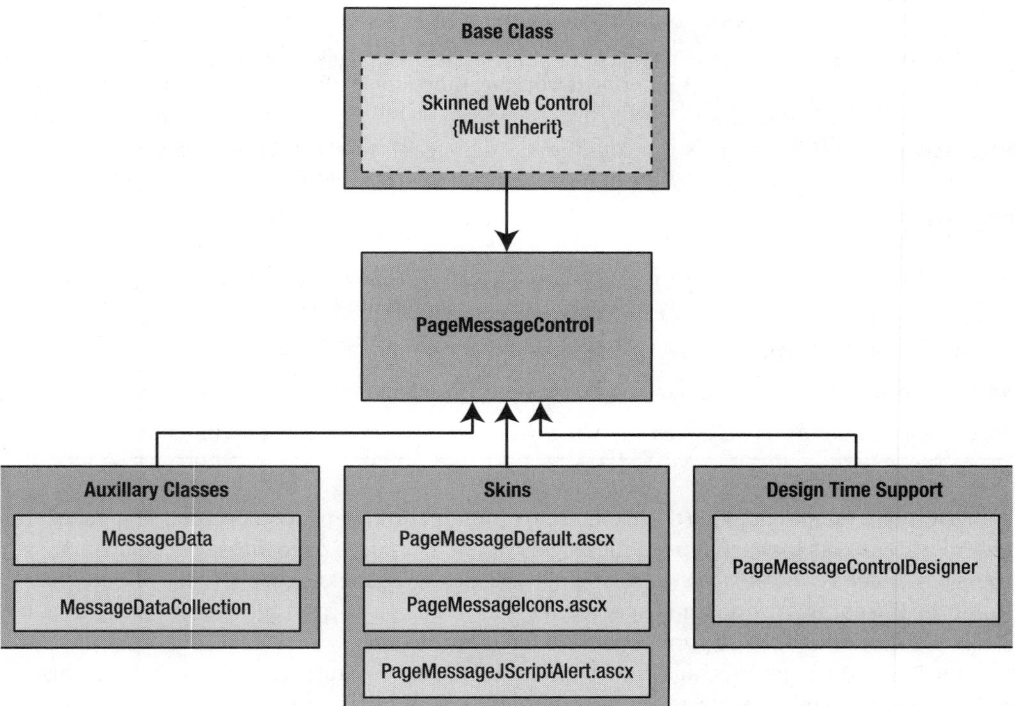

Figure 4-6. *Architecture diagram for the skinned page-message control*

Note The `UserControl` skin files for the `PageMessageControl` are located in the web application, not in the `Messaging` assembly.

Table 4-1. *Classes and Skins Used by the Skinned Page-Message Server Control*

Class/Skin	Description
`SkinnedWebControl`	An abstract (`MustInherit`) class that encapsulates the basic skinning functionality required by all skinned server controls.
`PageMessageControl`	Class containing the skinned page-messaging control logic. It inherits its skinning functionality from the `SkinnedWebControl` class.
`PageMessageControlDesigner`	Controls the way the `PageMessageControl` is displayed at design time in the Visual Studio IDE. It has no effect at runtime.
`MessageData`	Class that stores a single message that will be displayed via the `PageMessageControl`.
`MessageDataCollection`	Class that stores a collection of `MessageData` objects. Used by the `PageMessageControl` to maintain lists of messages.
`PageMessageDefault.ascx`	A very basic skin that displays messages.
`PageMessageIcons.ascx`	Like the default skin, but includes icons for each message type.
`PageMessageJScriptAlert.ascx`	Displays messages using the JavaScript alert function.

Each skin file should have three panel controls and three repeater controls. One panel and one repeater exists for each type of message: system messages, page messages, and error messages. Each repeater is nested inside of its associated panel. Figure 4-7 shows a diagram outlining the control layout and expected ID values for a page-message `UserControl` skin, and Table 4-2 describes each control in the skin file in more detail.

Basically, the page-message control maintains three separate lists containing messages. When the control renders, it determines whether a specific list has any messages in it and, if so, makes the panel associated with the list visible and data binds the corresponding message repeater to the list. I used a repeater to display the lists because the repeater is extremely flexible in terms of what it can output, whereas a `DataGrid` forces the list to be inside a table. As you'll see later when you implement the JavaScript alert skin for this control, the flexibility of the repeaters allows you to do some interesting things.

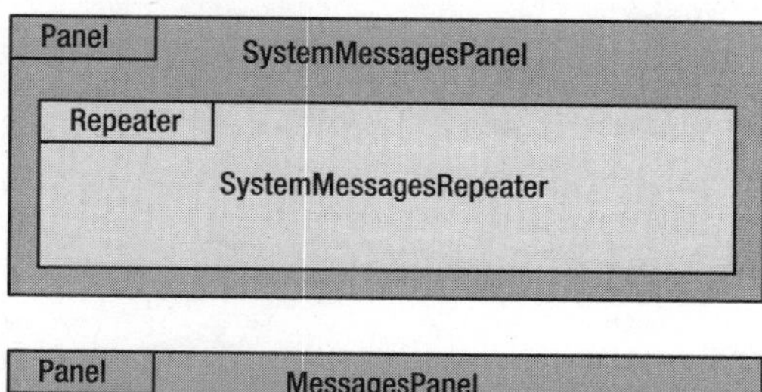

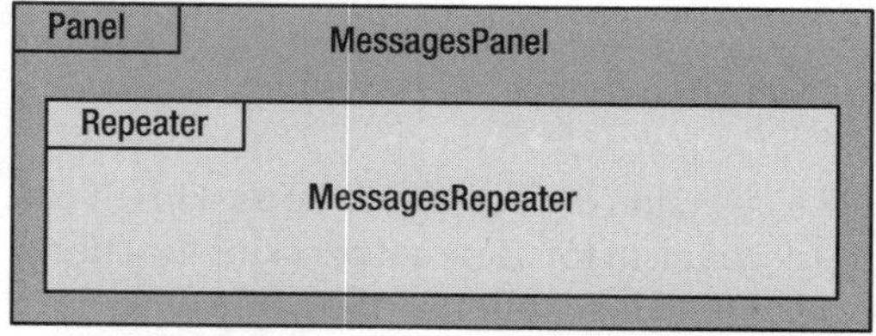

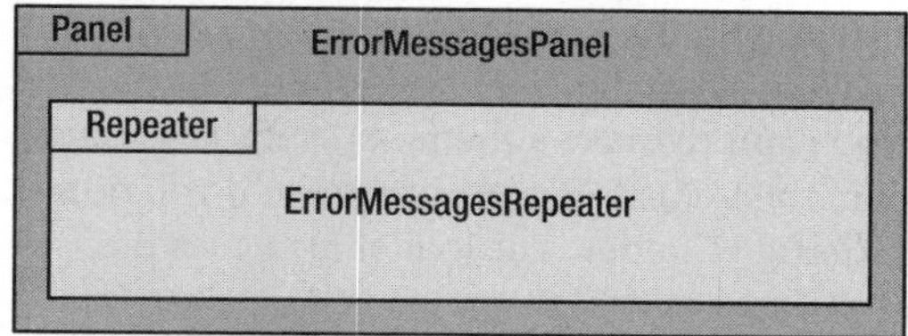

Figure 4-7. *Diagram of the page-message control's* `UserControl` *skin requirements*

Table 4-2. *Control and ID Requirements for Page-Message* `UserControl` *Skins*

Expected ID	Control Type	Description
`SystemMessagesPanel`	Panel	Visible when the control contains system messages
`SystemMessagesRepeater`	Repeater	Displays system messages
`MessagesPanel`	Panel	Visible when the control contains standard messages
`MessagesRepeater`	Repeater	Displays standard messages
`ErrorMessagesPanel`	Panel	Visible when the control contains error messages
`ErrorMessagesRepeater`	Repeater	Displays error messages

Storage Locations for UserControl Skins

In the example for this chapter, we'll store the `UserControl` skins under the `Skins` directory of the web application. The `Skins` folder is just an ordinary folder; it does not have a special meaning in ASP.NET 2.0. In the example application, you'll also see three subfolders in the `Skins` folder: `Default`, `GreenTheme`, and `RedTheme`. These folder names correspond to the theme folders from the `App_Themes` directory in the sample application, as shown in Figure 4-8.

Figure 4-8. *Subfolders in the* `Skins` *folder mimic the themes in the* `App_Themes` *folder*

This structure allows you to create theme-specific version of your `UserControl` skins, if you want to. Here's quick rundown of how the loading mechanism for `UserControl` skins functions. You tell the control the file name of the `UserControl` skin to load, but that file name does not have any path information. The control determines the path by checking to see if the page has a current theme. If so, it checks for the `UserControl` skin in the `Skins/<Theme>` directory. If the control finds the `UserControl` file in that location, it loads that file. If it does not find the file, the control looks in the `Skins/Default` folder. So, if you want to make a theme-specific version of the `UserControl` skin, you can build it and stick it in the `Skins/<Theme>` directory; if you don't, the loading mechanism reverts back to the `Skins/Default` folder. The loader also uses the default folder if the page does not have a theme.

Setting Up the Messaging Web Control Project

Custom server controls need to be defined in an assembly that can be referenced by a web project, so you need to create two projects for this example. First, create a new website by choosing **File ➤ New ➤ Website**. The **New Website** dialog box appears. Make sure you have selected **Visual Basic** as the project type and **ASP.NET Website** as the template. Enter the location where you want to store your website files and then click on the **OK** button.

After you've added the website, choose **File ➤ Add ➤** New Project. The **New Project** dialog box appears. Make sure **Visual Basic** is selected as the project type, and select **Web Control Library** from the list of templates. Name the new project **Messaging** and specify the location where you want your files to be stored. Click the **OK** button. The `Messaging` project is where you will place all the classes that make up the skinned page-messaging control.

The Skinned Web Control Class

All skinned server controls share a basic set of functionality for loading and coupling skin files, so you are going to create an abstract (`MustInherit`) class to encapsulate that behavior. This will allow you to use the abstract class as a base class when you build other skinned server controls in the future.

The entire code listing for the `SkinnedWebControl` abstract class is shown next, followed by a discussion about what each section of the code does.

```
Imports System.IO
Imports System.Web
Imports System.Web.UI
Imports System.Web.UI.WebControls
Imports System.Web.HttpContext

Public MustInherit Class SkinnedWebControl
    Inherits WebControl
    Implements INamingContainer

    '***********************************************************************
    Protected MustOverride Sub InitializeSkin(ByRef Skin As Control)

    '***********************************************************************
    Private _SkinFileName As String = String.Empty

    '***********************************************************************
    Public Property SkinFileName() As String
        Get
            Return _SkinFileName
        End Get
        Set(ByVal value As String)
            _SkinFilename = value
        End Set
    End Property

    '***********************************************************************
    Protected Function LoadSkin() As Control
        Dim Skin As Control
        Dim Theme As String = IIf(Page.Theme = String.Empty, "Default", Page.Theme)
        Dim SkinPath As String = "~/Skins/" & Theme & "/" & SkinFilename.TrimStart

        'Ensure that a skin file name has been provided
        If SkinFileName = String.Empty Then _
            Throw New Exception("You must specify a skin.")

        'Check if the skin exists before you try to load it up
        If Not File.Exists(Current.Server.MapPath(SkinPath)) Then
            SkinPath = "~/Skins/Default/" & SkinFileName.TrimStart
            If Not File.Exists(Current.Server.MapPath(SkinPath)) Then
                Throw New Exception("The skin file '" & SkinPath _
                                    & "' could be loaded.  This file must" _
                                    & " exist for this control to render.")
            End If
        End If
```

```
        'Attempt to load the skin now that you know it exists
        Try
            Skin = Page.LoadControl(SkinPath)
        Catch exSkinNotFound As Exception
            Throw New Exception("Error loading the skin file '" & SkinPath & "'")
        End Try

        Return Skin

    End Function

  '***************************************************************************
    Protected Overrides Sub CreateChildControls()
        Dim Skin As Control = LoadSkin()
        InitializeSkin(Skin)
        Controls.Add(Skin)
    End Sub

End Class
```

Class Definition

The `SkinnedWebControl` class represents a skinned web control, but it's a web control nonetheless. It inherits the basic web control functionality from the `WebControl` class and implements the `INamingContainer` marker interface. This interface does not require any methods to be implemented; it just marks the class as being a naming container. This lets the page know that the child controls in the `SkinnedWebControl` should be given a naming scope to help avoid naming conflicts with other controls on the page.

The InitializeSkin Abstract (MustOverride) Method

Skinned web controls need the capability to bind their variables and event handling to the controls and events from a skin file. This is accomplished via the `InitializeSkin` abstract method, which is passed a reference to a skin via the `Skin` parameter. Because each individual skinned web control needs to bind to its skin in a different manner, this method is left unimplemented. Its appropriate implementation is left up to the class that inherits from the `SkinnedWebControl` class.

The SkinFileName Property

Skinned web controls do not have a built-in UI; the interface is always provided via a skin file. Thus, skinned web controls need to know how to find that file. The `SkinFileName` property provides a location in which to store the name of the skin file that should be used to provide the control with a UI.

The LoadSkin Function

This function is responsible for using the SkinFileName property and any available theme information to load the appropriate UserControl skin for the control. It starts by creating a temp variable named Skin to hold the loaded control. It then determines the current page theme by checking the Theme property of the Page object. If the page does not have a theme, then the code uses Default as the theme.

Using the theme information, the LoadSkin method builds out the full path to the UserControl skin using Skins/<ThemeName>/<UserControlSkin>.ascx and stores it in the SkinPath variable. Next, the method checks to make sure that a nonempty SkinFileName value has been provided. If not, the code raises an exception because the control must have a UserControl skin file to load. After that, the method checks to see if the UserControl skin file exists in the theme directory using the File.Exists method from the System.IO namespace. Current.Server.MapPath converts the web-relative path into the full-path for use in the Exists function. If the file cannot be found, then the code rebuilds the path using the Skins/Default folder instead of Skins/<Theme> folder. It then checks to make sure the UserControl file exists in the default location. If not, the method throws an exception because the skin file is required. Otherwise, the method continues on.

After the SkinPath is known to exist, the method passes it into the Page.LoadControl function. The Page.LoadControl function accepts a virtual path to an .ascx file and returns a reference to the instantiated UserControl if the path and .ascx file are valid. That control reference is then returned as the value of the function.

Overriding the CreateChildControls Method

This method only has three lines of code, but they all play a very important role in the loading and initialization of a skin. The first line loads the skin using the LoadSkin method. The next line calls the abstract method InitializeSkin and passes in the skin that was loaded on the previous line. Remember, the InitializeSkin method couples the business logic of the custom server control to the UI of the skin file. Lastly, the instantiated skin control is added to the custom server control's control collection so it will be rendered to the browser. This is what gives the custom web control its UI.

The MessageData Class

The MessageData class exists, as the name implies, to store data about a message. This class may seem a bit superfluous considering that a message is only a string, but I wanted to show you how to add additional properties to the MessageData class in case the need arose. For instance, at some point, it may be helpful to add a help file link to a message so users can click on a message to get additional information.

Following you'll find the code for the MessageData class, followed by a brief discussion. This class is basic enough that it should be self explanatory:

```
Public Class MessageData

    '***************************************************************************
    Private _Message As String = String.Empty
```

```
    '***************************************************************************
    Public Sub New(ByVal Message As String)
        _Message = Message
    End Sub

    '***************************************************************************
    Public Property Message() As String
        Get
            Return _Message
        End Get
        Set(ByVal value As String)
            _Message = value
        End Set
    End Property

End Class
```

This class has a single string property named `Message`. The private class variable `_Message` is used to store the value of the `Message` property. There is also a constructor that initializes the `Message` property.

The MessageDataCollection Class

The `MessageDataCollection` is a strongly typed collection class designed to store `MessageData` objects. The `PageMessageControl` uses multiple `MessageDataCollections` to store system messages, page messages, and error messages before rendering those messages to the browsers.

```
Public Class MessageDataCollection
    Inherits System.Collections.CollectionBase

    '***************************************************************************
    Public Function Add(ByVal obj As MessageData) As Integer
        Return List.Add(obj)
    End Function

    '***************************************************************************
    Default Public Property Item(ByVal index As Integer) As MessageData
        Get
            ReturnList.Item(index)
        End Get
        Set(ByVal value As MessageData)
            List.Item(index) = value
        End Set
    End Property

End Class
```

MessageDataCollection inherits its basic collection functionality from the System.➥ Collections.CollectionBase class. It exposes two strongly typed functions: Add and Item. Add accepts a MessageData object and adds it to the List property. The List property is part of the basic functionality inherited from the CollectionBase class. The Item property allows you to get and set a MessageData object from the List property at the specified index.

Strongly typing your collections allows you to easily access object properties using IntelliSense in the Visual Studio IDE and avoid having to cast the objects before using them. Although it isn't absolutely necessary to strongly type a collection, it does make working with the collection a bit easier.

The PageMessageControl

In the PageMessageControl class, you'll find a great deal of code. Most of it is fairly simple, but there's a lot to go through. The following code listing contains the most significant portions of the PageMessageControl class, although some methods have been omitted to save space. Most of the omitted methods have names that closely describe their purpose, so I've included a comment containing the name of the method in place of the method itself.

```
Imports System.ComponentModel
Imports System.Web.UI
Imports System.Web.UI.WebControls

<ToolboxData("<{0}:PageMessageControl runat=server></{0}:PageMessageControl>"), _
 Designer(GetType(PageMessageControlDesigner))> _
Public Class PageMessageControl
    Inherits SkinnedWebControl

    '***************************************************************************
    Private Shared _SystemMessages As MessageDataCollection = Nothing
    Private _Messages As MessageDataCollection = Nothing
    Private _ErrorMessages As MessageDataCollection = Nothing

    Private MessagesPanel As Panel = Nothing
    Private ErrorMessagesPanel As Panel = Nothing
    Private SystemMessagesPanel As Panel = Nothing

    Private MessagesRepeater As Repeater = Nothing
    Private ErrorMessagesRepeater As Repeater = Nothing
    Private SystemMessagesRepeater As Repeater = Nothing

    '***************************************************************************
    'NOT SHOWN: Shared ReadOnly Property SystemMessages() As MessageDataCollection
    'NOT SHOWN: Shared Sub AddSystemMessage(ByVal Message As String)
    'NOT SHOWN: Shared Sub RemoveSystemMessage(ByVal Index As Integer)
    'NOT SHOWN: Shared Sub ClearSystemMessages()
```

```
'***************************************************************************
Public Sub New()
    If Me.SkinFileName = String.Empty Then _
        Me.SkinFileName = "PageMessageDefault.ascx"
End Sub

'***************************************************************************
'NOT SHOWN: Public ReadOnly Property Messages() As MessageDataCollection
'NOT SHOWN: Public ReadOnly Property ErrorMessages() As MessageDataCollection

'NOT SHOWN: Public Sub AddMessage(ByVal Message As String)
'NOT SHOWN: Public Sub AddErrorMessage(ByVal Message As String)

'NOT SHOWN: Public Sub ClearMessages()
'NOT SHOWN: Public Sub ClearErrorMessages()

'NOT SHOWN: Public ReadOnly Property HasMessages() As Boolean
'NOT SHOWN: Public ReadOnly Property HasErrorMessages() As Boolean
'NOT SHOWN: Public Shared ReadOnly Property HasSystemMessages() As Boolean

'***************************************************************************
Public Property AllowSetFocus() As Boolean
    Get
        If ViewState("AllowSetFocus") Is Nothing Then Return True
        Return CBool(ViewState("AllowSetFocus"))
    End Get
    Set(ByVal value As Boolean)
        ViewState("AllowSetFocus") = value
    End Set
End Property

'***************************************************************************
Protected Overrides Sub CreateChildControls()

    If Me.HasMessages Or Me.HasErrorMessages Or Me.HasSystemMessages Then

        If Me.AllowSetFocus Then
            'Add the focus anchor
            Dim AnchorLiteral As Literal = New Literal()
            AnchorLiteral.Text = "<a name='PageMessages'></a>"
            Controls.Add(AnchorLiteral)

            Page.ClientScript.RegisterStartupScript( _
                GetType(PageMessageControl), _
                "MsgFocus", _
                "window.location='#PageMessages';", _
                True)
        End If
```

```
            MyBase.CreateChildControls()

        End If

    End Sub

    '***************************************************************************
    Protected Overrides Sub InitializeSkin(ByRef Skin As System.Web.UI.Control)

        'Find Controls
        MessagesRepeater = Skin.FindControl("MessagesRepeater")
        MessagesPanel = Skin.FindControl("MessagesPanel")
        ErrorMessagesRepeater = Skin.FindControl("ErrorMessagesRepeater")
        ErrorMessagesPanel = Skin.FindControl("ErrorMessagesPanel")
        SystemMessagesRepeater = Skin.FindControl("SystemMessagesRepeater")
        SystemMessagesPanel = Skin.FindControl("SystemMessagesPanel")

        'Setup Messages
        SetupRepeaterAndPanel(MessagesRepeater, MessagesPanel, _Messages)
        SetupRepeaterAndPanel(ErrorMessagesRepeater, ErrorMessagesPanel, _
            _ErrorMessages)
        SetupRepeaterAndPanel(SystemMessagesRepeater, SystemMessagesPanel, _
            _SystemMessages)
    End Sub

    '***************************************************************************
    Private Sub SetupRepeaterAndPanel(ByRef R As Repeater, ByRef P As Panel, _
                                      ByRef Data As MessageDataCollection)
        If Not R Is Nothing Then
            R.DataSource = Data
            R.DataBind()
        End If

        If Not P Is Nothing Then
            If Data Is Nothing OrElse Data.Count = 0 Then
                P.Visible = False
            Else
                P.Visible = True
            End If
        End If

    End Sub

End Class
```

Class Definition

The PageMessageControl inherits its functionality from the SkinnedWebControl class. Remember that the SkinnedWebControl class inherits from the WebControl class, so the PageMessageControl has access to all the methods exposed by both WebControl and SkinnedWebControl. The ToolBoxData attribute that precedes the class definition tells the Visual Studio IDE what HTML markup should be added to the page when the control is placed on the form designer from the toolbox. The Designer attribute tells the Visual Studio IDE that the PageMessageControlDesigner class should be used to render the control in design time. You'll learn about design-time functionality later on in this chapter.

Private Class Variables

The next section contains all the private variables for the PageMessageControl class. Notice there are three sets of three items. The first set contains all the MessageDataCollection variables that store system messages, page messages, and error messages. Notice that the _SystemMessages collection has a Shared scope. This allows system messages to be saved indefinitely and shared by every PageMessageControl in the application. The next set of items contains the panel variables that will be set to visible or invisible depending on whether or not their respective MessageDataCollection variables contain any messages when the control is rendered. The last set contains the repeaters, to which the appropriate MessageDataCollection variables will be bound, assuming, once again, that they have messages.

Remember that the PageMessageControl does not have a UI of its own, but it has to declare variables that will reference controls in the skin file. These panel and repeater variables will reference those controls after they are appropriately bound in the InitializeSkin function.

System Message Functionality

Most of the system message functionality has been omitted from the code listing, but it still warrants some discussion. You can likely infer the purpose of each system message function by its name. The most notable thing is that all the system message functions are shared. They belong to the class, not to individual objects, because of the nature of system messages.

Page messages and error messages are displayed once and then forgotten, but system messages are more persistent. The best example of a system message is something to the effect of, "The system will be shutting down at 6:00 p.m. for maintenance." This message should appear on every PageMessageControl whenever it is rendered because it needs to be communicated to everyone on the system.

This also means that page messages must be explicitly removed before they stop displaying in the PageMessageControl. They will continue to display as long as they exist in the SystemMessages list. For reference, shutting down IIS causes the SystemMessages list to be lost.

The PageMessageControl Constructor

Although there is only a single line in the constructor for the PageMessageControl class, it performs a time-saving task. It assigns the SkinFileName property a default skin file name—in this case, PageMessageDefault.ascx. Chances are that you will *not* want to specify a skin file each time you drop a PageMessageControl on one of your web forms, and this keeps you from having to do so. You just have to make sure that you have a default page messaging skin file named PageMessageDefault.ascx in your skin directory.

Message Lists and Associated Functionality

After the constructor, you'll see a series of omitted listings representing most of the page messages and error messages functionality. These are methods and properties used to add messages, clear messages, and determine whether or not messages exist in a given message list. Notice that the `HasSystemMessages` property is a `Shared` property because it deals with the shared `SystemMessages` collection.

AllowSetFocus Property

One of the issues you'll inevitably encounter is that a web form will be redisplayed after a postback, and the message will be shown on a portion of the page that is not currently visible. This may be confusing to users because they may not notice an important message. To counteract this issue, the `PageMessageControl` can place an anchor just above the message list and launch a JavaScript function when the page loads that will scroll to that anchor.

Sometimes, however, you won't want to automatically scroll to the position where the anchor is located. For example, the `PageMessageAlert.ascx` skin outputs JavaScript to display an alert box when the page loads. The anchor, if used, would be placed before the JavaScript code block, which is invisible to the user. So, an alert would be issued, and then the page would scroll to a random location that does not display any useful information. To avoid issues like this, you can set the `AllowSetFocus` to `false`, and no JavaScript scrolling to the list will be allowed.

The code for the `AllowSetFocus` is fairly straightforward. It's a standard read-write property that uses `ViewState` to store its values and returns `True` by default if the property is not explicitly set.

Overriding the CreateChildControls Method

Most skinned web controls will not require you to override the `CreateChildControls` method because all the UI functionality is completely encapsulated in the skin file. The `PageMessage➥Control`, however, needs to implement the anchor and JavaScript scrolling functionality discussed in the preceding `AllowSetFocus` discussion. Because this functionality exists for all the skins, it makes sense to include it in the server control code instead of having to recreate it in each skin file.

In the `CreateChildControls` method, the code first determines whether or not any messages exist in any of the lists. If no messages exist, then no other action is required because nothing needs to be displayed.

If there are messages, then the code checks to see if the `AllowSetFocus` property is set to `true`. If so, the control knows it needs to add an anchor above the message lists and the JavaScript code that will automatically scroll the page after it loads. It does this by creating a literal control and populating it with the HTML to create an anchor named `PageMessages`. That literal control is then added to the `PageMessageControl`'s control collection.

After the anchor is added, the control registers a startup JavaScript on the page that will automatically scroll the page to the `PageMessages` named anchor:

```
AnchorLiteral.Text = "<a name='PageMessages'></a>"
Controls.Add(AnchorLiteral)

Page.ClientScript.RegisterStartupScript( _
    GetType(PageMessageControl), _
    "MsgFocus", _
    "window.location='#PageMessages';", _
    True)
```

The JavaScript output by the control is shown in bold. Also shown in bold is the name of the anchor. Notice how the anchor name matches the value assigned to `window.location` in the JavaScript. The # symbol means that the page is jumping to a named anchor in the page instead of to a new URL.

If you have worked with client-side scripting functions in ASP.NET, you may have noticed that there is a new way to access the client-side scripting functions. They are now exposed via the `ClientScript` property of the `Page` class. They also have a slightly different syntax as explained in Table 4-3.

Table 4-3. `RegisterStartupScript` *Parameter Reference*

Parameter Name	New to ASP.NET 2.0	Description
`type`	Yes	Represents the type name of the control that is registering the script. Passing in the type name helps avoid conflicts that arise when different types of controls registering a script with the same key.
`key`	No	Each script you register should have a unique key to identify it. If multiple scripts with the same key are registered for the same type, then only the first registered script for that type is output to the browser. No conflict occurs if you use a key that was used with another type. This helps avoid the same script being output to the browser multiple times.
`script`	No	This is the script that will be output to the page. It can include a surrounding `<script>` tag, but you may opt for ASP.NET to automatically create those tags for you by passing in `True` for the `addScriptTags` parameter.
`addScriptTags`	Yes	An optional parameter that is `False` by default. Setting this parameter to `True` tells ASP.NET to automatically surround your script with `<script>` tags so you do not have to do it directly in your script string.

The other scripting methods exposed by the `ClientScript` property tend to have the same parameters in case you ever happen to need them.

After the anchor has been added to the control and the JavaScript has been registered to the page, the control executes the `CreateChildControls` method in the base class, `SkinnedWebControl`, which is responsible for loading the appropriate skin and initializing it using the `InitializeSkin` method.

If the `AllowSetFocus` property is set to `false`, then the control doesn't bother adding the anchor or the JavaScript. Instead, it just calls the `CreateChildConrols` method from the base class.

Initializing the Skin

A reference to the loaded skin file is passed into the InitializeSkin method via the Skin parameter. The method then uses that reference to locate controls in the skin using the Skin.FindControl function:

```
MessagesRepeater = Skin.FindControl("MessagesRepeater")
```

The FindControl function searches through the skin looking for the appropriate control, and returns a reference to that control if it's found in the skin. If the control is not found, then Nothing is returned. The InitializeSkin method locates all three panels and repeaters in the control and stores a reference to them using the class-level panel and repeater variables. This is code that actually couples the UI in the skin to the business logic in the control. Notice that this server control is looking for specific ID's in the skin. There should be three panels: MessagesPanel, ErrorMessagesPanel, and SystemMessagesPanel. There should also be three repeaters: Messages, ErrorMessages, and SystemMessages.

After references to all the controls in the skin have been acquired, the InitializeSkin method calls the SetupRepeaterAndPanel function for each set of panels, repeaters, and MessageDataCollection lists.

■ **Note** The PageMessageControl does not need to respond to any events because the user does not interact with it after it has been displayed to the screen. If, however, you needed your control to respond to an event fired from a control in the skin, the InitializeSkin function is where you would want to set up any necessary event handle routines, for example:

```
AddHandler ControlReference.EventName, AddressOf➥
    EventHandlerInThePageMessageControl
```

SetupRepeaterAndPanel Method

This method accepts a repeater (R), a panel (P), and a MessageDataCollection (Data) as parameters. The method first checks to see whether or not the repeater was found. If so, it sets the repeater's data source and calls its DataBind method. This populates the repeater with any message information stored in the MessageDataCollection.

Next, the SetupRepeaterAndPanel method checks to see if the panel exists. If so, it then determines if the MessageDataCollection contains any messages. If it contains messages, the panel is set to visible. If the MessageDataCollection is Nothing or does not contain any messages, then the panel is set to invisible.

Checking for the existence of the controls in the skin before actually using them ensures that you won't get an error if one or more of the controls are missing. In effect, this means that the controls are not required and the skinned control gracefully handles their absence. This allows for a degree of flexibility because you could, for example, create a page-message UserControl skin that only displays one type of message. Of course, you may not want your skinned control to be so forgiving. If controls are required to be in the UserControl skin, then feel free to throw an exception if they are not present.

Defining a Standard Tag Prefix for Your Control Library

All server controls are required to have a tag prefix when they are added to a web form. You may have noticed how all the standard web control use asp as the tag prefix, as in <asp:label /> or <asp:textbox />. You may have also noticed when you drag a user control onto a web form, a registers directive is created for you defining a tag prefix of cc1, cc2, and so on, depending on how many custom controls (hence the cc) have been added to the page.

If you do not define a standard tag prefix for your custom control library, then Visual Studio automatically creates a tag prefix for your control library on a page-by-page basis. Thus, on one page, PageMessageControl may be defined as <cc1:PageMessageControl/> whereas on another page it may be defined as <cc3:PageMessageControl/>.

If you want to use a specific tag prefix for the controls in your library, then you can define it in the AssemblyInfo.vb file using the TagPrefix attribute. This helps ensure that the same prefix is used each time your control is added to a page.

Getting to the AssemblyInfo.vb, however, is confusing the first time around because it's obscured in Visual Studio 2005. If you look in your Solution Explorer, you'll see a special project item named My Project located directly under the Messaging project. The AssemblyInfo.vb file is actually displayed in this folder, but it isn't visible until you click the **Show All Files** icon in the Solution Explorer.

After the AssemblyInfo.vb file is visible, double-click it. It opens in the Visual Studio IDE. Make sure that Imports System.Web.UI appears at the top of the file. Below the imports statements, add the following code:

```
<Assembly: TagPrefix("Messaging", "msgControls")>
```

This informs the Visual Studio IDE to use msgControls as the tag prefix whenever it is adding a control from the Messaging namespace to a web form.

Design Time Rendering

If you drop a PageMessageControl onto a web form in design mode, that PageMessageControl won't render because it has no messages to display. If you want your PageMessageControl to display in design time, then you must implement your own design-time rendering capabilities by implementing your own ControlDesigner class.

The System.Web.UI.Design.ControlDesigner is a base class that defines design-time rendering capabilities for a control. By overriding the GetDesignTimeHtml function of this class, you can make your control appear however you want on the design surface. Here's the code for the class:

```
Imports System.Web.UI.Design

Public Class PageMessageControlDesigner
    Inherits System.Web.UI.Design.ControlDesigner
```

```
    '==========================================================================
    Public Overrides Function GetDesignTimeHtml() As String

        Const Style As String = "width:100%; padding:2px; " & _
                                "background-color:Gainsboro;" & _
                                "border:1px solid black;"

        Return String.Format("<div style='{0}'>Page Messages ({1})</div><br />", _
                             Style, ID)
    End Function

End Class
```

GetDesignTimeHtml returns a string containing the HTML that should be used to render the control on the designer's surface. In this case, the control appears as a gray-colored rectangle with a black border that contains the name of the control. The style was broken out on another line for readability; you can return the string from a single statement if you want to.

Now that you have this class defined, the Designer attribute on the PageMessageControl should make a bit more sense:

```
<ToolboxData("<{0}:PageMessageControl runat=server></{0}:PageMessageControl>"), _
 Designer(GetType(PageMessageControlDesigner))> _
Public Class PageMessageControl
```

Before the Visual Studio IDE renders the PageMessageControl, it checks to see if the control has a Designer associated with it. If so, it creates an instance of the Designer, calls the GetDesignTimeHtml function, and displays the resulting HTML on the design surface. If there is no designer, then the IDE instantiates an instance of your control and tries to render it as thought it were on an actual page

Referencing the PageMessageControl in Your Web Project

Before you can use the PageMessageControl in your web project, you must add a reference to the Messaging assembly. To do this, right-click on your web project and select **Add Reference** from the context menu. When the **Add Reference** dialog box appears, select the **Projects** tab. You should see **Messaging** listed in the selection area. Double-click the **Messaging** item and the project reference is added to your web project. Your web project will be updated automatically whenever you compile the Messaging assembly.

After adding the reference, the toolbox displays a new section called **Messaging Components** containing the controls in the assembly whenever you are viewing a web form. In Visual Studio 2003, you had to manually add controls to the toolbox even if your project already referenced those tools, so this is definitely a step up. In the **Messaging Components** section, you'll find the PageMessageControl, which you can drag and drop onto a web form just like any other server control.

Creating the PageMessageControl's Skin Files

Now that you've built the page-message server control, it's time to create the skin files that the control uses. As mentioned earlier, `UserControl` skin files are placed under the `Skins` folder of your web application. Inside the `Skins` folder, you should have subfolders that match the directory structure of your `App_Themes` folder as shown in Figure 4-9.

Figure 4-9. *As shown earlier in the chapter, subfolders in the* `Skins` *folder mimic the* `Themes` *in the* `App_Themes` *folder.*

You may look at the directory structure and, thinking that it looks a bit repetitive, wonder why you can't simply put your control skins in the `Themes` folder. ASP.NET does not allow any files, other than `.skin` and `.css` files for Themes to be placed in the `App_Themes` folder. Hence the reason why you need to build out the separate directory structure. You mimic the `App_Themes` directory because you use the theme information from the page to find the appropriate skin, for example, `/Skins/<ThemeName>/<UserControlSkin>.ascx`. You can see the code used to build the path to your skin file in the `LoadSkin` function of the `SkinnedWebControl` abstract class.

Over the course of the next few sections, you'll build the `UserControl` skin files for the page-message control. Figure 4-10 depicts how these controls will display in the browser when they are completely finished.

Creating the PageMessageDefault.ascx Skin

The first skin you need to create is the default skin file that your control will use if the `SkinFileName` property is not set. In this case, the name of the file is `PageMessageDefault.ascx`, but that name will be different for every control you make. The file should be placed in the `Skins/Default` folder of your website. By placing it in the folder, the `SkinnedWebControl` class will use it if no themed version of the skin can be found.

PageMessageDefault.aspx

- This is a page message!
- This is a second page message!
- An error occured!
- And another error occured!

PageMessageIcons.aspx

M - This is a page message!
- This is a second page message!

E - An error occured!
- And another error occured!

PageMessageJScriptAlert.ascx

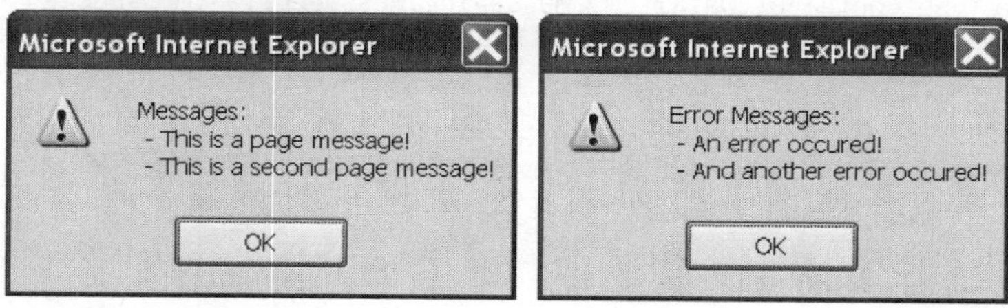

Figure 4-10. *Note how page messages and error messages are displayed using different skins. The* `PageMessageIcons.aspx` *skin is included in the sample code, although it isn't covered in this book.*

This skin displays the page messages in a tabular format inside of a rectangular `div` element with a gray (`Gainesboro` to be exact) background and `Black` border. Each message is displayed on its own row of the table. System message and page message text is shown in `DarkGreen` while error message text is shown in `DarkRed`. Each message is also prefixed with a dash (-). The panel and repeater controls that are used by the `PageMessageControl` have been bolded so they stand out:

```
<%@ Control Language="VB" %>
<div style="background-color:Gainsboro; width:100%;
            border:1px solid black;padding:5px;">
    <asp:Panel Runat=server ID=SystemMessagesPanel Visible=False>
        <asp:Repeater Runat=server id=SystemMessagesRepeater>
            <HeaderTemplate>
                <table cellspacing=0 cellpadding=2>
            </HeaderTemplate>
            <ItemTemplate>
                <TR>
                    <td style="width:5px;font-weight:bold;">-</td>
                    <td style='color:DarkGreen;'>
                     <%#CType(Container.DataItem, Messaging.MessageData).Message%>
                    </td>
                </TR>
            </ItemTemplate>
            <FooterTemplate>
                </table>
```

```
            </FooterTemplate>
        </asp:Repeater>
    </asp:Panel>
    <asp:Panel Runat=server ID=MessagesPanel Visible=False>
        <asp:Repeater Runat=server id=Messages>
            <HeaderTemplate>
                <table cellspacing=0 cellpadding=2>
            </HeaderTemplate>
            <ItemTemplate>
                <TR>
                    <td style="width:5px;font-weight:bold;">-</td>
                    <td style='color:DarkGreen;'>
                     <%#CType(Container.DataItem, Messaging.MessageData).Message%>
                    </td>
                </TR>
            </ItemTemplate>
            <FooterTemplate>
                </table>
            </FooterTemplate>
        </asp:Repeater>
    </asp:Panel>
    <asp:Panel Runat=server ID=ErrorMessagesPanel Visible=False>
        <asp:Repeater Runat=server id=ErrorMessages>
            <HeaderTemplate>
                <table cellspacing=0 cellpadding=2>
            </HeaderTemplate>
            <ItemTemplate>
                <TR>
                    <td style="width:5px;font-weight:bold;">-</td>
                    <td style='color:DarkRed;'>
                     <%#CType(Container.DataItem, Messaging.MessageData).Message%>
                    </td>
                </TR>
            </ItemTemplate>
            <FooterTemplate>
                </table>
            </FooterTemplate>
        </asp:Repeater>
    </asp:Panel>
</div>
<br />
```

After the PageMessageControl loads this skin file, assuming there are messages to output, the appropriate MessageDataCollection is bound to its corresponding repeater. This causes the HeaderTemplate of the repeater, which begins an HTML table, to be printed out. Then, the ItemTemplate is printed out for each message in the MessageDataCollection, filling the table with rows of messages. When all the messages have been output, the FooterTemplate is output, closing the table off. Refer to Figure 4-10 to see how this skin is displayed in the browser.

Creating the PageMessageJScriptAlert.ascx Skin

One of the reasons I chose to implement the `PageMessageControl` using `Repeater` controls instead of `DataGrid` controls is that the repeater allows for a greater deal of flexibility. This next example highlights that flexibility and shows you how you can use skins to completely change the UI of the control. Instead of outputting messages visibly on the page, as in the last example, the `PageMessageJScriptAlert.ascx` skin constructs a JavaScript message and calls the alert function to display the message to the user as an alert box:

```
<%@ Control Language="VB" %>
<asp:Panel Runat=server ID=SystemMessagesPanel Visible=False>
  <script language=javascript>
    var SystemMessages = "System Message\n";
    <asp:Repeater Runat=server id=SystemMessagesRepeater>
      <ItemTemplate>
        SystemMessages +=
          ' - <%#CType(Container.DataItem, Messaging.MessageData).Message%>\n';
      </ItemTemplate>
    </asp:Repeater>
    alert(SystemMessages);
  </script>
</asp:Panel>
<asp:Panel Runat=server ID=MessagesPanel Visible=False>
  <script language=javascript>
    var Messages = "Messages:\n";
    <asp:Repeater Runat=server id=Messages>
      <ItemTemplate>
        Messages +=
          ' - <%#CType(Container.DataItem, Messaging.MessageData).Message%>\n';
      </ItemTemplate>
    </asp:Repeater>
    alert(Messages);
  </script>
</asp:Panel>
<asp:Panel Runat=server ID=ErrorMessagesPanel Visible=False>
  <script language=javascript>
    var ErrorMessages = "Error Messages:\n";
      <asp:Repeater Runat=server id=ErrorMessages>
        <ItemTemplate>
          ErrorMessages +=
            ' - <%#CType(Container.DataItem, Messaging.MessageData).Message%>\n';
        </ItemTemplate>
      </asp:Repeater>
    alert(ErrorMessages);
  </script>
</asp:Panel>
```

If you look carefully, you'll notice that this skin contains three panels and three repeaters, exactly as the last example did. The difference is that this skin constructs JavaScript to output a message in an alert box. So, you can make anything you want with a `PageMessageControl` skin file, as long as you can do it with repeaters and panels. Refer to Figure 4-7 to see how this skin is displayed in a browser.

■ **Note** Check out the example application to see the `PageMessageIcons.ascx` skin, which places icons next to each set of messages.

Control Skins and Themes

Just to clarify, you can have multiple skins in a single theme. You do this by creating skins with different file names. That is why you have the `PageMessageDefault.ascx`, `PageMessageJScript➥Alert.ascx`, and the `PageMessageIcons.ascx` files all residing in the same `Skin` directory (`Skins/Default`).

You can also have themed skins. This requires creating a subfolder in your `Skins` folder with the same name as one of your themes (for example, `Skin/GreenTheme`). Then you can place a `Skin` file in the `Skin/GreenTheme` folder, and it will be used instead of the default skin when that particular theme is being employed by the page. So, you may have a directory structure that looks something like Figure 4-11 in your project.

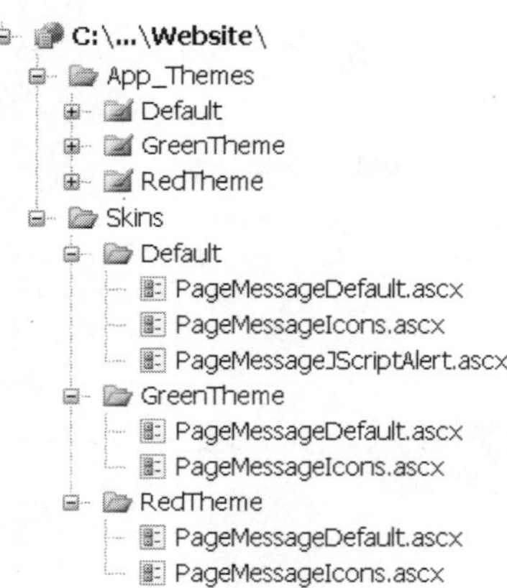

Figure 4-11. *File structure and contents of the* `Skin` *directory. Notice that it mimics the structure of the* `Themes` *folder. Also notice that the* `PageMessageJScriptAlert.ascx` *file only appears in the* `Default Skin` *folder.*

If the control finds a `UserControl` skin in the theme's directory, it uses that skin. If it does not find the skin, then it reverts to the skin located in the `Default` folder If no theme is specified for a given page, then the `SkinnedWebControl` looks for the control skin in the `Default` directory of the `Skins` folder.

Notice that the PageMessageJScriptAlert.ascx skin does not appear in the GreenTheme or RedTheme folders. Because it's a JavaScript alert box, there is very little you can do to change its UI. Thus, this skin is left unimplemented in these themes. If a themed page requires the PageMessageJScriptAlert.ascx skin, then the SkinnedWebControl reverts to the Default folder to find the skin.

There are many valid reasons for not implementing a themed version of a skin. If you need one, make it. If you don't, just let the SkinnedWebControl revert to the default skin.

■ **Note** The sample code (available in the Source Code area of the Apress Web site) includes themed skins for you to review. For the most part, they contain only cosmetic changes (different colors, backgrounds, and so on), which is why they are not shown in this text. You can see these themed skins in action from the MessagingDemo.aspx page.

Using the PageMessageControl

After you've added a project reference to the Messaging assembly, the PageMessageControl appears in the Visual Studio toolbox in a section titled Messaging Components. You can drag the PageMessageControl onto the surface of a web form and drop it wherever you want it to appear. The Visual Studio IDE uses the information from the ToolboxData attribute to automatically create the appropriate HTML markup to add to your web form. This includes both the control and the appropriate Register directive:

```
<%@ Register TagPrefix="msgControls" Namespace="Messaging" Assembly="Messaging" %>
<!-- Note: you could also make this a global registration tag if you wanted -->
...
<msgControls:PageMessageControl ID="PageMessageControl1" Runat="server" />
```

The only design-time change you can make to the PageMessageControl is to specify an alternative SkinFileName property. You can do this directly by adding the property to the control definition in HTML, or you can type in a new SkinFileName in the Visual Studio property editor. Either way, the HTML markup on the page is updated with the new SkinFileName property:

```
<msgControls:PageMessageControl ID="PageMessageControl1" Runat="server"
    SkinFileName="PageMessageIcons.ascx"/>
```

You can see a full-fledged demo of the PageMessageControl on the MessageDemo.aspx page in the Source Code area on the Apress website.

Using Page Messages and Error Messages

After you've added a PageMessageControl to your web form, you can add messages to it in code. Most messages originate in try/catch statements or in decision trees that determine whether an operation succeeded or failed.

```
Try
    'Some operation that may or may not succeed
    PageMessageControl1.AddMessage("Operation Succeeded.")
Catch ex as Exception
    PageMessageControl1.AddErrorMessage("Operation Failed.")
End Try
```

Although the need for it should be rare, you can also clear page messages and error messages:

```
PageMessageControl1.AddMessage("Operation Succeeded.")
PageMessageControl1.ClearMessages()

PageMessageControl1.AddErrorMessage("Operation Failed.")
PageMessageControl1.ClearErrorMessages()
```

Also know that you can add as many messages as you want to a page, and you can mix and match different types of messages. They all will be displayed when the page is rendered. Be conscious, however, of sending too many messages out at once. Information overload is just as much of a problem as no information at all.

Using System Messages

System messages are designed for ad-hoc messages that need to be disseminated to users of your application. Some good examples of system messages include notifications regarding a system shutdown or performance issues. For example, if you are running a database backup and you need to notify users that the system may be somewhat unresponsive during that period of time, you can use a system message to help users understand why their access times are slower than normal. This can reduce help calls while you are trying to get your backup completed.

Following is an example of how to add system messages to the `PageMessageControl`:

```
PageMessageControl.AddSystemMessage("System may be slow during backup.")
PageMessageControl.AddSystemMessage("System Message #2")
PageMessageControl.AddSystemMessage("System Message #3")
```

After you've added a system message, it continues to display until it is removed. You can remove system messages by clearing them out entirely or by removing a specific message using its index:

```
PageMessageControl.RemoveSystemMessage(2)
PageMessageControl.ClearSystemMessages
```

The `RemoveSystemMessage` method removes the system message at the specified index. Remember that the index is zero based, so the preceding code removes the third message in the list. The next line clears out the system messages entirely. Also remember that if you restart IIS, all system messages will be lost because they are stored in memory.

Summary

After reading this chapter, you should be aware of the potential reusable controls have for shaving time and effort off your overall project timeline. There are always benefits to spending a little bit of time upfront to design tools to help you during the entire life of your project. You also had a chance to look at some of the new features in ASP.NET 2.0, such as global tag registration, the design time rendering of `UserControls`, and the `ControlState` mechanism. And you finished it all off by implementing a skinned control that allows you to easily communicate status messages to the people who use your application. Let's finish up with a thought on skinned server controls.

Although the skinned page-message control is a very useful tool, it only scratches the surface in terms of the potential for skinned controls. You can see the full potential of skinned controls by taking a look at Community Server, a forum, gallery, and blogging application built by Telligent Systems. Community Server is built almost entirely from skinned controls, which allows you to customize the look and feel of the entire application to match the look and feel of an existing site. All the following sites look completely different, but use the same core Community Server blogging software to manage their content:

- `http://gearlog.com/blogs/gearlog/default.aspx`
- `http://microsoftgadgets.com/`
- `http://blogs.msdn.com/`

In effect, these companies rebranded the core Community Server application to visually integrate with the rest of their website. If you are building an application intended for use by multiple corporate clients, you can make your product much more attractive by building in rebranding capabilities using skinned controls. It takes time and effort, but clients are demanding more and more these days as web technology gets more sophisticated. You can pull down the C# source for Community Server from http://`www.CommunityServer.org` to see how it was put together.

CHAPTER 5

User Management Tools and Login Controls for Forms Authentication

Many business applications are intended solely for internal use and, as such, may rely on corporate domain controllers and Active Directory to maintain users and their login information. Of course, applications are not always solely intended for internal use; customers, suppliers, partners and other external users with no access to a corporate domain regularly need access to business applications. In fact, customer-facing business applications are often huge revenue generators for companies. Just think about how many average people sign in to eBay, PayPal, and Amazon every day. Smaller companies are also finding niche markets for outsourced services using web applications. Two consulting firms I worked for paid a fairly substantial monthly sum for an outsourced, web-based time-tracking and billing system. Supporting external users is undoubtedly a common need in business application development.

Microsoft was well aware of the need to support external users and designed ASP.NET with an authentication mechanism known as Forms Authentication, which derives its name from the fact that external users normally sign in to an application by entering their username and password in a web-based form (domain users log in via a browser dialog box). Forms Authentication relies on you, the developer, to manually authenticate a user against a data store and, upon successful authentication, use the `System.Web.Security.FormsAuthentication` class to issue the user an authentication ticket. On subsequent requests, ASP.NET automatically picks up that ticket, determines whether or not it's valid, loads the username and ticket information into an object, and places that object into the request context making it accessible from the executing page via `Context.User`. This enables you to see who is accessing your application.

Most applications, however, also rely on user roles to allow different people varying degrees of access to the system. Unfortunately, Forms Authentication does not automatically load role information into the `Context.User` object. If you want access to role information, you must manually set and parse that information out of the authentication ticket or access role information from a database or other data store. You're also completely responsible for setting up the database used to store user credentials and, as mentioned before, the code to authenticate users against the database. All in all, Forms Authentication is a great mechanism, but it does take a bit of setup and coding to actually use...at least it did before ASP.NET 2.0.

Microsoft augmented Forms Authentication by releasing a series of pretty spectacular providers and login controls that automatically handle all the grunt work associated with user management for your site. The membership provider can automatically create a user-management database capable of storing user and roles. The Web Site Administration Tool gives you a way to add, edit, and delete users and their respective roles in that database. The login controls automatically authenticate users from the database and load the appropriate user *and* their roles into the request context. In other words, you can implement an entire user-management system for your application without having to write a single line of code.

In this chapter, you'll explore the new user-management features of ASP.NET 2.0 and see the new login controls that are now available. Here's a synopsis of the chapter:

- *Forms Authentication in ASP.NET:* Describes how to manually implement Forms Authentication in your applications. Remember, all the new tools in ASP.NET 2.0 are augmentative in nature and are not meant to replace Forms Authentication. You can still implement Forms Authentication manually if your application requires.
- *Working with the* `Membership` *and* `RoleManager` *Objects:* Discusses the new providers that make the automated user-management features of ASP.NET possible.
- *Managing Users with the Web Site Administration Tool:* Demonstrates all the ins and outs of adding, editing, and deleting users, setting up roles, and assigning users to roles using the built-in web-based interface in ASP.NET.
- *Login Controls Overview:* Presents all the new login controls available in the Visual Studio Toolbox and how to use them in your applications.

Before you get too deep into all the new features in ASP.NET, let's take a minute to look at some Forms Authentication basics and how to manually implement Forms Authentication for your application.

Forms Authentication in ASP.NET

You can't fully appreciate how much time and trouble the new user-management features in ASP.NET 2.0 save you unless you understand how to manually implement Forms Authentication in your application. If you are already familiar with Forms Authentication from ASP.NET 1.x, everything you learned about Forms Authentication still applies because the Forms Authentication architecture is still in place. All the new features simply make it easier to use what is already there, and they do a lot of the grunt work for you. If you are not familiar with Forms Authentication, then this section will familiarize you with it and teach you how to implement it manually.

A manual implementation may be necessary for custom role and authentication schemes that break the mold of a normal user-management scenario or at least a normal user management scenario in the eyes of ASP.NET 2.0. I recently worked on an application designed to support multiple corporate clients. It runs as a single application, but each corporate client has a separate database in which to store application data. The new built-in user management features in ASP.NET 2.0 expect all user information to be stored in a single database, so that particular application required a manual Forms Authentication implementation. You never know what kind of quirky situation may arise, so it's best to be prepared for anything. In the sections that follow, you'll learn about a number of Forms Authentication topics. Pay careful attention because many of the topics discussed apply regardless of whether or not you are using the new ASP.NET 2.0 login tools.

Note Examples for everything we discuss about manually implementing Forms Authentication in an application can be found in the `ManualFormAuthWebsite` in the sample application in the Source Code area of the Apress website (http://www.apress.com).

Authentication Modes

Authentication is the process by which a system determines a user's identity, and no discussion about Forms Authentication is complete without a quick rundown of the other alternatives. Knowing your options helps you know if you have chosen the correct one.

ASP.NET allows you to configure your applications using any one of four different authentication modes: Windows, Forms, Passport, or None. The following sections provide a brief synopsis of each authentication mode and the situations for which they are intended. Understand, however, that a security architecture is operating behind the scenes when you use any of these authentication options. Chapter 12 covers security in much more detail.

Windows Authentication

Windows Authentication allows IIS to authenticate the user via Basic (clear text), Digest, or Integrated Windows Authentication. IIS checks the username and password acquired through this process against the local or domain (Active Directory) user accounts to determine their validity. If the username and password are not valid, then the browser prompts the user for a valid username and password using a generic login dialog box (not a page-based login form).

One of the greatest benefits of Windows Authentication is that the authentication process is highly transparent to Internet Explorer users. When people access an ASP.NET application that uses Windows Authentication, Internet Explorer automatically sends their Windows account information to the web server. Thus, Internet Explorer users do not have to continually reenter their login information to access web applications. Of course, this means that your users must be using Internet Explorer. Other browsers such as Firefox and Netscape lack the transparency because they do not automatically send account information to the web server. Instead, they start off by displaying the generic login dialog box mentioned previously.

Windows Authentication requires all the people who use your application to have a local Windows account or a domain (Active Directory) account. As such, internal business applications are most likely to use Windows Authentication because most businesses already have Windows accounts in place for their employees.

Note You cannot create Windows users via the ASP.NET 2.0 tools. You must use Active Directory to create domain accounts or the User Accounts applet in the Control Panel to create local accounts.

Internal business applications also have the most to gain in terms of the transparency provided by Internet Explorer. Employees normally do not enjoy having to log in to their computer when they first boot up, then when they access the sales system, then when they access customer information, and then again when they hit the HR application. And most businesses tend to standardize on a single platform, so you can be relatively assured that everyone is using the same browser, for example Internet Explorer.

Unless you have some compelling reason to do otherwise, you should not use Windows Authentication for public-facing applications. Home users have their own local accounts and cannot authenticate using that account on your web server. As such, they are forced to enter their login information (that is, their Windows login for your network, not their home computer) in that generic login dialog box discussed earlier, which is none to intuitive for the average computer user. Plus, maintaining Windows accounts for a large number of external users is a maintenance nightmare.

Forms Authentication

Forms Authentication allows people to identify themselves by entering their username and password in a web-based login form instead of the generic login dialog box generated by the browser. A person's username and password are validated against a user information data store (database, XML file, and so on). After being successfully authenticated, the system issues that person an authentication ticket that identifies the authenticated user on subsequent requests. People are considered authenticated as long as their authentication ticket is valid.

Public-facing sites typically use Forms Authentication for a couple of important reasons. First, the actual login experience is much more user friendly. The web-based form can include instructional text, graphics, and helpful links to quickly help people retrieve forgotten passwords or contact customer service. So the login look and feel can match your site and you can make it far more intuitive than the generic login dialog box associated with Windows Authentication. Second, Forms Authentication uses login credentials that are not tied to Windows accounts, so you can easily support and maintain a massive user base by storing login information in a database.

Many of the pitfalls associated with Forms Authentication were outlined in the opening of this chapter. What it boils down to is that you have to do some auxiliary work to get Forms Authentication up and running. This includes building a user-management database, developing code to validate user credentials against that database, and manually adding role information to the `Context.User` principal object (principal objects are discussed in more detail in Chapter 12).

When it comes to public-facing sites, Forms Authentication is definitely the route you want to take. You may also want to consider Forms Authentication if your company has standardized on something other than Internet Explorer because it at least provides you a bit of control over the login experience.

Passport Authentication

Passport Authentication is Microsoft's single-login framework, and it is supported in ASP.NET 2.0. This authentication method seems to be losing industry acceptance and is slowly disappearing from non-Microsoft sites.

No Authentication

Specifying None as the authentication type removes all authentication from your application. This is the best option if your application does not need to authenticate users because it removes the authentication overhead from your application.

Configuring an Authentication Mode for Your Application

You configure the authentication mode type for your application by setting the mode attribute in the <authentication> section of Web.config. The mode attribute can accept one of four settings, which correspond to the mode discussed earlier: Windows, Forms, Passport, or None. Windows Authentication is the default mode for new web applications. Listing 5-1 provides an example configuration that shows you how to enable Forms Authentication for your application.

Listing 5-1. *Configuring an Application to Use Forms Authentication*

```
<configuration>
   ...
   <system.web>
      ...
      <authentication mode="Forms" />
   </system.web>
</configuration>
```

Setting the mode attribute value to "Forms" enables Forms Authentication for your application, but that is only the beginning. A lot of work is still involved with manually implement Forms Authentication on an application.

Authentication Tickets in Concept

Conceptually, an authentication ticket is like a movie ticket. When you go to the movies you stop at the ticket booth, pay the attendee, and in return he gives you a ticket. That ticket means that you have paid for a movie and should be admitted to the movie theater. If you attempt to get into the movie theater without a ticket, then you are simply denied admittance. If you attempt to get into a movie using an outdated ticket, you will also be denied admittance.

Similarly, when you log in to an ASP.NET web application that uses Forms Authentication, ASP.NET issues you an authentication ticket. That ticket tells ASP.NET that you have already entered your username and password, that your username and password were valid, and that you should be considered authenticated as long as the ticket is valid. Authentication tickets also have expirations. If a ticket has expired, ASP.NET disregards the ticket because it is invalid, and the user must log in again.

Authentication Cookies

Most applications issue authentication tickets via authentication cookies, which is just a way of saying a cookie that contains an authentication ticket. This has some interesting implications when it comes to expirations. Although authentication tickets have expirations and cookies have expirations, they are two completely separate things.

If your authentication ticket expires before your cookie expires, then ASP.NET disregards the ticket because it has expired. If your cookie expires before your authentication ticket, then

ASP.NET never receives the authentication ticket because the browser simply deletes the cookie. Either way, you have to reauthenticate. This tends to cause a lot of problems when creating persistent authentication tickets (that is, the "Remember Me" functionality that allows users to remain logged in between browser session). If you make a persistent authentication ticket, make sure you place it in a persistent cookie.

Specifying a Default Login Page and Login Redirection URL

Although you can put a login form on any page you want, there should be one page that acts as the default login page. ASP.NET sends users to the default login page when they attempt to access a protected resource before logging in to the application. You configure the default login page via the `loginUrl` attribute of the `<forms>` element.

When ASP.NET redirects users to the default login page, it appends a query string variable named `ReturnUrl` containing the location to which the user was denied access. After the user successfully logs in, you can redirect them back to this page so they do not have to navigate to it again. Of course, users can also manually navigate to the default login page (by clinking on a link), in which case, there is no `ReturnUrl` variable. In this case, the user should be redirected to a default page for logged in users. You can specify this default login redirection URL via the `defaultUrl` attribute of the `<forms>` element. Tools in the `FormsAuthentication` class automatically determine whether the user should be redirected using the `ReturnUrl` in the query string or the `defaultUrl` in `Web.config`. You'll see examples of these shortly.

Listing 5-2 is an example showing how to configure a default login page and a default login redirection page.

Listing 5-2. *Configuring a Default Login Page and Login Redirection URL*

```
<configuration>
    ...
    <system.web>
        ...
        <authentication mode="Forms">
            <forms loginUrl="MyLoginForm.aspx" defaultUrl="SuccessfulLogin.aspx"/>
        </authentication>
    </system.web>
</configuration>
```

If you do not specify a default login page, then ASP.NET redirect the user to `Login.aspx` in the root folder of your application. And, in turn, if you do not have a `Login.aspx` page in your application root, then your users will see a 404 not found error because the page does not exist. So, it is in your best interest to define a default login page or make sure that the `Login.aspx` page exists in your application root.

Other Forms Authentication Configuration Options

Aside from defining the default login page and default login redirection URL, you can also configure a number of other Forms Authentication options within the `<forms>` element. Table 5-1 provides a quick rundown of the various attributes you can specify and what they do.

Table 5-1. `<forms>` *Element Attribute Descriptions*

Attribute Name	Default Value	Description
`loginUrl`	`login.aspx`	Defines the location relative to `Web.config` to which unauthorized users are redirected when they attempt to access a protected resource. When they are sent to this page, the redirection includes a query string value indicating the page they were attempt to access so they can be redirected there after logging in.
`defaultUrl`	`default.aspx`	Defines the default location to which users are redirected after successfully logging in. If the user was directed to the login page while trying to access a protected resource, then the user is returned to the protected resource, not to the location defined by this attribute.
`cookieless`	`UseDeviceProfile`	Forms Authentication can store a user's authentication data in a cookie or as a query string value. The query string is widely supported, but often results in authentication data being lost during navigation. Cookies are more reliable, but cookie support may be disabled by security-conscious users. The cookieless attribute has four settings that allow you to configure how Forms Authentication should store authentication data:

cookieless Values	Description
`UseCookies`	Forms Authentication always uses cookies. If the browser does not support cookies, or cookies have been disabled, the user is not allowed to access the application.
`UseUri`	Forms Authentication always stores authentication data in the query string and does not attempt to use cookies. This is good if your target users normally have cookies disabled or are using older browsers that do not support cookies.
`AutoDetect`	Browsers send information identifying the type and version of the browser, and ASP.NET maintains a repository of browser types, versions, and the features they support. If ASP.NET knows, based on that repository, that the browser supports cookies, then ASP.NET probes the browser to determine if cookies are enabled. If cookies are enabled, then ASP.NET writes authentication data to the cookie. Otherwise, ASP.NET writes data to the query string.
`UseDeviceProfile`	This works similarly to the `AutoDetect`, but the decision to use cookies is solely based on ASP.NET's browser feature repository. ASP.NET does not probe to check whether cookies are enabled. If the browser is known to support cookies, but the user has disabled cookies, the user is unable to access the application.

Table 5-1. `<forms>` *Element Attribute Descriptions (Continued)*

Attribute Name	Default Value	Description
`name`	`.ASPXAUTH`	Defines the name of the cookie that contains the user's Forms Authentication data. If you are running multiple applications on a single server and each one requires its own authentication cookie, then you'll need to change the name of this cookie for each individual application to avoid issues with overwriting authentication data.
`timeout`	`30`	Defines the length of time a cookie is valid (in minutes). Users who are idle for more than this time period must log in to the application again. The cookie timeout does not apply to permanent cookies.
`slidingExpiration`	`False`	Conventional logic dictates that cookie timeouts should be reset on every request. Using the default 30-minute timeout as a guide, this means that if a user accesses a page at page at 12:00 and then again at 12:10, the timeout will not occur until 12:40. Such is not the case because ASP.NET is optimized to reduce cookie setting to lessen network traffic and to avoid accosting users who have cookie alerts enabled. By default, ASP.NET only resets the timeout when more than half of the timeout time has passed. So, a user accessing a page at 12:00 and then again at 12:10, is still subject to a timeout at 12:30. You can force ASP.NET to reset the timeout on each request by setting the `slidingExplirationattribute` attribute to `True`.
`domain`		Defines the domain for which the cookie is valid. Before the browser requests a page, it checks to see if any cookies match the domain and path of the request. If so, it sends that cookie along with the request.
`path`	`/`	Defines the path in your application past which authentication cookies should be sent. For example, if you specify `/Protected/` as the path, then cookies are only sent to your application if the user requests something in the `/Protected/` folder or a subfolder of the `/Protected/` folder. Be wary of using this setting because case-sensitivity issues may result in a browser not sending the cookie.
`protection`	`All`	Defines the protection placed on Forms Authentication cookies.

Value	Description
Protection value	Cookies are not validated or encrypted. This has a slight performance benefit, but it means that malicious users could read and or alter cookie information. Only consider using this option if your application requires SSL (HTTPS) because cookies are encrypted along with all other communications over SSL connections.
Validation	Creates a message authentication code (MAC) by hashing the cookie data using a validation key. The resulting MAC hash is then appended to the cookie data. When ASP.NET receives the cookie on a subsequent request, it hashes the cookie data using the same validation key and checks the result against the MAC hash in the cookie. If both items match, then the data in the cookie has not been altered and the cookie is considered valid.
Encryption	Cookie data is encrypted using DES (Data Encryption Standard) or Triple-DES encryption and stored in the cookie. On subsequent requests, ASP.NET decrypts the cookie data. Validation is not used in this scenario, so the cookie may be susceptible to attacks. You specify the encryption algorithm in the `<machineKey>` element in `Machine.config` or `Web.config`.
All	Applies both `Validation` and `Encryption` to the cookie. `All` is the most secure option and is therefore both the recommended and default option as well.

Attribute Name	Default Value	Description
requireSSL	False	Defines whether an SSL connection is required to send the authentication cookie. When set to `True`, ASP.NET informs the browser that the cookie should only be sent over a secure connection.

Forms Authentication also supports a `<credentials>` section that allows you to hard-code users and passwords directly in `Web.config`. This was a quick and dirty way for developers to create users for a Forms Authentication application without having to use a database. It was seldom used in ASP.NET 1.1, and its use continues to decline because of the built-in membership and role providers in ASP.NET 2.0 (see Chapter 5).

All the configuration options from the Table 5-1 apply regardless of whether you are doing a manual implementation or using the new ASP.NET 2.0 login tools.

Manually Implementing Forms Authentication

All the information about Forms Authentication that you have read so far applies regardless of whether or not you are using the new ASP.NET 2.0 login controls. In this section, however, you'll be looking at how Forms Authentication was handled in ASP.NET 1.x. As mentioned before, Forms Authentication has not changed in ASP.NET 2.0, so you can still use this approach to manually implement Forms Authentication in your ASP.NET 2.0 applications if the new login tools do not fit your needs.

In the sections that follow, you'll see how to build a login form, authenticate users, construct an authentication ticket, fill that authentication ticket with role information, and parse that role information out on subsequent requests so you can use it on the pages in your application.

Building a Login Form

Before you can let people log in to your application, you need a login form, and almost every login page ever built has two text boxes to allow people to entire their username and password. Our login form has both of these entry controls as well as a **Remember Me** check box that allows users to decide whether they want the application to remember their login information when they close down the browser. This allows them to return to your application and use it without having to log back in.

The login form also has two login buttons. One demonstrates how to log in by placing role information directly in the authentication ticket, and the other demonstrates how to log in without placing role information in the authentication ticket. Listing 5-3 provides the definitions for the controls in the login form without any visual or layout formatting.

Listing 5-3. `Textbox` *Controls for a Username and Password*

```
<asp:TextBox runat="server" ID="txtUsername" />
<asp:TextBox runat="server" ID="txtPassword" TextMode="password" />
<asp:Button runat="server" ID="btnLogin" Text="Login with Roles" />
<asp:Button runat="server" ID="btnLoginNoRoles" Text="Login without Roles" />
```

After users enter their login credentials you have to authenticate those users by checking their credentials against a data store. We'll tackle that next.

Authenticating Users Against a Data Store

One aspect of manually implementing Forms Authentication is writing the code to authenticate users by validating their login credentials. Normally, you authenticate users against a database of usernames and passwords using a standard SQL query. For the sake of simplicity, the usernames and passwords are hard-coded directly in the sample application as shown in Listing 5-4.

Listing 5-4. *Example Authentication Method*

```
'*************************************************************************
Private Function AuthenticateUser(ByVal Username As String, _
  ByVal Password As String) As Boolean
    Select Case UCase(Username)
        Case "BOB" : Return CBool(Password = "bobpassword")
        Case "JANE" : Return CBool(Password = "janepassword")
        Case "MARK" : Return CBool(Password = "markpassword")
        Case Else : Return False
    End Select
End Function
```

This method accepts a username and password and then checks to see if the username and password match any of the three hard-coded users in the sample application. The username is not case sensitive because the method forces it into uppercase before checking it, but the passwords are case sensitive.

Determining User Roles

Your application is likely to store role information in a database along with the relationships that associates users to those roles. Figure 5-1 depicts a simple but commonly used database structure for storing users, roles, and user-role assignments. Normally, you pull role information out of the database by executing a query requesting roles for the authenticated user. Again, for simplicity, the example application uses hard-coded role information instead of accessing role information from a database as shown in Listing 5-5.

Listing 5-5. *Example User-Role Acquisition Method*

```
'***************************************************************************
Private Function GetUserRoles(ByVal username As String) As String
    Select Case UCase(username)
        Case "BOB" : Return "employee|sales"
        Case "JANE" : Return "executive|marketing"
        Case "MARK" : Return "contractor|support|admin"
        Case Else : Return ""
    End Select
End Function
```

The `GetUserRoles` function accepts a username as a string and returns a string containing a pipe-delimited list of roles for the user. Again, the username is not case sensitive because the method forces it into uppercase before comparing it to the hard-coded values.

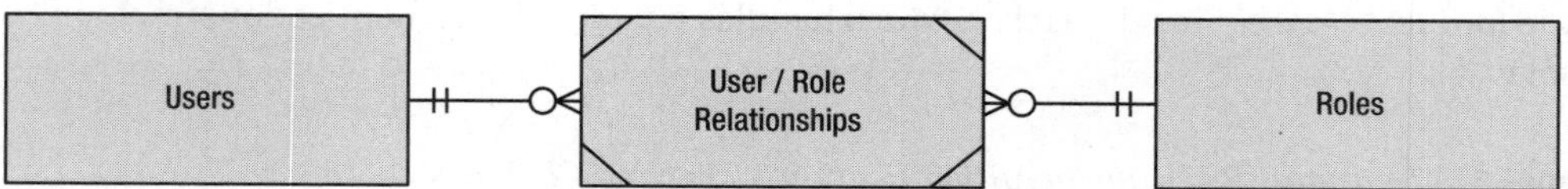

Figure 5-1. *Simple entity relationship diagram for storing users, roles, and role assignments in a database*

Issuing an Authorization Ticket Without Role Information

Authentication tickets must include a value that identifies the user and can optionally include role information. If your application does not require any role information, then you can issue an authentication ticket without too much hassle using the not intuitively named `Forms➥Authentication.RedirectFromLoginPage` method.

The `RedirectFromLoginPage` method accepts two parameters: `username` and `create➥PersistentCookie`. `Username` is the name of the authenticated user and `createPersistentCookie` denotes whether the cookie issued to the user is persistent (persists between browser sessions) or deleted when the user closes the browser. The method issues the user an authentication ticket in accordance with the configuration settings in the `<forms>` element in `Web.config` and then redirects the user to the `ReturnUrl` in the query string, if available, or the `defaultUrl` specified in `Web.config`. Listing 5-6 is the code from the `Click` event handler for the `btnLogin➥NoRoles` button, which demonstrates how to use the `RedirectFromLoginPage` method.

Listing 5-6. *Issuing an Authentication Ticket Without Role Information*

```
'***************************************************************************
Protected Sub btnLoginNoRoles_Click(ByVal sender As Object, _
  ByVal e As System.EventArgs) Handles btnLoginNoRoles.Click

    If AuthenticateUser(txtUsername.Text, txtPassword.Text) Then
        FormsAuthentication.RedirectFromLoginPage(txtUsername.Text, _
          chkRememberMe.Checked)
    End If

 End Sub
```

Notice that the event handler first authenticates the user information entered into the form and then calls the RedirectFromLoginPage method. Remember, the authentication ticket implies that you have authenticated the user already so you shouldn't issue it until the user has actually been authenticated.

Issuing an Authorization Ticket with Role Information

Authentication tickets have a string property that allows you to store custom user data along with the rest of the ticket information. This was not expressly designed to store roles, but it works well for the task. Unfortunately, the FormsAuthentication class does not give you a way to set that custom user data property from a convenient method such as RedirectFrom➥LoginPage, so you have to manually create the authentication ticket to get access to the custom user data property. You also have to manually create the authentication ticket that stores that authentication ticket.

Listing 5-7 is the code for the Click event handler for the btnLogin button, along with the code for CreateAuthenticationTicket, which handles building the authentication ticket and cookie.

Listing 5-7. *Manually Building an Authentication Ticket and Cookie*

```
'***************************************************************************
Protected Sub btnLogin_Click(ByVal sender As Object, _
  ByVal e As System.EventArgs) Handles btnLogin.Click

    If AuthenticateUser(txtUsername.Text, txtPassword.Text) Then
            CreateAuthenticationTicket(txtUsername.Text, chkRememberMe.Checked)
    End If

End Sub

'***************************************************************************
Private Sub CreateAuthenticationTicket(ByVal username As String, _
  ByVal isPersistent As Boolean)
```

```
    'Set up variables for authentication ticket
    Dim version As Integer = 1
    Dim issueDate As DateTime = Now
    Dim expirationDate As Date
    Dim userData As String = GetUserRoles(username)
    Dim cookiePath As String = "/"

    'Set the expirationDate
    If isPersistent Then
        expirationDate = Now.AddYears(1)
    Else
        expirationDate = Now.AddMinutes(60)
    End If

    'Set up the authentication ticket
    Dim FormAuthTicket As FormsAuthenticationTicket = _
          New FormsAuthenticationTicket(version, username, issueDate, _
          expirationDate, isPersistent, userData, cookiePath)

    'Encrypt the ticket content as a string so it can be stored in a cookie
    Dim encTicket As String = FormsAuthentication.Encrypt(FormAuthTicket)

    'Place the encrypted ticket in a cookie
    Dim AuthCookie As HttpCookie = _
          New HttpCookie(FormsAuthentication.FormsCookieName, encTicket)

    'Set cookie duration if necessary
    If isPersistent Then AuthCookie.Expires = Now.AddYears(1)

    'Send cookie back to user
    Response.Cookies.Add(AuthCookie)

    'Redirect user to the page from whence they came
    Response.Redirect(FormsAuthentication.GetRedirectUrl(username, isPersistent))

End Sub
```

As you can see the, the btnLogin_Click method simply authenticates the user and then calls the CreateAuthenticationTicket method. CreateAuthenticationTicket accepts two parameters: username identifies the user who has been authenticated, and isPersistent determines whether or not to issue a persistent authentication ticket. The isPersistent value comes from the **Remember Me** check box on the login form.

The CreateAuthentictionTicket method starts out by setting up a series of variables used to create the authentication ticket. Notice that issueDate is set to the current date and time using the Now() method, userData acquires a pipe delimited list of user roles using the GetUserRoles() method, and expirationDate is set to either 60 minutes or 1 year in the future depending on the value of the isPersistent method parameter (these are arbitrary values, you can make them shorter or longer depending on your particular needs). Next, the method creates a FormsAuthenticationTicket using the values it just defined. For reference, the version, cookiePath, and isPersistent values are informative in nature and have no bearing on the way ASP.NET handles an authentication ticket. In theory, you can use the version value to vary how your custom code handles authentication tickets, but it's rarely used. The cookiePath value has absolutely no bearing on the actual authentication cookie path. Nor does isPersistent value have any bearing on the expiration dates on the authentication ticket or the authentication cookie. They really are only there for reference.

After creating the FormsAuthenticationTicket object, the CreateAuthenticationTicket method encrypts the ticket by passing it into the FormsAuthentication.Encrypt method. The Encrypt method uses cryptographic settings from the <MachineKey> element in Machine.config to encrypt the ticket as a string. Web applications that reside on the same server encrypt their tickets using the same encryption settings, unless those settings are explicitly changed by creating a custom <MachineKey> section in your application's Web.config file (see the "Encrypted Passwords and the <MachineKey> Element" sidebar for information). Applications that use the same <MachineKey> settings can decrypt each other's encrypted authentication tickets, so it's possible to share authentication cookies between two different applications. You must also create matching <MachineKey> settings for applications hosted by a web farm. Any server in the farm could create an authentication ticket, and any other server in the farm could have to decrypt it. As such, they all need matching <MachineKey> settings to function properly. A full description about sharing authentication tickets is beyond the scope of this book. You should understand, however, that the <MachineKey> settings and authentication cookie names must be identical, and the cookie path must be set to a value that allows both applications to receive the cookie.

After the method encrypts the ticket, it creates an authentication cookie object using the value from FormsAuthentication.FormsCookieName as the cookie name. Remember, you configure the authentication cookie name in Web.config (refer to the name attribute in Table 5-1), so ASP.NET expects the authentication ticket to be in a cookie with that name. Also note that the cookie value uses the value from the encrypted ticket string.

After the cookie is created, the CreateAuthenticationTicket method checks to see if the authentication ticket is persistent. If so, it makes the cookie persistent by settings is expiration to one year in the future. You can make the cookie expiration date higher if you want, but normally a year is sufficient. The method then adds the cookie to the outgoing response so it will be sent back to the browser. Finally, it redirects the user via the FormsAuthentication.GetRedirectUrl method, which determines whether the user should be redirected to the default login page defined in Web.config or to the page specified in the ReturnUrl variable that comes in on the query string.

Caution When you implement your own authentication tickets, you lose the ability to configure cookie and ticket settings in Web.config because you are manually setting those values in code.

Making Role Information Available to Pages in Your Application

Placing role information into the authentication ticket does not automatically make it available to the application. Remember, the authentication ticket stores the role information in an ad-hoc user-data property, so it has no idea that it's supposed to be used to define roles. You have to manually parse out the role information, place it in a principal object, and then set the Context.User property equal to that principal object (principal objects are discussed in more detail in Chapter 12).

You need to complete these tasks in the AuthenticateRequest event of the application because the ASP.NET security model expects authentication information to be available immediately after the event fires. The code to make roles available to the pages in your application appears in the Global.asax file (see Listing 5-8).

Listing 5-8. *Making Role Information Availble to Pages in Your Application*

```
'***************************************************************************
Protected Sub Application_AuthenticateRequest(ByVal sender As Object, _
  ByVal e As System.EventArgs)

    Dim authCookie As HttpCookie
    Dim authTicket As FormsAuthenticationTicket
    Dim roles() As String
    Dim identity As FormsIdentity
    Dim principal As GenericPrincipal

    'Acquire the authorization cookie
    authCookie = Request.Cookies(FormsAuthentication.FormsCookieName)

    'Only process the authorization cookie if it is available
    If Not authCookie Is Nothing Then

        'Decrypt authorization cookie to acquire the authentication ticket
        authTicket = FormsAuthentication.Decrypt(authCookie.Value)

        'Make sure the authentication ticket has not expired
        If Not authTicket.Expired Then

            'Parse the pipe-delimited role string into a string array
            If Not authTicket.UserData = Nothing Then
            roles = authTicket.UserData.Trim.Split("|")
            Else
                roles = New String() {}
            End If

            'Create the principal object and assign it to Context.User
            identity = New FormsIdentity(authTicket)
            principal = New GenericPrincipal(identity, roles)
            Context.User = principal

        End If

    End If

End Sub
```

The Application_AuthenticateRequest method begins by acquiring the authentication cookie from the Request object. Assuming the cookie exists, the method acquires the authentication ticket by passing the cookie value into the `FormsAuthentication.Decrypt` method. The method then checks to make sure the authentication ticket has not expired. If the cookie is not present or the authentication ticket has expired, the user is not authenticated.

After determining the user has a valid authentication ticket, the method checks to see if there is any data in the `UserData` property of the authentication ticket. If so, it assumes the data is a pipe-delimited list of roles, splits them into a string array using the pipe as a delimiter, and stores them in the `roles` variable. If no data is present in the `UserData` property, then the method assigns `roles` an empty string array.

Finally, the method constructs a `FormsIdentity` object by passing in the authentication ticket to the `FormsIdentity` object constructor. This creates an object that represents the authenticated user. Then the method creates a new `GenericPrincipal` object by passing in the `FormsIdentity` object it just created along with the `roles` array to the `GenericPrincipal` constructor. This creates an object that represents an authenticated user and the roles to which that user belongs. Finally, the method assigns the `GenericPrincipal` object to the `Context.User` property. This makes the user and role information available to the page in your application.

■ **Tip** You do not have to store role information directly in the authentication ticket. You can use this same technique to acquire role information directly out of a database or other data store. Also, if your users tend to have a large number or roles (15–20), then you may want to shy away from storing them directly in an authentication ticket for performance purposes. The authentication ticket works best when storing a relatively limited number of roles (1–5).

Using Roles Information in Your Application

After you load the role information into the `Context.User` object, you access role information in your page via the `User.IsInRole` method. This method accepts a string containing a role name and checks through all the roles with which that user is associated. If the user is in the specified role, then the method returns `True`, otherwise, it returns `False`.

Listing 5-9 demonstrates the `User.IsInRole` method. `AddLabelText` is a utility method that appends the specified text to a label on the page.

Listing 5-9. `User.IsInRole` *Example*

```
AddLabelText("You are logged in as " & User.Identity.Name)
If User.IsInRole("admin") Then AddLabelText("You are in the admin role")
If User.IsInRole("contractor") Then AddLabelText("You are in the contractor role")
If User.IsInRole("employee") Then AddLabelText("You are in the employee role")
```

Now, it took a lot of work to make roles available to the application and you didn't even have to get into creating the database to store the user and role information or the database queries required to pull information out of a database. On top of that, you still need a way to maintain users, roles, and user-role assignments. Now let's shift focus and take a look at how ASP.NET 2.0 can take care of all the grunt work automatically.

Working with the Membership and Roles Objects

Microsoft designed many of the new features in ASP.NET 2.0 to be completely data-source independent by implementing those features using the provider model. In the provider model, you have a broker class that exposes properties and methods but does not have any logic to implement them, an abstract base class that defines the functionality required to implement the method and properties in the broker class, and a number of "provider classes" that provide various data-source specific implementations of the method and properties defined in the abstract class.

As a developer, you only interact with the properties and methods on the broker object, which, of course, do not contain any implementation logic. Behind the scenes, the broker object uses configuration settings in `Web.config` to load an appropriate provider class to actually do the work. This abstracts you from the implementation details. Behind the scenes, your application could be accessing SQL Server, Oracle, MySQL, Access, an XML file, or even an Excel spreadsheet, and you would never know the difference. Plus you have the added benefit of being able to change provider classes via the configuration without having to change your code.

The `Membership` and `Roles` are both "broker" objects that use the provider model to shield you from the nasty implementation details of user and role management. In this chapter, you'll see how to configure and use them in your applications.

The Membership Object

The `Membership` object exposes all the ASP.NET 2.0 user-management functionality from a single location. Because it uses the provider model, you can configure the `Membership` object to access any data source for which a membership provider exists. Out of the box, ASP.NET 2.0 only has two providers: the `SqlMembershipProvider`, which provides the `Membership` object with functionality for SQL Server, and the `AspNetActiveDirectoryMembershipProvider`, which provides support for Active Directory. You can expect other vendors and third-party software developers to create their own providers as the technology progresses. For reference, all membership providers inherit from the abstract `MembershipProvider` class in the `System.Web.Security` namespace.

A number of new tools and controls in ASP.NET rely on the `Membership` object for user-management functionality. The Web Site Administration Tool, for example, uses the `Membership` object extensively to support adding, editing, and deleting users. Many of the new login controls also rely on the `Membership` object to validate login credentials, look up email addresses, and add new users to the application.

Tables 5-2 and 5-3 list the more important properties and methods of the `Membership` object. Also understand that membership providers have many of the same properties and methods. Ultimately, the `Membership` object uses a membership provider for its functionality, so they naturally have a lot in common.

Table 5-2. `Membership` *Object Properties*

Property Name	Type	Description
`ApplicationName`	`String`	Name of the application. The membership provider may store data for multiple applications, so it needs to know the identify of the application.
`EnablePasswordReset` (Read-Only)	`Boolean`	True if the membership provider allows users to reset their password.
`EnablePasswordRetrieval` (Read-Only)	`Boolean`	True if the membership provider allows users to retrieve a forgotten password.
`MaxInvalidPasswordAttempts` (Read-Only)	`Integer`	Maximum number of times users may enter a password without being locked out of their account. The number of invalid attempts must occur in the time frame defined by the `PasswordAttemptWindow` property.
`MinRequiredNon➥AlphanumericCharacters` (Read-Only)	`Integer`	Minimum number of nonalphanumeric characters (not A–Z or 0–9) required for a user's password to be valid.
`MinRequiredPasswordLength` (Read-Only)	`Integer`	Minimum number of characters required for a user's password to be valid.
`PasswordAttemptWindow` (Read-Only)	`Integer`	Number of minutes in which the maximum number of invalid password attempts must occur for a user to be locked out.
`PasswordStrength➥RegularExpression`	`String`	Regular expression used to validate password strength. Password strength is usually dictated by length and presence of nonalphanumeric characters (for example, MyDogSkip vs. My_D0g_$k1p!). You can use this property to define a regular expression that forces users to have a minimum amount of numbers and nonalphnumeric characters for their password.
`Provider`	`MembershipProvider`	Returns a reference to the default `Membership➥Provider` for the application.
`Providers`	`MembershipProvider➥Collection`	Returns a collection of the `MembershipProviders` available to the application.
`RequiresQuestionAndAnswer` (Read-Only)	`Boolean`	True if the membership provider requires users to answer a security question before retrieving or resetting a password.
`UserIsOnlineTimeWindow` (Read-Only)	`Integer`	Number of minutes after the last user activity that the user is considered to be online. This affects the membership provider's `GetNumberOfUsersOnline` function.

You may have noticed that the overwhelming majority of the `Membership` object properties are read-only. You have to set them when you configure the provider. We'll discuss that shortly.

Table 5-3. `Membership` *Object Methods*

Method Name	Parameters	Returns	Description
`CreateUser`	`username` As String `password` As String `email` As String `passwordQuestion` As Stringpassword `Answer` As String `isApproved` As Boolean `providerUserKey` As Object `ByRef status As Membership CreateStatus`	`MembershipUser`	Adds a new user to the system and returns a `MembershipUser` object populated with the user information. Note that the status parameter is a `ByRef` value and contains an enumeration that indicates whether or not the user was added successfully when the function exists. The status enumeration contains a number of specific errors that may occur such as `DuplicateEmail`, `DuplicateUserName`, `InvalidEmail`, `InvalidPassword`, and so on.
`DeleteUser`	`username` As String `delete AllRelatedData` As Boolean	`Boolean`	Deletes the specified user and all data related to that user (assuming the `deleteAllRelatedData` value is `True`). Returns `True` if the deletion succeeds.

`FindUsers ByEmail`	`emailToMatch` As String
	`pageIndex As Integer`
	`pageSize As Integer`
	`ByRef totalRecords As Integer`
		`Membership UserCollection`	Locates all users in the system with the specified email address and returns a page of records based on the `pageIndex` and `pageSize` parameters. Notice that the `totalRecords` is a `ByRef` value that contains the total number of records located when the function exits.

`FindUsersByName`	`usernameToMatch As` String
	`pageIndex As Integer`
	`pageSize As Integer`
	`ByRef totalRecords As Integer`
		`Membership UserCollection`	Locates all users in the system with the specified username and returns a page of records based on the `pageIndex` and `pageSize` parameters.

`GetAllUsers`	`pageIndex As Integer`
	`pageSize As Integer`
	`ByRef totalRecords As Integer`
		`Membership UserCollection`	Locates all users in the system and returns a page of records based on the `pageIndex` and `pageSize` parameters.

`GetNumberOf UsersOnline`		`Integer`	Returns the number of users who are currently online. The provider calculates this number based on the last-activity timestamp of the user and the `UserIs➥ OnlineTimeWindow` value. Any users who have accessed the system within that time window are considered online.
`GetPassword`	`username` As String `answer` As String	`String`	Checks to see if the answer provided matches the user's security answer. If so, it returns the user's password. You should only call this method when the membership provider supports password retrieval, otherwise a `NotSupportedException` will be thrown.

Table 5-3. Membership *Object Methods (Continued)*

Method Name	Parameters	Returns	Description
GetUser	[userIsOnline As Boolean]	MembershipUser	Locates the currently logged in user and returns a MembershipUser object containing the user's information. If no user is found, then the method returns Nothing. If you are requesting the user in response to online activity, then set userIsOnline to True so the membership provider can keep track of which users are still online.
GetUser	username As String [userIsOnline As Boolean]	MembershipUser	Locates a user based on the username and returns a MembershipUser object containing the user's information. If no user is found, then the method returns Nothing. If you are requesting the user in response to online activity, then set userIsOnline to True so the membership provider can keep track of which users are still online.
GetUser	providerUserKey As Object [userIsOnline As Boolean]	MembershipUser	Locates a user based on the unique key the provider uses internally to identify users. Database providers, for example, may identify users via GUID values and not usernames. This allows you to search for a user with that native identifier and returns a MembershipUser object containing the user's information. If no user is found, then the method returns Nothing. If you are requesting the user in response to online activity, then set userIsOnline to True so the membership provider can keep track of which users are still online.
GetUserNameBy➥Email	email As String	String	Returns the username associated with the given email address.
UpdateUser	user As MembershipUser		Updates the membership provider data source with the information in the MembershipUser object. There is no return value from this method denoting whether the update succeeded or failed.
ValidateUser	username As String password As String	Boolean	Returns True if the username and password are valid.

If you work with these functions, you'll quickly notice that you never have to worry about passing them data store–specific parameters or settings. You just call the method or property, and the membership provider returns the appropriate data. Configuration settings for the membership provider are stored in Web.config, and the membership provider implementation is responsible for reading those settings and accessing a specific type of data store completely behind the scenes.

The Roles Object

The Roles object exposes role-management functionality in much the same way that membership functionality is exposed by the Membership object. The Web Site Administration Tool uses the Roles object to manage roles and user-role assignments, but the login controls do not user the Roles object directly. Some of the controls do access role information, but they do so via the Context.User.IsInRole function. The role provider is responsible, however, for setting up role information in the Context.User object on each request, so it does play an indirect part. Tables 5-4 and 5-5 list the more important properties and methods of the Roles object.

Table 5-4. Roles *Object Properties*

Property Name	Type	Description
ApplicationName	String	Name of the application. The role provider may store data for multiple applications, so it needs to know the identity of the application.
CacheRolesInCookie (Read-Only)	Boolean	True if the user's roles should be cached in a cookie.
CookieName (Read-Only)	String	Name of the cookie where roles are cached.
CookiePath (Read-Only)	String	Path of the cookie where roles are cached. The path tells the browser which pages of the application should receive the cookie. For example, a value of / means that the cookie should go to every page, whereas a value of /Secure means that the cookie should only go to pages located in the /Secure folder.
CookieProtection➥Value (Read-Only)	CookieProtection➥Value	Determines the level of protection on the role cookie. Possible values are All, Encryption, None, and Validation. Refer to Table 5-1 for more information on cookie protection.
CookieRequireSSL (Read-Only)	Boolean	True if the role cookie should only be sent over a secure communication channel (HTTPS).
CookieSliding➥Expiration (Read-Only)	Boolean	True if the expiration for the cookie should be updated on each request. Refer to Table 5-1 for more information on sliding expirations.
CookieTimeout (Read-Only)	Integer	Number of minutes before a cookie expires.
CreatePersistent➥Cookie (Read-Only)	Boolean	True if the cookie should not expire.
Domain (Read-Only)	String	Specifies the domain for which the cookie is valid.
Enabled	Boolean	True if role management is enabled for the application.
MaxCachedResults (Read-Only)	Integer	Maximum number of roles to cache for the user.
Provider (Read-Only)	RoleProvider	Returns a reference to the default RoleProvider for the application.
Providers (Read-Only)	RoleProvider Collection	Returns a collection of the RoleProviders available to the application.

Table 5-5. Roles *Object Methods*

Method Name	Parameters	Returns	Description
AddUsersToRole	usernames() As String roleName As String		Adds all the users in the usernames array to the specified role.
AddUsersToRoles	usernames() As String roleNames() As String		Adds all the users in the usernames array to all the roles in the roleNames array.
AddUserToRoles	username As StringroleNames() As String		Adds the specified user to all the roles in the roleNames array.
AddUserToRole	username As String roleName As String		Adds the specified user to the specified role.
CreateRole	roleName As String		Creates a new role with the specified name.
DeleteCookie			Deletes the cookie containing the cached roles for the currently logged on user.
DeleteRole	roleName As String [throw OnPopulatedRole as Boolean]	Boolean	Deletes the specified role and returns True if the delete succeeded. You can also tell the method to throw an exception if any users are assigned to the role by setting the throwOnPopulatedRole parameter to True.
FindUsersInRole	roleName As String usernameToMatch As String	String ()	Returns a list of users who are in the specified role and who match the usernameToMatch string. If you want to return all users in a role without using matching then use the GetUsersInRole method.
GetAllRoles		String()	Returns a list containing all the roles in the application.
GetRolesForUser	username As String	String()	Returns a list containing all the roles to which a user has been assigned.
GetUsersInRole	roleName As String	String()	Returns a list containing usernames for every user in the given role.
IsUserInRole	username As String roleName As String	Boolean	True if the specified user is in the specified role.
RemoveUserFromRole	username As String roleName As String		Removes the specified user from the specified role.
RemoveUserFromRoles	username As String roleNames() As String		Removes the specified user from all the roles in the roleNames array.
RemoveUsersFromRole	usernames() As String roleName As String		Removes all the users in the username array from the specified role.

Method Name	Parameters	Returns	Description
RemoveUsers➥FromRoles	usernames() As String roleNames() As String		Removes all the users in the username array from all the roles in the roleNames array.
RoleExists	roleName as String	Boolean	True if the specified role exists.

Programming with the Membership and Role Objects

Both the Membership and Role objects reside in the System.Web.Security namespace and are accessible from every page in your application. You do not have to reference any special assemblies or use any Imports statements because the System.Web.Security namespace is inherently available on web form pages. Listing 5-10 is a brief example showing how you can authenticate a user and determine if that user is in a specific role

Listing 5-10. Membership *and* Role *Object Usage Examples*

```
'***************************************************************************
Sub DeleteAllUsersInRole(ByVal roleName As String)

    Dim usernameList() As String = Roles.GetUsersInRole(roleName)

    For Each username As String In usernameList
        Membership.DeleteUser(username)
    Next

End Sub
```

This example function deletes all the users in the role passed in as a parameter of the function. It begins by getting a String array containing a list of all the users in the requested role using the Roles.GetUsersInRole method. Then it iterates over all the users it found and deletes them using the Membership.DeleteUser method. You can automate literally hundreds of different user-management tasks using the Membership and Roles objects.

Configuring the Membership and Role Providers

Both the Membership and Role objects rely on data-source–specific providers to "provide" their functionality. As such, you must configure the membership and role providers for your application so it knows which providers to use. One thing you need to be aware of is that a single provider class can have multiple provider configurations. The provider configurations define a provider, not the actual class itself. So, even though ASP.NET 2.0 only ships with a single membership provider class (SqlMembershipProvider), you can have multiple providers with various configurations using the class. This may seem a bit confusing at first, but you'll quickly get used to it as you use it.

Membership Provider Configuration

You can configure a membership provider for your application in the `<providers>` element of the `<membership>` section in `Web.config`. If the provider configuration is to be used for multiple applications, you can also define it in `Machine.config` so you can manage the provider from a single location.

Listing 5-11 shows a sample membership provider configuration. Remember all the read-only settings for the `Membership` object from Table 5-2? This is where you can set those values (see Listing 5-11).

Listing 5-11. *Membership Provider Configuration*

```
<configuration>
  ...
  <system.web>
    ...
    <membership defaultProvider="MySqlMembershipProvider">
      <providers>
        <add name="MySqlMembershipProvider"
          type="System.Web.Security.SqlMembershipProvider, System.Web,
                Version=2.0.0.0, Culture=neutral, PublicKeyToken=b03f5f7f11d50a3a"
          connectionStringName="LocalSqlServer"
          enablePasswordRetrieval="true"
          enablePasswordReset="true"
          requiresQuestionAndAnswer="true"
          applicationName="/"
          requiresUniqueEmail="true"
          passwordFormat="Hashed"
          maxInvalidPasswordAttempts="5"
          passwordAttemptWindow="10"
          passwordStrengthRegularExpression="" />
      </providers>
    </membership>
  </system.web>
</configuration>
```

There are a few key points to cover about this configuration. First, you can create multiple provider configurations in the `<providers>` element. This is helpful if you have different environments that require different provider configurations. However, the `Membership` object can only use one of the configurations, so you need to identify the default provider by specifying a value for the `defaultProvider` attribute in the `<membership>` element. In Listing 5-11, we created a new provider named `MySqlMembershipProvider` so we set up the `defaultProvider` value to use it.

Also notice that this provider has a connectionStringName attribute, but you won't find a connectionStringName attribute listed in Table 5-2. This is a custom attribute specific to the SqlMembershipProvider class. Each provider class may have its custom attributes, so you need to read the configuration instructions for new provider classes to see what kind of configuration options it exposes. This example uses the LocalSqlServer connection string. The LocalSqlServer connection string is defined in Machine.config and points to a database named ASPNETDB.mdf in the App_Data folder of the current application.

ASP.NET 2.0 ships with a single preconfigured membership provider named AspNetSqlMembershipProvider defined in Machine.config. This provider allows you to store user information in a SQL Server database. If you do not specify a value for the defaultProvider attribute in the <membership> section of Web.config, or you leave the <membership> section out entirely, then your application will default to AspNetSqlMembershipProvider. This provider also uses the LocalSqlServer connection string, so it employs the ASPNETDB.mdf database in the App_Data folder of the current application as its data source.

Role Provider Configuration

You can configure a role provider for your application in the <providers> element of the <roleManager> section in Web.config. You can also configure role providers in Machine.config if you want to centralize configuration for multiple applications. Listing 5-12 is a sample role provider configuration.

Listing 5-12. *Role Provider Configuration*

```
<configuration>
  ...
  <system.web>
    ...
    <roleManager enabled="true" defaultProvider="MySqlRoleProvider">
      <providers>
        <add name="MySqlRoleProvider"
             connectionStringName="LocalSqlServer"
             applicationName="/"
             type="System.Web.Security.SqlRoleProvider, System.Web,
                   Version=2.0.0.0, Culture=neutral,
                   PublicKeyToken=b03f5f7f11d50a3a" />
      </providers>
    </roleManager>
  </system.web>
</configuration>
```

The most important thing to know about the role provider for your application is that you must explicitly enable it by setting the enabled attribute of the <roleManager> element to True. Otherwise your application won't have access to any role-management functionality. You also need to specify the default provider via the defaultProvider attribute in the <roleManager> element. Unlike membership providers, role providers do not expose nearly as many configurable options, so you will probably not find yourself creating role providers nearly as often.

ASP.NET 2.0 comes with two preconfigured role providers defined in `Machine.config`. The first is the `AspNetSqlRoleProvider`, which provides the `role` object the capability to store role information in a SQL Server database. The second is the `AspNetWindowsTokenRoleProvider`, which is used for applications running Windows Authentication. The `AspNetSqlRoleProvider` uses the `LocalSqlServer` connection string so it uses the `ASPNETDB.mdf` database in `App_Data` folder of the current application as its data source. If you don't specify a default role provider, then your application will default to the `AspNetSqlRoleProvider`.

Your website needs to have a properly configured membership provider if you plan to administer users and roles via the Web Site Administration Tool and the `Membership` or `Roles` objects, or use many of the advanced features on the new ASP.NET 2.0 login controls.

The sample code for this chapter (in the Source Code area of the Apress website) uses the SQL Server membership provider to store all the user and role information, so you can learn all about membership provider configuration by setting it up. Create a new website (or open the Chapter 5 sample website) and click on **Website ➤ ASP.NET Configuration** to launch the Web Site Administration Tool.

Selecting a Provider in the Web Site Administration Tool

The **Provider** tab in the Web Site Administration Tool allows you to select which membership and role providers you want your application to use. First, you have to configure the providers in `Web.config`, however, before they appear in the **Provider** tab. If you need to use a custom provider in your application, you might as well configure it manually while you are in `Web.config`. If you want to use a preconfigured provider, you can use the Web Site Administration Tool to select it from a list. You'll learn more about the **Provider** tab shortly, when we discuss the Web Site Administration Tool.

ENCRYPTED PASSWORDS AND THE `<machineKey>` ELEMENT

You can configure the `SqlMembershipProvider` class to encrypt user passwords before storing them to the database, and you can expect that other providers will do the same as they are released. When dealing with encrypted password you may run across the following error when you visit the **Security** tab of the Web Site Administration Tool:

You must specify a non auto-generated machine key to store password in the encrypted format. Either specify a different passwordFormat or change machineKey configuration to use a nonauto-generated decryption key.

This means that you have an auto-generated `<machineKey>`, and that you need to specify a nonauto-generated `<machineKey>` for the password encryption to work. The `<machineKey>` element takes three parameters as listed in the following table.

<machineKey> *Parameters*

Attribute	Description	Format
validationKey	Key used to create validation hashes to ensure data has not been altered. An example would be the ViewState MAC generated to ensure the ViewState has not been altered at the client-side.	40–128 hex characters (0–9, A–F).
decryptionKey	Key used to encrypt and decrypt data.	16 hex characters when using DES encryption. 48 hex characters when using Triple DES encryption.
validation	The type of encryption used.	Can be either SHA1, MD5, or Triple DES.

Following is an example of a <machineKey> entry. You can place this either in Web.config or in Machine.config. If you place it in Machine.config, then you won't receive the error again when you are developing another website.

```
<configuration>
  ...
  <system.web>
    ...
    <!--The validation key and decryption key values CANNOT be
    split out
        on multiple lines. They need to be on a single line-->
    <machineKey
      validationKey="ba843845853defaba779d4637882706683bd2a7b795b7cbfab854a799➥
                    5435eb185e7a39f4d3a872bdbed21d592753a9b5bb6b798b9c5538038➥
                    dfb7665796fb75"
      decryptionKey="341a60c25c779d47d64697a55afd498ebff2584c28783115"
      validation="3DES"
  </system.web>
</configuration>
```

As the validationKey and decryptionKey are fairly long, you may be wondering about a good way to generate them. Discussing the generation of cryptographic strings is a bit outside of the scope of this book, but you can look at the sample application (in the Source Code area of the Apress website) or the website for this book to find helpful links to utilities that can help you generate cryptographic strings.

Tip If you ever find yourself developing a web-farm environment, you must ensure that the <machineKey> is the same across all the servers in the farm. This ensures that the encryption, decryption, and validation will work between machines.

Managing Users and Security with the Web Site Administration Tool

Applications that rely on Forms Authentication need some way to manage users, roles, and user-role assignments. When money is tight and time is running out, however, administration sections are normally the first feature that gets scrubbed because you can use preexisting database tools, such as Enterprise Manager, to keep the user-management database current. Although this approach works for developers and database administrators, you cannot expect (nor would you want) a business user to use a database administration tool for adding and removing information directly.

Microsoft leveraged the `Membership` and `Role` objects to build a standard Web Site Administration Tool. This tool allows you to configure a number of security and configuration options in your application, and it gives you web-based user- and role-management capabilities. In this section, you'll learn about each tab of the Web Site Administration Tool and how it can help manage users and security for your application.

Opening the Web Site Administration Tool

You can access the Web Site Administration Tool by clicking on the **Website ➤ ASP.NET Configuration** menu item in the Visual Studio IDE. The **Website** menu item is only available when you have an item under a web application project selected in the **Solution Explorer**, so you may not see it when you first open Visual Studio. After you click on the **ASP.NET Configuration** menu item, Visual Studio fires up a new browser instance and displays the **Home** tab of the Web Site Administration Tool.

Home Tab

When you first open the Web Site Administration Tool, it displays the **Home** tab. The **Home** tab is simply a starting point from which you can access other tabs of the application. The links on the page correspond to the tabs that run across the top of the page and contain additional text describing what you can do from that particular tab. Figure 5-2 shows the **Home** tab.

The Provider Tab

I highly recommend that you set up the membership and role providers before you start managing users from the Web Site Administration Tool, so we'll discuss the **Provider** tab first. The **Provider** tab allows you to choose from existing providers that you have configured in `Web.config` of the application or `Machine.config` for the system. I outlined how to do this earlier in the chapter in the "Configuring the Membership and Role Providers" section.

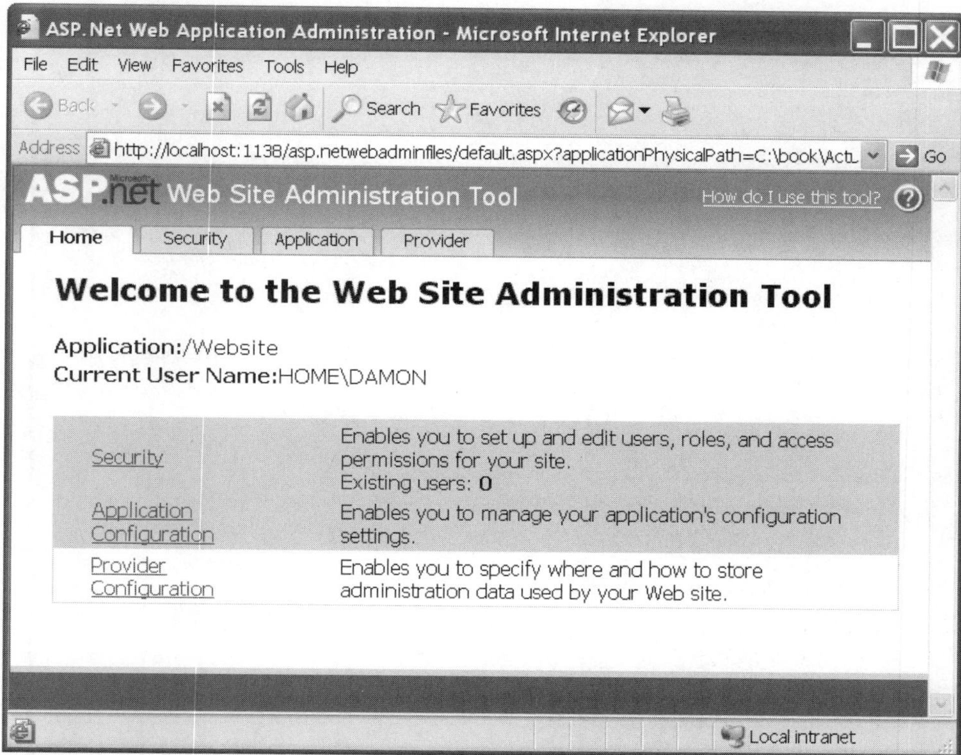

Figure 5-2. *Home tab of the Web Site Administration Tool*

When you open the **Provider** tab, you are greeted with two options presented as links in the middle of the page: **Select a single provider for all site management data** and **Select a different provider for each feature (advanced)** as shown in Figure 5-3.

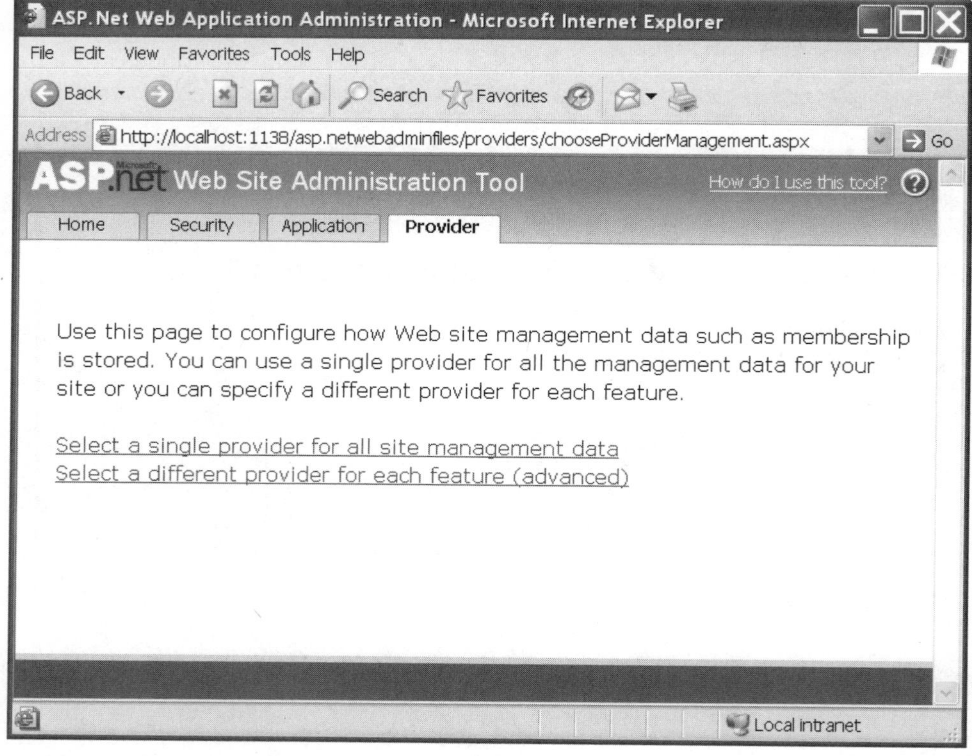

Figure 5-3. *Initial Provider tab page*

Selecting a Single Provider for All Site Management Data

If you want to use a single provider for all site management data, then you should choose the **Select single provider for all site management data** link from the initial **Provider** tab page. This takes you to a page that displays a list of providers that can handle all site management data. ASP.NET 2.0 only ships with the `AspNetSqlProvider`, so it's your only option when you visit this page. As more vendors provide complete provider solutions, this list should grow. To select a single provider, click on the option button next to the provider name. The Web Site Administration Tool updates the `<membership>` section to use the `SqlMembershipProvider` and `<roleManager>` section to use the `SqlRoleManager` in your `Web.config` in response to your selection. You can also click on the **Test** link to the right of the provider name to check if the provider has a valid configuration (as shown in Figure 5-4).

Selecting a Different Provider for Each Feature

You can also select individual providers for your application by clicking on the **Select a different provider for each feature (advanced)** link from the initial **Provider** tab page. This takes you to a page that lists features that use providers and the provider options under those features. The only features listed are the **Membership Provider** and **Role Provider** features (see Figure 5-5). To select the provider for a particular feature, click on the option button next to the provider name under that feature. The Web Site Administration Tool updates `Web.config` to reflect your selection. You should choose a provider for each component listed on the page. Once again, you can click on the **Test** link to right of the provider name to check if the provider has a valid configuration.

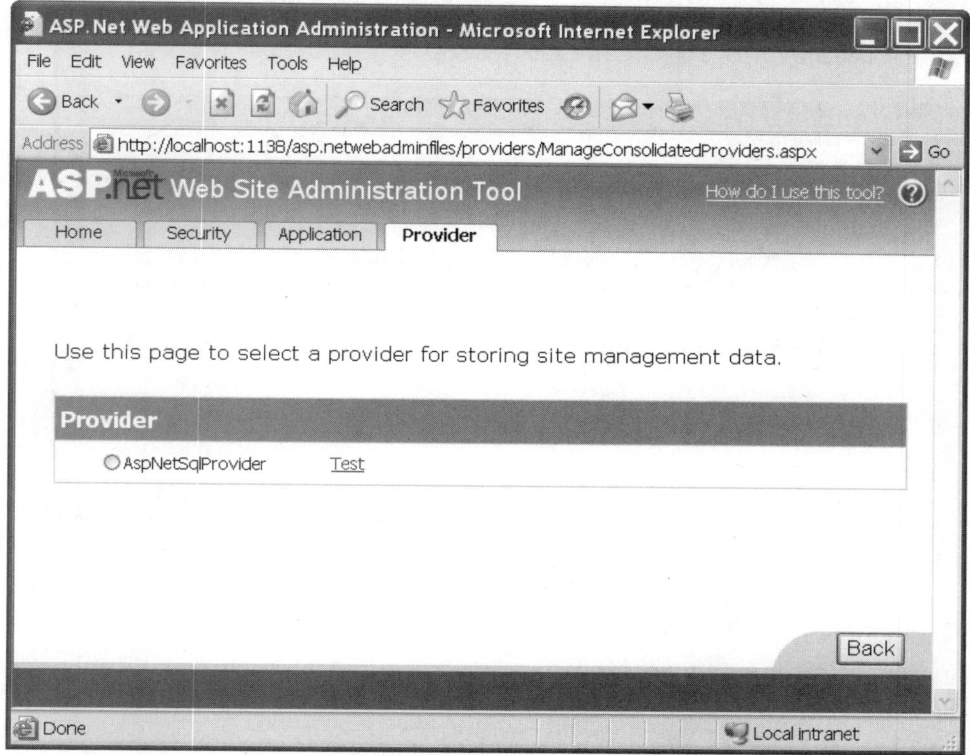

Figure 5-4. *Select a single provider for all site management data page*

The Security Tab

After you have determined which membership provider you want to use, you need to configure the security settings for your website. This entails choosing an authentication type, setting up roles, adding users, and defining access rules. All these tasks can be accessed from the **Security** tab of the Web Site Administration Tool, shown in Figure 5-6.

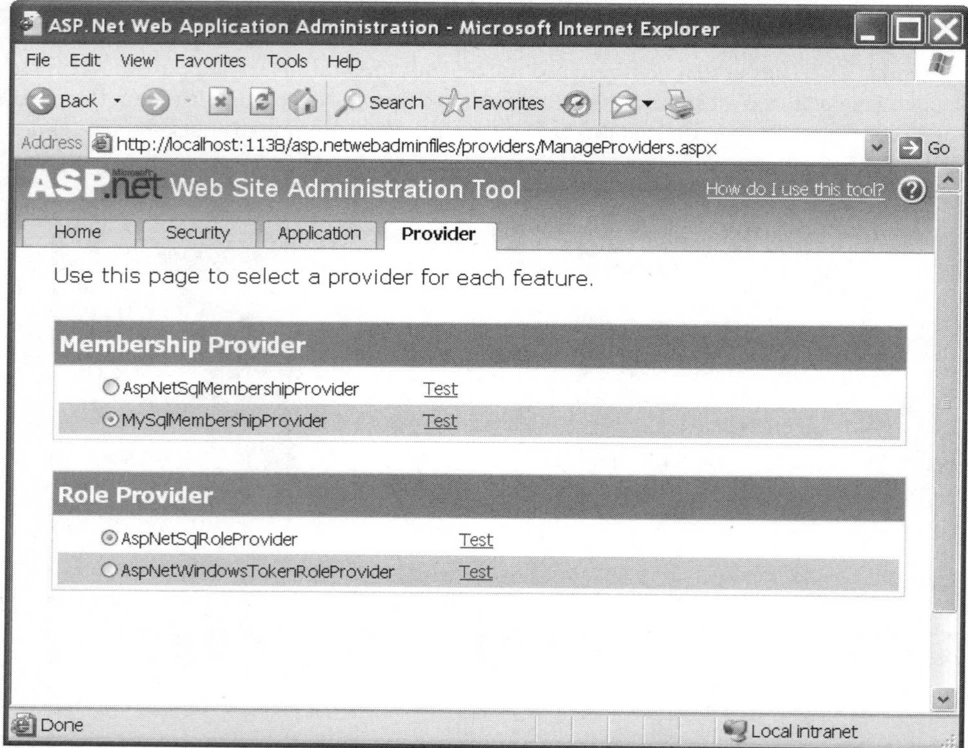

Figure 5-5. *Select a different provider for each feature page*

Configuring Security with the Security Setup Wizard

The easiest way to set up security for your web application is to use the Security Setup Wizard, a step-by-step process that guides you through security configuration. Each step of the Security Setup Wizard can be individually accessed from other areas of the **Security** tab, but the wizard ensures that you go through the configuration steps in the right order, and it skips over unnecessary sections depending on your configuration settings. You can launch the Security Setup Wizard by clicking on the **Use the security Setup Wizard to configure security step by step** link from the **Security** tab page.

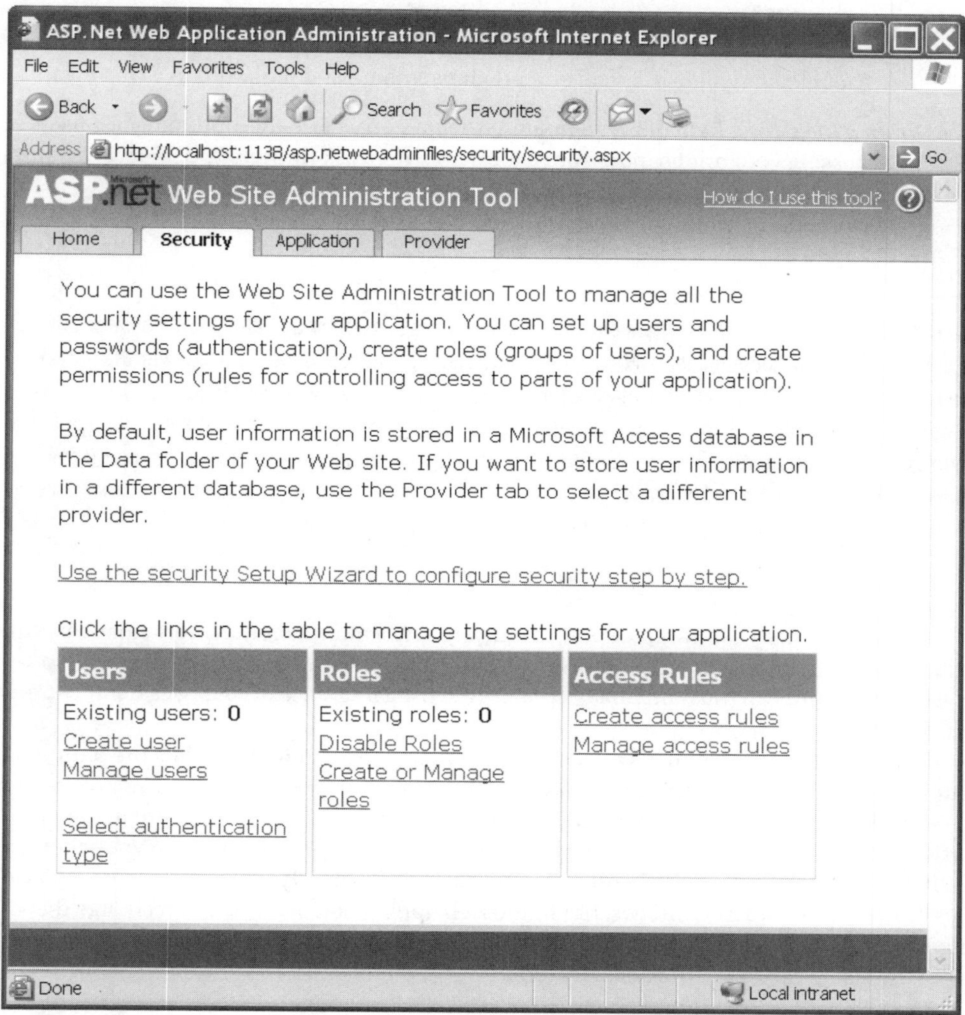

Figure 5-6. *Security tab of the Web Site Administration Tool*

Step 1: Welcome

The Welcome introductory screen gives you a brief overview of the capabilities of the Security Setup Wizard. It's basically fluff that you really don't need to read unless you're trying to kill some time. Click the **Next** button to move to Step 2.

Step 2: Select Access Method

This step allows you to define which authentication method you want ASP.NET to use when identifying users of your application. The wizard provides you two options:

- ***From the Internet*** *(Forms Authentication):* Use this option if you are building a public site that users will access over the Internet. ASP.NET will reroute users who have not yet logged in to a login page where they can enter their username and password in a web form.
- ***From a local area network*** *(Windows Authentication):* Use this option if your users will be accessing your application from a local area network (intranet). Users will be automatically identified by their Windows account information, so they won't have to manually enter a username and password to access your application.

■ **Note** There are certain circumstances when users have to enter their username and password manually when using Windows Authentication. For instance, say your application is mostly used over the corporate intranet but is still accessible via the Internet for those rare times when you need to access it from home. If you access the application from home, then the application tries to authenticate you using your home-based Windows account information, which likely does not match your corporate account information. Thus, Windows Authentication fails. This causes the browser to display a dialog box allowing you to manually enter your corporate username and password, which it then uses to try to authenticate you.

ASP.NET 2.0 does support passport and no authentication, but they were not deemed common enough for inclusion in Web Site Administration Tool. If you want to use passport or no authentication, you must manually configure setting it up in `Web.config` as demonstrated earlier in this chapter.

When you have determined which access method you want to use, select the option button next to its name. Then click on the **Next** button in the bottom-right corner of the Security Setup Wizard. The Web Site Administration Tool updates the `mode` attribute in the `<authentication>` section in `Web.config` with the appropriate option based on your choice.

If you choose Windows Authentication, you are taken directly to Step 6 because users and roles need to be set up in Windows, not in the web application. Also, you can change the authentication type without using the wizard by clicking on the **Select authentication type** link in the **Users** section of the **Security** tab.

■ **Caution** The Security Setup Wizard does not set up the `<forms>` element in `Web.config` that specifies a number of forms-related features such as the default login page or the default logged in user redirection URL. You need to manually configure these settings. Refer to the opening section of this chapter for information about manually configuring Forms Authentication.

Step 3: Data Store

This step simply tells you that you should configure your application providers before you start adding users and roles to your application and that you cannot change the provider from this page in Security Setup Wizard. You have to back out of the Security Wizard and click on the **Provider** tab of the Web Site Administration Tool to make provider configuration changes. If you've already configured your application providers, click on the **Next** button to move to Step 4.

Step 4: Define Roles

Defining roles is a two-step process. First you must determine whether or not you want to enable roles. Assuming that you enabled roles, you must then define the roles that exist in your application. The first page of Step 4 displays instructional text about the step and the **Enable roles for this Web site** check box. If you plan on using roles, you need to check this box. After you check or uncheck the box, the Web Site Administration Tool updates the `enabled` attribute of the `<roleManager>` section in `Web.config` to reflect your choice. After you make your selection, click on the **Next** button.

If you choose to enable roles in your application, you remain in Step 4 and the Security Setup Wizard displays an entry field allowing you to add roles to your application. To add a new role, type the name of the role in the **New Role Name** text box and click the **Add Role** button as shown in Figure 5-7. You'll see the role appear in the **Existing Roles** table below the entry section. When you are finished adding roles, click on the **Next** button to move to Step 5.

■ **Tip** Each user can have multiple roles, so you can actually use the roles functionality to set up "privileges" in your system. For instance, if you were creating an application that dealt with creating and submitting a form for approval, then you could have "privileges" such as Create Form, Edit Form, Delete Form, Approve Form, and so on.

Step 5: Add New Users

You can add users to your application by entering their user information in Step five (see Figure 5-8). To add a new user, enter the username, password, password confirmation, user email address, security question, and security answer in the provided text boxes. The `PasswordRecovery` control uses the security question and security answer to help determine whether the user should be sent his or her password via email. Finally, the **Active User** check box lets the membership provider know whether the user is active or inactive. Active users are granted access to the system according to their roles and whatever access rules you have defined for those roles. Inactive users are not allowed to log in to the system.

After you enter the appropriate information in the data entry section, click on the **Create User** button. A message appears informing you that the account has successfully been created. Click on the **Continue** button to add another user. When you are finished adding users, click on the **Next** button to go to Step 6.

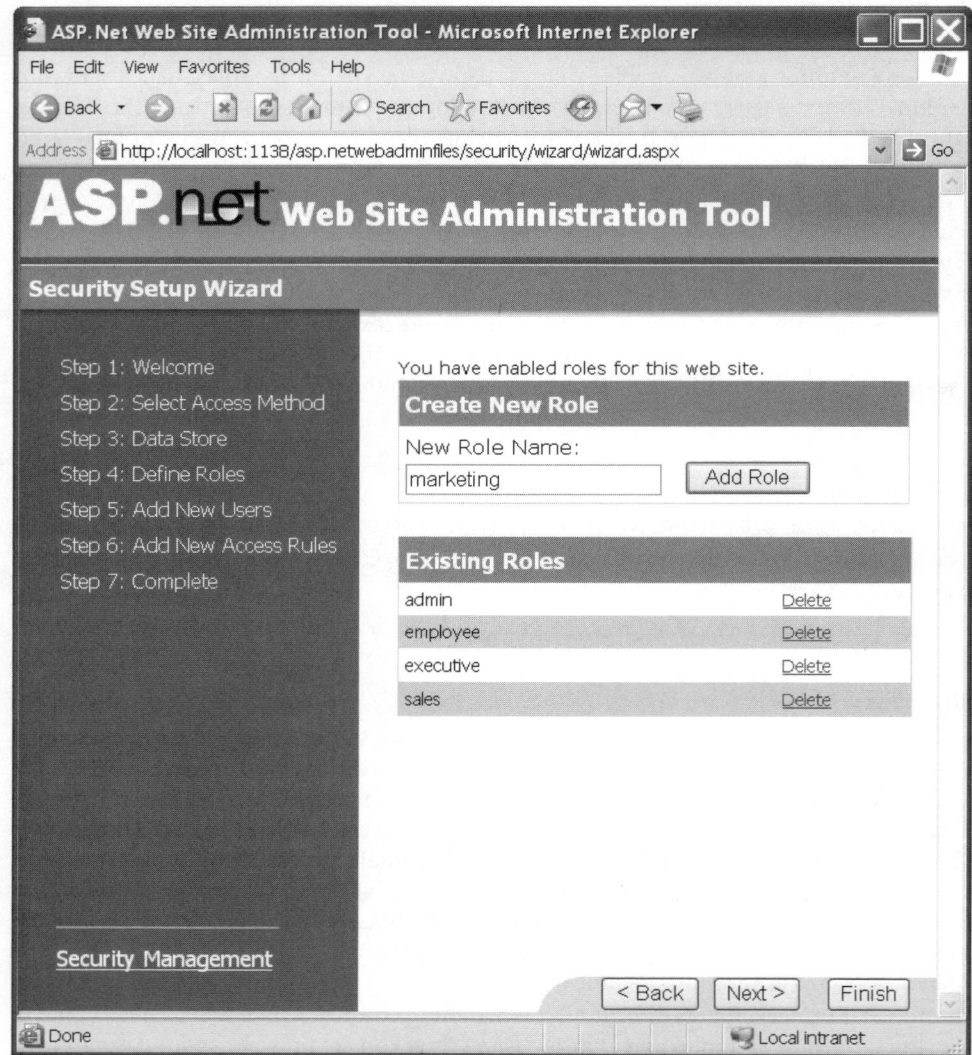

Figure 5-7. *Step 4 of the Security Setup Wizard—adding roles to your web application*

Adding a large number of users on this form can get tedious very quickly. If you have to enter a large number of users, you may want to automate the process by using the `Membership` object or by doing a manual database import against an existing set of user information. Another approach is to let users manually register for your application from a page that contains a `CreateUserWizard` control.

■ **Note** Unfortunately, you cannot add users to roles in the Security Setup Wizard. If you need to add users to roles, you can go back and edit users from the **Security** tab.

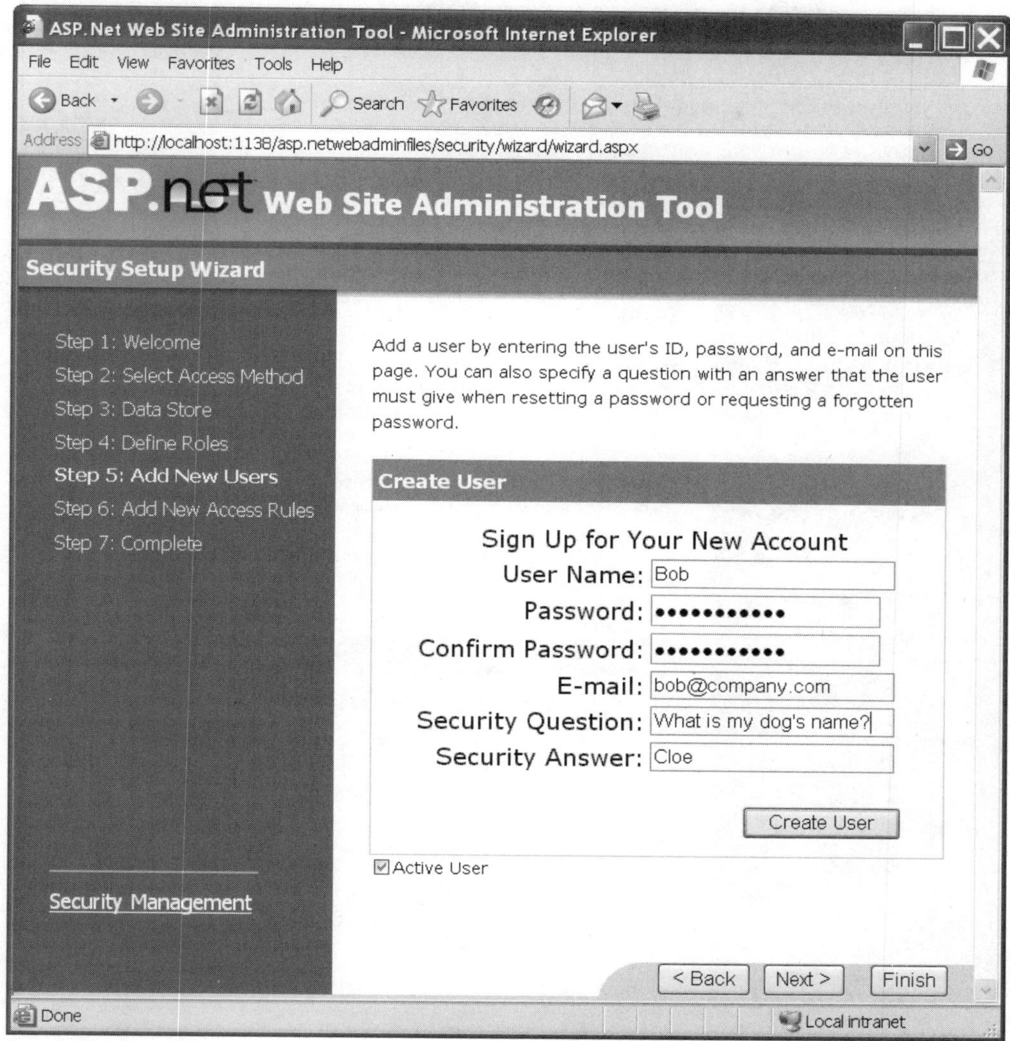

Figure 5-8. *Step 5 of the Security Setup Wizard—adding users to your web application*

Step 6: Add New Access Rules

Access rules are another name for the `<authentication>` entries in `Web.config` that control which users and roles are allowed access to certain folders in your web application. This step gives you a visual interface to set up those rules assuming that your folder structure is already built out. Figure 5-9 shows the interface for defining new access rules. You'll probably find it helpful to take a look at it before we continue.

To create a new access rule, select a folder from the folder tree. Then choose the role, user, or group (All Users/Anonymous Users) to which the rule should apply. You can click on the **Search for Users** link if you need help locating a user. Finally, choose whether the rule should allow or deny the chosen entity access to the selected folder. When you've made all your selections, click on the **Add This Rule** button. The Web Site Administration Tool adds the access rule to the `<authentication>` section of the `Web.config` file located in the folder you selected from the folder tree.

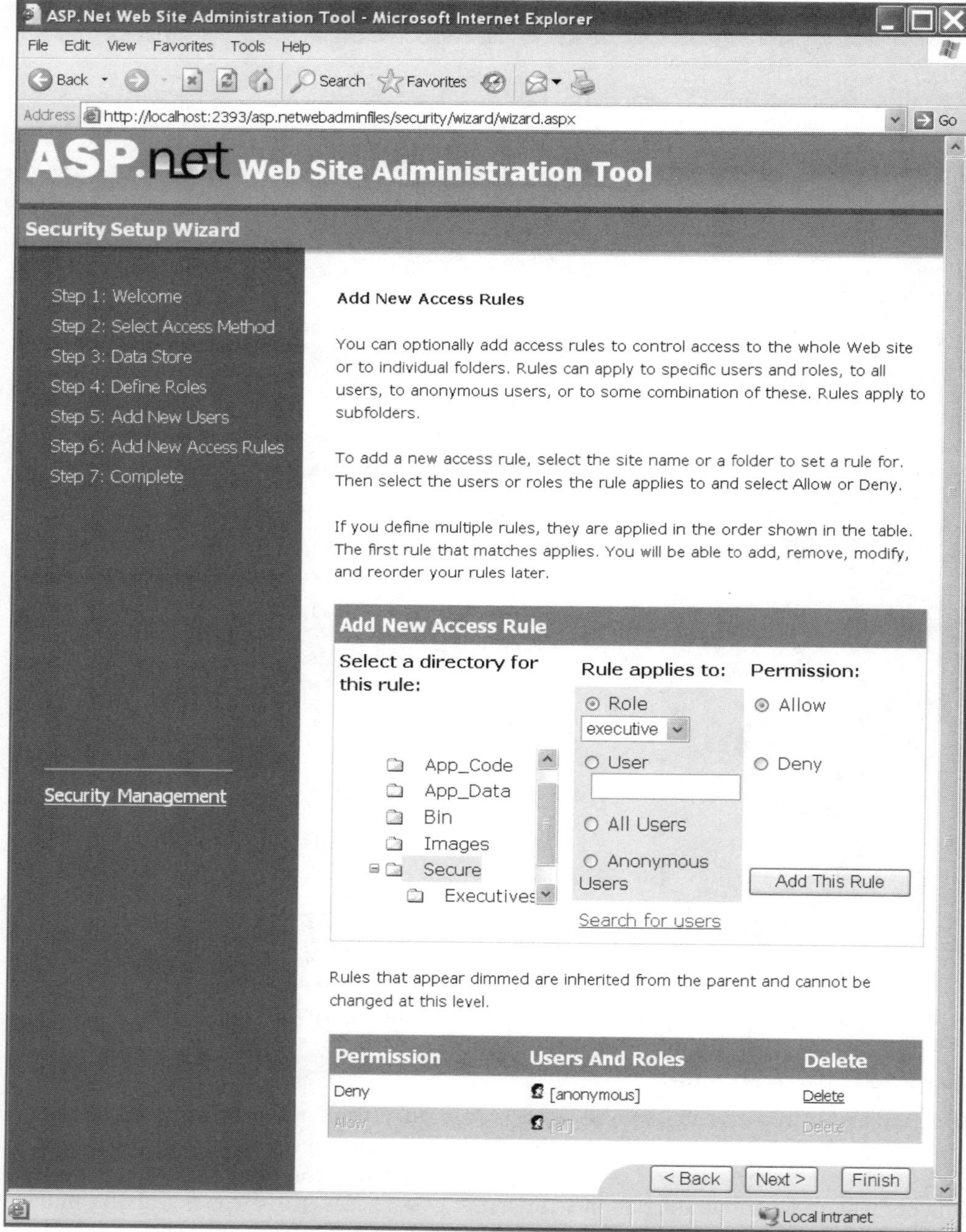

Figure 5-9. *Step 6 of the Security Setup Wizard—creating access rules*

Step 7: Complete

When you reach this step, you have completed the Security Configuration Wizard, but you still need to return to the **Security** tab to add users to specific roles. Look for the "Setting Up Roles" subsection within the next section for a quick and easy way to set up roles for users after you've added them to your application.

Adding, Editing, and Deleting Users

Although the Security Setup Wizard is helpful for setting up your web application initially, it wasn't designed to be used for ongoing maintenance. If you find yourself needing to add, edit, or delete a user, use the **Create user** or **Manage users** links in the **Users** section of the **Security** tab.

Adding a New User

Clicking on the **Create user** link in the **Users** section of the **Security** tab (refer to Figure 5-6) brings up the **Create User** screen shown in Figure 5-10, which is slightly different from the user screen displayed in the Security Setup Wizard. This **Create User** screen contains two sections: the first is for setting up user information, and the second for associating that user with specific roles.

To add a user, enter the appropriate user information in the **Create User** section. Remember, you may need a unique email address and a security question/answer depending on how the membership provider is set up. If you want the user to be active immediately, make sure the **Active User** check box is checked. After you enter the user information, select the roles the user should be in by checking the appropriate role names in the **Roles** section.

When you're finished, click on the **Create User** button. The page submits, and the user is added along with the role information. A new page displays indicating the successful addition of the user. You can click on the **Continue** button to add another user or the Back button to return to the **Security** tab.

Searching for Existing Users

If you need to edit or delete an existing user, click on the **Manage users** link in the **Users** section of the **Security** tab (refer to Figure 5-6). This brings up the **Search for Users** page shown in Figure 5-11. By default, the page lists all users, alphabetically, seven records at a time.

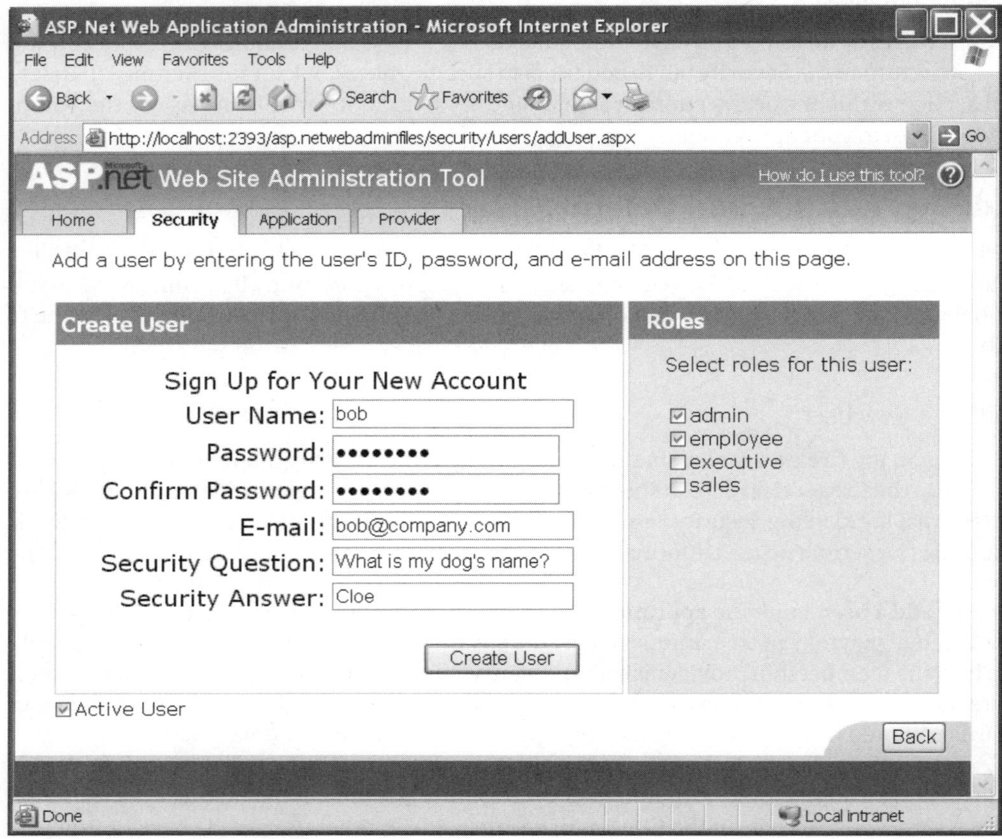

Figure 5-10. *Create User screen*

You have a couple of options for searching for users using this search page. If you only have a few users in your application, then you can use the pagination controls at the bottom of the list to jump through pages of records until you find the appropriate entry. The pagination controls only display if you have more than one page worth of data. And if your application has a fairly extensive number of users, then you'll likely want to use the A-Z selector or the search box to locate a user.

The A-Z selector displays all the letters of the alphabet as links. Clicking on a letter filters the list and displays only those users whose username begins with the selected letter. The search page still only lists seven records per page, so you may still need to use the pagination controls to page through results if you have more than seven usernames that begin with the same letter.

If you know any part of the username or email address of the user you are trying to locate, you can use the search box to locate a user. In the **Search by** drop-down list, select either **User name** or **E-Mail** depending on which item you know. Then enter the search term in the **for** text box. You can either search for an entire username/email address or you can use wildcards (*) to widen your search. When you click on the **Find User** button, the results of your search are displayed.

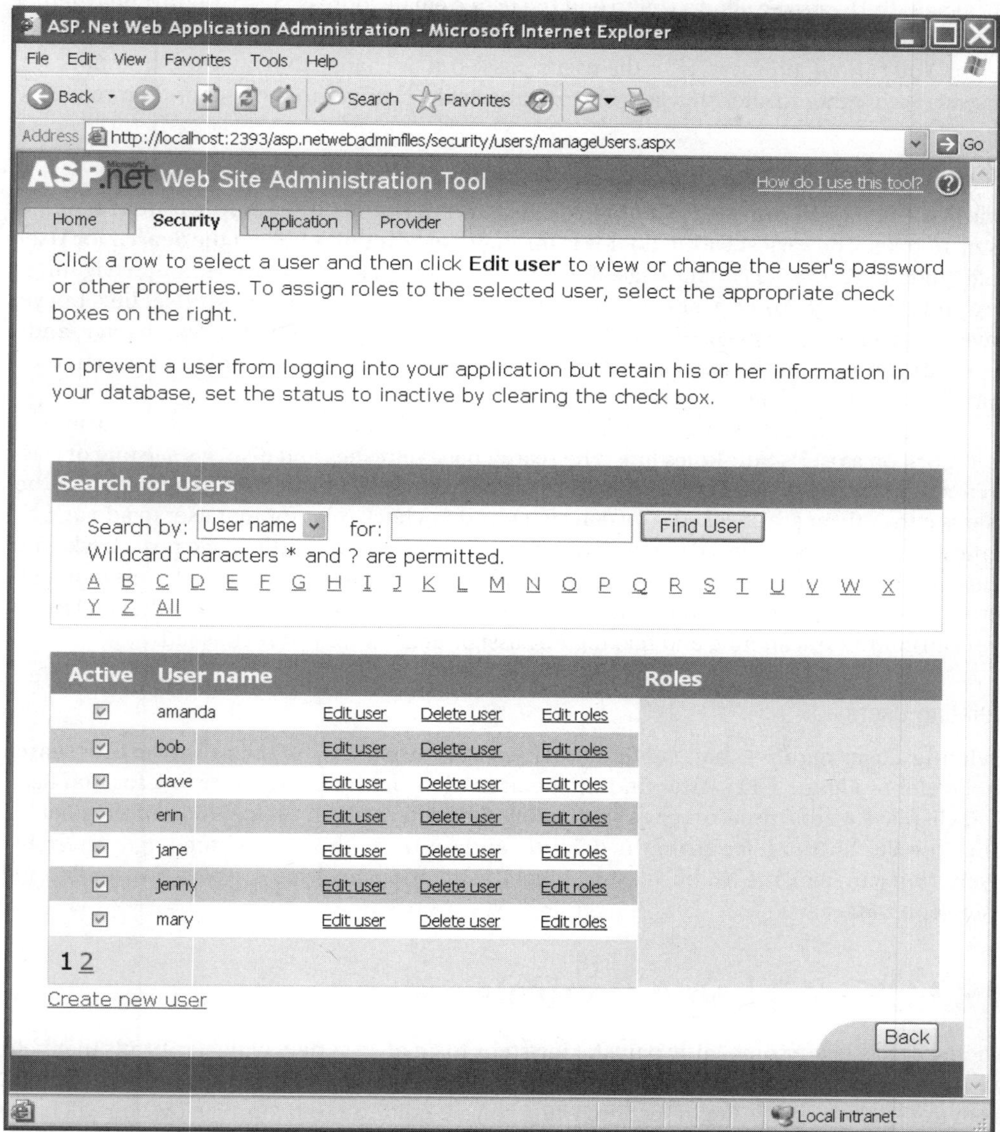

Figure 5-11. *Search for Users page*

Editing Users

Editing a user requires that you first find the user you want to edit using the user search tool (refer to Figure 5-11). After you find the user, click on the **Edit user** link for that user to launch the **Edit User** page.

The **Edit User** page allows you to edit the user's email address, description, and whether or not the user should be active. You can also add or remove the user from any roles that you desire. You cannot, however, alter the user's password or change the password question/ answer. Remember to click the **Save** button to save any changes to the user or their roles.

Setting Up Roles

One of the first tasks you need to complete after running the Security Setup Wizard is assigning users to roles. The easiest way to do this is through the **Edit Roles** link on the **Search for Users** page (refer to Figure 5-11). This page allows you to quickly set user roles without navigating away from the page. You can also assign users to roles by clicking on the **Edit User** link, but you have to navigate to the page, set the user roles, save the data, return to the search page, and repeat the process for the next user. Using the **Edit Roles** links is much quicker for a large number of role assignments.

Navigate to the user search page and locate the user (or users) whose roles you want to edit. Click on a user's **Edit Roles** link. The search page refreshes and displays a listing of roles on the right side of the screen along with check boxes to select those roles. Any roles that the user is currently in are checked. You can check and uncheck roles for that user to add or remove the user from roles. Each time you check or uncheck a role, the page posts back and adds or removes the user from the role. You do not have to explicitly save each time you make an update because the page automatically saves changes as you click on the individual items. You can continue searching and making role assignments until you're finished.

Deleting Users

Deleting a user requires that you first find the user you want to delete using the user search tool (refer to Figure 5-11). After finding the user, click on the **Delete user** link for that user. This displays a confirmation page requesting that you confirm the deletion of the user. Click the **Yes** button to confirm the deletion and return to the user search page. Alternatively, you can click the **No** button to cancel the deletion, and you are also returned to the user search page.

ASP.NET 2.0 Login Controls

Microsoft has taken some fairly painstaking steps to create a variety of new controls that help you with logins, lost passwords, and managing content based on roles. They are accessible from the Toolbox (in the Login section) when you are editing a web form. Below you will find a table that outlines the new controls, and gives you a brief overview of each one. Many of the controls are templated controls (more on that in a minute), and many of them are only designed to work with Forms Authentication. The **Type** and **Valid Auth. Method** columns express these two factors (see Table 5-6).

Table 5-6. *New Login Controls in ASP.NET 2.0*

Name	Type	Valid Auth. Method	Description
`Login`	Templated	Forms	Displays username and text box entry fields, and optionally a check box allowing the user to automatically log in the next time they visit. This control is responsible for automatically authenticating the user and setting up the Forms Authentication ticket used to identify the user when he or she returns.
`LoginView`	Templated	Forms/Windows	Allows you to control which content to display on the page based on user roles. Basically, the control contains a series of panels, and each panel is associated with a specific role. If the user is in that role, the panel displays; if not, the panel remains hidden. This keeps users from seeing content they are not intended to see.
`PasswordRecovery`	Templated	Forms	Allows users to recover lost passwords via email. This control automatically handles the security question and answer logic if it's required by the membership provider.
`LoginStatus`	Normal	Forms	Provides a link for users who are not logged in to go to the login page, and for users who are logged in to log out.
`LoginName`	Normal	Forms/Windows	Displays the username of the currently logged in user.
`CreateUserWizard`	Wizard/ Templated	Forms	Creates a basic entry form for adding users to your application. This control automatically communicates with your application's membership provider to create a new user.
`ChangePassword`	Templated	Forms	Allows users to change their password. This control automatically communicates with your application's membership provider to change the currently logged in user's password.

As you may have noticed, many of the controls are templated controls. Before jumping into the login controls, let's take a look at how to work with templated controls.

Templated Controls

Templated controls allow you to change the visual layout of the control's subcomponents without changing the way the control functions. They are very similar to the skinned controls discussed in Chapter 3, but the template for the control is defined directly in the control definition, not in an external file like a skinned control.

To really understand a templated control, you need to work with one. The `Login` control is a great example, so open up a web form designer and drag a `Login` control onto the designer's surface. You should see the control displaying a layout similar to the one shown in Figure 5-12.

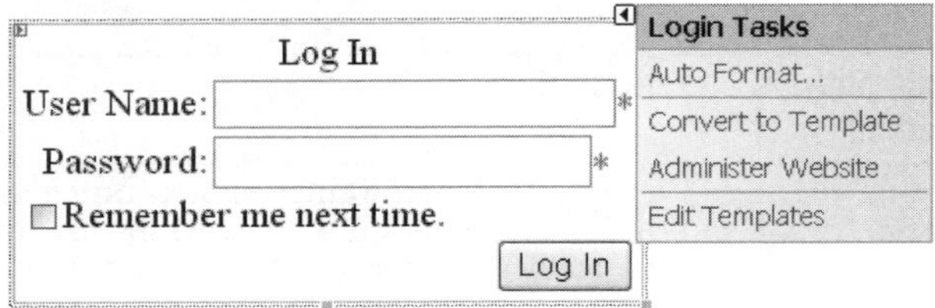

Figure 5-12. `Login` *control displaying the default login template (left) and the Common Tasks menu (right)*

Notice that the login control is comprised of text boxes, labels, validation controls, a check box, and a button. Also note that you did not have to define the layout of those subcontrols when you first placed the login control on your web form. Templated controls generate a layout when no template is explicitly defined. When you do not specify a template, the control definition for a templated control is fairly concise:

```
<asp:Login ID="Login1" Runat="server"></asp:Login>
```

You can use the generated layout, if it suits your needs, or you can create a template of your own. The basic idea behind creating a template is that all of the subcomponents in the template have a specific ID so the `Login` control can locate each subcomponent and use it. We used the same technique for the skinned page messaging control in Chapter 4. For example, the submit button always needs to have an ID of `Button`. The `Login` control will search through the template for a control with an ID of `Button`, and then add an event handler to the `Click` event of that control when it finds it. In the same way, the `Login` control stores references to the username text box by looking for a control named `UserName`, and the password text box by looking for a control named `Password`. Thus, when you click the `Button` subcomponent, the `Login` control can validate the username and password specified in the `UserName` and `Password` subcontrols.

Creating Templates

Templated controls may have one or more templates that you can edit. The `Login` control, for example, has a single template named `LayoutTemplate`, whereas the `PasswordRecovery` control has three templates named `UserName`, `Question`, and `Success`. The `PasswordRecovery` control has a three-step process for recovering a password, hence the three templates.

When you create a template, you need to know the names of all the subcomponents that are required to be in the template. Theoretically, the subcomponent names are buried somewhere in the MSDN documentation, but you don't want to sift through all that each time you need to build a template. Fortunately, you don't have to start completely from scratch. You have some options with the Common Tasks menu.

When you run your mouse over a templated control, you'll see a little box with an arrow appear to the upper right of the control. Clicking this tiny box brings up the Common Tasks menu (refer to Figure 5-12). Each Common Tasks menu will be slightly different, but they all revolve around making and editing content in the control. The `Login` control's Common Task menu has the following commands:

- *Auto Format:* Displays the Auto Format dialog box that allows you to select from a series of predefined login templates. When you select a template, the HTML for the template is placed in the `<LayoutTemplate>` element of the `Login` control.
- *Convert to Template:* Converts the layout generated by the control into a template. Choosing this option takes the HTML used to generate the layout and places it in the `<LayoutTemplate>` element of the `Login` control.
- *Reset:* Clears the `<LayoutTemplate>` and reverts back to the generated layout. This option is displayed after you click on the Convert to Template option.
- *Administer Website:* Displays the Web Site Administration Tool. This is just a quick link that lets you set up users, roles, and so on.
- *Edit Templates:* Places the templated control in Template Editing mode, which allows you to change the visual appearance of the control's templates in the designer (some controls support multiple templates). If you choose this option without first choosing a template from the Auto Format dialog box or choosing Convert to Template, you'll be presented with a blank designer (that is, you'll be creating the template from scratch).

Selecting either the **Auto Format** or the **Convert to Template** option from the Common Tasks menu provides you a basic template that contains all the controls with their appropriate names. Listing 5-13 is an example of markup that appears in your control definition after you select the **Convert to Template** option and edit the template. Note that all the control ID values have been bolded to stand out, and that all layout and styling information has been removed from the example for the sake of brevity.

Listing 5-13. `Login` *Control Definition*

```
<asp:Login ID="Login1" Runat="server">
  <LayoutTemplate>
    <asp:Label Runat="server" ID="UserNameLabel">User Name:</asp:Label>
        <asp:TextBox Runat="server" ID="UserName" />
        <asp:RequiredFieldValidator Runat="server" ID="UserNameRequired"
             ValidationGroup="Login1" ErrorMessage="User Name is required."
             ToolTip="User Name is required."
             ControlToValidate="UserName">*</asp:RequiredFieldValidator>
        <asp:Label Runat="server" ID="PasswordLabel">
             Password:</asp:Label>
        <asp:TextBox Runat="server" TextMode="Password" ID="Password" />
        <asp:RequiredFieldValidator Runat="server" ID="PasswordRequired"
             ValidationGroup="Login1" ErrorMessage="Password is required."
             ToolTip="Password is required."
             ControlToValidate="Password">*</asp:RequiredFieldValidator>
        <asp:CheckBox Runat="server" Text="Remember next time" ID="RememberMe" />
        <asp:Button Runat="server" ID="Button" Text="Log In"
             ValidationGroup="Login1" CommandName="Submit" />
        <asp:Literal Runat="server" ID="FailureText" EnableViewState="False" />
    </LayoutTemplate>
</asp:Login>
```

After you are finished acquiring a base template from which to start, you can edit the template using the **Edit Templates** option from the Common Tasks menu. This places the templated control in Template Editing mode, as shown in Figure 5-13. When a control is in Template Editing mode, the Common Tasks menu displays a drop-down list containing all the templates with which you can work (also shown in Figure 5-13). As mentioned before, the `Login` control only has a single template (`LayoutTemplate`), but if you were editing a `PasswordRecovery` control, the drop-down list would contain three entries. After you are finished editing the template, click on the **End Template Editing** link from the Common Tasks menu to exit Template Editing mode.

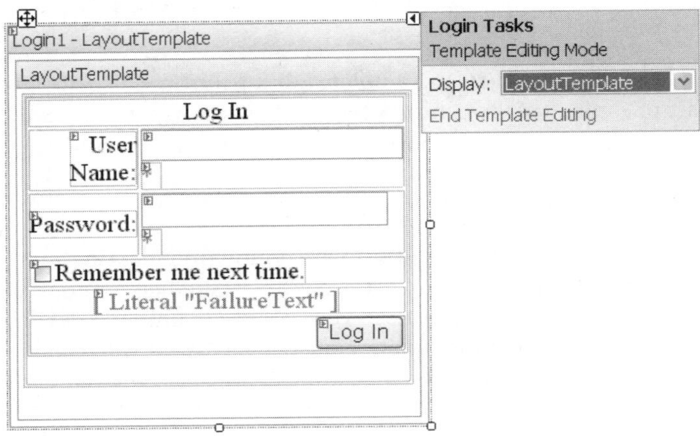

Figure 5-13. *The* `Login` *control (in Template Editing mode) after selecting the Convert to Template option (left) and the Common Login Tasks window after Edit Templates has been selected (right)*

The Login Control

Forms Authentication allows users to log in to an application by providing their username and password on a web-based form. Therefore, every application based on Forms Authentication requires some type of login form, username and password validation routine, and a way to build out the authentication ticket after a user has been authenticated. This can be quite a burden, especially if you are building a lot of smaller applications.

Enter the ASP.NET 2.0 `Login` control (Figure 5-12 and Figure 5-13), which tightly integrates with both the membership provider for your application and the authentication framework for ASP.NET. As long as you have a valid membership provider set up, you can drop a `Login` control onto a web form and have a fully functional login screen with zero coding. However, it also allows you to create your own validation routines when the need arises. It's a very flexible control. Table 5-7 contains a listing of the important `Login` control properties.

■ **Note** Most of the login controls expose an extensive list of properties, many of which deal with changing the appearance of the control's generated layout. I have *not* included those properties in any of the property lists that appear in this chapter. Feel free, however, to play around with those properties to see how they affect the layouts of the login controls

---

Table 5-7. *Important* Login *Control Properties*

Property Name	Description
DestinationPageUrl	This is the page where the user will be redirected upon successful login. If there is a value for the ReturnUrl in the query string (that is, a user was redirected from a secure page back to the main login page), then the page defined by the ReturnUrl is used instead of the page defined in DesintationPageUrl.
FailureAction	Specifies the action that will occur if the login attempt fails. You can only specify two actions: Refresh and RedirectToLoginPage. Refresh refreshes the page and displays a message that the login has failed. RedirectToLoginPage redirects the user to the default login page.
FailureText	Text that is displayed to the user when the login attempt fails.
Password	Sets or gets the password that appears in the **Password** text box.
RememberMeSet	Sets or gets whether or not the **Remember Me** check box is checked.
Username	Sets or gets the username that appears in the **UserName** text box.
VisibleWhenLoggedIn	Specifies whether or not the control will be visible if the user is already logged in.

■ **Tip** You can use the visual properties of the Login control to get its generated layout to closely resemble what you want. Then you can click on the **Convert to Template** option from the Common Tasks menu and convert what you see into a template. From there, you can fine-tune the content. Using this technique makes creating templates a bit easier.

Using the Login Control with its Built-in Authentication Functionality

Drop the control on the form. Make sure you have a properly configured membership provider. It's as simple as that. When users enter their login information, the Login control automatically uses the membership provider to validate usernames and passwords.

If the username and password is valid, the control generates the authentication ticket that will identify the user the next time he or she visits your site. The user is then redirected to the page specified in DestinationPageUrl or the ReturnUrl defined in the query string. If neither is defined, then the page simply refreshes and the user is logged in.

If the login fails, the login control determines what to do based on the FailureAction property. If FailureAction is set to refresh, then the page is refreshed and the FailureText message is displayed to the user. If FailureAction is set to RedirectToLoginPage, then the user is redirected to the default login page.

Coding Your Own Authentication Routines with the Login Control

Inevitably, there will be times when you want to code your own authentication routines. When those times come, you can still use the Login control for username and password entry purposes. You just need to handle the `Authenticate` event of the control so you can inject your own validation logic.

As an example, let's say that you want users to be able to log in using their normal username and password. You also want to be able to type in a username and a master password that allows you to log in as anyone. The membership providers do not support the concept of a master password, so you have to code your own validation logic. Luckily, you can use the built-in `Membership` object to interact with the web application's user information, so the validation code is still fairly simple (refer to Table 5-2 for more information regarding the `Membership` object's methods), as shown in Listing 5-14.

Listing 5-14. *Creating Custom Authentication Routines with the* `Login` *Control*

```
Imports System.Web.UI.WebControls
Imports System.Web.Security.FormsAuthentication
...

'**************************************************************************
Sub MyLogin_Authenticate(ByVal sender As Object, ByVal e As AuthenticateEventArgs)

    'Check to see if the master password is being used
    If MyLogin.Password = "MasterPassword" Then

        'Make sure the user exists
        If Not Membership.GetUser(MyLogin.UserName) Is Nothing Then
            SetAuthCookie(MyLogin.UserName, MyLogin.RememberMeSet)
            e.Authenticated = True
        End If

    Else

        'If there is no master password, just validate the user normally
        If Membership.ValidateUser(MyLogin.UserName, MyLogin.Password) Then
            SetAuthCookie(MyLogin.UserName, MyLogin.RememberMeSet)
            e.Authenticated = True
        End If

    End If

End Sub
```

The first line of Listing 5-14 checks to see if the master password was entered into the `Login` control's `Password` field. If so, it then uses the `Membership.GetUser` function to check if the username entered in the `Username` field exists in the membership database. If the member exists, then a `MembershipUser` object is returned. This code is not concerned with the actual object, only whether or not it was found. If the user was found, then the `SetAuthCookie` function creates the authentication cookie and sends it to the user to denote that they have successfully authenticated. Notice that the second parameter of the `SetAuthCookie` call is the `MyLogin.RememberMeSet` value (a Boolean value), which indicates whether or not the cookie should be persistent. Persistent cookies are saved between browser sessions, which allow the user to return and be automatically logged in. The code then sets `e.Authenticated` to `True`, which lets the `Login` control know that the user was successfully authenticated and that it should redirect the user to the appropriate page.

When you handle the `Authenticate` event, the `Login` control loses its capability to automatically authenticate users. Thus, if the master password is not used, then you become responsible for checking whether the user is attempting to log in normally. This is accomplished via the `Membership.ValidateUser` method. You just pass in the username and password, and the function returns a Boolean value indicating whether or not the username and password are valid. If so, an authentication cookie is created in the same manner as shown in the previous code listing, and `e.Authenticated` is set to `True`.

Although this code sample relies on the membership provider for authentication purposes, you are not required to use it. You can create login routines that directly access a database, XML file, or whatever data source you need to authenticate your users.

The LoginView Control

Users in a web application typically have different roles. As such, you may need a web form to display content one way for a certain role, and another way for a different role. `LoginView` provides a simple mechanism for defining what content should be displayed for which roles. You can think of the control as containing a series of panels, and each panel has content associated with a specific role, set of roles, or group (for example, anonymous or logged in users). You just drop content into the panel, and the `LoginView` control handles the logic for checking the role of the user and deciding which panel to display.

Working with RoleGroups, the LoggedInTemplate, and the AnonymousTemplate

Inside the `LoginView` control definition, you define a series of templates that dictate which user roles see what content. If the user has not logged in, then the `LoginView` displays the `AnonymousTemplate`. If you have not defined an `AnonymousTemplate`, then the `LoginView` does not display anything to the user.

If the user has logged in, the `LoginView` runs through all its `RoleGroup` entries checking to see if the user is authorized to view any of the `RoleGroup` templates. A `RoleGroup` definition contains two pieces of information: a template containing content, and a listing of the roles that are allowed to view that content. If the user is in *any* of the roles outlined by the `RoleGroup`, the `LoginView` displays that `RoleGroup` template. If the user is not authorized to view any of the `RoleGroups`, then the `LoginControl` displays the `LoggedInTemplate` (because the user *has* logged in). If you have not specified a `LoggedInTemplate`, then the `LoginControl` will not display anything.

Listing 5-15 shows the markup for a `LoginView` control and the various templates that it supports.

Listing 5-15. `LoginView` *Control Definition*

```
<asp:LoginView ID="LoginView1" Runat="server">
  <RoleGroups>
    <asp:RoleGroup Roles="Executive">
      <ContentTemplate>
```

```
        You are an executive
      </ContentTemplate>
    </asp:RoleGroup>
    <asp:RoleGroup Roles="Employee, Employee (Read Only)">
      <ContentTemplate>
        You are an employee
      </ContentTemplate>
  </asp:RoleGroup>
  </RoleGroups>
  <LoggedInTemplate>
    You are logged in, but you are not an employee or an executive.
  </LoggedInTemplate>
  <AnonymousTemplate>
    You are not logged in.  Please login using the form below:<br /><br />
    <asp:Login ID="Login1" Runat="server"/>
  </AnonymousTemplate>
</asp:LoginView>
```

Here's a rundown of how the LoginView processes all these RoleGroups and templates. First, it determines whether or not the current user is logged in. If the user is not logged in, LoginView displays the content from the AnonymousTemplate. In the preceding Listing 5-15, the AnonymousTemplate displays a Login control so the user can log in.

If the user is authenticated, the LoginView begins looking at each RoleGroup to see if any of the roles defined in the Roles parameter of the RoleGroup match any of the roles that the user is in. In Listing 5-15, the LoginView first checks to see if the user is in the Executive role. If so, the LoginView displays the content from the ContentTemplate associated with the RoleGroup. In this case, it displays **You are an executive**.

If the user is not an Executive, then the LoginView jumps to the next RoleGroup and starts the process over again. In this example, it checks to see if the user is in the Employee role *or* the Employee (Read Only) role, and displays **You are an employee** if so.

■ **Note** When you specify a list of roles, the content associated with those roles is displayed if the user is a member of any of those roles. It's an OR-based list, not an AND-based list.

If the LoginView runs through all the RoleGroups and does not find a match for the current user, it then defaults to the LoggedInTemplate content, which reads **You are logged in, but you are not an employee or an executive** in Listing 5-15.

One issue that may arise is when a user is assigned to multiple roles. For example, say a user is assigned to both the Employee and the Executive roles. The LoginView uses the first RoleGroup matches that it encounters to select the appropriate content for the user. Thus, the order of your RoleGroups is very important. In Listing 5-15, the Executive and RoleGroup appear before the Employee / Employee (Read Only) RoleGroup, so a user assigned to both groups would always see **You are an executive**.

You can define RoleGroup roles and edit RoleGroup templates directly in the Visual Studio IDE. Right-click on the LoginView control and select the **Edit RoleGroups** menu item from the context menu. This displays the **RoleGroup Collection Editor** dialog box, which allows you to add and remove roles from RoleGroups, and reorder RoleGroups in the LoginView control. You can edit the template for a particular role group by right-clicking on the LoginView control and selecting the appropriate RoleGroup from the **Edit Template** submenu.

Workarounds for AND-Based RoleGroups

As mentioned before, the list of roles associated with a RoleGroup is an OR-based list. So what happens when you need to know if a user is in both the Employee *and* Executive roles? You nest LoginView controls:

```
<asp:LoginView ID="LoginView1" Runat="server">
<RoleGroups>
  <asp:RoleGroup Roles="Executive">
    <ContentTemplate>
      <asp:LoginView ID="ExecLoginView" Runat="server">
        <RoleGroups>
          <asp:RoleGroup Roles="Employee">
            <ContentTemplate>
              You are an executive and an employee!
            </ContentTemplate>
          </asp:RoleGroup>
        </RoleGroups>
        <LoggedInTemplate>
          You are just an executive.
        </LoggedInTemplate>
      </asp:LoginView>
    </ContentTemplate>
  </asp:RoleGroup>
  <asp:RoleGroup Roles="Employee, Employee (Read Only)">
    <ContentTemplate>
      You are an employee
    </ContentTemplate>
</asp:RoleGroup>
</RoleGroups>
<! -- AnonymousTemplate / LoggedInTemplate -->
</asp:LoginView>
```

Here's how the nested LoginView works when a user who is both an Employee and an Executive visits the page. The outer LoginView notices that the user is an Executive, and uses the content from the Executive RoleGroup template. That content contains the inner LoginView, which only checks to see if the user is an Employee. If the user is an employee, then you know that they are both an Executive (because of the outer LoginView) AND an Employee (because of the inner LoginView). Although it makes for a bit more code, at least you can make the determination if you really have the need.

Displaying Mutually Exclusive Content

Another scenario that you may need to plan for, or rather avoid overplanning for, is when you want to display content for a role regardless of the other roles the user is in. For example, let's say that you have a page that needs to display a link to the Human Resources page if you are in the `Employee` role, and it also needs to display a link to visit the Executive Portal page if you are in the `Executive` role.

Do not make the mistake of trying to use nested `LoginViews` for this type of scenario because you'll only end up with a complicated jumble of code. Just use two independent `LoginViews`. One `LoginView` should have an `Employee RoleGroup` that displays the employee link. Another `LoginView` should have an Executive `RoleGroup` that displays the executive link. Keep them separate, and keep them simple.

The Password Recovery Control

Users forget their passwords. It's one of those inevitable things about dealing with people and the vast array of passwords they have to keep up with on a daily basis. ASP.NET 2.0's `PasswordRecovery` control (Figure 5-14) makes it exceptionally easy to reset or send a user their password if you are using a membership provider. If you are not using a membership provider, then you'll need to build your own password-recovery entry form from scratch because the `PasswordRecovery` control is not as flexible as the `Login` control. Table 5-8 contains a listing of the most important properties of the `PasswordRecovery` control.

Table 5-8. *Important* `PasswordRecovery` *Control Properties*

Property Name	Description
`GeneralFailureText`	Text that will be displayed if a nonroutine error occurs. This should be a general error message informing users that an error occurred and their password has not been retrieved.
`MailDefinition`	Defines the email message that will be sent to the user. This includes the subject, body, body format (text/HTML), email content file, priority, and so on.
`QuestionFailureText`	Text that will be displayed if the user fails to answer the security question correctly.
`SuccessPageUrl`	URL of the page to which the user will be redirected when the password is sent. If left blank, the page will refresh and the confirmation message will be displayed directly in the `PasswordRecovery` control.
`UserNameFailureText`	Text that will be displayed if the user enters a nonexistent username. This could be a potential security risk because it could let hackers know when they have stumbled upon a valid username.

The Password Recovery Process

Password recovery is two or three step process, depending on how you have configured your membership provider. The `PasswordRecovery` control has a total of three templates: the `UserNameTemplate`, the `QuestionTemplate`, and the `SuccessTemplate`. Each template represents a step of the process.

The first step of the process is to acquire the username of the user who is seeking their password. To accomplish this, the PasswordRecovery control displays a username entry field and a submit button (see Figure 5-14, left). The user enters the username, and then clicks on the **Submit** button. If the user is found, then the control moves to the second step. If not, the user is informed of the error.

The second step of the process depends on the configuration settings for your membership provider. One of the settings is whether or not to require a Question and Answer during the password recovery process. If no Question and Answer is required, then this step is skipped entirely and the user is just emailed the password. If it is required, then the user will see the security question that was entered when their account was setup and a field in which to enter the answer (Figure 5-14, center). If the user enters the correct answer, then the control moves on to step three. If not, the user is informed of the error.

The behavior of the third and final step is dictated by the enablePasswordRetrieval and enablePasswordReset properties of your membership provider configuration. If enablePasswordRetrieval is set to True, then the user will be emailed their existing password. If enablePasswordRetrieval is set to False and enablePasswordReset is set to True, then the user's password is cleared out and a new auto-generated password is emailed to the user. And if both properties are set to False, a nasty exception is thrown because you need to have one or the other enabled if you plan to use the PasswordRecovery control in your application.

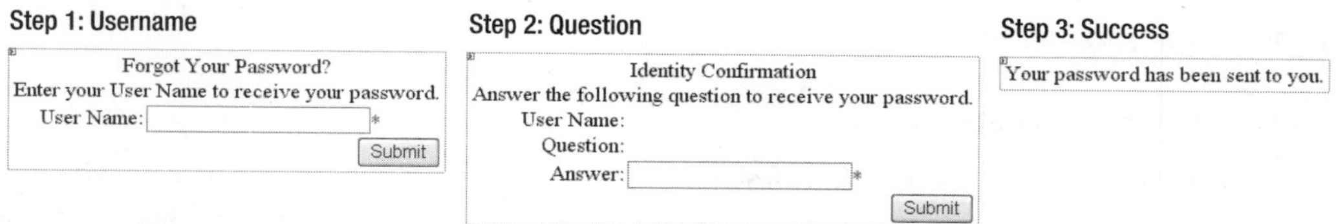

Figure 5-14. PasswordRecovery *control and the three steps of the password-recovery process: Username, Question, and Success*

Changing the Content of the Password Recovery Email

When a user completes the password-recovery process, an email is generated and sent to the user. By default, it contains a rather lack-luster messaging that informs the user that the password has been emailed. If you are shooting for mediocrity, then leave the message as-is.

If, however, you want a bit more pizzazz in your message, then you need to become familiar with the MailDefinition property of the PasswordRecovery control. Basically, the MailDefinition property exposes the most often used properties on a MailMessage object, so you can alter the content of your mail message to make it less generic. You should be relatively familiar with most of the properties such a BodyFormat (text/HTML), Cc, From, Priority, and Subject, so I won't cover them here. You may not, however, be familiar with the BodyFileName or EmbeddedObjects properties.

The EmbeddedObjects property is really just a bad way to say attachments. If you want to send a file (privacy agreement, for example) along with each email that goes out, then you can specify the files to attach using the EmbeddedObjects property editor. Basically, you just browse for a file, give it a name, and out it goes with your PasswordRecovery email.

BodyFileName is a helpful property that represents the path to a text file that contains the body content for your email. The PasswordRecovery control reads this file, if it is specified, and dumps the contents of the file into the body of the mail message before sending it off to a user. This is especially useful when you want to create an HTML email to send out to your users and makes it easier to maintain message content because you do not have to sift through a bunch of code to locate it. Just use the file selector from the property window to choose the file that contains your email body content and you will be all set to send emails.

Displaying the Username and Password in the Body Text

One issue you will run across rather quickly when you are creating your own email body text is how to get the user's username and password into the body of the text. Its static text, but you need to dynamically insert the username and password. This can be done using the `<% UserName %>` and `<% Password %>` tags in the body text, like this:

```
You requested that your password information be sent to you via email.
Following you will find your new login information:

Username: <% UserName %>
Password: <% Password %>
```

The `PasswordRecovery` control only parses through the email body looking for these two tags and replaces them with the actual username and passwords you are sending out. These are the *only* tags that you can use in the body text, so don't drop a bunch of ASP.NET code in there hoping that it will run.

Handling the SendingMail Event

The `PasswordRecovery` control exposes a single event named `SendingMail`, which fires right before an email is sent off to a user. This event passes in the `MailMessage` object that will ultimately be sent to the user, so you can programmatically manipulate the `MailMessage` object to suit your needs.

By the time the message reaches this event, the body content has been setup, the `<% UserName %>` and `<% Password %>` tags have been processed, and any subproperties from the `MailDefinition` property have been loaded into the message. It's basically ready to go, so make whatever alterations you need and then let the `PasswordRecovery` control send the message on its own. Do *not* send the message from inside the `SendingMail` event because the user will get it twice.

In the following example, you'll see how to set the `Bcc` field of the mail message. This is a descent example of when it's appropriate to use this event to modify a mail message because you cannot define a Bcc recipient using the `MailDefinition` property:

```
Sub PasswordRecovery1_SendingMail(ByVal sender As Object,
  ByVal e As System.Web.UI.WebControls.MailMessageEventArgs)
    e.Message.Bcc = "system@passwordRecovery.com"
End Sub
```

Notice that the email message variable is buried inside the `MailMessageEventArgs` parameter. You can access it using `e.Message`, as shown in the preceding code snippet.

The LoginStatus Control

Many websites display a link somewhere on their site that allows users to quickly log in or log out, depending on their current login status. The `LoginStatus` control is a simple control that exposes this functionality. Table 5-9 lists the important properties of the `LoginStatus` control.

Table 5-9. *Important* `LoginStatus` *Control Properties*

Property Name	Description
`LoginImageUrl`	URL of the image to display in the login link.
`LoginText`	Text displayed in the login link.
`LogoutAction`	Action that is to be taken when the logout link is clicked. The valid options are `Refresh`, `Redirect` (to `LogoutPageUrl`), and `RedirectToLoginPage`.
`LogoutImageUrl`	URL of the image to display in the logout link.
`LogoutPageUrl`	URL to where the user will be redirected when the logout button is clicked and the `LogoutAction` is set to Redirect.
`LogoutText`	Text displayed in the logout link.

Here's how the control works. Users who are not currently logged in see the login link and/or login image. When a user clicks on that login link, the user is redirected to the default login page. Users who have already logged in will see a logout link. This signs them off, and then redirects them or refreshes the page depending on the `LogoutAction` setting. That's the extent of the `LoginStatus` control.

The LoginName Control

The `LoginName` control is, by far, the simplest control of the bunch. It's really just a label that can display the username of the currently logged in user. If the user is not logged in, then it is completely invisible.

The only noteworthy property the `LoginName` control exposes is the `FormatString` property. If you have worked with the `String.Format` function before, then you will quickly recognize the syntax for using `FormatString`: you just place `{0}` wherever you want the username to appear in the string. Thus, the `FormatString` **You are logged in as {0}** would end up reading **You are logged in as JSmith** when it was displayed on a web form.

■ **Note** The `LoginName` control displays the login name of the user, not the actual user's name. So watch out when you use this because if you try to personalize something with it, it may end up reading something like "Thanks JSmith for visiting our website!"

The CreateUserWizard Control

Although the Web Site Administration Tool can serve as your primary means for adding users to a web application, you may also need to add users directly from a page inside your application. Many websites allow users to register for new accounts, or you may want to create a simple administrative interface so users who you don't want to give free reign on the Web Site Administration Tool can still do some simple admin tasks. In any case, the `CreateUserWizard` control (see Figure 5-15) gives you a quick and easy way to add users to your application. Table 5-10 contains a listing of the most important properties on the `CreateUserWizard` control.

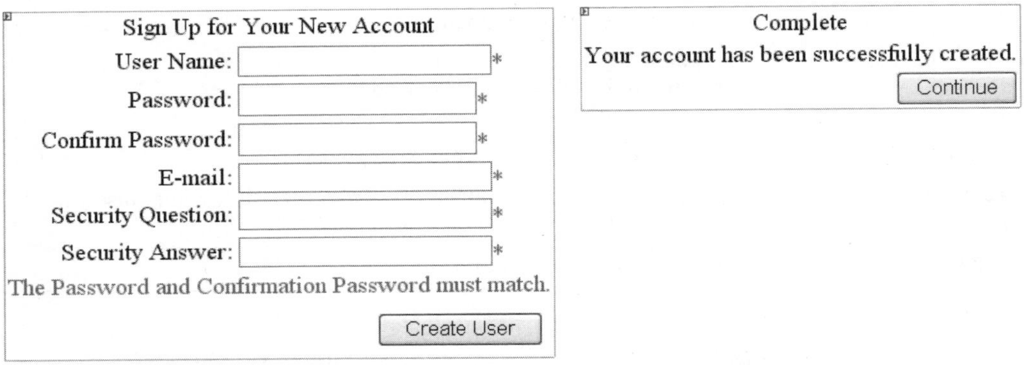

Figure 5-15. `CreateUserWizard` *control and its two steps: Sign Up for Your New Account (left) and Complete(right).*

Table 5-10. *Important* `PasswordRecovery` *Control Properties*

Property Name	Type	Description
`Answer`		Gets/sets the security answer field.
`AutoGeneratePassword`		Determines whether or not the password will be automatically generated for the user. If this is set to `True`, and a password was entered in the password field of the `CreateUserWizard` control, then the auto-generated password will overwrite the password field.
`CancelDestinationPageUrl`		Specifies the destination URL where users will be redirected if they click on the Cancel button.
`ContinueDestinationPageUrl`		Specifies the destination URL where users will be redirected if they click on the Continue button that appears in the `Complete` template (see Figure 5-16, bottom, later in this chapter).
`DisplayCancelButton`		Specifies whether or not to display a Cancel button on the control.
`DisableCreatedUser`		Specifies whether or not the user created by the control should be disabled.
`Email`		Gets/sets the email field.

Table 5-10. *Important* PasswordRecovery *Control Properties (Continued)*

Property Name	Type	Description
EmailRegularExpression		Regular expression used to validate the email address.
LoginCreatedUser		Determines whether or not the user entering the user information will be logged in after the user is created. This is most useful for "registrations" where the person creating the user account will also be the person using the account.
MailDefinition		Defines the new user notification email that will be sent to the user. This includes the subject, body, body format (text/HTML), email content file, priority, and so on. You *must* specify an email body content file for the BodyFileName in the MailDefinition if you want the CreateUserWizard to send notification emails. Refer to the PasswordRecovery control for information on how to customize the email and respond to the email event because all the same concepts apply to this control.
PasswordRegular➥Expression		Regular expression used to validate the password.
Question		Gets/sets the security question field.
RequireEmail		Determines whether or not an email address is required for the new user.
UserName		Gets/sets the UserName field.
WizardSteps		Steps that the user may go through to complete the wizard. By default, there are two steps: CreateUserWizardStep and CompleteWizardStep. You can add additional steps, and reorder the existing steps, using the WizardSteps property editor.

■ **Caution** If you want the CreateUserWizard control to send a notification email to the user containing that user's login information, then you *must* specify a BodyTextFile in the MailDefinition property. If you do not specify a BodyTextFile, then the CreateUserWizard will *not* send notification emails.

Using the CreateUserWizard Control in the Designer

Most of the Login controls you have worked with thus far are templated controls, but the CreateUserWizard is a special type of templated control known as a wizard. The wizard is a new addition to ASP.NET 2.0 that allows you to define steps in a process, and then create a "page" (in the form of a template) for each step. Navigation buttons on the wizard allow the user to move from step to step in an orderly fashion. This means that after you learn more about wizards (Chapter 10), you will be able to add custom steps to the CreateUserWizard and order those steps however you choose.

Another implication of the wizard is that the Common Tasks menu has a lot more options on it and so it appears to be a bit more complicated. Most of the options are standard wizard tasks that appear on all wizards. For now, you can disregard them. You should only pay attention to the options **Customize Create User Step** and **Customize Complete Step**. Clicking these options is synonymous to clicking the **Convert to Template** option on a normal templated control. After you click one of these options, you can click the **Edit Templates** option and change the layout of the Create User or Customize step, just as you would with a normal templated control.

The Create User Process

As is, the `CreateUserWizard` has two steps. The first step, `CreateUserWizardStep`, is to allow the entry and submission of user information. Depending on membership provider configuration, and your `CreateUserWizard` control configuration, the entry form for the user will require different fields. Clicking on the **Create User** button will submit the user information, and the membership provider will add the user to your application. At this point, the `CreatedUser` event (the only event this control exposes) is fired, and the notification email is sent to the user.

The second step, `CompleteWizardStep`, exists to display a confirmation message informing the user that their account was successfully added to the application, and a Continue button so you can redirect the user to some other location using the `ContinueDestinationPageUrl` property.

As mentioned before, you can add additional steps to the process by manipulating the `WizardSteps` property. This may be helpful if you want the user to fill out additional information during the registration process or if you want to force the user to fill out a questionnaire or survey before they register.

Handling the CreatedUser Event

Just after the user has been added to the application, and just before the control sends the notification email, the `CreateUser` event fires. This gives you the opportunity to set up routine user information that needs to be added to the database before the new user actually starts using your site. One scenario that may come up is that your users may need to be placed in a default role. The following example shows what you need to do if you want all new users created by this control to be a part of the "Customer" role:

```
'*****************************************************************************
Sub CreateUserWizard1_CreatedUser(ByVal sender As Object,
  ByVal e As System.EventArgs)
    Roles.AddUserToRole(CreateUserWizard1.UserName, "Customer")
End Sub
```

The ChangePassword Control

Users probably will want to change their passwords at some point in time, especially if you are auto-generating passwords that end up being 20 characters of random gibberish. Even if you're not auto-generating passwords, it's still a good idea to let users change their passwords for security reasons. The `ChangePassword` control (see Figure 5-16) gives users the ability to change their password from within your application, and it handles all the logic to do so automatically. Table 5-11 contains a listing of the most important properties in the `PasswordRecovery` control.

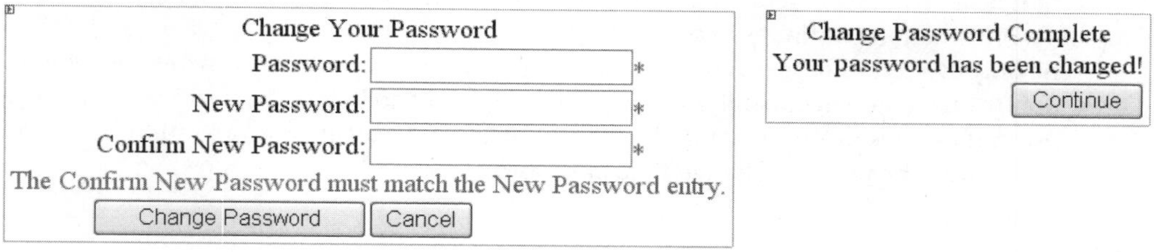

Change Your Password
Password: *
New Password: *
Confirm New Password: *
The Confirm New Password must match the New Password entry.
Change Password | Cancel

Change Password Complete
Your password has been changed!
Continue

Figure 5-16. *The* ChangePassword *control*

Table 5-11. *Important* PasswordRecovery *Control Properties*

Property Name	Type	Description
`AuthenticationFailureAction`		Action that is taken when a user who has not yet logged in attempts to change the password. The options are `RedirectToLoginPage` and `Refresh`.
`CancelDestinationPageUrl`		URL of the page where the user will be sent if the Cancel button is clicked.
`ContinueDestinationPageUrl`		URL of the page where the user will be sent if the Continue button is clicked.
`MailDefinition`		Defines the change password notification email that will be sent to the user. This includes the subject, body, body format (text/HTML), email content file, priority, and so on. You *must* specify an email body content file for the `BodyFileName` in the `MailDefinition` if you want the `ChangePassword` control to send notification emails. Refer to the `PasswordRecovery` control for information on how to customize the email and respond to an email event because all the same concepts apply to this control.
`PasswordRegularExpression`		Regular expression used to validate the password.
`SuccessPageUrl`		URL of the page where the control sends the user after the password change succeeds.

Using the `ChangePassword` control is as simple as placing it on a web form and ensuring that you have an appropriately configured membership provider. It takes care of all the logic required to update a user's password.

If you want to send a confirmation email to the user regarding the password change, create the email body and save it to a text file. Specify that text file as the `BodyTextFile` in the `MailDefinition` property in the control. When users successfully change their password, a notification email is fired off. If a `SuccessPageUrl is` defined, users are redirected to the specified location after the email has been sent.

If no email is sent, or the `v` is not defined, then the page refreshes and users see a confirmation note indicating that their password was successfully changed (refer to Figure 5-16, bottom). If users click on the **Continue** button on the confirmation page, they are redirected to the `ContinueDestinationPageUrl`, if it is has been specified. If it hasn't, the page just refreshes and the confirmation continues to be displayed.

The only event the `ChangePassword` control exposes is the `ChangedPassword` event, which is fired after the user has successfully changed the password and before the notification email is sent. You can use this event to manipulate the `v` object or to execute any operations that you need to run after the user has changed the password.

Summary

Developing login forms and user administration sections in ASP.NET 1.x used to be a time-consuming process, but you have seen in this chapter how the new user-management tool and features in ASP.NET 2.0 can help reduce that timeframe significantly. You have also seen how to effectively manipulate templated controls so you can fit them into any page layout or color scheme, and how to use the new `Membership` and `Roles` objects to easily access common user and role functions. Now you just need to figure out what to do with all that extra time you'll have when you finish your next project early.

CHAPTER 6

Managing Profiles

Hand tailored suits, custom made golf clubs, bath towels with embroidered names across the corner: people have a fascination with personalized items. The sense of attachment is stronger to something that you know was handcrafted just for you, and web pages are no different. Most major sites now have some degree of personalization that makes their customers feel more welcome. Content adjusts on an individual basis. Advertisements target specific groups of people. Upselling, cross-selling—it all falls under the category of personalization.

Whenever I need to buy movies tickets, I surf over to `Fandango.com` and it shows me all the theaters around my zip code. The news site I use knows my nearest affiliate and automatically displays local stories along with national headlines. `Amazon.com` graciously suggests products that it thinks I may like based on my past purchase history. These are all examples of targeted content. I live in Dallas, so it wouldn't do me much good to see movie listings in Atlanta or New York, and I'm not going to be nearly as attached to the Chicago news as I am Dallas news. And trust me, Amazon has a much better chance of selling me a technical gadget than a set of china. You can build targeted content into your applications by storing information about your users and using that information to output relevant content. For example, if you are building a company website, you can display department- or branch-specific news and information to your viewers. Or, if you know it has been a long time since a user logged in to an application, you can display additional help information to assist them through their tasks.

Another common use of profile information includes targeted selling. This is similar to targeted content, but the objective is to get products or services in front of the user that are most likely to be purchased. Have you noticed when you go to a search engine and type in a search term, that the advertisements closely parallel your search? I searched for Baseball on Google and it showed me advertisements for baseball equipment on eBay, a digital laser baseball that can clock your arm speed, tickets for baseball games, and a cake decorating kit that includes a sports pan for baking cakes in the shape of a baseball. My wife and I share a computer and she often searches for cake-decorating supplies, so I can only assume that the last item is linked to her search history. If you actively look for baseball, for example, you're probably interested in baseball. If you're interested in baseball, you'll probably be more likely to buy something related to it, such as tickets or equipment.

Personalization is based on user-specific information that outlines preferences or behaviors. You can use the new profile functionality in ASP.NET 2.0 to quickly and easily store information about the people who visit your website or use your application. You can then use that profile information to adjust the content of your site according to the specific information you have gathered about the visitors.

This chapter covers a wide range of topics related to using profiles, including the following:

- *Profile Basics:* Covers the basics of profile configuration, including how to define and work with profile properties, profile property groups, and the `ProfileManager` object.
- *Working with Anonymous Profiles:* Discusses the nuances of working with profiles and anonymous users, including how to define profile properties for anonymous users, avoid invalid profile property access, and migrate an anonymous profile to an authenticated profile using the `MigrateAnonymous` event.
- *Creating a Simple Targeted Advertisement:* Demonstrates how to use profiles to track user behavior and how to respond to target content based on the findings
- *The Shopping Cart Custom Property:* Illustrates the use of custom objects as profile properties by implementing a profile-based shopping cart. This also includes an example demonstrating how to migrate an anonymous profile to an authenticated profile.

Profile Basics

Microsoft, realizing the need for a simple mechanism to store information about the people who visit your site, added profile support to ASP.NET 2.0. A profile consists of a set of properties that helps define the demographics, behavior, configuration options, and just about anything else you want to store about an individual who accesses your web application. As people use your application, you set values for the profile properties based on their actions, their behaviors, and the information they enter into the system. You can then use that profile information in other parts of your application to customize the site based on user-specific profile information. Also understand that ASP.NET stores profile information between sessions (by default to a SQL Server database), so you can continually gather profile information over time as people continue to visit your application.

In this section, you'll learn about the `Profile` object, configuring profiles, defining profile properties and groups, and authenticated versus anonymous profile properties.

The Profile Object

ASP.NET 2.0 exposes its profile support via the `Profile` property of the `System.Web.HttpContext` object. Microsoft's implementation of profile support makes the `Profile` object very interesting because the properties on the `Profile` object change to reflect configuration settings you specify in `Web.config`. At its core, the `Profile` object is a `System.Web.Profile.ProfileBase` object. Like many features in ASP.NET, profile support relies on the provider model to abstract its implementation details from the developer. As such, the `ProfileBase` object defines the basic set of profile functionality the profile provider expects a profile object to expose.

■ **Note** You can get a brief description of providers in Chapter 5 in the section titled "Working with the Membership and Roles Objects."

You configure the names and types of properties the Profile object exposes in Web.config. I'll cover the exact details of how to do this shortly, so for now understand that you define the properties for the Profile object in a configuration file and not in code. Whenever ASP.NET runs your application, it looks at the profile property configuration in Web.config and automatically builds a new class named ProfileCommon that derives from the ProfileBase class and contains the properties you defined in Web.config. This gives you a strongly typed object that you can work with in your code. Also, although every application that uses profiles has a ProfileCommon class, each application has a unique ProfileCommon class that resides in the application's root namespace. So the ProfileCommon class in one application is not the same ProfileCommon class in another application.

When a user requests a page, ASP.NET uses the profile provider to load a ProfileCommon object for the user, and this object becomes the Profile object you can access on the various pages in your application. You can then use the information in the Profile object in your page code and set values as appropriate. When the page finishes processing, ASP.NET uses the profile provider to save any changes you made in the Profile object so you can access that information on subsequent visits by the user. ASP.NET handles the loading and saving of profile information entirely behind the scenes, so you never have to worry about manually saving or loading anything.

Because the Profile object depends on configuration settings to define its properties, profile configuration is covered next.

Enabling and Disabling Profiles

ASP.NET 2.0 enables profiles by default, so your application has access to the profile functionality unless you expressly disable profiles. A bit of overhead is associated with profiles because ASP.NET 2.0 loads user profile information on every request, regardless of whether you actually use the profile information on the page. As such, you should disable profiles entirely if you are not planning on using them in your application.

For reference, all profile configuration settings reside in the <profile> section of Web.config. Disabling profiles is a simple enough task; you just have to set the enabled attribute to false in the <profile> element as shown in Listing 6-1.

Listing 6-1. *Disabling Profile Support*

```
<configuration>
    <system.web>
        <profile enabled="false"></profile>
    </system.web>
</configuration>
```

When profiles are disabled, you will not have access to the Profile object in your application. Any calls to the Profile object result in an error and your application will not compile. You should only disable profiles if you do not use them anywhere in your application.

Defining Profile Properties in Web.config

You define properties for the Profile object by specifying them in the <properties> element of the <profiles> section in Web.config. You can create as many properties as you like, but keep in mind that ASP.NET has to load all of them into the `Profile` object on each request, so the more properties you add, the more time it takes to load them. Listing 6-2 is an example of how to define profile properties in `Web.config`.

Listing 6-2. *Defining Profile Properties in* `Web.config`

```
<configuration>
  <system.web>
    <profile>
      <properties>
        <add name="CustomerName" type="String" defaultValue="Valued Customer" />
        <add name="DateOfBirth" type="System.DateTime" defaultValue="8/20/1980" />
      </properties>
    </profile>
  </system.web>
</configuration>
```

■ **Note** If you are using the `SqlProfileProvider` (the default provider for profiles), you can add and remove properties from your profile without losing data from the existing properties. If you implement your own provider, or use a third-party provider, then be aware that you may lose data unless the provider has been specifically designed to handle changes to the profile data structure gracefully.

When you define a property, you must specify the property `name` and `type`. Optionally, you may define a default value using the `defaultValue` attribute. Specifying default values is a good idea because you may need to use a profile property value before you have a chance to capture the data from the person who visits your website. You can also define object property types, not just primitive types, as long as those types are serializable. You'll see an example of how to specify and use an object property type in the shopping cart example later in this chapter.

Creating Profile Property Groups

Property groups allow you to organize the properties in the `Profile` object by grouping related properties together. Groups make it easier to locate specific properties using IntelliSense in the Visual Studio IDE because ASP.NET creates a class for each group of properties and then uses that class to create a property of the `Profile` object that contains those profile properties. It's extremely useful when you have a large number of profile properties that you need to track.

For example, address information is usually made up of a street address, an apartment or suite number, a city, a state, and a zip code. Grouping these properties together using a property group keeps them from cluttering up the `Profile` object. Listing 6-3 shows how to group profile properties using the `<group>` element.

Listing 6-3. *Profile Property Group Definition Example in* `Web.config`

```
<profile>
    <properties>
        <add name="CustomerName" type="String" defaultValue="Valued Customer" />
        <add name="DateOfBirth" type="System.DateTime" defaultValue="8/20/1980" />
        <group name="Address">
            <add name="Address" type="String" />
            <add name="AptOrSuite" type="String" />
            <add name="City" type="String" />
            <add name="State" type="String" />
            <add name="Zip" type="String" />
        </group>
    </properties>
</profile>
```

All you have to do to define a property group is surround a set of properties with the `<group>` element and specify the group name via the `name` attribute. After you define a group, you access the group properties using the group name as a property of the `Profile` object as shown in Listing 6-4.

Listing 6-4. *Grouped Profile Property Access*

```
Profile.Address.Street = "5555 Main St."
Profile.Address.AptOrSuite = "Apt. 110"
Profile.Address.City = "Dallas"
Profile.Address.State = "Tx"
Profile.Address.Zip = "99999"
```

■ **Note** Profile groups can only be one level deep. Nested groups (subgroups) are not supported.

Implementing a Profile Property Class

You do not have to declare all your profile properties in `Web.config`. You can also define profile properties in a class that inherits from the `System.Web.Profile.ProfileBase` class, as shown in Listing 6-5

Listing 6-5. *Implementing a Profile Property Class*

```
Imports System.Web.Profile

Public Class MyProfile
    Inherits ProfileBase
```

```
    '***************************************************************
    Private _FirstName As String
    Private _LastName As String

    '***************************************************************
    Public Property FirstName() As String
        Get
            Return _FirstName
        End Get
        Set(ByVal value As String)
            _FirstName = value
        End Set
    End Property

    '***************************************************************
    Public Property LastName() As String
        Get
            Return _LastName
        End Get
        Set(ByVal value As String)
            _LastName = value
        End Set
    End Property

End Class
```

Notice that this class inherits its base functionality from the `ProfileBase` object in the `System.Web.Profile` namespace. Other than that, there is nothing special about the class, it simply contains two standard string properties called `FirstName` and `LastName`.

After you create your custom profile property class, you have to configure ASP.NET to use that custom class by specifying a value for the `inherits` attribute of the `<provider>` element as shown in Listing 6-6.

Listing 6-6. *Configuring ASP.NET to Use a Custom Profile Property Class*

```
<configuration>
  <system.web>
    <profile inherits="MyProfile">
      <properties>
        <add name="CustomerName" type="String" defaultValue="Valued Customer" />
        <add name="DateOfBirth" type="System.DateTime" defaultValue="8/20/1980" />
      </properties>
    </profile>
  </system.web>
</configuration>
```

Notice that you can specify a custom property class and still define properties in `Web.config`. ASP.NET simply compiles the `ProfileCommon` class using your custom class instead of `ProfileBase`, as shown in Figure 6-1.

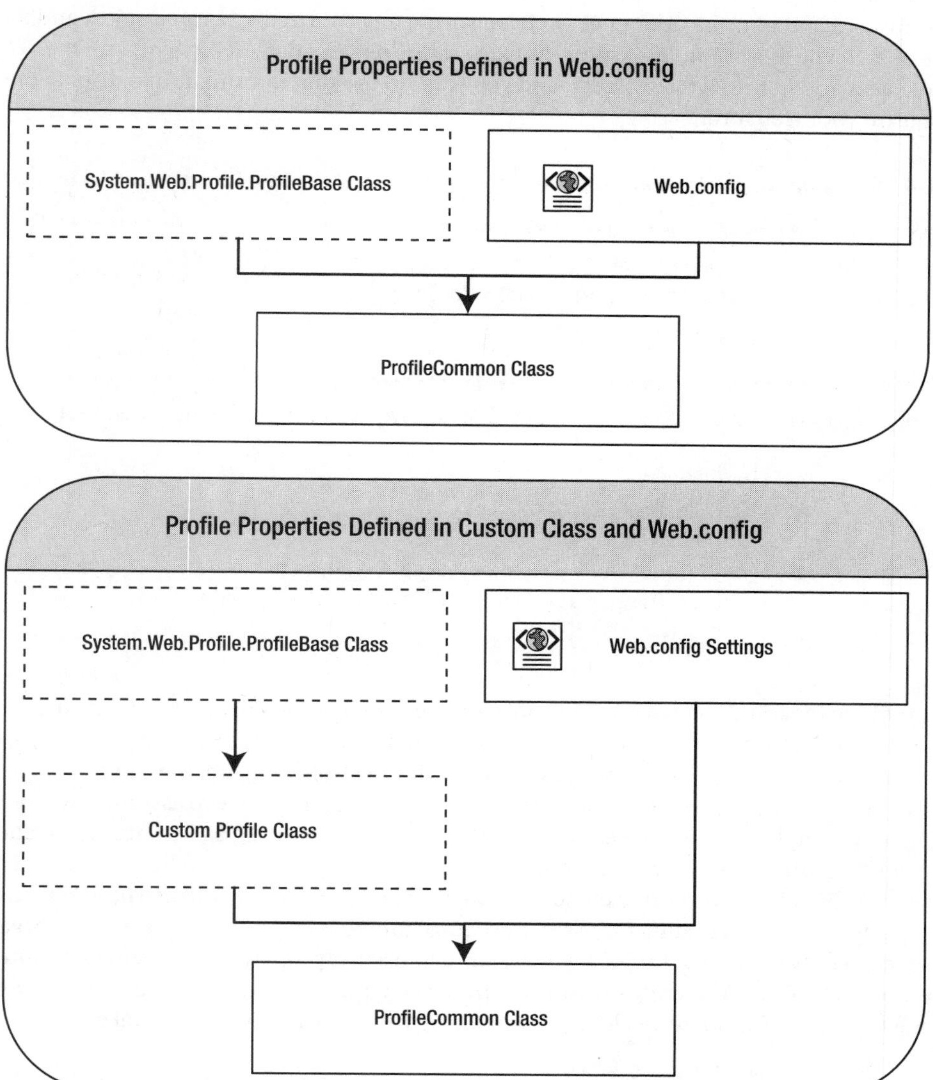

Figure 6-1. *ASP.NET compiles* `ProfileCommon` *using either* `ProfileBase` *or a custom class that you specify in* `Web.config`.

Strongly Typed Properties

Because ASP.NET actually compiles a class containing your profile properties, the `Profile` object exposes strongly typed properties. This is entirely different from what you have come to know from the `Session` object, which stores session data as nonstrongly typed key-value pairs.

Listing 6-7 highlights the differences between accessing data in the `Session` object and the `Profile` object. For this example, assume you are storing a user's date of birth in both the `Session` object and in the `Profile` object, and you want to use that information to display the user's age on your web form.

Listing 6-7. *Accessing Data Differences Between the* `Profile` *and the* `Session` *Objects*

```
'****************************************************************************
Private Function GetAge(ByVal DOB As Date) As Long
    Return DateDiff(DateInterval.Year, DOB, Now)
End Function

'****************************************************************************
Sub Page_Load(ByVal sender As Object, ByVal e As System.EventArgs) Handles Me.Load

    'Using the Profile
    Me.lblAge.Text = GetAge(Profile.DateOfBirth)

    'Using the Session: Notice that you have to cast the value to a Date Type
    Me.lblAge.Text = GetAge(DirectCast(Session("DateOfBirth"), Date))

End Sub
```

The `GetAge` function accepts a single date variable, which it then uses to calculate the user's age. You can see that to get the `DateOfBirth` value from the `Session` object you must use `Session("DateOfBirth")`. Because the `Session` object is not strongly typed, the call to `Session("DateOfBirth")` is only guaranteed to return an `Object`. You have to assume it will be a `Date`. If that assumption is wrong, i.e. the session happens to be storing a non `Date` type value in `Session("DateOfBirth")`, then an exception is thrown.

The `Profile` object, however, exposes a strongly-typed `Date` property called `DateOfBirth`. This property requires no casting for use in the `GetAge` function and poses no exception threat because it can only store a `Date` type. If you attempt to use the property inappropriately, you receive a compiler error. You are also protected from accidentally misspelling the item that you are trying to acquire. For instance, let's say you make the following spelling mistakes:

Listing 6-8. *Accidental Property Misspelling*

```
'Using the Session
    Me.lblAge.Text = GetAge(DirectCast(Session("DateOooofBirth"), Date))

'Using the Profile
    Me.lblAge.Text = GetAge(Profile.DateOooofBirth)
```

The line of code using the Session object compiles without any problems but experiences a logical error each time it runs because nothing is ever returned from the call. The line using the Profile object, however, fails to compile because no such property exists for the Profile object.

■ **Tip** If you use the session variable to store information, consider creating a strongly typed session class to help you manage your session variables. You can save a lot of hassle if you ever need to change a session variable name, define a default value, or eliminate a session variable from your code entirely. Chapter 2 has more information about strongly typed configuration classes, and you can apply the same technique to session variables.

ProfileManager Class

The System.Web.Profiles.ProfileManager class allows you to manage all the profiles in your application. Like the Membership and Roles objects discussed in Chapter 5, the ProfileManager acts as the proxy object for the provider model. You won't work with it nearly as much as the actual Profile object itself, but it has a number of methods that are very helpful for administrative tasks. Many of the methods, however, use a few components that we have yet to discuss, so let's cover those components first.

ProfileInfo Class

The ProfileInfo object is a very simple class that stores basic information about a profile. Many of the methods in the ProfileManager return a ProfileInfoCollection object, which simply contains a set of ProfileInfo objects. Table 6-1 outlines the properties of the ProfileInfo class.

Table 6-1. ProfileInfo *Properties*

Property Name	Type	Description
IsAnonymous	Boolean	True if the profile is an anonymous profile. False if the profile is an authenticated profile.
LastActivityDate	Date	Last date the profile was read or updated.
LastUpdatedDate	Date	Last date the profile was updated.
Size	Integer	Gets the size of the profile property data.
UserName	String	Identifies the user to whom the profile belongs.

ProfileAuthenticationOption Enum

Many of the methods in the ProfileManager also use the ProfileAuthenticationOption enumeration to let you filter results based on whether the profile is an anonymous or authenticated profile. The ProfielAuthentictionOption enumeration contains three values: All, Anonymous, and Authenticated.

ProfileManager Properties and Methods

Tables 6-2 and 6-3 provide a brief overview of the important properties and methods of the ProfileManager object.

Table 6-2. ProfileManager *Properties*

Property Name	Type	Description
ApplicationName	String	Name of the application. The role provider may store data for multiple applications, so it needs to know the identify of the application.
AutomaticSave➥ Enabled	Boolean (read only)	True if ASP.NET automatically saves changes to the profile when the page is finished executing. If this is false, then you must explicitly save the profile information by calling Profile.Save() after you change profile information.
Enabled	Boolean (read only)	True if profiles are enabled.
Provider	ProfileProvider	Returns a reference to the default ProfileProvider object for the application.
Providers	ProfileProviderCollection	Returns a collection of the ProfileProvider objects available to the application.

Table 6-3. ProfileManager *Methods*

Method Name	Parameters	Returns	Description
DeleteInactive➥ Profiles	authentication Option As Profile Authentication Option userInactive➥ SinceDate As DateTime	Integer	Deletes all profiles that have been inactive since the userInactive SinceDate. You can use the authenticationOption parameter to limit deletions to anonymous or authenticated users. Returns an Integer identifying the number of profiles deleted.
DeleteProfile	username As String	Boolean	Deletes the profile for the specified username. Returns True if the deletion succeeds.
DeleteProfiles	profiles As ProfileInfo Collection		Deletes all the profiles in the profiles parameter. Returns an Integer specifying the number of profiles deleted.
DeleteProfiles	usernames As String()	Integer	Deletes all the profiles for the specified usernames. Returns an Integer specifying the number of profiles deleted.

Method Name	Parameters	Returns	Description
FindInactiveProfilesByUserName	authenticationOption As ProfileAuthenticationOption usernameToMatch As String userInactiveSinceDate As DateTime	ProfileInfoCollection	Searches for inactive profiles based on authentication option, a username wildcard, and date of last activity. Returns a ProfileInfoCollection containing any matches.
FindProfilesByUserName	authenticationOption As ProfileAuthenticationOption UsernameToMatch As String	ProfileInfoCollection	Searches for profiles based on the authentication option and a username wildcard. Returns a ProfileInfoCollection containing any matches.
GetAllInactiveProfiles	authenticationOption As ProfileAuthenticationOption userInactiveSinceDate As DateTime	ProfileInfoCollection	Searches for inactive profiles based on authentication option and last activity date. Returns a ProfileInfoCollection containing any matches.
GetAllProfiles	authenticationOption As ProfileAuthenticationOption	ProfileInfoCollection	Searches for all profiles based on authentication option. Returns a ProfileInfoCollection containing any matches.
GetNumberOfInactiveProfiles	authenticationOption As ProfileAuthenticationOption userInactiveSinceDate As DateTime	Integer	Searches for InActiveProfiles based on authentication option and last activity date. Returns an Integer identifying the total number of records located.
GetNumberOfProfiles	authenticationOption As ProfileAuthenticationOption	Integer	Searches for all profiles based on authentication option. Returns an Integer identifying the total number of records located.

The FindInactiveProfilesByUserName, FindProfilesByUserName, GetAllInactiveProfiles, and GetAllProfiles methods all have overloads that allow you to request paged data.

Working with Anonymous Profiles

People who access your website will either be anonymous users or authenticated users, a distinction that adds a level of complexity to profiles. Authenticated users are easily identified because they have a unique username that identifies them each time they log in. As such, ASP.NET can easily store and track profile information for an authenticated user. Anonymous users, on the other hand, do not have a unique username. This makes storing and tracking anonymous profile information a bit more troublesome.

You do not have to do anything special to work with profile properties for an authenticated user because ASP.NET knows the identity of the user. Anonymous users, however, require a few special preparations. In this section, you'll learn about anonymous identification, anonymous profile properties, and all the caveats associated with using anonymous profiles.

Enabling Anonymous Profile Identification

ASP.NET acquires profile information for people based on their usernames. Authenticated users, by virtue of having been authenticated, have a valid, nonempty, unique username that identifies them to the web application. Each time an authenticated user visits your application, ASP.NET can easily acquire the user's profile information via the user's username.

Anonymous users do not have a unique username, but ASP.NET still needs a unique value by which to store and retrieve anonymous profiles. ASP.NET circumvents this issue using Anonymous Identification, a mechanism that assigns anonymous users a unique identifier. To do this, Anonymous Identification generates a random unique ID, stores that unique ID in a cookie, and then sends that cookie back to the user (or along with the URL depending on your Anonymous Identification configuration).

■ **Note** Anonymous Identification is *not* the same thing as a `SessionID`. Cookie-based Anonymous Identification is persistent and continues to identify the anonymous user over multiple browser sessions. URL-based Anonymous Identification only works as long as the URL contains the unique ID.

Each time the anonymous user requests a page from your site, the unique identifier accompanies the request. ASP.NET then uses the unique identifier to acquire the appropriate profile information for the anonymous user, even though they have never authenticated. ASP.NET stores profile information as though the anonymous user was actually an authenticated user, using the auto-generated ID as a username.

By default, Anonymous Identification is not enabled. To enable Anonymous Identification, set the enabled attribute of the `<anonymousIdentification>` section in `Web.config` to true, as shown in Listing 6-9.

Listing 6-9. *Enabling Anonymous Identification*

```
<configuration>
    ...
    <system.web>
        ...
        <anonymousIdentification enabled="true" />
        ...
    </system.web>
</configuration>
```

You can also configure a number of other Anonymous Identification settings if you so desire, but you can normally just enable the feature without any additional configuration required.

Table 6-4 outlines the various configuration options for the `<anonymousIdentification>` element if you happen to need it.

Table 6-4. `<anonymousIdentification>` *Section Attribute Descriptions*

Attribute Name	Default Value	Description
`enabled`	`False`	True if Anonymous Identification is enabled.
`cookieless`	`UseDeviceProfile`	Anonymous Identification can store a user's unique ID in a cookie or as a query string value. The query string is widely supported but often results in the unique ID being lost during navigation. Cookies are more reliable, but security-conscious users may disable cookie support. The cookieless attribute has four settings that allow you to configure how Anonymous Identification should store the unique ID:

cookieless Value	Description
`UseCookies`	Anonymous Identification always uses cookies. If the browser does not support cookies or cookies have been disabled, then the user will not be identified appropriately.
`UseUri`	Anonymous Identification always stores the unique ID in the query string and does not attempt to use cookie. This is good if your target users normally have cookies disabled or are using older browsers that do not support cookies.
`AutoDetect`	Browsers send information identifying the type and version of the browser, and ASP.NET maintains a repository of browser types, versions, and the features they support. If ASP.NET knows, based on that repository, that the browser supports cookies, then ASP.NET probes the browser to determine if cookies are enabled. If cookies are enabled, then ASP.NET writes the unique ID to the cookie. Otherwise, ASP.NET writes the unique ID to the query string.
`UseDeviceProfile`	This works similarly to `AutoDetect`, but the decision to use cookies is solely based on ASP.NET's browser feature repository. ASP.NET does not probe to check whether cookies are enabled. If the browser is known to support cookies, but the user has disabled cookies, the user will not be identified appropriately.

Table 6-4. `<anonymousIdentification>` *Section Attribute Descriptions (Continued)*

Attribute Name	Default Value	Description
`cookieName`	`.ASPXANONYMOUS`	Defines the name of the cookie that contains the user's unique ID. If you are running multiple applications on a single server, and each one requires its own Anonymous Identification cookie, then you'll need to change the name of this cookie for each individual application to avoid issues with overwriting the unique ID.
`cookiePath`	`/`	Defines the path in your application past which authentication cookies should be sent. For example, if you specify `/Protected/` as the path, then cookies are only sent to your application if the user requests something in the `/Protected/` folder or a subfolder of the `/Protected/` folder. Be wary of using this setting because case-sensitivity issues may result in a browser not sending the cookie.
`cookieProtection`	`All`	Defines the protection placed on Forms Authentication cookies. The `cookieProtection` attribute has four different settings that allow you to configure how to protect the authentication cookie:

cookieProtection Value	Description
`None`	Cookies are not validated or encrypted. This has a slight performance benefit, but it means that malicious users could read and/or alter cookie information. Only consider using this option if your application requires SSL (HTTPS), because cookies are encrypted along with all other communications over SSL connections.
`Validation`	Creates a MAC by hashing the cookie data using a validation key. The resulting MAC hash is then appended to the cookie data. When ASP.NET receives the cookie on a subsequent request, it hashes the cookie data using the same validation key and checks the result against the MAC hash in the cookie. If both items match, the data in the cookie has not been altered, and the cookie is considered valid.
`Encryption`	Cookie data is encrypted using DES or Triple-DES encryption and stored in the cookie. On subsequent requests, ASP.NET decrypts the cookie data. Validation is not used in this scenario, so the cookie may be susceptible to some attacks. You specify the encryption algorithm in the `<machineKey>` element in `Machine.config` or `Web.config`.
`All`	Applies both `Validation` and `Encryption` to the cookie. `All` is the most secure option and is therefore both the recommended and the default option as well.

Attribute Name	Default Value	Description
cookieRequireSSL	False	Defines whether an SSL connection is required to send the authentication cookie. When set to True, ASP.NET informs the browser that the cookie should only be sent over a secure connection.
cookieSliding Expiration	False	Conventional logic dictates that cookie timeouts should be reset on every request. Using the default 30-minute timeout as a guide, this means that if a user first accesses a page at 12:00 and then again at 12:10, the ticket timeout will not occur until 12:40. Such is not the case because ASP.NET is optimized to reduce cookie setting to lessen network traffic and to avoid accosting users who have cookie alerts enabled. By default, ASP.NET only resets the timeout when more than half the timeout time has passed. So, if a user first accesses a page at 12:00 and then again at 12:10, that user is still subject to a timeout at 12:30. If the user accesses the page past the halfway mark, then the timeout period is reset. For example, if the user first accesses the page at 12:00 and then again at 12:20, the timeout is set to 12:50. You can force ASP.NET to reset the timeout on each request by setting the slidingExpiration attribute to True.
domain		Defines the domain for which the cookie is valid. Before the browser requests a page, it checks to see if any cookies match the domain and path of the request. If so, it sends that cookie along with the request.

When to Use Anonymous Identification

Anonymous Identification should be used when you want to track profile information for a user before the user is authenticated. So, if you expect users to visit different areas of your website before logging in, you should consider using Anonymous Identification to track them in the interim.

One of the most common scenarios in which Anonymous Identification is used is for shopping cart applications. Most customers hate being forced to create an account before they can shop for products, so they should remain anonymous until the checkout process. During the checkout process, they either need to log in using an existing account or create a new one, at which point they become authenticated users.

■ **Tip** When an anonymous user logs in and becomes an authenticated user, the anonymous profile does not automatically turn into the authenticated profile. ASP.NET acquires the profile for the authenticated user (it may be a new or an existing profile) and, for a brief moment, the user has two profiles. ASP.NET then raises the MigrateAnonymous event, which you handle in Global.asax. This event allows you to port over any profile settings from the anonymous profile to the authenticated profile.

Drawbacks of Anonymous Identification

Anonymous Identification causes a few side effects that you should be aware of before you decide to enable it. Most of the side effects are very minor, but after you know what they are, you can decide how greatly they will impact your application.

The main cause of these side effects is that the unique ID generated by ASP.NET can easily be lost or dissociated from an anonymous user. The best-case scenario for the Anonymous Identification cookie is that the anonymous user always accesses your site from the same computer and never clears the cookie cache. If it always worked out this way, then Anonymous Identification would be virtually flawless. Unfortunately, users are likely to visit your site from their home computers, work computers, or their friends' computers. Some users delete their cookies on a regular basis. Other uses have cookies disabled entirely. Even registered users are considered anonymous until they actually log in. And with the growing trend of providing computer terminals at airports, hotels, cyber cafés, and libraries, you are likely to run into the issues that face anonymous profiles.

Accuracy Issues

An anonymous user logging in to your site from multiple locations ends up with multiple anonymous profiles, one for each location. Because each profile is tracked separately, you really only get to look at half the information on that person. The accuracy of anonymous profiles therefore depends on users always using the same computers and never clearing their cookie caches. Authenticated users do not have this issue because they use the same profile each time they log in.

Dissociated Profiles

While discussing accuracy issues, you saw that a user can have multiple active profiles. The possibility also exists for an anonymous user to have dissociated profiles. When the identification cookie is sent to the browser, it represents the only link between the anonymous user and the profile stored in the database. If that cookie is lost, the association between that user and the profile is effectively gone forever. The profile remains in the database, but it can no longer be accessed. This results in wasted disk space.

Disk Space Usage and Performance

Anonymous Identification ultimately results in the creation of extraneous profile records. This, in turn, wastes disks space and forces your database to search through more "junk" while looking for relevant profile information. Disk space issues will be most noticeable when you are hosting your site with an ISP that limits your database space, and performance issues will be most noticeable when you are running your application on slower hardware, or if you are trying to support a massive user base. Otherwise, the disk space and performance issues should be negligible.

■ **Tip** You can use the `ProfileManager` object discussed earlier to delete inactive profiles.

Defining Anonymous Profile Properties

By default, profile properties do not allow anonymous users write access. Attempting to do so will result in an exception. If you want a property to be write-accessible to an anonymous user, then Anonymous Identification should be enabled, and you must specifically mark that property as being an anonymous property in `Web.config`.

Listing 6-10 shows how an anonymous property named `PageHits` and a normal property named `CustomerName` would appear in `Web.config`.

Listing 6-10. *Defining Anonymous Profile Properties*

```
<configuration>
  ...
  <system.web>
    ...
    <anonymousIdentification enabled="true" />
    <profile>
      <properties>
        <add name="CustomerName" defaultValue="Valued Customer" type="String" />
        <add name="PageHits" type="Int64" allowAnonymous="True" />
        <add name="LastAdDate" type="DateTime" allowAnonymous="True" />
      </properties>
    </profile>
    ...
  </system.web>
</configuration>
```

■ **Note** The phrase *anonymous profile property* may seem to indicate that the property is only used for anonymous users, but that is not the case. Anonymous properties are used for both anonymous and authenticated users. Their name simply indicates that anonymous users have write access to the property.

Avoiding Anonymous Write Exceptions with IsAnonymous

Because anonymous users only have write access to anonymous properties, you need to avoid accidentally writing to nonanonymous properties with an anonymous user. The `IsAnonymous` property of the `Profile` object returns a Boolean value indicating whether or not the current user is an anonymous user, so you can use it to section off your nonanonymous profile properties in the following manner:

```
If Not Profile.IsAnonymous Then

    'Set nonanonymous profile properties in this If block
    Profile.CustomerName = GetCustomerName()

End If

'Set anonymous profile properties outside of the If block
Profile.PageHits += 1
```

As long as you cordon off nonanonymous profile properties using `Profile.IsAnonymous`, you should never run into a write exception.

The Importance of Default Property Values

Anonymous users cannot write to normal properties, but they can read from them. This is why default values for profile properties, especially normal properties, are so important. Initially, a profile property is populated with a default value. If the anonymous user cannot write to the property, then that property always contains the default value. So, you should always specify a sensible, generic default value for your normal properties.

This next example in Listing 6-11 should help to clarify. Assume that you want to output a message that uses the `CustomerName` property in your profile. The message will be something to the effect of "Dear [CustomerName], thank you for visiting our site!" `CustomerName` is a normal property, so anonymous users cannot write to it. If you do not specify a default value, then the message for an anonymous user will read "Dear , thank you for visiting our site!" This is definitely not a sentence that will win over the hearts of your customers. In fact, it will look like your site is faking the personalization experience and failing miserably at it.

If you specify a default value for the `CustomerName` property, then you can easily alleviate the grammatical mess. It should be something generic, but something that would make sense in most contexts where `CustomerName` will be used. The phrase "Valued Customer" seems like a good option.

Listing 6-11. *Defining Default Values*

```
<configuration>
  ...
  <system.web>
    ...
    <anonymousIdentification enabled="true" />
    <profile>
      <properties>
        <add name="CustomerName" type="String" defaultValue="Valued Customer" />
        <add name="PageHits" type="Int64" allowAnonymous="True" />
        <add name="LastAdDate" type="DateTime" allowAnonymous="True" />
      </properties>
    </profile>
    ...
  </system.web>
</configuration>
```

Well, at least it's better than an empty string. With the default value in place, anonymous users see "Dear Valued Customer, thank you for visiting our site!"

Default values are also important for authenticated users, as they will run into the same issue as anonymous users if the property has not yet been set. But they are extremely important for anonymous users.

Creating Profile Migration Code

When dealing with both anonymous users and authenticated users, there is the possibility that an anonymous user can log in and become an authenticated user. When this occurs, ASP.NET raises the `MigrateAnonymous` event. Inside the `MigrateAnonymous` event, two profiles exist: one belonging to the anonymous user and one belonging to the authenticated user. The event gives you a chance to copy profile values from the anonymous profile to the authenticated profile so they are not lost.

At first, you might think that the anonymous profile should just overwrite the authenticated profile, but that could result in loss of data. An anonymous user does not necessarily represent a user that has never been to your site before. An anonymous user may be someone who has been to your site, who has an account, and who has a profile, but who has not yet logged in. Take the shopping cart, for example. An existing user may come to your website and begin shopping. When the user goes to check out, he is asked to log in. When he does, his anonymous profile contains all the shopping cart information, and his authenticated profile contains all the personal information. If you were to simply copy over the authenticated profile, you would lose some fairly important information. So, you need to write profile migration code to get important data from the anonymous profile info the authenticated profile without overwriting existing data in the authenticated profile.

When an anonymous user authenticates, the `Profile_MigrateAnonymous` event handler in `Global.asax` is executed. You'll need to place your profile migration code in this procedure. For the next example in Listing 6-12, assume that your profile object has properties named `PageHits` and `LastAdDate`.

Listing 6-12. `MigrateAnonymous` *Event Handler Example*

```
'***************************************************************
Sub Profile_MigrateAnonymous(ByVal sender As Object,
                             ByVal e As ProfileMigrateEventArgs)

        Dim AnonymousProfile As ProfileCommon = Profile.GetProfile(e.AnonymousId)

        'Add the PageHits Values Together
        Profile.PageHits += AnonymousProfile.PageHits

        'Replace LastAdDate If More Recent
        If Profile.LastAdDate < AnonymousProfile.LastAdDate Then
            Profile.LastAdDate = AnonymousProfile.LastAdDate
        End If

End Sub
```

Before you can migrate data from the anonymous profile into the authenticated profile, you need to get a reference to the anonymous profile. This is accomplished by calling `Profile.GetProfile(e.AnonymousId)` and storing the resulting value in the `AnonymousProfile` variable. The authenticated profile is accessible via the `Profile` object. Next, you have to determine the most appropriate way to migrate data.

The `TotalPageHits` property represents the total number of pages this user has visited on the site. Because it represents a running total, it makes sense to add the values from the `Profile` and the `AnonymousProfile` together. If the user visited 50 pages as an authenticated user and then 5 pages as an anonymous user, you would definitely want the final `TotalPageHits` value to equal 55.

The `LastAdDate` property represents the last time the user was shown an advertisement. This profile property ensures that users are only accosted with full-page ads once every couple of days. This property should only be migrated over from the anonymous profile if `AnonymousProfile.LastAdDate` is greater than `Profile.LastAdDate`. This ensures that the most recent ad date will be used so that the customer is not accidentally shown another advertisement too early.

Basically, you need to analyze each profile property that has the `allowAnonymous` parameter set to `True`, and determine the best way that anonymous data should be merged with authenticated data. This may require that you append, add, subtract, average, or overwrite data, depending on what you are storing and why.

Creating a Simple Targeted Advertisement

Now that you know how to work with basic profile properties, you can create a simple targeted advertisement. Many websites have a ton of content, but most of that content can easily be categorized. A sports news site, for instance, may have thousands of stories, but those stories most likely fall into a category such as baseball, football, basketball, hockey, and so on.

If someone is always reading about baseball, chances are that person is a baseball fan. If a person is always reading about football, chances are that person is a football fan. This is important information, especially if you are selling sports-related items. You would prefer that an autographed basketball ended up on a basketball fan's screen instead of a hockey fan's screen. This is where *profile properties* come into play.

If you haven't already, go ahead and create a new web project in which to store the examples from this chapter. Or you can opt to open the sample application for this chapter, available from the Source Code area of the Apress website (http://www.apress.com), and just follow along.

Defining Profile Properties to Track Content Preferences

When you have categorized content, you can easily create profile properties to track which content categories a user is visiting most often. Let's continue with the sports site analogy, and say that your site really focuses on four main content areas: baseball, basketball, football, and hockey. You would then need to create four different profile properties to track page hits in each of those categories as shown in Listing 6-13.

Listing 6-13. *Content Tracking Properties*

```
<properties>
    <group name="CategoryTracking">
        <add name="Baseball" type="Int32" allowAnonymous="true"/>
        <add name="Basketball" type="Int32" allowAnonymous="true"/>
        <add name="Football" type="Int32" allowAnonymous="true"/>
        <add name="Hockey" type="Int32" allowAnonymous="true"/>
    </group>
</properties>
```

For organizational purposes, the four profile properties used to track content preferences have been created in a profile group named `CategoryTracking`. Notice that they are all anonymous properties, so you can still track content preferences for nonauthenticated users. After you have defined the profile properties, you can start using them to track user behavior.

Building the Targeted Advertisement Example Page

Obviously, you cannot build out hundreds of pages worth of content for this example, so you just have to fake it instead. You'll be creating a page with a series of link buttons and labels. Each link button will be named for a category: baseball, basketball, football, and hockey. Each time a user clicks one of the link buttons, the corresponding profile property that counts page hits in that category is incremented. The labels display the total number of hits each category has received.

Create a new page in your web project named `TargetedAdExample.aspx`. You need to add four link buttons, four labels, and an image control to the page. Place one link button and one label together on a line, and separate each line with a break. Under the arrangement of link buttons and labels, add the image control. Use Table 6-5 to help you set up the properties for these controls.

Table 6-5. *Properties for* `LinkButtons` *and* `Labels` *on the* `TargetedAdExample.aspx` *Page*

Control Type	ID	Text	ImageUrl
LinkButton	lnkBaseball	Baseball	
LinkButton	lnkBasketball	Basketball	
LinkButton	lnkFootball	Football	
LinkButton	lnkHockey	Hockey	
Label	lblBaseball	<empty>	
Label	lblBasketball	<empty>	
Label	lblFootball	<empty>	
Label	lblHockey	<empty>	
Image	imgAd		~/ProductImages/ Baseball.jpg

After you've placed all those link buttons and labels on your page, add the code in Listing 6-14 to the code-behind page.

Listing 6-14. *Tracking Content Preferneces*

```
'***************************************************************************
Sub lnkBaseball_Click(ByVal sender As Object, ByVal e As System.EventArgs) _
  Handles lnkBaseball.Click
    Profile.CategoryTracking.Baseball += 1
End Sub

'***************************************************************************
Sub lnkBasketball_Click(ByVal sender As Object, _
  ByVal e As System.EventArgs)  Handles lnkBasketball.Click
    Profile.CategoryTracking.Basketball += 1
End Sub

'***************************************************************************
Sub lnkFootball_Click(ByVal sender As Object, _
  ByVal e As System.EventArgs) Handles lnkFootball.Click
    Profile.CategoryTracking.Football += 1
End Sub

'***************************************************************************
Sub lnkHockey_click(ByVal sender As Object, ByVal e As System.EventArgs) _
  Handles lnkHockey.Click
    Profile.CategoryTracking.Hockey += 1
End Sub
```

These procedures effectively simulate page visits by incrementing the appropriate profile properties when a link button is clicked. Now you just need to implement the logic required to display different advertisements based on these profile properties. That is taken care of in the `Page_PreRender` method as shown in Listing 6-15.

Listing 6-15. *Adjusting Content Based on Content Preferences*

```
'***************************************************************************
Private Sub Page_PreRender(ByVal sender As Object,
                           ByVal e As System.EventArgs) Handles Me.PreRender

    With Profile.CategoryTracking

        'Determine which image to display
        If .Baseball >= .Basketball And _
            .Baseball >= .Football And _
              .Baseball >= .Hockey Then
            imgAd.ImageUrl = "~/ProductImages/Baseball.jpg"
        ElseIf .Basketball >= .Football And _
```

```
            .Basketball >= .Hockey Then
            imgAd.ImageUrl = "~/ProductImages/Basketball.jpg"
        ElseIf .Football >= .Hockey Then
            imgAd.ImageUrl = "~/ProductImages/Football.jpg"
        Else
            imgAd.ImageUrl = "~/ProductImages/Hockey.jpg"
        End If

        'Use labels to display hit counts next to each link button
        Me.lblBaseball.Text = String.Format("({0})", .Baseball)
        Me.lblBasketball.Text = String.Format("({0})", .Basketball)
        Me.lblFootball.Text = String.Format("({0})", .Football)
        Me.lblHockey.Text = String.Format("({0})", .Hockey)

    End With

End Sub
```

The `Page_PreRender` method has two main sections. The first section uses the `CategoryTracking` profile properties to determine which content category has the highest hit count and displays the image associated with that category. Granted, it's not the world's most elaborate algorithm, but it gets the point across.

The second section just outputs the number of hits each content category has. These numbers are displayed next to the link buttons for each content category. This helps when you are trying to figure out which link to click so you can see the advertisement change. Go ahead and run the `TargetedAdExample.aspx` page and see how clicking on different content categories result in a targeted advertisement at the bottom of the screen.

The Shopping Cart Custom Property

Profiles are not limited to primitive .NET data types such as integers, strings, or dates. You can actually store entire objects in a user profile, although working with objects requires a bit more finesse than working with native data types. One of the most common scenarios where you will want to store an object in a profile is a shopping cart application. Storing the shopping cart in the profile allows customers to shop, close their browser, and return to your site at a later time with all their items still intact. In this section, you'll implement a very basic shopping cart and store it in a user profile property.

■ **Note** This entire shopping cart example is located in the Chapter 6 sample application in the Source Code area of the Apress website. You may want to use the sample application for reference as you continue through this section.

Creating the Shopping Cart

The shopping cart you'll be implementing for this example is meant for demonstration purposes only and is not meant to be a full-fledged shopping cart component. You'll definitely want to create a more robust shopping cart for your own applications or purchase a third-party shopping cart that works with ASP.NET 2.0.

Creating the ShoppingCart Project

You'll be creating the shopping cart components in a new assembly named `ShoppingCart`, so you need to add a new class library to your web project. To do so, click on **File ➤ Add ➤ New Project**. The **Add New Project** dialog box appears. Select **Class Library** for the template and name the new project `ShoppingCart`. Click on the **OK** button. A new class library project named `ShoppingCart` is added to your solution.

The Product Class

The `Product` class is designed to store information about a product after it has been added to the cart. This example includes the product ID, product name, unit price, and quantity. If you are developing your own shopping cart application, you may also want to include properties to handle tax, color, size, discounts, and so on. Add a new class named `Product` to the `ShoppingCart` project and place the code in Listing 6-16 in the new file.

Listing 6-16. `ShoppingCart.Product` *Class*

```
<Serializable()> Public Class Product

    '***************************************************************************
    Private _productId As String
    Private _productName As String
    Private _unitPrice As Decimal
    Private _quantity As Integer

    '***************************************************************************
    Public Sub New(ByVal ProductID As String, ByVal ProductName As String, _
                   ByVal UnitPrice As Decimal, ByVal Quantity As Integer)
        _productId = ProductID
        _productName = ProductName
        _unitPrice = UnitPrice
        _quantity = Quantity
    End Sub

    '***************************************************************************
    Public Property ProductId() As String
        Get
            Return _productId
        End Get
        Set(ByVal value As String)
```

```
            _productId = value
        End Set
    End Property

    '***************************************************************************
    Public Property ProductName() As String
        Get
            Return _productName
        End Get
        Set(ByVal value As String)
            _productName = value
        End Set
    End Property

    '***************************************************************************
    Public Property UnitPrice() As Decimal
        Get
            Return _unitPrice
        End Get
        Set(ByVal value As Decimal)
            _unitPrice = value
        End Set
    End Property

    '***************************************************************************
    Public Property Quantity() As Integer
        Get
            Return _quantity
        End Get
        Set(ByVal value As Integer)
            _quantity = value
        End Set
    End Property

    '***************************************************************************
    Public ReadOnly Property TotalPrice() As Decimal
        Get
            Return _unitPrice * _quantity
        End Get
    End Property

End Class
```

The most notable part of this class is actually on the first line. It is marked with the `<Serializable()>` attribute, which lets serialization formatters know that it's safe to serialize the object. Any custom objects that you store directly or indirectly in a profile property must be marked with this attribute because they are serialized before being saved. `Product` objects are indirectly stored in the profile because the Cart object stores a list of products. Thus, serializing the Cart object results in the serialization of all its associated Product objects.

The rest of the code for the class is fairly routine and mostly devoted to defining class properties. The constructor accepts four parameters, named for the four properties in the class, and initializes the class properties using those parameter values. GetTotal returns the total price as calculated by Quantity * UnitPrice, which is helpful for displaying item totals or calculating shopping cart totals.

The Cart Class

The Cart class is responsible for remembering which items a user has added to the cart and for calculating the total price for all those items. In a full-fledged cart, the cart would also be responsible for calculating tax, shipping charges, and customer discounts. Listing 6-17 provides the code for the Cart class.

Listing 6-17. ShoppingCart.Cart *Class*

```
<Serializable()> Public Class Cart
    Inherits CollectionBase

    '*************************************************************************
    Function AddProduct(ByVal value As Product) As Integer
        If value.Quantity = 0 Then Return -1
        For Each P As Product In Me.List
            If P.ProductId = value.ProductId Then
                P.Quantity += value.Quantity
                Exit Function
            End If
        Next
        MyBase.List.Add(value)
    End Function

    '*************************************************************************
    Function AddProduct(ByVal ProductID As String, ByVal PRoductName As String, _
                        ByVal UnitPrice As Decimal, _
                        ByVal Quantity As Integer) As Integer
        AddProduct(New Product(ProductID, PRoductName, UnitPrice, Quantity))
    End Function

    '*************************************************************************
    Default Public Property Products(ByVal index As Integer) As Product
        Get
            Return DirectCast(MyBase.List.Item(index), Product)
        End Get
        Set(ByVal value As Product)
            MyBase.List.Item(index) = value
        End Set
    End Property
```

```
    '****************************************************************************
    Public Function GetTotal() As Decimal
        Dim total As Decimal = 0
        For Each p As Product In MyBase.List
            total += p.TotalPrice()
        Next
        Return total
    End Function

End Class
```

At its heart, the Cart class is an ArrayList that inherits the majority of its functionality from the abstract CollectionBase class. Notice, once again, that this class is marked with the <Serializable()> attribute because it is serialized when the profile is saved.

There are three methods in the Cart class: AddProduct, Products, and GetTotal. As mentioned before, this cart is meant for demonstration purposes only. A full-fledged cart would require a number of other methods to allow customers to remove items from the cart, update quantities, and so on. AddProduct is an overloaded method that allows Product objects to be added to the cart by either passing in a Product object or by specifying the ProductID, ProductName, UnitPrice, and Quantity of the product that is to be added. If the product being added already exists in the cart, the AddProduct method updates the quantity of the existing item instead of adding a new item. The Products property exposes the list of products that have been added to the cart. And the last function, GetTotal, iterates through each product in the product list and calculates the total price for all the items in the shopping cart.

Defining the ShoppingCart Property in Web.Config

Defining a custom profile property is not much different from defining a primitive one. The only real differences are that you have to specify the fully qualified type name of the property (that is, the namespace and class name, as in ShoppingCart.Cart), and you cannot specify a default value. Not being able to specify a default value means that your custom property is initialized to Nothing, so you must take caution not to access properties, methods, or functions on a custom property unless you are certain it has been instantiated.

Listing 6-18 is the code to add the ShoppingCart property to the Profile object. Of course, you need to reference the ShoppingCart assembly from your web application before adding the new property.

Listing 6-18. *Defining the* ShoppingCart *Profile Property*

```
<profile>
    <properties>
        <add name="ShoppingCart" serializeAs="Binary"
            type="ShoppingCart.Cart" allowAnonymous="true" />
    </properties>
</profile>
```

That's all there is to making a custom profile property. Just create the necessary classes, make sure they are marked as Serializable, and specify the fully qualified data type in the property definition in `Web.config`. The `serializeAs` attribute simply tells ASP.NET to serialize the property in binary form. You can also opt to serialize properties as XML or as a string, but binary tends to be faster. With the configuration in place, you can now use the `ShoppingCart` property in your application.

Building a Product Display Component to Add Products to the Cart

A shopping cart needs some mechanism for users to see and add products to the cart. This can be done in a number of different ways, but for this example, you'll be building a user control named `ProductDisplayer.ascx` that displays the picture, title, and price of a product. It also encapsulates all the controls and logic required to add a product to the shopping cart, so you just need to drag the user control onto a web form and set some product parameters, and the user control does the rest. Figure 6-2 shows how the `ProductDisplayer` will appear when it is output to the page.

Figure 6-2. *The* `ProductDisplayer.ascx` *file encapsulates all the logic for displaying an item on a web form and adding a product to the shopping cart. In this image, two such controls are displaying Apress books.*

Graphical Layout and Controls

In your web project, add a new web user control item named `ProductDisplayer`, and make sure it's using a code-behind file. Then replace the content of the `ProductDisplayer.aspx` file with the code in Listing 6-19.

Listing 6-19. `ProductDisplayControl` *Layout*

```
<%@ Control Language="VB" AutoEventWireup="false"
    CompileWith="ProductDisplayer.ascx.vb"
    ClassName="ProductDisplayer_ascx" EnableViewState="false" %>

<div style="text-align:center;width:200px;height:250px;border:1pxsolid black;
  padding:5px;">
    <asp:image Runat="Server" ID="imgProduct"></asp:image><br/><br/>
    <asp:Label Runat="Server" ID="lblProductName" Font-Bold="True"/><br/>
```

```
    <asp:Label Runat="Server" ID="lblPrice"></asp:Label><br/>
    Qnty <asp:TextBox Runat="Server" ID="txtQuantity" Width="27px"
            Height="22px">1</asp:TextBox>
    <asp:Button Runat="Server" ID="btnAdd" Text="Add" OnClick="btnAdd_Click"/>
</div>
```

This content defines the graphical layout of the `ProductDisplayer` and the controls that are available for use in the code-behind file. You can see that there is an image control to hold the product image, labels to hold the product name and product price, a text box to enter the total quantity to add to the cart, and a button to actually add the item to the cart.

Display and Product Adding Logic

The code-behind file for `ProductDisplayer` is responsible for a couple of things. First, it exposes properties that allow the page to tell the control how to display and which product to add to the cart if the Add Product button is clicked. It's also responsible for adding the correct quantity of the specified object to the `ShoppingCart` property. The code is shown in Listing 6-20.

Listing 6-20. `ProductDisplayControl` *Code Behind*

```
Partial Class ProductDisplayer
    Inherits System.Web.UI.UserControl

    '***************************************************************************
    Private _ProductId As String
    Public Property ProductID() As String
        Get
            Return _ProductId
        End Get
        Set(ByVal value As String)
            _ProductId = value
        End Set
    End Property

    '***************************************************************************
    Public Property ProductName() As String
        Get
            EnsureChildControls()
            Return Me.lblProductName.Text
        End Get
        Set(ByVal value As String)
            EnsureChildControls()
            Me.lblProductName.Text = value
        End Set
    End Property

    '***************************************************************************
    Public Property UnitPrice() As Decimal
```

```
        Get
            EnsureChildControls()
            Return CDec(Me.lblPrice.Text)
        End Get
        Set(ByVal value As Decimal)
            EnsureChildControls()
            Me.lblPrice.Text = FormatCurrency(value, 2)
        End Set
    End Property


    '****************************************************************************
    Public Property ImageUrl() As String
        Get
            EnsureChildControls()
            Return Me.imgProduct.ImageUrl
        End Get
        Set(ByVal value As String)
            EnsureChildControls()
            Me.imgProduct.ImageUrl = value
        End Set
    End Property

    '****************************************************************************
    Private ReadOnly Property Quantity() As Integer
        Get
            EnsureChildControls()
            If IsNumeric(Me.txtQuantity.Text) Then _
                Return CInt(Me.txtQuantity.Text)
            Return 0
        End Get
    End Property


    '****************************************************************************
    Sub btnAdd_Click(ByVal sender As Object, ByVal e As System.EventArgs)

        'Ensure shopping cart object exists before adding products to it
        If Profile.ShoppingCart Is Nothing Then _
            Profile.ShoppingCart = New ShoppingCart.Cart

        Profile.ShoppingCart.AddProduct(ProductID, ProductName, _
                                        UnitPrice, Quantity)
    End Sub

    '****************************************************************************
    Private Sub Page_PreRender(ByVal sender As Object, _
```

```
                                    ByVal e As System.EventArgs) Handles Me.PreRender

        'Return Quantity to Original State
        Me.txtQuantity.Text = "1"
    End Sub

End Class
```

First, let's discuss the two different types of properties this code-behind file exposes. The `ProductID` property is a standard property that uses a private class variable to store its value—nothing special, you've seen it before.

The `ProductName`, `UnitPrice`, `ImageUrl`, and `Quantity` properties, however, use control properties to store their values. Controls that make up a user control are not accessible from the page on which a user control is placed. So, assuming you had a page with a `ProductDisplayer` named `MyProduct`, you *cannot* make the following call:

```
MyProduct.lblProductName.Text = "Some Product"
```

The `lblProductName` control is not accessible from the `MyProduct` user control, so the previous statement won't even compile. But, the public property `ProductName` is accessible from `MyProduct`, so you *can* make the following call:

```
MyProduct.ProductName = "Some Product"
```

This executes the set portion of the `ProductName` property, which in turn saves the value "`Some Product`" to the `lblProductName.Text` property. So the `MyProduct` property is a good workaround for setting up the `lblProductName.Text` property.

One issue you may encounter when using controls to store property values is that the controls may not be instantiated yet, which can lead to null reference exceptions. To avoid this, make sure to call `EnsureChildControls` before you attempt to access a control in the user control. `EnsureChildControls` forces the user control to instantiate its child controls if it has not already done so.

Now it's on to the `btnAdd_Click` procedure, which contains all the logic to add a product to the cart. This procedure first checks to see if the `ShoppingCart` property of the Profile object is set to `Nothing`. Remember that custom objects are initially set to `Nothing` because they do not have a default value. If the `ShoppingCart` property is `Nothing`, the procedure creates a new `Cart` object and stores it in the `ShoppingCart` property. Finally, the procedure adds the item to the cart by calling `AddProduct` and passing in the values it has been set up with for `ProductID`, `ProductName`, `UnitPrice`, and `Quantity`.

Building the Shopping Cart Demo Page

Now that you have your reusable product display component, you can create a miniature shopping cart application to test out the `ShoppingCart` profile property. This application is actually going to display products, allow you to add products to your cart, and display your cart contents all from the same page.

Create a new web form in your web project and name it `ShoppingCartExample.aspx`. Make sure it uses a code-behind file. After you have done that, you are ready to display products on your page.

Displaying Products with the Product User Control

Open the `ShoppingCartExample.aspx` page and create a new table on the page that has four cells. Then, locate the `ProductDisplayer.aspx` file in the Solution Explorer. Drag a `ProductDisplayer` into each cell of your newly created table cells. They will all look a bit rough around the edges, even after you enter property values, but realize that when they are displayed to the user, they will look fine. Figure 6-3 shows how the `ProductDisplayer` appears at design time inside the IDE.

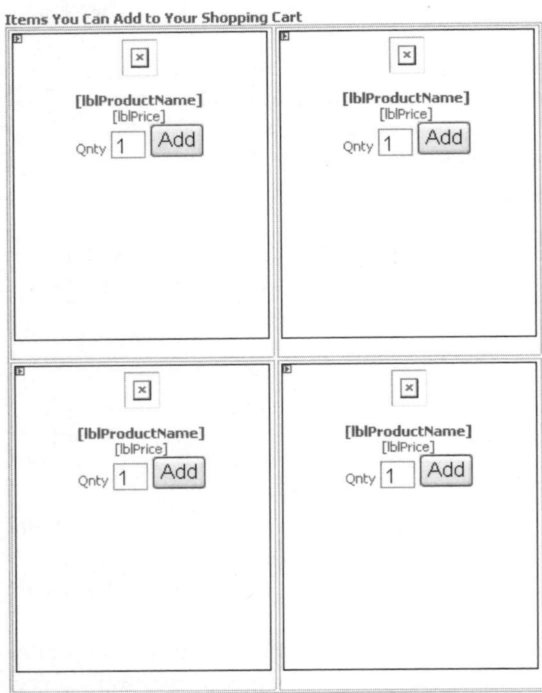

Figure 6-3. `ProductDisplayer` *controls as seen at design time in the Visual Studio IDE*

Now you need to set each `ProductDisplayer` control's `ProductID`, `ImageUrl`, `ProductName`, and `UnitPrice` properties, because these properties tell the `ProductDisplayer` control what image and text to display, and what product to add to the cart. Right-click on the top-left control and select **Properties** from the context menu. Visual Studio's **Properties** window should now be visible, and it should display a list of properties similar to those shown in Figure 6-4.

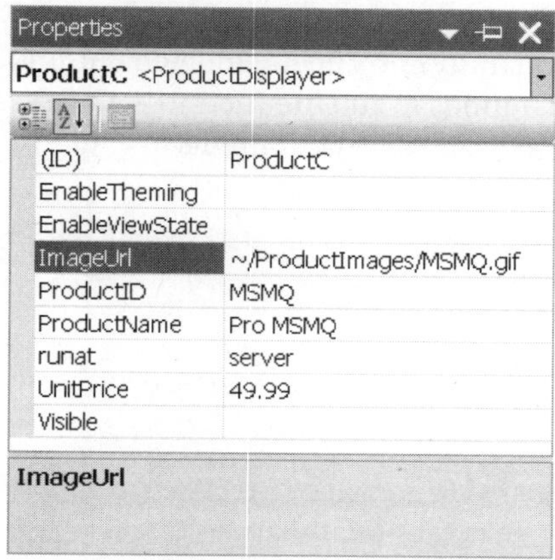

Figure 6-4. *The public properties you defined in the* `ProductDisplayer` *code-behind are displayed in the Properties window when you select a* `ProductDisplayer` *control.*

Use Table 6-6 as a reference for entering properties values for the four `ProductDisplayer` controls. These values are just for demonstration purposes, so feel free to make up your values if you so desire. The images referred to in this table are located in the sample application in the Source Code area of the Apress website.

Table 6-6. *Property Values for* `ProductDisplayer` *Controls on the* `ShoppingCartExample.aspx` *Page*

ID	ImageUrl	ProductID	ProductName	UnitPrice
ProductA	~/ProductImages/ Office2003.gif	Office2003	*Office 2003 Programming*	39.99
ProductB	~/ProductImages/ SharePoint.gif	SharePoint	*Advanced SharePoint*	59.99
ProductC	~/ProductImages/ SQLServer.gif	SQL2005	*Pro SQL Server 2005*	49.99
ProductD	~/ProductImages/ MSMQ.gif	MSMQ	*Pro MSMQ*	49.99

As you enter property values, they are saved in the `ProductDisplayer` tag, as shown in Listing 6-21.

Listing 6-21. `ProductDisplayControl` *Definition on a Web Form*

```
<uc1:ProductDisplayer ID="ProductA" Runat="Server"
    ImageUrl="~/ProductImages/Office2003Programming.gif"
    ProductID="Office2003"
    ProductName="Office 2003 Programming"
    UnitPrice="39.99"/>
```

When you finish, run the page. If you entered valid images URLs, you should see four product images, along with their product names, prices, quantity entry fields, and Add buttons (similar to Figure 6-5). You can click on the different Add buttons to add products to your cart, but you'll quickly realize that it's not much fun because you can't see the contents of your shopping cart.

Figure 6-5. `ProductDisplayer` *controls as seen in the browser*

Displaying the Contents of the Shopping Cart

Now that you can add products to your shopping cart, you need a way to see a listing of the cart's content. You can do this fairly easily by binding a `GridView` control to the `ShoppingCart` property. Most of the real work is in setting up the appropriate bindings on the `GridView` columns.

You'll be adding a `GridView` control to your web form named `gridShoppingCart`. The definition for this control is shown in Listing 6-22. It does not contain any formatting elements because it really clutters up the page in print. If you need to review the formatting elements, feel free to look at the sample application in the Source Code area of the Apress website.

Listing 6-22. *Creating the Layout for the Shopping Cart Display*

```
<asp:GridView ID="gridShoppingCart" Runat="server" AutoGenerateColumns="False"
  EnableViewState="False" ShowFooter="True" >

    <EmptyDataTemplate>
```

```
      There are no items in your shopping cart.  Please add some!
    </EmptyDataTemplate>

    <Columns>

      <asp:TemplateField HeaderText="Product Name">
        <ItemTemplate>
          <%#Container.DataItem.ProductName%>
        </ItemTemplate>
        <FooterTemplate>
          <B>Total</B>
        </FooterTemplate>
      </asp:TemplateField>

      <asp:BoundField HeaderText="Product ID" DataField="ProductID" />
      <asp:BoundField HeaderText="Unit Price" DataField="UnitPrice" />
      <asp:BoundField HeaderText="Quantity" DataField="Quantity" />

      <asp:TemplateField HeaderText="Total">
        <ItemTemplate>
          <%#FormatCurrency(Container.DataItem.TotalPrice, 2)%>
        </ItemTemplate>
        <FooterTemplate>
          <B><%=FormatCurrency(Profile.ShoppingCart.GetTotal(), 2)%></B>
        </FooterTemplate>
      </asp:TemplateField>

    </Columns>

  </asp:GridView>
```

One of the new features of the `GridView` control is the `EmptyDataTemplate`. This template allows you to specify content that should be displayed when the `GridView` control binds to an empty data source. In the preceding code, `EmptyDataTemplate` just informs the user that there are no items in the shopping cart and that the user should add some.

You should also note that the first and last columns in this `GridView` are `TemplateField` columns. Both of these columns require footers, so it was necessary to use a `TemplateField` column (which supports footers) instead of a `BoundField` column (which does not). The first column's footer just outputs bolded text that reads **Total**. The last column's footer outputs the total dollar amount of products in the shopping cart. The rest of the columns just output their bound property values. Figure 6-6 shows an approximation of what the `GridView` looks like after you add in some formatting.

Items in Your Shopping Cart

Product Name	Product ID	Unit Price	Quantity	Total
Office 2003 Programming	Office2003	39.99	2	$79.98
Advanced SharePoint	SharePoint	59.99	1	$59.99
Pro SQL Server 2005	SQL2005	49.99	1	$49.99
Pro MSMQ	MSMQ	49.99	1	$49.99
Total				$239.95

Figure 6-6. *This shows the formatted version of the* `gridShippingCart` *control after it has been data bound to the* `ShoppingCart` *property.*

After you define `GridView`, you need to bind the grid to your shopping cart data. You accomplish this in the `Page_PreRender` event handler as shown in Listing 6-23.

Listing 6-23. *Binding Cart Data to the Grid*

```
'**************************************************************************
Private Sub Page_PreRender(ByVal sender As Object, _
  ByVal e As System.EventArgs) Handles Me.PreRender
        Me.gridShoppingCart.DataSource = Profile.ShoppingCart
        Me.gridShoppingCart.DataBind()
End Sub
```

Now you can revisit the `ShoppingCartExample.aspx` page and watch as products are added to your cart and quantities are edged upward. Now, of course, you need a way to clear items from the cart.

Clearing the Shopping Cart

In theory, you could support removing individual items from the shopping cart. But, this is just a demonstration application and clearing the entire shopping cart is a much simpler task. To do so, add a link button to the `ShoppingCartExample.aspx` page, right under the `gridShoppingCart` control:

```
<asp:LinkButton ID="linkClearShoppingCart" Runat="server"
    OnClick="linkClearShoppingCart_Click">Clear Shopping Cart</asp:LinkButton>
```

Then add the code in Listing 6-24 to the code-behind file.

Listing 6-24. *Clearing the Shopping Cart*

```
'**************************************************************************
Sub linkClearShoppingCart_Click(ByVal sender As Object,
  ByVal e As System.EventArgs) Handles linkClearShoppingCart.Click

    If Not Profile.ShoppingCart Is Nothing Then Profile.ShoppingCart.Clear()

End Sub
```

When you click on the **Clear Shopping Cart** link button, all the products in the shopping cart are removed, and you can start adding products anew.

Profile Migration with the Shopping Cart

Remember that the `ShoppingCart` profile property is an anonymous property. That means users can add items to their shopping cart before they log in, and they may have items in their anonymous shopping cart and in their authenticated shopping cart when they do. Thus, you may need to do some profile migration.

In the example in Listing 6-25, you will be merging the contents of both carts together, which makes for a good demonstration. In reality, however, you would probably want to divert users to a page to inform them that their old shopping cart has items in it. You could then allow them to discard the old items, retain them, or choose which old items to retain and which ones to discard. But I will leave that up to you.

Listing 6-25. *Migrating Cart Data to the Authenticated Profile*

```
'*************************************************************************
Sub Profile_MigrateAnonymous(ByVal sender As Object,
                             ByVal e As ProfileMigrateEventArgs)

    Dim AnonymousProfile As ProfileCommon = Profile.GetProfile(e.AnonymousId)

    If AnonymousProfile.ShoppingCart Is Nothing Then Exit Sub
    If Profile.ShoppingCart Is Nothing Then _
        Profile.ShoppingCart = New ShoppingCart.Cart()

    For Each p As ShoppingCart.Product In AnonymousProfile.ShoppingCart
        Profile.ShoppingCart.AddProduct(p)
    Next

End Sub
```

The first thing this migration code does is acquire a reference to the anonymous profile. Then it checks to see if the anonymous profile even has a valid shopping cart. If not, it exits the procedure because no products need to be added to the authenticated profile. If there is an anonymous shopping cart, then the procedure knows that it must transfer items from the anonymous shopping cart into the authenticated shopping cart. Thus, it checks to make sure an authenticated cart exists before trying to make that transfer. If not, it will create one. Then the procedure iterates through each item in the anonymous cart and adds it to the authenticated cart, effectively merging them.

You can test out this profile migration code by adding a login control on the `ShoppingCartExample.aspx` page and creating a registered user for the website. Log in, add some items to your cart, and then log out. Then add some items to your cart as an anonymous user and log back in. You'll notice that the items you selected as an anonymous user are merged with the items you selected as an authenticated user.

Summary

This chapter has exposed you to a number of profile topics such as properties, profile groups, Anonymous Identification, and even profile migration. You were able to implement a targeted advertisement using profiles and even store an entire shopping cart in a custom property. You should have a solid enough foundation with profiles at this point to feel comfortable implementing some fairly advanced personalization tasks.

CHAPTER 7

Building Portals Using the Web Parts Framework

Portals have become an increasingly popular method for consolidating information from a variety of sources and for allowing people to customize the content and layout of websites and web applications. Public websites such as MSN and Yahoo! use portals to display links to and summaries of world news, technology, politics, investing, weather, traffic, shopping, and entertainment. When a particular article or category looks interesting, visitors can click on a link to drill into the actual content. The portal acts as a gateway, or starting point, for navigating the site. Both MSN and Yahoo! also allow you to customize the portal to your own personal liking. Never want to see political news? Just remove that section from the page. Want to see the technology section appear before the sports section? Just move it up. Need your daily comics? Add them to the page. The website remembers the content and layout changes you made when you return for a truly customized experience.

Corporate portals are also gaining popularity because they can help organize business information. Employees can go to the corporate portal to access information about customers, products, inventory, accounts receivable, sales pipeline, shipping, payroll, benefits, job openings, and company policies. Add the ability for employees to customize the portal for their particular role and tasks, and you can see the power of the technology. This is assuming, of course, that you have the time and money to build it. Building a portal is normally a costly endeavor because of the shear complexity of the project, which keeps many businesses from embracing the technology. Each page has to remember which users want what content in which location. There needs to be an editor to allow users to add, remove, relocate, and set custom properties for content on a page. And don't forget that the database must be designed and implemented to store all this information on a user-by-user basis. It seems like a fairly daunting task until you realize that ASP.NET 2.0 has an entire framework that takes care of all the hard stuff.

One of the most exciting additions to ASP.NET 2.0 is the Web Parts Framework, which allows you to build highly customizable portal applications without having to worry about all the little details that normally go into a portal. In this chapter, you'll explore how to use Web Parts in detail. The first two sections of the chapter contain a lot of theory and reference material, and the last two sections contain more detailed code examples. Feel free to jump around to find what you need:

- *Web Parts Framework Concepts:* Presents a high-level overview of Web Parts concepts including display modes, page scope, authorization, and how users interact with Web Parts on a page.
- *Web Part Interfaces, Classes, and Controls:* Describes the various components in the Web Part framework and how you can use them to complete various tasks.
- *Building Web Parts:* Demonstrates how to build Web Parts as user controls or as custom controls and covers personalizable Web Part properties.
- *Advanced Web Part Topics:* Explains how to create custom Web Part context-menu items, set up Web Part connections that allow Web Parts to communicate with one another, and export Web Part configuration files to ease the setup process for Web Parts with complicated configuration settings.

We'll get started by taking a look at some of the concepts surrounding the Web Parts framework.

Web Parts Framework Concepts

Microsoft created Windows SharePoint Services for Windows Server 2003 to act as a collaboration, document management, and portal framework for IIS. Included in the portal framework was the concept of a Web Part, a standalone component developed in ASP.NET that is capable of running from any page in the portal. Web Parts could be combined to create highly customized portal pages and allowed for a great deal of visual flexibility and personalization features. Because each Web Part is a standalone component, the page architecture was designed in such a way that Web Parts could be moved from one section of a page to another or reordered using a drag-and-drop interface. You could also add new Web Parts to a page or remove existing ones, and even set Web Part properties as desired. SharePoint Services maintained changes on a user-by-user basis, allowing for a truly personalized experience. For users, it was an awesome technology.

Developers, however, quickly found that creating and deploying Web Parts in SharePoint was a painstaking task. I remember having to read for a week before even figuring out where to begin, and the book I read admitted that a successful deployment was a very difficult and error-prone process. SharePoint was also tightly integrated with Active Directory, making it great for intranet applications but not for public-facing sites. And you were pretty much stuck with the look and feel of a SharePoint portal because the page template support was awkward at best. Something definitely needed to change.

Microsoft went back to the drawing board and revamped their portal framework. The result of that endeavor is the Web Parts Framework in ASP.NET 2.0, which was spectacularly implemented this time around. Building Web Parts is as simple as creating a user control or a custom server control. Deploying a Web Part is as easy as dropping the Web Part in a folder and adding the control definition to a Web Part catalog. All the drag-and-drop functionality for moving and reordering Web Parts is automatically added for you simply by dropping a `WebPartManager` control on your page. Because the portal framework is part of ASP.NET, it supports multiple authentication types and gives you complete control over page templates using Master Pages (see Chapter 3).

Note The `WebPartManager` is covered in detail when Web Parts controls are discussed later in this chapter. Every page that uses Web Parts is required to have one (and only one) `WebPartManager` control to coordinate interactions between Web Parts and to manage all the Web Parts settings on the page.

Understand, however, that the Web Parts technologies in ASP.NET 2.0 and SharePoint have not yet merged. They are distinct and very different items. Rumor has it that Microsoft plans to use ASP.NET 2.0 Web Parts in the next release of SharePoint, but for the time being, SharePoint developers have to work in both worlds.

Using the Web Parts Framework in ASP.NET 2.0 is mostly a matter of adding the appropriate controls to the page. Once in place, they handle the majority of the grunt work. You still have to do a little bit of coding, but in the grand scale of building a portal, it's fairly minor. So, let's begin by taking a look at some of the concepts you need to know about when working with Web Parts.

Web Parts in Concept

Any control in ASP.NET can be a Web Part, so nailing down the definition of a Web Part is pretty difficult. Most Web Parts either implement the `IWebPart` interface or derive from the `WebPart` control in the `System.Web.UI.WebCotrols.WebParts` namespace. Controls that do not meet either of these criteria can still participate in the Web Parts Framework because ASP.NET automatically wraps with the `GenericWebPart` class at runtime, giving the control all the basic functionality of a normal Web Part.

Web Parts normally allow individual users to create personalized settings that dictate their appearance and behavior, allowing users to tailor the Web Part functionality to their particular need. How useful would a weather Web Part be if it only told you the forecast for one city? It would be great it if happened to be the city in which you lived, but it would be pretty useless if it wasn't. Allowing users to personalize a weather display Web Part to show a forecast relevant to their home city is critical for its use. The same holds true for many Web Parts. People can also personalize their experience by dynamically adding, removing, and repositioning Web Parts on the page. You'll be glad to know that the Web Parts Framework automatically handles the storage and retrieval of personalized settings using the provider model, which makes your life easier by abstracting you from the implementation details.

Onscreen, a Web Part consists of a title bar, border, menu, and the Web Part content. When you create a Web Part control, you only need to worry about the content because the Web Part Framework automatically generates the title bar, border, and the menu. The menu allows the user to access a list of actions (called *verbs*). By default, each Web Part has a basic set of verbs allowing users to minimize, restore, close, edit, delete, and set up connections for the Web Part. Verbs are display-mode sensitive, so not all verbs appear at all times. You can also create custom verbs for a Web Part if you want the user to have access to additional features in your Web Part via the menu.

Figure 7-1 is an example of a simple Web Part that allows users to search the Apress Web site. The control itself is only composed of an image, a text box, and a button. Take a good look at it to get an idea of the basic Web Part layout.

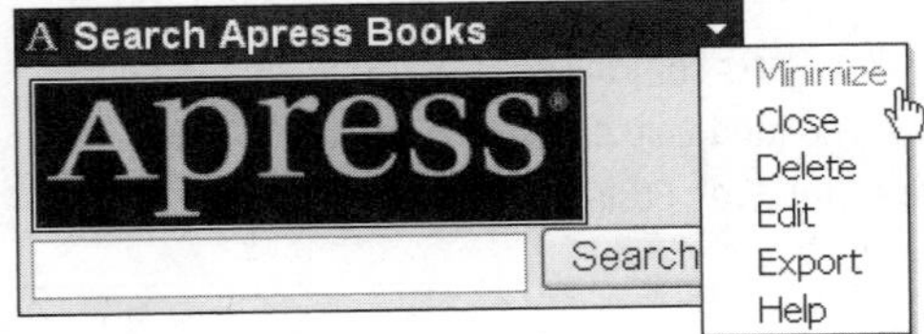

Figure 7-1. *Basic Web Part showing the title bar, border, menu, and content*

Note In the same manner that you have classes and instances, you have Web Parts and Web Part instances. What you, as the developer, create is the actual Web Part itself. Users are interacting with Web Part instances when they add, reposition, edit, or delete Web Parts.

Web Part Connections

As you work through this chapter, you'll see a number of references to Web Part connections. Web Part connections allow Web Parts to communicate important information with one another. You may find this useful when you want one Web Part to change in response to an action on another Web Part. For example, let's say you have a Web Part that allows you to select an employee from a list and a Web Part that displays an employee's photo. You can create a connection between the two and pass the selected employee information from the selector Web Part into the photo Web Part so the photo display changes in response to the currently selected employee.

By default, a Web Part is a standalone component that does not support connections. If you plan on connecting two Web Parts, then you have to create a custom message interface that defines the data passed along the connection, a Provider Web Part that supplies that data, and a Consumer Web Part that uses the data to accomplish some task. And that only allows the Web Parts to support connections; it does not actually create a connection.

A Web Part connection defines the relationship between a Provider Web Part and a Consumer Web Part on a page. In essence, a Web Part connection tells the Web Part Framework to acquire the custom message object from the Provider Web Part and send it to the Consumer Web Part where it can be used to accomplish some task. For a connection to exist between two Web Parts, both of the Web Parts must be present and active on the same page (they may be hidden but cannot be closed). Also understand that a Provider Web Part can participate in many connections, but a Consumer Web Part can only participate in one. This ensures that data is not sent to the Consumer twice, which could result in an accidental overwrite.

Note Creating custom message interfaces, creating Provider and Consumer Web Parts, and setting up static and dynamic Web Part connections are all covered in the "Advanced Web Part Topics" later in this chapter.

Portal Page Display Modes

Although the Web Parts Framework allows people to add, remove, reposition, reorder, and edit Web Parts on a portal page, the majority of people's time will be spent looking at the page content, not manipulating it. As such, a page does not always need to load the components required to drag and drop Web Parts from one place to another, to add new Web Parts from a catalog, or to edit custom properties on a Web Part.

Display modes are simply a way of telling the Web Part Framework what type of functionality the user needs for a particular task. There are five different display modes, each of which exposes a different set of functionality:

- `BrowseDisplayMode`: This mode is designed for browsing a portal page and looking at the page content. In this mode, users may minimize, restore, and close Web Parts.
- `DesignDisplayMode`: This mode allows users to move and reorder Web Parts using a drag-and-drop interface and to delete Web Parts. In this mode, Web Part zones are outlined and have title bars to define where Web Parts may be dropped. Also, if you have configured a Web Part to hide its title bar, the title bar is displayed in this mode to give you access to its menu. You can only switch to this mode if you have defined at least one `WebPartZone` control on the page. A `WebPartZone` is a container (like a `Panel`) that defines a section of the page that displays Web Parts.
- `EditDisplayMode`: This mode has all the functionality found in `DesignDisplayMode` and also enables the Edit verb (menu item) on each Web Part's menu. Users may click on the Edit item from the menu to display any `EditorZone` controls on the page. Editor zones contain controls that allow the user to edit properties Web Parts at runtime. You can only switch to this mode if you have defined at least one `EditorZone` control on the page.
- `CatalogDisplayMode`: This mode has all the functionality found in `DesignDisplayMode` and also displays any Catalog Zones on the page. *Catalog Zones* contain controls that allow the user to add Web Parts to the page. You can only switch to this mode if you have defined at least one `CatalogZone` control on the page.
- `ConnectionDisplayMode`: This mode has all the functionality found in `DesignDisplayMode` and allows users to set up dynamic connections between Web Parts. Because you can add Web Parts dynamically at runtime, you also need a way to dynamically create connections for those added Web Parts. As such, the `ConnectionDisplayMode` exists to let users define those dynamic connections. You can only switch to this mode if you have at least one `ConnectionsZone` on the page.

You can change the page display mode by setting the `DisplayMode` property of the `WebPartManager` control. You'll learn a bit more about the `WebPartManager` control later, but for the time being, know that every page that uses the Web Parts Framework must have one of these controls. Assuming you have a `WebPartManager` control named `WebPartManager1` on the page, you can set the various display modes as shown in Listing 7-1.

Listing 7-1. *Changing Display Modes*

```
'Change to Browse Mode
WebPartManager1.DisplayMode = WebPartManager.BrowseDisplayMode

'Change to Design Mode
WebPartManager1.DisplayMode = WebPartManager.DesignDisplayMode

'Change to Edit Mode
WebPartManager1.DisplayMode = WebPartManager.EditDisplayMode

'Change to Catalog Mode
WebPartManager1.DisplayMode = WebPartManager.CatalogDisplayMode

'Change to Connection Mode
WebPartManager1.DisplayMode = WebPartManager.ConnectDisplayMode
```

■ **Caution** Only authenticated users can access design, edit, catalog, and connection display mode. So make sure your users have logged in before allowing them access to these features. Attempting to change to one of these modes with an unauthenticated user results in an `ArgumentException` being thrown at runtime.

Display mode changes normally come in response to a user action, so you should provide links, buttons, menu options, or some other means of allowing the user to switch between display modes. Just include one of the aforementioned lines of code in the event handler of the control. With that out of the way, let's take a look at zones.

Defining Portal Regions with Zones

Zones are special containers designed to hold specific types of portal controls and to define regions of the page that should be displayed in certain display modes. You use zones to define the page layout and location where certain portal elements should appear. Four different types of zones are used in the Web Parts Framework:

- `WebPartZone`: These zones define the regions where Web Parts may appear on the page, and there can be more than one `WebPartZone` on a page. People can add new Web Parts to a `WebPartZone`, reorder Web Parts within the zone, or drag and drop Web Parts from one zone to another. Web Part zones are always present, but they are not necessarily "visible" in the `BrowseDisplayMode`, and they may appear to be normal content. Other display modes outline the `WebPartZone` and give it a title bar so the region can be easily identified on the page.
- `CatalogZone`: The Catalog Zone exists to give users a way to browse through available Web Parts that may be added to the page, for example, a catalog of Web parts from which users can pick and choose. The Catalog Zone becomes visible when the page enters `CatalogDisplayMode` and can only contain Catalog Part controls. ASP.NET 2.0 has

two Catalog Parts: the DeclarativeCatalogPart and the PageCatalogPart. The DeclarativeCatalogPart allows you to specify a set of Web Parts that the user may dynamically add to a Web Part page. The PageCatalogPart allows users to redisplay Web Parts that exist on the page but are closed. We'll discuss these in more detail later on in this chapter. You cannot switch into CatalogDisplayMode if you do not have a CatalogZone.

- EditorZone: The Editor Zone exists to give users a way to edit the appearance, behavior, layout, and custom properties of a Web Part. Editor zones become visible when the page is in EditDisplayMode and the user has selected a Web Part to edit. When the user first enters edit mode, the EditorZone will not be visible because no Web Part is selected. This zone can only hold Editor Parts, of which there are four types: the AppearanceEditorPart, BehaviorEditorPart, LayoutEditorPart, and PropertyGridEditorPart controls. These editor parts are covered in detail later in this chapter. You must have an EditorZone defined to switch to the EditDisplayMode.
- ConnectionsZone: The Connection Zone exists to give users a way to set up a dynamic connection between a Consumer Web Part that consumes data and the Provider Web Part. The Connection Zone becomes visible when the page is in ConnectionDisplayMode and the user has chosen to modify a Web Part that supports connections. Not all Web Parts support connections, so you may not need to include a Connection Zone in your portal page. This zone automatically creates the controls needed to modify connections for a Web Part, so there are no "Connection Zone parts" with which to work.

Most portal page layouts include multiple Web Part zones because people enjoy having a couple positioning options when adding Web Parts to a page. Technically, you can have multiple Catalog, Editor, and Connection Zones as well. More than likely, however, you'll want to restrict these types of zones to a single instance so users can see their editing, catalog, and connection functionality in a single location instead of having it strewn all over the page.

User and Shared Scope

Authenticated users can edit a Web Parts page in user scope, assuming customization of the Web Parts on that page has not been explicitly disabled by an administrator. Changes made in user scope apply specifically to that user and do not affect the experience of other users. Changes are persisted using the personalization features of the Web Parts Framework and are only retrieved and redisplayed when that particular user accesses the page. Other users do not see those changes because changes made in the user scope are not shared between users. As such, this is the default mode in which the Web Parts Framework operates.

Administrative users can edit a Web Part page in either user scope (their personal scope) or in shared scope. Alterations made in shared scope are visible to all users. Add a Web Part to the page in shared scope, and everyone will see that new Web Part the next time they view the page. Remove a Web Part, and it disappears for everyone. Change properties and the properties change for everyone. The idea behind the shared scope is to give administrators a simple interface for defining the default content and layout of a portal page. We'll explore how to edit the content of a Web Part page a bit later. For now, let's take a look at the shared scope behavior.

Behavior of Shared Scope Items

Although shared scope items affect everyone, that does not necessarily mean that everyone is stuck with those shared scope items. Portal technology is all about personalization, and user scope changes actually take precedence over shared scope items. So you can override the default settings on a Web Part page by editing the page in user scope.

Here is an example of how this situation works. An administrator enters shared scope and adds a new Web Part. As such, that Web Part is now visible to all users who access the page. Roger logs in and visits the portal page. He notices the new Web Part that has been added to the page. After using it for a while, he determines that he does not like the new Web Part and wants to remove it. He switches to design mode, closes the Web Part, and then returns to browse mode. The Web Part does not appear. Even though shared scope is saying to add the item to the page, his user scope is saying hide the item, and his user scope wins out over the shared scope. Individual properties on Web Parts work the same way. User scope settings are applied over the shared scope setting. Even if an administrator goes back and changes a setting, the user scope setting still overrides it.

At first glance, it may seem that this gives the individual user more power than the administrator, but this is not the case. Administrators can set properties on shared Web Parts that make it impossible to hide the Web Part, move the Web Part to another zone, or edit the Web Part. In that case, the user cannot set user scope settings; therefore, the shared scope item has no user scope settings with which to contend. You'll see how to set these types of properties on a Web Control when we discuss the `EditorZone` and Editor Parts in greater detail later on in this chapter.

■ **Tip** Setting a shared scope item to uneditable simply disables user editingfor that item from that point on. Any edits they have already made are still applied. The easiest way to ensure nobody has personal settings on the item is to delete it entirely, and then add it back to the page. This gets rid of any user scope settings that may have existed on the previous item.

Default Content and Immutable Web Parts

Before people make user changes to a page, that page only displays items that were defined in shared scope. Thus, shared scope defines the default content and layout when people first visit a portal page. By default, users are allowed to make user scope changes to shared Web Parts, so default content is helpful for new users because it gives them a starting point from which to make those changes.

Another use of shared scope is to create immutable Web Parts. You can set behavioral properties on a Web Part in shared scope to deny people the ability to close, connect, edit, hide, minimize, or move that Web Part. This is a useful tactic to ensure a specific Web Part always appears on your users' screens. For example, if you have a Web Part that disseminates important company news and you don't want users to be able to remove it from the screen, you can alter its behavioral properties to make it immutable.

Note No behavioral properties can stop a user from reordering Web Parts in a particular zone. If you always want a specific Web Part to appear in a specific location within a zone, you must programmatically check and reposition the Web Part.

Shared Scope Authorization

By default, nobody can enter shared scope to make changes. Any attempt by a user to switch into shared mode without authorization results in an `InvalidOperationException` being thrown. You must explicitly define which users and roles have access to enter into shared scope by adding them to the Web Part authorization section in `Web.config`. The syntax for setting up share scope authorization is analogous to that of creating ASP.NET authorization settings as shown in Listing 7-2.

Listing 7-2. *Authorizing Users and Roles to Enter Shared Scope*

```
<configuration>
  <system.web>
    <webParts>
      <personalization>
        <authorization>
          <deny users="Richard, Anna" verbs="enterSharedScope"/>
          <allow roles="admin" verbs="enterSharedScope"/>
        </authorization>
      </personalization>
    </webParts>
  </system.web>
</configuration>
```

As you can see, the `<authorization>` section is within the `<personalization>` element, which itself is inside the `<webParts>` element. You can allow or deny user access to shared scope by creating `<allow>` or `<deny>` entries for the `enterSharedScope` verb. In this particular example, Richard and Anna are denied access to the shared scope while all users who are part of the `admin` role are allowed access. Remember, order matters when defining authorization items. Even if Richard and Anna are administrators, they will be denied access because the deny rule based on username appears before the allow rule based on role.

Checking Authorization and Toggling Scope

Switching from personal to shared scope requires toggling the scope from the page's `WebPartManager` control. It's also a good idea to check whether or not the current user is authorized to enter shared scope, because attempting the switch without proper authorization results in an exception. You can use the code in Listing 7-3 to check user authorization and toggle the scope.

Listing 7-3. *Checking Authorization and Toggling Scope*

```
If WebPartManager1.Personalization.CanEnterSharedScope Then
    WebPartManager1.Personalization.ToggleScope()
End If
```

Notice that the `ToggleScope()` method does not take any parameters. The method simply switches from one scope to the other and does not allow you to specify the scope you want to enter. You can, however, determine the current scope of the page using the `PersonalizationScope` enumerator as shown in Listing 7-4.

Listing 7-4. *Determining Mode*

```
Select Case WebPartManager1.Personalization.Scope

    Case PersonalizationScope.Shared
        'Shared scope code

    Case PersonalizationScope.User
        'Personal scope mode

End Select
```

The `Personalization.Scope` property on the page's `WebPartManager` control stores an enumeration defining the page scope. You'll see this code used later on to set the text on the button used to toggle between page scopes. You can also use it to run scope-specific code. `Personalization.Scope` is a read-only property, so you can only use it to check the page scope, not change it.

Closing vs. Deleting a Web Part

Deleting a Web Part removes it from the page permanently and destroys all its personalization settings. After you delete a Web Part instance, it will not appear in the `PageCatalogPart`. You'll have to create a new instance of the Web Part and reconfigure its settings if you want to add it back to the page.You should be aware of the distinction between closing and deleting a Web Part, and you should make the distinction known to the people who'll be using your Web Part application. Closing a Web Part removes it from the page visually. Behind the scenes, however, the Web Part is still associated with the page and retains all its personalized settings. You can think of closing a Web Part as hiding it or making it invisible. After closing a Web Part, you can make it visible via the `PageCatalogPart`, which maintains a listing of all the closed Web Parts on a page. When retrieved, the item retains all the settings it had before it was closed.

Hiding vs. Closing a Web Part

You can also hide Web Parts, which makes them invisible in browse display mode. When you switch into design, catalog, edit, or connection mode, hidden Web Parts reappear so you can edit them accordingly. The main difference between hiding and closing a Web Part is that a hidden Web Part is still an active participant in the Web Part Framework. You'll find this helpful when you need a Web Part to participate in a connection, but you do not want it visible on the page. Closed Web Parts cannot participate in a connection, but hidden Web Parts can.

Web Part Interfaces, Classes, and Controls

You will encounter a variety of interfaces, classes, and controls as you work with Web Parts in ASP.NET 2.0. Creating a Web Part page requires an understanding of the various Web Part controls, where they fit on the page, and how they interact with one another. Building an actual Web Part requires knowledge of the interfaces and controls that house the core Web Part functionality. In this section, you'll learn all about the various components that make up the Web Parts. Figure 7-2 shows a graphical overview of the classes we are about to discuss.

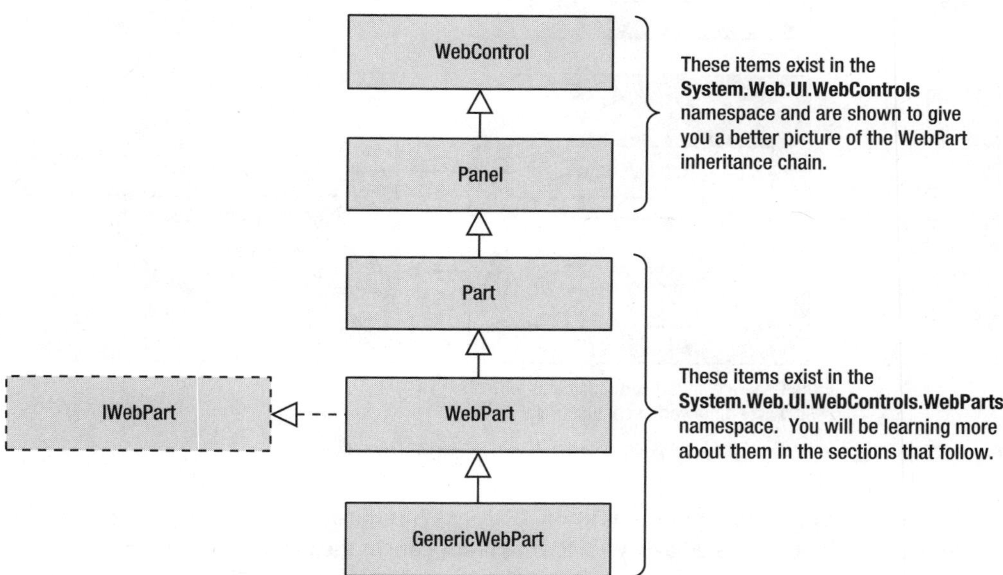

Figure 7-2. *The relationship between various Web Part components*

IWebPart Interface

Any ASP.NET control can participate in the Web Parts Framework because ASP.NET automatically wraps non-Web Part controls with Web Part functionality at runtime using the aptly named `GenericWebPart` class. The `GenericWebPart` class provides the bare minimum Web Part functionality required for the control to participate in the framework, but all the Web Part properties in the `GenericWebPart` are set to nondescript values. This makes it pretty confusing when users look at the Web Part catalog because all your Web Parts are named "Untitled" and have a similarly useless description.

You can avoid this confusion by implementing the `IWebPart` interface on user controls and server controls that you plan to use in the Web Parts Framework. The `IWebPart` interface exposes a set of properties that help define the most important properties on a Web Part, and it gives the `GenericWebPart` class a way to pass property values back and forth between the Web

Part Framework and the control. In other words, changes made to an IWebPart property within the control propagate up to the Web Parts Framework, and changes made in the Web Parts Framework propagate back down to the control. Figure 7-3 diagrams how the GenericWebPart class wraps standard controls (top) and those that implement the IWebPart interface (bottom).

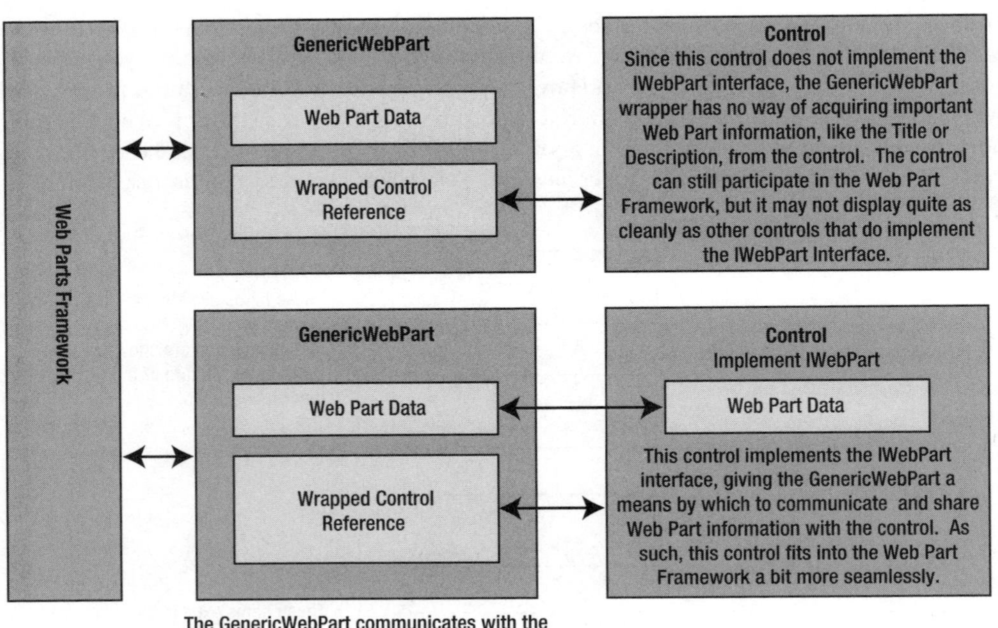

Figure 7-3. *The `GenericWebPart` control and the `IWebPart` Interface*

Table 7-1 outlines the properties in the IWebPart Interface. You may find it useful to refer to Figure 7-1, which shows a basic Web Part as it appears in the browser.

Table 7-1. `IWebPart` *Interface Properties*

Property	Type	Description
`CatalogIconImageUrl`	`String`	Specifies which image, if any, the Web Part catalog should display next to the Web Part in the catalog. If this is an empty string, then no icon will appear in the catalog.
`Description`	`String`	Brief description of the Web Part. Whenever someone hovers the mouse over a Web Part title on the page or in the Web Part catalog, the description is displayed as a tooltip to provide an idea of what the Web Part is and how it can be used.
`Subtitle (Read Only)`	`String`	When a Web Part displays in the browser, the title bar displays the `Title` of the Web Part and the `Subtitle` if it exists. The `SubTitle` allows you to specify additional title information in the title bar. For example, you may have a Weather Web Part whose title is "Weather" with a subtitle that read "Dallas" to denote which city's weather the Web Part is displaying.

Property	Type	Description
`Title`	`String`	Name of the Web Part as it should appear in the title bar and in the Web Part catalog.
`TitleIconImageUrl`	`String`	Specifies which image, if any, should be displayed in the title bar of the Web Part on the page. If this is an empty string, then no icon will appear in the title bar.
`TitleUrl`	`String`	Specifies which URL, if any, users should be redirected to when they click on the title of the Web Part in the title bar. If this is an empty string, then the title will not link to another page.

These properties give the Web Parts Framework a way of communicating the point and purpose of your web control to the user, so you'll definitely need them if you want your Web Parts to be user friendly.

Later in this chapter, you'll learn about the `BehaviorEditorPart`, which allows users to edit Web Part properties exposed by the `IWebPart` interface. For now, however, know that you must implement the `IWebPart` interface using properties. Listing 7-5 is an example of a static property that cannot be changed.

Listing 7-5. *UnchangeableProperty Implementation*

```
'***************************************************************************
Public Property Title() As String _
  Implements System.Web.UI.WebControls.WebParts.IWebPart.Title
    Get
        Return "Web Part Title"
    End Get
    Set(ByVal value As String)
        'Do nothing
    End Set
End Property
```

No matter what you do, the `Title` property shown in Listing 7-5 will always return the same value. Attempting to set the property will not affect anything because the `Set` portion of the property simply disregards incoming values. Naturally, this affects the `BehaviorEditorPart` control's capability to make changes to a Web Part. If your end goal is to have the Web Part disregard changes to a property, then by all means use an unchangeable property. If you want the changes made by the `BehaviorEditorPart` control to save, then you need to use standard properties for the `IWebPart` implementation as shown in Listing 7-6.

Listing 7-6. *Field-Backed Property Implementation*

```
'***************************************************************************
Private _Title as String = "Web Part Title"

'***************************************************************************
Public Property Title() As String _
  Implements System.Web.UI.WebControls.WebParts.IWebPart.Title
    Get
        Return _Title
    End Get
    Set(ByVal value As String)
        _Title = value
    End Set
End Property
```

In Listing 7-6, the private `_Title` field backs the `Title` property. Whenever the `Title` property changes, the property stores the new value in the `_Title` field where it can later be retrieved when the `Title` property is read. You can specify a default value for the property by specifying a default value for the field that backs it. In this example, the `Title` property has a default value of "Web Part Title".

Later in the chapter, I'll show you a simple way of creating user controls that inherit their `IWebPart` implementation from a base class.

Part Class

As you read through this chapter, you'll see information about `WebPart`, `EditorPart`, and `CatalogPart` controls. All the parts in the Web Part Framework inherit a common set of visual properties from the `Part` class. This allows the Web Parts Framework to render parts in a consistent manner. Table 7-2 is an overview of those common properties.

Table 7-2. `Part` *Class Properties Common to All Parts in the Web Part Framework*

Property Name	Type	Enum Values	Description
`ChromeState`	`PartChromeState`	`Minmized`	`Normal` Determines whether the page renders the entire part (`Normal`) or just the part's title bar (`Minimized`).

`ChromeType`	`PartChromeType`	`BorderOnly`
		`Default`
		`None`
		`TitleAndBorder`
		`TitleOnly`
			Determines whether the page renders a title and border around the part. A value of `Default` means the part inherits settings from its zone.

`Description`	`String`		Brief explanation of the control and what it does. The Web Parts Framework displays this information to the user when applicable.
`Title`	`String`		Displayed in the part's title bar.

WebPart Class

You can use the WebPart class as a base for building custom Web Part controls that can be packaged into an assembly. This is extremely useful if you need to create a set of reusable Web Parts to use over a series of projects or if you want to build a commercial Web Part.

If you have experience building custom server controls, then you'll feel right at home building custom Web Parts because the WebPart ultimately derives from a WebControl. For those who are interested, the WebPart class's inheritance chain looks something like this: WebPart ➤ Part ➤ Panel ➤ WebControl. As such, it has the same rendering architecture as any other custom server control and requires that you adhere to many of the same design principles. Later in this chapter, you'll see how to build a simple custom Web Part that derives from the WebPart class; however, a full discourse on custom control development is far beyond the scope of this text.

The WebPart class provides an implementation for the IWebPart interface, along with a host of additional properties used in the Web Parts Framework. Table 7-3 provides a rundown of some of the more important WebPart class properties.

Table 7-3. *Important* WebPart *Members*

Property Name	Type	Enum Values	Description
AllowClose	Boolean		True if users may close the Web Part.
AllowConnect	Boolean		True if users may create dynamic connections for the Web Part.
AllowEdit	Boolean		True if users may edit the Web Part.
AllowHide	Boolean		True if users may hide the Web Part.
AllowMinimize	Boolean		True if users may minimize the Web Part.
AllowZoneChange	Boolean		True if users may move the Web Part from one zone to another.
AuthorizationFilter	String		Provides a location where you can define and store an authorization string for use in a custom authorization scenario. There is *no* default behavior associated with this property. You may find it useful to use this property in conjunction with custom authorization code in the AuthorizeWebPart event of the WebPartManager. For example, you could specify a comma-delimited list of roles in the AuthorizationFilter property, and then have custom code in the AuthorizeWebPart event check to make sure the user is in one of those roles before authorizing the display of the Web Part.
CatalogIconImageUrl	String		Specifies which image, if any, the Web Part catalog should display next to the Web Part in the catalog. This property is part of the IWebPart interface.
ConnectErrorMessage	String		Error message displayed to the user if the Web Part experiences a connection error with another Web Part.

Table 7-3. *Important* WebPart *Members (Continued)*

Property Name	Type	Enum Values	Description
Direction	Content➥ Direction	LeftToRight NotSet RightToLeft	Specifies the text orientation for languages requiring left-to-right support. The default value is NotSet.
DisplayTitle	String		Read-only property that returns a string containing the actual value displayed in the title bar. The value is a concatenation of the Title and the Subtitle properties. If the actual Title property is an empty string, then DisplayTitle returns "Untitled"; if multiple Web Parts have the same title, then DisplayTitle adds a numeric index to the title to distinguish the Web Parts.
ExportMode	WebPart➥ ExportMode	All None NonSensitive➥ Data	Determines whether all, none, or only the properties that have been marked as nonsensitive may be exported from a web control. The default value is None.
HasSharedData	Boolean		Read-only property that returns true if the Web Part has shared (all-user) personalization data.
HasUserData	Boolean		Read-only property that returns true if the Web Part has personal (user-specific) personalization data.
Height	Unit		Desired height of the Web Part. Web Part height is determined by the Web Part content, so your Web Part content must take this desired height into account for it to have any meaning. Although it seems like this would control the height of the Web Part container, it does not.
HelpMode	WebPartHelp➥ Mode	Modal Modeless Navigate	Determines how the help page specified in the HelpUrl property displays. Modal displays a modal web page dialog box (popup). Modeless displays a nonmodal popup window. Navigate uses the current window to display the help, that is, it takes the user away from page. The default value is Modal.
HelpUrl	String		URL where help for the Web Part may be found. The Help verb in the Web Part menu is enabled when the HelpUrl property has a value.
Hidden	Boolean		True if the Web Part should be hidden.
ImportErrorMessage	String		Error message displayed to the user if the Web Part experiences an error while trying to import settings.
IsClosed	Boolean		Read-only property that returns true if the Web Part is closed.
IsShared	Boolean		Read only property that returns true if the Web Part is a shared, that is, visible to all users.
IsStandalone	Boolean		Read-only property that returns true if the Web Part is not shared, that is, visible only to a single user.

Table 7-3. *Important* WebPart *Members (Continued)*

Property Name	Type	Enum Values	Description
IsStatic	Boolean		Read-only property that returns true if the Web Part is defined directly in the page markup. False if the Web Part was added to the page programmatically or dynamically via the declarative page Catalog Part.
SubTitle	String		Displays additional text on the title bar of a Web Part when displayed on the page. The Web Part catalog does not display subtitles. This property is part of the IWebPart interface.
TitleIconImageUrl	String		Specifies which image, if any, should be displayed in the title bar of the Web Part on the page. This property is part of the IWebPart interface.
TitleUrl	String		Specifies which URL, if any, users should be redirected to when they click on the title of the Web Part in the title bar. This property is part of the IWebPart interface.
Verbs	WebPartVerb➥ Collection		Read-only collection of custom verbs associated with the web control.
WebBrowsableObject	Object		Read-only property that returns a reference to the WebPart instance. EditorPart controls use this property to load the Web Part into the editor.
WebPartManager	WebPart➥ Manager		Read-only property that gets a reference to the WebPartManager for the current page.
Width	Unit		Desired width of the Web Part. Web Part width is determined by the Web Part content, so your Web Part content must take this desired width into account for it to have any meaning. Although it seems this would control the width of the Web Part container, it does not.
Zone	WebPartZone➥ Base		Read-only property providing a reference to the zone that houses the Web Part.
ZoneIndex	Integer		Read-only property identifying the order position of the Web Part in the zone.

It's definitely a lot to take in, but these properties make it simple to modify the behavior and appearance of Web Parts programmatically. Custom Web Parts that inherit the WebPart class have direct access to all these properties by virtue of inheritance. You can also access all the WebPart class properties from inside a user control that does not inherit the WebPart class, but you have to do it indirectly through the GenericWebPart wrapper class.

GenericWebPart Wrapper Class

User controls inherit their base functionality from the UserControl class and, therefore, cannot inherit Web Part functionality from the WebPart class. This is problematic because the Web

Parts Framework needs the information exposed by the WebPart class to manage a Web Part. Enter the GenericWebPart class, which allows controls that do not inherit Web Part functionality from the WebPart class to participate in the Web Parts Framework by "wrapping" the control with the necessary functionality.

In essence, the GenericWebPart acts as a stand-in for the user control because it is the GenericWebPart that has all the Web Parts functionality. Whenever the Web Part Framework appears to be interacting with the user control, it is in fact interacting with the GenericWebPart that is there on behalf of the user control. Of course, the GenericWebPart relies on the user control it represents for nongeneric implementation details. For example, when the time comes to render the Web Part content (that is, the content below the title and inside the border of the Web Part), the GenericWebPart passes execution off to the user control so it can render itself. Whatever the user control renders is what appears as the Web Part content. Also, the user control handles any event arising from user interaction with the Web Part. Figure 7-4 outlines the structure of implementing a custom Web Part vs. a Web Part based on a user control.

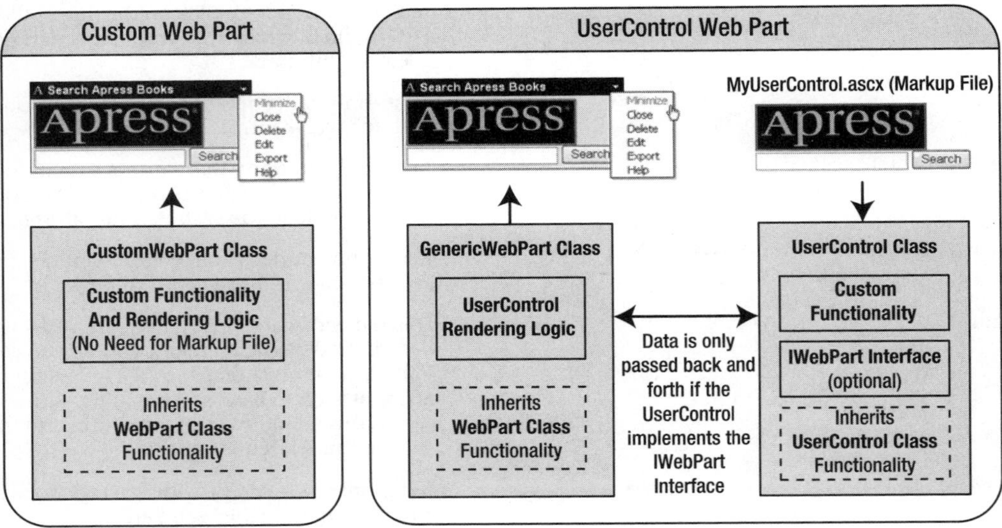

Figure 7-4. *Web Part implemenation using the* WebPart *and* GenericWebPart *classes*

The WebPartManager class exposes a shared method named GetCurrentWebPartManager, which returns a reference to the WebPartManager control on the current page. You can then acquire a reference to the GenericWebPart object, which represents the user control via the GetGenericWebPart function of the WebPartManager control. This allows you to access and manipulate Web Part functionality in a user control even though the user control does not inherit from the WebPart class. This will be explored in more detail when you learn how to build Web Parts, but Listing 7-7 gives a quick look at how to get the reference in your user control.

Listing 7-7. *Acquiring a Reference to a User Control's* `GenericWebPart`

```
Public Class MyUserControl
    Inherits UserControl

    '**************************************************************************
    Private WebPartData As GenericWebPart

    '**************************************************************************
    Private Sub Page_Load(ByVal sender As Object, _
      ByVal e As System.EventArgs) Handles Me.Load
        WebPartData = _
          WebPartManager.GetCurrentWebPartManager(Page).GetGenericWebPart(Me)

        'You can then access Web Part data
        Dim Title As String = WebPartData.Title
        Dim Description As String = WebPartData.Description
        Dim AllowMinimize As Boolean = WebPartData.AllowMinimize
        'etc...

    End Sub

End Class
```

In Listing 7-7, `WebPartManager.GetCurrentWebPartManager(Page)` acquires a reference to the `WebPartManager` for the page. Notice that you pass the current instance of the user control into `GetGenericWeb` via the `Me` reference. The `WebPartManager` searches through all the `GenericWebPart` objects on the page looking for the one that represents the user control. The return reference is then stored in the `WebPartData` field for future reference.

■ **Note** You can also use `GenericWebPart` to represent server controls. User controls were specifically discussed in this section because developers are more likely to use the `GenericWebPart` in conjunction with user controls.

WebPartManager Control

Web Part pages must load content based on personalized settings and have an assortment of controls that need to interact with others based on the page mode, scope, and connections to other Web Parts. The `WebPartManager` control acts as the master coordinator for all the Web Parts and Web Part functionality on a Web Part page.

Every page that uses Web Parts must have one (and only one) `WebPartManager` control, and it must appear before any Web Part controls on the page. Inside the `WebPartManager` definition you can set up static connections between Web Parts and define personalization settings for the page as shown in Listing 7-8 and 7-9.

Listing 7-8. *Defining a* `WebPartManager`

```
<!-- Definition without personalization or connection settings -->
<asp:WebPartManager ID="WebPartManager1" runat="server" />
```

Listing 7-9. *Defining a* `WebPartManager` *with Providers and Static Connections*

```
<!-- Definition with personalization and connection settings -->
    <Personalization Enabled="True" <asp:WebPartManager ID="WebPartManager1"
        runat="server">
        InitialScope="User"
        ProviderName="MyPersonalizationProvider" />
    <StaticConnections>
        <asp:WebPartConnection ID="StaticConnection1”
                               ConsumerID="ConsumerControl1_ID"
                               ProviderID="ProviderControl1_ID"
                               ConsumerConnectionPointID="PointA"
                               ProviderConnectionPointID="PointA" />

        <asp:WebPartConnection ID="StaticConnection2"
                               ConsumerID="ConsumerControl2_ID"
                               ProviderID="ProviderControl2_ID"
                               ConsumerConnectionPointID="PointB"
                               ProviderConnectionPointID="PointB" />
    </StaticConnections>
</asp:WebPartManager>
```

In the preceding example, you can see how to set personalization settings and define static connections in the `WebPartManager` control definition. On the personalization side, you can enable or disable personalization by setting the `Enabled` property, defining the initial scope of the page by setting the `InitialScope` property, and specifying a personalization provider in the `ProviderName` property. If you want to use the default personalization provider, then leave off the `ProviderName` property. Also, the `InitialScope` property is smart enough to check whether the user can enter shared scope before it attempts to enter it, so you can set this without fear of getting exceptions. If users can enter shared scope, then they will start in shared scope, if not, they will stay in personal scope. We'll discuss Web Part connection in greater detail later on in this chapter, but for now, just know that static Web Part connections are defined in the `WebPartManager` control.

The `WebPartManager` control does not have a UI, so you won't "see" it on the page, but you can use it in code. As the coordinator for Web Part interactions on the page, it maintains all pagewide information, such as the current display mode, scope, a list of all Web Part zones on the page, and a list of all the Web Parts in those zones. You've already seen how to use the `WebPartManager` to change scope and display mode, but it also allows you to manipulate Web Parts programmatically. Anything you can do in design, edit, catalog, or connection display mode can also be accomplished using methods on the `WebPartManager`.

■ **Note** Changes made in code are applied to the current page scope. Thus, if the page is in personal scope, the change is applied specifically to that user. If the page is in shared scope, the change is applied to all users.

Table 7-4 provides a brief list of the important, properties, methods, and events of the `WebPartManager` control. For a more exhaustive listing check out the MSDN website.

Table 7-4. *Important* `WebPartManager` *Properties*

Property	Type	Description
`CloseProvider➥ Warning`	`String`	When someone attempts to close a Web Part that is acting as a connection provider for another Web Part, the `CloseProviderWarning` informs the user of the possible effects and requests confirmation. You can change that warning via this property.
`DeleteWarning`	`String`	When someone attempts to delete a Web Part, the `DeleteWarning` displays and requests a confirmation. You can change the default deletion warning via this property.
`DisplayMode`	`WebPartDisplayMode`	Determines the current page display mode. You can set this property equal to one of five static `WebPartDisplay➥ Mode` objects defined in the `WebPartManager` class: `BrowseDisplayMode`, `CatalogDisplayMode`, `Connect➥ DisplayMode`, `DesignDisplayMode`, and `EditDisplayMode`. For more information about display modes, see "Portal Page Display Modes" earlier in this chapter.
`DynamicConnections`	`WebPartConnection➥ Collection`	Users can define dynamic connections between Web Parts on a page. This collection contains a listing of all those dynamic connections.
`ExportSensitive➥ DataWarning`	`String`	Some Web Parts may have properties that contain sensitive data and are marked as such in the `Personalizable` property attribute (discussed later in the "Defining Web Part Properties" section). When someone attempts to export settings on a Web Part marked as having sensitive data, the `ExportSensitiveDataWarning` message displays informing the user of the potential security risk. You can change the default warning via this property.
`Personalization`	`WebPart➥ Personalization`	Used to interact with the personalization provider for the Web Part Framework.
`SelectedWebPart`		When a user selects a verb from the Web Part menu, it "selects" that Web Part. This property provides an object reference to the currently selected Web Part. It returns `Nothing` when a Web Part has not been selected. This is a read-only property.
`StaticConnections`	`WebPartConnection➥ Collection`	Developers can define static connections between Web Parts on a page. This collection contains a listing of all those static connections.

Table 7-4. *Important* `WebPartManager` *Properties (Continued)*

Property	Type	Description
`WebParts`	`WebPartCollection`	Collection of all the Web Parts on the page regardless of the Web Part zone in which they reside. This *only* includes Web Parts and not Catalog or Editor Parts.
`Zones`	`WebPartZoneCollection`	Collection of all the Web Part zones on the page. This *only* includes Web Part zones and not Catalog, Editor, or Connection Zones

Most of the methods for the `WebPartManager` control mimic the functionality found in the UI for the various display modes, so they should be somewhat familiar (see Table 7-5).

Table 7-5. *Important* `WebPartManager` *Methods*

Method	Parameters	Returns	Description

`AddWebPart`	`WebPart As WebPart`
	`zone As WebPartZoneBase`
	`zoneIndex As Integer`
		`WebPart`	Adds a Web Part to a Web Part zone at the given zone index. Zone indices are zero-based, so you'll need to use an index of 0 to make the Web Part the first item in the zone. The `WebPart` added is returned as the result of the function.

`CloseWebPart`	`webPart As WebPart`		Closes the specified Web Part.

`ConnectWebParts`	`provider As WebPart`
	`providerConnection➥Point as Provider➥ConnectionPoint`
	`consumer As WebPart`
	`consumer➥ConnectionPoint➥As Consumer➥ConnectionPoint`
	`[transformer as WebPartTransformer]`
		`WebPartConnection`	Connections are used to transmit data from one Web Part to another. This method creates a `WebPart➥Connection` object representing the connection between the Provider Web Part and Consumer Web Part. The `transformer` parameter, (shown in [] brackets because it appears on an overloaded version of this method) is a custom object that translates data from the provider into a format the consumer can read.

`CreateWebPart`	`control As Control`	`GenericWebPart`	Wraps the given control in a `GenericWebPart` and returns it as the result of the function. Wrapping controls in a `GenericWebPart` allows any user controls or server control to participate in the Web Parts Framework. After you create a `Generic➥WebPart`, you need to add it to a zone before users may view it.
`DeleteWebPart`	`webPart as WebPart`		Deletes the specified Web Part.
`DisconnectWebPart`	`webPart as WebPart`		Disconnects a Web Part from its connection provider.

Method	Parameters	Returns	Description
DisconnectWebParts	connection As WebPartConnection		Disconnects all Web Parts who use the given connection.
ExportWebPart	webPart As WebPart writer as XmlWriter		Populates XmlWriter with property names and values from the given Web Part. You can use the ImportWebPart method with this XML definition to initialize a WebPart with the appropriate settings.
ImportWebPart	reader as XmlReader➥ ByRef errorMessage As String	WebPart	Reads the property names and values from XmlReader and initializes a WebPart with the appropriate configuration settings. Notice that the errorMessage parameter is a ByRef parameter, meaning that the variable value may change inside the function. You should pass an empty string variable into the method and check to see if it's still blank when the method exits. If the variable contains a message, then an error occurred. If not, the method succeeded.
GetGenericWebPart	control as Control	GenericWebPart	This retrieves the GenericWebPart wrapper for a user control or server control that is already participating in the Web Parts Framework. You normally use this inside of a control definition to get a reference to that control's corresponding GenericWebPart.
MoveWebPart	webPart As WebPart zone As WebPart➥ ZoneBase zoneIndex As Integer		Moves the given Web Part to the specified Web Part zone at the given zone index.

■ Note When you "import" a Web Part, you are really only importing a Web Part's configuration. You can only successfully import Web Part configurations for Web Part controls that exist in your application. If you find a Web Part in another application, export its configuration to a file and then import that configuration into your application, the import will fail because your application does not have access to the Web Part the configuration references.

All the WebPartManager events are represented by pairs. Events that end in ing fire right before an action occurs, which allows you to alter the action before it's actually executed. Events that end in ed fire after an action has been performed. All the events have a sender parameter, which is always the WebPartMangaer for the page, and e, which contains important information regarding the event. Table 7-6 contains a listing of WebPartManager events.

Table 7-6. *Important WebPartManager Events*

Event	Description
ConnectionsActivating, ConnectionsActivated	Fires before and after all the connections on the page have been activated. When the connections are activated, Provider Web Parts send data to Consumer Web Parts via the connections.
DisplayModeChanging, DisplayModeChanged	Fires before and after the display mode changes.
SelectedWebPartChanging, SelectedWebPartChanged	Fires before and after the selected Web Part changes.
WebPartAdding, WebPartAdded	Fires before and after a user adds a Web Part to the page.
WebPartClosing, WebPartClosed	Fires before and after a user closes a Web Part.
WebPartDeleting, WebPartDeleted	Fires before and after a user deletes a Web Part.
WebPartMoving, WebPartMoved	Fires before and after a user moves a Web Part.
WebPartConnecting, WebPartConnected	Fires before and after a user establishes a connection between two Web Parts.
WebPartDisconnecting, WebPartDisconnected	Fires before and after a user removes the connection between two Web Parts.

Most of the events allow you to modify the action by setting properties in the event handler arguments parameter (e). For example, you can cancel a Web Part deletion by setting e.Cancel = True in the WebPartDeleting event. Or you can force a Web Part to be added to the top of a zone by setting e.ZoneIndex = 0 in the WebPartAdding or WebPartMoving events. Also understand that you can set up event handlers for these events from within your Web Part control. This means that individual Web Parts can respond to these events directly in their code. You'll see examples of this later on in this chapter.

ProxyWebPartManager Control

The ProxyWebPartManager allows you to define static connections from a content page when the WebPartManager control is located on the Master Page (see Chapter 3). If you plan on having Web Parts on multiple pages in your website, then you make your life a lot easier by implementing most of your Web Part functionality in a Master Page. Any page that needs to use Web Parts can inherit that Master Page's features. To do so, you need to place your WebPartManager control in the Master Page. This presents a problem for static connections.

Static connections are defined in the WebPartManager control, but most static connections are needed on a page-by-page basis and should not be defined in the Master Page. To get around this issue, you can place a ProxyWebPartManager on the actual content page itself and define static connections in the ProxyWebPartManager. Listing 7-10 is an example of what this looks like on the content page.

Listing 7-10. *Defining Static Connections Using the* ProxyWebPartManager

```
<asp:Content ContentPlaceHolderID="ContentPlaceHolder1" runat="server">
    <asp:ProxyWebPartManager ID="ProxyWebPartManager1" runat="server">
        <StaticConnections>
            <asp:WebPartConnection ID="StaticConnection1"
                                   ConsumerID="ConsumerControl1_ID"
                                   ProviderID="ProviderControl1_ID" />
            <asp:WebPartConnection ID="StaticConnection2"
                                   ConsumerID="ConsumerControl2_ID"
                                   ProviderID="ProviderControl2_ID" />
        </StaticConnections>
    </asp:ProxyWebPartManager>
</asp:Content>
```

All the static connections defined in the ProxyWebPartManager control appear as though they were defined in the WebPartManager control itself, and calling StaticConnections on the WebPartManager returns the connections defined in the ProxyWebPartManager.

Web Part Zones

All Web Part zone controls act as containers for their respective type of Web Parts and automatically hide or become visible depending on the current display mode. In the IDE, zones look like and act like any other container control, allowing you to drag and drop in items from the toolbox and work with them right on the screen.

Zones inherit a basic set of functionality from the WebZone base class, so all the zone controls share a common set of text and style properties that govern their appearance when displayed in the browser. Table 7-7 provides an overview of those properties and their purpose.

Table 7-7. WebZone *Properties*

Property Name	Type	Description
EmptyZoneText	String	Text to display when the zone is displayed but has no content. The WebPartZone will *not* display the EmptyZoneText while the page is in browse display mode.
EmptyZoneTextStyle	Style	Style applied to the EmptyZoneText.
ErrorStyle	Style	Style applied to error messages shown in the zone.
FooterStyle	TitleStyle	Style applied to the zone footer (although no zone seem to have footers).

Table 7-7. WebZone *Properties (Continued)*

Property Name	Type	Description
HeaderStyle	TitleStyle	Style applied to the zone header. This is synonomous with the title bar of a Web Part.
HeaderText	String	Text displayed in the zone header. This is synonomous with the Title property of the Web Part.
Padding	Integer	Amount of padding between Web Parts in the zone.
PartChromeStyle	Style	Style applied to the border and background of the parts in the zone.
PartChromeType	PartChromeType	Specifies whether the parts in the zone will have a border, title, or both.
PartStyle	TableStyle	Style applied to the content of the parts in the zone.
PartTitleStyle	TitleStyle	Style applied to the title of parts in the zone.
VerbButtonType	ButtonType	Specifies whether the actions buttons (verbs) in the zone will be links, buttons, or images. The VerbButtonType property is not available on the WebPartZone because the WebPartZone does not have any verbs.
VerbStyle	Style	Style applied to the verbs in a zone.

You will be looking at zone controls over the next few sections, so remember that these properties also apply to those controls.

WebPartZone Control and Static Web Parts

You use the WebPartZone to create a region on the page to display and manage Web Parts. In browse mode, the region is invisible and the title bar is hidden. When you switch into catalog, design, edit, or connection mode, you'll see a bounding region around the WebPartZone along with a title bar displaying the HeaderText, assuming of course that you have not explicitly disabled the border and title bar for the zone. Figure 7-5 shows a WebPartZone in design mode with three Web Parts.

Figure 7-5. `WebPartZone` *with Three Web Parts*

The `WebPartZone` has a lot of properties that help define the visual appearance and behavior of the Web Parts in the zone. Table 7-8 is a quick reference for those properties.

Table 7-8. *Important* `WebPartZone` *Properties*

Property Name	Type	Description
`AllowLayoutChange`	`Boolean`	True if the user may reorder Web Part within the zone.
`CloseVerb`	`WebPartVerb`	Reference to the verb that closes the Web Part.
`ConnectVerb`	`WebPartVerb`	Reference to the verb that allows users to set up connections for the Web Part.
`DeleteVerb`	`WebPartVerb`	Reference to the verb that deletes the Web Part.
`DragHighlightColor`	`Color`	Color of the drag position indicator bar displayed when a user drags a Web Part from one location to another. The default color is blue.
`EditVerb`	`WebPartVerb`	Reference to the verb that allows the user to edit the Web Part.
`ExportVerb`	`WebPartVerb`	Reference to the verb that allows the user to export the Web Part.
`HelpVerb`	`WebPartVerb`	Reference to the verb that displays help for the Web Part.
`LayoutOrientation`	`Orientation`	Specifies whether the Web Part in the zone should appear on top of one another (`Vertical`) or side by side (`Horizontal`). The default is `Vertical`.
`MenuCheckImageStyle`	`Style`	Style applied to the check mark image used on the verb that has been selected (checked).

Table 7-8. *Important* WebPartZone *Properties (Continued)*

Property Name	Type	Description
MenuCheckImageUrl	String	URL of the image used as the check mark image on a verb that has been selected (checked).
MenuLabelHoverStyle	Style	Style applied to the drop-down menu label in the title bar when the mouse hovers over the text.
MenuLabelStyle	Style	Style applied to the label containing the MenuLabelText and drop-down arrow for the verb menu.
MenuLabelText	String	Text that appears in the title bar of a web control next to the drop-down arrow for the verb menu. The default value is an empty string meaning that nothing is shown next to the drop-down arrow (refer to Figure 7-1).
MenuPopupImageUrl	String	URL of the image to use as the drop-down image for the verb menu. By default, the MenuPopupImageUrl points to a small drop-down arrow.
MenuPopupStyle	WebPartMenuStyle	Style applied to the popup menu containing the list of verbs for a Web Part.
MenuVerbHoverStyle	Style	Style applied to a verb in the popup menu when the mouse is hovering over that verb.
MenuVerbStyle	Style	Style applied to a verb in the popup menu.
MinimizeVerb	WebPartVerb	Reference to the verb that minimizes the web control.
RestoreVerb	WebPartVerb	Reference to the verb that restores a minimized web control.
SelectedPart➥ChromeStyle	Style	Style applied to the border of the selected Web Part.
ShowTitleIcons	Boolean	True if the zone should display the Web Part's title icon.
TitleBarVerb➥ButtonType	ButtonType	Determines the type of button (Link, Button, or Image) to display on the title bar when the WebPartVerbRenderMode is set to TitleBar.
TitleBarVerbStyle	Style	Style applied to the title bar verb buttons when the WebPartVerbRenderMode is set to TitleBar.
WebParts	WebPartCollection	List of the Web Part in the zone.
WebPartVerb➥RenderMode	WebPartVerb➥RenderMode	Specifies whether the verbs for the Web Part should appear in a menu (Menu) or as buttons in the title bar (TitleBar). The default value is Menu. Also know that the MenuXXX properties are applied when this value is set to Menu, and the TitleXXX properties are applied when this value is set to TitleBar.
ZoneTemplate	ITemplate	A template containing the static Web Part that should appear in the zone. Dropping controls into the zone from the IDE populates the ZoneTemplate in the page markup.

All the Verbs and Style properties are defined as child <elements> *in the control definition. Notice in Listing 7-11 that* DragHighlightColor *is defined as an attribute whereas* HeaderStyle *is defined as an* <element>

To create a new Web Part zone, just drag the WebPartZone control from the toolbox to the location where you want it to appear on the web form. You'll see the zone appear in the IDE, and the following control definition will be added to the page markup:

```
<asp:WebPartZone ID="WebPartZone1" runat="server"></asp:WebPartZone>
```

Of course, you'll probably want to set the HeaderText attribute to give the zone an appropriate title, define some visual styles, and possibly specify a few static Web Part controls to display in the zone. Listing 7-11 is a more detailed example of the WebPartZone control definition.

Listing 7-11. WebPartZone *Control Definition*

```
<asp:WebPartZone SkinID="" Runat="server" DragHighlightColor="0, 0, 255">
    <HeaderStyle CssClass="WebPartZoneHeader" />
    <PartTitleStyle CssClass="WebPartTitle"  />
    <PartStyle CssClass="WebPartContent" CellSpacing="5"  />
    <PartChromeStyle BorderWidth="1px" BackColor="#CCCCCC" />
    <MenuPopupStyle BackColor="#FFFFFF"     BorderColor="#000000"
                    BorderStyle="Solid"     BorderWidth="1px"
                    ShadowColor="#AAAAAA"   GridLines="Horizontal"
                    Font-Names="Tahoma"     Font-Size="9pt" />
    <MenuLabelStyle ForeColor="White" />
    <MenuVerbStyle ForeColor="Black" />
    <MenuVerbHoverStyle ForeColor="Red" />
    <ZoneTemplate>
        <cc1:MyWebPartA runat=server id=StaticWebPart1 />
        <cc1:MyWebPartB runat=server id=StaticWebPart2 />
    </ZoneTemplate>
</asp:WebPartZone>
```

Because Web Parts have many visual aspects, you end up having to set a fairly large number of stylistic properties for the Web Part zones. If you have multiple zones over multiple pages, then you should use control skins to make your task a bit easier and more maintainable. Control skins allow you to apply a set of properties to controls across the entire application by defining the control properties in a .skin file. Check out Chapter 3 for more information on how to implement control skins.

■ **Note** You can check out the skin files for the example application in the App_Themes\Bravo\ folder of the web application in the Source Code area of the Apress website (http://www.apress.com).

Also notice the controls in the <ZoneTemplate> element of the control definition. These are called static Web Parts because they are defined directly in the page markup. Static Web Parts act similarly to shared scope Web Parts in that they appear for all users but allow individual users to create personalized settings. The biggest difference is that static Web Parts cannot be removed from the page dynamically, that is, administrators cannot enter shared scope and delete the Web Part. You have to manually remove the item from the page markup to delete it.

CatalogZone Control and Related Catalog Parts

You use the `CatalogZone` to create a region on the page to display Catalog Parts, which in turn allows the user to add or restore Web Parts on the page. Figure 7-6 shows an example `CatalogZone` that contains three Catalog Parts. Although the `CatalogZone` holds multiple `CatalogPart` controls, it only displays one of those controls at a time. You can select which `CatalogPart` to display by clicking on one of the links located at the top of the `CatalogZone`.

Figure 7-6 shows a Web Part Catalog control that displays 11 Web Parts (the 11 items with check boxes next to them). Notice that the number **(11)** appears next to the **Web Part Catalog** item in the list identifying the total number of Web Parts in the catalog. Also remember that the `CatalogZone` only appears when the page is in catalog display mode, so your page must provide some means of switching modes before users can see the `CatalogZone`.

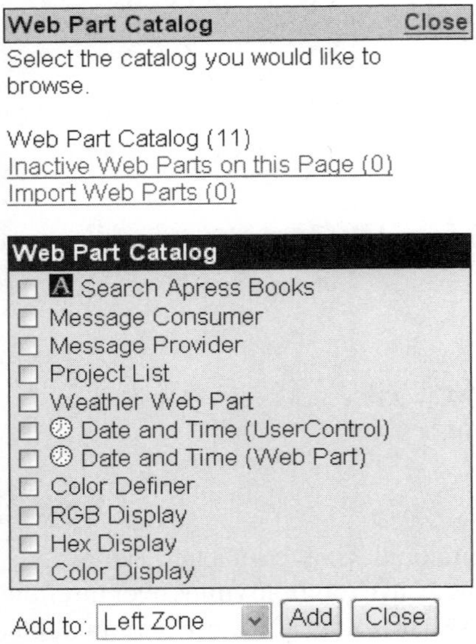

Web Part Catalog Close
Select the catalog you would like to browse.

Web Part Catalog (11)
Inactive Web Parts on this Page (0)
Import Web Parts (0)

Web Part Catalog
☐ Search Apress Books
☐ Message Consumer
☐ Message Provider
☐ Project List
☐ Weather Web Part
☐ Date and Time (UserControl)
☐ Date and Time (Web Part)
☐ Color Definer
☐ RGB Display
☐ Hex Display
☐ Color Display

Add to: Left Zone Add Close

Figure 7-6. `CatalogZone` *drop-down box and the **Add** button*

Like the `WebPartZone`, there are a few control-specific properties you need to know about when working with a `CatalogZone`. Table 7-9 gives a quick listing of those properties.

Table 7-9. *Important* `CatalogZone` *Properties*

Property Name	Type	Description
`AddVerb`	`WebPartVerb`	Read-only reference to the verb that adds the selected Catalog Parts to the page. This verb appears at the bottom of the page.
`CatalogParts`	`CatalogPartCollection`	List of the Catalog Parts in the zone.

Property Name	Type	Description
CloseVerb	WebPartVerb	Read-only reference to the verb that closes the CatalogZone and switches the page back into browse display mode. This verb appears at the bottom of the page.
EditUIStyle	Style	Style applied to the form elements (text boxes, check boxes, and so on) on the Catalog Parts in the zone.
HeaderCloseVerb	WebPartVerb	Read-only reference to the verb in the header that closes the CatalogZone and switches the page back to browse display mode.
HeaderVerbStyle	Style	Style applied to any verbs that appear in the header, such as the HeaderCloseVerb.
InstructionText	String	Brief description of how to use the catalog to add Web Parts to the page. This text may contain HTML markup.
Instruction➥ TextStyle	Style	Style applied to the InstructionText.
LabelStyle	Style	Style applied to labels that appear throughout the Catalog Parts in the zone.
PartLinkStyle	Style	Style applied to the links in the Catalog Part list for the unselected Catalog Parts.
SelectedCatalog➥ PartID	String	ID of the selected Catalog Part.
SelectedPartLink➥ Style	Style	Style applied to the text in the Catalog Part list for the selected (visible) Catalog Part.
ShowCatalogIcons	Boolean	True if the catalog should display the catalog icon next to available Web Part.
VerbButtonType	ButtonType	Determines the type of button (Link, Button, or Image) used to display verbs in the zone. This style is applied to the Add and Close verbs at the bottom of the control.
VerbStyle	Style	Style applied to verbs in the zone.
ZoneTemplate	ITemplate	A template containing the Catalog Parts to display in the zone. Dropping controls into the zone from the IDE populates the ZoneTemplate in the page markup.

To create a new Catalog Zone, just drag the CatalogZone control from the toolbox to the location where you want it to appear on the web form. You'll see the zone appear in the IDE, and the following control definition will be added to the page markup:

```
<asp:CatalogZone ID="CatalogZone1" runat="server"></asp:CatalogZone>
```

Once again, you'll likely want to add stylistic properties to the CatalogZone control definition, and you may want to define those properties in a .skin file. You also need to include

Catalog Part items in the `<ZoneTemplate>` element so your Catalog Zone will have tools to help the user add Web Parts to the page. Listing 7-12 is a more detailed example of a `CatalogZone` control definition.

Listing 7-12. `CatalogZone` *Control Definition*

```
<asp:CatalogZone runat="server" ID="CatalogZone1" CssClass="CatalogZone"
  VerbButtonType="Button" Width="100%" >
    <HeaderStyle CssClass="WebPartZoneHeader" />
    <PartTitleStyle CssClass="WebPartTitle"  />
    <PartStyle CssClass="WebPartContent" CellSpacing=5  />
    <PartChromeStyle BorderWidth="1px" BackColor="#CCCCCC"></PartChromeStyle>
    <ZoneTemplate>
        <asp:DeclarativeCatalogPart ID="DeclarativeCatalogPart1"
            runat="server" Title="Web Part Catalog"
            WebPartsListUserControlPath="~/WebParts/WebPartCatalog.ascx" />
        <asp:PageCatalogPart ID="PageCatalogPart1" runat="server"
            Title="Inactive Web Parts on this Page" />
        <asp:ImportCatalogPart ID="ImportCatalogPart1" runat="server"
            Title="Import Web Parts" />
    </ZoneTemplate>
</asp:CatalogZone>
```

As shown in the `ZoneTemplate` declarations, three different Catalog Parts ship with ASP.NET 2.0. Of course, you can make your own Catalog Parts by creating a class that derives from the `CatalogPart` class, but that is beyond the scope of this book. Next, we'll take a look at `DeclarativeCatalogPart`, `PageCatalogPart`, and `ImportCatalogPart`.

DeclarativeCatalogPart

`DeclarativeCatalogPart` allows users to add new Web Parts to the page by selecting them from a list of available web controls. As such, you need to identify which controls you want to be available to the user. You can accomplish this task in one of two ways.

Your first option is to define the available Web Part list directly in the `DeclarativeCatalogPart` definition by means of the `<WebPartsTemplate>`. Any controls appearing in the `<WebPartsTemplate>` are made available to the user as shown in Listing 7-13.

Listing 7-13. `DeclarativeCatalogPart` *Definition with Web Part List*

```
<asp:CatalogZone runat="server" Width="100%" >
    <ZoneTemplate>
        <asp:DeclarativeCatalogPart ID="DeclarativeCatalogPart1" runat="server"
            Title="Web Part Catalog"
            Description="Add new Web Part to the page">
            <WebPartsTemplate>
                <cc1:MyFirstWebPart runat="server" id="MyFirstWebPart1" />
                <cc1:MySecondWebPart runat="server" id="MySecondWebPart1" />
                <cc1:MyThirdWebPart runat="server" id="MyThirdWebPart1" />
```

```
            </WebPartsTemplate>
        </asp:DeclarativeCatalogPart>
    </ZoneTemplate>
</asp:CatalogZone>
```

Your second option is to place the Web Part list in a user control, then point the `WebPartsListUserControlPath` at that user control as shown in Listing 7-14 and 7-15.

Listing 7-14. *Catalog Parts Defined in a* `UserControl` *(*`~/WebParts/WebPartCatalog.ascx`*)*

```
<%@ Register Src="C1.ascx" TagName="MyFirstWebPart" TagPrefix="CC1" %>
<%@ Register Src="C2.ascx" TagName="MySecondWebPart" TagPrefix="CC1" %>
<%@ Register Src="C3.ascx" TagName="MyThirdWebPart" TagPrefix="CC1" %>

<cc1:MyFirstWebPart runat="server" id="MyFirstWebPart1" />
<cc1:MySecondWebPart runat="server" id="MySecondWebPart1" />
<cc1:MyThirdWebPart runat="server" id="MyThirdWebPart1" />
```

Listing 7-15. `DeclarativeCatalogPart` *that Employs the* `UserControl` *for its Catalog Listing*

```
<!-- Control Definition -->
<asp:CatalogZone runat="server" Width="100%" >
    <ZoneTemplate>
        <asp:DeclarativeCatalogPart ID="DeclarativeCatalogPart1" runat="server"
            Title="Web Part Catalog"
            Description="Add new Web Part to the page"
            WebPartsListUserControlPath="~/WebParts/WebPartCatalog.ascx" />
    </ZoneTemplate>
</asp:CatalogZone>
```

Placing your Web Part list in a user control means that you can maintain that list in a single location if you have multiple pages that share a common set of Web Parts. You can also use a hybrid approach and have a default set of Web Parts defined in a user control and have page-specific items defined directly in the markup. Refer to Figure 7-6 for an example of a `DeclarativeCatalogPart` as it appears on screen.

To use `DeclarativeCatalogPart`, users simply choose which Web Parts they want to add to the page, select which `WebPartZone` to place the Web Parts in from the zone drop-down located at the bottom of the `CatalogZone`, and click on the Add button. The page refreshes, and the selected Web Parts then appear in the chosen zone.

PageCatalogPart

When users close a Web Part, the Web Part is no longer active but it's still associated with the page and retains all of its personalized settings. The `PageCatalogPart` lists all the closed items on the page, thus giving users a way to add them back to the page. Because the `PageCatalogPart` automatically generates its list of Web Parts based on the inactive Web Parts in the page, there is not much setup required to use this control (see Listing 7-16).

Listing 7-16. PageCatalogPart *Control Definition*

```
<asp:CatalogZone ID="CatalogZone1" runat="server" HeaderText="Web Part Catalog">
    <ZoneTemplate>
        <asp:PageCatalogPart ID="PageCatalogPart1" runat="server"
            Title="Hidden Web Parts"  />
    </ZoneTemplate>
</asp:CatalogZone>
```

In the browser, the PageCatalogPart is both visually and behaviorally identical to the DeclarativeCatalogPart. Users select which Web Parts they want to add to the page from the list of available Web Parts, choose a zone to place them in, and then click on the **Add** button. The page refreshes, and the selected Web Parts then appear in the chosen zone. After the Web Part has been added back to the page, it no longer appears in PageCatalogPart because it has been reactivated.

ImportCatalogPart

ImportCatalogPart allows users to add Web Parts to the page by uploading and importing a Web Part definition file. This gives administrators a convenient way to create Web Part setup files that can configure complex Web Parts. Instead of having to go through a complicated configuration process, users can just import the definition file. It also gives users a way to copy a Web Part from one page to another within the same application, although it does require exporting the definition file from the original page to the user's machine and then reuploading the definition on the target page.

■ **Note** When you "import" a Web Part you are really only importing a Web Part's configuration. You can only successfully import Web Part configurations for Web Part controls that exist in your application. If you find a Web Part in another application, export its configuration to a file and then import that configuration into your application, the import will fail because your application does not have access to the Web Part the configuration references.

Like the PageCatalogPart, you can't do much in the way of configuration for the ImportCatalogPart, so the control definition is fairly straightforward (see Listing 7-17). Figure 7-7 shows an example of the control as it appears after the user has uploaded a definition file.

Listing 7-17. ImportCatalogPart *Defintion*

```
<asp:CatalogZone ID="CatalogZone1" runat="server" HeaderText="Web Part Catalog">
    <ZoneTemplate>
        <asp:ImportCatalogPart ID="ImportCatalogPart1" runat="server"
            Title="Import Web Parts"
            Description="Import a Web Part from a Web Part Definition File"
            UploadButtonText="Upload" />
    </ZoneTemplate>
</asp:CatalogZone>
```

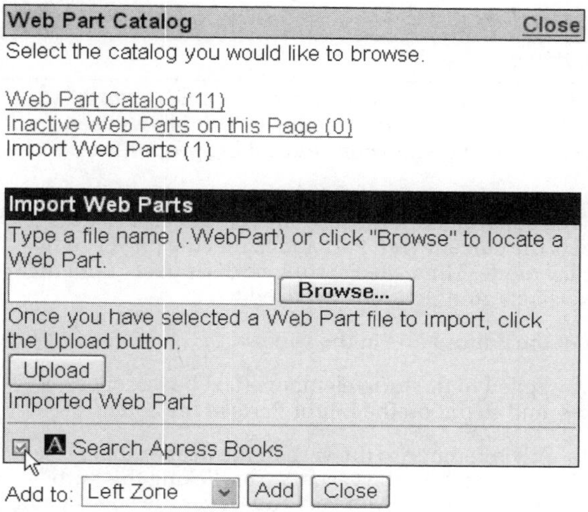

Web Part Catalog Close
Select the catalog you would like to browse.

Web Part Catalog (11)
Inactive Web Parts on this Page (0)
Import Web Parts (1)

Import Web Parts
Type a file name (.WebPart) or click "Browse" to locate a Web Part.
Browse...
Once you have selected a Web Part file to import, click the Upload button.
Upload
Imported Web Part
Search Apress Books
Add to: Left Zone Add Close

Figure 7-7. `ImportCatalogPart`

Initially, the `ImportCatalogPart` displays a file upload input, an **Upload** button, and some informative text describing how to use the import features of the control. Users can browse for a Web Part file and then upload it using the **Upload** button. After uploading the file, the control displays the name of the uploaded Web Part along with a check box. To add the item to the page, the user selects the check box next to the Web Part name, chooses a zone to place it in, and then clicks on the **Add** button. The page refreshes, and the selected Web Part then appears in the chosen zone.

EditorZone Control and Related Editor Parts

You use the `EditorZone` to create a region on the page to display Editor Parts. Editor Parts allow users to edit different sets properties on a Web Part. ASP.NET ships with fours standard Editor Parts: the `AppearanceEditorPart`, `BehaviorEditorPart`, `LayoutEditorPart`, and the `PropertyGridEditorParty`. Each of these Editor Parts is responsible for displaying a different set of properties for a single Web Part. The `EditorZone` only appears when the page is in `EditDisplayMode` *and* the user has selected a Web Part to edit by clicking the Web Part's **Edit** verb from its menu.

Unlike the `CatalogZone`, the `EditorZone` displays all the Editor Parts at the same time. This allows you to edit all the properties for a Web Part without having to switch back and forth between Editor Parts using a series of links. The `EditorZone` properties closely resemble those of the `CatalogZone`, with the most notable difference being the verb references. Table 7-10 provides a breakdown of those properties.

Table 7-10. *Important* EditorZone *Properties*

Property Name	Type	Description
ApplyVerb	WebPartVerb	Read-only reference to the verb that applies changes to the Web Part without deselecting it. This allows users to save their changes and continue ediing properties.
CancelVerb	WebPartVerb	Read-only reference to the verb that cancels editing on the current Web Part. Clicking on the cancel verb deselects the current Web Part and leaves the page in edit display mode. Thus, the EditorZone disappears until the user selects another Web Part to edit.
EditorParts	EditorPartCollection	List of the Editor Parts in the zone.
EditUIStyle	Style	Style applied to the form elements (text boxes, check boxes, and so on) on the Editor Parts in the zone.
HeaderCloseVerb	WebPartVerb	Read-only reference to the verb in the header that closes the EditorZone. Like the CancelVerb, clicking this verb deselects the current Web Part and leaves the page in edit display mode.
HeaderVerbStyle	Style	Style applied to any verbs that appear in the header, i.e. the HeaderCloseVerb.
InstructionText	String	Brief description of how to use the Editor Parts to modify Web Part properties. This text may contain HTML markup.
Instruction➥TextStyle	Style	Style applied to the InstructionText.
LabelStyle	Style	Style applied to labels that appear throughout the Editor Parts in the zone.
OKVerb	WebPartVerb	Read-only reference to the verb that applies changes to the Web Part and deselects it. Users can click on the OK verb to save their changes and end editing on the selected Web Part.
VerbButtonType	ButtonType	Determines the type of button (Link, Button, or Image) used to display verbs in the zone. This style is applied to the Apply, Cancel, and OK verbs at the bottom of the control.
VerbStyle	Style	Style applied to verbs in the zone.
ZoneTemplate	ITemplate	A template containing the Editor Parts to display in the zone. Dropping controls into the zone from the IDE populates the ZoneTemplate in the page markup.

To create a new Editor Zone, drag the EditorZone control from the toolbox to the location where you want it to appear on the web form. You'll see the zone appear in the IDE, and the following control definition is added to the page markup:

```
<asp:EditorZone ID="EditorZone1" runat="server"></asp:EditorZone>
```

Although the EditorZone supports all the stylistic properties found in the other zones, you may not want to use them. Each Editor Part is surrounded by a <FieldSet> HTML tag that looks good without much styling. You will, however, need to include Editor Part items in the

`<ZoneTemplate>` element so your Editor Zone will have tools to help the user edit Web Parts on the page. Listing 7-18 is a more detailed example of an `EditorZone` control definition.

Listing 7-18. `EditorZone` *Control Definition*

```
<asp:EditorZone runat="server" SkinID="" CssClass="EditorZone"
  HeaderText="Editor Zone" Width="100%" >
    <HeaderStyle CssClass="WebPartZoneHeader" />
    <ZoneTemplate>
        <asp:AppearanceEditorPart ID="AppearanceEditor1" runat=server />
        <asp:BehaviorEditorPart ID="BehaviorEditorPart1" runat=server />
        <asp:LayoutEditorPart ID="LayoutEditorPart1" runat=server />
        <asp:PropertyGridEditorPart ID="PropGridEditor1" runat="server"  />
    </ZoneTemplate>
</asp:EditorZone>
```

As shown in the `ZoneTemplate` declarations, there are four different Editor Parts that ship with ASP.NET 2.0. Once again, you can create your own Editor Parts by creating a class that derives from the `EditorPart` class, but that is also beyond the scope of this book. Next, we'll take a look at all the Editor Parts.

AppearanceEditorPart

The `AppearanceEditorPart` allows users to set the appearance properties of the Web Part. Specifically, they can set the title text, title and border display options (Chrome Type), language orientation (Direction), height, width, and whether or not the Web Part should be hidden.

No configuration is required to use the `AppearanceEditorPart`. Just drag it from the toolbox into the `EditorZone` where you want it to appear, and the following control definition is added to the `<ZoneTemplate>` of the `EditorZone` definition:

```
<asp:AppearanceEditorPart ID="AppearanceEditor1" runat=server />
```

By default, the `Title` property of this Editor Part is `"Appearance"`. You can set a different `Title` value in the control definition if you wish. Figure 7-8 shows an example of the `AppearanceEditorPart` as it appears in edit display mode in the browser.

Figure 7-8. `AppearanceEditorPart`

BehaviorEditorPart

The `BehaviorEditorPart` allows users to set behavioral properties of the Web Part. Administrators will find this part very useful for setting up shared scope Web Parts because it allows them to define how users interact with the Web Part. Normal users will probably not find the `BehaviorEditorPart` very useful, and some may just find it confusing, so you may only want to display it to administrators. Table 7-11 is a quick rundown of the behavior properties exposed by the `BehaviorEditorPart`:.

Table 7-11. *Editable Properties in the* `BehaviorEditorPart`

Item Name	Description
`Allow Close`	Checked if the user may close the Web Part.
`Allow Connect`	Checked if the user may set up dynamic connections using the Web Part.
`Allow Edit`	Checked if the user may edit the Web Part.
`Allow Hide`	Checked if the user may hide the Web Part.
`Allow Minimize`	Checked if the user may minimize the Web Part.
`Allow Zone Change`	Checked if the user may move the Web Part from one zone to another.
`Authorization Filter`	Ad-hoc string that can be used in custom authorization scenarios.
`Catalog Icon Image Link`	URL of the image to use as the catalog icon.
`Description`	Description of the Web Part.
`Export Mode`	Determines whether or not users can export all the Web Part data, none of the Web Part data, or nonsensitive portions of the Web Part.
`Help Link`	URL of the help file for the Web Part.
`Help Mode`	Determines whether help is displayed in a modal popup window, a nonmodal popup window, or if the user is redirected to the help using the current browser window.
`Import Error Message`	Text displayed if an error occurs importing the Web Part to another page. This requires the Web Part to be exported first.
`Title Icon Image Link`	URL of the image to use as the Web Part title bar icon.
`Title Link`	URL where users are taken when the click on the Web Part title.

The `BehaviorEditorPart` is smart enough to keep you from locking yourself out of the Web Part. Permission properties are only applied to shared scope items for normal users. If you can enter shared scope, you can edit a shared scope Web Part even if the Allow Edit option has been unchecked.

No configuration is required to use `BehaviorEditorPart`. Just drag it from the toolbox into the `EditorZone` where you want it to appear, and the following control definition is added to the `<ZoneTemplate>` of the `EditorZone` definition:

```
<asp:BehaviorEditorPart ID=" BehaviorEditorPart1" runat=server />
```

By default, the `Title` property of this Editor Part is `"Behavior"`. You can set a different `Title` value in the control definition if you wish. Figure 7-9 shows an example of the `BehaviorEditorPart` as it appears in edit display mode in the browser.

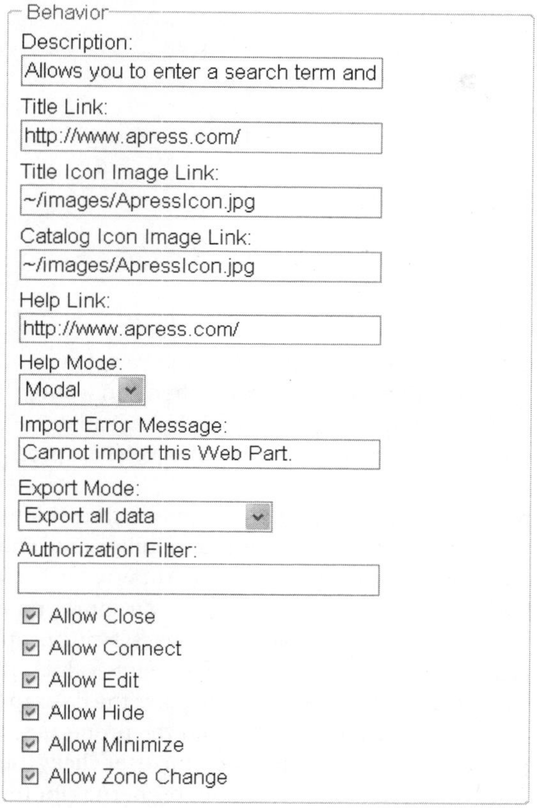

Figure 7-9. `BehaviorEditorPart`

LayoutEditorPart

The `LayoutEditorPart` allows users to set layout properties of the Web Part, such as whether the Web Part should be minimized, which zone it should be in, and which position it should appear at in that zone. Internet Explorer users will probably be baffled by this Editor Part because Internet Explorer allows you to drag and drop Web Parts to reorder them within a zone or move them from one zone to another. Other browsers, however, may not support drag-and-drop functionality, so they need to use the `LayoutEditorPart` to help facilitate moving a Web Part from place to place.

No configuration is required to use the `LayoutEditorPart`. Just drag it from the toolbox into the `EditorZone` where you want it to appear and the following control definition is added to the `<ZoneTemplate>` of the `EditorZone` definition:

```
<asp:LayoutEditorPart ID="LayoutEditor1" runat=server />
```

By default, the Title property of this Editor Part is "Layout". You can set a different Title value in the control definition if you wish. Figure 7-10 shows an example of the LayoutEditorPart as it appears in edit display mode in the browser.

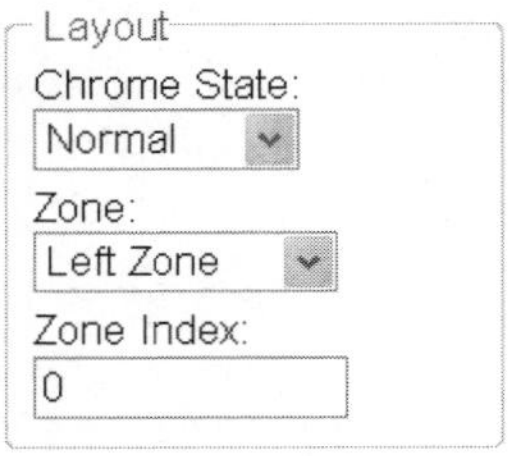

Figure 7-10. LayoutEditorPart

PropertyGridEditorPart

Web Parts can expose personalizable properties specific to that particular Web Part. For example, if you create a Web Part to display weather information to a user, then you would likely need a custom zip code property so the Web Part would know which city's weather to display. Which brings up the question, how does the user configure a custom Web Part property? The answer is a PropertyGridEditorPart.

Each custom property in a Web Part is marked with the <Personalizable> attribute identifying it as such. There are also additional attributes that give the property a friendly name and description. The PropertyGridEditorPart uses reflection to locate a custom property by searching for these attribute values. When it finds a custom property, it displays an appropriate entry field for the property based on its type. Boolean properties have check boxes, string properties have text boxes, and enumerations have a drop-down list containing possible values. It also displays the friendly name of the property above the entry field and displays the description if you hover over the name long enough. Users can then enter values for the properties, and PropertyGridEditorPart syncs the changes back to the Web Part when the user clicks the **OK** or **Apply** buttons at the bottom of the Editor Part. If there are no custom properties for the Web Part being edited, then the PropertyGridEditorPart does not display.

Like the other Editor Parts, there is no configuration required to use the PropertyGrid➥EditorPart. Just drag it from the toolbox into the EditorZone where you want it to appear and the following control definition is added to the <ZoneTemplate> of the EditorZone definition:

```
<asp:PropertyGridEditorPart ID="PropertyGridEditor1" runat=server />
```

By default, the Title property of this Editor Part is "Property Grid". You should set a different Title value in the control definition because the default value is fairly nondescript. Figure 7-11 shows an example of the PropertyGridEditorPart as it appears in edit display mode in the browser.

ConnectionsZone Control

You use the ConnectionsZone to create a region on the page to display connection information and to allow users to create connections between Provider Web Parts and Consumer Web Parts. The ConnectionsZone only appears when the page is in ConnectionDisplayMode *and* the user has selected a Web Part to connect by clicking on the Web Part's **Connect** verb from its verb menu.

Custom Web Part Properties
Date Format String:
M/dd/yyyy
Date Prefix:
Date:
☑ Show the Date
☑ Show the Time
Time Format:
StandardTime
Time Prefix:
Time:

Figure 7-11. `PropertyGridEditorPart`

One of the first things you'll notice about the `ConnectionZone` is that there are no "Connection Parts" to drop in it. The zone automatically displays the appropriate controls for setting up Web Part connection so you do not need to add any parts for this zone to function. Also notice that there are two ways to set up connections in the `ConnectionZone`: from a Provider to a Consumer or from a Consumer to a Provider. This determination is based on whether you click on a Provider Web Part's **Connect** verb or a Consumer Web Part's **Connect** verb. If you edit a Provider's connections then the `ConnectionZone` displays the connections for the Provider (if it has any) and allows you to connect the Provider to any number of consumers. If you edit a Consumer's connections, then the `ConnectionZone` displays the connection for the Consumer (if it has one) and lets you set up a single connection to a Provider. You can only set up one connection if you edit the Consumer because it only allows one connection.

There are a lot of properties for the `ConnectionZone` because it allows you to customize many of the controls it automatically displays. A total of eight different screens could display as you work with a `ConnectionZone`. You'll see three of those screens here. Why only three? It goes back to the fact that you can set up connections either from a Provider to a Consumer or from a Consumer to a Provider. Both ways have four screens each, but they are virtually identical aside from a couple of textual differences and the fact that a Provider allows you to create multiple connections and a Consumer only allows you to create one. So that leaves you with four screens: the No Active Connections Screen, the Manage Existing Connections Screen, the Add Connection Screen, and the Edit Connection Screen. And the Add and Edit connection screens are also similar aside from a few textual differences. So, let's take a look at those three screens:

■ **Note** On the screenshots that follow, you'll see numeric references to various pieces of text. These numbers correspond to the Reference column in Table 7-12 and help you identify which `ConnectionZone` properties change which text values on what screens. All the screenshots shown display the screens you see when you click on a Provider Web Part's Connect verb.

No Active Connections Screen

This screen displays when there are no existing connections to manage (see Figure 7-12). It displays a link allowing you to create a new connection and displays a title and instructional text for establishing a connection.

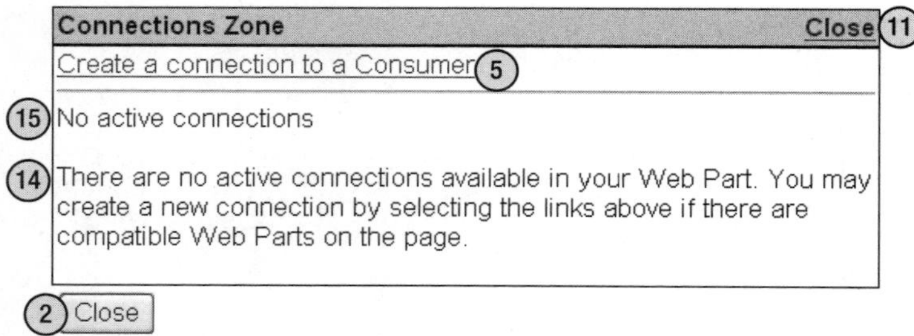

Figure 7-12. *No existing connections screen of the* `ConnectionZone`

Manage Existing Connections Screen

This screen displays when the Web Part has existing connections and allows you to disconnect or edit those connections (see Figure 7-13). The Provider version of the screen allows you to set up multiple connections using the link at the top of the page. It also displays a list of existing connections. The Consumer version only displays a single connection and does not allow you to add additional connections. You can also set up a title and instructional text on the screen as well.

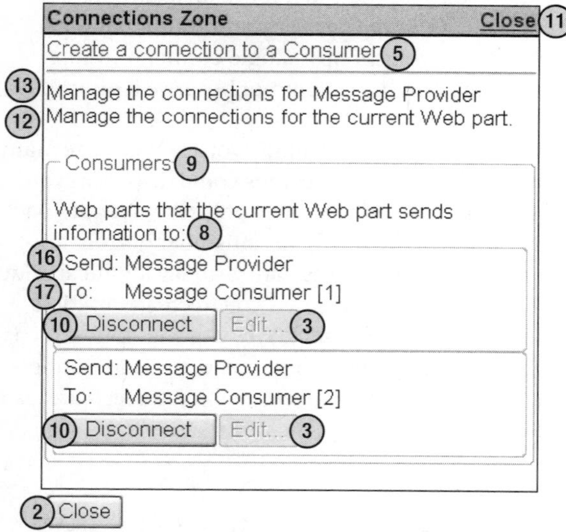

Figure 7-13. *Manage existing connecitons screen of the* `ConnectionZone`

Add Connection Screen

This screen displays when you click on the link to set up a new connection (see Figure 7-14). It provides you with a drop-down list showing all the Consumers (or Providers) to which a connection may be established. Creating a new connection is as easy as selecting an item from the drop-down list and clicking on the **Connect** button.

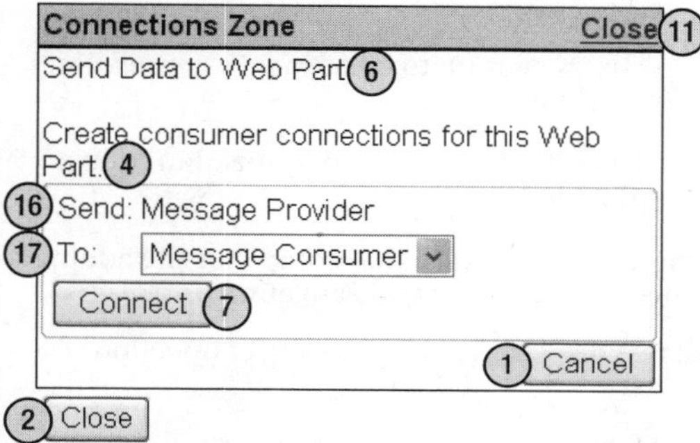

Figure 7-14. *Add connection screen (similar to the edit connection screen)*

ConnectionZone Properties

Table 7-12 is a listing of the more important properties on the `ConnectionsZone` control. Many of the properties have numeric references back to locations on the images shown above so you can see exactly where they appear on the various screens. Most of the properties without references are the Consumer-screen versions and exist in the same location as the Provider-screen variants. For example, the `ConnectToProviderTitle` and `ConnectToConsumerTitle` properties are synonymous with one another on their respective screens.

Table 7-12. *Important* `ConnectionsZone` *Properties*

Reference	Property Name	Type	Description
1	`CancelVerb`	`WebPartVerb`	Read-only reference to the verb that cancels the creation of a new connection.
2	`CloseVerb`	`WebPartVerb`	Read-only reference to the verb that closes the `ConnectionsZone`. The page is left in connection display mode after clicking the Close verb.
	`ConfigureConnectionTitle`	`String`	Title displayed when configuring an existing connection.
3	`ConfigureVerb`	`WebPartVerb`	Read-only reference to the verb that allows users to configure an existing connection.
4	`ConnectToConsumerInstructionText`	`String`	Instructional text displayed when setting up a connection from a provider to a consumer.
5	`ConnectToConsumerText`	`String`	Text for the link users click on to create a new connection from a provider to a consumer.

Table 7-12. *Important* ConnectionsZone *Properties (Continued)*

Reference	Property Name	Type	Description
6	ConnectTo➥ ConsumerTitle	String	Title displayed when setting up a new connection from a provider to a consumer.
	ConnectTo➥ Provider➥ InstructionText	String	Instructional text displayed when setting up a connection from a consumer to a provider.
	ConnectTo➥ ProviderText	String	Text for the link users click on to create a new connection from a consumer to a provider.
	ConnectTo➥ ProviderTitle	String	Title displayed when setting up a new connection from a consumer to a provider.
7	ConnectVerb	WebPartVerb	Read-only reference to the verb that completes the adding of a new connection by saving and activating it.
8	Consumers➥ InstructionText		Instructional text displayed above existing connections for a provider.
9	ConsumersTitle	String	Title displayed for the existing consumers for a provider.
10	DisconnectVerb	WebPartVerb	Read-only reference to the verb that disconnects a connection.
11	HeaderCloseVerb	WebPartVerb	Read-only reference to the verb in the header that closes the CatalogZone and switches the page back to browse display mode.
	HeaderVerbStyle	Style	Style applied to any verbs that appear in the header, such as the HeaderCloseVerb.
	Existing➥ Connection➥ ErrorMessage	String	Error text displayed if the user attempts to create a connection between two Web Parts that are already connected.
	GetFromText	String	Label text appearing next to the data provider name. Corresponds to the SendToText property for the Consumer screens (reference label 17 in the images).
	GetText	String	Label text appearing next to the type of data the consumer receives. Corresponds to the SendText property (reference label 16 in the images).
12	InstructionText	String	Brief description of how to use the catalog to add Web Parts to the page. This text may contain HTML markup.
	Instruction➥ TextStyle	Style	Style applied to the InstructionText and NoExistingConnectionInstrucitonText.
13	InstructionTitle	String	Title text that appears over the InstructionText.
	LabelStyle	Style	Style applied to labels that appear throughout the Catalog Parts in the zone.
	NewConnection➥ ErrorMessage	String	Error message displayed when an error occurs creating a new connection.

Reference	Property Name	Type	Description
14	NoExisting➥ Connection➥ InstructionText		Instructional text displayed when there are no existing connections.
15	NoExisting➥ ConnectionTitle	String	Title displayed when there are no existing connections.
	Providers➥ InstructionText	String	Instructional text display above existing connections for a consumer.
	ProvidersTitle	String	Title displayed for the existing providers for a consumer.
16	SendText	String	Label text appearing next to the type of data the provider is sending.
17	SendToText	String	Label text appearing next to the data consumer name.
	VerbButtonType	ButtonType	Determines the type of button (Link, Button, or Image) used to display verbs in the zone. This style is applied to the Cancel, Close, Configure, Connect, and Disconnect verbs at the bottom of the control.
	VerbStyle	Style	Style applied to verbs in the zone.

To create a new Connection zone, drag the ConnectionsZone control from the toolbox to the location where you want it to appear on the web form. You will see the zone appear in the IDE, and following control definition will be added to the page markup:

```
<asp:ConnectionsZone ID="ConnectionsZone1" runat="server"></asp:EditorZone>
```

There are no Connection Zone parts for the ConnectionZone control. All the connection screens are managed internally by the control itself, hence the reason for the high number of title and instructional properties. You'll learn about connections in a bit more detail later on in this chapter.

Building an Example Web Part

You've already taken a conceptual look at Web Parts and seen a couple of useful Web Part code snippets, but now its time to actually build a functioning Web Part. The question is what to build? Web Part content is limited only by your imagination. You can create consolidated reports, take surveys, show graphs or charts, display inspirational quotes, exhibit images, create advertisements, list important news or information, or do any one of a thousand other things you can think of specific to your application or business need.

To keep things simple, let's look at how to implement a Date/Time Display Web Part, which displays the server's current date and time in the browser. Users are allowed to set personalized properties on the Web Part to dictate whether to show the time and date, just the time, or just the date. They can also format the date using a format string and choose whether to view time in standard or 24-hour format. Users can also specify the labels that appear before the time and date as well. Although it seems fairly trivial, this example showcases the various aspects of building a Web Part. Figure 7-15 shows the Date/Time Display Web Part as it appears in the browser.

Figure 7-15. *Date/Time Display Web Part as seen in the browser*

As mentioned before, you can create Web Parts in two ways. If you are building an application-specific Web Part, you should opt for the simplicity of Web Part based on a user control. If you need to build a Web Part for use in multiple applications, you should opt for a custom Web Part. You'll see the Date/Time Display implemented as both, but first you need to learn a little bit about personalizable Web Part properties.

Defining Web Part Properties

Web Parts can expose personalizable properties that allow users to tailor the Web Part to their particular needs. For example, if you build a Web Part that allows users to search the Internet, you may want that Web Part to have a personalizable property allowing the user to specify which search engine to use. Or if you build a stock price display Web Part, then you'll need to create a personalizable property allowing individual users to enter the stock symbols they want to display.

Creating a personalizable property is, for the most part, just like creating any other property. The only difference is that you need to tack on a couple of property attributes that identify the property as personalizable and allow you to specify the name and description of the property when displayed in the `PropertyGridEditorPart`. Remember, the `PropertyGridEditorPart` allows users to edit personalizable properties. You can see the attributes for defining a personalizable property in Listing 7-19.

Listing 7-19. *Personalizable Property Example*

```
'***************************************************************************
    Private _ShowDate As Boolean = True

'***************************************************************************
<Personalizable(PersonalizationScope.User, False), _
 WebBrowsable(), _
 WebDisplayName("Show the Date"), _
 WebDescription("Determines whether or not to display the current date")> _
Public Property ShowDate() As Boolean
    Get
        Return _ShowDate
    End Get
    Set(ByVal value As Boolean)
        _ShowDate = value
    End Set
 End Property
```

Notice that this is a standard property aside from the property attributes. Table 7-13 provides a quick rundown of each attribute and what it does.

Table 7-13. *Personalizable Property Attributes*

Attribute	Description
`Personalizable`	Marks the property for inclusion in the personalization framework. As such, changes to the property are automatically saved and retrieved on a user-by-user basis. This attribute also allows you to mark the property as having a specific scope (Shared or User) and whether the data should be considered sensitive or nonsensitive. Marking the property as sensitive lets the Web Parts Framework know that it should restrict the export of that setting or display a sensitive data-export message to the user. The determination to display a message or restrict export is based on the `ExportMode` property of the Web Part containing the sensitive data.
`WebBrowsable`	Marks the property so it will be picked up and displayed by the `PropertyGrid➥EditorPart`. If you've marked an item as being a shared scope item in the `Personalizable` attribute, then the `PropertyGridEditorPart` only displays the property when the page is in shared scope mode.
`WebDisplayName`	Allows the `PropertyGridEditorPart` to display a user-friendly name for the property.
`WebDescription`	Allows the `PropertyGridEditorPart` to display a description of the property when the user hovers the mouse over the property name.

You can use these attributes to define personalizable properties for `UserControl`-based Web Parts and custom Web Parts alike. Now that you know how to define personalizable properties, let's take a look at the `UserControl` based Web Part implementation.

Implementing a UserControl Based Web Part

Implementing the `IWebPart` interface is by no means a difficult task, but that still doesn't mean you want to continually implement it for each Web Part you make. Simple as it may be, repetition tends to make things real old, real quick. So, as part of this example in building `UserControl`-based Web Parts, you'll also learn how to create a base class that implements the `IWebPart` interface. You can then use the base class to quickly build `UserControl`-based Web Parts without having to continually reimplement the `IWebPart` interface. We'll start by looking at the `WebPartUserControl` base class and then move on to the actual `UserControl` implementation.Any user control can participate in the Web Parts Framework by means of the `GenericWebPart`, but only user controls that implement the `IWebPart` interface can do so gracefully. As such, you should make it a priority to implement the `IWebPart` interface in your `UserControl` so it can seamlessly participate in the Web Parts Framework.

WebPartUserControl Base Class

Listing 7-20 is the entire code listing for the `WebPartUserControl` base class. For the most part, the class consists of simple property implementations for the `IWebPart` interface, but pay careful attention to `MustOverride` functions and the default values for the class fields:

Listing 7-20. `WebPartUserControl` *Base Class*

```
Imports System.Web.UI.WebControls.WebParts

Public MustInherit Class WebPartUserControl
    Inherits UserControl
    Implements IWebPart

    '**************************************************************************
    Public MustOverride Function DefaultCatalogIconImageUrl() As String
    Public MustOverride Function DefaultDescription() As String
    Public MustOverride Function DefaultSubTitle() As String
    Public MustOverride Function DefaultTitle() As String
    Public MustOverride Function DefaultTitleIconImageUrl() As String
    Public MustOverride Function DefaultTitleUrl() As String

    '**************************************************************************
    Private _WebPartData As GenericWebPart
    Private _CatalogIconImageUrl As String = DefaultCatalogIconImageUrl()
    Private _Description As String = DefaultDescription()
    Private _SubTitle As String = DefaultSubTitle()
    Private _Title As String = DefaultTitle()
    Private _TitleIconImageUrl As String = DefaultTitleIconImageUrl()
    Private _TitleUrl As String = DefaultTitleUrl()

    '**************************************************************************
    Public ReadOnly Property WebPartData() As GenericWebPart
        Get
            Try
                If _WebPartData Is Nothing Then
                    _WebPartData = WebPartManager.GetCurrentWebPartManager( _
                      Page).GetGenericWebPart(Me)
                End If
                Return _WebPartData
            Catch
                Return Nothing
            End Try
        End Get
    End Property

    '**************************************************************************
    Public Property CatalogIconImageUrl() As String _
      Implements IWebPart.CatalogIconImageUrl
        Get
            Return _CatalogIconImageUrl
        End Get
        Set(ByVal value As String)
            _CatalogIconImageUrl = value
```

```
        End Set
    End Property

    '*************************************************************************
    Public Property Description() As String Implements IWebPart.Description
        Get
            Return _Description
        End Get
        Set(ByVal value As String)
            _Description = value
        End Set
    End Property

    '*************************************************************************
    Public ReadOnly Property Subtitle() As String Implements IWebPart.Subtitle
        Get
            Return _SubTitle
        End Get
    End Property

    '*************************************************************************
    Public Property Title() As String Implements IWebPart.Title
        Get
            Return _Title
        End Get
        Set(ByVal value As String)
            _Title = value
        End Set
    End Property

    '*************************************************************************
    Public Property TitleIconImageUrl() As String _
      Implements IWebPart.TitleIconImageUrl
        Get
            Return _TitleIconImageUrl
        End Get
        Set(ByVal value As String)
            _TitleIconImageUrl = value
        End Set
    End Property

    '*************************************************************************
    Public Property TitleUrl() As String Implements IWebPart.TitleUrl
        Get
            Return _TitleUrl
        End Get
        Set(ByVal value As String)
```

```
            _TitleUrl = value
        End Set
    End Property

End Class
```

First off, notice that the WebPartUserControl class inherits its base functionality from the UserControl class and implements all the properties in the IWebPart interface. This means that the class has all the functionality of a UserControl plus the capability to interact with the Web Parts Framework, at least to the extent provided by the IWebPart properties. Having this base class is helpful when it's time to make a new UserControl-based Web Part because you just inherit all the necessary functionality from the WebPartUserControl class. You don't have to worry about implementing all the properties for the IWebPart interface all over again.

Also notice that the WebPartUserControl is a MustInherit class containing a series of MustOverride functions, each of which retrieves a default value for one of the IWebPart properties. The WebPartUserControl class uses these functions to assign default values to the property fields, thus giving each IWebPart property a default value. You have to set default values for the user control when it instantiates because the Web Part Framework sets the IWebPart properties on the control right after it instantiates. It comes down to a timing issue. If you set default values after the Web Part Framework sets the IWebPart properties, then your properties will always have default values because any changes made to the properties by the Web Part Framework would be overridden by the default values.

When you use the WebPartUserControl as a base for making a new Web Part, the Visual Studio IDE automatically stubs out the MustOverride members for you in the new Web Part. All you have to do is run though and return an appropriate default value from each one of the functions, and you'll have a working IWebPart interface implementation, complete with default values specific to your Web Part. This is a whole lot easier than having to continually set up the same properties and fields in a Web Part.

Finally, the WebPartUserControl also gives you access to the GenericWebPart object that represents the UserControl in the Web Part Framework by means of WebPartData property. This property gives you access to a variety of other Web Part properties outside of the IWebPart interface, such as the desired Width and Height, HelpUrl, Zone, ZoneIndex, and so on. To acquire a reference to the GenericWebPart, the WebPartData property uses WebPartManager.Get➥ CurrentWebPartManager(Page) to locate the WebPartManager control for the page. Then the property calls GetGenericWebPart(Me), passing in a reference to the current UserControl. The WebPartManager looks through all the GenericWebParts on the page until it finds the one representing the current UserControl and returns the GenericWebPart as a result of the function or nothing if no match was found.

Other than that, the rest of the class is just a series of simple property implementations.

DateTimeWebPart.ascx (UserControl Markup)

Because the Date/Time Display Web Part is extremely simple, it does not require many controls to implement. Listing 7-21 is the entire markup for the DateDisplayWebPart.ascx file.

Listing 7-21. DateTimeWebPart.ascx *Markup*

```
<%@ Control Language="VB" CodeFile="DateTimeWebPart.ascx.vb"
    Inherits="DateTimeWebPart" AutoEventWireup="false"%>
<asp:Label runat=server ID=lblDate />
<asp:Label runat=server ID=lblTime />
```

As you can see, the DateDisplayWebPart UserControl contains two label controls. One label displays the date whereas the other displays the time. That's the extent of the markup; now let's take a look at the code-behind file for the UserControl. Figure 7-15 earlier in the chapter shows the Date/Time Display Web Part as it appears in the browser.

DateTimeWebPart.ascx.vb (UserControl Code-Behind File)

There is a bit more substance to the code behind because it must provide default values for the IWebPart interface, contains a number of personalizable properties for configuring the date and time display settings and has rendering logic that makes use of those settings. As you look through the listing, remember that all the Overrides functions appearing in the "MustOverride Functions from WebPartUserControl" region were automatically stubbed out by the IDE, making it extremely easy to set default values for the IWebPart properties.

Listing 7-22. DateTimeWebPart *Class* (DateTimeWebPart.ascx.vb)

```
Partial Class DateTimeWebPart
    Inherits WebPartUserControl

    '***************************************************************************
    Public Enum TimeFormatEnum
        StandardTime
        TwentyFourHour
    End Enum

    '***************************************************************************
    'These define the default settings for the properties in the class
    Private _ShowDate As Boolean = True
    Private _ShowTime As Boolean = True
    Private _DateFormat As String = "M/dd/yyyy"
    Private _TimeFormat As TimeFormatEnum = TimeFormatEnum.StandardTime
    Private _DatePrefix As String = "Date: "
    Private _TimePrefix As String = "Time: "

#Region "Mustoverride Functions from WebPartUserControl"

    '***************************************************************************
    Public Overrides Function DefaultCatalogIconImageUrl() As String
        Return "~/images/ClockIcon.gif"
    End Function
```

```
    '***************************************************************************
    Public Overrides Function DefaultDescription() As String
        Return "Example Web Part that displays the date and time"
    End Function

    '***************************************************************************
    Public Overrides Function DefaultSubTitle() As String
        Return String.Empty
    End Function

    '***************************************************************************
    Public Overrides Function DefaultTitle() As String
        Return "Date and Time (UserControl)"
    End Function

    '***************************************************************************
    Public Overrides Function DefaultTitleIconImageUrl() As String
        Return "~/images/ClockIcon.gif"
    End Function

    '***************************************************************************
    Public Overrides Function DefaultTitleUrl() As String
        Return String.Empty
    End Function

#End Region

#Region "Personalizable Properties"

    '***************************************************************************
    <Personalizable(PersonalizationScope.User, False), _
     WebBrowsable(), WebDisplayName("Show the Date"), _
     WebDescription("Determines whether or not to display the current date")> _
    Public Property ShowDate() As Boolean
        Get
            Return _ShowDate
        End Get
        Set(ByVal value As Boolean)
            _ShowDate = value
        End Set
    End Property

    '***************************************************************************
    <Personalizable(PersonalizationScope.User, False), _
     WebBrowsable(), WebDisplayName("Show the Time"), _
     WebDescription("Determines whether or not to display the current time")> _
```

```
Public Property ShowTime() As Boolean
    Get
        Return _ShowTime
    End Get
    Set(ByVal value As Boolean)
        _ShowTime = value
    End Set
End Property

'***************************************************************************
<Personalizable(PersonalizationScope.User, False), _
 WebBrowsable(), WebDisplayName("Date Format String"), _
 WebDescription("Formatting string used to display the current date")> _
Public Property DateFormat() As String
    Get
        Return _DateFormat
    End Get
    Set(ByVal value As String)
        Try
            Format(Now, value)
        Catch ex As Exception
            Exit Property
        End Try
        _DateFormat = value
    End Set
End Property

'***************************************************************************
<Personalizable(PersonalizationScope.User, False), _
 WebBrowsable(), WebDisplayName("Time Format"), _
 WebDescription("Determines whether to display normal or 24-hour format")> _
Public Property TimeFormat() As TimeFormatEnum
    Get
        Return _TimeFormat
    End Get
    Set(ByVal value As TimeFormatEnum)
        _TimeFormat = value
    End Set
End Property

'***************************************************************************
<Personalizable(PersonalizationScope.User, False), _
 WebBrowsable(), WebDisplayName("Date Prefix"), _
 WebDescription("Prefix that appears before the date display")> _
Public Property DatePrefix() As String
    Get
        Return _DatePrefix
```

```
        End Get
        Set(ByVal value As String)
            _DatePrefix = value
        End Set
    End Property

    '**************************************************************************
    <Personalizable(PersonalizationScope.User, False), _
     WebBrowsable(), WebDisplayName("Time Prefix"), _
     WebDescription("Prefix that appears before the time display")> _
    Public Property TimePrefix() As String
        Get
            Return _TimePrefix
        End Get
        Set(ByVal value As String)
            _TimePrefix = value
        End Set
    End Property

#End Region

    '**************************************************************************
    Protected Sub Page_Load(ByVal sender As Object, _
      ByVal e As System.EventArgs) Handles Me.Load

        If WebPartData.HelpUrl = String.Empty Then _
            WebPartData.HelpUrl = "~/Help/DateDisplayWebPart.htm"

    End Sub

    '**************************************************************************
    Protected Sub Page_PreRender(ByVal sender As Object, _
      ByVal e As System.EventArgs) Handles Me.PreRender

        If ShowDate Then
            Me.lblDate.Text = DatePrefix & Format(Now, DateFormat)
        Else
            Me.lblDate.Visible = False
        End If

        If ShowTime Then
            Select Case TimeFormat
                Case TimeFormatEnum.TwentyFourHour
                    Me.lblTime.Text = TimePrefix & Format(Now, "HH:mm")
                Case TimeFormatEnum.StandardTime
                    Me.lblTime.Text = TimePrefix & Format(Now, "hh:mm tt")
            End Select
```

```
            If ShowDate Then lblTime.Text = "<br/>" & lblTime.Text
        Else
            Me.lblTime.Visible = False
        End If

    End Sub

End Class
```

The DateDisplayWebPart class inherits its base functionality from the MustInherit WebPartUserControl class, which means it inherits the IWebPart interface implementation. It also means that the DateDisplayWebPart class must override all the default property functions defined as MustOverride in the WebPartUserControl class. You can see that each overridden function only takes three lines of code, and two of them are automatically stubbed out for you. You just have to write the return <value> portion in the middle.

There are also six personalizable properties in the class, all of which allow the user to set display settings for the Web Part. Table 7-14 provides a listing of each personalizable property and its purpose.

Table 7-14. *Personalizable* DateDisplayWebPart Properties

Property Name	Type	Enum Values	Description
ShowDate	Boolean		True if the user wants to see the date displayed.
ShowTime	Boolean		True if the user wants to see the time displayed.
DateFormat	String		Date format string that dictates the date format.
TimeFormat	TimeFormatEnum	StandardTime TwentyFourHour	Determines whether time displays in a standard or 24-hour format.
DatePrefix	String		Prefix appearing before the date.
TimePrefix	String		Prefix appearing before the time.

Each property also has a corresponding field used to store the property value, and that field has a default value. There are a couple of different property data types in this Web Part so you can see how the PropertyGridEditorPart handles them accordingly.

The Page_Load event handler demonstrates how you can set a default value for a Web Part property not exposed by the IWebPart interface. All you need to do is check to see whether the value is empty and, if so, assign it a default property. If the property is not empty, then you can assume it has been set and therefore needs no default value. If you just set a value without checking to see whether or not a value already exists, it's tantamount to defining a static value for the property. Then again, if you want to make the property value static, then set the property and disregard the initial check.

Finally, the Page_PreRender event handler uses the personalized properties to make display decisions for the Web Part. If the user has configured the Web Part to view the date, then the date is output using the appropriate prefix and format. If the user chooses to view the time, then the time is output with the appropriate prefix and format. It also checks to make sure that the items are spaced out on separate lines.

Deploying and Using DateTimeWebPart

After you build the `DateTimeWebPart`, you need to add it to a `WebPartZone` or the `DeclarativeCatalogPart` so people can access and use it. Remember, if you add a Web Part directly to a `WebPartZone`, then it becomes a static Web Part, which you cannot delete from the web-based interface. Either way, you need to register the `UserControl` at the top of the page. Assuming that the catalog and the user control are in the same directory:

```
<%@ Register Src="DateTimeWebPart.ascx" TagPrefix="WebParts"
    TagName="DateTimeWebPart" %>
```

Then you can declare an instance of the `DateTimeWebPart` just like any other user control using the `TagPrefix` and `TagName` defined in the control registration as shown in Listing 7-23.

Listing 7-23. `DateTimeWebPart` *Control Defined in a* `DeclarativeCatalogPart`

```
<asp:CatalogZone runat="server" Width="100%" >
  <ZoneTemplate>
    <asp:DeclarativeCatalogPart ID="DeclarativeCatalogPart1" runat="server"
      Title="Web Part Catalog"
      Description="Add new Web Part to the page">
        <WebPartsTemplate>
          <WebParts:DateTimeWebPart ID="MyDateTimeWebPart1" runat="server" />
        </WebPartsTemplate>
    </asp:DeclarativeCatalogPart>
  </ZoneTemplate>
</asp:CatalogZone>
```

After placing the `DateTimeWebPart` in the catalog, users can add it to the page to see the current date and time. They can also alter the `DateTimeWebPart` control's appearance by setting personalizable properties using the `PropertyGridEditor`. Figure 7-16 shows the `DateTimeWebPart` control in the catalog, on the page, and how the `PropertyGridEditor` looks when displaying the personalizable properties from the control.

Implementing a Custom Web Part

Consequently, the crux of building a custom Web Part is to internalize the UI and output it from a procedure within your Web Part class. You can accomplish this in one of two ways. One way is to override the `Render` method of the Web Part and manually construct the HTML for your Web Part using the provided `HtmlTextWriter` object. Listing 7-24 is a simplistic example of how this may look.You implement a custom Web Part by inheriting from and extending the functionality contained in the `WebPart` base class. Any controls deriving from the `WebPart` class are capable of directly participating in the Web Parts Framework without an intermediary `GenericWebPart` wrapper. Custom Web Parts also follow a custom server control rendering model, meaning that the control has self-contained logic for rending its UI. In other words, you have to programmatically add all the child controls and HTML layout required to work with and display the control without using an external markup file (for example, the `.ascx` file for a user control). Self-contained rendering logic allows the control to be packed and deployed in an assembly without the need for any additional files.

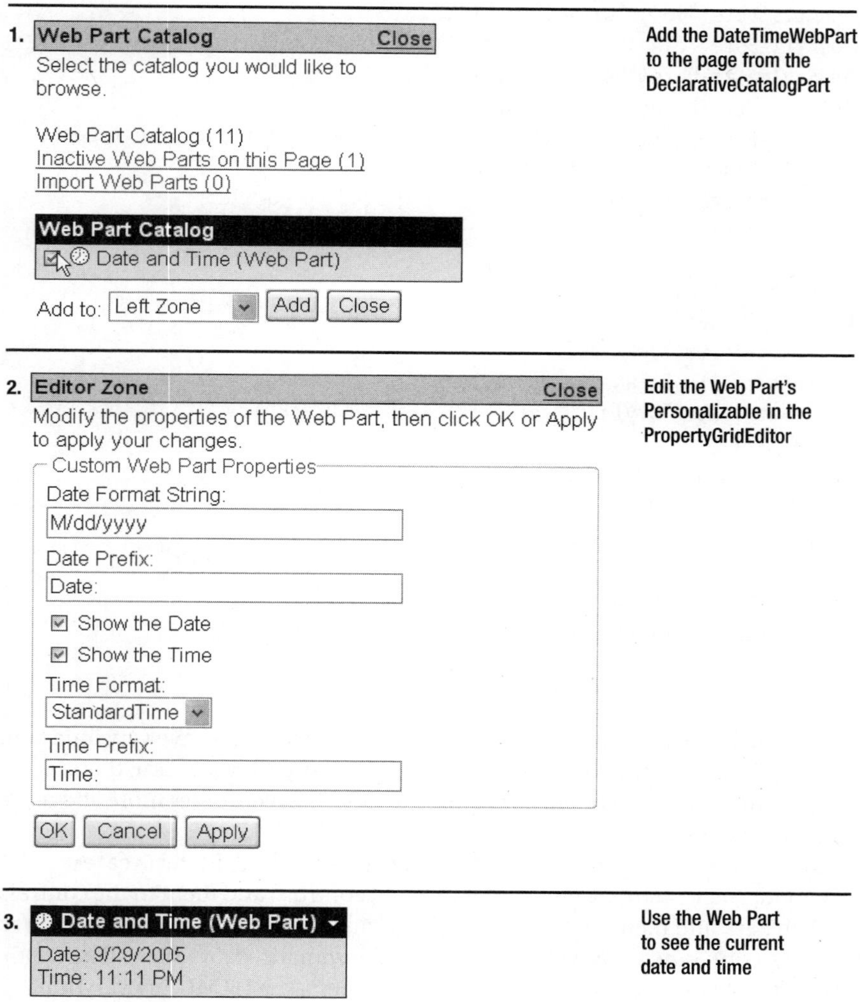

1. Web Part Catalog Close
Select the catalog you would like to browse.

Web Part Catalog (11)
Inactive Web Parts on this Page (1)
Import Web Parts (0)

Web Part Catalog
Date and Time (Web Part)

Add to: Left Zone Add Close

Add the DateTimeWebPart to the page from the DeclarativeCatalogPart

2. Editor Zone Close
Modify the properties of the Web Part, then click OK or Apply to apply your changes.
Custom Web Part Properties
Date Format String:
M/dd/yyyy
Date Prefix:
Date:
Show the Date
Show the Time
Time Format:
StandardTime
Time Prefix:
Time:
OK Cancel Apply

Edit the Web Part's Personalizable in the PropertyGridEditor

3. Date and Time (Web Part)
Date: 9/29/2005
Time: 11:11 PM

Use the Web Part to see the current date and time

Figure 7-16. *Date and Time Web Part in the catalog, its custom properties as seen in the* `PropertyGridEditor` *and on the page*

Listing 7-24. *Overriding the Render Method to Output a Custom Web Part UI*

```
'**************************************************************************
Protected Overrides Sub Render(ByVal writer As System.Web.UI.HtmlTextWriter)
  MyBase.Render(writer)

    'Fully Object Oriented Approach
      writer.AddAttribute("id", "Div1")
      writer.AddAttribute("class", "MyDivClass")
      writer.AddStyleAttribute("border", "1px solid black")
      writer.AddStyleAttribute("font-weight", "bold")
      writer.RenderBeginTag(HtmlTextWriterTag.Div) 'Renders attributes in tag
      writer.Write("This appears in the 1st div")
      writer.RenderEndTag() 'Closes off the DIV tag started earlier
      writer.WriteBreak()

    'Object Oriented/Text Approach
      writer.WriteBeginTag("div ")
      writer.WriteAttribute("id", "Div2")
      writer.WriteAttribute("class", "MyDivClass")
      writer.WriteAttribute("style", "border: 1px solid black")
      writer.Write(">")
      writer.Write("This appears in the 2nd div")
      writer.WriteEndTag("div")

    'Text-Based Approach
      writer.Write("<br><div id=Div3 class=MyDivClass style=" & _
        "'border: 1px solid black'>This appears in the 3rd div</div>")

End Sub
```

Outputting content using the HtmlTextWriter is a good idea when you have very little and/or simple content requirements. It's also very fast, so if performance is a concern, this is the way to go as well. As complexity and content size grow, this approach becomes more and more unwieldy and difficult to maintain.

Your second option is to override the CreateChildControls method. In the Create➥ChildControls method, you instantiate and configure child controls, add them to the controls collection of the Web Part, and then use those controls as you respond to page events (such as Load, PreRender, and so on). When the Web Part renders, it automatically renders all its child controls, so you don't have to worry about manually constructing the HTML for everything. Plus you have the added benefit of being able to leverage events and functionality from existing controls such as combo boxes, data grids, validators, and so on.

■ **Tip** To respond to events for child controls, you have to declare a class-level field for the control using the WithEvents keyword. You must then set up event handlers in the WebPart class to respond to events from that control.

Truth be told, the Date/Time Display Web Part is simple enough to implement by overriding the `Render` method and using the `HtmlTextWriter`. In this example, however, it's implemented by overriding the `CreateChildControls` method so you can see how to use this technique.

DateTimeWebPart2.vb

Listing 7-25 contains all the code for the `DateTimeWebPart2` Web Part. You'll find that the code for the "`Personalizable Properties`" region is not displayed because personalizable properties have identical implementations in both `UserControl`-based and custom Web Part classes.

Listing 7-25. `DateTimeWebPart2` *Class*

```
Namespace CustomWebParts

    Public Class DateTimeWebPart2
        Inherits WebPart

        '**************************************************************************
        'If you wanted to respond to events for a control, you would need to define
        'that control using the "WithEvents" keyword in the section below and
        'create event handlers for those events in the Web Part class
        '**************************************************************************
        Private lblDate As Label      'Holds reference to lblDate child control
        Private lblTime As Label      'Holds reference to lblTime child control

        #Region "Personalizable Properties"
          'All of the personalizable properties, their fields, and their attributes
          'are identical to those listed in the UserControl implementation
        #End Region

        '**************************************************************************
        Sub New()
            'All Web Part Properties are inherited from the WebParts class
            'so you can set up default property values in the constructor
            CatalogIconImageUrl = "~/images/ClockIcon.gif"
            Description = "Example Web Part that displays the date and time"
            Title = "Date and Time (Web Part)"
            TitleIconImageUrl = "~/images/ClockIcon.gif"
            HelpUrl = "~/Help/DateDisplayWebPart.htm"
        End Sub

        '**************************************************************************
        Protected Overrides Sub CreateChildControls()

            'Create new child label controls and maintain a reference to them
            lblDate = New Label
            lblTime = New Label
```

```
            'Set up child control properties
            lblDate.ID = "lblDate"
            lblTime.ID = "lblTime"

            'Add child controls to the Controls collection
            Controls.Add(lblDate)
            Controls.Add(lblTime)

            MyBase.CreateChildControls()

        End Sub

        '**************************************************************************
        Protected Overrides Sub OnPreRender(ByVal e As System.EventArgs)

            'Notice that this code is identical to that of the UserControl
            If ShowDate Then
                Me.lblDate.Text = DatePrefix & Format(Now, DateFormat)
            Else
                Me.lblDate.Visible = False
            End If

            If ShowTime Then
                Select Case TimeFormat
                    Case TimeFormatEnum.TwentyFourHour
                        Me.lblTime.Text = TimePrefix & Format(Now, "HH:mm")
                    Case TimeFormatEnum.StandardTime
                        Me.lblTime.Text = TimePrefix & Format(Now, "hh:mm tt")
                End Select
                If ShowDate Then lblTime.Text = "<br/>" & lblTime.Text
            Else
                Me.lblTime.Visible = False
            End If

            MyBase.OnPreRender(e)

        End Sub

    End Class

End Namespace
```

Like user controls, you must register custom controls on the page in which they are used (or for the entire application in the `Web.config`). Either way, the `Register` directive needs to know which namespace houses the control. In this case, the `DateTimeWebPart2` class is in the `CustomWebParts` namespace.

Being that the definition of a custom Web Part is that it derives from the `WebPart` class, it should come as no shocker that the `DateTimeWebPart2` inherits `WebPart`. This means that the class has direct access to all the Web Part properties without having to go through the GenericWebPart class or manually implementing the IWebPart interface. Because the class has direct access to the properties, you can set defaults for those properties in the New constructor without fear that your default properties will overwrite the values acquired from personalization setting stored by the Web Part Framework.

All the controls required by the DateTimeWebPart2 control are instantiated and configured in the CreateChildControls method. In this example, the task only entails creating two label controls, setting their ID values, and adding them to the Controls collection. Also note that you'll need access to these controls in the OnPreRender method, so references to the labels are stored at the class level in the lblDate and lblTime fields. In essence, this is what you'll do for more complex controls, but the configuration portion will likely be more intensive.

That brings us to OnPreRender, which is fairly anticlimactic. Notice that you have references to the lblDate and lblTime labels. This is effectively the same situation you had in the user control, the only difference being that the labels are generated in code and not defined in a markup file. As such, the OnPreRender code for the UserControl implementation and the custom Web Part implementation are nearly identical. The only difference is the call to MyBase.OnPreRender(e) at the bottom of the method, which ensures that the base control's original OnPreRender runs. It's a good habit to let the base function run as long as it isn't affecting anything negatively.

Deploying and Using DateTimeWebPart2

You also need to deploy custom Web Parts to a WebPartZone or a DeclarativeCatalogPart to allow users to access it on the page. This requires a minor change to the Register directive:

```
<%@ Register Namespace="CustomWebParts" TagPrefix="WebParts" %>
```

Then you can declare an instance of the DateTimeWebPart2 using the TagPrefix defined in the control registration and the class name (which is DateTimeWebPart2) as shown in Listing 7-26.

Listing 7-26. DateTimeWebPart2 *Control Defined in a* DeclarativeCatalogPart

```
<asp:CatalogZone runat="server" Width="100%" >
  <ZoneTemplate>
    <asp:DeclarativeCatalogPart ID="DeclarativeCatalogPart1" runat="server"
      Title="Web Part Catalog"
      Description="Add new Web Part to the page">
        <WebPartsTemplate>
          <WebParts:DateTimeWebPart2 ID="MyDateTimeWebPart2" runat="server" />
        </WebPartsTemplate>
    </asp:DeclarativeCatalogPart>
  </ZoneTemplate>
</asp:CatalogZone>
```

In the browser, DateTimeWebPart2 behaves no differently than its UserControl-based counterpart. They both have the same properties and the same UI logic, so they are, for all intents and purposes, identical. The only visual difference is the title text, which was only used to distinguish them from one another.

Now that you have an idea of how to build simple Web Parts, we'll build upon that knowledge and take a brief look at some advanced Web Part topics.

Advanced Web Part Topics

There are a couple of advanced Web Part techniques that you won't necessarily use all the time, but they definitely come in handy when you need them. In this section, you'll look at custom Web Part verbs, building Web Parts that can provide data to and consume data from other Web Parts, and importing and exporting Web Part settings.

Adding Custom Verbs to Your Web Part

Web Part verbs are action items that appear on the menu of a Web Part. Out of the box, Web Part verbs provide users with an easy way to access common functionality such as minimizing, restoring, deleting, editing, exporting, and connecting a Web Part. If you are building a custom Web Part control, then you can also create your own Web Part verbs that execute custom actions for your Web Part.

The process for adding a custom Web Part is simple. First, you need to create a Web Part that derives from the `WebPart` class. Then you create verb handlers for the verbs you are adding to the Web Part. A verb handler is a method that executes when a user clicks on the verb. After defining your verb handlers, you can override the `Verbs` property and set up your custom verbs. The `Verbs` property only has to account for the custom verbs in your Web Part. The Web Part Framework generates the standard verbs automatically. Setting up custom verbs entails creating new `WebPartVerb` objects that point to their appropriate verb handlers, configure the `WebPartVerb` property values, and return a `WebPartVerbCollection` containing all your newly created `WebPartVerb` objects. The Web Part Framework automatically adds your new verbs to the Web Part's menu and, when users click on the menu item, executes the appropriate handler.

In Listing 7-27, you'll see how to add the Next Zone and Previous Zone verbs to the `DateTimeWebPart2` class. These verbs allow users to move the Web Part around the page without having to switch into design mode. For the sake of brevity, only the applicable portions of code are shown.

Listing 7-27. *Adding Custom Verbs to a Web Part*

```
Namespace CustomWebParts

    Public Class DateTimeWebPart2
        Inherits WebPart

        '... Code Not Shown for the Sake of Brevity ...

        '***********************************************************************
        Public Overrides ReadOnly Property Verbs() _
          As System.Web.UI.WebControls.WebParts.WebPartVerbCollection
            Get

                'Instantiate two new verb objects
                Dim MoveNextZone As New WebPartVerb("v1", _
                  New WebPartEventHandler(AddressOf MoveNextZoneClick))
```

```
        Dim MovePrevZone As New WebPartVerb("v2", _
          New WebPartEventHandler(AddressOf MovePrevZoneClick))

        'Set up Verb Properties
        MoveNextZone.Text = "Next Zone"
        MoveNextZone.Description = "Moves Web Part to the next zone"
        MoveNextZone.ImageUrl = "~/Images/NextIcon.gif"

        MovePrevZone.Text = "Previous Zone"
        MovePrevZone.Description = "Moves Web Part to the previous zone"
        MovePrevZone.ImageUrl = "~/Images/PrevIcon.gif"

        'Create and return a WebPartVerbCollection
        Dim PartVerbs As WebPartVerb() = {MoveNextZone, MovePrevZone}
        Return New WebPartVerbCollection(PartVerbs)

    End Get
End Property

'***************************************************************************
Private Sub MoveNextZoneClick(ByVal sender As Object, _
  ByVal e As WebPartEventArgs)

    'Moves Web Part to the next zone
    Dim CurrentZoneIndex As Integer = WebPartManager.Zones.IndexOf(Zone)
    Dim MaxZoneIndex As Integer = WebPartManager.Zones.Count - 1

    If CurrentZoneIndex < MaxZoneIndex Then
        WebPartManager.MoveWebPart(Me, _
          WebPartManager.Zones(CurrentZoneIndex + 1), 0)
    Else
        WebPartManager.MoveWebPart(Me, _
          WebPartManager.Zones(0), 0)
    End If

End Sub

'***************************************************************************
Private Sub MovePrevZoneClick(ByVal sender As Object, _
  ByVal e As WebPartEventArgs)

    Dim CurrentZoneIndex As Integer = WebPartManager.Zones.IndexOf(Zone)
    Dim MaxZoneIndex As Integer = WebPartManager.Zones.Count - 1

    'Moves Web Part to the previous zone
    If CurrentZoneIndex > 0 Then
```

```
                WebPartManager.MoveWebPart(Me, _
                  WebPartManager.Zones(CurrentZoneIndex - 1), 0)
            Else
                WebPartManager.MoveWebPart(Me, _
                  WebPartManager.Zones(MaxZoneIndex), 0)
            End If

        End Sub

        '... Code Not Shown for the Sake of Brevity ...

End Class
```

Inside the overridden Verbs property, you can see the constructor syntax for a new WebPartVerb object. It accepts two parameters: a string containing an arbitrary unique ID for the verb and a WebPartEventHandler object that points to the appropriate verb handler. You specify which method you want to use as the verb handler by passing it into the WebPartEventHandler constructor behind the AddressOf keyword. All verb methods share a common method signature, so the method you specify has to accept an object as the first parameter and a WebPartEventArgs object as the second parameter. Notice that both the MoveNextZoneClick and the MovePrevZoneClick methods adhere to the method signature.

After creating the WebPartVerb objects, you should define values for the Name and Description properties. You can also opt to specify an icon for the verb by setting the ImageUrl property. The icon appears to the left of the verb text in the menu.

Lastly, you need to create a WebPartVerbCollection object. You do this by first creating an array containing your WebPartVerb objects, and then you pass that array into the WebPartVerbCollection constructor to initialize the collection. Then you return the collection as the result of the function, and the Web Parts Framework places the new verbs at the top of the menu in the order you passed them in. The default verbs (for example, Minimize, Restore, Close, and so on) appear at the bottom of the menu.

As for the verb handler methods, both are relatively simple and do not require a lot of explanation. Basically, they determine the index of the zone containing the control and move the control to the next or previous index. If the index surpasses the high or low bounds of the zone collection, then it logically "wraps" to the next or previous zone. Figure 7-17 shows the DateTimeWebPart2 menu as seen in the browser with the newly added **Next Zone** and **Previous Zone** verbs.

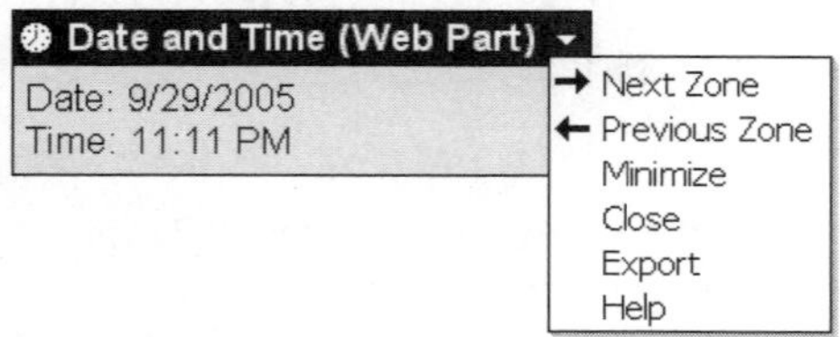

Figure 7-17. *Custom verbs with icons in the* DateTimeWebPart2 *class*

Connection Providers and Consumers

Most Web Parts are self-contained components that run independently of other Web Parts on the page, but occasionally, you'll want Web Parts to interact with one another. For example, you may want to display a list of records in one Web Part and display a more detailed view of the selected record in a second Web Part (or sets of details in a series of other Web Parts). The Web Parts Framework enables Web Parts to communicate with other Web Parts on the page through connections.

Connecting two Web Parts requires a connection interface, connection provider, connection consumer, and connection instance. Figure 7-18 gives an overview of how to create connections and the various pieces of components are described in more detail in the list that follows.

- *Connection Interface:* A custom interface you create to define how the two Web Parts in the connection share information and communicate with one another. There are no restrictions on what you can define in the interface, so feel free to put whatever properties, methods, and functions you feel are useful.
- *Connection Provider Web Part:* Responsible for exposing a function marked with the `ConnectionProvider` attribute and returning an object that implements the appropriate connection interface as the result of that function. The Web Part Framework uses the marked function to acquire the connection interface object before passing it off to the connection consumer.
- *Connection Consumer Web Part:* Responsible for exposing a function marked with the `ConnectionConsumer` attribute, which accepts an appropriate incoming connection interface object. The Web Part Framework passes the connection interface object acquired from the connection provider into the connection consumer via the marked method. The consumer is then responsible for storing a reference to and/or using the connection interface object accordingly.
- *Connection Instance:* After creating a connection interface, a connection provider, and a connection consumer, you have Web Parts that are capable of participating in a connection. But, you still have to create Web Part instances to go on pages and a connection instance that connects those Web Part instances. You will explore how to set up connection instances later on in this section.

In the following sections, you'll learn about all these topics as you implement the `MessageProvider` and `MessageConsumer` Web Parts. These are simple controls that really demonstrate how to set up connections without the clutter of auxiliary functionality.

■Note The Web Parts in this section are implemented as `UserControl`-based Web Parts, but you can apply the same connection techniques to custom Web Parts.

Defining the IMessage Connection Interface

These controls are both built to send and receive a single string-based message, so the `IMessage` interface is extremely simple. In the next section, you'll see how the `MessageProvider` passes a message to the `MessageConsumer` using the interface. Your connection interface will probably need a few more properties, but the concept is still the same (see Listing 7-28).

1. Create a Custom Message Interface that defines the data you need to pass between the Web Parts (ICustomMessage is only an EXAMPLE name).

2. Create a Provider Web Part that exposes an ICustomMessage property. That property should return an object that implements the ICustomMessage Interface (normally the Provider Web Part implements this interface and just returns a reference to itself).

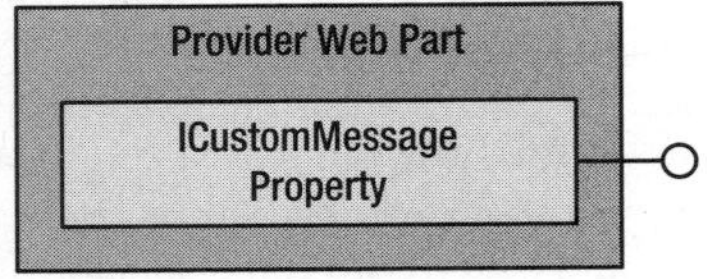

3. Create a Consumer Web Part that exposes a property that accepts an object that implements the Custom Message Interface. You can then use the data in the ICustomMessage object to accomplish a task in your Web Part

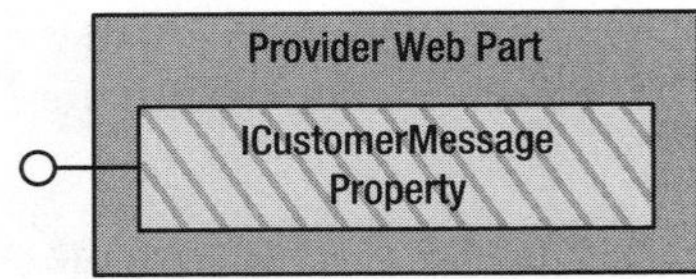

4. Define a Connection Between the Two Web Parts (either Statically or Dynamically).

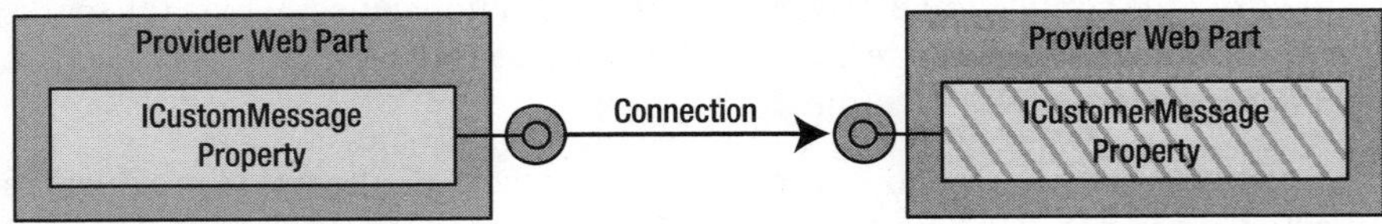

5. The Web Part Framework passes the ICustomMessage object from the Provider to the Consumer Web Part. The Consumer then uses it accordingly.

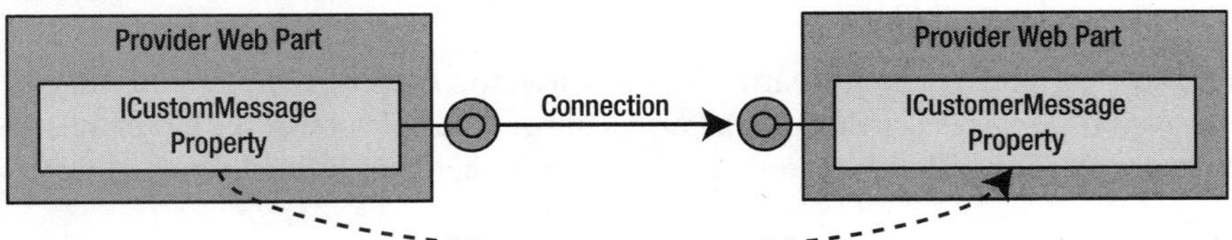

Figure 7-18. *Creating a Web Part connection*

```
Public Interface IMessageListing 7-28. IMessage Interface
    ReadOnly Property Message() As String
    Sub PassBackConsumerData(ByVal ConsumerName As String)
End Interface
```

One thing you need to realize about Web Part connections is that you *can* pass information from the consumer Web Part back into the provider Web Part using the connection interface object. When you first hear the provider and consumer terminology, it makes a connection sound very one directional. Later, you'll see a demonstration showing how to use the `PassBackConsumerData` on the connection interface object to send data from the `MessageConsumer` Web Part to the `MessageProvider` Web Part.

Creating the MessageProvider Web Part

The `MessageProvider` Web Part allows users to enter a text message and submit it, then takes that message and "provides" it to "consumer" Web Parts where it can be displayed. Onscreen, the control only has two inputs, a text box and a button. A list at the bottom of the control also identifies all the consumers to which the Web Part sends data. I'll use this list later on to demonstrate how a Consumer Web Part can pass information back to the Provider Web Part over the Custom Message Interface. Figure 7-19 shows the `MessageProvider` UI as it appears in the browser.

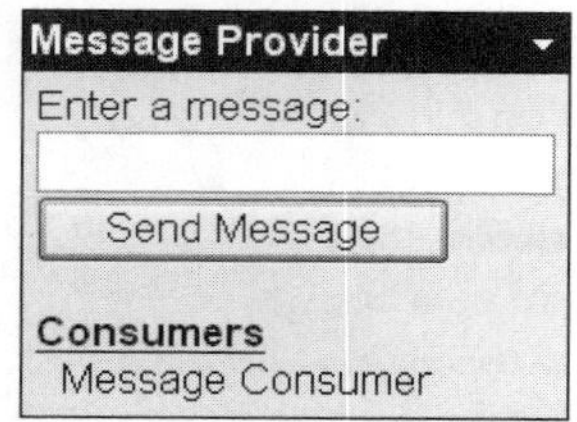

Figure 7-19. `MessageProvider` *Web Part*

Next, Listing 7-29 and 7-30 show the markup and code used to create the `MessageProvider` Web Part. Because you've already seen how to use the `WebPartUserControl` class to help implement a `UserControl` based Web Part, I'll omit the default property overrides to save space. Pay careful attention to the `ConnectionProvider` attribute on the `ProvideInterface` function as you look over the listing, because this attribute marks the function (and therefore the class) as being a Provider Web Part.

Listing 7-29. `MessageProvider.ascx` *(Markup)*

```
<%@ Control Language="VB" AutoEventWireup="false"
            CodeFile="MessageProvider.ascx.vb"
            Inherits="MessageProvider" %>
Enter a message:<br />
<asp:TextBox runat=server ID=txtMessage />
<asp:Button runat=server ID=btnSubmit Text="Send Message" /><br />
<asp:Label runat=server ID=lblConsumers EnableViewState=false/>
```

Listing 7-30. `MessageProvider.ascx.vb` *(Code Behind)*

```
Partial Class MessageProvider
    Inherits WebPartUserControl
    Implements IMessage

#Region "WebPartUserControl Overrides"
    'Not Displayed for the Sake of Brevity
#End Region

    '***************************************************************************
    Public ReadOnly Property Message() As String Implements IMessage.Message
        Get
            Return Me.txtMessage.Text
        End Get
    End Property

    '***************************************************************************
    Public Sub PassBackConsumerData(ByVal ConsumerName As String) _
      Implements IMessage.PassBackConsumerData

        If lblConsumers.Text = String.Empty Then _
            lblConsumers.Text &= "<br/><b><u>Consumers</u></b>"

        lblConsumers.Text &= "<br/>  " & ConsumerName

    End Sub

    '***************************************************************************
    <ConnectionProvider("Message Provider","MyProviderConnectionPoint")> _
    Public Function ProvideInterface() As IMessage

      'Since the MessageProvider class implements the IMessage Interface, it
      'passes a reference of itself to the consumer

        Return Me

    End Function

End Class
```

Aside from inheriting its base functionality from `WebPartUserControl`, the `MessageProvider` also implements the `IMessage` interface. As such, the `MessageProvider` can pass itself as the connection interface object to connection consumers, which it does in the `ProvideInterface` function. Another tactic is to create a third object that supports the connection interface and pass that object to the consumer. It comes down to a matter of necessity or preference. If you need to do it a particular way or prefer one way over the other, then feel free to choose whichever one suits your needs because either one is valid.

Attached to the `ProvideInterace` function you'll see the `ConnectionProvider` attribute. This marks the function as being a provider connection point. A provider connection point is a function capable of returning a connection interface object. Inside the `ConnectionProvider` attribute, you give the provider connection point a friendly name (**Message Provider**) to help identify the connection point when it displays in the `ConnectionsZone`. You can also opt to define a connection point ID (**MyProviderConnectionPoint**), which is used to reference that particular connection point when setting up connections programmatically. If you do not specify the connection point ID, it defaults to "default".

A single provider connection point can participate in multiple connections, so you can think of it as a one-to-many relationship. In other words, a single `MessageProvider` Web Part can act as the connection provider for multiple `MessageConsumer` Web Parts. You can also define multiple provider connection points within a Web Part. This allows you to support separate connection interfaces from a single Web Part. This would be helpful if, for example, you wanted to define two messages in the `MessageProvider` and allow `MessageConsumers` to connect to one message or the other. When you have multiple connection points in a Web Part, the friendly names and connection point ID values make it possible to locate or specify a particular connection point.

Notice that the `Message` property of the `IMessage` interface acquires its value from the text in the `txtMessage` text box control. Thus, when you enter text into the message text box, that text becomes the value of the `Message` property in the `IMessage` interface. Because the `MessageProvider` sends a reference of itself as the connection interface object, connection consumers can get or set the text from the text box in the `MessageProvider`. This is an example of the two-way communication between a provider and a consumer. Another example is the `PassBackConsumerData` function, which accepts the consumer name as a parameter. This function builds a list of all the consumers who use the `MessageProvider` Web Part in a connection. Because this function is part of the `IMessage` interface, it means that the consumer has access to the method and can call it across the connection.

Creating the MessageConsumer Web Part

The `MessageConsumer` Web Part is a connection consumer that uses the `IMessage` connection interface object from the `MessageProvider`. Its UI consists of a single label that displays the incoming text messaged. Figure 7-20 shows the `MessageConsumer` as it appears in the browser.

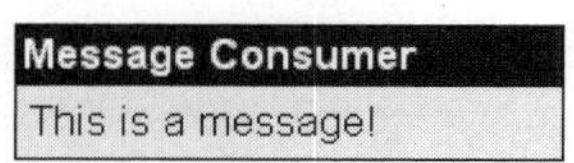

Figure 7-20. `MessageConsumer` *Web Part*

Listing 7-31 is the code for the `MessageProvider` class. Once again, the overrides for the inherited `WebPartUserControl` class have been omitted.

Listing 7-31. `MessageConsumer` *Web Part*

```
Partial Class MessageConsumer
    Inherits WebPartUserControl

#Region "WebPartUserControl Overrides"
    'Not Displayed for the Sake of Brevity
#End Region

    '***************************************************************************
    Private MessageData As IMessage

    '***************************************************************************
    <ConnectionConsumer("Message Consumer","MyConsumerConnectionPoint")> _
    Sub AcquireInterface(ByVal MessageDataIn As IMessage)
        MessageData = MessageDataIn
        MessageData.PassBackConsumerData(Me.Title)
    End Sub

    '***************************************************************************
    Protected Sub Page_PreRender(ByVal sender As Object, _
      ByVal e As System.EventArgs) Handles Me.PreRender

        If (MessageData) Is Nothing Then
            lblMessage.Text = "No connection available"
        Else
            If MessageData.Message = String.Empty Then
                lblMessage.Text = "&lt;No Message&gt;"
            Else
                lblMessage.Text = MessageData.Message
            End If
        End If

    End Sub

End Class
```

Here's a quick rundown of how the `MessageConsumer` works. First, it defines a private field named `MessageData` in which to store the connection interface object. Notice that `MessageData` is an `IMessage` variable, meaning that the variable can store a reference to any object that implements the `IMessage` interface. That's good, because that's what the `MessageProvider` Web Part provides.

Next, the class contains a method named `AcquireInterface` that accepts an incoming `IMessage` connection interface object. Notice that the `AcquireInterface` function is tagged with the `ConnectionConsumer` attribute. This marks the function as being a consumer connection point capable of accepting an interface object from a provider. You use the `ConnectionConsumer` attribute to give the consumer connection point a friendly name (**Message**

Consumer), which helps identify the connection point when it displays in the ConnectionsZone. You can also opt to define a connection point ID (**MyConsumerConnectionPoint**), which is used to reference that particular connection point when setting up connections programmatically. If you do not specify the connection point ID, it defaults to "default".

Unlike provider connection points, consumer connection points can only be involved in a single connection. In other words, a MessageConsumer Web Part instance can only receive its message information from a single MessageProvider Web Part. Of course, you can still define multiple consumer connection points inside of your Web Part if you really need to pull from multiple providers, but each individual consumer connection point is still subject to that one-to-one relationship.

When the Web Parts Framework passes an IMessage object into the MessageConsumer Web Part via the AcquireInterface function, the function stores a reference to the object using the MessageData field variable. It then calls PassBackConsumerData(Me.Title) to demonstrate how you can execute functions on the Provider Web Part from the Consumer Web Part using the connection interface. This call forces the MessageProvider to display the name of the MessageConsumer Web Part in its list of active consumers.

Finally, the render method uses the MessageData field to determine what to display in the MessageConsumer Web Part's label. Notice that it checks to see if it has a valid reference to the connection interface object before using it. When the connection interface object is not present, it means that the Web Part is not participating in a connection, and the label text is updated to reflect this situation. Otherwise, the label text can be set to the Message property of the MessageData field. If the message is blank, the code displays <No Message> as a visual indicating that the connection is working, but the message is blank. Remember, the Message property pulls the message text directly from the text box field on the MessageProvider Web Part.

Caution Web Parts that are not yet part of a connection are displayed on the page but will not have a reference to the connection interface object. You should always check to make sure you have a valid reference to the connection interface object before you attempt to use it.

Creating Static Connections

Defining a consumer connection point and a provider connection point in a pair of Web Parts simply sets them up to accept connections; it does not actually create the connection itself. To create the actual connection, you have to define which Web Part instances and what connection points in those instances are involved in the connection.

Connections are considered static or dynamic depending on how they are defined. Static connections appear directly in the page markup in the <StaticConnections> section of the WebPartManager and ProxyWebPartManger controls. Because the connection is hard-coded, it cannot change, and is therefore static. Listing 7-32 is a quick example showing how to create a static connection between a MessageProvider and a MessageConsumer.

Listing 7-32. *Creating a Static Connection*

```
<!-- Define static connections in the Web Part Manager -->
<asp:WebPartManager ID="WebPartManager1" runat="server">
    <StaticConnections>
        <asp:WebPartConnection ID="StaticConnection1"
            ProviderID="MessageProvider1"
            ConsumerID="MessageConsumer1"
            ProviderConnectionPointID="MyProviderConnectionPoint"
            ConsumerConnectionPointID="MyConsumerConnectionPoint"
        />
    </StaticConnections>
</asp:WebPartManager>

<!-- Define static Web Part in a WebPartZone -->
<asp:WebPartZone ID="zoneLeft" runat="server" HeaderText="Left Zone">
    <ZoneTemplate>
        <uc1:MessageProvider ID="MessageProvider1" runat="server" />
        <uc2:MessageConsumer ID="MessageConsumer1" runat="server" />
    </ZoneTemplate>
</asp:WebPartZone>
```

To define a connection, you must specify values for the `ID`, `ProviderID`, and `ConsumerID` properties. You can leave off the `ProviderConnectionPointID` and the `ConsumerConnectionPointID` properties, but the values will default to “default”. That’s all there is to it. When you run this page, the `MessageConsumer` Web Part receives message information from the `MessageProvider` Web Part.

Creating Dynamic Connections

In this section, you’ll learn how to set up dynamic connections as we walk through connecting the `MessageConsumer` Web Part to the `MessageProvider` Web Part. Defining a dynamic connection is done entirely using the browser-based interface, so there are illustrations to help you visualize what happens onscreen.

The process begins when you place the page into connection display mode. When the page switches into this mode, the Web Parts Framework iterates through all the Web Part controls on the page and determines which ones are capable of taking part in a connection, that is, any Web Parts that have connection points. As the framework encounters Web Parts that can support connections, it enables the **Connect** verb in the Web Part’s menu as shown in Figure 7-21.

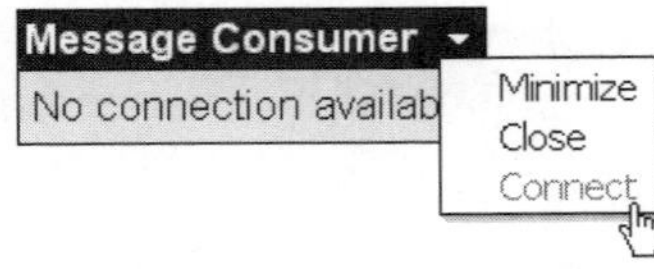

Figure 7-21. *Click the **Connect** verb on the Web Part context menu.*

Selecting the **Connect** verb from the menu causes the `ConnectionsZone` to display the connection information about the Web Part. If the Web Part is new, then the `ConnectionsZone` informs you that there are no active connections and gives you a link at the top of the zone to allow you to create a connection as shown in Figure 7-22.

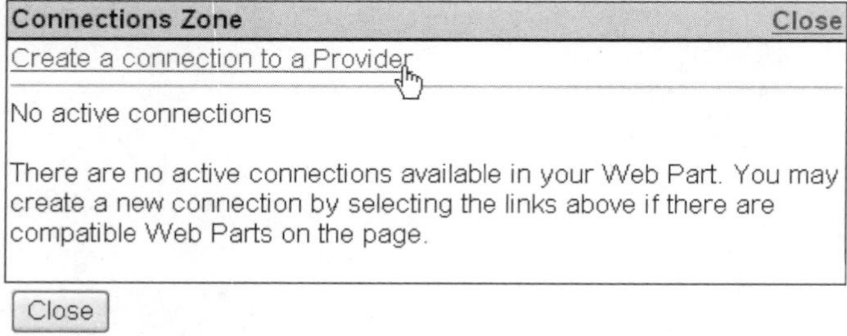

Figure 7-22. *Click on the **Create a connection to a Provider** link at the top of the Connection Zone.*

Clicking on that link takes you to the connection definition screen, which displays a list of possible provider connection points for the provider in a drop-down list (see Figure 7-23. The list displays the friendly name specified in the `ConnectionProvider` attribute and is intelligently designed, so it only displays provider connection points that match the connection interface for your consumer. In other words, if your Web Part expects an `IMessage` object, then only provider connection points that return `IMessage` objects show up in the list. If one provider exposes multiple connection points, then all those connection points show up in the list.

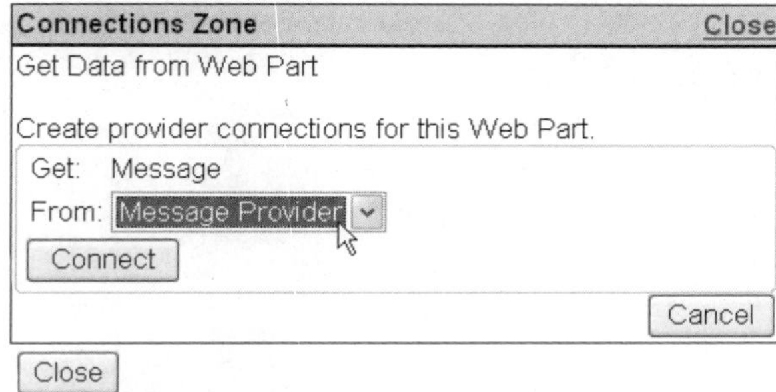

Figure 7-23. *Choose a provider connection point from the provider drop-down list, and then click the **Connect** button to create a Web Part connection.*

After you select the provider from the drop-down list, click on the **Connect** button to create the connection. After creating the connection, follow the screen that allows you to disconnect the connection as shown in Figure 7-24.

This is also the screen you would have seen after clicking on the **Connect** verb if the Web Part had an existing connection. Clicking on the **Disconnect** button removes the connection and data is no longer sent to the `MessageConsumer` Web Part.

When you set up the connection from the consumer to the provider, you can only define one connection. Remember, consumers can only have one provider. Providers, however, can have many consumers. As such, providers can display all their connections to consumers when you choose **Connect** from their verb menu. Figure 7-25 shows the connection screen for a `MessageProvider` that is providing data to three `MessageConsumer` Web Parts.

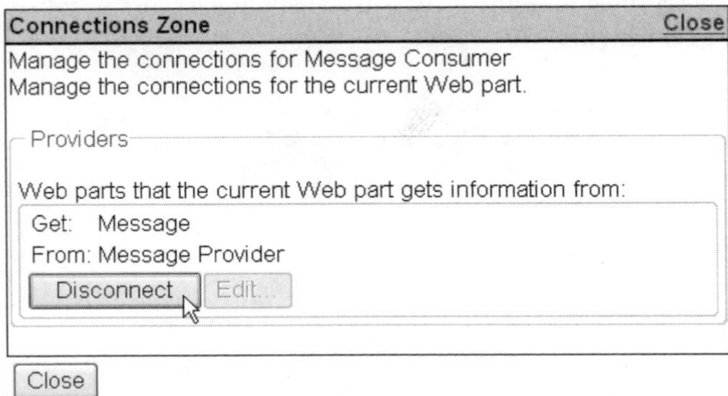

Figure 7-24. *The Consumer Web Part's Manage Existing Connections screen allows you to disconnect a Web Part connection by clicking on the **Disconnect** button. You can only create one connection at a time for a Consumer Web Part.*

Notice that you can manage all the connections at once from the provider. You can also specify new connections to the provider by clicking on the link at the top of the `ConnectionsZone`, but you'll choose a consumer from the drop-down list this time around instead of a provider (see Figure 7-26).

Connections Zone
Close
Create a connection to a Consumer
Manage the connections for Message Provider
Manage the connections for the current Web part.
Consumers
Web parts that the current Web part sends information to:
Send: Message Provider
To: Message Consumer [1]
Disconnect
Edit...
Send: Message Provider
To: Message Consumer [2]
Disconnect
Edit...
Send: Message Provider
To: Message Consumer [3]
Disconnect
Edit...
Close

Figure 7-25. *The Provider Web Part's Manage Existing Connections screen displays multiple connections because a Provider Web Part can acts as the provider for multiple consumers.*

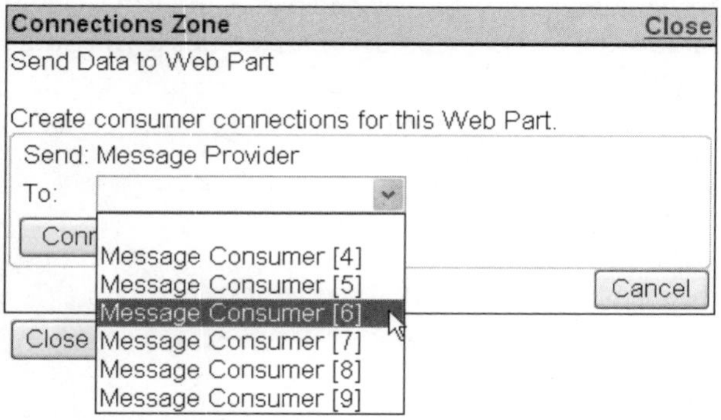

Figure 7-26. *Choosing a consumer connection point from the consumer drop-down list*

Exporting Web Part Configuration Files

Earlier in the chapter, you learned how you can add Web Parts to a page by uploading and importing a Web Part configuration file using the `ImportCatalogPart` control. Naturally, this raises the question, how do you get a Web Part definition file? The answer is that you export them using the built-in export functionality in the Web Parts Framework.

Before you can export a Web Part file, however, you must enable exporting for the application in the `Web.config`. ASP.NET takes security very seriously, and because the possibility exists for Web Part configurations to contain confidential information, exports are disabled by default. To enable exporting, you set the `enableExport` attribute in the `<webParts>` section to true as shown in Listing 7-33.

Listing 7-33. *Enabling Web Part Configuration File Exporting*

```
<configuration>
    ...
    <system.web>
        ...
        <webParts enableExport="true">
            ...
        </webParts>
    </system.web>
</configuration>
```

After you have enabled exporting in general, you must also set the `ExportMode` for the Web Part. By default, the `ExportMode` property on a Web Part is set to `None`, meaning that it does not allow users to export the Web Part. You need to set the `ExportMode` to `All` or `NonSensitiveData`. `All` means that all the data in the Web Part is exported regardless of whether or not it has been marked as sensitive. `NonSensitiveData` means that all the data is exported except properties marked as sensitive. Remember, you can mark a Web Part property as sensitive using the `Personalizable` attribute discussed earlier in the chapter.

You set the `ExportMode` for a custom Web Part either by initializing it along with all the other Web Part properties in the constructor or by overriding the `ExportMode` property and returning a static value. The option you choose depends on what you are trying to accomplish.

If you specify a default value in the constructor, then the value you choose is simply the default. In other words, users can change that value using the BehaviorEditorPart. If this is your intention, then use the approach shown in Listing 7-34.

Listing 7-34. *Setting a Configurable* ExportMode *on a Custom Web Part*

```
Namespace CustomWebParts

    Public Class DateTimeWebPart2
        Inherits WebPart
        ...

        '**************************************************************************
        Sub New()
            CatalogIconImageUrl = "~/images/ClockIcon.gif"
            Description = "Example Web Part that displays the date and time"
            Title = "Date and Time (Web Part)"
            TitleIconImageUrl = "~/images/ClockIcon.gif"
            HelpUrl = "~/Help/DateDisplayWebPart.htm"
            ExportMode = WebPartExportMode.All
        End Sub

        ...
    End Class

End Namespace
```

If, however, your objective is to enforce a specific ExportMode value for all Web Part instances, then you should override the ExportMode property and return a static value from the get portion of the property as shown in Listing 7-35.

Listing 7-35. *Setting a Nonconfigurable* ExportMode *on a Custom Web Part*

```
Imports System.Web.UI.WebControls.WebParts
Namespace CustomWebParts

    Public Class DateTimeWebPart2
        Inherits WebPart
        ...

        '**********************************************************************
        Public Overrides Property ExportMode() _
          As System.Web.UI.WebControls.WebParts.WebPartExportMode
            Get
                Return WebPartExportMode.NonSensitiveData
            End Get
            Set(ByVal value As WebPartExportMode)
                'Do nothing here
```

```
            End Set
        End Property

        ...
    End Class

End Namespace
```

You can also set the ExportMode value in a UserControl-based Web Part, but it effectively becomes a static value because there is no effective way to check for a blank value before setting the default (see Listing 7-36).

Listing 7-36. *Setting a Nonconfigurable* ExportMode *on a* UserControl-*Based Web Part*

```
Partial Class DateTimeWebPart
    Inherits WebPartUserControl
    ...

    '*************************************************************************

    Protected Sub Page_Load(ByVal sender As Object, _
      ByVal e As System.EventArgs) Handles Me.Load
        WebPartData.ExportMode = WebPartExportMode.NonSensitiveData
    End Sub

    ...
End Class
```

After specifying either All or NonSensitiveData for the ExportMode, exporting is extremely simple. The WebPartFramework automatically adds the Export verb to the Web Part's verb menu.

When a user clicks on the Export verb, the Web Part Framework collects all the configuration data for the Web Part and returns it as an XML file with the .webpart file extension. The user can then save that file to their hard drive, switch pages, and use the ImportCatalogPart to add the exported Web Part to the page.

Summary

Portals are a very popular means of displaying a wide variety of information to people in a consolidated fashion, and many people are already fairly comfortable with portal technology because of its adoption on major websites. As such, you can rest assured that you'll be seeing more and more application requirements focusing on portal technology.

In this chapter, you have had a chance to see the pieces of the Web Part Framework and how they fit together. You've built Web Parts, created custom verbs for Web Parts, connected Web Parts to other Web Parts, and learned how to manage Web Parts using the Catalog, Editor, and Connection Zones. You should be well equipped to start implementing portal technology into your own applications, and you'll probably have a jump on SharePoint developers when SharePoint starts using the ASP.NET Web Part Framework as well.

CHAPTER 8

Effective Search Tools and Techniques for Your Business Applications

Searching has become a daily activity because of the sheer volume of information available in the world today. You need the Yellow Pages to sift through thousands of business phone numbers. Search engines sift through billions of web pages and bring back relevant content. Radios have a scan button to help search through stations. Even this book has an appendix and index to help you locate specific topics.

Business applications are no different. After information is entered into a system, users appreciate the ability to find that information without having to page through hundreds and hundreds of records. Too many applications have "display" pages that dump countless rows of data to the screen and rely on the user to employ the browser's built-in search functionality to locate a specific item. These "display" pages start out innocently enough, usually because the number of records being returned in the application's infancy is low enough to warrant dumping everything to the page. As the application matures, however, more and more data is input, so more and more data appears on the screen. Before long, the page is timing out before all the data can be output, and users lose their patience with incredible load times.

From a business perspective, one of the biggest benefits of searching is application usability. Sites with little or no searching functionality usually generate a greater number of complaints and help requests than sites where searching is well thought out and implemented. People who can easily find information are happy. People who cannot find information are not happy and can quickly become irate depending on the deadlines under which they are working. Usually these people end up calling someone for help or just to complain about their dilemma. If the person they are calling happens to be you, then just think about how much time you can save yourself in the future by implementing appropriate search features now.

Searching provides other "technical" benefits as well, such as reduced database load and reduced bandwidth requirements. A search that sends back 50 results is far more efficient than a dump of 50,000. These technical benefits actually map to business benefits when you think about not having to spend more money on hardware and network infrastructure, or in the amount of time you are saving individual employees by eliminating lengthy wait times.

I have worked on a number of different search forms, and this chapter is the result of my learning experiences with those endeavors. A couple of very powerful searching techniques are discussed in the following pages. Following is a breakdown of what you will find:

- *Creating the `SqlQuery` Tool:* The overwhelming majority of this chapter details the design and implementation of a tool that provides an object-oriented approach to writing SQL queries in code. This section also details how to build paged queries using SQL Server 2005.
- *Commonly Used Search Functions:* Keywords and date-range searching are two of the most common search types you will encounter. This section outlines how to build an advanced keyword-searching mechanism that handles `AND`/`OR` logic and complex grouping scenarios, and how to easily add date-range searches to your SQL queries.
- *Displaying Basic and Advanced Searches:* Another powerful searching option for your application is to display a basic search form for routine searches, but offer an advanced search form for more detailed search requirements. This section discusses how to build a common search-form interface that allows you to easily switch between search forms on a page.

The `SqlQuery` component, which uses an object-oriented approach to creating SQL queries, is used in both this chapter and the next. Make sure you have a thorough understanding of the component and how it works before moving on.

Creating the SqlQuery Tool

After working with searches over the course of a few projects, I realized that searching is all about building queries. People enter search criteria, the criteria are converted into a SQL query, the query is executed against a database, and the matched results are returned. I also realized that I constantly implemented two types of searches over and over again. Date range searches and keyword searches tend to be fairly popular for searching through business data.

Keeping with the mantra that if you plan to reuse it, encapsulate it, I decided to build an object-oriented query tool to help create search queries. The `SqlQuery` class is the end result of that endeavor. As you'll see in later sections of this chapter, it really makes creating search queries quick and painless. All the sample code for the `SqlQuery` class is located in the `Reporting` class library project in this chapter's example application in the Source Code area of the Apress website (http://www.apress.com).

Objectives and Architecture Overview

The primary objective of the `SqlQuery` class is to encapsulate common query-building logic into a reusable component to provide an object-oriented approach to creating search queries. SQL queries have a number of different keywords and clauses, but not all of them are represented in the `SqlQuery` class. For example, the `COMPUTE` and `HAVING` clauses as well as the `WITH` qualifier for the `GROUP BY` clause were left out for the sake of brevity, but you can easily add them to the class on your own after you learn how it works. The concepts outlined in this chapter should make it easy for you to implement any SQL features that you want. One feature that we are interested in, however, is paging functionality. The `SqlQuery` class provides basic paging functionality to reduce the total amount of data that needs to be pulled down from the database server.

Figure 8-1 shows a diagram outlining the properties and methods of `SqlQuery`, and where many of the auxiliary classes and enumerations fit into the overall pictures (auxiliary classes and enumerations are shown in bold).

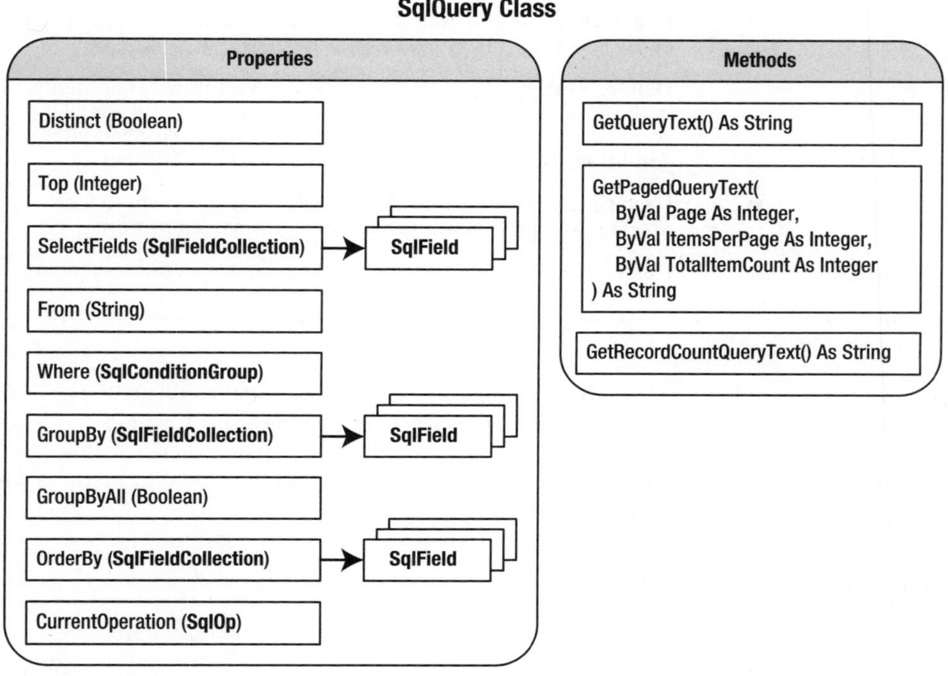

Figure 8-1. `SqlQuery` *Properties and Methods*

Implementing the `SqlQuery` class requires four auxiliary classes, one interface, and four enumerations. Each of these items and a description of their purpose are listed in Table 8-1.

Table 8-1. `SqlQuery` *Class and Auxillary Components*

Item Name	Type	Description
`SqlQuery`	`Class`	Main class that encapsulates all query-building logic.
`SqlField`	`Class`	Defines information about an individual field in the query. This class helps define which fields are selected by the query and which fields appear in the `GROUP BY` and `ORDER BY` clauses.
`SqlFieldCollection`	`Class`	Contains a collection of `SqlField` objects.
`ISqlConditional`	`Interface`	Defines a common interface for conditional statements used in the `WHERE` clause of the query.
`SqlCondition`	`Class`	Defines an individual condition in the `WHERE` clause of the query.

Table 8-1. SqlQuery *Class and Auxillary Components (Continued)*

Item Name	Type	Description
SqlConditionGroup	Class	Defines a group of SqlCondition objects in the WHERE clause of the query.
SqlSortDirection	Enum	Defines the sort direction (ASC/DESC) used in the ORDER BY clause of the query.
SqlOperation	Enum	Defines the operation (AND/OR) used for conditional statements in the WHERE clause of the query. You can create simple or complex queries by applying the SqlOperation to individual conditions and to groups of conditions in the WHERE clause.
SqlConditionalType	Enum	Used by the ISqlConditional interface to identify whether an object is an individual condition or a group of conditions.
SqlEvaluationType	Enum	Determines whether values should be inclusive (greater than or equal to) or exclusive (greater than but not equal to).

The sections that follow cover each component in more detail. First, you'll get the details on the enumerations and simpler auxiliary classes such as the SqlField and SqlFieldCollection, and then you'll move into the more complicated items such as the ISqlConditional interface and the classes that implement it. Finally, you'll see how to use those auxiliary objects to create the actual SqlQuery class itself.

Enumerations in Globals.vb

Throughout this chapter, you'll see enumerations that define values for certain items. All these enumerations are stored in the Globals.vb file in the Reporting project in the sample code (in the Source Code area of the Apress website). Listing 8-1 provides all the enumerations and their corresponding values.

Listing 8-1. Globals.vb

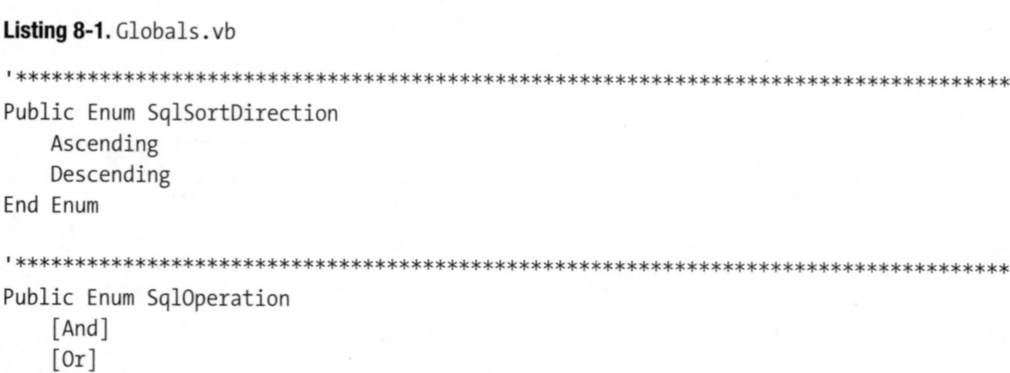

```
'********************************************************************************
Public Enum SqlSortDirection
    Ascending
    Descending
End Enum

'********************************************************************************
Public Enum SqlOperation
    [And]
    [Or]
End Enum
```

```
'*****************************************************************************
Public Enum SqlConditionType
    Condition
    Group
End Enum

'*****************************************************************************
Public Enum SqlEvaluationType
    Exclusive
    Inclusive
End Enum

Public Module Globals

    '*************************************************************************
    Public Function SqlString(ByVal text As String) As String
        Return text.Replace("'", "''")
    End Function

End Module
```

Refer to Table 8-1 for commentary on each enumeration and what the values represent. The `SqlString` function listed in the `Globals` module replaces any apostrophe in a string with two apostrophes. This ensures strings are appropriately formatted for a SQL statement and helps avoid SQL injection attacks because this tool does not use parameterized queries.

SqlField Class

The `SqlField` class is designed to store information for fields (a.k.a. columns) that appear in the `SELECT`, `ORDER BY`, and `GROUP BY` clauses of a SQL query. Each of these clauses has a slightly different syntax, but when you get right down to it, they are all lists of fields. Here are the main differences between them:

- `SELECT` *clause:* Field list that defines which fields are returned from the query. This clause allows you to rename fields using the `AS` keyword (if desired), such as `SELECT Field1 AS AliasA, Field2, Field3 AS AliasB`, and so on.
- `GROUP BY` *clause:* Field list that defines result groupings for aggregate data (`MAX`, `MIN`, `SUM`, `AVG`, and so on). This clause is simply a field list without any additional properties, such as `GROUP BY Field1, Field2`, and so on.
- `ORDER BY` *clause:* Field list that determines the sort order of the returned data. This clause allows you to specify sort directions (if desired) along with field names, such as `ORDER BY Field1, Field2 ASC, Field3 DESC`, and so on.

You could implement a different field class for each one of these three clauses, but in the interest of time and space, I've created a single class that supports properties for all three. The very simple `SqlField` class consists of three properties and three constructors as shown in Listing 8-2.

Listing 8-2. `SqlField` *Class*

```
Public Class SqlField

    '***************************************************************************
    Private _Name As String
    Private _Alias As String
    Private _SortDirection As SqlSortDirection = SqlSortDirection.Ascending

    '***************************************************************************
    Sub New(ByVal Name As String)
        _Name = Name
    End Sub

    '***************************************************************************
    Sub New(ByVal Name As String, ByVal [Alias] As String)
        _Name = Name
        _Alias = [Alias]
    End Sub

    '***************************************************************************
    Sub New(ByVal Name As String, ByVal SortDirection As SqlSortDirection)
        _Name = Name
        _SortDirection = SortDirection
    End Sub

    '***************************************************************************
    Public Property Name() As String
        Get
            Return _Name
        End Get
        Set(ByVal value As String)
            _Name = value
        End Set
    End Property

    '***************************************************************************
    Public Property [Alias]() As String
        Get
            Return _Alias
        End Get
        Set(ByVal value As String)
            _Alias = value
        End Set
    End Property
```

```
    '****************************************************************************
    Public Property SortDirection() As SqlSortDirection
        Get
            Return _SortDirection
        End Get
        Set(ByVal value As SqlSortDirection)
            _SortDirection = value
        End Set
    End Property

End Class
```

Notice the three constructors in the class, and remember that there are three different SQL clauses in which the fields may be used (SELECT, GROUP BY, and ORDER BY). This is no coincidence. Each constructor is designed to initialize a SqlField object with the appropriate properties for a specific clause. Table 8-2 outlines each clause and which properties and constructors the clauses may use.

Table 8-2. *SQL Clauses and the* SqlField *properties and Constructors They Rely On*

Clause	Name	Alias	SortDirection	Constructor
SELECT	X	X		Public Sub New(ByVal Name As String)Sub New(ByVal Name As String, ByVal [Alias] As String)
GROUP BY	X			Public Sub New(ByVal Name As String)
ORDER BY	X		X	Public Sub New(ByVal Name As String) Sub New(ByVal Name As String, ByVal SortDirection As SqlSortDirection)

You can initialize a SqlField object for any field type just by specifying the field Name. For a SELECT field, it means that no alias will be defined. For an ORDER BY field, it means that the sort direction will default to ASC (ascending).

If any unused properties are specified for a field, they are simply disregarded by the method that uses the SqlField object. For instance, if you specify an Alias property for an ORDER BY or GROUP BY field, it will *not* affect the GROUP BY or ORDER BY clause when the SQL statement is written out.

SqlFieldCollection Class

A single SqlField object by itself is of little value because SQL queries usually deal with lists of fields, not just individual fields. The SqlFieldCollection is a strongly typed collection class designed to store a list of SqlField objects as shown in Listing 8-3.

Listing 8-3. `SqlFieldCollection` *Class*

```
Public Class SqlFieldCollection
    Inherits CollectionBase

    '*****************************************************************************
    Public Function Add(ByVal name As String) As Integer
        Return List.Add(New SqlField(name))
    End Function

    '*****************************************************************************
    Public Function Add(ByVal name As String, ByVal [alias] As String) As Integer
        Return List.Add(New SqlField(name, [alias]))
    End Function

    '*****************************************************************************
    Public Function Add(ByVal name As String, _
      ByVal SortDirection As SqlSortDirection) As Integer
        Return List.Add(New SqlField(name, SortDirection))
    End Function

    '*****************************************************************************
    Default Public ReadOnly Property Item(ByVal Index As Integer) As SqlField
        Get
            Return List.Item(Index)
        End Get
    End Property

    '*****************************************************************************
    Public Function Find(ByVal name As String) As SqlField
        name = UCase(name)  'Only uppercase the name once

        'Iterate through each field name looking for a match
        For index As Integer = 0 To Count - 1
            If UCase(Item(index).Name) = name Then Return Item(index)
        Next

        Return Nothing
    End Function

    '*****************************************************************************
    Public Sub Remove(ByVal item As SqlField)
        List.Remove(item)
    End Sub
```

```
    '****************************************************************************
    Public Sub Remove(ByVal name As String)
        Dim item As SqlField = Find(name)
        If Not item Is Nothing Then List.Remove(item)
    End Sub

End Class
```

Like most collection classes, `SqlFieldCollection` exposes strongly typed collection properties and methods such as `Item`, `Add`, and `Remove` that help make working with the `SqlField` objects in the collection more intuitive. Notice that there are three different `Add` functions for the class. Each `Add` function maps to its equivalent `SqlField` constructor discussed in the previous section.

The only real noteworthy method is the `Find` function. It accepts `name` as a parameter and iterates through the list of fields looking for a `SqlField` with a matching `Name` property. If it finds a suitable match, the matched `SqlField` object is returned. Otherwise, `Nothing` is returned. The `Find` function is used inside the `Remove(byval name as string)` method to remove a field from the list based on its name.

Analyzing the WHERE Clause in Search of an Object Model

Now that the `SELECT`, `GROUP BY`, and `ORDER BY` clauses have been accounted for with the `SqlField` and `SqlFieldCollection` classes, we can now focus on a bit more complicated issue: the `WHERE` clause. In a query, the `WHERE` clause defines a set of conditions that a row of data must meet in order to be returned by the query. For example, if you have a table containing first names, last names, and phone numbers of employees in your organization, and you want to find Joe Smith, then you can use `WHERE FirstName='Joe' AND LastName='Smith'` to filter out all the other names. Of course, this is just a simple example.

Our goal is to create an object model that can successfully define a `WHERE` clause, so we need to take a look at all the different parts of a `WHERE` clause. Following is an example SQL statement containing a `WHERE` clause. Table 8-3 describes the various parts of the `WHERE` clause.

```
SELECT * FROM [MyTable]
WHERE A=1 OR (B=2 AND C>3 AND (D=4 OR E<=5)) OR NOT (Y=5 AND LEN(Z)=6)
```

Table 8-3. *Parts of a* `WHERE` *Clause*

Part Name	Description	Examples

`Expression`	An expression is an item can be reduced into a value. SQL functions, user-defined functions, variables, and constants can all be used as expressions.	`A` (a field)
		`LEN(Z) (a function)`
		`6 (a constant)`

`Evaluation Operator`	The operator used to evaluate one expression against another expression.	= (equal) < (greater than) > (less than) >= (greater than or equal) <= (less than or equal) <> (not equal)

Table 8-3. *Parts of a* `WHERE` *Clause (Continued)*

Part Name	Description	Examples

`Condition`	A condition consists of an expression, an evaluation operator, and another expression. Conditions evaluate to a value of `True` or `False` and represent requirements that must be met in order for a row of data to be returned by the query.	`A=1`
		`C>3`
		`E<=5`
		`LEN(Z)=6`

`Condition Operator`	Defines `AND`/`OR` logic for multiple conditions.	`A=1 AND B=2 AND C=3` `D=4 OR E=5 OR F=6`

`Condition Group`	A condition group contains a set of conditions enclosed by parentheses. Condition groups return a value of `True` or `False` based on the conditions and condition operators in the condition group. You can create groups inside of groups.	`(D=4 OR E<=5)`
		`(B=2 AND C>3 AND (D=4 OR E<=5))`
		`(Y=5 AND LEN(Z)=6)`

`Negation`	Negation allows you to reverse the value returned for a condition or a condition group using the `NOT` keyword. For example, `NOT(True)` evaluates to `False` and `NOT(False)` evaluates to `True`	`NOT (Y=5 AND LEN(Z)=6)`

Note The entire `WHERE` clause is a condition group even though it may not be enclosed by parentheses.

I can tell you from experience that you do not want a SQL query object model to drill down into the expression and expression operator level because it is far too granular. It makes defining a simple condition such as `A=B` into a three-line statement:

```
'This would be a ridiculous waste of time and space...
Query.Where.AddExpression("A")
Query.Where.AddExpressionOperator("=")
Query.Where.AddExpression("1")

'This is a much more succinct way to go about it...
Where.AddCondition("A=1")
```

In reality, the condition is where the object model should start because you'll mostly be adding and manipulating entire conditions in a `WHERE` clause, not individual expressions and expression operators. The condition group should also be included in the object model because it represents a collection that stores a mix of conditions and conditions groups. These two classes are named `SqlCondition` and `SqlConditionGroup`, respectively.

Condition operators, however, are not represented by independent objects. I attached condition operators directly to the `SqlCondition` and `SqlConditionGroup` objects. This requires a bit of explaining. Logically, a condition operator should only exist on the `SqlConditionGroup` object because operators, by definition, operate on two conditions (for example, `D=4 OR E<=5`). And if you have more than one condition, then it's a group, and a group is stored in a `SqlConditionGroup`. Logically, a group always contains the same operator, as in `(A=1 AND B=2 AND C=3)`. Ah, but what about a group like `(A=1 AND B=2 OR C=3)`? Doesn't it have different operators? No, because implicit groups are defined by order of operations. SQL server automatically applies order of operations to an implicit group, so the statement really executes as though it was written like `((A=1 AND B=2) OR (C=4))`. So a group with more than one operator is a perfectly valid statement because SQL "fixes" it for you before executing the statement, which is why I opted to attach condition operators directly to the `SqlCondition` and `SqlConditionGroup` objects. Also know that implicit grouping makes keyword searching significantly easier because the SQL statements can be built word by word without having to worry about grouping constructs.

The only issue with defining the condition operator at the `SqlCondition` level is that not all `SqlCondition` objects actually use the condition operator. Look at the following example:

```
(A=1 AND B=2 OR C=3)
```

Notice that there are three conditions (`A=1`, `B=2`, `C=3`) but only two condition operators (`AND`, `OR`). In my implementation, the condition operator on a `SqlCondition` object represents the condition operator that precedes the condition. As such, the operator on the first condition inside a group is disregarded.

Figure 8-2 shows a `WHERE` clause represented as a string and as a set of `SqlCondition` and `SqlConditionGroup` objects. This should help you visual how a `WHERE` clause will be stored in a `SqlQuery` object. Notice that the condition operation is defined inside the individual `SqlCondition` and `SqlConditionGroup` objects.

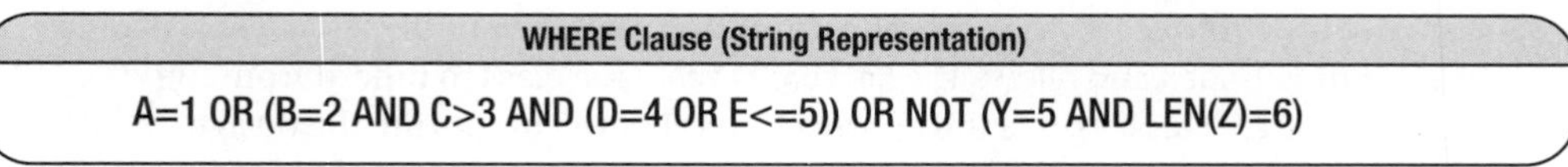

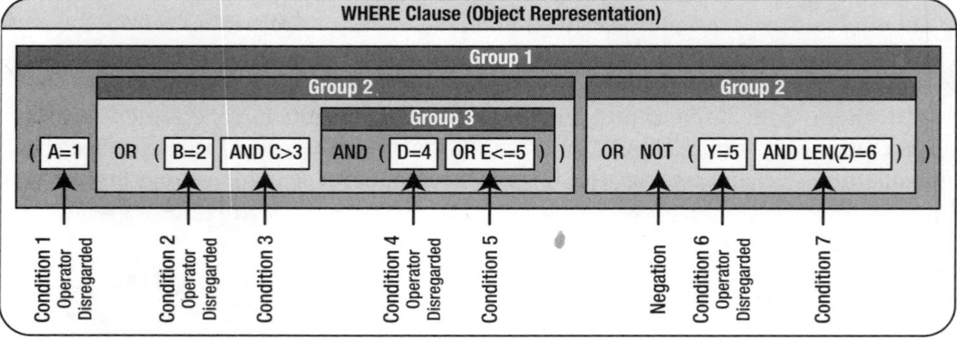

Condition operators (AND / OR) are attached directly to conditions and condition groups.
The first condition operator in a group is ignored.

Figure 8-2. *String and object representations of a* `WHERE` *clause*

Note The `SqlQuery` tool automatically surrounds groups with brackets.

ISqlCondition Interface

As mentioned earlier, the `SqlConditionGroup` needs to store a mix of `SqlCondition` and other `SqlConditionGroup` objects. Thus, it must store and reference two completely different objects. When you need to refer to two completely different objects from within one collection class, you have to find some common ground between the objects so you can find a generic way to reference them. To do this, you have three options:

- *Refer to items by using* `System.Object`: All objects inherit from the `System.Object` base class, so you can refer to any object using `System.Object`. This is not an ideal solution because it requires late binding to access any properties or methods, which slows down performance.
- *Inherit from a common base class:* Because both the condition and condition group share common properties (`Name` and `Type`), you can define a base class and have both objects inherit from that base class. You can then use the base class as the common ground to reference both classes, and any properties and methods in base class can be accessed from both objects without having to resort to late binding. This is a perfectly valid solution. One consideration, however, is that `SqlConditionGroup` is a collection class. You can save a significant amount of coding time if you inherit basic collection class functionality from the `CollectionBase` base class. The .NET Framework does not support multiple inheritance, so you have to choose which base class is more important for your particular situation.
- *Implement a common interface:* You can also define a common set of properties and methods in an interface and have both classes implement that interface. You can then use the interface as the common ground to reference both classes. This avoids late-binding issues and allows the `SqlConditionGroup` class to inherit from the `CollectionBase` class. This is the approach that I opted for during the design.

So, we'll end up with two classes, `SqlCondition` and `SqlConditionGroup`, both of which implement the `ISqlCondition` interface. In addition, `SqlConditionGroup` inherits from the `CollectionBase` object and is designed to store objects that implement the `ISqlCondition` interface, thus allowing it to store both `SqlCondition` and `SqlConditionGroup` objects. Figure 8-3 diagrams both the conceptual and the physical representation of this model. Notice that you can recursively store `SqlConditionGroup` objects inside `SqlConditionGroup` objects. So, be aware that the `SqlConditionGroup` uses recursive functions for searching and printing out SQL text.

ISqlCondition Interface and Implementations

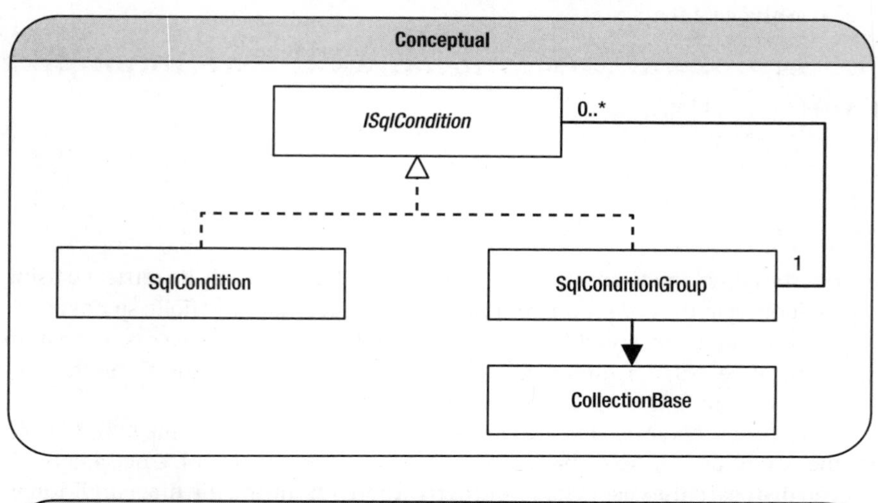

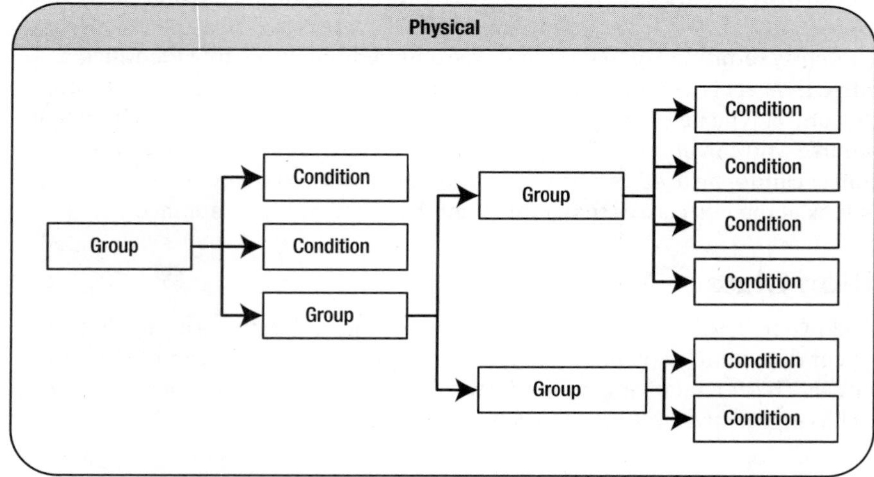

Figure 8-3. *Conceptual and physical model of the* `ISqlCondition` *interface and the* `SqlCondition` *and* `SqlConditionGroup` *classes*

Take a look at the `ISqlCondition` interface in Listing 8-4, and then we'll discuss each property in the interface and why it was included.

Listing 8-4. `ISqlCondition` *Interface*

```
Public Interface ISqlCondition

    '***************************************************************************
    Property Name() As String
    Property ConditionOp() As SqlOperation
    ReadOnly Property Type() As SqlConditionType

End Interface
```

The `Name` property allows you to create named conditions that can easily be retrieved using the find functions defined in the condition group object. It's not a required field, so not all conditions have to be named. You should use named items if you plan on reaccessing an item in your query. For instance, you may find it convenient to build a complex query and then remove or change certain named items based on some criteria.

The `ConditionOp` property represents the condition operation (refer to Table 8-3). It determines whether the condition should be preceded with `AND` or `OR` when output. Once again, remember that you disregard the `ConditionOp` property when outputting the first condition in a condition group.

The `Type` property returns a `SqlConditionalType` enumeration value that identifies whether the current object is a condition (`Condition`) or a condition group (`Group`). It's important to know the object type before attempting to cast it from an `ISqlCondition` to its actual data type. Of course, you can also use `GetType()` to determine the object type, but the `System.Type` object cannot be used as easily as a property in a `Case` statement.

Next, let's look at the two classes that implement the `ISqlCondition` interface.

SqlCondition Class

When it comes down to it, the `SqlCondition` class has two objectives: store a string that contains a SQL condition and implement the `ISqlCondition` interface so it can be stored in a `SqlConditionGroup`. This is a relatively straightforward class because it just exposes simple properties and has no methods or functions (see Listing 8-5).

Listing 8-5. `SqlCondition` *Class*

```
Public Class SqlCondition
    Implements ISqlCondition

    '***************************************************************************
    Private _Condition As String

    '***************************************************************************
    Public Sub New(ByVal condition As String, ByVal operation As String)
        _Condition = condition
        _ConditionOp = Operation
    End Sub
```

```
    '**************************************************************************
    Public Sub New(ByVal condition As String, ByVal operation As String, _
      ByVal name As String)
        _Condition = condition
        _ConditionOp = operation
        _Name = name
    End Sub

    '**************************************************************************
    Public Property Condition() As String
        Get
            Return _Condition
        End Get
        Set(ByVal value As String)
            _Condition = value
        End Set
    End Property

#Region "ISqlConditional Implementation"

    '**************************************************************************
    Private _Name As String
    Private _ConditionOp As SqlOperation

    '**************************************************************************
    Public Property Name() As String Implements ISqlCondition.Name
        Get
            Return _Name
        End Get
        Set(ByVal value As String)
            _Name = value
        End Set
    End Property

    '**************************************************************************
    Public Property Operation() As SqlOperation _
      Implements ISqlCondition.ConditionOp
        Get
            Return _ConditionOp
        End Get
        Set(ByVal value As SqlOperation)
            _ConditionOp = value
        End Set
    End Property
```

```
    '*************************************************************************
    Public ReadOnly Property Type() As SqlConditionType _
      Implements ISqlCondition.Type
        Get
            Return SqlConditionType.Condition
        End Get
    End Property

#End Region

End Class
```

You can see that this class has two constructors. The first allows you to pass in a value for the condition, and the second allows you to pass in a value for the condition and give the condition a name. The `condition` parameter is a string representing the condition text (for example, `A=B` or `DateField=GetDate()`). The `name` parameter allows you to specify a unique string that identifies the condition. Later on, you can use the name to search for the condition inside of a condition group. The `operation` parameter is the condition operator that should be associated with the `SqlCondition` object (`AND`/`OR`). Also notice that the read-only `Type` property from the `ISqlCondition` interface returns the value associated with `SqlConditionType.➥ Condition` because this class represents a condition.

■Note Condition objects do not have a negation property. If you want to negate condition, you must do so by passing in the negation operation as text, that is, `"NOT A=1"`.

SqlConditionGroup Class

On top of being a multiobject collection class and implementing the `ISqlCondition` interface, the `SqlCondition` class also exposes a number of methods that allow you to add, locate, modify, and remove conditions and conditions groups. Needless to say, the code for this class is a bit more detailed than the classes you've seen thus far. If you look back at Figure 8-1, you'll notice that the `Where` property is actually a `SqlConditionGroup` object, so this class contains all the `WHERE` clause building logic. Listing 8-6 shows most of the code for the `SqlConditionGroup` class.

■Note Two functions, `CreateKeywords` and `CreateDateRange`, will be covered a bit later when we discuss defining common search queries. For now, their function definitions are included so you'll know where they appear in the listing when we get to them later.

Listing 8-6. `SqlConditionGroup` *Class*

```
Imports System.Text.RegularExpressions

Public Class SqlConditionGroup
    Inherits CollectionBase
    Implements ISqlCondition

    '***************************************************************************
    Private _Not As Boolean
    Private _NextOperation As SqlOperation = SqlOperation.And

    '***************************************************************************
    Public Property [Not]() As Boolean
        Get
            Return _Not
        End Get
        Set(ByVal value As Boolean)
            _Not = value
        End Set
    End Property

    '***************************************************************************
    Public Sub New(ByVal operation As SqlOperation, ByVal [not] As Boolean)
        _ConditionOp = operation
        _Not = [not]
    End Sub

    '***************************************************************************
    Public Sub New(ByVal operation As SqlOperation, ByVal [not] As Boolean, _
      ByVal name As String)
        _ConditionOp = operation
        _Not = [not]
        _Name = name
    End Sub

    '***************************************************************************
    Public Sub [And]()
        _NextOperation = SqlOperation.And
    End Sub
```

```
'***************************************************************************
Public Sub [Or]()
    _NextOperation = SqlOperation.Or
End Sub

'***************************************************************************
Public Function AddCondition(ByVal condition As String) As SqlCondition
    Return AddCondition(condition, String.Empty)
End Function

'***************************************************************************
Public Function AddCondition(ByVal condition As String, _
  ByVal name As String) As SqlCondition
    Dim item As New SqlCondition(condition, _NextOperation, name)
    List.Add(item)
    Return item
End Function

'***************************************************************************
Public Function AddGroup() As SqlConditionGroup
    Return AddGroup(String.Empty)
End Function

'***************************************************************************
Public Function AddGroup(ByVal name As String) As SqlConditionGroup
    Dim item As New SqlConditionGroup(_NextOperation, False)
    item.Name = name
    List.Add(item)
    Return item
End Function

'***************************************************************************
Public Function AddNotGroup() As SqlConditionGroup
    Return AddNotGroup(String.Empty)
End Function

'***************************************************************************
Public Function AddNotGroup(ByVal name As String) As SqlConditionGroup
    Dim item As New SqlConditionGroup(_NextOperation, True)
    item.Name = name
    List.Add(item)
    Return item
End Function
```

```
'**************************************************************************
Private Function GetNamedItem(ByVal name As String, _
  ByVal requestType As SqlConditionType) As ISqlCondition

    Dim item As ISqlCondition
    Dim tempItem As ISqlCondition

    'Ensure there are items before setting item to the first one in the list
    If Me.Count = 0 Then Return Nothing

    item = List.Item(0)

    'Only UCase the name once
    name = UCase(name)

    'Iterate through all items in the list looking for a match
    For Each item In List
        If UCase(item.Name) = name And item.Type = requestType Then
            Return item
        End If
    Next

    'If no match is found, then search subgroups
    For Each item In List

        'If the current item is a group, search through it recusively
        If item.Type = SqlConditionType.Group Then
            tempItem = DirectCast(item, _
                       SqlConditionGroup).GetNamedItem(name, requestType)
            If Not tempItem Is Nothing Then Return tempItem
        End If

    Next

    Return Nothing

End Function

'**************************************************************************
Public Function GetNamedGroup(ByVal name As String) As SqlConditionGroup
    Return GetNamedItem(name, SqlConditionType.Group)
End Function

'**************************************************************************
Public Function GetNamedCondition(ByVal name As String) As SqlCondition
    Return GetNamedItem(name, SqlConditionType.Condition)
End Function
```

```
'***************************************************************************
Public Sub Remove(ByVal item As ISqlCondition)
    Me.List.Remove(item)
End Sub

'***************************************************************************
Public Sub RemoveNamedCondition(ByVal name As String)
    Dim item As SqlCondition = GetNamedCondition(name)
    If Not item Is Nothing Then Me.List.Remove(item)
End Sub

'***************************************************************************
Public Sub RemoveNamedGroup(ByVal name As String)
    Dim item As SqlConditionGroup = GetNamedGroup(name)
    If Not item Is Nothing Then Me.List.Remove(item)
End Sub

'***************************************************************************
Public Function WriteStatement() As String

    Dim firstItemFlag As Boolean = True
    Dim statement As String = String.Empty
    Dim tempStatement As String = String.Empty

    'Run through each item (may be condition or condition group) in list
    For Each item As ISqlCondition In List

        'Determine the condition type
        Select Case item.Type

            Case SqlConditionType.Condition
                'Acquire the statement from the condition property
                tempStatement = DirectCast(item, SqlCondition).Condition

            Case SqlConditionType.Group
                'Recursively call the WriteStatement function
                Dim group As SqlConditionGroup = _
                  DirectCast(item, SqlConditionGroup)

                tempStatement = group.WriteStatement

                'Ensure statement returned text before adding parentheses
                If Not tempStatement = String.Empty Then _
                  tempStatement = "(" & tempStatement & ")"
```

```
                'If this is a "NOT" group, add the NOT keyword
                If group.Not Then tempStatement = "NOT" & tempStatement

        End Select

        'Ensure statement contains text before appending condition operation
        If Not tempStatement = String.Empty Then

            If firstItemFlag Then
                'Do not add condition operation for first item in group
                firstItemFlag = False
            Else
                'Determine condition operation and add appropriate SQL
                Select Case item.ConditionOp
                    Case SqlOperation.And
                        tempStatement = " AND " & tempStatement
                    Case SqlOperation.Or
                        tempStatement = " OR " & tempStatement
                End Select
            End If

            statement &= tempStatement

        End If

    Next

    Return statement

End Function

#Region "ISqlConditional Implementation"

    '***************************************************************************
    Private _Name As String
    Private _ConditionOp As SqlOperation

    '***************************************************************************
    Public Property Name() As String Implements ISqlCondition.Name
        Get
            Return _Name
        End Get
        Set(ByVal value As String)
            _Name = value
        End Set
    End Property
```

```
    '***************************************************************************
    Public Property ConditionOp() As SqlOperation _
      Implements ISqlCondition.ConditionOp
        Get
            Return _ConditionOp
        End Get
        Set(ByVal value As SqlOperation)
            _ConditionOp = value
        End Set
    End Property

    '***************************************************************************
    Public ReadOnly Property Type() As SqlConditionType _
     Implements ISqlCondition.Type
        Get
            Return SqlConditionType.Group
        End Get
    End Property
#End Region

#Region "Common Queries"

    '***************************************************************************
    Public Function CreateKeywords(ByVal keywords As String, _
      ByVal column As String, ByVal defaultOp As SqlOperation) _
      As SqlConditionGroup

        'This code will be discussed in a later section, so return Nothing for now
        Return Nothing

    End Function

    '***************************************************************************
    Public Function CreateDateRange(ByVal startDateStr As String, _
      ByVal endDateStr As String, ByVal column As String, _
      ByVal evalType As SqlEvaluationType, ByVal dateFormat As String) _
      As SqlConditionGroup

        'This code will be discussed in a later section, so return Nothing for now
        Return Nothing

    End Function

#End Region

End Class
```

Because this is a fairly lengthy code listing, we'll discuss it in sections.

Class Definition and Imports Statement

The SqlConditionGroup inherits basic collection functionality from the CollectionBase base class, and it implements the ISqlCondition interface. You saw a collection class earlier in this chapter when we discussed the SqlFieldCollection. Although this implementation is similar, there are a few differences because the collection will be storing two different object types (SqlCondition and SqlConditionGroup) instead of just a single object type.

■ **Note** If you take a good look at the code, you'll see that there is an import statement for the System.Text.RegularExpressions namespace, but there aren't any regular expressions used anywhere in the code listing. Regular expressions are used in the CreateKeywords function, but that code is not shown until later on in this chapter. So, know that it's there for a reason, we just haven't gotten there yet.

Class Level Variables

There are two class-level variables. The _Not variable stores a Boolean value for the Not property, which determines whether the group needs to be negated in the SQL query. _NextOperation stores a SqlOperation enumeration value (And/Or) and determines which condition operator to apply to the next condition added to the group. For example, say the group contains a condition A=1, and the _NextOperation is set to And. When you then add another condition to the group, say B=2, then the group sets that condition's condition operator to the value stored in the _NextOperation variable. Thus, the condition group effectively contains A=1 AND B=2. You control the _NextOperation value from the And and Or methods on the class. This allows you to have an object-oriented approach to building SQL statements that mimics SQL syntax, as you'll see in the Add and Or method descriptions next.

■ **Note** Do not confuse the _NextOperation value with the ISqlCondition.ConditionOp implementation for the SqlConditionGroup object. The ConditionOp property stores the condition operation for the SqlConditionGroup itself. The _NextOperation field defines the condition operation values for the conditions and conditions groups that are added to the SqlConditionGroup.

Not Property

Expressing NOT in a SqlCondition is easy because you can define it directly in the condition text itself. For example, you can create a condition like IntField!=5 or even NOT IntField=5 to specify a condition where IntField is not equal to 5.

The SqlConditionGroup also needs negation functionality because you can have a statement like NOT (A=1 AND B=2). This is accomplished by setting the Not property to True when the group should be prefixed with the NOT keyword. In this text, a group whose Not property is set to True is referred to as a negated group. You'll see this property used in the AddNotGroup, and WriteStatement functions.

Class Constructors (Sub New)

Creating a new SqlConditionGroup object requires passing in two parameters to the constructor: operation and not. The operation parameter initializes the ConditionOp property defined in the ISqlCondition interface. Remember that this property determines which operator (And/Or) to output before the group when building the SQL query. The not parameter simply sets the Not property, which was just covered. You can, optionally, specify a unique name for the group using the overloaded constructor. Later on, you can use the unique name to search for this group in the query.

And/Or Methods

Both of these methods set the _NextOperation variable to each method name's respective value. Thus, the And method sets _NextOperation to And and the Or method sets _NextOperation to Or. These two functions help make using the SqlConditionGroup more intuitive in code. For example, if you wanted a group containing a statement like A=1 AND B=2 OR C=3, then the code would look something like this:

```
Group.AddCondition("A=1")
Group.And()
Group.AddCondition("B=2")
Group.Or()
Group.AddCondition("C=3")
```

Because the _NextOperation is retained after calling the And or Or functions, you only have to call And or Or once when adding a series of conditions. Thus, the statement (A=1 OR B=2 OR C=3 OR D=4 AND E=5 AND F=6 AND G=7 AND H=8) could be written like this in code:

```
Group.AddCondition("A=1")
Group.Or()                    'You could also place this line first, if you wanted
Group.AddCondition("B=2")
Group.AddCondition("C=3")
Group.AddCondition("D=4")
Group.And()
Group.AddCondition("E=5")
Group.AddCondition("F=6")
Group.AddCondition("G=7")
Group.AddCondition("H=8")
```

The intricacies of using the SqlQuery and SqlConditionGroup are covered later in this chapter.

■ **Note** The And/Or functions are surrounded by [ ] brackets because VB .NET recognizes them as keywords. The [ ] brackets let the compiler know not to process the term as a keyword.

AddCondition, AddGroup, and AddNotGroup Functions

You need the ability to add conditions and condition groups to the WHERE clause to use the SqlQuery tool effectively, and the AddCondition, AddGroup, and AddNotGroup methods make it easy to do just that. Each Add function instantiates a new SqlCondition or a new SqlConditionGroup object and adds the new object to the List property of the current SqlConditionGroup object. Remember, the SqlConditionGroup class inherits the List property from the CollectionBase class.

Each Add function is overloaded so you can create named and unnamed conditions and groups. To create a named item, just pass a name into the function. Named items are useful because you can use the name to search for the object. Also, all the Add functions will return the object that gets added to the list. This allows you to keep a reference to an item without having to search for it. The following code shows both features in action:

```
Dim C1 as SqlCondition = Group.AddCondition("x=1")                'Unnamed condition
Dim C2 as SqlCondition = Group.AddCondition("x=1", "Condition1") 'Named condition
Dim G1 as SqlConditionGroup = Group.AddGroup()                    'Unnamed group
Dim G2 as SqlConditionGroup = Group.AddGroup("group1")            'Named group
```

If you take a close look at the code, you'll notice the "named" version of each function contains the actual list-adding and property-setting code. The "unnamed" version of each function simply calls the "named" version and passes in String.Empty as the name.

Finally, the AddNotGroup function is exactly the same as the AddGroup function, but it also sets the Not property of the SqlConditionGroup it creates to True. This makes it a bit easier to create negated groups by saving you the hassle of setting the Not property yourself.

Note A Not property is not included on the SqlCondition because you can define negation directly in the condition text, for example, "NOT A=1". Groups have no such text, so they require the Not property. If you want a Not property on your SqlCondition objects, then feel free to add it to the class.

GetNamedItem Function (Private Function)

All the search logic for locating named conditions and named groups resides in the private GetNamedItem function. It returns a generic ISqlCondition object, allowing it to return either a SqlCondition or a SqlConditionGroup object. It accepts two parameters: a string value called name that identifies the name of the item for which you are searching, and a SqlConditionType enumeration value called requestType that identifies the type of object being sought.

This function starts by checking the count to ensure there are items through which to search. If there are not, the function returns Nothing. Then the function uppercases the name parameter using the UCase method because we want to look for case-insensitive matches. Uppercasing it outside of the loops avoids the recurrent cost of uppercasing the name inside the loop.

GetNamedItem then iterates through each ISqlCondition item in the list. Inside the loop, it runs UCase on the Name property of the item and compares it to the name parameter passed into the function. It also checks the Type property of the item and compares it to the requestType to determine if the object type matches the object type being sought. If both the name and the object type match, then that item is returned. If not, the loop continues until all items in the current group have been checked.

If no match is made in the current group, then the GetNamedItem iterates through all the items again, this time checking for SqlConditionGroup objects in the collection. When a SqlConditionGroup object is encountered, it casts the item into a SqlConditionGroup and recursively calls the GetNamedItem method on the subgroup. The result of the recursive call is stored in a temporary variable, which is then checked to see if it contains a valid object or Nothing. If it contains a valid object, then that object is returned. If it contains Nothing, then the loop continues and the next group in the list is checked.

Finally, if a match is never made, the function simply returns Nothing.

GetNamedGroup and GetNamedCondition Functions

These two functions allow you to search for a named SqlCondition or named SqlConditionGroup object, respectively. Each function accepts one parameter, name, which identifies the name of the item being sought. Both functions call the GetNamedItem and pass in the name parameter as well as a hard-coded SqlConditionType enumeration value identifying the object type being sought. The result of the GetNamedItem function is implicitly cast into a strongly typed SqlCondition or SqlConditionGroup when it is returned.

Note You may have noticed that you can search for conditions or for groups, but no generic search exists that will return a named item regardless of its type. You can implement this function on your own if you want by modifying the GetNamedItem function, but I've never run across the need for it.

Remove, RemoveNamedCondition, and RemoveNamedGroup Methods

Each of these methods uses functionality inherited from the CollectionBase class to remove an item from the collection. Remove accepts an ISqlCondition object and removes that object from the collection if it's present.

RemoveNamedCondition and RemoveNamedGroup also remove items from the collection, but they accept a name parameter instead of an ISqlCondition object. These methods search for the name using GetNamedCondition and GetNamedGroup, respectively. If the item is located, then it is removed from the collection.

WriteStatement Function

At some point, all the conditions and condition groups in the SqlConditionGroup object must be converted from their object representations into text suitable for use in a SQL query. WriteStatement is responsible for iterating through all the items in its collection and building a text representation of itself.

Building the string for condition groups that only contain conditions is easy because it simply requires concatenating all the condition text and adding a couple of operator keywords. However, a condition group can also contain child condition groups. And of course, that child condition group may have condition groups of its own, and so on. How do you return all the text for a condition group? Interestingly enough, the function we're talking about right now handles just that sort of thing. To acquire the text for a child-condition group, the Write➥Statement method recursively calls that child group's WriteStatement method. At some point, the condition groups only contain conditions, the recursion stops, and the method can build a string by aggregating the output form its child groups.

The WriteStatement function starts by defining three variables:

- firstItemFlag: Boolean value that identifies whether or not the current item is the first item in the group because the first item requires special processing. This is initially set to True.
- Statement: Maintains the SQL statement as it's being built.
- TempStatement: Holds the condition from an item or the result of the recursive call to the WriteStatement method to ensure valid SQL is present before appending it to the actual statement variable.

WriteStatement begins by jumping into a loop that iterates through each item in the group's collection. Inside the loop, it checks the Type property of the item to determine whether it's a Condition or a Group. If the item is a Condition, then WriteStatement casts the item into a SqlCondition and sets tempStatement equal to the SqlCondition's condition property.

If the item is a Group, then the function casts the item into a SqlConditionGroup and stores the reference in the group variable. It then recursively calls group.WriteStatement and assigns the return value to the tempStatement variable. When a group is output as a SQL query, the group should be surrounded by parentheses. Of course, you do not want to have a set of parentheses with no inner content, so WriteStatement checks to make sure tempStatement contains text before surrounding the text with those parentheses. It also checks the Not property of the group to determine whether the NOT keyword should appear before the group, and adds the NOT keyword if necessary.

Next, the function needs to add the condition operator (AND/OR) to the SQL string. There are two conditions for adding the condition operator. First, tempStatement must contain some text to ensure a condition operator is not added without having a condition on which to operate. Second, the condition operator should *not* be added to the first item in the group.

So, WriteStatement first checks to see if tempStatement contains text. If it does not contain any text, then the loop continues on to the next item. If it does, then the function determines whether this item is the first item in the group using the firstItemFlag variable. If it is the first item, then the firstItemFlag is cleared by setting it to False. If it isn't the first item, then WriteStatement reads the item.ConditionOp property and adds the appropriate SQL text to the front of tempStatement. The function then appends tempStatement to the statement and moves on to the next item in the collection.

When all the items in the list have been processed, WriteStatement returns the value that has been built and stored in the statement variable.

Implementing the ISqlCondition Interface

SqlConditionGroup implements the ISqlCondition interface. This interface was covered in detail in the SqlCondition section, so you may refer to that class for more details. The only difference between the two implementations is that the Type property of the SqlConditionGroup returns a value of SqlConditionType.Group instead of SqlCondition➥Type.Condition.

Building the SqlQuery Class

All the components you have seen so far are auxiliary classes that provide support functionality for the SqlQuery class. The SqlQuery class is an object representation of a SQL SELECT statement and exposes a variety of properties to help you build queries in code using a simple programmatic interface. When the time comes to execute the query, the SqlQuery builds the SELECT statement based on its object representation. In addition to being able to build out normal queries, the SqlQuery class also can build paged queries that only return a subset of the entire set of data.

Before we get too far into the SqlQuery class code, let's take a minute to discuss paging and some of the new features in SQL Server 2005 that make paging a lot simpler than in previous versions.

What Is Paging?

Paging is the practice of breaking up large sets of data into smaller, more manageable sets, known as pages. Instead of being inundated by all the data at once, users can look through large amounts of data one page at a time, like flipping through the pages of a book. When implemented appropriately, paging helps reduce database and web server loads, increases response times, and reduces bandwidth requirements.

Google provides a great example of paging. When you search for "ASP.NET" in Google, there are more than 7 million results. Nobody in their right mind would want to be shown a page with 7 million links on it, and Google certainly does not have the bandwidth to constantly serve up pages with 7 million links. Instead, Google displays 10 results on a page and lets the searcher go to the next page to see the next 10 results. Rarely do people make it past the first few pages in a search, so Google saves a lot of bandwidth and processing power by only showing 10 results at a time.

Paging with Previous Version of SQL Server

My experience with paging in SQL Server 2000 started on a project where I needed to implement paging functionality on a variety of different reports. What I quickly learned is that paging in SQL Server 2000 is not an easy task.

You can limit the search results using the TOP keyword, but that only restricts the total number of rows returned. This is helpful for paging because you do not return extra data beyond what you need. But you do return all the data up to what you need. For example, say you have 100 items and you want to use paging to show 10 items per page over 10 pages. On the first page, you can use TOP 10 to limit the number of items to 10 (items 1–10) and avoid returning 90 extra results (items 11–100). On the second page, however, your only option is to use TOP 20. This avoids sending 80 extra results (items 21–100), so it's better than sending back everything, but you do send 10 results (1–10) unnecessarily. As you get further and further along in the page count, you send back more and more extraneous data until you reach the last page, which returns all the data. So the TOP keyword is helpful but not a great solution. Unfortunately, it's the only keyword previous versions of SQL Server had to help with paging.

To overcome the paging limitations in previous versions of SQL Server, many developers turned to stored procedures. The basic idea behind the stored procedure is to create a temporary table with an identity field, populate that table with records, and then use the auto-generated identify field as a row number. To select results 51 to 60, the statement reads something like

```
SELECT  * FROM #TempTable WHERE ResultRow > 50 and ResultRow < 61
```

Of course this is done programmatically, so the values 51 and 60 are actually variables in the stored procedure whose values are based on the current page and page size. Stored procedures overcome the issue of returning extraneous data, and they are very fast, but they require a lot of development time to write because you have to write one for every query you want to make (you may be able to consolidate a few of them). So it's a good solution, but it takes a lot of extra time and effort to build.

MySQL, a very well known open-source database, allows you to offset results and specify a page size using the LIMIT keyword. Returning results 51 to 60 is as easy as adding LIMIT 50,10 to the query (that is, skip 50 results and then return the next 10). And it has had this built-in paging functionality for at least the last 5 years (if not longer). Unfortunately, Microsoft did not follow suit and make a similar paging mechanism in SQL Server 2005. Next, let's take a look at what we did get.

Paging in SQL Server 2005 Using the ROW_NUMBER() Function

One of the new features in SQL Server 2005 is the ROW_NUMBER() function, which allows you to sequentially number the rows returned by a query. This alleviates you from having to build stored procedures for your paging needs. Understand, however, that stored procedures are faster than ad-hoc queries, and they are the way to go if you need to build super-high-performance applications.

You have to use the ROW_NUMBER() function in conjunction with the OVER() construct, which accepts an ORDER BY clause as a parameter. For example, if you want to select all the customer records from the Northwind database and give them each a row number, the query and subsequent results look something like Listing 8-7.

Listing 8-7. *SQL Query Demonstrating the* ROW_NUMBER *Function*

```
SELECT      ROW_NUMBER() OVER (ORDER BY CustomerID) AS RowNum, *
FROM        Customers
ORDER BY    RowNum

-- Returns the following results
```

RowNum	CustomerID	CompanyName	...
1	ALFKI	Alfreds Futterkiste	...
2	ANATR	Ana Trujillo Emparedados y helados	...
3	ANTON	Antonio Moreno Taquería	...
4	AROUT	Around the Horn	...
5	BERGS	Berglunds snabbköp	...
6	BLAUS	Blauer See Delikatessen	...

Although you specify an ORDER BY clause in the OVER() construct, that is not the ORDER BY clause for your query. In Listing 8-7, the ORDER BY clause for the query uses the RowNum alias to sort the results so you see the row's number values in sequential order. The ROW_NUMBER() function assigns sequential numbers to rows based on the ORDER BY clause in the OVER() construct. But you don't have to order your query using the same ORDER BY clause as defined in the OVER() construct. This means that the rows may be reordered by the actual ORDER BY clause after the row numbers have been assigned, leading to a result set with nonsequential `ROW_NUMBER()` values as shown in Listing 8-8.

Listing 8-8. *SQL Query Demonstrating Nonsequential* `ROW_NUMBER` *Values*

```
SELECT     ROW_NUMBER() OVER (ORDER BY CustomerID) AS RowNum, *
FROM       Customers
ORDER BY   City

-- Returns the following results
```

RowNum	CustomerID	CompanyName	City	...
17	DRACD	Drachenblut Delikatessen	Aachen	...
65	RATTC	Rattlesnake Canyon Grocery	Albuquerque	...
55	OLDWO	Old World Delicatessen	Anchorage	...
83	VAFFE	Vaffeljernet	Arhus	...
29	GALED	Galería del gastrónomo	Barcelona	...
46	LILAS	LILA-Supermercado	Barquisimeto	...

This is behavior by design. It seems a bit odd, but there is probably some great use for nonsequential row numbers that eludes me. At any rate, queries that return sequential row numbers are an awesome addition to SQL Server 2005, and they make paging a lot easier because you don't have to rely on stored procedures.

SqlQuery Class

Everything discussed so far is brought together in the `SqlQuery` class. This function exposes nine properties and three functions that provide you with an object-oriented approach to building SQL queries. Table 8-4 provides a brief overview of the properties and class-level variables found in the class and the role each property/variable plays.

Table 8-4. `SqlQuery` *Properties* and Class-Level Variables*

Name	Type	Description
`CurrentPage`	`Integer`	Defines which page of data should be returned.
`Distinct`	`Boolean`	Denotes whether or not the `DISTINCT` keyword should be used in the query.
`From`	`String`	Contains the `FROM` clause text.
`GroupBy`	`SqlFieldCollection`	Field list specifying aggregate data grouping constructs.
`GroupByAll`	`Boolean`	Denotes whether or not the `GROUP BY` clause should use include the `ALL` keyword.
`ItemsPerPage`	`Integer`	Defines the number of items that exist on a single page of data.

Name	Type	Description
`OrderBy`	`SqlFieldCollection`	Field list specifying which fields and what directions the query should use to sort the results.
`SelectFields`	`SqlFieldCollection`	Field list specifying those fields that should be returned by the query. If none are specified, then * is assumed.
`Top`	`Integer`	Specifies the number of rows that should be returned by a query. If `Top` is `0`, then all rows are returned. `Top` is disregarded during a reverse sort query.
`Where`	`SqlConditionGroup`	Set of conditions and condition groups that make up the `WHERE` clause.

** All properties have corresponding class-level variables named* `_<property name>` *to store their values*

Now that you have a basic understanding of each property, let's take a look at the `SlqQuery` class code. The first part of the code mainly consists of variable and property declarations described previously. It then moves into the SQL query-building functions, which are a bit more complicated. After you look at Listing 8-9, we'll consider these functions.

Listing 8-9. `SqlQuery` *Class*

```
Imports System.Text

Public Class SqlQuery

    '***********************************************************************
    Private _Distinct As Boolean
    Private _From As String
    Private _GroupBy As SqlFieldCollection
    Private _GroupByAll As Boolean
    Private _SelectFields As SqlFieldCollection
    Private _Top As Integer
    Private _OrderBy As SqlFieldCollection
    Private _Where As SqlConditionGroup

    'Paged Query Variables
    Private _ItemsPerPage As Integer
    Private _CurrentPage As Integer

    '***********************************************************************
    Public Property Distinct() As Boolean
        Get
            Return _Distinct
        End Get
        Set(ByVal value As Boolean)
```

```
            _Distinct = value
        End Set
    End Property

    '**************************************************************************
    Public Property SelectFields() As SqlFieldCollection
        Get
            If _SelectFields Is Nothing Then _
                _SelectFields = New SqlFieldCollection
            Return _SelectFields
        End Get
        Set(ByVal value As SqlFieldCollection)
            _SelectFields = value
        End Set
    End Property

    '**************************************************************************
    Public Property From() As String
        Get
            Return _From
        End Get
        Set(ByVal value As String)
            _From = value
        End Set
    End Property

    '**************************************************************************
    Public Property GroupBy() As SqlFieldCollection
        Get
            If _GroupBy Is Nothing Then _GroupBy = New SqlFieldCollection
            Return _GroupBy
        End Get
        Set(ByVal value As SqlFieldCollection)
            _GroupBy = value
        End Set
    End Property

    '**************************************************************************
    Public Property GroupByAll() As Boolean
        Get
            Return _GroupByAll
        End Get
        Set(ByVal value As Boolean)
            _GroupByAll = value
        End Set
    End Property
```

```
'***************************************************************************
Public Property OrderBy() As SqlFieldCollection
    Get
        If _OrderBy Is Nothing Then _OrderBy = New SqlFieldCollection
        Return _OrderBy
    End Get
    Set(ByVal value As SqlFieldCollection)
        _OrderBy = value
    End Set
End Property

'***************************************************************************
Public Property Where() As SqlConditionGroup
    Get
        If _Where Is Nothing Then _Where = _
          New SqlConditionGroup(SqlOperation.And, False)
        Return _Where
    End Get
    Set(ByVal value As SqlConditionGroup)
        _Where = value
    End Set
End Property

'***************************************************************************
Public Property Top() As Integer
    Get
        Return _Top
    End Get
    Set(ByVal value As Integer)
        _Top = value
    End Set
End Property

'***************************************************************************
Public Property ItemsPerPage() As Integer
    Get
        Return _ItemsPerPage
    End Get
    Set(ByVal value As Integer)
        _ItemsPerPage = value
    End Set
End Property

'***************************************************************************
Public Property CurrentPage() As Integer
    Get
        Return _CurrentPage
    End Get
```

```
        Set(ByVal value As Integer)
            _CurrentPage = value
        End Set
    End Property

    '**************************************************************************
    Private Function BuildQuery(ByVal countOnly As Boolean, _
     ByVal pagedQuery As Boolean) As String

        Dim sql As New StringBuilder(128)
        Dim seperator As Boolean
        Dim whereClause As String

        'Create the beginning of the SELECT statement
        sql.Append("SELECT")
        If Distinct Then sql.Append(" DISTINCT")

        'Append the TOP
        If pagedQuery Then
            sql.Append(" TOP ") : sql.Append(_ItemsPerPage * _CurrentPage)
        Else
            If top > 0 Then sql.Append(" TOP ") : sql.Append(top)
        End If

        'Determine if this is a normal or a count only query
        If countOnly Then
            sql.Append(" COUNT(*) AS TotalRecords")
        Else
            seperator = False
            If pagedQuery And _CurrentPage > 1 Then
                sql.Append(" ROW_NUMBER() OVER(ORDER BY ")
                For Each field As SqlField In OrderBy
                    If seperator Then sql.Append(", ") Else seperator = True
                    sql.Append(field.Name)

                    'Check to see if the order of the field is DESC
                    If field.SortDirection = SqlSortDirection.Descending Then
                        sql.Append(" DESC")
                    End If

                Next
                sql.Append(") as RowNum")
                seperator = True
            End If

            'Append SELECT fields
            If Me.SelectFields.Count = 0 Then
```

```
            If seperator Then sql.Append(", ") Else seperator = True
            sql.Append(" *")
        Else
            seperator = False
            sql.Append(" ")
            For Each field As SqlField In SelectFields
                If seperator Then sql.Append(", ") Else seperator = True
                If field.Alias = String.Empty Then
                    sql.Append(field.Name)
                Else
                    sql.Append(field.Name)
                    sql.Append(" AS ")
                    sql.Append(field.Alias)
                End If
            Next
        End If

    End If

    'Create the FROM clause
    If Not From = String.Empty Then
        sql.Append(" FROM ")
        sql.Append(From)
    End If

    'Create the WHERE clause
    whereClause = Where.WriteStatement()
    If Not whereClause = String.Empty Then
        sql.Append(" WHERE ")
        sql.Append(whereClause)
    End If

    'Create the GROUP BY clause
    If Not countOnly Then
        If GroupBy.Count > 0 Then
            sql.Append(" GROUP BY ")
            If GroupByAll Then sql.Append("ALL ")
            seperator = False
            For Each field As SqlField In GroupBy
                If seperator Then sql.Append(", ") Else seperator = True
                sql.Append(field.Name)
            Next
        End If

        If pagedQuery And Not CurrentPage = 1 Then
```

```
            'Order by the RowNum
            sql.Append(" ORDER BY RowNum")

        Else

            'Create the ORDER BY clause
            If OrderBy.Count > 0 Then
                sql.Append(" ORDER BY ")
                seperator = False

                For Each field As SqlField In OrderBy
                    If seperator Then sql.Append(", ") Else seperator = True
                    sql.Append(field.Name)

                    'Check to see if the query should be reverse sorted
                    If field.SortDirection = SqlSortDirection.Descending Then
                        sql.Append(" DESC")
                    End If

                Next

            End If

        End If

    End If

    Return sql.ToString

End Function

'***************************************************************************
Public Function GetQuery() As String
    Return BuildQuery(False, False)
End Function

'***************************************************************************
Public Function GetCountQuery() As String
    Return BuildQuery(True, False)
End Function

'***************************************************************************
Public Function GetPagedQuery()
    Return GetPagedQuery(CurrentPage, ItemsPerPage)
End Function
```

```
    '***************************************************************************
    Public Function GetPagedQuery(ByVal currentPage As Integer, _
     ByVal itemsPerPage As Integer) As String

        If currentPage < 1 Then currentPage = 1
        If itemsPerPage < 1 Then itemsPerPage = 10
        _CurrentPage = currentPage
        _ItemsPerPage = itemsPerPage

        Dim PagedQuery As String = BuildQuery(False, True)

        If _CurrentPage > 1 Then
            PagedQuery = String.Format( _
              "SELECT * FROM ({0})innerSelect WHERE RowNum > {1}", _
              PagedQuery, _
              _ItemsPerPage * (_CurrentPage - 1))
        End If

        Return PagedQuery

    End Function

End Class
```

As you can see, most of the complexity lies in the query-building functions, specifically, the `BuildQuery` function. Let's take a look at the query-building functions to see how they convert the properties of the `SqlQuery` class into a usable SQL query.

BuildQuery Function (Private)

`BuildQuery` may be called upon to create three different types of queries. All are very similar, but each has its own minor variation that makes it slightly different.

- *Regular query:* Builds out a normal SQL `SELECT` statement based on the properties of the `SqlQuery` class.
- *Count query:* The count query is the regular query with the `SELECT` fields replaced by `COUNT(*) AS TotalRecords`, and no `GROUP BY` or `ORDER BY` clauses. This query determines how many records the normal query returns when executed and is useful for paging scenarios when you need to calculate the total number of pages required to display a set of data. You'll see this query used in the next chapter when we discuss paging in more detail.
- *Paged query:* Builds a query that uses the `ROW_NUMBER()` function to sequentially order the rows and limits the overall rows based on the page size and current page. This query is used in conjunction with the `GetPagedQuery` method to build a query capable of returning a single page worth of data.

BuildQuery accepts two Boolean parameters, countOnly, and pagedQuery, which it uses throughout the function to determine which query to output. If neither of the parameters are True, then the method outputs the regular. If countOnly is True, then the method outputs the count query. And if the pagedQuery parameter is True, then the method knows to output the paged query.

Immediately after the function declaration, BuildQuery creates three variables. The sql variable is a StringBuilder object that holds the text of the query as it is built out; separator helps determine whether or not to use a comma in field lists; and whereClause temporarily holds the WHERE clause after it has been built using the WriteStatement function.

Now we get into the actual query construction. BuildQuery always outputs the SELECT portion of the statement because it's used by all the query types. Then it adds the DISTINCT keyword if the Distinct property is set to True.

Next, it determines whether or not to output a TOP keyword and value. This is where we see our first distinction between query types. BuildQuery checks to see if this query is a paged query and, if so, appends a TOP value calculated based on the number of items per page and the current page. This limits the total amount of data that must be assigned sequential numbers by the ROW_NUMBER() function. If the method is not building a paged query, it checks to see if the normal TOP property has a value greater than zero and appends the TOP keyword and value if needed.

BuildQuery then determines whether or not the query is a count query. If it is a count query, then the method appends COUNT(*) AS TotalRecords to the field list. In doing so, the query will only return a single numeric value indicating how many total records are returned by the query. If the query is not a count query, then the method has to do a little more work. First, it checks to see if the query is a paged query. If so, it uses the ROW_NUMBER() function to create a sequentially numbered field named RowNum. To build the OVER() construct, the method iterates through and outputs all the fields in the OrderBy property. Notice that it uses the separator variable to determine whether or not to put a comma in the field list, and it checks each field object's SortDirection property to see if the field requires the DESC keyword.

Next, BuildQuery constructs the field list for the SELECT statement for both the normal and the paged query. If no fields are defined in the SelectFields property, then the method appends * to return all available fields. If fields are defined, then BuildQuery iterates through them and builds the field listing using the field name and, if it's available, the field's alias. You'll also see the separator variable used in this section to help create commas to separate fields in the list.

After building the select field list, the function appends the FROM statement to the query if a FROM statement has been defined. You won't encounter many queries that do not have a FROM clause, but it can happen on rare occasions if you only need to select a value from a function (for example, SELECT GetDate() AS DatabaseDate).

BuildQuery then executes Where.WriteStatement() and stores the result of the function in the whereClause variable. Remember, the WriteStatement method of the SqlConditionGroup is responsible for returning a string containing all the conditions and condition groups used in the WHERE clause. If there are no conditions to apply, the method simply returns an empty string. If the whereClause variable contains a string, then BuildQuery knows to append the WHERE clause to the query. Otherwise, the method skips the WHERE clause.

After appending the WHERE clause, BuildQuery appends the GROUP BY and ORDER BY clauses for the normal and paged queries. Notice that the method skips this section for the count query. The count query only returns a single value so it doesn't need any grouping or ordering clauses. BuildQuery constructs the GROUP BY clause by iterating through all the fields in the GroupBy property and outputting them as a comma-separated list. BuildQuery then checks to see whether it's building a normal or paged query. If a paged query, then it uses `ORDER BY RowNum` as the `ORDER BY` clause because the `RowNum` contains sequential values based on the `ORDER BY` clause supplied to the `OVER` construct, so you might as well use that to your advantage and avoid rewriting a duplicate `ORDER BY` clause. Depending on how SQL optimizes the query, there may be a slight performance gain by using this method because it's easier to sort a single numeric field than say, for example, three text fields. Worst-case scenario is that it reduces the size of the `SELECT` statement. If the build query is creating a normal query, it outputs the `ORDER BY` clause by iterating through all the fields in the `OrderBy` property and appending the field names and sort directions as a comma-separated list.

Finally, the function returns `sql.ToString()`, which contains the query text that was built out over the course of the function.

GetQuery and GetQueryCount Functions

These two functions both use the `BuildQuery` function to return their respective queries. `GetQuery` returns the regular query. `GetQueryCount` returns the count query. The only differences between the two functions are their names and the parameters used to call `BuildQuery`.

GetPagedQuery Functions

This function is responsible for building a query that returns data from the requested page. It's an overloaded method, so you can call it with or without any parameters. `GetPagedQuery` uses two parameters named `currentPage` and `itemsPerPage`, which help determine which page of data to return. You can specify this by calling `GetPagedQuery` and passing the current page and items per page in as parameters, or you can set the `CurrentPage` and `ItemsPerPage` properties on the `SqlQuery` object and call `GetPagedQuery` without any parameters. The parameterless version of the function simply calls the parameterized version and passes in the property values.

The first couple of lines in the method ensure that there are valid values for the `currentPage` and `itemsPerPage` parameters. If either one of the values is invalid, it's assigned a valid value. You can also throw an exception here if you want to.

`GetPagedQuery` then calls `BuildQuery(False,True)`, which tells `BuildQuery` to return a paged query and stores that paged query in the `PagedQuery` variable. If the requested page is the first page, then no more work needs to be done because the `TOP` value returns the correct amount of data for the first page. On subsequent pages, however, a bit more work needs to be done to hack off the extraneous data returned at the beginning of the result set. To get rid of that data, `GetPagedQuery` wraps the query in `PagedQuery` in another `SELECT` statement that operates on the data returned by `PagedQuery`. Remember, the data in `PagedQuery` contains a column named `RowNum` that identifies the rows returned by the query in sequential order. Also remember that the `BuildQuery` method limits the amount of data returned for a paged query using the `TOP` keyword. So, to get the right data, the second `SELECT` statement only selects rows whose `RowNum` value is higher than `_ItemsPerPage * (_CurrentPage - 1)`.

Here's an example. Say you are trying to get data for page 6 of a query, and you are showing 10 items per page. This means that you are trying to display row numbers 51–60. `BuildQuery` ensures that only 60 rows of data come back, so you only have to worry about getting rid of the extraneous data before row 51. So, the outer `SELECT` statement created by `GetPagedQuery` selects rows whose `RowNum` values are greater than 50. You acquire this value using the equation `_ItemsPerPage * (_CurrentPage - 1) = 10 * (6-1) = 10 * 5 = 50`. And that's how the `SqlQuery` class builds normal and paged queries. Next, you'll learn how to use the `SqlQuery` class in code.

Using a SqlQuery Object to Build Queries

Creating the `SqlQuery` tool took a bit of work, but now you can see how all that work can really pay off when you need to manipulate SQL queries in code. This section runs through a series of scenarios, working from simple to complex, and illustrates how to use a `SqlQuery` object to help you create a SQL query for each scenario. The table names and columns come from the Northwind sample database in case you want to try the queries out on your own.

■ **Note** You can find the Northwind sample database on the Microsoft website. Unfortunately, the link to the page consists mostly of random characters and is far from intelligible. The easiest way to locate the Northwind database is to search Google for "Northwind and Pubs Sample Databases." You can also find a link to the sample database in the Links section of the sample application in the Source Code area of the Apress website.

Scenario 1: Building a Simple Query

If you are building static queries that will not change, then you use a `String` to store the query, not a `SqlQuery` object. This example is just a demonstration of how to use some of the simple properties of the `SqlQuery` object. The scenario is that you want to build a query that allows your users to see a customer phone list that shows the customer ID, name, city, phone number, and fax number. You also want to rename the `Phone` column to read `PhoneNumber`, and the `Fax` column to read `FaxNumber`. Listings 8-10 and 8-11 show the SQL and `SqlQuery` representations of this scenario's query.

Listing 8-10. *Scenario #1* `SQL` *Representation*

```
SELECT CustomerID, CompanyName, City, Phone AS PhoneNumber, Fax as FaxNumber
FROM   Customers
ORDER BY CompanyName
```

Listing 8-11. *Scenario #1* `SqlQuery` *Representation*

```
'***************************************************************************
Public Shared Function Scenario1() As String

    Dim SqlQueryObj As New Reporting.SqlQuery

    SqlQueryObj.SelectFields.Add("CustomerID")
    SqlQueryObj.SelectFields.Add("CompanyName")
    SqlQueryObj.SelectFields.Add("City")
    SqlQueryObj.SelectFields.Add("Phone", "PhoneNumber")
    SqlQueryObj.SelectFields.Add("Fax", "FaxNumber")
    SqlQueryObj.From = "Customers"
    SqlQueryObj.OrderBy.Add("CompanyName")
    Return SqlQueryObj.GetQuery()

End Function
```

This is a very simple and straightforward example that has no conditional logic. The function simply builds the query and returns it as the value of the function.

Scenario 2: Building Conditional WHERE Clauses

In this scenario, you run the same query as specified in Scenario 1, but with a `WHERE` clause that filters the results by a specific city name. If no city is specified, then you want to include all cities. This effectively means that no `WHERE` clause should appear when the city name is unspecified. The city name is passed in via the `CityName` parameter in the function definition. Listings 8-12 and 8-13 show the SQL and `SqlQuery` representations of this scenario's query.

Listing 8-12. *Scenario #2* SQL *Representation*

```
SELECT   CustomerID, CompanyName, City, Phone AS PhoneNumber, Fax as FaxNumber
FROM     Customers
WHERE    City='<City Name>'    -- line is optional based on city value
ORDER BY CompanyName
```

Note Items that appear in < > brackets represent SQL terms that vary from query to query.

Listing 8-13. *Scenario #2* `SqlQuery` *Representation*

```
'***********************************************************************
Public Shared Function Scenario2(ByVal CityName As String) As String

    Dim SqlQueryObj As New Reporting.SqlQuery

    SqlQueryObj.SelectFields.Add("CustomerID")
    SqlQueryObj.SelectFields.Add("CompanyName")
    SqlQueryObj.SelectFields.Add("City")
    SqlQueryObj.SelectFields.Add("Phone", "PhoneNumber")
    SqlQueryObj.SelectFields.Add("Fax", "FaxNumber")
    SqlQueryObj.From = "Customers"

    If Not CityName = String.Empty Then
        SqlQueryObj.Where.AddCondition("City='" & CityName & "'")
    End If

    SqlQueryObj.OrderBy.Add("CompanyName")
    Return SqlQueryObj.GetQuery()

End Function
```

This example has conditional logic, highlighted in bold, that appends a `WHERE` clause condition if the city name is specified in the `CityName` variable. You can make the conditional logic for your `WHERE` clause as simple or as complicated as you need.

Scenario 3: Building Conditional FROM, SELECT, WHERE, and ORDER BY Clauses

Next, we have a more complicated scenario that gives the user multiple ways to view data and the ability to specify the order in which the results are returned. The first way to view the data mimics the data from Scenario 2. The second option returns all the data from Scenario 2 along with the total amount of money each customer has spent on products in the last six months. Acquiring the sales totals for customers requires joining the `Customers`, `Orders`, and `Order Details` tables, adding aggregate columns to the select fields list, and additional `WHERE` clause items to limit the orders to those in the last six months. Listing 8-14 and 8-15 show the SQL and `SqlQuery` representations of this scenario's query.

Note You can extend the `SqlQuery` tool to programmatically create joins between tables if you want to. For now, we'll manually define the joins and assign them to the `From` property.

Listing 8-14. *Scenario #3* SQL *Representation*

```
SELECT   CustomerID, CompanyName, City, Phone AS PhoneNumber, Fax as FaxNumber
FROM     Customers
WHERE    City='<City Name>'    -- line is optional
ORDER BY <Sort Order Field List> -- line is optional
SQL Representation (Option 2):
SELECT     Customers.CustomerID, Customers.CompanyName,
           Customers.Phone AS PhoneNumber, Customers.Fax AS FaxNumber,
           Customers.City,
           SUM([Order Details].UnitPrice * [Order Details].Quantity) AS TotalSpent
FROM       Customers INNER JOIN Orders ON
             Customers.CustomerID = Orders.CustomerID INNER JOIN [Order Details] ON
               Orders.OrderID = [Order Details].OrderID
WHERE      (Orders.OrderDate > '<Six Months Ago>')
           AND (Customers.City = '<City Name>') -- line is optional
GROUP BY  Customers.CustomerID, Customers.CompanyName, Customers.Phone,
          Customers.Fax, Customers.City
ORDER BY  <Sort Order Field List> -- line is optional
```

Listing 8-15. *Scenario #3* SqlQuery *Representation*

```
'***************************************************************************
Public Shared Function Scenario3(ByVal CityName As String, _
  ByVal ShowTotalSpent As Boolean, ByVal SortColumn As String, _
  ByVal SortDir As Reporting.SqlSortDirection) As String

    Dim SqlQueryObj As New Reporting.SqlQuery

    SqlQueryObj.SelectFields.Add("Customers.CustomerID")
    SqlQueryObj.SelectFields.Add("Customers.CompanyName")
```

```
SqlQueryObj.SelectFields.Add("City")
SqlQueryObj.SelectFields.Add("Customers.Phone", "PhoneNumber")
SqlQueryObj.SelectFields.Add("Customers.Fax", "FaxNumber")

If Not CityName = String.Empty Then
    SqlQueryObj.Where.AddCondition("Customers.City='" & CityName & "'")
End If

If ShowTotalSpent Then

    'Set up the additional Select Field
    SqlQueryObj.SelectFields.Add( _
        "SUM([Order Details].UnitPrice * [Order Details].Quantity)", _
        "TotalSpent")

    'Set up the FROM clause with the Joined tables
    SqlQueryObj.From = "Customers INNER JOIN Orders ON " & _
        "Customers.CustomerID = Orders.CustomerID INNER JOIN " & _
        "[Order Details] ON Orders.OrderID = [Order Details].OrderID"

    'Add the WHERE clause to limit orders to the last 6 months
    SqlQueryObj.Where.And()
    SqlQueryObj.Where.AddCondition("Orders.OrderDate > '" & _
        Format(CDate(Now.AddMonths(-6)), "MM/dd/yyyy") & "'")

    'Set up the GROUP BY clause
    SqlQueryObj.GroupBy.Add("Customers.CustomerID")
    SqlQueryObj.GroupBy.Add("Customers.CompanyName")
    SqlQueryObj.GroupBy.Add("Customers.Phone")
    SqlQueryObj.GroupBy.Add("Customers.Fax")
    SqlQueryObj.GroupBy.Add("Customers.City")

Else
    'Set up the single table FROM clause
    SqlQueryObj.From = "Customers"
End If

'Build out ORDER BY based on SortColumn value
Select Case UCase(SortColumn)
    Case "CUSTOMERID"
        SqlQueryObj.OrderBy.Add("CustomerID", SortDir)
    Case "TOTALSPENT"
        SqlQueryObj.OrderBy.Add("TotalSpent", SortDir)
        SqlQueryObj.OrderBy.Add("CompanyName", SortDir)
    Case Else
        SqlQueryObj.OrderBy.Add("CompanyName", SortDir)
End Select
```

```
    Return SqlQueryObj.GetQuery()
End Function
```

As you can see, the SqlQuery class allows you to focus more on building queries and less on string manipulation. Scenario3 begins by adding the common fields to both queries to SqlQueryObj. Notice that the SELECT field names are fully qualified; that is, they contain both the table and the column name in their definition. It always helps to fully qualify fields because SQL Server does not have to do any extra work to determine which table the field belongs to. And you are required to fully qualify field names that appear in more than one of the tables you are joining because SQL has no way of resolving the name otherwise.

Both queries use the CityName filter in the WHERE clause if it's specified, so Scenario3 runs the conditional logic to determine if the clause should be added.

Then the function determines whether or not the user wants to see the total amount each customer has spent in the last six months by checking the ShowTotalSpent flag parameter of the function. If the flag is set to True, then Scenario3 sets up an additional SELECT column that calculates the sum of all items ordered, and sets up an alias for that column named TotalSpent.

Next, assuming that the ShowTotalSpent flag is True, the function sets up the appropriate FROM clause because the Customers, Orders, and Order Detail tables all need to be joined before the TotalSpent column can be calculated. To do this, we join the Customer table to the Order table, which contains a record of an individual order, but not the details of that order. We then join the Order table to the Order Details table, which contains a listing of the items included in the order and their purchase price. This gives us a relationship between customers and order details that we can use to calculate the total amount of money each customer has spent. After the FROM clause has been set up, Scenario3 calculates a date value six months in the past using Now.AddMonths(-6) and adds the condition to the WHERE clause to ensure only orders from the last six months are included in the TotalSpent calculation. Finally, the method adds a series of GROUP BY items to the query. These are required by SQL syntax because they are nonaggregate columns (that is, not calculated using an aggregation function such as SUM or AVG).

If the ShowTotalSpent flag is not set, then Scenario3 assigns "Customers" to the FROM clause because no joins are required and continues on to the ORDER BY section.

The last thing the function does before returning the query is to set up the appropriate ORDER BY clause based on the sortColumn and SortDir parameters of the function. The function uses a case statement to determine which column was specified and then adds the appropriate items to the OrderBy property based on that determination.

■ **Tip** You can add a field list parser or an alternative string property to your SqlQuery class if you would rather specify your SELECT, GROUP BY, and ORDER BY items as a single string instead of as a series of individual items.

Executing Queries with the SqlQuery Class

Building a query is only one part of the equation; you also have to execute that query. Because a normal query is just like any static query that you would create with a string, you just have to create the appropriate database objects and execute it as shown in Listing 8-16.

Listing 8-16. *Executing a Normal Query*

```
Imports System.Data.SqlClient
...

Private Sub RunQuery()
    Dim SqlQueryObj As New Reporting.SqlQuery
    Dim dbConn As New SqlConnection( _
      ConnectionStrings("Northwind").ConnectionString)
    Dim dbCmd As SqlCommand
    Dim dr As SqlDataReader

    'Build SQL Query (SELECT * FROM CUSTOMERS)
    SqlQueryObj.From = "Customers"

    'Execute the query
    dbConn.Open()
    dbCmd = New SqlCommand(SqlQueryObj.GetQuery, dbConn)
    dr = dbCmd.ExecuteReader()

    'Do what you need to with the data reader
    '    ... Code ...

    dr.Close()
    dbConn.Close()
End Sub
```

This should not look much different than another database access routine that you have seen. It creates a connection object and a command object, opens the database, and executes the command. The command initializes a data reader that can then be used for whatever purpose you need. Then you close the data reader and the database connection.

Executing Paged Queries with the SqlQuery Class

Executing a paged query is just as simple as executing a normal query, but you must specify an ORDER BY clause, the number of items to display on a page, and which page of data you want the query to return. Listing 8-17 provides an example outlining the differences.

Listing 8-17. *Executing a Paged Query*

```
Imports System.Data.SqlClient
...

'****************************************************************************
Private Sub RunQuery(ByVal currentPage as Integer, ByVal itemsPerPage as Integer)
    Dim SqlQueryObj As New Reporting.SqlQuery
    Dim dbConn As New SqlConnection( _
      ConnectionStrings("Northwind").ConnectionString)
```

```
    Dim dbCmd As SqlCommand
    Dim dr As SqlDataReader

    'Build SQL Query (SELECT * FROM CUSTOMERS)
    SqlQueryObj.From = "Customers"
    SqlQueryObj.OrderBy.Add("CustomerID")

    'Execute the query
    dbConn.Open()
    dbCmd = New SqlCommand( _
            SqlQueryObj.GetPagedQuery(currentPage, itemsPerPage), dbConn)
    dr = dbCmd.ExecuteReader()

    'Do what you need to with the data reader
    '   ... Code ...

    dr.Close()
    dbConn.Close()
End Sub
```

These examples have given you a good demonstration of the basic usage of the SqlQuery class. You can use it to create as simple or as complex of a query as you desire, and it's especially handy when working with the ORDER BY and WHERE clauses, and for paging data. In the next chapter, you'll learn a lot more about the paging features of the SqlQuery class and how to use the count query to display detailed paging information like the total number of records returned and the overall page count.

In this next section, you'll see how easy it is to build out common search clauses using the SqlConditionGroup object.

Commonly Used Search Functions

As you work with search and query features, you may find yourself building out the same WHERE clauses over and over again. The most common ones are usually date range and keyword searches, both of which are fairly generic. You may also have less-generic ones that align themselves more with your core business. For instance, you may repetitively use certain customer, product, category, or other clauses that are more tightly linked to your company's business processes. If you continually use it over and over again, then you might as well make it easier to use over the long haul by creating a commonly used search function.

There are two options for building out commonly used search functions. If the search function is fairly generic and thus can be reused on almost every one of your projects, then you can add the function directly to the SqlConditionGroup class. Adding the function in this location makes it easy to call the function from a logical place when you are using a SqlQuery object.

```
sqlQueryObj.SelectFields.Add("OrderID")
sqlQueryObj.SelectFields.Add("OrderDate")
sqlQueryObj.From = "Order"
sqlQueryObj.Where.CreateDateRange("1/1/2004", "1/1/2005", "Order Date", _
  Exclusive, "MM/dd/yyyy")
```

Notice that the `CreateDateRange` function can be called from the `Where` property of the `SqlQuery` object because it resides in the `SqlConditionGroup` class. This makes your code fairly easy to read.

The other option is to create a function in a separate library, and pass the function a reference to a `SqlQuery` object. Then you can manipulate the `SqlQuery` object accordingly inside the function. This option is useful when you have a function that will be common in a single project but not necessarily in all your projects.

```
sqlQueryObj.SelectFields.Add("OrderID")
sqlQueryObj.SelectFields.Add("OrderDate")
sqlQueryObj.From = "Order"
ProjectLibrary.CustomSearchQuery(sqlQueryObj,Param1,Param2)
```

This approach helps keep your `SqlConditionGroup` class from becoming cluttered with code that cannot be ported from one project to the next.

Because both the `CreateDateRange` and `CreateKeyword` functions are generic, they will be placed in the `SqlConditionGroup` class. You can see their function definitions and location in the class by looking near the end of Listing 8-6 earlier in this chapter.

Date Range Search

Searching for records in a specific date range is one of the most common ways to search for records because time is very important when it comes to data. It may be important to find data created in the past few days so it can be processed appropriately. It may be important to exclude data beyond a certain date because the data is no longer applicable. Whatever the case, it's a situation that is very likely to come up in your searching and querying endeavors.

The idea behind the `CreateDateRange` function is simple. It acts like the `AddGroup` function, but it adds a group containing date-range conditions. It also returns the `SqlConditionGroup` that it creates as the result of the function, just like the `AddGroup` function, in case you want to store a reference to it. You'll notice that there are two function definitions for the `CreateDateRange` function. The first allows you to create a date-range group without a unique group name, and the second allows you to specify a unique group name for searching purposes. This discussion is limited to the second function because the first one just calls the second one and passes in an empty string for the unique name (see Listing 8-18).

Listing 8-18. `CreateDateRange` *Function*

```
'***************************************************************************
Public Function CreateDateRange(ByVal startDateStr As String, _
  ByVal endDateStr As String, ByVal column As String, _
  ByVal evalType As SqlEvaluationType, ByVal dateFormat As String) _
  As SqlConditionGroup

    Return CreateDateRange(startDateStr, endDateStr, column, evalType, _
      dateFormat, String.Empty)

End Function
```

```
'*************************************************************************
Public Function CreateDateRange(ByVal startDateStr As String, _
  ByVal endDateStr As String, ByVal column As String, _
  ByVal evalType As SqlEvaluationType, ByVal dateFormat As String, _
  ByVal name As String) As SqlConditionGroup

    Dim group As SqlConditionGroup
    Dim startDate As Date
    Dim endDate As Date

    'Make sure that there is at least one date specified before continuing
    If IsDate(startDateStr) Then startDate = CDate(startDateStr)
    If IsDate(endDateStr) Then endDate = CDate(endDateStr)
    If startDate = Nothing And endDate = Nothing Then Return Nothing

    'Specify a date format string if none was supplied
    If dateFormat = String.Empty Then dateFormat = "MM/dd/yyyy"

    'Create new group. Specify that all conditions in group must be met
    group = New SqlConditionGroup(_NextOperation, False, name)
    group.And()

    'Append the start date criteria, if applicable
    If Not startDate = Nothing Then

        Select Case evalType

            Case SqlEvaluationType.Exclusive
                group.AddCondition(String.Format("{0}>'{1}'", column, _
                                         Format(startDate, dateFormat)))

            Case SqlEvaluationType.Inclusive
                group.AddCondition(String.Format("{0}>='{1}'", column, _
                                         Format(startDate, dateFormat)))

        End Select
    End If

    'Append the end date criteria, if applicable
    If Not endDate = Nothing Then
        Select Case evalType

            Case SqlEvaluationType.Exclusive
                group.AddCondition(String.Format("{0}<'{1}'", column, _
                Format(endDate, dateFormat)))
```

```
                Case SqlEvaluationType.Inclusive
                    group.AddCondition(String.Format("{0}<='{1}'", column, _
                    Format(endDate, dateFormat)))

            End Select
        End If

        List.Add(group)
        Return group

    End Function
```

CreateDateRange accepts a number of parameters. Before we go any further, Table 8-5 clarifies what those parameters are and what they represent.

Table 8-5. CreateDateRange *Parameters*

Parameter Name	Type	Description
startDateStr	String	Start date.
endDateStr	String	End date.
column	String	Name of the column containing the date information.
evalType	SqlEvaluationType	Defines whether the actual date should be included or excluded in the query results. If inclusive is specified then, >= and <= will be used. If exclusive is specified then > and < will be used.
dateFormat	String	Allows you to specify a format for the date string in the SQL query. If no format string is specified, then MM/DD/yyyy is used. This is helpful if you want to specifically include the time portion of a date in the query or you need to specify a different date format for your locale.
name	String	Allows you to give the group created by the method a unique ID.

The CreateDateRange function begins by creating a series of variables that will be used throughout the function. The group variable is a SqlConditionGroup that stores the statement as it's being built. Both startDate and endDate are Date variables used to store the actual Date representation of the startDateStr and endDateStr parameters, respectively. The code to check and convert the strings into dates is shown directly under the variable declarations.

If neither startDate nor endDate is a valid date, then there is no reason to continue. The function simply returns Nothing, and nothing is added to the statement. If there is at least one valid date, then the function continues.

Because at least one date exists, the function initializes the group object so it can store conditions as they are added to the statement. Notice that the method passes _NextOperation, False, and name into the group constructor. You pass _NextOperation into the group to assign the group its ISqlCondition.ConditionOp value to determine which condition operator precedes the group when it is output as a string. The second parameter, False, simply means that the group should not be negated. And the last parameter gives the group a unique name, assuming a unique name was provided (it could be an empty string). The method then calls group.And() because all the conditions in the group must be met for the date to fall within the date range. Remember, you do not need to repeatedly call group.And() because it sets an internal value that will continue to use AND with conditions until you explicitly change it.

Next, if startDate contains a valid date, CreateDateRange checks to see which evaluation method should be used by checking the evalType parameter. If the exclusive evaluation type is being used, then the function will use > in the condition. If inclusive is being used, then the function will use >= in the condition. In either case, String.Format is used to create a condition containing the column named and appropriately formatted startDate information. That condition is then added to group.

The following section behaves similarly, but it applies to the end date. Thus, it uses < and <= in the condition.

At the end of the function, group is added to the collection of ISqlCondition objects stored in the List property of the SqlConditionGroup, and then returned as the result of the function.

Using the DateRangeSearch

You may be wondering why the DateRangeSearch function accepts string representations of the start and end dates instead of actual date types. The reasoning is that this function is designed for use with web-based applications, and web-based applications usually acquire dates as strings. Thus, the DateRangeSearch function encapsulates the logic for converting those strings into dates.

Listing 8-19 is a simple example of how to use the DateRangeSearch function. Assume there are three text boxes named txtCustomerID, txtStartDate, and txtEndDate; a GridView control named myGrid; and a button named btnDateRangeQuery:

Listing 8-19. CreateDateRange *Function Example*

```
'***************************************************************************
Protected Sub btnDateRangeQuery_Click(ByVal sender As Object, _
  ByVal e As System.EventArgs) Handles btnDateRangeQuery.Click

    Dim sqlQueryObj As New Reporting.SqlQuery
    Dim dbConn As New SqlConnection( _
      ConnectionStrings("Northwind").ConnectionString)
    Dim dbCmd As SqlCommand
    Dim dr As SqlDataReader

    sqlQueryObj.From = "Orders"

    If Not Me.txtCustomerID.Text = String.Empty Then
        sqlQueryObj.Where.AddCondition( _
          String.Format("CustomerID='{0}'", txtCustomerID.Text))
    End If

    sqlQueryObj.Where.And()
    sqlQueryObj.Where.CreateDateRange(Me.txtStartDate.Text, _
      Me.txtEndDate.Text, "OrderDate", _
      Reporting.SqlEvaluationType.Inclusive, "MM/dd/yyyy")
```

```
    dbConn.Open()
    dbCmd = New SqlCommand(SqlQueryObj.GetQuery(), dbConn)
    dr = dbCmd.ExecuteReader()

    myGrid.DataSource = dr
    myGrid.DataSource.DataBind()

    dr.Close()
    dbConn.Close()

End Sub
```

Listing 8-19 demonstrates how you can pass text directly into the `CreateDateRange` function, and how you can apply conditional logic to the `SqlConditionGroup` added by function. Take note of the `sqlQueryObj.Where.And()` call in the code. This means that if both the `CustomerID` and a date range are specified, then only rows matching the `CustomerID` AND the date range will be returned. If the `sqlQueryObj.Where.Or()` had been called, then `OR` logic would apply.

Now let's move on to another useful search feature, the `CreateKeywords` function.

Keyword Search

Keyword searching should be a more common search tool in business applications. I say should because most of the applications I run across either do not have keyword searching, or it's implemented very poorly. The following keyword search allows you to search for multiple keywords in multiple columns, and it allows you to employ conditional and parenthetical operators. This means that if your users are, for example, searching for a particular employee, they can enter complex text-based keyword queries like `(Smith OR Abrams) AND NOT (Manager)` to help narrow down searches. Notice that the text for the keyword search is totally free form. You pass the text entered by the user directly into the method and it sorts out the details, so it's very simple to use. Plus, the search mechanism uses `LIKE` searching with wildcards that matches on substrings. For example, a search for "Jo" returns matches on "Joe", "Joseph", "Jonathan", and so on.

Although keyword searching may seem like a complicated task, it's actually fairly simple because of the `SqlQuery` tool's architecture, and actually requires a few less lines of code than the `CreateDateRange` function. Listing 8-20 is the code for the function.

Listing 8-20. `CreateKeywords` *Function*

```
Imports System.Text.RegularExpressions
...

'*********************************************************************
Public Function CreateKeywords(ByVal keywords As String, _
  ByVal column As String, ByVal defaultOp As SqlOperation) As SqlConditionGroup

    Dim group As New SqlConditionGroup(_NextOperation, False)
    Dim groupStack As New Stack
    Dim keywordList As String()
```

```
    Dim [not] As Boolean
    Dim hasCondition As Boolean

    If Trim(keywords) = String.Empty Then Return Nothing
    keywords = Regex.Replace(keywords, "\(|\)", " $0 ")
    keywords = Regex.Replace(keywords, "\s{2,}", " ")
    keywordList = Split(UCase(Trim(keywords)))

    For Each keyword As String In keywordList
        Select Case keyword
            Case "AND"
                group.And()
            Case "OR"
                group.Or()
            Case "NOT"
                [not] = True
            Case "("
                groupStack.Push(group)
                group = group.AddGroup()
                group.Not = [not]
                [not] = False
            Case ")"
                If groupStack.Count > 0 Then group = groupStack.Pop
            Case ""
                'Do nothing
            Case Else
                group.AddCondition(String.Format( _
                    "{0}{1} like '%{2}%'", IIf([not], "NOT ", ""), _
                    column, SqlString(keyword)))
                [not] = False
                hasCondition = True
        End Select
    Next

    If hasCondition Then
        'Make sure you end up with the top level group
        While groupStack.Count > 0
            group = groupStack.Pop()
        End While
        List.Add(group)
        Return group
    Else
        Return Nothing
    End If

End Function
```

`CreateKeywords` has eight different parameters and variables used throughout the function. For reference, they are outlined in Table 8-6.

Table 8-6. `CreateKeyword` *Variables*

Name	Type	Description
`keywords`	`String`	Contains the free-form keyword text entered by the user. The bolded text in this section's introduction is an example of the text that may be coming in via the `keywords` parameter.
`column`	`String`	Parameter containing the name of the column to search. You can search multiple columns at the same time by passing in a column name like "Column1 + Column2 + Column3". At runtime, SQL concatenates the column values together and allows you to search through all the column text at once. You will see an example of this trick later on in the chapter.
`defaultOp`	`SqlOperation`	Parameter defining the default conditional logic (`AND`/`OR`) applied when no conditional logic is explicitly defined; that is, if the keywords are BILL SMITH, `defaultOp` defines whether it means BILL AND SMITH or BILL OR SMITH.
`group`	`SqlConditionGroup`	Holds a reference to the active `SqlConditionGroup` to which conditions are being added.
`groupStack`	`Stack`	Maintains a stack of `SqlConditionGroup` objects to help build out the parenthetical logic defined in the keyword text. When you encounter an open parenthesis in the keyword string, you create a new group and set it as the active group. But you need a way to return to the parent group when you encounter the end parenthesis. Because the `SqlConditionGroup` object does not have a property identifying its parent, you need the `groupStack` to maintain parent references. When you encounter the end parenthesis, you simply pop a group off the stack because it is the parent of the current group. You can then continuing processing the keyword text.
`keywordList`	`String()`	Holds the resulting string array when the keywords parameter is split into an individual word list.
`[not]`	`Boolean`	When the `NOT` keyword is encountered, this flag is set so the next condition can be negated.
`hasCondition`	`Boolean`	This flag is set when a condition is encountered. This helps the function avoid returning a completely empty `SqlConditionGroup`.

After defining and initializing its function variables, `CreateKeywords` checks to make sure `keywords` is not empty. If `keywords` is empty, then the function immediately returns `Nothing`. Otherwise, it runs two regular expressions that ensure keywords can be split appropriately.

The first regular expression adds a space before and after any parenthesis in the string. Thus, ((A OR B)AND(C OR D)) becomes ((A OR B) AND (C OR D)) . This is important because we want each parenthesis to be recognized as its own item in the keyword list, and the list is split using the space character as a delimiter. Without this regular expression, the list would look like this: `{((A, OR, B)AND(C, OR, D))}` (5 items). With the regular expression, the list looks like this: `{(,(,A,OR,B,),AND,(,C,OR,D,),)}` (13 items). You'll see why this is important in a minute.

The second regular expression looks for any parts of the string where there are two or more spaces and replaces those spaces with a single space. Because the keyword list is delimited by spaces, two spaces in a row will create a blank item in the list. Removing extra spaces reduces these blank items.

After the keyword string has been checked and processed, it is forced into uppercase, trimmed to remove leading and trailing spaces, and then split into a string array that is stored in the `keywordList` variable.

■ **Caution** If your SQL Server is set up to do case-sensitive text searching, then you will *not* want to `UCase` the entire keyword string. You may want to just use a regular expression to uppercase the `AND`, `OR`, and `NOT` keywords in the string instead, or add additional `Case` statements to handle the different spellings of those keywords.

Next, the `CreateKeywords` function iterates through each `keyword` string in `keywordList` and checks the `keyword` against a series of options in a `Select Case` statement. Following is a list of the `Case` options and what happens if `keywords` matches that particular `Case`:

- `Case` "AND": When this keyword is encountered, the next condition or group added to the current group should be added with `AND` conditional logic, so this `Case` simply calls `group.And()`.
- `Case` "OR": When this keyword is encountered, the next condition or group added to the current group should be added with `OR` conditional logic, so this `Case` simply calls `group.Or()`.
- `Case` "NOT": When this keyword is encountered, the next condition or group added to the current group should be negated. This `Case` sets the `[Not]` flag to `True`. The actual negation is handled when the next condition or group is added.
- `Case` " (": When this keyword is encountered, a new child group should be added to the current group. This `Case` begins by pushing the current group to the `groupStack`. It then adds a new child group to the current group using the `group.Add()` method. Remember, `group.Add()`returns the newly created group object, which you assign back to the group variable on the same line. This makes the new child group the active group. Also, the `group.Not` property is set to the `[Not]` flag, which negates the group if the `[Not]` flag has been set. The `[Not]` flag is then cleared.
- `Case` ")": When this keyword is encountered, the active group has been closed, and the parent of the active group should become the new active group. The parent of the active group is always the topmost item on the stack because it was pushed to the stack before the child group was created. This `Case` first checks to make sure the stack contains an item, then pops the value from the stack and stores it in the `group` variable. Checking the

stack for an item avoids issues that could arise if a user accidentally enters too many closing parentheses, such as (A AND B))). You do not have to worry about users entering too many opening parentheses either because parentheses are automatically closed by the SqlQuery object when it writes out the query.

- Case "": If this case is encountered, it is simply skipped.
- Case Else: If none of the other cases are matched, then a new condition should be added to the active group that searches the column for the keyword. You can see that the String.Format function is used to construct a condition using the [Not] flag, column, and the keyword. The condition uses the SQL LIKE operator and surrounds the keywords with % wildcard characters, so the operation checks to see if the keyword exists anywhere in the specified column or columns. It also sets the [Not] flag to False and the has➥ Condition flag to True.

Tip You can modify the wildcard functionality by allowing your users to include wild cards directly in their searches and removing the automatic wild-card insertion in the code if you so desire.

Finally, the CreateKeywords function checks to see if the hasCondition flag has been set to True. If not, then it knows that it never encountered an actual keyword, so it returns Nothing. Otherwise, it pops any items still remaining on the stack off the stack, which ensures the group contains the topmost SqlConditionGroup. It then adds that topmost group to the collection of ISqlCondition items in the List property (that is, the function adds the group to the current SqlQuery object) and returns a reference to the newly created keyword text group as the result of the function.

Using the CreateKeywords Function

You can use the CreateKeywords function in a couple of different ways, most of which revolve around how many fields you have on your search form and how many columns you want to search. For example, let's say that you want to create a search form that allows your users to search for a customer by CustomerID. You would create a text box named txtCustomerID where users would enter keywords. Then you would use the following code to create a query using that keyword information:

```
sqlQueryObj.Where.CreateKeywords(Me.txtCustomerID.Text, "CustomerID",
   Reporting.SqlOperation.And)
```

You just pass in the search text, the column to search, and default operator to use if multiple keywords exist. In this case, And is the default operator so the CustomerID must match all the keywords specified. This reduces the number of values returned (because it is more restrictive than an Or search). If you want to maximize the number of values returned, then use Or as the default operator instead.

Later on, let's say you wanted to add two more text box fields to your search form to expand the search functionality. One allows for a keyword search on the FirstName column (txtFirstName), and the other allows for a keyword search on the LastName column (txtLastName). Your code would then look like this:

```
sqlQueryObj.Where.And()
sqlQueryObj.Where.CreateKeywords(Me.txtCustomerID.Text, "CustomerID", _
   Reporting.SqlOperation.And)
sqlQueryObj.Where.CreateKeywords(Me.txtFirstName.Text, "FirstName", _
   Reporting.SqlOperation.And)
sqlQueryObj.Where.CreateKeywords(Me.txtLastName.Text, "LastName", _
   Reporting.SqlOperation.And)
```

Then let's say that your users come back to you and say they don't like tabbing through all the fields on the form, and they would prefer to just have one field for the keyword entry. They still want it to search through the CustomerID, FirstName, and LastName fields, however. You can do this by having a single text box named txtKeywords and running this code:

```
sqlQueryObj.Where.CreateKeywords(Me.txtKeywords.Text, _
   "FirstName + ' ' + LastName + ' ' + CustomerID", _
   Reporting.SqlOperation.And)
```

Notice that the "column" specified in this code is really three columns that are concatenated together (with spaces placed in-between). When the SqlQuery object outputs the text to build the query, it places FirstName + ' ' + LastName + ' ' + CustomerID directly in the SQL query. When SQL encounters this text, it concatenates the value of the columns together to produce a large string value that you can search all at once.

There are, of course, some performance considerations. For the most part, you should not see many issues, but if you do, here are some things you may want to check. As you use more and more CreateKeywords functions (as in the second example), your SQL query will become longer and longer and take longer and longer to process. Along the same lines, as you concatenate more and more columns together (as in the third example), your SQL query will have to process more and more text before it can search through it. If you are experiencing issues, you may want to reduce the number of columns on which you are searching. Also, the number of keywords specified has an impact on performance, so you may want to limit the number of keywords users may enter if you notice any performance issues.

Displaying Basic and Advanced Searches

Everyone has their own preferences when it comes to searches. Some people may want to see a simple search with only a few fields. Others may want to see an advanced search that allows for a more detailed query. Fortunately, you don't have to choose one over the other. You can let your users choose their preferred option by providing the ability to switch between a simple and an advanced search. The next few sections walk you through a simple architecture for switching out search forms.

In the examples that follow, you'll see the implementation of a simple and advanced search form, both of which generate queries for the Employee table in the Northwind database. The basic idea behind this solution is that you want to create a generic interface that a search form can implement, then use that interface to allow different search forms to communicate with the actual search page. Because the actual search form is abstracted through the interface, you can implement any type of search form you want and the page can still work with it. That means simple forms, advanced forms, or even different forms for different security levels. You are not just limited to simple and advanced forms under this architecture.

There are a total of four components in this example. The `ISearchControl` interface defines a common set of search functionality for search forms. The `SimpleForm.ascx` and `AdvancedForm.ascx` are two search forms that implement the `ISearchControl` form and expose varying levels of searching functionality. And lastly, the `EmployeeSearch.aspx` page demonstrates how you can easily switch back and forth between search forms that implement the `ISearchControl` interface. All these components can be found in the Chapter 8 sample application in the Source Code area on the Apress website.

ISearchControl Interface

The `ISearchControl` interface exists to abstract the functionality of a search form so there can be a single generic way to extract data from the form. The objective of a search form is to take user search criteria and build a query from those criteria. Because the actual fields change from form to form, the only piece of data we are really interested in acquiring from a search form is the actual query it constructs based on that user input. Take a look at the `ISearchControl` interface, which is housed in the `Reporting` project of the sample application as shown in Listing 8-21.

Listing 8-21. `ISearchControl` *Interface*

```
Public Interface ISearchControl
    Function GetSqlQuery() As SqlQuery
End Interface
```

Notice that this interface only requires the implementation of a single function. `GetSqlQuery` is designed to return a `SlqQuery` object containing the query built out by the form. This `SqlQuery` object can then be used by the main page to pull back search results from a database.

Creating the Basic Search Form (SimpleForm.ascx)

Search forms are user controls that implement the `ISearchControl` interface. Like any user control, you can drag ASP.NET controls onto the user control, and use the code-behind file to execute code in response to any events fired by the controls on the form.

In this example, the simple form allows users to enter keywords into a text box control named `txtEmployeeInfo` as shown in Figure 8-4. In the code behind, it builds a query that searches for those keywords in the `FirstName`, `LastName`, and `Title` columns in the `Employees` database. Listing 8-22 is code behind for the simple form.

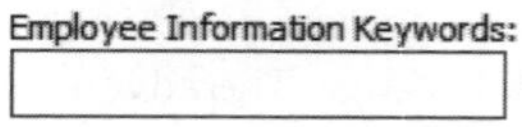

Employee Information Keywords:

Figure 8-4. *Screenshot of* `SimpleForm.ascx`

Listing 8-22. `SimpleForm.ascx.vb` *(Code-Behind File)*

```
Imports Reporting

Partial Class SimpleForm
    Inherits System.Web.UI.UserControl
    Implements ISearchControl

    '*************************************************************************
    Public Function GetSqlQuery() As Reporting.SqlQuery _
      Implements Reporting.ISearchControl.GetSqlQuery

        Dim SqlQueryObj As New SqlQuery

        SqlQueryObj.From = "Employees"
        SqlQueryObj.Where.CreateKeywords(Me.txtEmployeeInfo.Text, _
          "FirstName + ' ' + LastName + ' ' + Title", SqlOperation.And)

        Return SqlQueryObj

    End Function

End Class
```

You can see that the only function the user control has is the `GetSqlQuery` function required by the `ISearchControl` interface. Inside the `GetSqlQuery` function, a `SqlQuery` object named `SqlQueryObj` is instantiated, it's `From` property is set to the `Employees` table, and a keyword condition is added to the `WHERE` clause using the keywords from the `txtEmployeeInfo` text box control. Then `SqlQueryObj` is returned as a result of the function so it can be used in the main search page.

You'll get to see how the form interacts with the actual page in a minute, but for now, let's also take a quick look at the advanced form.

■ **Note** Both the simple and the advanced forms are located in the `SearchForms` folder of the website project in the sample application in the Source Code area of the Apress website.

Creating the Advanced Search Form (AdvancedForm.ascx)

The advanced form allows people to create more granular searches. Users can search for a specific employee ID, for keywords in the employee's first and last name, for keywords in the employee's title, and even for employees who were born in a specific date range. The advanced form is shown in Figure 8-5. Although the form is more advanced, it still implements the `ISearchControl` interface, just like the simple form. Listing 8-23 shows the code behind.

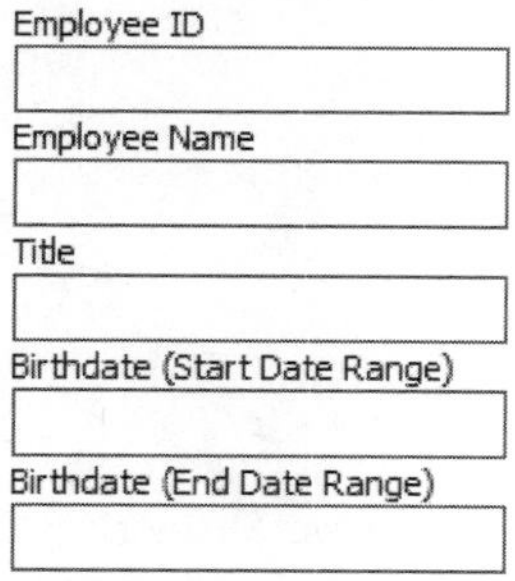

Employee ID

Employee Name

Title

Birthdate (Start Date Range)

Birthdate (End Date Range)

Figure 8-5. *Screenshot of* `AdvancedForm.ascx`

Listing 8-23. `AdvancedForm.ascx.vb` *(Code-Behind File)*

```
Imports Reporting

Partial Class AdvancedForm
    Inherits System.Web.UI.UserControl
    Implements ISearchControl

    '***************************************************************************
    Public Function GetSqlQuery() As Reporting.SqlQuery _
      Implements Reporting.ISearchControl.GetSqlQuery

        Dim sqlQueryObj As New SqlQuery
        sqlQueryObj.From = "Employees"

        'This query will use AND conditional logic
        sqlQueryObj.Where.And()

        'Set up the employee ID condition if applicable
        If Me.txtEmployeeID.Text <> String.Empty Then _
          sqlQueryObj.Where.AddCondition("EmployeeID=" & _
          SqlString(Me.txtEmployeeID.Text))

        'Set up the employee name keywords
        sqlQueryObj.Where.CreateKeywords( _
          Me.txtEmployeeName.Text, "FirstName + ' ' + LastName", SqlOperation.And)

        'Set up the title keywords
        sqlQueryObj.Where.CreateKeywords( _
         Me.txtTitle.Text, "Title", SqlOperation.And)

        'Set up the birth date date range
        sqlQueryObj.Where.CreateDateRange( _
```

```
            Me.txtBirthDateStart.Text, Me.txtBirthDateEnd.Text, "BirthDate", _
            SqlEvaluationType.Inclusive, "MM/dd/yyyy")

        Return sqlQueryObj

    End Function

End Class
```

Once again, the only method this user control implements is the `GetSqlQuery` function required by the `ISearchControl` interface. The `GetSqlQuery` function instantiates a `SqlQuery` object, sets the `FROM` property to the `Employee` table, and proceeds to add conditions to the `WHERE` clause for the employee ID (if applicable), name keywords, title keywords, and the birth date range. Remember, you do not have to check for the existence of the value before calling the `CreateKeywords` or `CreateDateRange` functions. They will not add entries to the `Where` property unless there are valid entries to add. When all is said and done, it returns the `SqlQuery` object as a result of the function. Now let's see how to switch back and forth between these types of forms on the actual search page.

Implementing the Main Search Page (EmployeeSearch.aspx)

The main search page contains all the logic for loading a default search form, switching back and forth between forms, for acquiring the query from the form, and for actually using the query after it has been received. Before we get into the code, however, you need to know about four controls on the main search page as listed in Table 8-7.

Table 8-7. *Relevant Controls on* `EmployeeSearch.aspx`

Control Name	Type	Description
`phForm`	`PlaceHolder`	Acts as a placeholder for the actual form that will be loaded by the search page. You should position the placeholder in the location where you want the form to appear.
`btnDisplayQuery`	`Button`	Action button. When the viewer clicks this button, the search page acquires the `SqlQuery` object from the form and displays the query on the page. You always need some form of action control to kick off the query, but it doesn't have to be a button.
`lnkToggleForm`	`LinkButton`	Toggle button. When the viewer clicks this button, the search page toggles between the simple and the advanced form. You normally display a toggle button to change between search forms. The exception is if you are using some other mechanism, such as security permissions, to determine which form to display. Like the action button, this does not have to be a `LinkButton`.
`lblQueryOutput`	`Label`	Displays the query after the action button has been clicked. Normally you would use the query to execute a database search, but this example just outputs the query to this label.

Now that you have an idea about some of the page components, lets take a look at the code behind for the EmployeeSearch.aspx page (see Listing 8-24).

Listing 8-24. EmployeeSearch.aspx.vb *(Code-Behind File)*

```
Imports Reporting
Imports System.Data.SqlClient
Imports System.Configuration.ConfigurationManager

Partial Class EmployeeSearch
    Inherits System.Web.UI.Page

    '**********************************************************************
    Private SearchControl As ISearchControl

    '**********************************************************************
    Private Property FormName() As String
        Get
            'You could also use the profile here if you wanted
            If Session("SearchForm") Is Nothing Then
                Return "simpleForm.ascx"
            Else
                Return CStr(Session("SearchForm"))
            End If
        End Get
        Set(ByVal value As String)
            Session("SearchForm") = value
        End Set
    End Property

    '**********************************************************************
    Private Sub SetupForm()

        Dim SearchForm As Control = LoadControl("~/SearchForms/" & FormName)
        SearchControl = CType(SearchForm, ISearchControl)
        SearchForm.ID = "ucSearchForm"
        phForm.Controls.Clear()
        phForm.Controls.Add(SearchForm)

        If FormName = "SimpleForm.ascx" Then
            Me.lnkToggleForm.Text = "Advanced Search"
        Else
            Me.lnkToggleForm.Text = "Simple Search"
        End If

    End Sub
```

```
    '***************************************************************************
    Protected Sub lnkToggleForm_Click(ByVal sender As Object, _
      ByVal e As System.EventArgs) Handles lnkToggleForm.Click
        If FormName = "SimpleForm.ascx" Then
            FormName = "AdvancedForm.ascx"
        Else
            FormName = "SimpleForm.ascx"
        End If
        SetupForm()
    End Sub

    '***************************************************************************
    Protected Sub Page_PreLoad(ByVal sender As Object, _
      ByVal e As System.EventArgs) Handles Me.PreLoad
        SetupForm()
    End Sub

    '***************************************************************************
    Protected Sub btnDisplayQuery_Click(ByVal sender As Object, _
      ByVal e As System.EventArgs) Handles btnDisplayQuery.Click

        Dim SQL As String = SearchControl.GetSqlQuery.GetQuery()
        Me.lblQueryOutput.Text = SQL

        Dim SqlQueryObj As New Reporting.SqlQuery
        Dim dbConn As New SqlConnection( _
          ConnectionStrings("Northwind").ConnectionString)
        dbConn.Open()

        Dim dbCmd As New SqlCommand(SQL, dbConn)
        Dim dr As SqlDataReader = dbCmd.ExecuteReader()

        MyGrid.DataSource = dr
        MyGrid.DataBind()

        dr.Close()
        dbConn.Close()

    End Sub

End Class
```

There are five methods in the `EmployeeSearch.aspx.vb` code-behind file, and a single class-level variable named `SearchForm`. `SearchForm` holds a reference to the appropriate form (simple or advanced) so the page can acquire the `SqlQuery` from the form.

FormName Property

When you allow users to switch back and forth between two forms, you need a way to determine which form they want to use. This example uses the FormName property to make that determination. FormName returns the file name of the search form (user control) that is to be loaded. The property uses the Session object to actually store the information, so the user only needs to change the setting once per login. You can make this a profile setting if you want the information to be retained between logins. Also, if the user has not specifically selected a form—that is, Session("SearchForm") returns Nothing—then the property returns "Simple➥orm.ascx" by default.

SetupForm Method

SetupForm is responsible for loading the appropriate search form and adding it to the phForm placeholder. It does this by calling LoadControl("~/SearchForms/" & FormName), which loads the user control at the specified file name and stores the resulting object in the SearchForm variable. Then it casts the SearchForm into to an ISearchControl and stores a reference to the ISearchControl in a class-level variable named SearchControl. The page uses SearchControl later on in the btnDisplayQuery_Click event handler to acquire the SQL query.

It then sets the ID of the user control to ensure that it has a well-defined name. If you do not set the ID on the user control, then ASP.NET automatically generates an ID for the control. This may result in lost data and events if ASP.NET does not reassign your control the same ID on the next postback, so we always give this control the same name to ensure data reaches it appropriately. After setting the ID, SetupForm clears any controls in phForm, and adds Search➥Form to the PlaceHolder.

The last section of code in SetupForm makes sure the toggle link text reads "Advanced Search" if the simple search form is being shown and "Simple Search" if the advanced search form is being shown.

lnkToggleForm_Click Method

Clicking the toggle button causes the advanced form to be displayed if the simple one is currently being shown, or the simple one to be displayed if the advanced one is being shown. This method uses an If statement to check the FormName property and switches the FormName property accordingly. Then it calls SetupForm(), which removes the current form from the PlaceHolder and adds the new one.

Page_PreLoad Event Handler

The Page_PreLoad method simply calls the SetupForm() method, which loads the selected form into the placeholder. Loading the form into the page during the Page_PreLoad event handler also means that the search form data is automatically loaded back into the user control on a postback.

btnDisplayQuery_Click Method

When the action button is clicked, the SqlQuery object is acquired from the search form referenced by the SearchForm variable. The GetQuery() function of that object is then called, and the resulting SQL statement is stored in a label so it can be displayed on the page. Normally, you would execute the query, but this is just an example.

Benefits of User Control–Based Search Forms

Now that you understand how to implement interchangeable search forms, let's consider some of the benefits of implementing search forms in this fashion. I've worked on numerous projects where search forms are used in multiple locations. An employee search form may be used directly on the employee management page, and it could also be used to help search for an employee while filling out a form. When you implement your forms as user controls, it increases the likelihood that you can easily reuse those forms in other areas of your project.

Another benefit comes from implementing your search forms with the `ISearchControl` interface. This makes your search forms interchangeable and allows you to manage their display more effectively. Without the `ISearchControl` interface, you usually end up managing the form displays by showing and hiding panels and using a lot more code.

Summary

We spent a great deal of time discussing the `SqlQuery` tool in this chapter, but I think you'll find that an object-oriented SQL query builder can definitely save you a lot of time and hassle in certain situations. As mentioned before, the `SqlQuery` tool is by no means a complete solution. There are still certain keywords and clauses that it does not support, and you can always add more common search functionality to it as you find the need.

You also learned a great deal about paging using the new features in the features in SQL Server 2005, which should help you make your data applications more efficient. Paged data can definitely boost performance for most applications, and the `SqlQuery` tool makes using paged data a breeze. It also makes it easier for your users to look through large sets of data.

Finally, you learned how to build search forms and how to make interchangeable forms to give users advanced and simple search options. People definitely appreciate flexibility, so these types of features can help boost user acceptance and the overall usability of an application.

CHAPTER 9

Building a Reusable Reporting Framework

Searching and reporting are tied together because one naturally leads to the other. So, it should come as no surprise that this chapter on reporting follows the chapter on searching. My experience with reporting began on my very first project where I was assigned to create a series of reports for a workflow system. There were about a dozen reports in all, all of which had the same requirements: allow users to filter the data with a search form, display the data as rows in a table, and allow users to sort the columns in ascending and descending order by clicking on the column name in the table header. Sound familiar?

After writing the first couple of reports, I noticed that I was using the same query-building logic, the same database connection and command-execution logic, the same paging logic, and the same column-sorting logic on every page. Instead of repeating that sequence 10 more times, I made a reusable reporting framework to simplify the report-creation process. Thinking through and building out that framework took about as much time as creating one or two reports, but it allowed me to build subsequent reports in a fraction of the time. It was definitely worth the effort.

On the business side, there are three reasons for developing against a reporting framework: speed, accuracy, and consistency. All the tedious reporting logic is written once and encapsulated in a reusable reporting component. You can then leverage the component whenever needed instead of copying and pasting code from page to page or starting over from scratch. This speeds up report creation significantly, which ultimately helps meet deadlines and keep projects on time and on budget.

As speed increases, accuracy normally decreases. Think about it. If you have five days to develop a report or one day to develop the same report, which one is going to be more error prone? Coding against a framework allows you to create reports faster, without adverse effects on accuracy. The speed increase is a function of efficiency, not of cutting corners or short-changing the development process. In fact, because the complex reporting logic is encapsulated in a component, you are actually less likely to encounter errors because you are touching less code.

Finally, using a reporting framework means that each of your reporting pages will be consistent. I remember looking at an application that was coded by a team of developers, and each developer had a different way of creating a Report Page. Some pages supported column sorting, others did not. Some pages supported pagination; some just dumped the content directly to the screen. And those that did have pagination had different ways to navigate through the pages. Consistency is imperative for the user experience.

This chapter outlines how to create and use a reporting framework. You can feel free to use it as-is or as a basis for your own framework. Here's how the chapter breaks down:

- *Building the Reporting Framework:* Discusses the design and implementation of a reporting framework to encapsulate the more complex aspects of reporting. The framework simplifies the database connection, query execution, result sorting, pagination, and loading of `ISearchControl` and `IPaginationControl` components.
- *Creating a Report Using the Reporting Framework:* Demonstrates how to use the reporting framework to create a feature-rich Report Page. This includes the construction of multiple search forms, a paging navigation component, and the actual Report Page itself. You'll also learn how to use the framework to easily toggle between an advanced search form and a simple search form.

Just to forewarn you, the reporting framework discussed in this chapter uses many of the tools and concepts discussed in the pervious chapter. Make sure you are familiar with the `SqlQuery` class and the `ISearchControl` interface from the last chapter before continuing.

Building the Reporting Framework

Reporting is a complicated subject because it has so many pieces. Report pages need to build a query, connect to a database, execute the query, display the query results, handle pagination, and allow users to sort data by clicking on a column header. Performance is also a consideration, so it would be nice to use a `DataReader` to acquire report data, and it should take steps to limit the size of the `ViewState` as much as possible.

■ Note `DataReaders` are faster than `DataSets` in terms of raw reading performance; however, `DataSets` can outperform `DataReaders` if you have complex calculations in your reports. Why? Because `DataSets` acquire data, close the database connection, and then operate on the data. `DataReaders` operate on the data while the connection is still open. If you're doing your reporting calculations on the database side (recommend), then a `DataReader` should perform well. If you need to do complex calculation in code, then you may get a performance increase using a `DataSet`.

If you're familiar with the data controls that ship with ASP.NET 2.0, then you may say that most of the requirements described previously can be implemented using the `GridView` control. The `GridView` control in ASP.NET 2.0 is the next generation of the `DataGrid` control from ASP.NET 1.x. Although the `GridView` control does support paging and column sorting, some restrictions limit those features. Paging with `GridView` requires the use of a `DataSet` because `DataReader` objects do not inherently support server-side paging. Even if you could use a `DataReader` with the paging features, the built-in paging navigation leaves much to be desired. You can use a `DataReader` with the sorting capabilities of the `GridView` as long as you are using an intermediary `SqlDataSource` as the `GridView`'s data source, you've specified that the `SqlDataSource` should return a `DataReader`, the `SqlDataSource` is using a stored procedure to acquire that `DataReader`, the stored procedure has a parameter that allows the `SqlDataSource` to specify a sort column. Needless to say, I'm not a fan of the built-in paging and sorting functionality from the GridView control.

To circumnavigate these issues, you'll learn how to build a reporting framework that allows you to create feature-rich reports in no time at all.

Abstract Class Primer

You'll implement a good chunk of the reporting framework as an abstract (MustInherit) class named ReportFramework, so it's imperative that you understand how abstract classes work. An abstract class consists of both concrete and abstract (MustOverride) members. Concrete members are defined and written directly in the abstract class. They look and act just like any other properties or methods in a normal class (for example, they contain code, you can override and overload them in a derived class, and so on). Abstract members are defined in the abstract class, but no code for the member is written in the abstract class. The code for abstract members must be provided by whatever class inherits the abstract class.

To illustrate the point, think about two household objects: a glass vase and a book. All household objects have a status that identifies how the object is doing. It could be fine, old, worn, broken, and so on. All household objects can also be dropped; however, the result of the item being dropped differs between each object, so each object will have a different post-drop status. Listing 9-1 shows how these objects would be represented in code.

Listing 9-1. Example\HouseHoldItem.vb *(Reporting Project)*

```
Public MustInherit Class HouseHoldItem

    MustOverride Function PostDropStatus() As String
    Private _Status As String

    '***************************************************************************
    Public ReadOnly Property Status() As String
        Get
            Return _Status
        End Get
    End Property

    '***************************************************************************
    Public Sub Drop()
        _Status = PostDropStatus()
    End Sub

End Class
```

This is the HouseHoldItem abstract class. For the most part, it looks like a normal class. You can see it has a property named Status and a method named Drop. Both of these items are considered concrete because the code for the items exists directly in the HouseHoldItem abstract class. If you look at the PostDropStatus method, however, you'll notice that it isn't normal. It's an abstract method that is defined, but for which no code exists. This method is marked as MustOverride, which lets the inheriting class know that it needs to provide the actual code for the PostDropStatus method. Notice, however, that you can still call the PostDropStatus method in the abstract class, even though no code for the method exists. The Drop method uses the PostDropStatus method to determine the status of the household item after it has been dropped.

Because the PostDropStatus method is marked MustOverride, the class is incomplete. It has no code for that method. Thus, the class must be marked as MustInherit; otherwise, you get a build error. This lets the inheriting class know that it must "complete" the abstract class by providing code for any of the abstract methods; in this case, it's just the PostDropStatus method. Because abstract classes are incomplete, you cannot instantiate them directly. So calling New HouseHoldItem()gives you a build error.

Now let's take a look at the Book class, which inherits its household item functionality from the HouseHoldItem class (see Listing 9-2).

Listing 9-2. Example\Book.vb *(Reporting Project)*

```
Public Class Book
    Inherits HouseHoldItem

    '***************************************************************************
    Public Overrides Function PostDropStatus() As String
        Return "OK"
    End Function

End Class
```

Because a book is a household item, the Book class inherits its base household item functionality from the HouseHoldItem class. In doing so, the Book class is obligated to override the PostDropStatus method because it's marked as MustOverride in the HouseHoldItem class. You can see that the overridden PostDropStatus method in the Book class returns "OK", because books can survive a short drop without any damage. Thus, if you were to call BookObject.Drop(), then BookObject.Status would be "OK" after the drop method completed. Now let's take a look at the GlassVase class in Listing 9-3.

Listing 9-3. Example\GlassVase.vb *(Reporting Project)*

```
Public Class GlassVase
    Inherits HouseHoldItem

    '***************************************************************************
    Public Overrides Function PostDropStatus() As String
        Return "Shattered into a thousand pieces"
    End Function

End Class
```

Once again, the GlassVase class inherits its household item functionality from the HouseHoldItem class, and it's obligated to override the PostDropStatus method. This time, however, the method returns "Shattered into a thousand pieces" because a vase behaves a bit differently than a book when dropped. When the Drop method is called, the Status of the vase indicates that it has shattered.

So, you can alter the outcome of the Drop method on a class-by-class basis by changing the PostDropStatus method. When a book is dropped, it's okay. When a glass vase is dropped, it shatters. Two different outcomes occur with only one Drop method.

If you think about the implications of this, you should begin to understand the usefulness of abstract classes. The ReportFramework abstract class, for instance, needs to connect to a database and execute a query, but it does not always connect to the same database nor execute the same query. So, you can create a concrete method with code to query the database and execute a query that uses abstract properties to acquire the connection string and SQL statement. Then, when you need to create a reporting page, you inherit the majority of the reporting functionality and implement a few basic abstract members to make the reporting page work.

Of course, there is a lot more to it than just abstract members, but you should now have a basic understand of where all this is heading as we take a high-level look at the reporting framework architecture.

Solution Architecture

The design goals for the reporting framework described in this chapter are to maximize visual flexibility and to minimize repetitive coding. Most of the Report Pages I create use a search form and paging navigation, so I build support for those components directly into the reporting framework. The ISearchControl interface from the last chapter is used for the search support, and a new interface named IPaginationControl is used for the paging navigation. You'll notice the SqlQuery tool from the last chapter as well because it's very useful for building out paged queries.

In the end, six components work together to make the reporting framework. The most prominent component is the ReportFramework abstract class, which was mentioned briefly in the previous section. It acts as a coordinator between the other components and really drives the entire framework. Figure 9-1 shows how all the components fit into the reporting framework, and Table 9-1 outlines the components and their purpose in the overall design.

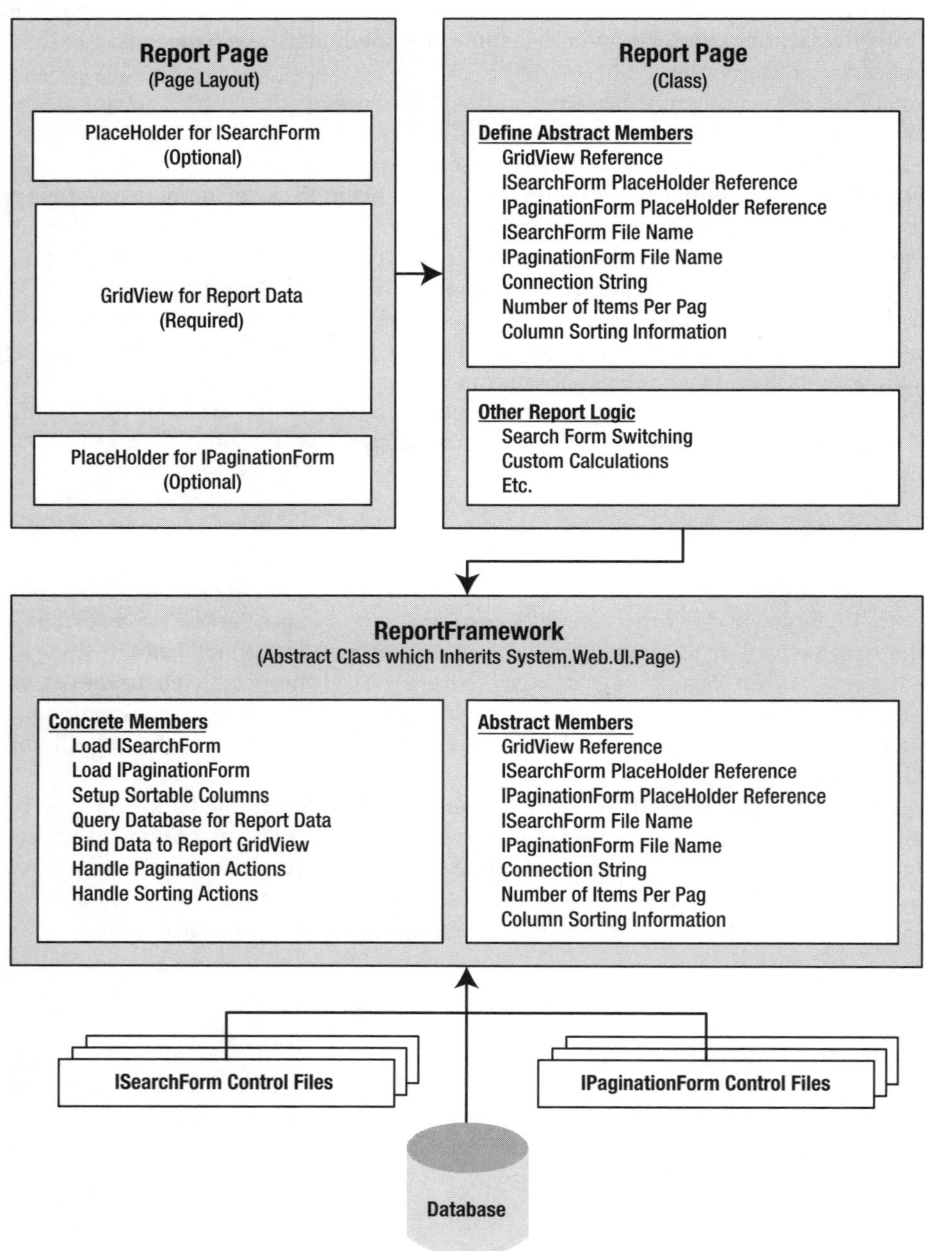

Figure 9-1. *Reporting framework architecture*

Table 9-1. *Reporting framework components and descriptions*

Component	Description
Database	Contains the report data ultimately displayed by the Report Page.
ISearchControl	Interface for a search form used to create a query for the database.
IPaginationControl	Interface for a navigation form that allows the user to page through data (next page, last page, go to specific page, and so on).
ReportFramework	Abstract class that coordinates all data access, data display, pagination, and sorting functionality for a Report Page. The ReportFramework inherits its base functionality from the Page class because it needs to respond to page-level events such as PreLoad and PreRender. This also makes it easy to build Report Pages because your .ASPX page inherits from the ReportFrameworkClass instead of the Page class. All you have to do then is complete the abstract members from the ReportFramework class in the Report Page code behind. The abstract members of this class identify connection string information, number of items to display per page, the search form to use, and so on.
Report Page (Layout)	Defines the look and feel of the report, that is, which columns of data should be displayed, how that data is formatted, how the page around the data should appear, and so on. The Report Page layout is required to have at least one GridView control to which the ReportFramework can output its report data. There are also two optional PlaceHolders that identify where an ISearchControl control can appear and where an IPaginationControl control can appear.
Report Page (Class)	Inherits the ReportFramework abstract class and completes all abstract members required by ReportFramework. The completed members identify the setting and controls with which the ReportFramework functionality will interact (for example, the connection string used to connect to the database, the number of items to display per page, the search form to use, and so on).

When you look at the sample application, you'll notice that the Reporting class library project looks very similar to the Reporting class library in the previous chapter. The Reporting class library in this sample application contains the SqlQuery tool and auxiliary classes that you looked at in the last chapter, plus some new components from the reporting framework discussed in this chapter.

Database

Ultimately, the objective of the reporting framework is to display data; therefore, you need a data source containing the data that you want to display. Most projects use databases for their primary data store, so the reporting framework is designed around acquiring data from a database.

In this example, you'll acquire data from the Customers table in the Northwind database. The Northwind database is in the App_Data folder of the sample application in the Source Code area of the Apress website (http://www.apress.com), and a connection string entry named "Northwind" for the Northwind database is in the <connectionStrings> section of the Web.config. If you installed the sample applications to the default location, then this connection string should work. If not, then you may need to change the AttatchDbFilename parameter to match your custom location. Refer to the introduction for this book for more information on the Northwind database and setting up connections with SQL Server Express. Table 9-2 outlines the fields in the Customers table.

Table 9-2. Customer *Table in the* Northwind *Database*

Field	Type	Description
CustomerID	nchar(5)	Primary key; Nonnullable; unique customer identifier
CompanyName	nvarchar(40)	Nonnullable; company name
ContactName	nvarchar(30)	Nullable; name of the primary company contact
ContactTitle	nvarchar(30)	Nullable; title of the primary company contact
Address	nvarchar(60)	Nullable; address of the company
City	nvarchar(15)	Nullable; city of the company address
Region	nvarchar(15)	Nullable; region of the company address
PostalCode	nvarchar(10)	Nullable; postal (zip) code of the company address
Country	nvarchar(15)	Nullable; country of the company address
Phone	nvarchar(24)	Nullable; company phone number
Fax	nvarchar(24)	Nullable; company fax number

You do not need to create this table or populate it with data. The Northwind *sample database already contains the* Customer *table and sample customer data.*

The ISearchControl Interface

This interface was introduced in the previous chapter as a generic way to define search forms and to acquire the SQL queries generated by those forms. Notice, however, that the interface exposes a new event named SearchButtonClicked. The new event helps ReportFramework know when the user executed a search from the form. Because it is a rather brief interface, it is shown in Listing 9-4.

Listing 9-4. Interfaces\ISearchControl.vb *(Reporting Project)*

```
Public Interface ISearchControl

    Function GetSqlQuery() As Reporting.SqlQuery
    Event SearchButtonClicked()

End InterfaceSecond
```

The ISearchControl must be implemented by a user control because the ReportFramework is specifically designed to load user controls into the Report Page. One side benefit is that user controls make the search forms reusable if you ever need them for another page or project. The objective of a user control that implements ISearchControl is twofold. The first objective is to display search fields so the user may enter search criteria, and the second is to build out a

SqlQuery object based on the entered criteria when the ReportFramework calls GetSqlQuery. The user control also raises the SearchButtonClicked event when the user clicks the Search button, alerting the ReportFramework that it should run the query.

Pagination and the IPaginationControl Interface

Pagination is the process of dividing large sets of data into smaller more manageable pages, which can help make your application more responsive and user friendly. To understand how it makes an application more responsive and user friendly, let's look at an extreme example.

Most people use search engines to help find information on the Internet, and if you look at the total number of matches for a search, you can see why. A search for "ASP.NET" on a couple of major search engines nets between 9 and 12 million results. Luckily, each search engine only showed 10 results at a time. Now, image what would happen if they tried to return all 12 million results on one page. The page would be huge. It would take forever to load (assuming that it did not time out). About 12 million results would have been unnecessarily sent because most people rarely look beyond the first 20 matches. And all the search engines would grind to a halt because fulfilling requests would take hours instead of milliseconds. So, paging has some descent benefits.

When you display data using pagination, you also need to display paging navigation controls to allow users to jump from one page to the next. The GridView control has built-in support for paging navigation, but you have very little control of its appearance and behavior. Basically, it looks like Figure 9-2.

<< ... 11 12 13 14 15 16 17 18 19 20 ... >>

Figure 9-2. *Paging navigation for the* GridView *control*

Each individual link is a separate command: << means jump to the first page and >> means jump to the last page. The ellipses (. . .) allow you to jump to the next or previous set of pages. Notice how pages 11–20 are displayed in the Figure 9-2. Clicking the first ellipsis takes you to page 10 and displays pages 1–10 in the navigation. Clicking on the second ellipsis takes you to page 21 and displays pages 21–30 in the navigation. And lastly, clicking on a number takes you to that specific page.

There are three usability issues with the GridView's paging navigation. First, it requires a lot of clicking. If you want to get to page 50, you have to click about five times because only 10 page links are displayed. You can increase the total number of page links displayed, but you still run into the same problem, and the navigation becomes jumbled with tons of links. Granted, most of the time you'll have fewer than 10 pages, but when you do end up with more, it can be a burden on your users. Second, the GridView does not display the total number of pages or the total number of records in the result set, which users often want to know. You can display this information, but you'll have to set up the appropriate controls and code the display routines. And lastly, the pagination features of the GridView control don't work with DataReader objects and, of course, the reporting framework relies on DataReader objects. For these reasons, we'll forgo the GridView's built-in paging support.

Because we can't use the GridView's paging mechanism, we have to come up with our own. But, we don't want to create another rigid and inflexible component, so care should be taken to make the component flexible enough to support a variety of visual designs while exposing a standard set of functionality common to all paging navigation. This definitely sounds like a job for an interface (see Listing 9-5).

Listing 9-5. `Interfaces\IPaginationControl.vb` *(Reporting Project)*

```
Public Interface IPaginationControl

    Sub SetInfo(ByVal currentPage As Integer, ByVal totalPages As Integer, _
      ByVal totalRecords As Integer, ByVal itemsPerPage as Integer, _
      ByVal recordStart as Integer, ByVal recordEnd as Integer)
    Event NextPageRequested()
    Event PrevPageRequested()
    Event NewPageRequested(ByVal page As Integer)

End Interface
```

Communication between the reporting framework and the paging navigation component takes place via the `IPaginationControl` interface shown in the preceding listing. The reporting framework initializes the paging navigation component by calling the `SetInfo` method and passing in important information, such as the current page, total number of pages, total number of records, the number of items displayed on each page, and the starting and ending record numbers currently being displayed (for example, 1–10, 11–20, and so on). The paging navigation component can then display that information in any way it chooses.

When a user interacts with the paging navigation component, the component raises different events that the reporting framework can listen for and handle. There are three events the `IPaginationControl` can raise:

- `NextPageRequested`*:* Raised when the user wants to jump to the next page.
- `PrevPageRequested`*:* Raised when the user wants to jump to the previous page.
- `NewPageRequested`*:* Raised when the user wants to jump to a specific page. This event accepts a single integer parameter identifying the page to which the user wants to jump.

You may have realized, after looking at all the events, that you could get away with only exposing the `NewPageRequested` event. The others are included because it simplifies jumping to the next and previous pages, which is a very common feature of paging navigation. You could also include events such as `JumpToFirstPage` or `JumpToLast` page if you so desired, or you could handle them by raising the `NewPageRequested` event and passing in `1` (which is always the first page) or the total page count (which is always the last page) as the requested page.

Now that you have an understanding of the `IPaginationControl` interface, let's take a look at the `ReportFramework` class.

ReportFramework Abstract Class

Most of the reporting functionality exposed by the reporting framework is contained in the `ReportFramework` abstract class. As mentioned before, it has routines to load the search and paging controls, acquire a query, connect to a database, retrieve data, display data in a `GridView`, paginate through the data, and handle sorting data. Needless to say, it takes a lot of code to make all that happen.

Listing 9-6 includes the entire code listing for the ReportFramework class. In all, there are about 400 lines of code. It's a lot to take in all at once, but each part of the class is covered in more detail in the sections that follow.

■ **Note** You need to add a project reference to the System.Configuration and System.Web assemblies for this code listing to build.

Listing 9-6. ReportFramework.vb *(Reporting Project)*

```
Imports System.Configuration.ConfigurationManager
Imports System.Data.SqlClient
Imports System.Web.UI
Imports System.Web.UI.WebControls

Public MustInherit Class ReportFramework
    Inherits System.Web.UI.Page

    '***************************************************************************
    'View State Name (VSN) Constants
    '***************************************************************************
    Const CurrentPageVSN = "1"
    Const LastSqlVSN = "2"
    Const SearchFormIndexVSN = "3"

    '***************************************************************************
    'Private Class Variables
    '***************************************************************************
    Private WithEvents _SearchForm As ISearchControl
    Private WithEvents _PaginationForm As IPaginationControl
    Private _TotalRecords As Long
    Private _SortClicked As Boolean
    Private _SortExpression As String
    Private _SortDirection As SqlSortDirection

    '***************************************************************************
    'MustOverride Methods and Properties
    '***************************************************************************
    Protected MustOverride Function ConnectionStringKey() As String
    Protected MustOverride Function ReportGrid() As GridView
    Protected MustOverride Function ItemsPerPage() As Integer
    Protected MustOverride Function SearchFormFileName() As String
    Protected MustOverride Function SearchFormPH() As PlaceHolder
```

```
    Protected MustOverride Function PaginationFormFileName() As String
    Protected MustOverride Function PaginationFormPH() As PlaceHolder
    Protected MustOverride Sub SetSortOrder(ByVal query As SqlQuery, _
      ByVal sortExpression As String)

    '***************************************************************************
    'Overridable Methods
    '***************************************************************************
    Protected Overridable Function GetSqlQuery() As SqlQuery
        If _SearchForm Is Nothing Then
            Return Nothing
        Else
            Return _SearchForm.GetSqlQuery
        End If
    End Function

    '***************************************************************************
    Protected Overridable Sub OnReportError(ByVal ex As Exception)
        Throw ex
    End Sub

    '***************************************************************************
    Protected Overridable ReadOnly Property BindInPreLoad() As Boolean
        Get
            Return False
        End Get
    End Property

'***************************************************************************
    'Class Properties
    '***************************************************************************
    Protected Property LastSql() As String
        Get
            If ViewState(LastSqlVSN) Is Nothing Then
                Return String.Empty
            Else
                Return ViewState(LastSqlVSN)
            End If
        End Get
        Set(ByVal value As String)
            If value = String.Empty Then
                ViewState.Remove(LastSqlVSN)
            Else
                ViewState(LastSqlVSN) = value
            End If
        End Set
    End Property
```

```
'***************************************************************************
Protected Property SearchFormIndex() As Short
    Get
        If ViewState(SearchFormIndexVSN) Is Nothing Then
            Return 0
        Else
            Return ViewState(SearchFormIndexVSN)
        End If
    End Get
    Set(ByVal value As Short)
        If value = 0 Then
            ViewState.Remove(SearchFormIndexVSN)
        Else
            ViewState(SearchFormIndexVSN) = value
        End If
    End Set
End Property

'***************************************************************************
Protected Property CurrentPage() As Long
    Get
        If ViewState(CurrentPageVSN) Is Nothing Then
            Return 1
        Else
            Return ViewState(CurrentPageVSN)
        End If
    End Get
    Set(ByVal value As Long)
        If value <= 1 Then
            ViewState.Remove(CurrentPageVSN)
        Else
            ViewState(CurrentPageVSN) = value
        End If
    End Set
End Property

'***************************************************************************
Protected ReadOnly Property TotalPages() As Long
    Get
        If ItemsPerPage() = 0 Then
            Return 1
        Else
            Return (_TotalRecords \ ItemsPerPage()) + _
                     CInt(IIf(_TotalRecords Mod ItemsPerPage() = 0, 0, 1))
        End If
    End Get
End Property
```

```
'***********************************************************************
'Page Event and Related Methods
'***********************************************************************
Private Sub Page_PreLoad(ByVal sender As Object, _
  ByVal e As System.EventArgs) Handles Me.PreLoad

    If ReportGrid() Is Nothing Then
        OnReportError(New Exception("ReportGrid cannot be Nothing"))
        Exit Sub
    End If

    If Page.IsPostBack Then AcquireHiddenFieldValues()
    LoadSearchForm()
    LoadPaginationForm()

    If _SortClicked Then
        CurrentPage = 1
        SetupSearchSql()
    End If

    If BindInPreLoad() Then BindReport()

End Sub

'***********************************************************************
Private Sub AcquireHiddenFieldValues()

    _SortClicked = CBool(Request.Form("sortClicked") = "1")
    _SortExpression = Request.Form("sortExp")

    If CBool(Request.Form("sortDir") = "1") Then
        _SortDirection = SqlSortDirection.Descending
    Else
        _SortDirection = SqlSortDirection.Ascending
    End If

End Sub

'***********************************************************************
Protected Sub LoadSearchForm()
    If SearchFormPH() Is Nothing Then Exit Sub
    Try
        _SearchForm = LoadControl(SearchFormFileName())
        DirectCast(_SearchForm, UserControl).ID = "SearchFormControl"
        SearchFormPH.Controls.Clear()
        SearchFormPH.Controls.Add(_SearchForm)
    Catch ex As Exception
```

```
        OnReportError(New Exception("Error loading search form", ex))
    End Try
End Sub

'*****************************************************************************
Protected Sub LoadPaginationForm()
    If PaginationFormPH() Is Nothing Then Exit Sub
    Try
        _PaginationForm = LoadControl(PaginationFormFileName())
        DirectCast(_PaginationForm, UserControl).ID = "PaginationFormControl"
        PaginationFormPH.Controls.Clear()
        PaginationFormPH.Controls.Add(_PaginationForm)
    Catch ex As Exception
        OnReportError(New Exception("Error loading pagination form", ex))
    End Try
End Sub

'*****************************************************************************
Private Sub SearchButtonClicked() Handles _SearchForm.SearchButtonClicked
    CurrentPage = 1
    _SortExpression = String.Empty
    _SortDirection = SqlSortDirection.Ascending
    SetupSearchSql()
    If BindInPreLoad() Then BindReport()
End Sub

'*****************************************************************************
Private Sub SetupSearchSql()

    Dim SqlQueryObj As SqlQuery = GetSqlQuery()
    If SqlQueryObj Is Nothing Then ClearSearch() : Exit Sub

    SetSortOrder(SqlQueryObj, _SortExpression)

    If _SortDirection = SqlSortDirection.Descending Then _
      ReverseOrderBy(SqlQueryObj)

    If _PaginationForm Is Nothing Then
        LastSql = SqlQueryObj.GetQuery()
    Else
        LastSql = SqlQueryObj.GetPagedQuery( _
                     CurrentPage, ItemsPerPage) & ";" & _
                     _SearchForm.GetSqlQuery.GetCountQuery()
    End If

End Sub
```

```
'***************************************************************************
Private Sub ReverseOrderBy(ByVal Query As SqlQuery)
    For Each field As SqlField In Query.OrderBy
        If field.SortDirection = SqlSortDirection.Ascending Then
            field.SortDirection = SqlSortDirection.Descending
        Else
            field.SortDirection = SqlSortDirection.Ascending
        End If
    Next
End Sub

'***************************************************************************
Protected Sub ClearSearch()
    LastSql = String.Empty
End Sub

'***************************************************************************
Private Sub BindReport()

    If LastSql = String.Empty Then Exit Sub

    Dim dbConn As SqlConnection
    Dim dbCmd As SqlCommand
    Dim dbDr As SqlDataReader
    Dim RecordStart As Integer
    Dim RecordEnd As Integer

    Try
        dbConn = New SqlConnection( _
           ConnectionStrings(ConnectionStringKey).ConnectionString)
        dbCmd = New SqlCommand(LastSql, dbConn)
        dbConn.Open()
        dbDr = dbCmd.ExecuteReader()
        ReportGrid.DataSource = dbDr
        ReportGrid.DataBind()
        If Not _PaginationForm Is Nothing _
          AndAlso dbDr.NextResult AndAlso dbDr.Read Then
            _TotalRecords = dbDr.Item(0)

            'Ensure page bounds are correct
            If CurrentPage < 1 Then CurrentPage = 1
            If CurrentPage > TotalPages Then CurrentPage = TotalPages

            'Calculate the Starting and Ending Records
            RecordStart = ((CurrentPage - 1) * ItemsPerPage()) + 1
            If CurrentPage = TotalPages Then
                RecordEnd = _TotalRecords
            Else
```

```
                RecordEnd = RecordStart + ItemsPerPage() - 1
            End If

            'Initialize the Paging Component
            _PaginationForm.SetInfo(CurrentPage, TotalPages, _
              _TotalRecords, ItemsPerPage, RecordStart, RecordEnd)

        End If
        dbConn.Close()

    Catch ex As Exception
        OnReportError(ex)
    End Try

End Sub

'***************************************************************************
Private Sub Page_PreRender(ByVal sender As Object, _
  ByVal e As System.EventArgs) Handles Me.PreRender

    If Not BindInPreLoad() Then BindReport()
    SetupHiddenFields()
    SetupJavaScript()
    If Not _PaginationForm Is Nothing Then _
      If ReportGrid.Rows.Count = 0 Then Me.PaginationFormPH.Controls.Clear() _
        Else SetupSortableColumns()

End Sub

'***************************************************************************
Private Sub SetupHiddenFields()
    ClientScript.RegisterHiddenField("sortClicked", "0")
    ClientScript.RegisterHiddenField("sortExp", _SortExpression)
    ClientScript.RegisterHiddenField("sortDir", _
      IIf(_SortDirection = SqlSortDirection.Ascending, 0, 1))
End Sub

'***************************************************************************
Private Sub SetupJavaScript()
    Dim script As String = _
          "   function setSortExp(sortExp){" & _
          "     var sortExpField = document.getElementById('sortExp');" & _
          "     var sortDirField = document.getElementById('sortDir');" & _
          "     if(sortExpField.value==sortExp){" & _
          "       if(sortDirField.value==0){" & _
          "         sortDirField.value=1;" & _
```

```
            "       }else{" & _
            "         sortDirField.value=0;" & _
            "       }" & _
            "     }else{" & _
            "       sortExpField.value=sortExp;" & _
            "       sortDirField.value=0;" & _
            "     }" & _
            "     document.getElementById('sortClicked').value = '1';" & _
            "  }"
        ClientScript.RegisterClientScriptBlock(Me.GetType, "sortExp", script, True)
    End Sub

    '***************************************************************************
    Private Sub SetupSortableColumns()

        Dim sortButton As LinkButton
        Dim columnHeading As Label

        For index As Integer = 0 To ReportGrid.Columns.Count - 1
            'If neither the header text, nor the sort expression are defined
            'then do not place anything in the header
            If ReportGrid.Columns.Item(index).SortExpression = String.Empty _
              And ReportGrid.Columns.Item(index).HeaderText <> String.Empty Then
                'Do not allow sorting on the column
                columnHeading = New Label
                columnHeading.Text = ReportGrid.Columns.Item(index).HeaderText
                ReportGrid.HeaderRow.Cells.Item(index).Controls.Add(columnHeading)
            Else
                'Allow sorting on the column
                sortButton = New LinkButton
                sortButton.Text = ReportGrid.Columns.Item(index).HeaderText

                sortButton.Attributes.Add("onclick", String.Format( _
                    "setSortExp('{0}');", _
                    ReportGrid.Columns.Item(index).SortExpression))

                ReportGrid.HeaderRow.Cells.Item(index).Controls.Add(sortButton)
            End If
        Next

    End Sub

    '***************************************************************************
    'Pagination Methods
    '***************************************************************************
    Protected Sub RequestNextPage() _
      Handles _PaginationForm.NextPageRequested
        CurrentPage += 1
```

```
        SetupSearchSql()
        If BindInPreLoad() Then BindReport()
    End Sub

    '***************************************************************************
    Protected Sub RequestPrevPage() _
      Handles _PaginationForm.PrevPageRequested
        CurrentPage -= 1
        SetupSearchSql()
        If BindInPreLoad() Then BindReport()
    End Sub

    '***************************************************************************
    Protected Sub RequestNewPage(ByVal page As Integer) _
      Handles _PaginationForm.NewPageRequested
        CurrentPage = page
        SetupSearchSql()
        If BindInPreLoad() Then BindReport()
    End Sub

End Class
```

As mentioned before, that is definitely a lot to take in all at once. The sections that follow discuss each portion of the code in more detail. It will help to reference the code as you look through the commentary.

Class Definition

Notice that the ReportFramework inherits the System.Web.UI.Page class. Because of this, any class inheriting the ReportFramework class also inherits the System.Web.UI.Page class. This is a necessity because the Report Pages that use the ReportFramework class for their base functionality are actually ASP.NET web forms, and ASP.NET web forms must, at some point, derive from the System.Web.UI.Page class.

Reducing the ViewState with ViewState Name (VSN) Constants

Items stored in the ViewState are referenced by a string-based key. Ideally, you want the key to be long enough to describe the item it references, but the key actually gets stored in the ViewState along with the data. So, long key names translate into a larger overall ViewState.

You can get around this issue by using ViewState Name (VSN) constants. The idea is that you can make the constant name very descriptive, but leave its value very short. Then you use the constant in your code when you need to reference an item in the ViewState:

```
Const SomeViewStateValue as String = "1"
ViewState(SomeViewStateValue)      'Instead of ViewState("SomeViewStateValue")
```

It's a small step to take, but it's those small steps that really help keep the ViewState size down to a minimum. You'll see the VSN constants used a bit later in the LastSql, CurrentPage, and TotalPages properties.

Declaring the Private Class Variables

Throughout the ReportFramework class, you'll see six different class-level variables used to store various pieces of information. Table 9-3 outlines each variable and its purpose in the class.

Table 9-3. ReportFramework *private class variables*

Name	Type	Description
_SearchForm	ISearchControl	Stores a reference to the ISearchControl displayed on the actual Report Page (if a search form is displayed). Declared WithEvents so ReportFramework can respond to the control's SearchExecuted event.
_PaginationForm	IPaginationControl	Stores a reference to the IPaginationControl displayed on the actual Report Page (if paging navigation is displayed). Declared WithEvents so the ReportFramework can respond to the control's NextPageRequested, PrevPageRequested, and NewPageRequested events._SearchForm
_TotalRecords	Long	Stores the total number of records returned by the query.
_SortClicked	Boolean	Flag indicating whether or not the current postback was caused by the user clicking on a sort column. When this value is True, ReportFramework knows to save the new _SortExpression and _SortDirection values for the report.
_SortExpression	String	Stores the sort expression of the column the users wants to sort on. ReportFramework saves the _SortExpression value in a hidden field to ensure that it's available on subsequent request. The value only changes when the user sorts on a different column.
_SortDirection	SqlSortDirection	Stores a value indicating the sort direction (ascending or descending) used in conjunction with _SortExpression.➥ ReportFramework saves the SortExpression value in a hidden field to ensure that it's available on subsequent requests. The value only changes when the user sorts on a different column.

You'll be seeing more of these as we go through more code, so keep them in the back of your mind as we continue along.

Reviewing the MustOverride Methods

After the private class definitions, you'll see a series of MustOverride members. These members are declared here, in the ReportFramework abstract class, but they must be overridden in each Report Page that inherits from the ReportFramework abstract class. This allows the Report Page to control certain functionality in the ReportFramework abstract class. Table 9-4 provides a brief description of each MustOverride method and its purpose in the class.

Table 9-4. *Description of* MustOverride *members in the* ReportFramework *abstract Class*

Name	Type	Description
ConnectionStringKey	Function	Returns a connection string key used to acquire a connection string from the <connectionStrings> section of Web.config. That connection string is ultimately used to open a database connection to acquire the report data.
ReportGrid	Function	Returns a reference to the GridView control where the report data is output. You must always return a valid GridView control from this function.
ItemsPerPage	Function	Returns an Integer value indicating how many items should appear on each page.
SearchFormPH	Function	Returns a PlaceHolder control into which an ISearch➥Control control may be loaded. If no SearchFormPH is returned (for example, the function returns Nothing), the page doesn't use an ISearchControl (and you must override the GetQuery function—by default it relies on the ISearchControl).
SearchFormFileName	Function	Returns a String containing the path to the ISearch➥Control user control (.ascx file) that is to be loaded into the SearchFormPH control.
PaginationFormPH	Function	Returns a PlaceHolder control into which an IPaginationControl control may be loaded. If no PaginationFormPH is provided (for example, it is Nothing), the page does not use an IPaginationControl.
PaginationForm➥FileName	Function	Returns a String containing the path to the IPaginationControl user control (.ascx file) that is to be loaded into the PaginationFormPH control.
SetSortOrder	Sub	Users can click on the column headers over the data displayed on a Report Page to sort the data according to that column. To do this, however, the query needs to know which sort orders to use for which column. The SetSortOrder method accepts a query and a sort expression value and expects the overridden SetSortOrder method in the Report Page to set up the appropriate sort orders for the query based on the sort expression. The SortDirection is not used in this method because ReportFramework automatically reverses the sort direction, if needed, before executing the query.

All the MustOverride members must be overridden in the Report Page, so each of these items will be discussed in more detail a bit later when we get to the actual Report Page. For now, let's continue on with the ReportFramework class.

The GetQuery and OnReportError Overridable Methods

You just looked at all the MustOverride methods, but you can also choose to override a few other methods in the ReportFramework class. They are the GetSqlQuery method and the OnReportError method. These members have been created with default functionality, but you can opt to override them with your own code if you so choose.

The GetSqlQuery method returns a SqlQuery object containing the query used to pull report data from the database. You may recall that the ISearchControl interface also has a GetSqlQuery method that returns a SqlQuery object as well. One of the key features of the ReportFramework is that it can easily load an ISearchControl component, so the GetSqlQuery method in the ReportFramework class uses the GetSqlQuery method from the loaded ISearchControl component to acquire the SqlQuery for the report. Listing 9-7 shows what it looks like in code.

Listing 9-7. GetSqlQuery *method*—ReportingFramework.vb

```
Protected Overridable Function GetSqlQuery() As SqlQuery
    If _SearchForm is Nothing then Return Nothing
    Return _SearchForm.GetSqlQuery
End Function
```

Here's the problem. Although the ReportFramework class can use an ISearchControl to provide searching functionality to users, it does not have to use one. If that is the case, then the code in Listing 9-7 will return Nothing, and the report will not display any search results. So, if you do not use an ISearchControl, then you need to override the ReportFramework's GetSqlQuery method on the ReportPage and then build out and return a SqlQuery object from that overridden method.

The same holds true for the OnReportError method. With its default code, it simply throws an exception when an error occurs in the ReportFramework class as shown in Listing 9-8.

Listing 9-8. OnReportError *method*—ReportingFramework.vb

```
Protected Overridable Sub OnReportError(ByVal ex As Exception)
    Throw ex
End Sub
```

You can override the method and log the error, or execute some other error-handling code of your own liking. Refer to Chapter 2 for information on structured error handling and error logging.

Boosting Performance with the BindInPreLoad Property

One notable aspect of the ReportFramework is that it implements sorting using client-side script and hidden form variables instead of relying on the postback sorting events in the GridView control. Here's why. If you want to use the sorting events in the GridView, then you *must* data bind the report data to the GridView during the PreLoad or Load events, otherwise, the paging and sorting events will not fire. More than likely, Report Pages are posted-back when users want to display another page of data or need to sort the results differently. This means that you have to reload the old report to get the events to fire, and then load the new report data to display to the end user. As such, you regularly execute two round trips to the database, which is inefficient. The client-side sorting functionality allows the `ReportFramework` to sort report data without needing to data bind the `GridView` in the page load. You can actually load the data in the `PreRender` event, which ensures you will only make one round trip to the database.

There is a catch, however. If you do not data bind the `GridView` to its data in the page load, many of its postback events will *not* fire. This is a problem if you like the row editing, updating, and deleting functionality of the `GridView` control. The problem of where to put the data binding is solved by putting it in both places and using the `Overridable` `BindInPreLoad` property to control whether or not the framework binds the report during the `PreLoad` or the `PreRender` event. If `BindInPreLoad` returns `True`, then the data binding occurs in the `PreLoad` event and the `GridView` control's postback events should fire without any problems.

Data binding also occurs in other methods when the report data changes to ensure the `GridView` control displays the most current data. If `BindInPreLoad` returns `False`, then the data binding is a bit more efficient and only occurs in the `PreRender` event and only one round trip to the database occurs. By default, `BindInPreLoad` returns `False` to take advantage of the performance gain. You may override the method on the Report Page and return `True` if you need to bind the data in the `PreRender` event.

Calculated and ViewState Based Class Properties

Directly following the `Overridable` methods section, you'll find four class property definitions. Table 9-5 provides a brief overview of the class properties and their purpose in the `ReportFramework` class.

Table 9-5. `ReportFramework` *class properties*

Name	Type	Description
`LastSql`	`String`	Uses the `ViewState` to store and retrieve the SQL statement that needs to be executed. When this is empty, no search will be executed.
`SearchFormIndex`	`Short`	Allows you to store a value indicating which search form the user has elected to use on the page. This is *not* used directly by the `ReportFramework` class, it simply exists to give you a predefined location to store data about which form the user wants to view when your page has multiple search-form options. It is intended for use in the overridden `SearchFormFileName` method in your Report Page. You'll see an example outlining its use later in the chapter when you learn how to implement an actual Report Page.
`CurrentPage`	`Long`	Uses the `ViewState` to store and retrieve a value that identifies which page the user is currently viewing.
`TotalPages`	`Long`	Uses the private class variable `_TotalRecords` and the `MustOverride` `ItemsPerPage` property to calculate the total number of data pages required to show the result set.

Three of the properties listed in the preceding table are used to store and retrieve information from the `ViewState`. These properties follow the same basic structure and use the VSN constants discussed earlier to reduce the overall `ViewState` size. Listing 9-9 shows the `LastSql` property, following by a brief description regarding the code for a `ViewState`-based property.

Listing 9-9. `LastSql Property—ViewState` *property example*

```
Protected Property LastSql() As String
    Get
        If ViewState(LastSqlVSN) Is Nothing Then Return String.Empty Else _
          Return ViewState(LastSqlVSN)
    End Get
    Set(ByVal value As String)
        If value = String.Empty Then ViewState.Remove(LastSqlVSN) Else _
          ViewState(LastSqlVSN) = value
    End Set
End Property
```

In the `Get` section, the property first determines whether or not a value for the property has been saved in the `ViewState`. Notice that it uses the VSN constant as the `ViewState` key. If a value for the property does not exist (that is, it's `Nothing`), then the property returns a default value. If a value does exist, then the property returns that value.

In the Set section, the property determines if the incoming values is the default value used in the Get section. If so, the property will clear the value from the `ViewState` to save space. If the value is not the default value, the value is stored to the `ViewState`. Once again, notice that the VSN constant is used as the `ViewState` key.

Setting Up the Report Framework with the Page_PreLoad Method

One of the new events in the ASP.NET 2.0 page model is the `PreLoad` event, which is useful when you are loading dynamic controls into a page. Any static controls you declare directly on the page are initialized and loaded with their `ViewState` and postback data by the time `PreLoad` fires. This means `PreLoad` can use the values in those controls.

In turn, any controls you add to the page in the `PreLoad` event are initialized with their `ViewState` and postback data by the time the `Load` event fires. So, if you add dynamic controls in the `PreLoad` event, all the controls on the page are initialized and ready for use by the time the `Load` event fires. Also, any events tied to those controls fire, assuming the control has been initialized with all its data. This is why you have to bind the `GridView` in a report back to its original data source in the `PreLoad` event if you want its events to fire correctly.

Note `ReportFramework` does not need to work with the dynamic controls in the `Load` event because it completes everything it needs to do in the `PreLoad` and `PreRender Page` events; however, it's a good habit to start putting dynamically created controls into your page in the `PreLoad` event so they are available when `Load` fires.

`ReportFramework` uses the `PreLoad` event to load both the `ISearchControl` and the `IPaginationControl` into the page and to do a couple of other setup routines. The code in the

PreLoad event references a number of other members that will be discussed in more detail momentarily.

Here's how it works. First, the Page_PreLoad method checks to make sure the MustOverride ReportGrid method returns a non Nothing reference. Remember, the ReportGrid is the only required element. If the ReportGrid method returns Nothing, then a new Exception is generated and passed into the OnReportError method, and then the method exits. If it does not return Nothing, then the method continues on normally.

After that, the Page_PreLoad method determines whether or not the current request is a PostBack. If so, it calls the AcquireHiddenFieldValues() method, which acquires sort values stored in hidden fields. If not, the method simply continues onward.

Next, the Page_PreLoad method calls the LoadSearchForm() and LoadPaginationForm() methods. LoadSearchForm determines whether or not an ISearchControl user control needs to be added to the page, and does so if necessary. LoadPaginationForm() does the same thing with an IPaginationControl user control. By adding these items during the PreLoad event, it ensures that the events associated with the ISearchControl and the IPaginationControl are raised and handled accordingly.

The Page_PreLoad method then determines whether or not the user clicked on a column heading to sort the data. It does this by checking the _SortClicked variable that is set during the AcquireHiddenFieldValues() method mentioned earlier. If the user clicked on a column heading, then the method sets the CurrentPage value to 1, and calls the SetupSearchSql method. Reordering a query is similar to creating a new query altogether, and because it makes little sense to start the user off in the middle of a new query, you should set CurrentPage to 1. SetupSearchSql then prepares the Report Page to display the reordered query.

Finally, if BindInPreLoad is True, then the method calls BindReport to ensure the GridView postback events fire. BindReport contains all the logic for connecting to a database, retrieving data, and binding that data to the GridView control on Report Page.

Determining Sorting Values with the AcquireHiddenFieldValues Method

Sorting values stored in the _SortClicked, _SortExpression, and _SortDirection class variables are determined on the client side using JavaScript and hidden form values. When the browser submits the web form, those hidden field values are sent back as well, but those values are not automatically stored in class-level variables. The AcquireHiddenFieldValues method pulls those hidden field values from the Request.Form collection and stores them in appropriate variables so they can be easily referenced.

AcquireHiddenFieldValues is fairly straightforward. It checks form variables and sets the corresponding class variables to the appropriate value. You will see where these hidden variables and client-side JavaScript are sent to the browser momentarily.

Loading an ISearchControl Component with the LoadSearchForm Method

LoadSearchForm is responsible for determining whether or not to load an ISearchControl component, and if so, loading the component into the appropriate PlaceHolder control on the Report Page. It starts off by checking the SearchFormPH virtual method to see if it returns Nothing. If it does, then the method knows not to load an ISearchControl into the page and it simply exits. If SearchFormPH returns a PlaceHolder, then the rest of the method continues.

The remainder of the method is surrounded in a Try Catch block. If any errors occur, the error is caught and passed into the OnReportError method. LoadSearchForm actually loads the search from on the first line in the Try Catch block using the LoadControl method. LoadControl accepts a URL to a user control, loads the user control found at that URL, and returns a reference to the loaded control as the value of the method. If any issues are encountered loading the control, an exception is thrown—hence the `Try Catch` block. The method assigns the `LoadControl` return value to the `_SearchForm` class variable.

After loading the component, the method casts `_SearchForm` into a `UserControl` to set the component's `ID` property. Setting the `ID` property ensures that controls inside the `ISearchControl` component retain their appropriate values from postback to postback. If you do not specify an `ID` property, then an `ID` is auto-generated for the control, which can cause data loss issues or events not being fired appropriately because ASP.NET may not auto-generate the same `ID` each time.

Finally, `LoadSearchForm` clears all the controls in the `PlaceHolder` control returned by the `SearchFormPH` virtual method and then adds the component referenced by `_SearchForm` into that `PlaceHolder`'s controls collection. This makes the `ISearchControl` component appear on the page.

Loading an IPaginationControl Component with the LoadPaginationForm Method

Loading the `IPaginationControl` follows the same logic as the `LoadSearchForm`, although it uses the `PaginationFormPH` and `PaginationFormFileName` virtual methods instead of the `LoadSearchForm` equivalents. Review the previous section for more information on how this method works.

Responding to the SearchButtonClicked Event with the SearchButtonClicked Method

Remember that that `ISearchControl` component exposes an event named `SearchButton➥ Clicked`. Any time a user clicks on a Search button located directly on an `ISearchControl` component, the component raises this event. When the event is raised, the `ReportFramework` must set up a new query to be executed. The `SearchButtonClicked` method handles the `SearchButtonClicked` event and contains the code for the query setup.

Because a new query is being executed, the method begins by setting certain query variables back to their default settings. `CurrentPage` is set to `1`, `_SortExpression` is set to an empty string, and `_SortDireciton` is set to `Ascending`. After setting the default values, the method calls `SetupSearchSql`, which prepares the SQL query for execution. If `BindInPreLoad` is `True`, then it calls `BindReport` to execute the new query and overwrite any existing data loaded into the Report Page during the `PreLoad` event. If `BindInPreLoad` is `False`, then the report is data bound in the `PreRender` method, and it does not need to be executed in this method.

■ **Note** If you do not use an `ISearchControl` component on your Report Page, then you must create a search button directly on the Report Page. In the click event of that button, make sure to call the `SearchButtonClicked` method directly so the `ReportFramework` can set up the query for execution.

Preparing the SQL Query with the SetupSearchSql Method

Later on in the `BindReport` method, the `ReportFramework` class executes a SQL statement to acquire the report's result set. It stores that SQL statement in the `LastSql` property as a string, but that string is built using the SqlQuery object returned by the GetSqlQuery method. The SetupSearchSql method acquires the SqlQuery object and uses it to build out a SQL statement to store in the LastSql property.

First, the SetupSearchSql method declares a variable named SqlQueryObj to store the SqlQuery object. It assigns the variable the result of the GetSqlQuery method in the declaration, and then checks the SqlQueryObj to ensure that it's not Nothing. If the variable is Nothing, then the method calls ClearSearch and then exits; no data is displayed when this occurs.

After acquiring the SqlQuery object, the SetupSearchSql method passes the object and the _SortExpression variable into the SetSortOrder method. The SetSortOrder is a MustOverride method and determines and sets up the appropriate ORDER BY clause for the SqlQuery object using the value in _SortExpression. You'll see the code for the SetSortOrder method when we get to the Report Page.

Next, SetupSearchSql checks the _SortDirection variable to determine whether the overall order of the search results should be ascending or descending. The SetSortOrder method always returns the SqlQuery object in ascending mode. If the overall results are to be shown in descending order, then the method calls ReverseSortOrder and passes in the SqlQuery object. This "flips" all the SortDirection properties on the ORDER BY fields in the SqlQuery object, effectively reversing the direction of the query from ascending to descending.

Finally, the method checks the _PaginationForm variable to determine whether or not it contains an IPaginationControl control. If not, the method assumes that no paging is being used and assigns LastSql the result of the SqlQuery object's GetQuery method. If an IPaginationControl control is found, then the method assumes paging is being used, concatenates the result from the GetPagedQuery and GetCountQuery together using a semicolon to separate the two queries, and saves the query to the LastSql property. Placing two queries together in the same SQL statement allows you to execute both statements without the overhead of needing to execute two individual commands. You'll see how to retrieve the data from both commands in the BindReport method.

Reversing the Sort Order with the ReverseOrderBy Method

As mentioned in the previous section, ReverseOrderBy flips the overall sort order of a SqlQuery object. It accomplishes this by iterating through each of the SqlField objects in the SqlQuery object's OrderBy collection. The method checks each SqlField object's SortDirection property and then reverses its value. If the SortOrder is ascending, it is changed to descending. If the SortOrder is descending, it is changed to ascending. This effectively flips the overall order of the query.

Clearing the Search Query with the ClearSearch Method

At some point, you may want to clear the search so the Report Page does not display any data. You can do this using the ClearSearch method, which sets the LastSql variable equal to an empty string. The page does not attempt to execute a query when the LastSql variable does not contain text, so this effectively clears the search. This is a protected method so you can access it from the Report Page if you need to use it.

Acquiring and Displaying Report Data with the BindReport Method

Inside the BindReport method, you'll find all the logic for connecting to a database, querying data, outputting the data to the Report Page, and setting up the paging navigation controls. The BindReport method is called from a number of different locations. The ReportFramework class calls the BindReport method in the Pre_Load event so the appropriate GridView events fire. Whenever the user executes a new search or navigates to another page, then the ReportFramework class must set up the new query and call BindReport to ensure that the Report Page displays the appropriate information.

BindReport starts out by determining whether or not the LastSql property is an empty string. If so, then the method exits; otherwise, the method continues on and declares a number of method variables. Three of the variables, dbConn, dbCmd, and dbDr, store references to database objects used to connect to the database, execute a command, and retrieve the results, respectively. RecordStart and RecordEnd store the beginning and ending record numbers of the items displayed during a paged query.

A Try Catch block surrounds most of the code in the BindReport method. Following suit with other Try Catch blocks in the ReportFramework class, it catches any exception that occurs and sends it to the OnReportError method.

Inside the Try Catch block, the method creates a new SqlConnection object. The connection string for the SqlConnection object comes from the <connectionString> section of Web.config and is acquired by passing the value from the ConnectionStringKey method—implemented in the derived class—into the ConnectionStrings property. The resulting ConnectionStringSettings object contains the appropriate connection string in its ConnectionString property.

After creating the database connection, the method then creates a new SqlCommand object, passing in LastSql as the query and dbConn as the database connection. After the SqlCommand object is created, BindReport opens the database connection, executes the SqlCommand using the ExecuteReader method, and stores the resulting SqlDataReader in the dbDr variable. The method then assigns dbDr to the DataSource property of the ReportGrid, and calls DataBind to bind the ReportGrid to its data source. All the data from the SqlDataReader then populates the ReportGrid according to its display templates defined on the Report Page.

After the ReportGrid has been data bound, the BindReport uses an IF statement and a series of AndAlso conditionals to check whether or not it should set up the paging navigation controls. This IF statement uses AndAlso because one condition must be met before the next condition can be safely checked. The IF statement starts out by checking whether or not the _PaginationForm variable is set to Nothing. If not, it assumes that paging is being used and continues on to the next condition.

The next condition in the IF statement is AndAlso dbDr.NextResult. Remember back to the SetupSearchSql method, and you'll recall that paged queries contain two SQL statements. The first statement returns a result set with a single page of data, and the second statement returns a scalar value containing the total number of records across all pages of data. Calling dbDr.NextResult makes dbDr move from the first statement's result set to the second statement's result set. If it successfully moves to the next result set, then the call returns True, which is required to meet the second condition of the If statement.

The last condition in the IF statement is AndAlso dbDr.Read. After dbDr has moved to the next result set, you call the Read method to determine if any data has been returned and to prepare that data to be read. If data has been returned, then the data reader moves to the first record in the result set and returns True to indicate that the data is ready to be read.

Assuming all three of the If statement conditions are met, then the BindReport method sets up the paging navigation controls. The method begins by assigning the value in dbDr.Item(0), which contains an integer value identifying the total number of records located by the query, to the TotalRecords variable. Then method runs some validation on the CurrentPage property to ensure that it's within the appropriate page range. The validation occurs after TotalRecords is set because TotalRecords is used in the TotalPages property calculation.

After the validation routines, BindReport calculates the starting and ending record numbers. RecordStart, which holds the starting record number, is always calculated using the equation ((CurrentPage - 1) * ItemsPerPage()) + 1. Multiplying (CurrentPage - 1) by ItemsPerPage gives you the total number of items on previous pages (that is, page 1 has 0 records before it). Adding 1 gets you to the first records on the current page (that is, page 1 starts at record 1). RecordEnd, which holds the ending record number, is calculated differently depending on whether or not the current page is the last page. If the current page is the last page, then the last record should be the same as the value stored in TotalRecords because it is the last record being shown. If it isn't the last page, then the calculation for RecordEnd is simply the RecordStart plus the value stored in ItemsPerPage minus 1. Remember, you added 1 to acquire the RecordStart value, so now you have to subtract it to make the math work out.

After all the paging calculations have been made, BindReport calls PaginationForm.➥
SetInfo and passes the appropriate values into the method. Recall that the SetInfo method of the IPaginationControl interface sets up the visual display of the paging navigation form.

Finally, regardless of whether or not paging navigation was set up, the BindReport method calls dbConn.Close to close the database connection.

Rendering Data and Client-Side Functionality with the Page_PreRender Method

Right before ASP.NET generates the output for a page, the PreRender event fires, and the event is handled by the Page_PreRender method. Inside Page_PreRender, a series of method calls helps output client-side sorting functionality.

First, if BindInPreLoad is False, then the method calls BindReport to populate the GridView with the report data.

Then the method calls SetupHiddenFields which outputs a series of hidden fields to store the sort expression, sort direction, and whether or not the user clicked on a column heading to sort the result set. Next, it calls SetupJavaScript, which outputs a JavaScript method that helps set sorting values when the user clicks on a column heading. Then the method checks to see whether or not PaginationForm references a valid IPaginationControl component.

If _PaginationForm references a valid IPaginationControl component, then the method checks to see if the ReportGrid contains any data by checking its row count. If the row count is 0, then no data is present, and the method removes the paging navigation controls by calling PaginationFormPH.Controls.Clear(). If data is present, then the method calls SetupSortableColumns, which runs through all the column headings and creates column headers that use the client-side sorting functionality output earlier.

Storing Client-Side Sort Settings with the SetupHiddenFields Method

The ReportFramework maintains three different sort values to help determine how to sort the report. You should remember SortClicked, SortExpression, and _SortDirection from the section covering class variables and the AcquireHiddenFieldValues method. The values for these variables are stored on the client-side between postbacks, and their values change on the client side based on which column header the user clicks. `SetupHiddenFields` is the method that builds out the hidden fields and places them on the page.

`SetupHiddenFields` uses the `ClientScript.RegisterHiddenField` method to create three hidden fields named `sortClicked`, `sortExp`, and `sortDir`. The `RegisterHiddenField` method accepts two parameters, a name and a value, and outputs the name and value as a hidden field directly under the `<form>` tag when ASP.NET renders the page. The `sortClicked` value is always set to `0` when the page is output. If the user clicks on a column header, then the client-side scripts change the `sortClicked` value to `1` to denote that the user clicked on a column heading, set `sortExp` to the sort expression value associated with the column, and set the `sortDir` based on whether or not the user clicked on the same column more than once (allowing users to reverse the sort by clicking on a column twice in succession). `SetupHiddenFields` outputs both the `sortExp` and the `sortDir` with their current values because those values are used in the `setSortExp` client-side method. We'll talk about it next.

Creating Client-Side Sorting Functionality with the SetupJavaScript Method

The `SetupJavaScript` method constructs a JavaScript method as a string, and then outputs that method using the `Page.ClientScript.RegisterClientScriptBlock` method. The `RegisterClientScriptBlock` method accepts four parameters.

The first parameter is the object type of the object requesting to add the client script block. This gives the key a context and helps avoid issues with different components overwriting each other's scripts because they use the same key. In this example, `me.GetType()` provides the type. The key is the unique identifier for the script that ensures your component does not output a single script multiple times. You can name it anything you want, but in this case it's `sortExp`. The script string is a string containing the client-side code to output to the page. You can see that the lines above the call to `RegisterClientScriptBlock` are devoted to building out the script string. We'll discuss it a bit more in a second. The last parameter tells `RegisterClientScriptBlock` whether or not to add `<script>` tags around the client-side script. Because the script does not include `<script>` tags, the parameter is set to `True` so the tags will be included.

Next, Listing 9-10 provides the client-side JavaScript used to set the hidden variables that store the sorting values. Remember that the `SetupHiddenFields` method creates the hidden fields used in this method.

Listing 9-10. `setSortExp` *client-side JavaScript method*

```
function setSortExp(sortExp){
    var sortExpField = document.getElementById('sortExp');
    var sortDirField = document.getElementById('sortDir');
    if(sortExpField.value==sortExp){
        if(sortDirField.value==0){
            sortDirField.value=1;
        }else{
            sortDirField.value=0;
        }
    }else{
```

```
        sortExpField.value=sortExp;
        sortDirField.value=0;
    }
    document.getElementById('sortClicked').value = '1';
}
```

The setSortExp method executes when a user clicks on a column heading to sort the report. We'll take a look at exactly how this works in the next section. For now, know that each column heading passes a different sortExp value into the method denoting which column heading was clicked. Inside the method, setSortExp first acquires a reference to the sortExp and sortDir hidden fields, and stores those references in sortExpField and sortDirField, respectively. The sortDirField contains the last sort expression value, and sortDirField contains the last sort direction value.

The first if statement in the method checks to see if the incoming value, sortExp, matches the last sort expression value in sortExpField. If so, the method knows that the column has been clicked two or more time in a row. When an item is clicked more than once, the sort order reverses. If the sort direction is 0, which represents ascending, then it becomes 1. If 1, which represents descending, then it becomes 0. If it's the first time the user clicked the column, then the method sets the sortExpField value to the incoming sortExp value, and sets sortDirField to be ascending, or 0.

At the very end of the code, the method sets the sortClicked hidden field to 1, indicating that the user clicked on a sort heading.

Creating Sorting Functionality with the SetupSortableColumns Method

With ViewStateEnabled set to False, the default sorting mechanism of the GridView does not fire its Sorting postback event. This means the column headers that generate the Sorting postback event are useless. To circumvent this issue, the ReportFramework creates its own set of column headers and sets up each one to execute the setSortExp client-side method with a different sort expression for each column. When the user clicks on a column header to sort the query, the LinkButton executes the setSortExp client-side method, stores the appropriate sort expression and direction, and then posts the page back.

SetupSortableColumns begins by declaring two variables named sortButton and columnHeading, a LinkButton and Label control, respectively. The method then iterates over each column in the ReportGrid.Columns collection. Inside that loop, SetupSortableColumns checks the SortExpression and HeaderText properties of the column to determine which control it should place in the column header. If the column does not provide a SortExpression but does provide a HeaderText, then the method places a Label containing the HeaderText value in the column header.

If the column provides a SortExpression, then the method builds out a LinkButton that displays the HeaderText. It then adds an attribute for the client-side onClick event specifying that the setSortExp client-side method should execute—using the appropriate SortExpression for the column—when the user clicks on the column header.

Paging Through Data with the Pagination Methods

The final three methods in the ReportFramework handle pagination. RequestNextPage handles the NextPageRequested event of the _PaginationForm, RequestPrevPage handles the PrevPageRequested event, and RequestNewPage handles the NewPageRequested event.

Each method follows the same logic and structure. First, the method adjusts the CurrentPage value. RequestNextPage increments CurrentPage by one, RequestPrevPage decreases CurrentPage by one, and RequestNewPage assigns CurrentPage the incoming page value. Then each method calls SearchSearchSql to create a new query to acquire the new data page. Finally, if BindInPreLoad is True, then the method calls BindReport and overwrites any data placed in the GridView control during the PreLoad event.

This concludes the code for the reporting framework. Next, you will implement reporting framework components and make a working Report Page.

Creating a Report Using the Reporting Framework

Now that you have a reporting framework at your disposal, you can use it to create a Report Page. In this example, you'll create a Report Page named CustomerSearch.aspx to search for and display customer records from the Northwind database. This will allow users to easily locate contact information for customers. The search is paginated to avoid dumping too much data to the screen, and it has a simple and advanced search form to allow users searching flexibility. Figure 9-3 shows the CustomerSearch.aspx page when it is fully output to the browser.

ID	Company	Contact	Title	Phone
FAMIA	Familia Arquibaldo	Aria Cruz	Marketing Assistant	(11) 555-9857
FISSA	FISSA Fabrica Inter. Salchichas S.A.	Diego Roel	Accounting Manager	(91) 555 94 44
FOLIG	Folies gourmandes	Martine Rancé	Assistant Sales Agent	20.16.10.16
FOLKO	Folk och fä HB	Maria Larsson	Owner	0695-34 67 21
FRANK	Frankenversand	Peter Franken	Marketing Manager	089-0877310
FRANR	France restauration	Carine Schmitt	Marketing Manager	40.32.21.21
FRANS	Franchi S.p.A.	Paolo Accorti	Sales Representative	011-4988260
FURIB	Furia Bacalhau e Frutos do Mar	Lino Rodriguez	Sales Manager	(1) 354-2534
GALED	Galería del gastrónomo	Eduardo Saavedra	Marketing Manager	(93) 203 4560
GODOS	Godos Cocina Típica	José Pedro Freyre	Sales Manager	(95) 555 82 82

Figure 9-3. CustomerSearch.aspx

The sections that follow outline the implementation of all the components required to put a Report Page together. This includes a couple of ISearchControl components to show you how to switch back and forth between search forms, IPaginationControl to demonstrate paging navigation, and the actual Report Page layout and code behind that inherits the ReportFramework abstract class.

Building Search Forms Using the ISearchControl Interface

One feature the reporting framework boasts is the capability to automatically load an `ISearchControl` component into the Report Page and to use the `SqlQuery` object it creates to populate the report. You can use this built-in functionality to easily toggle between different types of search forms with ease. To see this functionality in action, you need to create a couple of `ISearchControl` components for your Report Page.

Creating the CustomerSimple.ascx UserControl

First, let's look at the simple search form. Because this is a simple form, it only contains a text box named `txtCustomerInfo` and a button named `btnSearch`. The text box is where users enter keywords to search through the `CustomerID`, `CompanyName`, `ContactName`, and `ContactTitle` fields of the `Customers` table. Figure 9-4 shows the `CustomerSimple.ascx` control, and the code for the `CustomerSimple` class is shown in Listing 9-11.

■ **Tip** If you are using the Visual Studio IDE, make sure you type `Implements ISearchControl` and then press the Enter key. The IDE automatically creates the definitions for all members of the `ISearchControl` interface. You can then fill them out.

Listing 9-11. `SearchForms\CustomerSimple.ascx.vb` *(Web Project)*

```
Imports Reporting

Partial Class CustomerSimple
    Inherits UserControl
    Implements ISearchControl

    '***************************************************************************
    Public Event SearchExecuted() Implements ISearchControl.SearchButtonClicked

    '***************************************************************************
    Public Function GetSqlQuery() As SqlQuery Implements ISearchControl.GetSqlQuery
        SqlQueryObj.From = "Customers"         Dim SqlQueryObj As New SqlQuery
        SqlQueryObj.Where.CreateKeywords(Me.txtCustomerInfo.Text, _
          "CustomerID + ' ' + CompanyName ' ' + ContactName + ' ' + " & _
          "ContactTitle", SqlOperation.And)
        Return SqlQueryObj
    End Function
```

```
    '***************************************************************************
    Protected Sub btnSearch_Click(ByVal sender As Object, _
      ByVal e As System.EventArgs) Handles btnSearch.Click
        RaiseEvent SearchExecuted()
    End Sub

End Class
```

You've seen an ISearchControl implementation before, so the main thing you need to know about this listing is that the SqlQuery object created by the GetSqlQuery method creates a query to pull data from the Customers table, and it uses a single CreateKeywords with four concatenated database fields to build out the WHERE clause of that query. This allows the query to search for any keywords entered in the text box across all those concatenated fields. Also, the Search button used to execute the search functionality of the reporting framework is located directly on the UserControl, so clicking btnSearch raises the SearchExecuted event.

Simple Search Form
Please enter customer keywords in the textbox below. Those keywords will be used to match items in the CustomerID, CompanyName, ContactName, and ContactTitle fields.

Customer Information Keywords:
Search

Figure 9-4. CustomerSimple.ascx *search form*

Creating the CustomerAdvanced.ascx User Control

Next, you need to see the advanced customer search form that allows users a bit more control in regards to their search criteria. This search form actually displays four text boxes and uses the keywords from those text boxes to search specific fields in the Customers table, which can be helpful when you're getting too many accidental matches from the simple search form.

For example, let's say a user needs to search for a CompanyID that has "Ana" in it. A search using the simple form yields 35 results. Searching specifically through the CompanyID field in the advanced search yields 2 results, so it definitely helps narrow the search down.

You'll see four text boxes in the CustomerAdvanced.ascx UserControl: txtCustomerID, txtCompanyName, txtContactName, and txtContactTitle. Each text box allows a user to enter keywords for a specific field, CustomerID, CompanyName, ContactName, and ContactTitle, respectively. Figure 9-5 shows the CustomerAdvanced.ascx UserControl, and the code for the component is in Listing 9-12.

Listing 9-12. SearchForms\CustomerAdvanced.ascx.vb *(Web Project)*

```
Imports Reporting

Partial Class CustomerAdvanced
    Inherits UserControl
    Implements ISearchControl
```

```
    '***************************************************************************
    Public Event SearchExecuted() Implements ISearchControl.SearchButtonClicked

    '***************************************************************************
    Public Function GetSqlQuery() As SqlQuery Implements ISearchControl.GetSqlQuery
        Dim SqlQueryObj As New SqlQuery
        SqlQueryObj.From = "Customers"
        SqlQueryObj.Where.And()
        SqlQueryObj.Where.CreateKeywords(Me.txtCustomerID.Text, _
          "CustomerID", SqlOperation.And)
        SqlQueryObj.Where.CreateKeywords(Me.txtCompanyName.Text, _
          "CompanyName", SqlOperation.And)
        SqlQueryObj.Where.CreateKeywords(Me.txtContactName.Text, _
          "ContactName", SqlOperation.And)
        SqlQueryObj.Where.CreateKeywords(Me.txtContactTitle.Text, _
          "ContactTitle", SqlOperation.And)
        Return SqlQueryObj
    End Function

    '***************************************************************************
    Protected Sub btnSearch_Click(ByVal sender As Object, _
      ByVal e As System.EventArgs) Handles btnSearch.Click
        RaiseEvent SearchExecuted()
    End Sub

End Class
```

The CustomerAdvanced UserControl is similar to the CustomerSimple UserControl because both implement the ISearchControl interface, both build queries that pull data from the Customers table, and both contain a button that begins the searching process when clicked. Really, the main difference is in how the SqlQuery object constructs the WHERE clause of the query. Instead of using a single CreateKeywords call that spans four database fields, the advanced version of the form uses four CreateKeywords calls and only reference one field in each of those calls. This allows specific keywords to be targeted to specific fields, instead of the more general search across all fields.

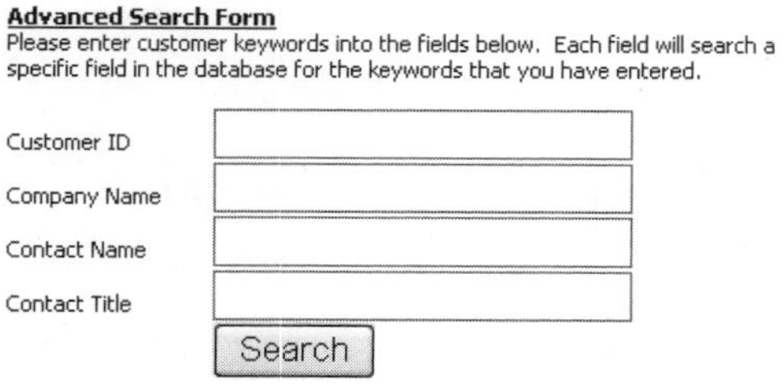

Figure 9-5. CustomerSimple.ascx *search form*

Creating a Paging Navigation Component

You are about to look at one way paging navigation controls can appear, but you can make your own pagination component look and behave however you want. That's the beauty of generalizing the component using the `IPaginationControl` interface. This version of a pagination control displays links to easily navigate to the next and previous pages and a text box that allows you to enter the page to which you want to jump. It also displays the current page, total pages, which records are currently being displayed, and the total number of records in the result set as shown in Figure 9-6.

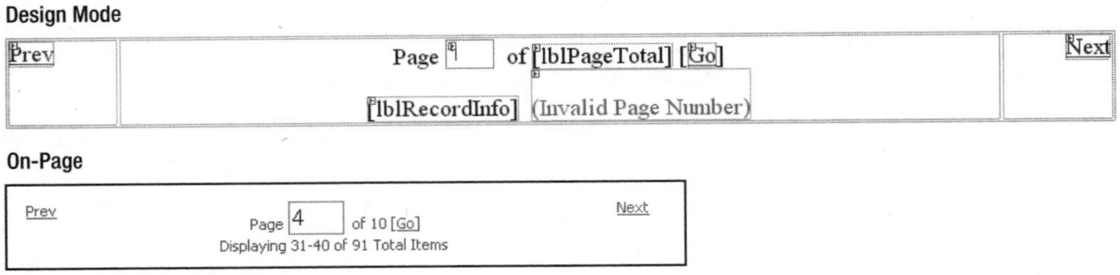

Figure 9-6. `Pagination.ascx UserControl` *shown in design mode and as it appears onscreen*

The paging navigation component shown in Figure 9-6 contains the controls in Table 9-6.

Table 9-6. *Controls in the* `Pagination.ascx UserControl`

ID	Type	Description
`lnkPrev`	`LinkButton`	Clicking this link takes the user to the next page of data.
`lnkNext`	`LinkButton`	Clicking this link takes the user to the previous page of data.
`txtCurrentPage`	`TextBox`	Displays the current data page when the web form first loads. It also allows the user to enter the page to which they want to be taken after clicking the `lnkGotoPage LinkButton`.
`lnkGotoPage`	`LinkButton`	Clicking this link takes the user to the page specified in the `txtCurrentPage TextBox`.
`lblPageTotal`	`Label`	Displays the total number of pages in the result set.
`lblRecordInfo`	`Label`	Displays information about the current records being displayed and the total number of records in the result set.
`rngPageNumber`	`RangeValidator`	Ensures the page number entered into the `txtCurrentPage TextBox` is valid.

Refer to the `PagingControl.ascx UserControl` *in the web project of the sample application in the Source Code area of the Apress website for exact control settings and layout.*

Now that you know which controls appear in the `PagingControl`, let's take a look at how they are used and how the control implements the `IPaginationControl` interface (see Listing 9-13).

Listing 9-13. PaginationForms\PagingControl.ascx.vb *(Web Project)*

```
Imports Reporting
Partial Class PagingControl
    Inherits System.Web.UI.UserControl
    Implements IPaginationControl

    'IPaginationControl Events
    '***************************************************************************
    Public Event NewPageRequested(ByVal page As Integer) _
      Implements IPaginationControl.NewPageRequested

    Public Event NextPageRequested() _
      Implements IPaginationControl.NextPageRequested

    Public Event PrevPageRequested() _
      Implements IPaginationControl.PrevPageRequested

    '***************************************************************************
    Public Sub SetInfo(ByVal currentPage As Integer, ByVal totalPages As Integer, _
      ByVal totalRecords As Integer, ByVal itemsPerPage As Integer, _
      ByVal recordStart as Integer, ByVal recordEnd as Integer) _
      Implements IPaginationControl.SetInfo

        'Set up current page, total page, and record display labels
        Me.lblPageTotal.Text = totalPages.ToString
        Me.txtCurrentPage.Text = currentPage.ToString
        Me.lblRecordInfo.Text = String.Format( _
          "Displaying {0}-{1} of {2} Total Items", _
          recordStart, recordEnd, totalRecords)

        'Set up validation for jumping to another page
        rngPageNumber.MinimumValue = "1"
        rngPageNumber.MaximumValue = totalPages.ToString

        'Disable
        If currentPage = totalPages Then Me.lnkNext.Enabled = False
        If currentPage = 1 Then Me.lnkPrev.Enabled = False
        If totalPages = 1 Then Me.lnkGotoPage.Enabled = False

    End Sub

    '***************************************************************************
    Protected Sub lnkPrev_Click(ByVal sender As Object, _
      ByVal e As System.EventArgs) Handles lnkPrev.Click
        RaiseEvent PrevPageRequested()
    End Sub
```

```
    '***************************************************************************
    Protected Sub lnkNext_Click(ByVal sender As Object, _
      ByVal e As System.EventArgs) Handles lnkNext.Click
        RaiseEvent NextPageRequested()
    End Sub

    '***************************************************************************
    Protected Sub lnkGotoPage_Click(ByVal sender As Object, _
      ByVal e As System.EventArgs) Handles lnkGotoPage.Click
        If Not IsNumeric(Me.txtCurrentPage.Text) Then Exit Sub
        RaiseEvent NewPageRequested(CInt(Me.txtCurrentPage.Text))
    End Sub

End Class
```

The `PagingControl` class inherits from `System.Web.UserControl` because it is a `UserControl`, and it implements the `IPaginationControl` interface. Remember, three events and one method make up the `IPaginationControl` interface. The events for the interface are defined immediately after the class definition; there is no code involved with the definition of the events.

After the reporting framework loads the paging navigation component, it passes in important initialization data to the component's `SetInfo` method. You can see from the code listing above that the `SetInfo` method for this component uses this data to accomplish three things. First, it displays the information so the user can see the current page, total pages, and record count information. Second, it sets up validation for the `txtCurrentPage` text box. This ensures that users can only attempt to jump to valid pages. Lastly, it disables the `lnkPrev` control when the first page is being displayed, disables the `lnkNext` control when the last page is being displayed, and disables the **Go** link if there is only one page. Like the validation on `txtCurrentPage`, this ensures users cannot request pages that do not exist.

Below the `SetInfo` method, the `PagingControl` contains a series of methods that handles the click events of the `lnkPrev`, `lnkNext`, and `lnkGotoPage` controls. When clicked, each one of these buttons raises one of the `IPaginationControl` events. So, `lnkPrev` causes the `PrevPageRequested` event to fire, `lnkNext` causes the `NextPageRequested` event to fire, and `lnkGotoPage` causes the `NewPageRequested` event to fire. Note that the requested page value in `txtCurrentPage.text` is converted into an integer and passed into the raised `NewPageRequested` event.

That's the extent of a paging navigation component that implements the `IPagination➥Control` interface. Most of the code you write will be to display information passed into the `SetInfo` method and raise the `IPaginationControl` events in response to user actions. Next, you'll see the `ReportFramework` abstract class that brings everything together that we've talked about so far.

Building the Report Page Layout

The Report Page is, for the most part, just like any other ASP.NET web form. The only real difference is that is inherits additional reporting functionality from the `ReportFramework` abstract class. Remember, `ReportFramework` inherits `System.Web.UI.Page`, so the Report Page still has all the normal web-form functionality that you have come to expect in ASP.NET.

Because it is a normal ASP.NET page, it means you are free to use any ASP.NET technologies you want to create the page layout and behavior. You can employ Master Pages, themes, user controls, server controls, or anything else you would normally use.

From the beginning of the chapter, recall that there are three controls that have special meaning to the `ReportFramework`. The first is the `GridView` control where the framework displays data. This is mandatory for all Report Pages. The other two controls are `PlaceHolder` controls. One defines the position where the `ISearchControl` should appear, and the other defines the position where the `IPaginationControl` should appear. These are optional components. If you don't want them on a Report Page, you don't have to have them.

Listing 9-14 shows the page layout code from `CustomerSearch.aspx`. Because the page uses both an `ISearchControl` and an `IPaginationControl`, it contains two `PlaceHolder` controls defining the locations where these items should be inserted. It also has the mandatory `GridView` control. You may name these controls anything you like because references to the controls are returned by the overridden virtual members defined in the Report Page code behind; it has nothing to do with their actual names. Figure 9-7 shows the layout as it appears in design mode.

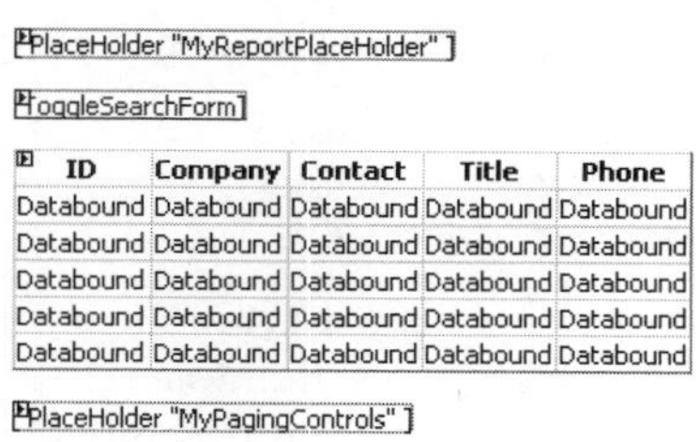

Figure 9-7. `CustomerSearch.aspx` *design time*

Listing 9-14. `CustomerSearch.aspx` *(Web Project)*

```
<asp:PlaceHolder ID="MyReportPlaceHolder" runat="server"
     EnableViewState=false /><br /><br />
<asp:LinkButton ID="ToggleSearchForm" runat="server" EnableViewState=false />
<br /><br />
<asp:GridView ID="MyReportGrid" runat="server" ShowHeader=true
     EnableViewState=False AutoGenerateColumns="False" Width="100%">
    <Columns>
        <asp:BoundField DataField="CustomerID"   HeaderText="ID"
             SortExpression="CustomerID" />
        <asp:BoundField DataField="CompanyName"  HeaderText="Company"
             SortExpression="CompanyName" />
        <asp:BoundField DataField="ContactName"  HeaderText="Contact"
             SortExpression="ContactName" />
        <asp:BoundField DataField="ContactTitle" HeaderText="Title"
             SortExpression="ContactTitle" />
        <asp:BoundField DataField="Phone"        HeaderText="Phone"
             SortExpression="Phone" />
```

```
        </Columns>
        <EmptyDataTemplate>
            Your search did not return any results
        </EmptyDataTemplate>
    </asp:GridView><br />
    <asp:PlaceHolder ID="MyPagingControls" runat="server" EnableViewState=false />
```

This page has a total of four controls: two PlaceHolder controls, one LinkButton, and one GridView. The LinkButton is used to toggle between the simple and advanced ISearchControl components. Both PlaceHolders define the location where ReportFramework should insert the ISearchControl and IPaginationControl components. Set EnableViewState to False on all these items to keep the ViewState size to a minimum, unless there is a compelling reason to do otherwise.

Make sure you take advantage of the GridView control's visual properties, styles, and column templates to format the report data as you see fit. Remember, the field names of the data coming into the report will match the field names defined in the SqlQuery you created in the ISearchControl component used on the page (or in the overridden GetSqlQuery method if no ISearchControl exists). Also remember to define the HeaderText property if you want the column to have a heading, and to define the SortExpression if you want the user to be able to sort the report based on that column.

Developing the Report Page Code Behind

Developing a Report Page is a fairly easy process because the ReportFramework class encapsulates most of the complex reporting logic. You just need to override a series of simple MustOverride methods to make the Report Page work. Many of the methods only require a single line of code, so you can hopefully begin to appreciate how easy a reporting framework can make the report-creation process. Listing 9-15 shows the CustomerSearch.aspx.vb code behind.

Listing 9-15. CustomerSearch.aspx.vb *(Code-Behind File)*

```
Imports Reporting
Imports System.Web.UI.WebControls

Partial Class CustomerSearch
    Inherits ReportFramework

    '***************************************************************************
    ' Search Form Toggling Functionality
    '***************************************************************************
    Protected Sub ToggleSearchForm_Click(ByVal sender As Object, _
      ByVal e As System.EventArgs) Handles ToggleSearchForm.Click
        If SearchFormIndex = 1 Then SearchFormIndex = 0 Else SearchFormIndex = 1
        LoadSearchForm()
    End Sub
```

```
'***************************************************************************
Protected Sub Page_PreRender(ByVal sender As Object, _
  ByVal e As System.EventArgs) Handles Me.PreRender
    Select Case SearchFormIndex
        Case 0
            Me.ToggleSearchForm.Text = "Advanced Search"
        Case Else
            Me.ToggleSearchForm.Text = "Simple Search"
    End Select
End Sub

'***************************************************************************
' ReportFramework Virtual Member Overrides
'***************************************************************************
Protected Overrides Function SearchFormFileName() As String
    Select Case Me.SearchFormIndex
        Case 0
            Return "~/SearchForms/CustomerSimple.ascx"
        Case Else
            Return "~/SearchForms/CustomerAdvanced.ascx"
    End Select
End Function

'***************************************************************************
Protected Overrides Function PaginationFormFileName() As String
    Return "~/PaginationForms/PagingControl.ascx"
End Function

'***************************************************************************
Protected Overrides Function ConnectionStringKey() As String
    Return "Northwind"
End Function

'***************************************************************************
Protected Overrides Function ItemsPerPage() As Integer
    Return 10
End Function

'***************************************************************************
Protected Overrides Function ReportGrid() As GridView
    Return MyReportGrid
End Function

'***************************************************************************
Protected Overrides Function SearchFormPH() As PlaceHolder
    Return MyReportPlaceHolder
End Function
```

```
    '*************************************************************************
    Protected Overrides Function PaginationFormPH() As PlaceHolder
        Return MyPagingControls
    End Function

    '*************************************************************************
    Protected Overrides Sub SetSortOrder(ByVal queryObj As SqlQuery, _
      ByVal sortColumn As String)

        Select Case sortExpression
            Case "CompanyName"
                queryObj.OrderBy.Add("CompanyName")
                queryObj.OrderBy.Add("ContactName")
            Case "ContactName"
                queryObj.OrderBy.Add("ContactName")
            Case "ContactTitle"
                queryObj.OrderBy.Add("ContactTitle")
                queryObj.OrderBy.Add("ContactName")
            Case "Phone"
                queryObj.OrderBy.Add("Phone")
            Case Else
                queryObj.OrderBy.Add("CustomerID")
        End Select
    End Sub

End Class
```

■ **Tip** If you are using the Visual Studio IDE, make sure you type `Inherits ReportFramework` and then press the Enter key. The IDE automatically creates definitions for all the virtual members in the `ReportFramework` abstract class. You can then fill them out.

There are two distinct sections in the code-behind file. The first section deals with the `ToggleSearchForm` `LinkButton` control and toggling the `ISearchControl` component between the simple and advanced mode. The second section contains all the overridden virtual methods defined in the `ReportFramework` abstract class.

Toggling Between ISearchControl Components

Creating the togging functionality is a fairly simple process. You already know there is a `LinkButton` named `ToggleSearchForm` on the Report Page. When the user clicks this `LinkButton`, the Report Page posts backs and executes the `ToggleSearchForm_Click` method. This method changes the `SearchFormIndex` from `0` to `1`, or from `1` to `0`, depending on the current value of `SearchFormIndex`. You'll see how the Report Page uses the `SearchFormIndex` to determine which `ISearchControl` component to load when we discuss the overridden

SearchFormFileName method. For reference, when the SearchFormIndex is set to 0, the page displays the simple form. When it is 1, the page displays the advanced form. After setting the SearchFormIndex, the method calls LoadSearchForm because the SearchFormIndex changed and the ReportFramework needs to load the new ISearchControl component into the page.

The Pre_Render method looks at the SearchFormIndex value and assigns Toggle➥ SearchForm.Text a value describing the opposite search form. If the page is displaying the simple form, then the ToggleSearchForm.Text contains "Advanced Search"; if the advanced form is shown, then ToggleSearchForm.Text contains "Simple Search". This allows the user to either fill out the current form or click on the appropriately named LinkButton to take them to the other form.

Overriding ReportFramework's Virtual Members

Overriding the virtual members from ReportFramework is a fairly painless process because the Visual Studio IDE creates the member definitions for you. On top of that, many of the members only require one line of code, so you can begin to appreciate how easy it is to create reports using a reporting framework.

The first overridden method is SearchFormFileName. This method returns the file name of the ISearchControl component to the LoadSearchForm method in the ReportFramework class. Remember, the LoadSearchForm method uses the file name provided by SearchFormFileName to load the search form into the Report Page. You can see that SearchFormFileName uses the SearchFormIndex to determine which ISearchControl component file name to return. If the SearchFormIndex is 0, it returns the file name for the simple search form. Otherwise, it returns the file name for the advanced search form. This, along with the toggling functionality used to set the SearchFormIndex, is all you need to toggle between ISearchControl components.

The next six overridden methods are all one-liners that return a specific value or control reference.

PaginationFormFileName returns a string containing the file name of the IPagination➥ Control to load into the page. If you want to allow your users to select a different paging navigation form based on a profile setting or some other value, then you'll need to account for that setting in this method.

SearchFormPH returns a reference to the PlaceHolder control where you want to display your ISearchControl component. If you do not want to use an ISearchControl component on the Report Page, then return Nothing as the value of this method. Also remember to override the GetSqlQuery method because it relies on the ISearchControl component to acquire the search query for the report.

PaginationFormPH returns a reference to the PlaceHolder control where you want to display your IPaginationControl component. If you do not want to use pagination, then return Nothing as the value of this method and the ReportFramework will not use pagination.

ReportGrid returns a reference to the GridView control where the ReportFramework outputs the report data. This is a required control. Returning Nothing as the value of this method causes an exception to be thrown.

ConnectionStringKey returns the key associated with the connection string that you want to use to connect the Report Page to the database. If the key is invalid, or the key points to an invalid connection string, it causes an exception to be thrown.

ItemsPerPage returns an Integer defining how many items should be shown per page. This is only applicable for reports using pagination. If each page should contain 10 items, then return 10. If each page should contain 20 items, then return 20.

The last method, SetSortExpression, accepts a SqlQuery object and a sort expression. Its job is to set up the appropriate ORDER BY clause for the SqlQuery object. It doesn't need to worry about reversing the sort order based on the sort direction because ReportFramework handles that automatically. The easiest way to set up the ORDER BY clause is to use a SELECT CASE statement to determine the CASE of the incoming sortExpression and to set the ORDER BY clause accordingly. You can see in the preceding code that each case has its own unique ORDER BY clause. Also, you should always include a default CASE in the event the sortExpression is an invalid value. In the preceding example, the query uses the sort order in the default case when a user clicks on the CustomerID column because the CustomerID column's sort expression is *not* handled by any other Case statements.

Running the Report Page

Now you have a working Report Page, so go ahead and run it so you can play around with the different pieces of functionality. The simple search form appears by default, but you can toggle between the simple and advanced search forms by using the link button that appears under the search form.

Click on the **Search** button. The results of the search are displayed in sets of 10 on the Report Page. Use the paging navigation to move to the next page, the previous page, and to a page in the middle. You can enter criteria in the search form to filter the search. Make sure to take a look at the total number of records being displayed and the page count information as you update the query.

You should also click on a couple of column headings to see the sorting capabilities. Make sure you click on a column heading twice to see the report sort by the column in ascending and descending order. You may also want to view the page source and look at the ViewState size. Notice that it does have some data, but it remains fairly manageable as you navigate through the report.

If you happen to have a utility that shows the total number of database requests being processed, then you can see how overriding the BindInPreLoad property can help database performance. Run a search and make sure you navigate through each page of data. Take note of how many database requests were processed. Then override the BindInPreLoad property and make sure it returns False. Execute the same search and navigate through each page of data. Compare the number of database requests.

Summary

In this chapter, you learned that developing against a reporting framework helps you make reports quicker, more accurately, and with more consistency. You learned how to make search forms and how to toggle between a simple and advanced search form using the reporting framework. You also built a reusable paging component that is far superior to the built-in paging component available on the GridView control. Plus, you explored the performance to functionality trade-offs regarding data binding in the PreLoad versus the PreRender method, and you saw how to allow for either scenario using the BindInPreLoad property.

Creating a reusable reporting framework takes a lot of time, effort, and thought, but it definitely pays off in the long run. No doubt, you'll continue to create search pages reports, so you might as well not reinvent the wheel each time you do. This chapter has given you a better understanding of the thought process and design considerations that go into building reusable components and frameworks for reporting.

CHAPTER 10

Web-Based Wizards: Avoiding Duplicate Data Entry

Complete disarray. People in the injury compensation department for a large fulfillment company had been entering employee information for years with no process in place to avoid data duplication. A claim for Beth Smith is sent in, for example, and she is added to the system. All the information relating to her claim, injury information, eyewitness accounts, and insurance data are all captured in the system. Later on, more information comes in regarding the incident, but this time the name on the form is Elizabeth Smith. You can see where this is going. Someone looks for Elizabeth Smith, doesn't find her, and creates a new record even though Beth Smith is already in the system. The new information is entered into a new record, so the old record has no new data, and the new record has no old data. To make matters worse, sometimes information would come in and users would simply enter it as new without ever even trying to determine whether or not it had previously been entered. As a result of the duplicated data and duplicated effort, their systems and processes were inefficient, ineffective, and in complete disarray.

Data entry will be a part of just about any business application you develop, so you must consider how you'll keep people from unnecessarily entering data. Many developers create search pages that allow users to check for a record before entering it into the system; however, those search pages are not an integral part of the record-adding process. Users are supposed to go and check for the record, but the responsibility for doing so rests entirely on the user. As such, the step is often skipped when the user is in a hurry.

ASP.NET 2.0 features a new web-based `Wizard` control that allows you to guide a user through a well-defined, step-by-step process. You can use wizards for just about anything that you want, including searching, reporting, and displaying information. This chapter shows you how to use a web-based wizard that forces users to search for duplicates as part of the adding process. Here's what you can expect in this chapter:

- *Wizard Control Overview:* Gives a basic description of the `Wizard` control, features, properties, and how to work with one in the IDE.

- *Phonetic Searching:* Exact match searching isn't very effective when trying to avoid data duplication because it assumes the user know exactly how to spell someone's name and that an alternate spelling isn't being used. SQL soundex functions allow you to search for close matches based on the phonetics of a word instead of the exact spelling and can be very useful in avoiding data duplication.

- *Creating the Add Employee Wizard:* Demonstrates how to use web-based wizards and SQL soundex searching functionality to create a step-by-step process for adding employees to a system and avoid data duplication.

Let's start by taking a quick look at the new `Wizard` control.

Wizard Control Overview

Over the past few years, wizards have gained in popularity because they provide a simple step-by-step interface for walking users through detailed processes. Most users are familiar and comfortable with wizards, so it should come as no surprise that wizards have made their way into the web-based world to help walk users through web-based processes. Creating wizards in ASP.NET 1.x either took multiple pages or complex page logic to sequence items on a single page. ASP.NET 2.0 ships with a new user control called the `Wizard`, which simplifies the creation of web-based wizards on a single page.

You can find the `Wizard` control near the bottom of the **Standard** tab in the Visual Studio IDE's toolbox. Adding a `Wizard` to your page is easy; just drag the control from the toolbox to the location where you want the `Wizard` on your page. By default, the IDE creates a `Wizard` control with two steps, as shown in Listing 10-1.

Listing 10-1. *Default Wizard Control Definition*

```
<asp:Wizard ID="Wizard1" runat="server">
    <WizardSteps>
        <asp:WizardStep ID="WizardStep1" runat="server" Title="Step 1">
        </asp:WizardStep>
        <asp:WizardStep ID="WizardStep2" runat="server" Title="Step 2">
        </asp:WizardStep>
    </WizardSteps>
</asp:Wizard>
```

Before we get into how to create and modify steps in the wizard, let's take a moment to look at the layout of the `Wizard` control and pieces that make it up.

Layout and Parts of a Wizard Control

`Wizard` controls are responsible for displaying the number of steps in the wizard, handling navigation between those steps, and displaying the actual step content. As such, there are three distinct sections to a `Wizard` control. Figure 10-1 shows the layout and appearance of all three steps in a three-step wizard. You can see how each section of the wizard appears throughout the various steps.

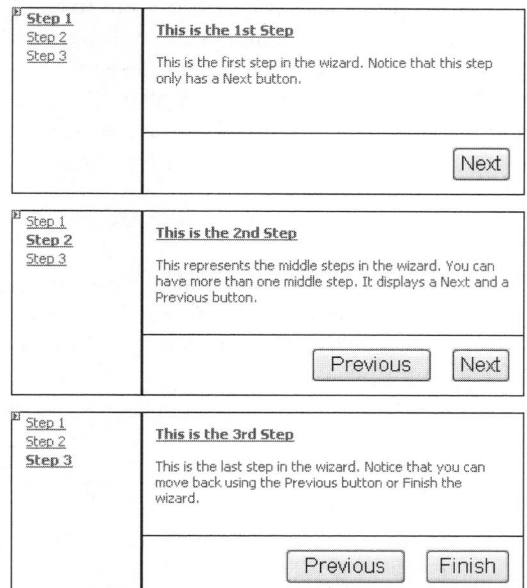

Figure 10-1. *Displays the layout and appearance of all three steps in a three-step wizard*

■ Note `BasicWizard.aspx` in the example application for this chapter (in the Source Code area of the Apress website at `http://www.apress.com`) contains the markup for `Wizard` shown in Figure 10-1. For now, we are only focusing on the visual layout of a wizard.

The first section is the sidebar, which appears on the left side of the wizard. The sidebar is responsible for displaying a list of steps in the wizard and identifying which step the user is currently on. Users can click on a step name in the sidebar to jump to that step. Of course, events in the `Wizard` control allow you to stop users from jumping to a step prematurely or returning to a step after it has been completed. You can use the default sidebar template or create a custom template for the sidebar by editing the `SideBarTemplate` in the control.

The second section of a wizard is the actual step content. It appears in the upper-right section of the wizard and is normally the largest section in the control. You can enter content for a step directly in the IDE by selecting the appropriate step in the sidebar and then selecting the content area in the `Wizard` control. You can drag ASP.NET controls into that section or enter any HTML you desire. The content you place in the step appears between the `<asp:WizardStep>` and `</asp:WizardStep>` elements inside the `<WizardSteps/>` section of a `Wizard` control (see Listing 10-1).

The last section of a wizard is the navigation section. This section displays navigational buttons allowing the user to move to the next and previous steps in the wizard, and a **Finish** button to finish out the wizard on the last step. It can also display a **Cancel** button to exit the wizard without finishing. You can modify the appearance of the navigation section by editing the `StartNavigationTemplate`, `StepNavigationTemplate`, and the `FinishNavigationTemplate`.

There are three navigation templates because there are three different types of steps in a wizard all requiring different navigation options. The StartNavigationTemplate only displays on the first step of a wizard. It shows a **Next** button but no **Previous** button because no previous step exists on the first step. The StepNavigationTemplate displays on all middle steps of a wizard and shows both a **Next** and a **Previous** button. The FinishNavigationTemplate displays on the last step of the wizard and shows a **Previous** button and a **Finish** button.

Important Wizard Properties and Events

You can control the appearance and behavior of a wizard by modifying any of its 75-plus properties. Many of the properties you've already seen—such as the EnableViewState, TabIndex, and Visible properties—so they don't require discussion. The Table 10-1 outlines the most pertinent properties and gives a description as to their purpose.

Table 10-1. *Important Wizard Properties*

Property Name	Type	Description
ActiveStep	ActiveStepBase (Read-only)	Gives you a reference to the ActiveStepBase object, which represents the current step displayed in the wizard. You use the ActiveStepBase object to get or set step-specific properties.
ActiveStepIndex	Integer	Identifies the active wizard step. This is a zero-based index.
CancelDestination➥ PageUrl	String	URL where the user is redirected when the Cancel button is clicked.
DisplayCancelButton	Boolean	Determines whether to display a Cancel button in the navigation section.
DisplaySideBar	Boolean	Determines whether or not to display the sidebar.
FinishDestination➥ PageUrl	String	URL where the user is redirected after the wizard completes.
NavigationStyle	TableItemStyle	Defines various style elements dictating the visual appearance of the navigation section.
SideBarStyle	TableItemStyle	Defines various style elements dictating the visual appearance of the sidebar section.
StepStyle	TableItemStyle	Defines various style elements dictating the visual appearance of the step section (that is, the main content area of the wizard).
WizardSteps	WizardStepCollection	Maintains an ordered listing of the various steps in the wizard as a collection of WizardStepBase objects.

There are 24 wizard properties that deal specifically with button appearance in the various navigation templates. Their names and descriptions are highly repetitive, so they aren't listed here in their entirety; however, they are important, and you need to know how to use them. The properties appear in the form <ButtonName><Property>. A total of six different buttons are exposed by templates in the wizard and each of the buttons has four properties (6 buttons

* 4 properties = 24 total properties). Tables 10-2 and 10-3 outline the different button names and properties.

Table 10-2. *The Six Buttons Exposed by Templates in the Wizard*

Button Property Prefix	Description
`CancelButton`	Cancel button that may appear on all templates in the wizard
`FinishCompleteButton`	Finish button that appears in the `FinishNavigationTemplate`
`FinishPreviousButton`	Previous button that appears in the `FinishNavigationTemplate`
`StartNextButton`	Next button that appears in the `StartNavigationTemplate`
`StepNextButton`	Next button that appears in the `StepNavigationTemplate`
`StepPreviousButton`	Previous button that appears in the `StepNavigationTemplate`

Each of these buttons listed in Table 10-2 has four different properties as shown in Table 10-3.

Table 10-3. *Button Properties*

Property Name	Type	Description
`Type`	`ButtonType`	Defines whether the button appears as a button, link, or image
`Text`	`String`	Defines the text that appears on the button when it is a button or a link
`ImageUrl`	`String`	URL of the image displayed when the button is an image
`Style`	`Style`	Defines various style elements dictating the visual appearance of the button

So, if you combine the button name from Table 10-2 with a property name from Table 10-3, then you end up with a property name on the `Wizard` control. The `StepNextButtonType` property, for instance, defines the button type of the **Next** button that appears in the `Step➥NavigationTemplate`. The `FinishCompleteText` property defines the text that appears on the **Finish** button in the `FinishNavigationTemplate`, and so on.

`Wizard` controls also expose a number of events that allow you to respond to certain user actions and programmatic changes to the control. Most of the events revolve around navigation because the wizard is really a means of navigating a user through a predefined series of steps. Table 10-4 contains a listing of the events the `Wizard` control raises.

Table 10-4. *Wizard Events*

Event Name	Description
ActiveStepChanged	Fires when the user navigates to another step in the wizard.
CancelButtonClick	Fires when a user clicks on the Cancel button. This signifies that the user wants to exit the wizard.
FinishButtonClick	Fires when the user clicks the Finish button. This signifies that the user has completed the wizard, and you can run any code that you need to run to finalize the wizard process.
NextButtonClick	Fires when the user clicks the Next button. You can use this event to manage the way users navigate forward through the wizard.
PreviousButtonClick	Fires when the user clicks the Previous button. You can use this event to manage the way users navigate backwards through the wizard.
SideBarButtonClick	Fires when the user clicks on a step link in the sidebar. You can use this event to manage the way users navigate through the wizard.
*Activate	Fires after the wizard deactivates the last step. You can use this event to set up resources that are required by the step and to implement step-skipping logic.
*Deactivate	Fires when the user navigates away from a step. You can use this event to release resources that are no longer required and to run validation logic on the step.

** These events are attached to each* `WizardStep` *in the* `Wizard`.

As you move from one step to another in the Wizard, the events listed in the preceding table fire in the following sequence. First, one of the `NextButtonClick`, `PreviousButtonClick`, or `SideBarButtonClick` events occur (only one). After the click event has been processed, the `Deactivate` event of the old step fires, followed by the `Activate` event of the new step. Lastly, the `ActiveStepChanged` event fires indicating that the new step has been activated successfully. If you click on the **Cancel** or **Finish** buttons, the `CancelButtonClick` or the `FinishButtonClick` events fire, but none of the other events are ever raised (not even the deactivate events). As mentioned before, most of the events exposed by the wizard are useful for controlling navigation. You'll learn about that after we discuss how to actually add steps to a wizard.

Adding Steps to the Wizard

Your first task when making a wizard is determining how you want to lead your users through the task at hand. This requires that you think through which screens to make available and the sequence in which those screens should be displayed. After you have determined how many steps you want and where they should be, you need to add them to the wizard.

There are two ways you can add steps to a `Wizard` control. The easiest way is to use the `WizardStep` collection editor. It provides you with an intuitive interface for creating and rearranging steps. You can access the collection editor by clicking on the ellipsis next to the

WizardSteps property in the property editor, by right-clicking on the Wizard control and selecting Add/Remove Wizard Steps from the context menu, or by choosing Wizard Tasks ➤ Add/Remove Wizard Steps. You can see an example of the WizardStep Collection Editor in Figure 10-2.

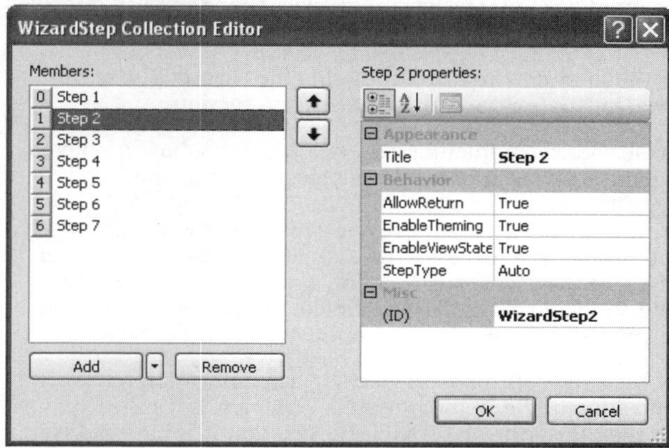

Figure 10-2. WizardStep *Collection Editor*

Using the WizardStep Collection Editor should be fairly intuitive. You can add new WizardStep items by clicking the **Add** button, and you can remove the selected WizardStep item by clicking the **Remove** button. The arrows to the right of the WizardStep listing allow you to rearrange the steps by moving the selected item up and down. On the right side of the collection editor, you'll see the properties for the selected WizardStep. The WizardStep properties are shown in Table 10-5, and the WizardStepType descriptions are given in Table 10-6.

Table 10-5. WizardStep *Properties*

Property Name	Type	Description
Title	String	Descriptive title of the step. This text is displayed in the sidebar along with the titles of all the other steps.
AllowReturn	Boolean	Defines whether or not the user may return to this step from subsequent steps or from the sidebar. Setting this value to False causes subsequent steps to hide the Previous button and renders the sidebar link useless (although it's still clickable), so the user can't navigate back to the step. The user *can* navigate forward to the step if they can somehow get to a previous step in the sequence. If you want to avoid this, simply set the AllowReturn value for all the steps to False.
StepType	WizardStepType	This property determines which navigation to display for the step. There are five different WizardStepType enumerations: Start, Step, Finish, Complete, and Auto.

Table 10-6. `WizardStepType` *Properties*

WizardStepType	Description
`Start`	Identifies the step as the starting step. The wizard displays the `StartNavigationTemplate` in the navigation section.
`Step`	Identifies the step as a middle step. The wizard displays the `StepNavigationTemplate` in the navigation section.
`Finish`	Identifies the step as the final step before completing the wizard. The wizard displays the `FinishNavigationTemplate` in the navigation section.
`Complete`	Identifies the step as the wizard completing step. When the user has completed the wizard, you can opt to send the user to another location using the `FinishDestinationPageUrl`, or you can allow the Wizard to display the "Complete" step. The Complete step is a means by which you can display a message to the user indicating the success of the wizard, provide links to other locations, or otherwise give the user some direction as to what to do now that the wizard is complete. When displaying the Complete step, the wizard does not display navigation buttons in the navigation section.
`Auto`	When a step is set to `Auto`, the control determines which navigation template to use based on the position of the step in the step sequence. If it's the first step in the sequence, then the control displays the `StartNavigationTemplate`. If it's the last step in the sequence, the control displays the `FinishNavigationTemplate`. If it's anything else, the control displays the `StepNavigationTemplate`.

■ **Caution** You should always specify a title for your wizard steps. If you fail to provide a title, the wizard uses the `ID` of the template as its name in the sidebar. If you fail to provide both a title and an `ID`, then the wizard does not display anything in the sidebar, but displays the step when users click on the **Next** or **Back** buttons. This can be *very* confusing, so make sure you always specify a title.

When you're finished adding, editing, and removing steps from the wizard, click the **OK** button to save your changes. The HTML in the page is updated to reflect your changes. You can also opt to manually add a `WizardStep` by adding a new `<asp:WizardStep>` element under the `<WizardSteps>` element as shown in Listing 10-2.

Listing 10-2. `WizardStep` *Elements in the UI*

```
<asp:Wizard ID="Wizard1" runat="server" ActiveStepIndex="0">
    <WizardSteps>
        <asp:WizardStep ID="WizardStep1" runat="server" Title="Step 1">
            <!-- Step 1 Html and ASP.NET Controls -->
        </asp:WizardStep>
        <asp:WizardStep ID="WizardStep2" runat="server" Title="Step 2">
            <!-- Step 2 Html and ASP.NET Controls -->
        </asp:WizardStep>
        <asp:WizardStep ID="WizardStep3" runat="server" Title="Step 3">
            <!-- Step 3 Html and ASP.NET Controls -->
```

```
        </asp:WizardStep>
    </WizardSteps>
</asp:Wizard>
```

After adding a WizardStep to the page, you can add content for the WizardStep visually in the IDE or manually in the HTML. To switch between steps in the IDE, click on the step links in the sidebar of the wizard. Clicking these links changes the ActiveStepIndex property of the Wizard control and displays the selected step in the IDE. You can also manually set the ActiveStepIndex in the property editor.

■ **Tip** Whatever step is shown in the IDE will be shown when the page displays to the user. You may want to set the ActiveStepIndex to 0 when the page first loads to avoid accidentally displaying the wrong starting step.

Any content you add to the step appears between the <asp:WizardStep> and </asp:WizardStep> elements of that particular step, as denoted in Listing 10-2. You can also manually edit the HTML in the section if you so desire. Now that you know how to create steps, let's take a look at how to control navigation between those steps.

Controlling Wizard Navigation

Navigation is a central theme in Wizard controls because they exist to intelligently guide people through a task. You have complete control over how users may navigate through the steps in your wizard. Your wizard can require users to go through the wizard one step at a time, restrict users from going backwards after they have completed a step, or allow your users to jump forwards and backwards at will.

You control wizard navigation by responding to the navigation events exposed by the Wizard control. The navigation events include the FinishButtonClick, NextButtonClick, Previous➥ButtonClick, and SideBarButtonClick events. All these events have a WizardNavigationEventArgs parameter, which is, by default, named e. This parameter identifies the index of the current step via e.CurrentStepIndex and the index of the step to which the user is attempting to move via e.NextStepIndex. It may help to think of e.NextStepIndex as the requested index because it could be the next step, a previous step, or a couple of steps backward or forward in the sequence. You can also use the e parameter to cancel navigation by setting e.Cancel to True or change the step to be shown by setting e.ActiveStepIndex to the required step. The Activate and Deactivate events also play a key role in running validation for specific steps.

The following couple sections describe various navigation scenarios that you may encounter and how to code for those scenarios.

Only Allow Users to Move Forward One Step at a Time or Back to Any Step

Users are limited to moving one step at a time from the Next and Previous buttons. The only location from which a user can jump forward multiple steps is from the sidebar links. You have a couple of options for dealing with this issue. The first option is to set the DisplaySideBar property to False, which takes away the user's ability to see and use the sidebar. This effectively solves the problem, but the sidebar is very useful for users who want to know where they are in the process and how many steps remain.

Another option is to add code to the SideBarButtonClick that keeps the user from moving forward more than one step at a time as shown in Listing 10-3.

Listing 10-3. *Only Allow Users to Move Forward One Step at a Time*

```
'***************************************************************************
Protected Sub SideBarButtonClick(ByVal sender As Object, _
  ByVal e As System.Web.UI.WebControls.WizardNavigationEventArgs) _
  Handles Wizard1.SideBarButtonClick

    If e.NextStepIndex > e.CurrentStepIndex + 1 Then e.Cancel = True

End Sub
```

This code checks to see if the NextStepIndex is more than one step away and, if so, cancels navigation. You could also just move the user ahead one step, but that may be confusing if the user clicks on one step and gets another. Users can still navigate back to any step in the step sequence using this code because all previous step indexes will be less than the CurrentStepIndex.

Skip an Unnecessary Step When the User Clicks the Next Button

You can skip an unnecessary step by placing skip code in the NextButtonClick event handler. The code should determine the step to which the user is attempting to navigate and then whether or not to skip the step. In Listing 10-4, Step 2 is skipped when the chkSkipStep2 check box is checked.

Listing 10-4. *Skipping an Unncessary Step*

```
'***************************************************************************
Protected Sub Wizard1_NextButtonClick(ByVal sender As Object, _
  ByVal e As System.Web.UI.WebControls.WizardNavigationEventArgs) _
  Handles Wizard1.NextButtonClick

    'Remember, step indexes are zero-based so index 1 represents step 2
    Select Case e.NextStepIndex
        Case 1 'Skip logic for step #2
            If Me.chkSkipStep2.Checked Then Wizard1.ActiveStepIndex = 2
        Case 2 'Skip logic for step #3
        Case 3 'Skip logic for step #4
    End Select

End Sub
```

This code uses a Select Case statement to determine which step the user is requesting, and then runs step-skipping logic for each step in the individual Case statements. You can see that when chkSkipStep2 is checked, the event handler sets the ActiveStepIndex to 2, which represents step 3 in the sequence. Notice that you don't set e.Cancel = True when you change the index to which the user should navigate. Setting e.Cancel cancels all navigation, even if you set the ActiveStepIndex in code.

Skip an Unnecessary Step When the User Clicks the Previous Button

If you implement logic to skip steps in the `NextButtonClick` event handler, it seems like you would also have to implement similar logic to skip steps in the `PreviousButtonClick` event handler. But such isn't the case because the `Wizard` control actually maintains a list of the steps the user has visited and automatically routes the user to the last visited step. Therefore, if a step was skipped going forward, it's also skipped going backward, without any additional coding required.

Of course, this can also be very awkward if you allow your users to jump all over the place using the sidebar. Let's say a user visits Step 1, then Step 5, then Step 8, then Step 3, and lastly Step 6. From Step 6, the user clicks the previous button trying to get back to Step 5. Instead of being taken to Step 6, the user will actually be taken to Step 3, then Step 8, and then Step 5, because that's the order in which the user originally visited the pages. This brings us to our next navigation scenario.

■ **Note** You can acquire an `ICollection` object containing the listing of previously visited steps using the `GetHistory()` function of the `Wizard` control.

Removing an Unnecessary Step Completely

One problem with placing step-skipping logic in the `NextButtonClick` event handler is that users can still access the skipped step from the sidebar. At times, you'll want users to be able to get back to skipped steps, but sometimes you'll want to completely remove a step even from the sidebar.

Removing a step in its entirety is very easy because the steps exist as a collection exposed from the `WizardSteps` property of the `Wizard` control. To remove an item, you simply use the collection's `Remove` function and pass in the appropriate `WizardStep` object. Listing 10-5 shows you how to remove a step from the `Wizard` control.

Listing 10-5. *Completely Removing Steps from the Wizard*

```
'***************************************************************************
Protected Sub Wizard1_Load(ByVal sender As Object, _
  ByVal e As System.EventArgs) Handles Wizard1.Load

    If Me.chkRemoveStep2.Checked Then
        Wizard1.WizardSteps.Remove(WizardStep2)
        Me.chkSkipStep2.Checked = False
    End If

End Sub
```

Inside the event handler for the wizard's load event, the code checks to see if the `chkRemoveStep2` check box is checked. If so, then the method removes `WizardStep2` from the

WizardSteps collection. When the Wizard control renders, Step 2 no longer appears in the sidebar, and users can't reach it using the navigation buttons.

Always Navigate to the Previous Step in the Step Sequence Using the Previous Button

If you want to avoid the awkwardness of jumping around using the step history, you can force the **Previous** button to always move to the previous step in the sequence. To do this, explicitly set the ActiveStepIndex to e.CurrentStepIndex - 1 as shown in Listing 10-6.

Listing 10-6. *Force Previous Button to Return User to Previous Step in the Sequence*

```
'***************************************************************************
Protected Sub Wizard1_PreviousButtonClick(ByVal sender As Object, _
  ByVal e As System.Web.UI.WebControls.WizardNavigationEventArgs) _
  Handles Wizard1.PreviousButtonClick

    Wizard1.ActiveStepIndex = e.CurrentStepIndex - 1

End Sub
```

This forces the ActiveStepIndex to be one less than the CurrentStepIndex, which effectively displays the previous step in the sequence.

Remain on a Step If the Step Contains Invalid Data

First, you should always try to validate data on the client side if at all possible. Of course, there are times when client-side validation isn't an option, such as when you need to check data in a database. In these situations, you can use the Deactivate event of a step to validate data and force the user back to the step if the data is invalid (see Listing 10-7).

Listing 10-7. *Validating Data in Wizard Step*

```
'***************************************************************************
Protected Sub WizardStep1_Deactivate(ByVal sender As Object, _
  ByVal e As System.EventArgs) Handles WizardStep1.Deactivate

    If Not chkStep1IsValid.Checked Then
        Wizard1.ActiveStepIndex = Wizard1.WizardSteps.IndexOf(WizardStep1)
    End If

End Sub
```

This code determines the validity of Step 1 by checking whether or not the chkStep1IsValid check box has been checked. Obviously, your code will have more complicated logic to determine whether or not the input is valid. If the data isn't valid, the step acquires its step index by passing itself into the `WizardSteps.IndexOf` method, then assigns that step index back to the `Wizard1.ActiveStepIndex` property, forcing the wizard to redisplay the step where the invalid data was entered. In this situation, you would also want to display a message to the user indicating which data is invalid and how to change it.

■ **Note** If you're using client-side validation, you should also use `Page.IsValid` to confirm the user input is valid before allowing navigation events to occur.

Determining Which Button Was Clicked in the ActiveStepChanged Event

Although the need should be rare, you may find occasions when it's helpful to know which navigation button was clicked in the `ActiveStepChanged` event. Unfortunately the `ActiveStepChanged` event does not contain any arguments identifying which button the user clicked, the current step or the next step. But there is nothing stopping you from setting page-level variables to help you with that determination. Listing 10-8 shows how you can store information during the `Click` events for later use in the `ActiveStepChanged` event.

Listing 10-8. *Validating Data in Wizard Step*

```
'***************************************************************************
Private NextButtonClicked = false
Private PrevButtonClicked = false
Private SideBarClicked = false
Private MyEventArgs As WizardNavigationEventArgs

'***************************************************************************
Protected Sub Wizard1_NextButtonClick(ByVal sender As Object, _
  ByVal e As System.Web.UI.WebControls.WizardNavigationEventArgs) _
  Handles Wizard1.NextButtonClick

    NextButtonClicked = true
    MyEventArgs = e

End Sub

'***************************************************************************
Protected Sub SideBarButtonClick(ByVal sender As Object, _
  ByVal e As System.Web.UI.WebControls.WizardNavigationEventArgs) _
  Handles Wizard1.SideBarButtonClick

    PrevButtonClicked = true
    MyEventArgs = e

End Sub
```

```
'*************************************************************************
Protected Sub Wizard1_PreviousButtonClick(ByVal sender As Object, _
  ByVal e As System.Web.UI.WebControls.WizardNavigationEventArgs) _
  Handles Wizard1.PreviousButtonClick

    SideBarClicked = true
    MyEventArgs = e

End Sub

'*************************************************************************
Protected Sub AddWizard_ActiveStepChanged(ByVal sender As Object, _
  ByVal e As System.EventArgs) Handles AddWizard.ActiveStepChanged

    'You can use NextButtonClicked, PrevButtonClicked, SideBarClicked, and
    'EventArgs from this method (or any other method) to help determine
    'navigational requirements

End Sub
```

By now you should have a fairly good understanding of how to control navigation in a `Wizard` control. Next, you'll learn about creating custom content using templates.

Working with Templates

The `Wizard` is one of the many controls in ASP.NET 2.0 that supports templates (see the "Templated Controls" section in Chapter 5). Templates allow you to alter the visual layout of a control while still retaining the control's built-in functionality. Basically, a control expects certain types of child controls with specific names to be present inside a template, but allows you to place those controls anywhere in the template that you want. This gives you a great degree of visual flexibility and allows you to respond to events to which you would normally not have access.

Here is the scenario for this example. You want to add a title to the sidebar section of the wizard because you think it will make the wizard look more professional. Because there are no properties on the wizard allowing you to define a title bar, you have to manually edit the `SideBarTemplate` to create it. You have also received complaints from some users who say it's confusing for the sidebar to displays links to future steps if you can't navigate to those future steps by clicking on the links. Currently, you allow users to move forward using the **Next** button and back using the **Previous** button or the links on the sidebar. You want to make the sidebar navigation more intuitive for the user by only showing links for the current and previous items. Future items should be displayed in the sidebar but not as links.

First, create a new `Wizard` control by dragging the control from the toolbox onto a page. Add six or seven steps to the control and give them descriptive titles. You can also take this time to familiarize yourself with creating content for the steps. When you're finished adding steps and step content, right-click on either the sidebar or the navigation section of the wizard to display the control context menu. Near the bottom of the context menu, you'll see a section specifically for the `Wizard` control. There are four **Convert to Template** menu options. These menu items convert the control's default output for a template into an editable format that you can use as a base for creating a template. Click the **Convert to SideBarTemplate** menu item as shown in Figure 10-3.

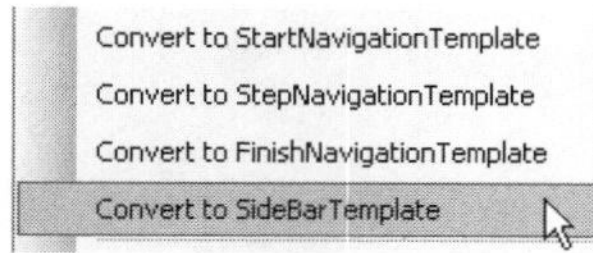

Figure 10-3. *Converting a template from the control's context menu*

After you click the menu item, the IDE acquires the `Wizard` control's default output for the `SideBarTemplate` and places the template in your control. The code it adds looks like Listing 10-9.

Listing 10-9. *Converted* `SideBarTemplate` *(Appears in the Wizard Control Definition)*

```
<SideBarTemplate>
    <asp:DataList ID="SideBarList" runat="server"
      OnItemDataBound="SideBarListBound">
        <SelectedItemStyle Font-Bold="True" />
        <ItemTemplate>
            <asp:LinkButton ID="SideBarButton" runat="server" />
        </ItemTemplate>
    </asp:DataList>
</SideBarTemplate>
```

Notice that the template contains a single ASP.NET `DataList` named `SideBarList`, and that `SideBarList` has a `LinkButton` child control named `SideBarButton`. Behind the scenes, the `Wizard` control binds its `WizardSteps` collection to the `DataList` and sets the `Text` property of the `LinkButton` to the `WizardStep` object's `Title` property. It also sets the `CommandName` property of the `LinkButton` to identify which step the user clicks.

Now that you have a `SideBarTemplate`, you can edit it directly in the IDE or in the source. To edit a template in the IDE, right-click on the `Wizard` control to display the control's context menu. Locate the **Edit Template** menu item and move your mouse over it. Allow it to display its submenu, and then click on the `SideBarTemplate` menu item in the submenu as shown in Figure 10-4.

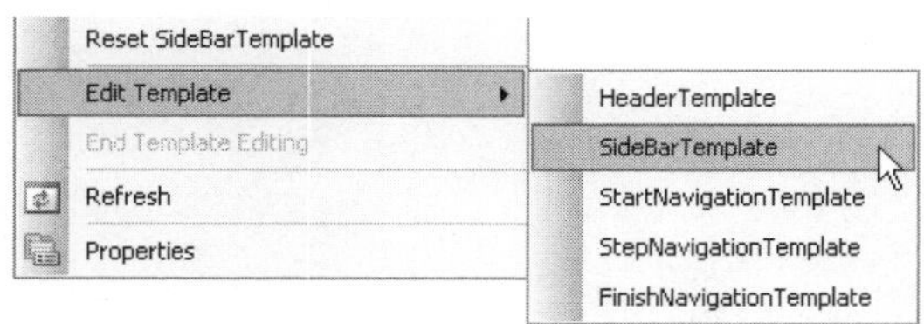

Figure 10-4. *Navigating to the* `SideBarTemplate` *context menu item*

This displays the `SideBarTemplate` in the IDE where you can edit it. Of course, the only item in the `SideBarTemplate` is a `DataList` with a blank button, so the `SideBarTemplate` looks a bit empty when you first see it (see Figure 10-5).

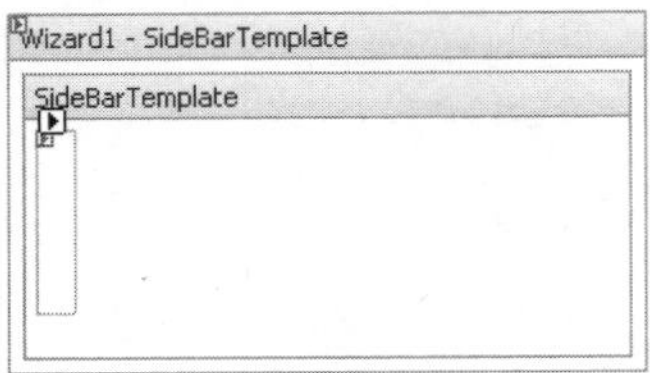

Figure 10-5. *Editing the* `SideBarTemplate` *in the IDE*

At this point, you can add the sidebar title to the `SideBarTemplate` using the graphical template editor just as you would normally in the Visual Studio IDE. The title should be a `<div>` tag with a 100% width, Gainsboro background, and bold text that reads `Wizard Steps`. After you create it, it should look like Figure 10-6 in the template editor.

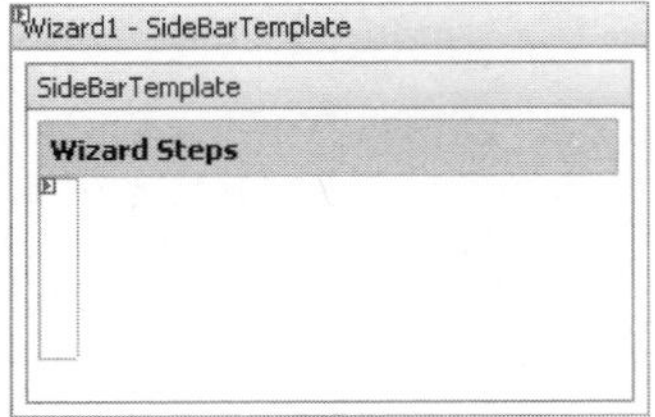

Figure 10-6. *Adding a sidebar title in the IDE*

While you have the template open, go ahead and set the event handler for the `Item➥ DataBound` event to `SideBarListBound`. You'll be using this momentarily to manipulate the links displayed in the sidebar. To set the `ItemDataBound` event handler in the IDE, select the `DataList` in the template. In the property window, click on the **Events** button (with the lightning bolt) near the top of the window. This displays a list of control events and allows you to define event handlers for the events. Double-click the `ItemDataBound` event. The IDE automatically creates a method stub for the event named `SideBarList_ItemDataBound` with the appropriate event arguments (see Figure 10-7).

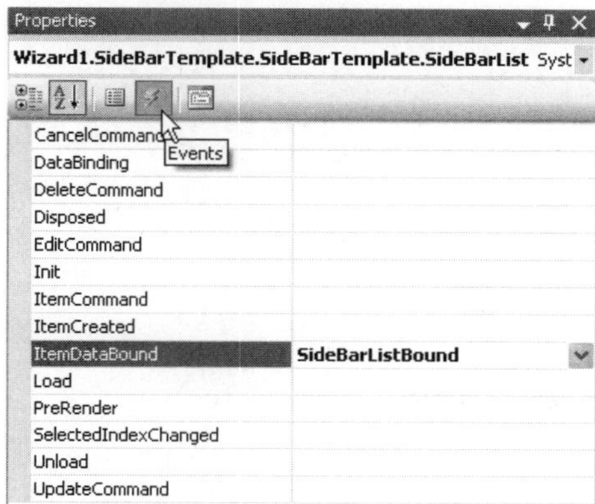

Figure 10-7. *Setting the event handler for the* `ItemDataBound` *event to* `SideBarListBound`

When you're done editing the template, right-click on the template and select **End Template Editing** from the context menu. This allows the control to redisplay using the updated template.

Before moving on to dealing with the links in the sidebar, let me reiterate that you can also manually edit the templates in the page source. In fact, it can sometimes be easier to work with the source than the template in the IDE. Following, you'll find the `SideBarTemplate` source. If you have already edited the `SideBarTemplate` in the IDE, make sure your source matches up with what is shown. Or you can manually enter the text shown in Listing 10-10 into the `SideBarTemplate`.

Listing 10-10. *Modified Sidebar Template (Appears in the* `Wizard` *Control Definition)*

```
<SideBarTemplate>
    <div style="width:100%; background-color:Gainsboro;padding:5px;
      color:Black;font-weight:bold;">Wizard Steps</div>
    <asp:DataList ID="SideBarList" runat="server"
      OnItemDataBound="SideBarListBound">
        <SelectedItemStyle Font-Bold="True" />
        <ItemTemplate>
              <asp:LinkButton ID="SideBarButton" runat="server"/>
        </ItemTemplate>
    </asp:DataList>
</SideBarTemplate>
```

Now let's focus on disabling future step links in the sidebar. You can see in Listing 10-10 that the `SideBarList_ItemDataBound` method handles the `ItemDataBound` event of the `DataList` in the sidebar. You just need to code the method in such a way that it disables any links for steps that are greater than the current step. Listing 10-11 provides the code for the method.

Listing 10-11. *Modifying Links in the Sidebar*

```
'***************************************************************************
    Protected Sub SideBarList_ItemDataBound(ByVal sender As Object, _
      ByVal e As System.Web.UI.WebControls.DataListItemEventArgs)

        If e.Item.ItemType = ListItemType.Item Or _
          e.Item.ItemType = ListItemType.AlternatingItem Then

            Dim btnLink As LinkButton = _
              DirectCast(e.Item.FindControl("SideBarButton"), LinkButton)

            Dim linkStepIndex As Integer
            linkStepIndex = Wizard1.WizardSteps.IndexOf(e.Item.DataItem)

            If linkStepIndex > Wizard1.ActiveStepIndex Then
                btnLink.Enabled = False
            End If

        End If

End Sub
```

SideBarListBound accepts a DataListItemEventArg object named e that contains important information about the DataListItem being created, such as its type and the data item being bound. The function begins by using an If statement on e.Item.ItemType to ensure the link disabling code only runs when an Item or AlternatingItem type is created.

Next, the function uses e.Item.FindControl("SideBarButton") to locate the LinkButton control where the step title is output. The Wizard control binds the DataList to the WizardSteps collection, so e.Item.DataItem points to a single WizardStep object from that collection. The function determines the exact index of the item in the WizardSteps collection using the IndexOf method and stores the index in the linkStepIndex variable. Finally, SideBarListBound compares linkStepIndex to the ActiveStepIndex of the wizard. If linkStepIndex is greater than the ActiveStepIndex, then the function disabled the link button. The link text still appears when a LinkButton is disabled, but users can't click the link. This alleviates user frustration with clicking on links only to find out they don't work.

By now, you should have a fairly good understanding of the Wizard control. Next, you'll learn about SQL soundex functions, which play a big role in reducing duplicate information entry.

Phonetic Searching

One of the most important aspects of reducing data duplication is intelligent searching functionality. Searching is often the first line of defense against data duplication because users are expected to check to see if data exists before entering it into a system. The problem is that most searches use exact-match searches. This can be detrimental in terms of data duplication because it requires the user to enter search criteria exactly as they appear in the database, which is problematic because data can have alternate spellings, abbreviated forms, or be entered incorrectly.

SQL soundex functions allow you to search using phonetics instead of exact spelling. In other words, you can use soundex functions to search for words that sound like the word entered. For example, say you have a database full of U.S. presidents. One of your users is searching for *Harry Truman* in the database. Because the user is a horrible speller, they are actually searching for *Hairy Trueman*. If your system uses exact-match searching, then the search won't turn up any results. If your system uses phonetic searching with the SQL soundex functions, then a search for *Hairy Trueman* will match on *Harry Truman* because *Hairy* and *Harry* are phonetic matches, and *Trueman* and *Truman* are also phonetic matches.

You should become familiar with two SQL soundex functions if you want to use phonetic searching. One is the `Soundex` function, and the other is the `Difference` function. They are covered next.

Phonetic Codes and the Soundex Function

Phonetic searching actually uses exact-match searching, but the exact match is based on the phonetic code of a string instead of the string itself. You can acquire the phonetic code of a string by passing the string into the `Soundex` function. The `Soundex` function processes the string and returns a four-digit alphanumeric code identifying the phonetics of the string. Strings that match phonetically return the same phonetic code. For example, `Soundex('Harry')` and `Soundex('Hairy')` both return the phonetic code `H600`.

The phonetic code generated by the `Soundex` function always consists of the uppercased version of the first letter of the string, followed by three digits. When calculating the digits, the `Soundex` function disregards all vowels, double letters, and the consonants Y and H (unless the letter is the first letter of the word). Thus, **Hairy** and **Harry** are reduced to **Hr** and **Hr**, respectively, before the `Soundex` function generates their phonetic code.

You can use the `Soundex` function anywhere you could normally use a function in SQL, but it mostly appears in the `WHERE` clause. Following is an example that selects `'Phonetic Match'` if the two `Soundex` functions return the same phonetic code:

```
SELECT 'Phonetic Match' WHERE Soundex('Hairy') = Soundex('Harry');
```

You can also learn a lot about the phonetic codes returned from the `Soundex` function by thinking of random words and seeing what phonetic code they generate:

```
SELECT Soundex('Pie'), Soundex('Fly'), Soundex('Rye')
```

As you look at different words, you'll quickly find that exact matching with phonetic codes suffers from similar problems to exact-match searching. For example, *Larry* and *Harry* are closely related phonetic words, but their phonetic codes will never match because the words start with different letters. The phonetic code for *Larry* is `L600` and the phonetic code for *Harry* is `H600`. They are close to one another, but definitely not an exact match.

Phonetic Proximity Matching with the Difference Function

Knowing that exact matching on phonetic codes has its limitations, SQL Server also includes the `Difference` function. The `Difference` function accepts two strings whose phonetic codes you want to compare, acquires the phonetic codes for each string, runs a comparison on the two codes, and returns a value between 0 and 4 indicating how closely the phonetic codes match. Table 10-7 outlines the various return codes and what they mean.

Table 10-7. `Difference` *Return Value Meanings*

Value	Meaning	Example
0	Not a Phonetic Match	`Difference('Elizabeth', 'Beth')`
1	Highly Unlikely Phonetic Match	`Difference('Raquel', 'Bob')`
2	Unlikely Phonetic Match	`Difference('Steve', 'Sam')`
3	Possible Phonetic Match	`Difference('Mike', 'Michael')`
4	Perfect or Near Perfect Phonetic Match	`Difference('Rachael', 'Raquel')`

Obviously, the `Difference` function is by no means foolproof. You can see from the preceding examples that the function returns 0 when comparing Elizabeth and Beth even though Beth is a substring that appears in Elizabeth. Remember, it only works with phonetics when doing its comparisons.

You can use the `Difference` function in your `WHERE` clause to return approximate phonetic matches. You should only return values where the `Difference` function returns 3 or 4, and you should also order your results by the `Difference` value as well so more likely matches appear at the top of the results. Anything less than that and you could be returning some pretty sketchy results. Following is an example SQL statement using the `Difference` function:

```
SELECT 'Phonetic Match' WHERE Difference('Mike','Michael') >= 3;
```

Now that you have an understanding of phonetic searching and wizards, you can apply that knowledge to build the Add Employee Wizard.

Creating the Add Employee Wizard

In a perfect world, users would always use the search page in an application to check whether or not the data they are about to enter already exists. In the real world, users to tend to skip nonrequired steps because it saves time and energy, at least in the short term. As a developer, you need to understand that no amount of training or threats from supervisors will change human behavior, so your applications need to enforce proper data-entry techniques. You can use web-based wizards to assist you in this endeavor.

In the example that follows, you'll learn how to create a web-based wizard that guides users through adding an employee. Instead of seeing one massive employee entry screen, the employee information is filled out in sections as the wizard progresses. Part of the process also includes an automatic search for existing information using phonetic searching. The user is shown a list of possible matches and given the option of backing out of the add process if the information already exists.

This example uses the `Northwind` database. You'll be adding employee records to the `Employee` table. All the source code for the example can be found in the Chapter 10 sample application in the Source Code area of the Apress website. Business objects can be found in the App_Code folder in the website, AddEmployee.aspx contains the actual wizard, and the database can be found in the App_Data folder. Let's begin by taking a look at the business objects that handle searching and writing employee data to the database.

■ **Note** Make sure the Northwind connection string entry in the <connectionStrings> section of the Web.config points to the Northwind.mdf file in the App_Data folder of the sample application. For more information about connection strings, see Chapter 1.

Business Objects and Utility Functions

As you look through the Add Employee Wizard, you'll encounter two business classes that help the wizard interact with employee data from the database: the Employee class and the EmployeeCollection class. You'll also encounter the Data class, which contains a number of database-related utility functions used by both business objects to acquire a database connection and handle various types of data.

In the sections that follow, you'll look at the code for these classes and gain a bit of insight as to what each one does. Make sure you pay careful attention to the GetEmployeeMatches function in the EmployeeCollection because it uses phonetic searching on employee names to locate possible duplicates.

Data Class

The Data class is responsible for holding common database access functions shared by the Employee and EmployeeCollection classes. Most of the functions in the class only have one or two lines of code, so it should be fairly easy to determine their purpose, but I'll briefly describe what each function does after Listing 10-12.

Listing 10-12. *Data Class*

```
Imports System.Data.SqlClient
Imports system.Web.Configuration.WebConfigurationManager

Public Class Data

    '**************************************************************************
    Public Shared Function GetConnectionString() As String
        Return ConnectionStrings("Northwind").ConnectionString
    End Function

    '**************************************************************************
    Public Shared Function GetOpenConnection() As SqlConnection
        Dim conn As New SqlConnection(GetConnectionString)
        conn.Open()
        Return conn
    End Function
```

```
    '***************************************************************************
    Public Shared Function SQLEncode(ByVal sqlString As String) As String
        Return sqlString.Replace("'", "''")
    End Function

    '***************************************************************************
    Public Shared Function GetInteger(ByVal obj As Object) As Integer
        If IsDBNull(obj) Then Return 0 Else Return CInt(obj)
    End Function

    '***************************************************************************
    Public Shared Function GetDate(ByVal obj As Object) As Date
        If IsDBNull(obj) Then Return Nothing Else Return CDate(obj)
    End Function

    '***************************************************************************
    Public Shared Function GetString(ByVal obj As Object) As String
        If IsDBNull(obj) Then Return String.Empty Else Return CStr(obj)
    End Function

    '***************************************************************************
    Public Shared Function StringToDate(ByVal dateString As String) As Date
        If IsDate(dateString) Then Return CDate(dateString)
        Return Nothing
    End Function

    '***************************************************************************
    Public Shared Function NullableDate(ByVal dateIn As Date) As String
        If dateIn = Nothing Then
          Return "null"
        Else
          Return "'" & Format(dateIn, "MM/dd/yyyy") & "'"
        End If
    End Function

End Class
```

The first function in the class, `GetConnectionString`, is responsible for acquiring the `Northwind` database connection string from `Web.config`. For more information on acquiring connection strings from `Web.config`, see Chapter 2.

`GetOpenConnection`, the next function in the class, uses the `GetConnectionString` function to create a new connection to the database. It creates and opens a new `SqlConnection` before returning it so the connection is ready to be used immediately.

`SQLEncode` replaces all the apostrophes in a string with double apostrophes. In SQL, you need to escape an apostrophe with double apostrophes because SQL uses apostrophes as its string delimiter. You should use `SQLEncode` any time you're placing a user-entered string into a SQL statement to help avoid SQL injection attacks.

You can use GetInteger, GetDate, and GetString to ensure a null database value does not cause your application to thrown an exception. These functions return an appropriate value for their respective data types upon encountering a null database value. If the value isn't null, it returns the value acquired from the database.

StringToDate converts a date-based-string value into an actual date value. You can use this to convert string-based dates entered into text boxes into actual dates used by the date properties in the Employee class. If the string is empty or invalid, the function simply returns nothing (an empty date).

Lastly, NullableDate assists in the insertion of null date values into the database. If the date provided to the function is nothing, it returns the string null. If the date is valid, then it returns the date string surrounded by apostrophes, for example, '7/21/2001'.

Employee Class

The Employee class is an object representation of the Employees table in the Northwind database. The class has a number of properties that map to fields in the table and contains all the logic for adding a record to the database.

All 15 properties in the class are standard property definitions and would only serve to take up space in this text. For the sake of brevity, I've taken the property definitions and their respective fields out of the code listing. You can review Table 10-8 to see all the properties in the Employee class or check out the source code in the sample application in the Source Code area of the Apress website.

Table 10-8. *Employee Properties (Properties Are Not Shown in the Listing)*

Property Name	Type	Description
EmployeeID	Integer	Number that uniquely identifies the employee (this is autogenerated by the database)
LastName	String	Last name
FirstName	String	First name
Title	String	Business title (for example, Sales Manager, Assistant, and so on)
TitleOfCourtesy	String	Courtesy title (for example, Mr., Mrs., Ms., Dr., and so on)
BirthDate	Date	Date employee was born
HireDate	Date	Date employee was hired
Address	String	Street name and number of the employee's home address
City	String	City of the employee's home address
Region	String	State (or Region) of the employee's home address
PostalCode	String	Zip code of the employee's home address
Country	String	Country of the employee's home address
HomePhone	String	Phone number where employee may be reached at home
Extension	String	Extension where employee may be reached at work
Notes	String	Additional information about the employee

With the properties excluded, only two functions are left in the class as shown in Listing 10-13.

Listing 10-13. Employee *Class*

```
Imports System.Data.SqlClient
Imports System.Data.SqlDbType
Imports Data

Public Class Employee

    '*************************************************************************
    ' Fields and property definitions for EmployeeID, LastName, FirstName,
    ' Title, TitleOfCourtesy, BirthDate, HireDate, Address, City, Region,
    ' PostalCode, Country, HomePhone, Extension, and Notes have been
    ' omitted to save space. Please review the sample code for full listing.

    '*************************************************************************
    Public Sub PopulateObject(ByVal DR As SqlDataReader)
        EmployeeID = GetInteger(DR("EmployeeID"))
        LastName = GetString(DR("LastName"))
        FirstName = GetString(DR("FirstName"))
        Title = GetString(DR("Title"))
        TitleOfCourtesy = GetString(DR("TitleOfCourtesy"))
        BirthDate = GetDate(DR("BirthDate"))
        HireDate = GetDate(DR("HireDate"))
        Address = GetString(DR("Address"))
        City = GetString(DR("City"))
        Region = GetString(DR("Region"))
        PostalCode = GetString(DR("PostalCode"))
        Country = GetString(DR("Country"))
        HomePhone = GetString(DR("HomePhone"))
        Extension = GetString(DR("Extension"))
        Notes = GetString(DR("Notes"))
    End Sub

    '*************************************************************************
    Public Function Add() As Boolean

        Dim SQL As String

        SQL = "INSERT INTO [Employees] (" & _
              "   LastName, FirstName, Title, " & _
              "   TitleOfCourtesy, BirthDate, HireDate, Address, " & _
              "   City, Region, PostalCode, Country, HomePhone, " & _
              "   Extension, Notes) " & _
              " VALUES (" & _
              "   @LastName, @FirstName, @Title, " & _
```

```
            "   @TitleOfCourtesy, @BirthDate, @HireDate, @Address, " & _
            "   @City, @Region, @PostalCode, @Country, @HomePhone, " & _
            "   @Extension, @Notes)"

        Dim conn As SqlConnection = GetOpenConnection()

        Dim cmd As New SqlCommand(SQL, conn)
        cmd.Parameters.Add("@LastName", VarChar).Value = LastName
        cmd.Parameters.Add("@FirstName", VarChar).Value = FirstName
        cmd.Parameters.Add("@Title", VarChar).Value = Title
        cmd.Parameters.Add("@TitleOfCourtesy", VarChar).Value = TitleOfCourtesy
        cmd.Parameters.Add("@BirthDate", DateTime).Value = BirthDate
        cmd.Parameters.Add("@HireDate", DateTime).Value = HireDate
        cmd.Parameters.Add("@Address", VarChar).Value = Address
        cmd.Parameters.Add("@City", VarChar).Value = City
        cmd.Parameters.Add("@Region", VarChar).Value = Region
        cmd.Parameters.Add("@PostalCode", VarChar).Value = PostalCode
        cmd.Parameters.Add("@Country", VarChar).Value = Country
        cmd.Parameters.Add("@HomePhone", VarChar).Value = HomePhone
        cmd.Parameters.Add("@Extension", VarChar).Value = Extension
        cmd.Parameters.Add("@Notes", VarChar).Value = Notes

        cmd.ExecuteNonQuery()
        cmd.CommandText = "SELECT @@IDENTITY;"
        Me.EmployeeID = CInt(cmd.ExecuteScalar())
        conn.Close()

    End Function

End Class
```

Both of the methods shown here accomplish relatively simple things. PopulateObject pulls database field information out of a SqlDataReader and places that information into the appropriate Employee properties. Notice that it uses the GetInteger, GetString, and GetDate functions defined in the Data class to ensure that the properties are populated correctly even if a null database value is encountered. You'll see the PopulateObject method used in the EmployeeCollection class.

Add is responsible, you may have guessed, for adding an employee record to the database. It builds out a parameterized INSERT statement containing the database field names and their respective value parameters. After creating the INSERT statement, the Add function opens up a connection to the database using the GetOpenConnection method from the Data class. It then sets up a SqlCommand object using the parameterized INSERT statement in the SQL variable, adds the appropriate parameters to the command object, and executes a command to add the record. After inserting the record, the function immediately reuses the command object to acquire the auto-generated EmployeeID from the database. The statement SELECT @@IDENTITY; selects the latest auto-generated number, and the ExecuteScalar() command bypasses the DataReader and just returns the EmployeeID value directly from the function. The value returned is an object, so it must be cast to the correct type, an integer, using CInt.

Up next, we have the `EmployeeCollection` class.

EmployeeCollection Class

`EmployeeCollection` is a strongly typed collection class responsible for maintaining a collection of `Employee` objects and loading collections from the database. It also exposes the `GetEmployeeMatches` function, which uses phonetic searching to locate possible duplicates based on an employee's name. Listing 10-14 is the code for the class, followed by some brief commentary on its methods.

Listing 10-14. `EmployeeCollection` *Class*

```
Imports System.Data.SqlClient
Imports System.Data.SqlDbType
Imports Data

Public Class EmployeeCollection
    Inherits CollectionBase

    '***************************************************************************
    Default Public Property Item(ByVal index As Integer) As Employee
        Get
            Return DirectCast(List.Item(index), Employee)
        End Get
        Set(ByVal value As Employee)
            List.Item(index) = value
        End Set
    End Property

    '***************************************************************************
    Public Function Add(ByVal item As Employee) As Integer
        Return List.Add(item)
    End Function

    '***************************************************************************
    Private Shared Function PopulateCollection(ByVal SQL As String) _
      As EmployeeCollection

        Dim EmployeeCol As New EmployeeCollection
        Dim EmployeeObj As Employee
        Dim conn As SqlConnection = GetOpenConnection()
        Dim cmd As New SqlCommand(SQL, conn)
        Dim dr As SqlDataReader = cmd.ExecuteReader()

        While dr.Read
            EmployeeObj = New Employee
            EmployeeObj.PopulateObject(dr)
            EmployeeCol.Add(EmployeeObj)
        End While
```

```
        conn.Close()

        Return EmployeeCol

    End Function

    '***********************************************************************
    Public Shared Function GetEmployeeMatches(ByVal LastName As String, _
      ByVal FirstName As String) As EmployeeCollection

        Dim SQL As String = String.Format( _
                "SELECT * FROM [Employees] " & _
                " WHERE   (DIFFERENCE(LastName, '{0}') >= 3 " & _
                "          OR LastName LIKE '%{0}%' " & _
                "          OR '{0}' LIKE '%' + LastName + '%')" & _
                "     AND (DIFFERENCE(FirstName,'{1}') >= 3 " & _
                "          OR FirstName LIKE '%{1}%' " & _
                "          OR '{1}' LIKE '%' + FirstName + '%')" & _
                " ORDER BY DIFFERENCE(LastName, '{0}'),  " & _
                "         DIFFERENCE(FirstName,'{1}')", _
                SQLEncode(LastName), SQLEncode(FirstName))

        Return PopulateCollection(SQL)

    End Function

End Class
```

Employee Collection inherits most of its collection functionality from the CollectionBase class. Both the Item and Add functions shown in the code are strongly-typed implementations of the standard Item and Add functions associated with most collections.

PopulateCollection is responsible for executing a SELECT statement and populating an EmployeeCollection with the results from the query. It is a Public Shared function so you can use it without having to instantiate an EmployeeCollection object. The function begins by creating a new EmployeeCollection object named EmployeeCol, which will ultimately be returned as the result of the function. It also defines an Employee object named EmployeeObj, which helps populate the EmployeeCollection with Employee objects. After that, Populate➥Collection acquires an open SQL connection using the GetOpenConnection method and creates a SqlCommand object named cmd to execute the query passed into the function via the SQL parameter. The call to cmd.ExecuteReader() returns a SqlDataReader containing the results of the query. PopulateCollection iterates through the SqlDataReader using a While loop. Inside the loop, the function creates a new Employee object and passes the SqlDataReader into the object's PopulateObject method. Remember, this method populates the properties of the object from the data in the SqlDataReader. The function then adds the object to EmployeeCol. If the SQL query does not return data, then no Employee objects are added to the EmployeeCol. Finally, the function closes the database connection and returns EmployeeCol.

GetEmployeeMatches returns a collection of possible duplicates given a first name and a last name. This function simply constructs a SQL statement, passes it to the PopulateCollection function, and returns the resulting `EmployeeCollection`. The big part of this function is the actual SQL statement itself. One issue noted earlier with phonetic searching is that it can miss substring matches. Remember, the names *Elizabeth* and *Beth* are not phonetic matches, but they are obviously related because *Beth* is a substring of *Elizabeth*. Thus, the SQL statement in the function uses both phonetic and substring searching to locate results. An example SQL statement may look like Listing 10-15 when searching for *Elizabeth Smith*.

Listing 10-15. *Example SQL Statement Used in* `GetEmployeeMatches`

```
SELECT * FROM [Employees]

WHERE   (DIFFERENCE(LastName, 'Smith') >= 3
          OR LastName LIKE '%Smith%'
          OR 'Smith' LIKE '%' + LastName + '%')
        AND
        (DIFFERENCE(FirstName,'Elizabeth') >= 3
          OR FirstName LIKE '%Elizabeth%'
          OR 'Elizabeth' LIKE '%' + FirstName + '%')

ORDER BY DIFFERENCE(LastName, 'Smith'),DIFFERENCE(FirstName,'Elizabeth')
```

Notice that the query uses four `LIKE` statements to search for substrings, two for each name. This ensures that if either the search criteria or the database value is a substring of the other, the result is returned. For example, if you have a *Beth* in the database and search for *Elizabeth*, the first `LIKE` statement determines that *Elizabeth* isn't a substring of *Beth*, however, the second one determines that *Beth* is a substring of *Elizabeth*. It also tries to intelligently order the duplicate listings using the return values from the `DIFFERENCE` functions.

■ **Tip** You can also use the `LIKE` functions in the `WHERE` clause to help intelligently sort the results.

Add Employee Wizard

Before you build a wizard, you should sit down and think about which steps you want to include in the wizard and how to guide the user through the task at hand. The Add Employee Wizard has two objectives. First, it should force users to look at the list of existing employees with similar names to the name being entered to avoid duplicate data entry. Second, it should split up the data entry for an employee into logical sections over several screens.

Each of the properties in the `Employee` class fits into one of three logical categories: personal information, business information, and notes. Personal information contains properties such as name, date of birth, address, and home phone number. Business information contains information such as hire date, title, and extension. Notes is in a category by itself because it could contain business or personal notes about the employee. Because of these categories, the wizard needs to contain three different steps for data entry.

Of course, you don't want users to enter a lot of employee information only to find out after the fact that they are entering duplicate data. You want the existing record search to happen first. Thus, the Add Employee Wizard will have an initial screen where the user can enter an employee name followed by a screen that displays possible matches on that name. If there are no matches, then the screen is skipped. The wizard then displays a step to enter personal information, a step for business information, and a step for notes. Each of these steps is outlined in more detail in the sections that follow.

Following you'll find a brief summary of each step in the wizard as well as a screenshot showing the layout of the screen. Refer to the sample application in the Source Code area of the Apress website for more information about the visual design and styles used for the wizard layout.

Step 1 – Enter an Employee Name

In the initial screen of the Add Employee Wizard, users can enter the first name and last name of the employee they want to add to the system (see Figure 10-8). Both the first name and the last name are required fields, so users will see an error message if they attempt to move to the next step without entering either one.

Figure 10-8. *Step 1—Enter an employee name*

Step 2 – Check for Existing Data

In this step, the user can review existing employees whose names closely match the name of the employee the user wants to enter (see Figure 10-9). By quickly scanning the list, users can see if there are any possible duplicates. Optionally, users can click on the `View` link to get a more detailed listing about a particular individual to help make an informed decision as to whether or not the employee being entered is a duplicate. If there are no possible matches, then the wizard skips this screen and the user is automatically taken to the data-entry screen.

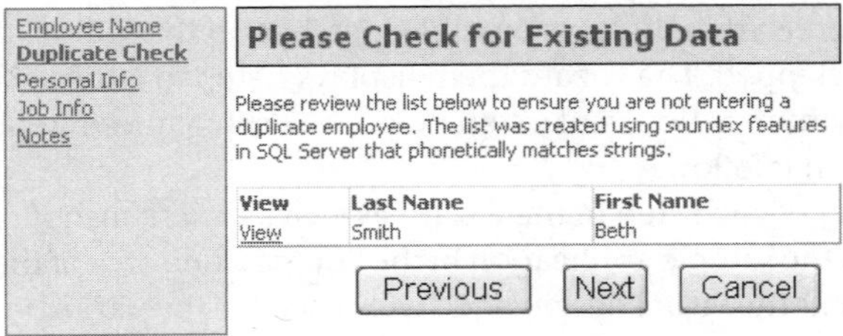

Figure 10-9. *Step 2—Check for existing data*

Step 3 – Enter Personal Information

At this point in the wizard, the user enters any known personal information about the employee. Although it isn't visible from Figure 10-10, there is a range validator on the **Birth Date** field to ensure that the date entered is in an appropriate format. You should also note that the **First Name** and **Last Name** text box values are automatically set to the values entered on the first step of the process to help reduce data entry for the user.

Employee Name
Duplicate Check
Personal Info
Job Info
Notes

Please Enter the Employee's Personal Info

Use the fields below to fill out personal information regarding this employee. First and Last name are required.

Title of Courtesy: Mr.
First Name: Elizabeth
Last Name: Smith
Birth Date: 5/15/79
Address: 777 Street Dr.
City: Frisco
State: TX
Postal Code: 75078
Country: United States
Home Phone: 555.555.5555

Previous Next Cancel

Figure 10-10. *Step 3—Enter personal information*

Step 4 – Enter Business Information

This screen is very similar to the personal information screen, but it deals with business information (see Figure 10-11). It exists to show how you can split out data entry into multiple sections, which is very helpful when you have large items with many fields.

Employee Name
Duplicate Check
Personal Info
Job Info
Notes

Please Enter the Employee's Job Information

Use the fields below to enter the employee's job information

Hire Date: 8/1/2005
Job Title: Sales Manager
Extension: 8722

Previous Next Cancel

Figure 10-11. *Step 4—Enter job information*

Step 5 – Enter Notes

Finally, the notes screen allows the user to enter ad-hoc information about the employee (see Figure 10-12). Because this is the last screen in the wizard, it displays the **Finish** button, which the user can click to commit the operation and save the employee to the database.

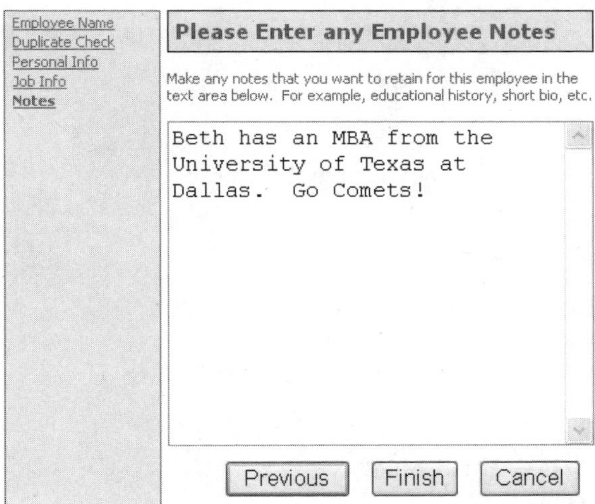

Figure 10-12. *Step 5—Enter employee notes*

Add Employee Wizard Code

Next, you'll find the code for the Add Employee Wizard (see Listing 10-16). Nothing in the code should come as a shock to you because it is simply an implementation of what we have been discussing throughout this entire chapter.

Note You can find the markup for the Add Employee Wizard in `AddEmployee.aspx` in the sample application in the Source Code area of the Apress website.

Listing 10-16. *Add Employee Wizard Code (*AddEmployee.aspx*)*

```
Partial Class AddEmployee
    Inherits System.Web.UI.Page

    '*************************************************************************
    Private SideBarClicked As Boolean = False
    Private PrevButtonClicked As Boolean = False

    '*************************************************************************
    Protected Sub Page_Load(ByVal sender As Object, _
      ByVal e As System.EventArgs) Handles Me.Load

        If Not IsPostBack Then
            AddWizard.ActiveStepIndex = 0
        End If

    End Sub

    '*************************************************************************
    Protected Sub WizardStep2_Activate(ByVal sender As Object, _
      ByVal e As System.EventArgs) Handles WizardStep2.Activate

        If PrevButtonClicked Then
            'Always return to step 1 if the previous button is clicked
            AddWizard.ActiveStepIndex = 0
        Else

            Dim EmployeeCol As EmployeeCollection
            EmployeeCol = EmployeeCollection.GetEmployeeMatches( _
                            txtSearchLastName.Text, txtSearchFirstName.Text)

            If EmployeeCol.Count > 0 Then
                GridDuplicates.DataSource = EmployeeCol
                GridDuplicates.DataBind()

                Me.pnlHasResults.Visible = True
                Me.pnlNoResults.Visible = False

            Else
                If SideBarClicked Then
                    Me.pnlHasResults.Visible = False
                    Me.pnlNoResults.Visible = True
                Else
                    'Skip the step
                    AddWizard.ActiveStepIndex = 2
                End If
```

```
            End If

        End If

    End Sub

    '**************************************************************************
    Protected Sub WizardStep3_Activate(ByVal sender As Object, _
      ByVal e As System.EventArgs) Handles WizardStep3.Activate

        If Me.txtFirstName.Text = String.Empty Then _
            Me.txtFirstName.Text = Me.txtSearchFirstName.Text
        If Me.txtLastName.Text = String.Empty Then _
            Me.txtLastName.Text = Me.txtSearchLastName.Text

    End Sub


    '**************************************************************************
    Protected Sub AddWizard_PreviousButtonClick(ByVal sender As Object, _
      ByVal e As System.Web.UI.WebControls.WizardNavigationEventArgs) _
      Handles AddWizard.PreviousButtonClick

        PrevButtonClicked = True
        Me.AddWizard.ActiveStepIndex = e.CurrentStepIndex - 1

    End Sub

    '**************************************************************************
    Protected Sub AddWizard_SideBarButtonClick(ByVal sender As Object, _
      ByVal e As System.Web.UI.WebControls.WizardNavigationEventArgs) _
      Handles AddWizard.SideBarButtonClick

        SideBarClicked = True
        If e.CurrentStepIndex < 2 And e.NextStepIndex > e.CurrentStepIndex + 1 Then
            e.Cancel = True
            Page.ClientScript.RegisterStartupScript(Me.GetType, "noJump", _
              "alert(' You cannot jump over Step 2');", True)
        End If

    End Sub
```

```
'***************************************************************************
Protected Sub AddWizard_FinishButtonClick(ByVal sender As Object, _
  ByVal e As System.Web.UI.WebControls.WizardNavigationEventArgs) _
    Handles AddWizard.FinishButtonClick

    Dim EmployeeObj As New Employee
    EmployeeObj.FirstName = txtFirstName.Text
    EmployeeObj.LastName = txtLastName.Text
    EmployeeObj.TitleOfCourtesy = ddlTitleOfCourtesy.SelectedValue
    EmployeeObj.BirthDate = Data.StringToDate(txtBirthDate.Text)
    EmployeeObj.Address = txtAddress.Text
    EmployeeObj.City = txtCity.Text
    EmployeeObj.Region = Me.txtCountry.Text
    EmployeeObj.PostalCode = Me.txtPostalCode.Text
    EmployeeObj.Country = Me.txtCountry.Text
    EmployeeObj.HomePhone = Me.txtHomePhone.Text

    EmployeeObj.HireDate = Data.StringToDate(txtHireDate.Text)
    EmployeeObj.Title = ddlJobTitle.SelectedValue
    EmployeeObj.Extension = txtExtension.Text

    EmployeeObj.Notes = txtNotes.Text

    If Not EmployeeObj.Add() Then
        e.Cancel = True
        ClientScript.RegisterStartupScript(Me.GetType, "AddFail", _
         "alert('Could not add employee to database');", True)
    End If

End Sub

End Class
```

Private Members for Storing Button Click Flags

SideBarClicked and PrevButtonClicked are Boolean variable store flags indicating which navigation button the user clicked. Storing these values makes it possible to determine which button the user clicked from inside the WizardStep2_Activate event. For more information on this tactic, review the "Determining Which Button Was Clicked in the ActiveStepChanged Event" section earlier in the chapter.

Page_Load: Resetting the ActiveStepIndex

When the page loads for the first time (for example, not on a postback), the Page_Load event sets the ActiveStepIndex to 0. When you edit the Wizard control in the IDE, it automatically sets the ActiveStepIndex of the wizard to whatever step you're currently editing. Setting it to 0 in the Page_Load ensures that the user starts on the first step of the wizard even if you accidentally leave the Wizard control on a different step in the IDE.

WizardStep2_Activate: Searching for Existing Records

When the user navigates to the second step, the WizardStep2_Activate method executes. This method is responsible for populating a data grid with existing employees who matched the employee name entered by the user. It is also responsible for skipping the step if no matches were located, and the user is coming to the step via the **Next** button because there's no point in showing a list of no results. If the user is coming via the **Previous** button, then the step is skipped because it's highly likely the user is backing up to enter a different name. If the user clicks on the sidebar navigation, the step is displayed. This allows curious or overly cautious users to see a message that indicates they are in no danger of adding a duplicate.

The method begins by checking to see if the user came via the **Previous** button. If so, the method sets the ActiveStepIndex to 0, which returns the user to the first step. This is the only code that runs when users came to this step via the **Previous** button.

If they come from the **Next** button or the sidebar navigation, then the method acquires an EmployeeCollection using the GetEmployeeMatches function and the first and last name of the employee entered from Step 1. Next, the method determines whether or not the Employee➥Collection contains any data. If so, it binds the GridView control to the EmployeeCollection, displays the pnlHasResults panel, and hides the pnlNoResults panel. A message in pnlHasResults informs users to look through the results to ensure they don't add a duplicate.

If the EmployeeCollection does not have any data, then the method checks to see if the user came to the step via the SideBarButton. If so, it displays pnlNoResults, hides pnlHas➥Results, and allows the step to be displayed. If a user is fearful of missing a step, the message in pnlNoResult reassures that everything is fine and there is no danger of adding a duplicate record. If the user arrived at the step via the **Next** button, then the method skips forward one step, effectively skipping Step 2.

WizardStep3_Activate: Copying the Employee Name Values

When the user navigates to the third step, the WizardStep3_Activate method executes. It is responsible for copying the first and last name of the user from Step 1 into Step 3 so the user does not have to retype it. The method checks to see if the **First Name** or **Last Name** text boxes in Step 3 are blank and, if so, copies the values from Step 1 into the text boxes.

AddWizard_PreviousButtonClick: Logical Backward Navigation

This method is responsible for setting the PrevButtonClicked flag so other methods know which navigation button the user clicked to change steps. It also forces the wizard to navigate backwards logically one step at a time instead of using the history.

AddWizard_SideBarButtonClick: Disallow Users Jumping over the Second Step

This method is responsible for setting the SideBarClicked flag so other methods know which navigation button the user clicked to change steps. It also ensures that users cannot skip the second step. If users attempt to skip the second step, the method registers a startup script that displays a popup box stating that users cannot jump over Step 2.

AddWizard_FinishButtonClick: Saving the Employee Record

When the user clicks on the **Finish** button, the `AddWizard_FinishButtonClick` event fires, signifying that the user wants to save the employee records to the database. The method proceeds to create an employee object, populate that employee object with the various fields from the wizard (the values have been stored in the `ViewState` until this point), and then saves the `Employee` object using the `Add` method. If the `Add` method is unsuccessful, the method cancels navigation and registers a startup script that displays a popup box telling the user that the save failed.

If the employee record successfully saves to the database, then the user is redirected to the URL in the `FinishDestinationPageUrl`. In the case of the sample application, the `Finish➥DestinationPageUrl` is set to `AddSucess.aspx` page, which displays a message informing the user that the add operation succeeded. If you don't want to redirect the user to another page, then you should add another step to the end of the wizard and set its `StepType` property to `Complete`. You can then place your confirmation message in the step content and the wizard will display it when the wizard finishes.

Trying It All Out

You can see the Add Employee Wizard in action by navigating to the `AddEmployee.aspx` page in the sample application in the Source Code area of the Apress website. Try adding a couple of similarly named employees to the database and see what kind of matches you get on them using phonetic searching. You should quickly see that it does a great job of giving you some wiggle room for typos and alternate spellings.

Summary

Web-based wizards are great for breaking down complicated tasks into smaller, more manageable chunks. They make it easy to display instructions, help enforce business processes, and gather data in an appropriate sequence. Plus, most people are very familiar with wizards because of their growing popularity over the past few years so they will feel right at home when they see one in your web application.

CHAPTER 11

Uploading Files

Businesses generate millions of documents every day, so naturally business applications need to work with files. Workflow systems allow people to upload supplemental documents and reports to help in decision-making processes. Employee directories may use uploaded images to help people put names with faces. Collaboration systems allow team members to upload shared information to a centralized storage system. Even web-based email clients use file uploads when working with attachments. Although not every web application allows file uploads, many do, so it's an important topic to understand.

One of my clients manages conference speakers and their presentations. Speakers show up at events with presentation files on floppy disks, CDs, DVDs, thumb drives, flash cards, mini discs, and any other obscure type of media you can imagine. Loading all the files into the client's system the day of the event was becoming a daunting task because of the sheer number of speakers and files. I helped the client build a presentation-management system to expedite the process by allowing speakers to upload their presentation files from home via the web.

During the design of the system, we struggled through a few questions that tend to come up on every project involving uploaded files. How do you allow users to upload multiple files at once? Should the system store files in a database or in the file system? And how do you allow users to download files if they are in a database? In this chapter, you'll explore all these topics:

- *Database vs. File System Debate:* Discusses general guidelines for determining whether or not to store files on the file system or in a database.
- *Uploading Files:* Describes the basics of file uploading in ASP.NET.
- *Uploading Multiple Files:* Shows how to combine JavaScript and VB .NET to allow multiple file uploads.
- *Storing Uploaded Files in a Database:* Demonstrates how to save files directly to a database instead of the file system.
- *Retrieving Uploaded Files from the Database:* After you get data into a database, you need to get it out again. This demonstrates how to retrieve uploaded files from the database.

We'll begin by taking a look at an ongoing debate between storing files in the file system or in a database.

Database vs. File System Debate

Should you store uploaded files in a database or on the file system? It's a question that comes up all the time when dealing with uploaded files and, unfortunately, there is no clear winner one way or the other. One side claims that if you want to maintain atomicity, consistency, isolation, and durability (ACID) principles, then you need to store files in a database. The other side claims that if you want better performance, you should store files on the file system because databases just add overhead. Each way has benefits and drawbacks, so you need to make a case-by-case decision based on the situation at hand.

The sections that follow describe some of the distinguishing factors between both storage options. Although not an exhaustive list, the discussion should help you make an informed decision about which method to use in a particular situation. I default to storing files on the file system unless there is an otherwise compelling reason to choose a database, but remember to weigh the decision carefully in each situation.

Transactional Support

Many advocates of database file storage are quick to point out that databases support ACID principles and the file system does not. The ACID acronym describes the principles of a transaction, so "supporting ACID principles" is really just a suave way of saying "databases support transactions." Transactional support is useful when saving multiple pieces of information because the transaction saves all the data or none of the data; that is, there are no partial saves.

Say, for example, you need to save an employee record along with an image file of the employee. Also say that the web server stores files on the file system and not in a database. You enter the employee information on a web form, specify an image file, and send it off to the server for processing. The server creates a new employee record in the `Employee` table with the information you entered in the form. One field in the employee record is a string identifying the path to the employee image file the system is about to write to the file system (you have to link the record to the file somehow). It successfully adds the record to the database, but, before it can save the image file to the file system, a glitch kills the application. Now there is a record in the database linking to a file that does not exist. Alternatively, you could wait until the image file is successfully written before committing the employee record to the database, but then you run the risk of having a file without a record. Both situations result in a partial save.

Now, say the server stores files in the database. Chances are that an employee image would be stored directly in the `Employee` table, but let's say it gets stored in a separate table named `EmployeeImages` for the sake of the example. You submit the employee information and image file. The server adds an employee record to the `Employee` table, but encounters an error adding the image file to the `EmployeeImages` table. At this point, the transaction has failed, and all changes in the transaction roll back. Therefore, the employee record is not committed to the database, so you do not have a partial save problem.

Does transactional support justify always using the database to save files? Not really. Applications are data driven, so the biggest issue that could arise from a partial save is when a record is written to the database, but an associated file is not written to the file system. Why? In such a scenario, the data driving the application is incorrect, so the application could try to use nonexistent file references. You can avoid this by writing files to the file system before saving records to the database. This ensures that the data driving the application is correct. If a partial save does occur, then you have an orphaned file sitting out in a folder somewhere taking up some space but not doing any harm. And remember, if a partial save does occur, it's due to an exception. Thus, the user should be informed that the save did not work so the user can try it again. This means that the orphaned file is likely to be overwritten and associated with a valid record on the next attempt, or that an administrator will be looking at the problem if a user has continued issues with adding a record.

Enforcing Referential Integrity and Avoiding Broken File Links

Enforcing referential integrity is one of the most compelling reasons to use database file storage over file-system storage. You can think of referential integrity as the status of relationships between two pieces of data. In the previous example, an employee record and an employee image share a one-to-one relationship, meaning every employee record is required to have an employee image. One should not exist without the other. If one does exist without the other, then the data has lost its referential integrity.

Databases continually enforce relationships between related data in a database. The relationships are maintained during inserts, updates, and deletes, so the relationships are guaranteed to be protected at all times. If you attempt to insert, update, or delete an item that would cause a referential integrity issue, the operation fails.

Such is not the case with the file system. If you have a record in a database that points to a file on the file system, the database cannot enforce the relationship. There is nothing stopping someone from moving the file to another location or deleting the file outright. Moving or deleting the file results in a broken file link, meaning that the record no longer has a valid link to the file.

Referential integrity is a compelling reason to use database file storage, but it does not win hands down in every situation. You need to weigh the costs of having broken file links associated with the file system against the performance issues associated with database file storage. If you are storing uploaded images for a gallery, then you may opt for performance and risk a couple of broken file links. If you are storing files for compliance with the Sarbane Oxley Act, then you may want to opt for enforced referential integrity so you don't end up with a jail sentence for missing documents.

Security Considerations

A proponent of database file storage offers this helpful advice: if your *file system* is compromised, then it's a good idea to have your files in a *database*. To which, I offer this reply: if your *database* is compromised, then it's a good idea to have your files in the *file system*. Sarcasm aside, the reality is that databases do afford you an additional layer of protection.

People have become relatively comfortable with the file system. Navigating through folders, searching for documents, opening files, moving files, copying files, and deleting files are second nature to most. That means more people are capable of stealing or damaging files on a file system. If an irate employee gains access to the file system, he knows just what he needs to do to wreak havoc.

Files in a database, however, are much more difficult to manipulate. Writing file data from the database to disk requires programmatic intervention. Modifying a file is nearly impossible without writing it to disk, editing it, and sending it back to the database. Moving a file or searching for a file is also unlikely without an understanding of SQL. Suffice it to say that a number of barriers prevent hackers from working with files stored in a database, which makes them inherently more secure.

You can use database users, roles, and permissions to limit access to files stored in a database. Similarly, you can use .NET authorization and NTFS file permissions to protect files in the file system. Both are fairly comparable in terms of protection when configured appropriately. Some people find it easier to maintain permissions solely in the database instead of worrying about the database and the file system. You can define .NET authorization and NTFS permissions on a file-by-file and folder-by-folder basis, however, which gives you much more granular control over application security.

Performance

The file system was designed from the ground up for optimized file storage and retrieval. It's the whole reason the file system exists, so it should come as no surprise that the file system outperforms a database when it comes to file storage and retrieval.

Databases are optimized for storing relatively small records, not large files. SQL Server, for example, stores records in a structure known as a database page, which is approximately 8KB in size. Most files, however, are significantly larger than 8KB, so SQL Server splits the file up into 8KB chunks and stores the file over multiple pages. Thus, you incur a performance cost when saving a file because the file has to be broken up, and you incur a performance cost when retrieving a file because it has to be pieced back together. You also incur a performance cost when SQL Server returns the data to the calling application because it uses the tabular data stream (TDS) protocol, which is not as optimal as the native data transfer capabilities inherent in the file system.

You also need to consider how storing files in a database will affect your database connections and database server load. Remember, if someone is downloading a 200MB file, then you'll need an open connection for the duration of the download. This can be problematic if you have connection-based licensing for your SQL Server, and it can cause performance issues if you end up with too many connections open at once.

Although the file system outperforms database file storage, some factors can narrow the performance gap. If you are working with relatively small files, you'll see less of a performance hit. Smaller files use few database pages so they are easier to reassemble, and they won't hold database connections open as long as larger files. Infrequently accessed files also make for better performance because the biggest hits you incur happen when files are saved and retrieved. You can also always upgrade the hardware in your database server if you're not getting the kind of performance you desire.

Data Backup and Replication

Database backups automatically include files stored in the database because those files are treated just like any other database data. This makes backing up files stored in a database easier in the sense that you do not have to set up any additional routines to back up those files. Of course, most backup applications can easily backup files on the file system as well, so it's not an overly compelling reason to choose one way or the other.

The same goes for database replication. Files in a database are automatically replicated just like any other data in a database, but it isn't too difficult to set up file replication between two servers.

Programmatic Complexity

Storing files in a database requires a bit more coding than just saving files directly to the file system. You have to write more code to upload the file, and you have to write all the code to retrieve the file from the database and send it back to the user. You may also find yourself coding workarounds for database file storage because components naturally assume files are stored on the file system. Programmatic complexity, although a bit more work, gives you complete control over serving files. This means that you can create advanced security and authorization schemes to control which users have access to what files.

Future Considerations

Microsoft has been developing a database-driven file system for inclusion in a future operating system for quite some time. It was slated for released with Windows Vista but was pushed back because the technology was not ready. Many proponents of database file storage see this as a confirmation that database technology will close the performance gap and become the standard for storing files.

As such, you may hear some people saying that you should start putting files in a database now so your application will be ready to take advantage of the new technology when it's fully ready. Although I agree that database technology will definitely close the performance gap, I don't think it's a compelling enough reason by itself to choose database file storage. If you need the additional referential integrity or security, then go ahead and use a database to store files. But, it may be years before database technology outperforms the file system, and you never know how compatible database file storage 5 or 10 years in the future will be with what you write today. Chances are that you'll have to rewrite parts of your application anyway and your initial effort will be for naught.

By now, you should have a good understanding of the pros and cons associated with the file system and database file storage. Next, you'll see the various file upload implementations. We'll start with uploading files to the file system to get the fundamentals down, and then we'll move into multiple file uploads and storing files in a database.

Uploading Files

HTML forms support a variety of different input elements. You can enter text into a text box, check a check box, select an option button, or choose an item from a drop-down list. HTML forms also allow you to upload files using a file-input element, which appears in the browser as a text box and a browse button, as shown in Figure 11-1.

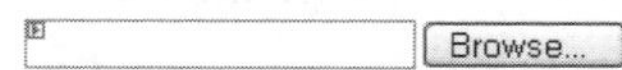

Figure 11-1. *File input control*

Users can either type a file name directly into the text box or use the **Browse** button to select a file using a file-selection dialog box. When the user submits the form, the browser appends the contents of the specified file to the outgoing form data and sends it to the server for processing. Prior to ASP.NET, working with file uploads was difficult because you had to parse out the incoming file information, open a file, and write the data out to disk. ASP.NET, however, shields you from most of the grunt work.

The FileUpload Control

One of the new controls in ASP.NET 2.0 is the `FileUpload` control. In the same way that an ASP.NET `TextBox` control represents an HTML text input, the `FileUpload` control represents an HTML file input. The control exposes properties and methods that help take the guesswork out of file uploads, and it allows you to save incoming files with merely a few lines of code.

■ **Note** If you worked with file uploads in previous versions of ASP.NET, then you should feel fairly comfortable with the `FileUpload` control because it is basically a server control version of the `HtmlInputFile` control from ASP.NET 1.x.

The `FileUpload` control appears on the Standard tab of the toolbox in Visual Studio .NET 2005. To add a `FileUpload` control to your web form, simply drag the item from the toolbox to the location where you want it to appear on the form. Visual Studio automatically creates the following control definition on your web form:

```
<asp:FileUpload ID="FileUpload1" runat="server" />
```

You can opt to change the `ID` or set visual and stylistic properties of the `FileUpload` control, but aside from that, it requires no configuration to function. The control is ready to go the moment you drop it on your form. Note, however, that the control does not have any auto postback capabilities, so you need a submit button or some other means of submitting the form.

■ **Caution** Be careful about using controls that cause auto-postbacks when working with files. Auto-postbacks cause the file input to upload its file, so a file dramatically reduces the responsiveness of the application. The file will also *not* be reuploaded on subsequent post backs.

The `FileUpload` control exposes a number of properties and methods that make it easy to work with an uploaded file in code (see Table 11-1).

Table 11-1. *FileUpload Properties/Method*

Name	Type	Description
`FileBytes`	`Byte()`	Byte array containing the binary content of the uploaded file.
`FileContent`	`System.IO.Stream`	Stream object that points to the uploaded file.

Name	Type	Description
FileName	String	File name of the uploaded file. This does not include any extraneous path information from the client (for example, if c:\directory\file.txt is uploaded, this returns file.txt).
HasFile	Boolean	Specifies whether or not a file was uploaded. If the file input is left blank on the form, then no file is sent with the request.
PostedFile	HttpPostedFile	Gets a reference to the underlying HttpPostedFile object from which the FileUpload control acquires its property information. You can use this object to acquire additional information about the uploaded file such as its length and its MIME (Multipurpose Internet Mail Extension) type.
SaveAs(filename as String) method		Saves the uploaded file to the location specified by filename.

As you work with file uploads, you'll routinely encounter HttpPostedFile objects that give you access to information about a file the user has uploaded. The PostedFile property of the FileUpload control is one example. Table 11-2 outlines the various members of the Http➥PostedFile class.

Table 11-2. HttpPostedFile *Properties/Method*

Name	Type	Description
ContentLength	Integer	Size (in bytes) of the uploaded file.
ContentType	String	MIME type of the uploaded file. This defines the type of file being uploaded (for example, text/html, application/msword, image/jpeg, and so on).
FileName	String	Raw file name from the client that includes client-path information. Unlike the FileName property on the FileUpload control, you need to manually parse the file name out of this property before you can use it.
InputStream	Stream	Gives you direct access to the stream containing the uploaded file data.
SaveAs(filename as String) method		Saves the uploaded file to the location specified by filename.

Now let's actually get into some code and see how to save an uploaded file.

Saving Files with the FileUpload Control

Based on the fact that the FileUpload control has a method called SaveAs, saving an uploaded file seems a trivial process at best. Listing 11-1 assumes you have a web form with a FileUpload control named FileUploader and a button named btnUpload that the user clicks to submit the file.

Listing 11-1. *Saving a File with the* `FileUpload` *Control*

```
Imports System.IO

...

'***************************************************************************
Protected Sub btnUpload_Click(ByVal sender As Object, _
  ByVal e As System.EventArgs) Handles btnUpload.Click

    If FileUploader.HasFile Then
            FileUploader.SaveAs( _
              Path.Combine(Server.MapPath("Files"), FileUploader.FileName))
    End If

End Sub
```

First, the code checks to make sure a file was actually submitted using the `HasFile` property. If you attempt to save a nonexistent file, then the `SaveAs` method will throw an exception. After checking to make sure the file exists, the code uses the `SaveAs` method to save the file to the file's folder of the web application using the file name of the uploaded file. The `Server.MapPath` function converts the web-relative file's path into a fully qualified path on the file system (for example, `c:\inetpub\wwwroot\application\files\`), and the `Path.Combine` method from the `System.IO` namespace combines the path with the file name and adds an appropriate folder separator between the two if you do not already have one. Of course, you are not required to use the name of the uploaded file when you save it. Many applications rename incoming files using special naming conventions to make the files easier to identify and to avoid accidentally overwriting other files. You can see this sample run by opening the `FileUpload.aspx` page in the sample application in the Source Code area of the Apress website (`http://www.apress.com`).

Caution The `SaveAs` method automatically overwrites a file if the file already exists. If you don't want to overwrite existing files, then you must explicitly check for an existing file in your code and avoid calling the `SaveAs` method.

So, saving a file using the `FileUpload` control is reduced to two steps. First, use the `HasFile` property to ensure a file was actually uploaded and then use the `SaveAs` method to save the file to disk. It really is that simple.

Uploading Multiple Files

Frequently, you'll want users to upload multiple files to your application. The presentation-management system discussed in the opening of this chapter is a great example. Presenters who use the system upload anywhere from 5 to 10 documents per conference with the average file size hovering in the 1MB to 2MB range. Naturally, users prefer to upload all the files at once instead of having to wait to upload one file, then the next, and then the next.

You have a variety of options when it comes to multiple file uploads from a single page. The first option is to use a third-party control to handle the file uploads for you. There are some pretty snazzy controls out there that include file-upload status bars and great file-selection interfaces (check out ABCUpload from `http://www.websupergoo.com` or visit the `http://www.ASP.net` control gallery). Of course, you may have to pay for some of them, and others rely on technologies that are not supported by all browsers.

Another option involves adding multiple `FileUpload` controls to the page. HTML forms are not limited to the number of files you can upload, so you can add as many file-input elements on a page as you want (within reason). If you have five `FileUpload` controls on the page, then the user can upload up to five files at a time. But, this still runs into the fundamental issue arising from having a static number of file inputs on the page: what happens when the user has one more file than there are file-input elements?

You could tackle the issue by asking the user upfront how many files will be uploaded and then create a page with that many `FileUpload` controls. Although possible, it's annoying to force users to predetermine how many files they need to upload before they get to the upload page. And what happens if they make a mistake and need to upload one or two more than they had originally planned?

What you really need is to give the user the ability to dynamically add file inputs to the form using client-side JavaScript. This ensures that users will always have enough input elements because, if they don't, they can always create another one by clicking on a button. In the example that follows, you'll learn how to dynamically vary the number of file-input elements on the client side and how to handle those incoming files.

Multiple File Uploads on the Client Side

Adding file-input elements to a page requires two things: an HTML page with easily locatable containers where the file inputs are to be added and the actual JavaScript that locates the container and adds the file-input elements.

We'll begin by examining the HTML page, because you need to know the HTML element names before you can use them in the JavaScript code. Listing 11-2 is the relevant HTML for this example.

Listing 11-2. *HTML Definition for Dynamically Adding File Inputs*

```
<div id=files>
    <input type=file name=fileUpload1 /><br />
</div>
<input type=button value="Add File" onclick="AddFileInput();"/>
<asp:Button runat=server ID=btnUpload Text="Upload Files" />
```

In Listing 11-2, there are four important HTML elements. The first is the opening `<div>` tag, which acts as the container for the file-input elements. Notice that the `id` attribute is set to `files`, but there is no `runat="server"` element. You only ever need to access this container using client-side JavaScript, so there's no need for the server to even know that the `<div>` exists.

Inside the `<div>` container, you'll see a single file input. Because this is an upload page, you can assume that the user wants to upload at least a single file, so one input element has been predefined so it will appear when the page first loads. You can predefine more input elements if you think your users would prefer to have more. Notice that each of these file-input elements are HTML elements, not FileUpload server controls. All the files uploaded from the page end up in the Request.Files collection, so the server doesn't need to explicitly know about the file-input elements.

Under the <div> tag is the Add File input button. When the user clicks this button, the client-side JavaScript AddFileInput() method executes in response to the onclick event. You'll see momentarily that the AddFileInput() method adds a new input file element to the <div> container.

And lastly, you have the Upload button. This is a server control used to submit all the files the user wants to upload from the page. Now that you have seen the HTML, let's take a look at the JavaScript that manipulates it in Listing 11-3.

Listing 11-3. *JavaScript for Dynamically Adding File Inputs to a Page*

```
<script language=javascript>
<!--
    ////////////////////////////////////////////////////////////////////////
    var fileCount = 1;

    ////////////////////////////////////////////////////////////////////////
    function AddFileInput(){

        var fileSectionDiv = document.getElementById("files");
        var fileItemDiv = document.createElement("div");

        //Increment the file counter
        fileCount++;

        //Set up the HTML content
        var content = "<input type=file name=fileUpload" +
              fileCount + "> <a href='javascript:RemoveFile(" +
              fileCount + ");'>Remove</a>"


        //Set up the fileItemDiv properties and append element
        fileItemDiv.id = "fileItemDiv" + fileCount;
        fileItemDiv.innerHTML = content;
        fileSectionDiv.appendChild(fileItemDiv);
    }

    ////////////////////////////////////////////////////////////////////////
    function RemoveFile(fileIndex){
        var fileSectionDiv = document.getElementById("files");
        var fileItemDiv = document.getElementById("fileItemDiv" + fileIndex);
        fileSectionDiv.removeChild(fileItemDiv);
    }
-->
</script>
```

At the top of the script is the fileCount variable declaration. This variable maintains the total count of file-input elements in the <div> container. Because the HTML has one predefined file-input element, the variable starts out with a value of 1. If you had five predefined file-input elements, then you would want to start it out with a value of 5. Although the variable keeps a count of the number of file-input elements, the real point of the variable is to give new file-input elements a unique name, a task for which the total count comes in handy.

Under the fileCount declaration is the AddFileInput method, which, is responsible for adding a new file-input element to the page. Remember that the id attribute of the <div> container that holds all the file-input is files. The method begins by acquiring an object reference to that <div> container using document.getElementById("files") and stores the resulting reference in the fileSectionDiv variable. The method needs this reference later on when adding the file-input element to the page.

After that, the AddFileInput method calls document.createElement("div") to create a new <div> element and stores a reference to that new element in the fileItemDiv variable. Each time a user adds a new file-input element, a couple of HTML elements are actually added to the page: a file-input element, some spacing characters, and a Remove link so the user can get rid of the file-input element if necessary. The newly created <div> tag acts as a container for the file-input and associated elements. If the user opts to remove the file-input element, the <div> container is removed, effectively clearing everything associated with the file-input element and making for cleaner deletion code.

To ensure each file-input element and its surrounding <div> container end up with a unique ID, the method increments the fileCount variable by one.

After the counter variable has been incremented, the content of the new <div> element is created—you can see that the HTML contains a definition for a file-input element, a spacing character, and a Remove link that executes the client-side JavaScript RemoveFileInput function when clicked. It looks something like this when output to the page:

```
<input type=file name=fileUpload2> 
<a href='javascript:RemoveFileInput(2);'>Remove</a>
```

After creating the content for the new <div> element, fileDivItem is assigned a unique ID and the innerHTML property is set to the content string that was created earlier.

Finally, AddFileInput appends the fileDivItem element to fileSectionDiv using the appendChild method. Appending the element places it at the bottom of any existing elements, so the new file-input element appears at the bottom of the file-input list. Figure 11-2 shows how everything looks after adding a few new file-input elements to the page.

Figure 11-2. *Dynamically adding file-input elements to a page*

The final method in the script is the `RemoveFile` method. This is called from the `Remove` link, passing in the `ID` of the upload control to remove. An object reference to the `<div>` container is again acquired using `document.getElementById("files")`, as is a reference to the `<div>` element that you want to remove using the `fileIndex` value that is passed into the method. Finally, `RemoveFile` removes the `fileDivItem` element from `fileSectionDiv` using the `removeChild` method.

With this code in place, you should have a fully functional page on the client side. Now you just need to get it to save files on the server side.

Saving Multiple Files on the Server Side

Allowing users to add multiple file-input elements on the client side gives them some serious flexibility for file uploads, but it also means that you can't use the `FileUpload` control on the server side. This may seem like a major setback at first, but ASP.NET has some great file-upload handling functionality outside of the `FileUpload` control. You do have to do a bit more work, but not much. Listing 11-4 is the code that you'll need to save multiple incoming files.

Listing 11-4. *Multiple File Upload Code Behind*

```
Partial Class MutlipleFileUpload
    Inherits System.Web.UI.Page

    '***************************************************************************
    Protected Sub Page_Load(ByVal sender As Object, _
      ByVal e As System.EventArgs) Handles Me.Load
        Page.Form.Enctype = "multipart/form-data"
    End Sub

    '***************************************************************************
    Protected Sub btnUpload_Click(ByVal sender As Object, _
      ByVal e As System.EventArgs) Handles btnUpload.Click

        For index As Integer = 0 To Request.Files.Count - 1
            If Request.Files(index).FileName <> String.Empty Then
                Request.Files(index).SaveAs(Server.MapPath("Files/") + _
                  System.IO.Path.GetFileName(Request.Files(index).FileName))
            End If
        Next

    End Sub

End Class
```

■ Note You can't use a `For Each` loop to iterate over the `HttpPostedFiles` in the `Request.Files` collection because it results in an exception.

Any time you want to submit a file from a form, the form must have its EncType attribute set to multipart/form-data. This attribute tells the form how to format the file information so the server can process it. Without this attribute, the form will not send the file information to the server correctly. One of the nice things about the FileUpload control is that it automatically takes care of the EncType property behind the scenes. You are not using the FileUpload in this situation, however, so you must manually set the Page.Form.Enctype property before the page renders (you can do it in the PreLoad, Load, PreRender, directly in the <form> element of the markup, and so on).

Inside the Request object, you'll find a property called Files. The Files property holds a collection of HttpPostedFile objects representing all the files that were uploaded to the page. If a user uploads 10 files, then there will be 10 objects in the collection. If there were no files uploaded, there will be 0 files in the collection. As an added bonus, the HttpPostedFile object supports a SaveAs method, once again making it relatively easy to save files to disk. You can see inside the btnUpload_Click method that the code simply loops through each item in the collection and saves all the files to disk.

There are, however, two major differences between using the items in the file's property and a file in the FileUpload control. First, the HttpPostedFile object does not support a HasFile property. To test whether or not the HttpPostedFile contains a file, you need to check the FileName or ContentLength properties. Browsers do not let users upload nonexistent files. This means that when the FileName property has a value, a file was uploaded. Users can, however, upload zero-byte files. So you can use the ContentLength property to check for that if you would prefer to keep empty files off your server. It's up to you.

Saving files to disc is really easy because ASP.NET does most of the work for you. Uploading files to a database, however, takes a bit more effort on your part. We'll take a look at that next.

Storing Files in a Database

You've looked at the situation and determined that the benefits of using database file storage outweigh the costs. Now you have to get those files into the database. Most developers are comfortable with database-storage techniques involving numeric- and text-based data, but the concept of cramming a data file into a database field is foreign to most. Where do you start? What do you need? How do you do it?

Storing files in a database is a three-step process. First, define a database table with an appropriate structure to hold the file. Second, get the file or files from the client to the server. And third, create a byte array containing the content of the file and insert it into the table. It may sound like a lot to do, but it's really simple.

Creating a Database Table to Store Files

SQL Server has three fields capable of storing binary data: binary, varbinary, and the image data types. The binary and varbinary data types are synonymous with the char and varchar data types: binary stores a fixed-length byte array and varbinary stores a variable-length binary array. Both data types also max out at 8,000 bytes, making them suitable for relatively small files. The image data type can store up to a 2GB file, which should be sufficient for any files with which you are working.

Note The image data type only stores data. When you save a "file" into a database, you are really just saving the data in the file. Other information—such as the file name, file attributes, creator, last modified date, and so on—is not saved with that data. If you need to retain this information, make sure you write it to other fields in the database.

For the examples in this book, you'll create a new table named Files with three fields: FileName, FileSize, and FileData. Their names should be fairly descriptive of their purpose, so I won't go into much detail. Listing 11-5 is the SQL table and primary-key creation script.

Listing 11-5. *Create Table SQL*

```
CREATE TABLE [dbo].[Files] (
    [FileName] [varchar] (50) NOT NULL ,
    [FileSize] [int] NOT NULL ,
    [FileData] [image] NOT NULL
) ON [PRIMARY] TEXTIMAGE_ON [PRIMARY]

ALTER TABLE [dbo].[Files] ADD
    CONSTRAINT [PK_Files] PRIMARY KEY  CLUSTERED
    (
        [FileName]
    )  ON [PRIMARY]
```

The sample application for Chapter 12 includes a sample database with the Files table precreated. Feel free to use that database or create your own using the table-creation script.

Getting Files from the Client to the Server

You don't need to do anything differently on the client side to get files up to the server. Thus, everything you learned about single and multiple file uploads from earlier in the chapter still applies. If you want to allow a single file upload, then use the FileUpload control. If you want to allow multiple file uploads, then use JavaScript to dynamically create file-input elements. Understand, of course, that the code-behind file will change dramatically because you can no longer use the SaveAs function on the FileUpload control or the HttpPostedFile object to save your data, but we'll take a look at what you do need to do next.

Saving a Single File to the Database

Whether you are saving a file to disk or to a database, you should use a FileUpload control if your users only need to upload a single file from a page. Listing 11-6 shows how to acquire the content of the file from the FileUpload control and how to add it to a database.

Listing 11-6. *Saving a Single File to the Database*

```
Imports System.Data.SqlClient

Partial Class DatabaseFileUpload
    Inherits System.Web.UI.Page

    '*************************************************************************
    Protected Sub btnUpload_Click(ByVal sender As Object, _
      ByVal e As System.EventArgs) Handles btnUpload.Click

        If FileUploader.HasFile Then

            'Create the database objects we need
            Dim dbConn As SqlConnection = Nothing
            Dim dbCmd As SqlCommand = Nothing

            'Open the connection and set up the SQL statement
            dbConn = Data.GetConnection()
            dbCmd = New SqlCommand( _
               "DELETE FROM [Files] WHERE [FileName]=@FileName;" & _
               "INSERT INTO [Files] VALUES (@FileName, @FileSize, @FileData);", _
               dbConn)

            'Add values using parameters
            dbCmd.Parameters.AddWithValue("@FileName", _
              System.IO.Path.GetFileName(FileUploader.FileName))
            dbCmd.Parameters.AddWithValue("@FileSize", _
              FileUploader.FileContent.Length)
            dbCmd.Parameters.AddWithValue("@FileData", FileUploader.FileBytes)
            'Execute and close
            dbConn.Open()
            dbCmd.ExecuteNonQuery()
            dbConn.Close()

        End If

    End Sub

End Class
```

When a user clicks on the **Upload** button, the `btnUpload_Click` event handler executes. Its purpose is to save the file in the `FileUploader` control to the database. The method starts out by checking the `HasFile` property of the `FileUploader` control to determine if the user uploaded a file. If so, the method acquires a new database connection using the `Data.GetConnection()` utility function. This function acquires a connection to a SQL database connection using the "Database" connection string from the `Web.config` file. You can look at the source code for the function in the sample application in the Source Code area of the Apress Web site.

After it has established a database connection, the method creates a SQL command with multiple statements. The first statement deletes existing file information, if any is present, and the second inserts the new file information into the table using a simple `INSERT` statement. Notice that the SQL statements contain three different parameters: `@FileName`, `@FileSize`, and `@FileData`. Also notice that the `@FileName` parameter is used in two locations: once in the `DELETE` statement and once in the `INSERT` statement.

After defining the parameterized command, the method adds parameters to the command object using the `Parameters.AddWithValue` function. This function accepts the name of the parameter and the parameter value; it automatically determines the data type based on the incoming value. The `@FileName` parameter is fairly straightforward because it passes in a string property on the `FileUploader` control. Next in line is the `@FileSize` parameter. You can determine the file size using `FileUploader.FileContent.Length`. The `FileContent` property of the `FileUpload` control returns a reference to the `IO.Stream` containing the file. You can safely read properties from the `FileContent` property without flushing the file data from the stream. Do *not* use `FileUploader.FileBytes.Length` to determine the file size.

■ **Caution** The first time you access the `FileBytes` property, it flushes all the data from the `FileContent` `IO.Stream` and returns a byte array containing the data. This leaves the `FileContent IO.Stream` in an unusable state. Thus, after you access the `FileBytes` property, you can no longer rely on the `FileBytes` property or the `FileContent` property to point to valid data. Also be wary about running your mouse over the `FileBytes` property while debugging because it's just like accessing the property in code and results in the same unusable state.

And lastly, you have the `@FileData` parameter. You need to pass the content of the file into this parameter. To do so, use the `FileBytes` property of the `FileUpload` control. `FileBytes` returns a byte array containing the content of the file upload, and it maps to the image data type (as well as the `binary` and `varbinary` types) in SQL.

Right before closing the database, the method calls the `ExecuteNonQuery` method on the command object. This causes the command object to build out the actual command using the parameterized command text and the parameter values you have provided. It then executes the command against the database, which deletes any conflicting file and inserts your file and its related information.

Saving Multiple Files to the Database

As was the case with a single file upload, you don't need to change anything on the client side to handle multiple uploads to a database. You can use the same JavaScript with the same HTML so users are always guaranteed to have as many file-input elements as they need to upload their files. In Listing 11-7, you'll see how to save those files without resorting to the `FileUpload` control.

Listing 11-7. *Saving Multiple Files to a Database*

```
Imports System.Data
Imports System.Data.SqlClient

Partial Class DatabaseMultipleFileUpload
    Inherits System.Web.UI.Page

    '*************************************************************************
    Protected Sub Page_Load(ByVal sender As Object, _
      ByVal e As System.EventArgs) Handles Me.Load
        Page.Form.Enctype = "multipart/form-data"
    End Sub

    '*************************************************************************
    Protected Sub btnUpload_Click(ByVal sender As Object, _
      ByVal e As System.EventArgs) Handles btnUpload.Click

        For index As Integer = 0 To Request.Files.Count - 1

            Dim postedFile As HttpPostedFile = Request.Files(index)

            If Not postedFile.FileName = String.Empty Then

                Dim fileBytes(CInt(postedFile.InputStream.Length)) As Byte
                postedFile.InputStream.Read(fileBytes, 0, _
                  CInt(postedFile.InputStream.Length))

                Dim dbConn As SqlConnection = Data.GetConnection()
                Dim dbCmd As SqlCommand = New SqlCommand( _
                  "DELETE FROM [Files] WHERE [FileName]=@FileName;" & _
                  "INSERT INTO [Files] VALUES (@FileName, @FileSize, " & _
                  "  @FileData);", dbConn)

                dbCmd.Parameters.AddWithValue("@FileName", _
                  System.IO.Path.GetFileName(postedFile.FileName))
                dbCmd.Parameters.AddWithValue("@FileSize", fileBytes.Length)
                dbCmd.Parameters.AddWithValue("@FileData", fileBytes)

                dbConn.Open()
                dbCmd.ExecuteNonQuery()
                dbConn.Close()

            End If

        Next

    End Sub

End Class
```

Any time you work with file uploads and you're not using the FileUpload control, you need to manually add the enctype attribute to the form containing the file-upload elements. Otherwise, the form won't know to send the files back to the server for processing. In Listing 11-7, this is taken care of in the Page_Load method.

When the user clicks on the **Upload** button, the btnUpload_Click event handler executes. This method is responsible for uploading files to the database without using the FileUpload control. It begins with a For loop that iterates through each HttpPostedFile in the Request.Files collection. Inside that loop, the method defines a variable named postedFile to hold a reference to the HttpPostedFile currently being processed. This makes the code easier to read because it's harder to refer to the file as Request.Files(Index). Next, the method checks to see if the postedFile actually has a file by checking its FileName property to see if it's empty. If the FileName property is empty, there is no file, and the method does not attempt to add anything to the database.

After determining that the user actually uploaded a file, the method needs to create a byte array containing file content. This is where you'll see the most difference between saving a single file to a database and saving multiple files to a database because the HttpPostedFile object does not have a ByteArray property like the FileUpload control. Instead, it has an InputStream property with a reference to the IO.Stream containing the file content.

You use InputStream to accomplish two things. First, you use it to determine how large the file is using InputStream.Length. This allows you to redimension the fileBytes byte array so it's long enough to accommodate all the file data. You also use the InputStream.Read method to transfer the file content from the IO.Stream into a buffer. In this case, the buffer is fileBytes. You also need to pass in the start position and the read length into the Read method. The start position is 0 because you want to start at the beginning of the file data, and the length is InputStream.Length because you want to read the entire stream. After the Read method executes, fileBytes contains all the file data.

After the byte array containing the file data has been acquired, the method acquires a database connection using the Data.GetConnection() utility function. It then creates a parameterized SQL query to delete the file name if it already exists and insert the uploaded file into the database. Next, the method adds the appropriate parameters and parameter values to the command object, opens the database, executes the query, closes the database, and then moves on to process the next file.

Retrieving Uploaded Files from the Database

Now that you can store files in a database, the question quickly turns to how can you get them out again? IIS can't natively serve files out of a database, so the answer lies in coding your own file-download page.

Listing 11-8 allows users to request a file from the database by specifying the file name in the FileName parameter of the query string. The page searches through the FileName field of the database for a match on that file name. If the page locates a match, it returns the content of the file and writes it back to the user. If the page cannot locate a match, it generates a 404-Not Found error telling the user that the requested files does not exist.

Listing 11-8. *Downloading a File Stored in the Database*

```
Imports System.Data.SqlClient

Partial Class GetDBFile
    Inherits System.Web.UI.Page

    '***************************************************************************
    Private ReadOnly Property FileName() As String
        Get
            Return Request.QueryString("FileName")
        End Get
    End Property

    '***************************************************************************
    Protected Sub Page_Load(ByVal sender As Object, _
      ByVal e As System.EventArgs) Handles Me.Load

        Dim dbConn As SqlConnection
        Dim dbCmd As SqlCommand
        Dim fileData As Byte()

        'Acquire file data
        dbConn = Data.GetConnection()
        dbCmd = New SqlCommand( _
          "SELECT FileData FROM [Files] WHERE [FileName]=@FileName", dbConn)
        dbCmd.Parameters.AddWithValue("@FileName", FileName)
        dbConn.Open()
        fileData = DirectCast(dbCmd.ExecuteScalar(), Byte())
        dbConn.Close()

        If fileData Is Nothing Then
            Response.StatusCode = 404
        Else
            Response.AddHeader("Content-Disposition", _
              "attachment; filename= """ & FileName & """")
            Response.BinaryWrite(fileData)
        End If

        Response.End()

    End Sub

End Class
```

■ **Caution** This example is intended to demonstrate how to retrieve a file from the database. It does not, however, take into account any security restrictions you may want to put on file access. You should always check to make sure the user making the request has the appropriate permissions to access the file. You may find the `User.IsInRole` method helpful for making this determination. For more on security, check out Chapter 12.

At the top of the Listing 11-8, you'll find the `FileName` property. This read-only property makes it easy to reference the value for `FileName` passed to the page via the query string.

Whenever someone accesses the page to download a file, the `Page_Load` event handler executes and connects to the database, locates the requested file, pulls back the file data, and outputs that data so the user can download the file. And it really doesn't take much to do it. The method begins by acquiring an open connection to the database using the `Data.GetConnection` utility function. After that, it sets up a command object with a very simple SQL `SELECT` statement to acquire the data for the requested file:

```
SELECT FileData FROM [Files] WHERE [FileName]=@FileName
```

The only field returned by the query is the `FileData` field, which contains the file content, and it's only returned when the `@FileName` parameter matches a file in the database. Immediately after the command object declaration, the method passes in the `FileName` property as the value for the `@FileName` parameter value. Then the method executes the database command using the `ExecuteScalar` function. If the requested file was located, `ExecuteScalar` returns a byte array containing the file content. If not, it returns nothing. Either way, the result is directly cast into a byte array and stored in the `fileData` byte-array variable.

Next, the method determines whether or not `fileData` contains any data. If `fileData` does not contain data, then the method sets the Response status code to 404, indicating that the file was not found. If the file was found, then the page adds a `Content-Disposition` header to the page indicating that the incoming data is an attachment meant to be saved or opened, not displayed in the browser. It then uses `Response.BinaryWrite` to write the content of `fileData` out to the user.

■ **Caution** The Content-Disposition: attachment technique has a few drawbacks because it does not work with all browsers, and it can misbehave in the ones that do support it. Check out Chapter 13, which covers HTTP handlers, for file-download techniques that work across all browsers.

So now you can save files to the database and retrieve them too.

Summary

From reports, spreadsheets, and documents to images, videos, and presentations, companies routinely depend on files for business. Inevitably, you'll work on a project where uploading files is an important feature, and this chapter has prepared you for that encounter. You've learned the pros and cons of storing files in the file system versus a database. You implemented single-file and multiple-file upload pages. You also saw an example of how to serve files from a database. There are countless reasons that you may need to upload files in an application, but now you should be able to handle anything you come across.

CHAPTER 12

Security and Encryption

I recently spoke with Craig Bell, owner of the networking services firm Momentium Technologies, about a new client engagement. The client, called Bravo Corp. for this discussion, had just reviewed its security and data backup guidelines and determined that security was too lax, and they were not making any backups of important company information. Bravo Corp. took the right step in hiring Momentium to revamp its network security and to put the appropriate data backup routines in place, but they did it about a week too late. Before Momentium got a chance to even look at the network infrastructure, an irate ex-employee hacked into Bravo Corp.'s systems and deleted their entire data repository. There's an FBI investigation into the incident, but even if they find the culprit, Bravo Corp. can't recover its lost data.

The University of Texas Center for Research on Information Systems published a study outlining the devastating impact of a catastrophic data loss. Only 6% of companies survive, 43% never reopen after the data loss, and 51% fail within two years. And that's only data loss. According to a study by ASIS International, PricewaterhouseCoopers, and the U.S. Chamber of Commerce, data theft costs businesses in the United States upwards of $60 billion annually. Imagine your company's research and development, business plans, product pricing and information, or customer lists in the hands of your competitors. Protecting your business information from loss or theft is an absolute necessity when it comes to business viability.

Security, however, tends to be an afterthought in business application development, even though many applications contain login information for important business systems. In the rush to get functionality out to users, security is often forgotten, neglected, or slapped together at the end. In reality, security needs to be part of the upfront design so it can be thought out appropriately. This chapter covers some of the security topics that I've run across and ways to address them. Here's what you'll find inside:

- *Basic Security Concepts:* Defines basic terminology and security principles discussed throughout the chapter.
- *ASP.NET Security Architecture Overview:* Gives a high-level overview of how IIS and ASP.NET handle security.
- *Encrypting Configuration Data:* Shows how to use some of the new ASP.NET 2.0 configuration encryption features to secure configuration data.
- *Encrypting Application Data:* Discusses how to create one- and two-way encryption routines to protect data from unauthorized use.

We'll begin by taking a look at some of the basic concepts and terminology discussed in the chapter.

Basic Security Concepts

Security in ASP.NET begins at the operating system level and hits a number of different components and processes along the way. You'll see as you read this chapter that IIS, ASP.NET, the file system, network shares, enterprise services, and databases all have different security measures in place, but most share some common concepts. This section is geared toward getting you familiar with some of the terminology and concepts that you'll see throughout this chapter.

Security Terminology

Whenever you discuss Windows security and ASP.NET, you end up throwing around a security phrases such as authentication, authorization, token, principal, identity, and ticket. If you haven't seen these terms before, they can be rather confusing. Table 12-1 contains a list of terms and definitions that you'll see throughout this chapter.

Table 12-1. *Security Terms and Definitions*

Term	Definition
Account	Represents a single person, service application, or computer system for which security and access information is defined. Accounts contain identifying information about the entity (name and description), authentication information (credentials), and information outlining any roles to which the account belongs.
Security Principal	Represents the identity and role information about an entity and is usually referred to as just the *principal*. The .NET Framework contains the `IPrincipal` interface that describes classes representing security principals. This term is interchangeable with the term *account*.
Roles	Represents a logical grouping of accounts. Roles allow you to specify security settings for the role, but apply those security settings to all the accounts that are members of that role. For example, you may have 10 accounts that belong to managers in your company. You want to grant all managers access to a specific folder on the network, so you create a Manager role and create a security setting giving the Manager role access to that folder. Then you make the 10 accounts members of the Manager role. This effectively gives them access to the folder. An added benefit of using roles is maintenance. If you create a new account and assign it to the Manager role, that account will also have access to the folder without you having to specifically set up access permissions for the account. Plus, if you ever have to change access permissions for all the managers, then you can make the change once in the Manager role instead of editing permissions on each individual user account.

Term	Definition
Permissions	Permissions allow you to specify whether a given account or role will be granted or denied access to a specific resource. Different resources allow different sets of permissions. The file system, for example, lets you to set permissions allowing or denying users to read, write, modify, list, and execute files. SQL Server lets you set permissions allowing or denying users to create databases, create tables, edit rows of data, and so on.
Authentication	Process by which an entity provides credentials as proof of its identity. The system checks the credentials and determines whether the entity really is who it says it is.
Credentials	Information used for authentication purposes normally containing the name of the account and some piece of information that only the account holder should know or possess. Credentials are normally supplied as a username/password pair, but may be certificate- or biometrically based.
Authorization	Process by which the system determines whether an authenticated user has permissions to access a specific resource.
Access Token	After Windows authenticates an entity, the operating system creates an object known as an *access token* containing identification and role information for the authenticated entity. Windows attaches a copy of the access token to every running process to give the process a security context under which to run.
Security Context	Applications run under different accounts. Accounts have different security permissions. As such, application permissions are dependent on the account running the application. Security context simply refers to the permissions the application is subject to based on the account running the application.
Ticket	You can think of this as an access token for web applications using Forms Authentication. A Forms Authentication ticket contains user and role information for an authenticated entity. An authenticated entity passes the ticket along with every web request as a cookie or a parameter on the query string. ASP.NET then uses that ticket to create an `IPrincipal` object identifying the entity and the roles to which the entity belongs so the web request may be processed with an appropriate security context.
Impersonation	Allows a process to access a resource using a different security context than the one specified in the access token. In ASP.NET, you can opt for an application to impersonate individual users as they access the application, or you can opt for the entire application to impersonate one specific user. By default, impersonation is disabled, and ASP.NET runs using the ASPNET account in IIS 5 and the Network Service account in IIS 6. You'll learn about impersonation in more detail later in the chapter.
Delegation	Delegation is a form of impersonation that works across a network. When you want to impersonate an account on a network resource, the network resource must be able to authenticate the credentials you're trying to impersonate. Delegation requires that you impersonate an account whose credentials can authenticate on both machines.

Authentication vs. Authorization

There is a subtle but notable difference between authentication and authorization that you need to fully understand before moving on. Authentication determines if you are in fact who you say you are. Authorization determines if you have the appropriate permissions to complete some action. Authentication occurs before authorization and is responsible for ensuring that the system knows who is making the request. If a user cannot be authenticated, then the user is considered anonymous.

Authorization occurs after authentication because the system needs to know who is making a request before it can determine whether or not the request can be authorized. For example, if Amy has access to a resource, but Robert does not, then the system needs to know whether Amy or Robert is requesting the resource. If authorization fails, then the user is denied access to the resource. Depending on how you have a web application set up, this may come in the form of an HTTP 403 error (unauthorized) or by redirecting the user to a login page or an access denied page.

Least Privileged Access

The concept of least privileged access means that you give roles and accounts enough permission to do their jobs, but no more. If a user needs the ability to read documents, then give the user the ability to read documents, but not to create or modify documents. If the user needs to create new documents, then give the user the ability to create new documents, but not to read or modify existing documents. Also make sure to add accounts only to those groups to which they belong. If someone needs to be in the Manager group, don't add him or her to the Administrator group also.

Creating accounts and roles with least privileged access helps keep gaping holes from developing in your security. I saw one inexperienced network administrator give his users administrator level access to the entire network because they were having permissions issues accessing a single network share. Instead of looking into and fixing a small problem, he created a giant new one. He assumed it was okay to give everyone administrative rights because everyone in the small company was trustworthy, but failed to realize if any of those accounts were compromised by a hacker, the hacker would have free reign on the network. And you can never rule out the possibility of an irate employee using an internal account to sabotage a company resource before leaving.

So make sure that your security only allows users and accounts to do what they need to do, nothing more. Next, let's take a look at how ASP.NET handles security.

Processes, Threads, and Tokens

A process is the memory space in which an executable program runs. When you launch Word, Visual Studio, or even Minesweeper, you're running a process. Inside of a process, there may be one or more threads of execution, or simply threads, running various tasks. IIS, for example, is a single process running on a server, but it creates numerous threads inside that single process to handle incoming requests.

An access token is a Windows security object containing the security context of an authenticated account. Windows attaches an access token to each running process on the system to give the application a security context under which to run. As the process accesses resources, those resources use the security context in the access token for authorization purposes. This ensures that the application can't access any resources that the account does not normally have privileges to access (see Figure 12-1).

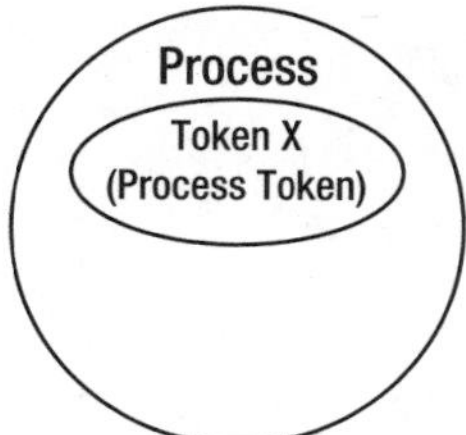

Figure 12-1. *Process and process level*

Although processes run using an overall security context, each thread inside of a process also has its own access token defining the security context under which that individual thread may run. By default, a process creates a new thread, builds a copy of its process-level access token, and then assigns that copied access token to the thread. Thus, most threads run using the same security context as the process in which they run (see Figure 12-2).

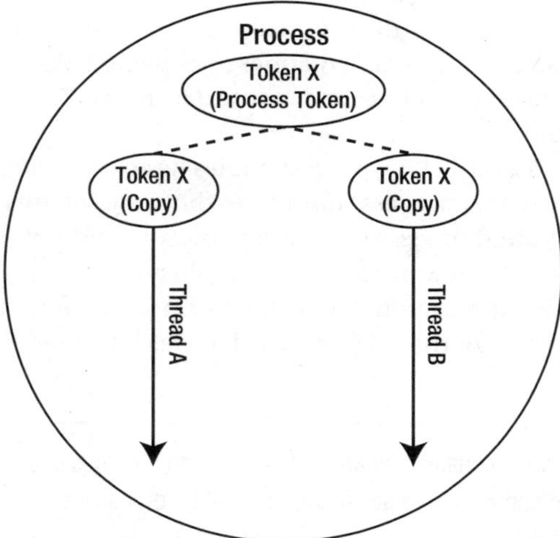

Figure 12-2. *Process with two threads, both of which contain copies of the process-level token*

Processes may, alternatively, create threads that run using a different security context than the process itself. ASP.NET uses this type of thread creation for impersonation. In this scenario, the process authenticates an account using that account's credentials, uses the authenticated account to create a new access token, and associates the newly created access token with a thread in the process. This allows that particular thread to access resources using a different security context than the process itself and to access resources to which access would otherwise be denied (see Figure 12-3).

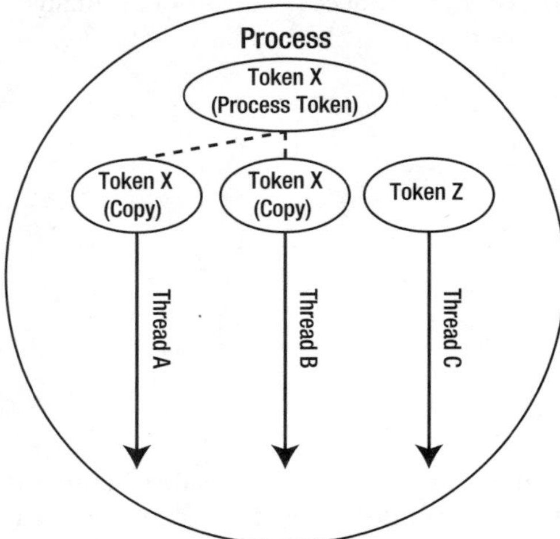

Figure 12-3. *Three threads in a process and their associated access tokens*

Figure 12-3 shows an example of a threaded process and the access tokens assigned at the process and thread level. Notice that the process is running under the security context in Token X. You can see from the diagram that the process has three threads running inside it, and that the process created Thread A and Thread B in the default manner by copying Token X to the individual threads. Thread C, however, runs under the security context of Token Z, giving it different permissions than Threads A and B.

Whenever a process launches another process, the calling process copies its access token to the new process. This ensures that the newly created process runs under the same security context of the parent process. Like threads, the parent process has the capability to authenticate an account and create a new access token for the new process. You should rarely be creating an entirely new process from an ASP.NET application, but if you do, understand that it runs using the same security context of the process or thread from which it was launched.

■ **Tip** Executing processes from an ASP.NET application is usually indicative of bad design. Process execution is not very scalable, so think about redesigning the application to avoid calling external processes.

You can alter the security context for an ASP.NET applications or individual users by implementing impersonation. A general overview of impersonation and delegation are given next, and configuring impersonation and delegation are discussed later in the chapter.

Impersonation

Impersonation allows you to run a process or thread using the security context of a different account instead of inheriting the security context from the current process or thread. This can be very useful in ASP.NET because ASP.NET normally runs under the least privileged ASPNET account in IIS 5 and Network Service in IIS 6, which has limited access to system resources.

ASP.NET supports application-level and user-level impersonation. Application-level impersonation allows you to specify an account used to process requests for the application. ASP.NET ensures that any thread used to process a request for that application has an access token using the security context of that particular account.

User-level impersonation allows ASP.NET to authenticate the user, acquire an access token with that user's security context, and process the request using that individual user's security context. This means that ASP.NET can access any resources to which the user has been granted access.

Delegation

Discussions on delegation and impersonation can sometimes be confusing because it seems like impersonation and delegation are two different concepts even though they aren't. Delegation is a form of impersonation involving an account that can be authenticated on a remote machine.

Here's how it works. Impersonating an account requires that you provide credentials for the account you want to impersonate. After successfully authenticating that account, Windows associates an access token containing the security context of the account with the process or thread on which you're running the impersonation. Access tokens only contain the security context for an authenticated account, so the security context remains valid on the local machine and no further authentication is ever required.

The real question is what happens when that process or thread attempts to access a resource on a remote machine? Remote machines don't blindly accept access tokens from other machines, so the remote machine wants to verify the credentials of the security context contained in the access token. If you're using an account that is only available on the local machine, then the remote machine has no way of authenticating the request, and the account can't be used for delegation. When both the local and remote computers can authenticate the credentials from an account, the account supports delegation, and the request may be processed by the remote machine.

■ **Note** Delegation requires appropriately configured accounts and authentication mechanisms, which are discussed in further detail in the "Configuring Delegation" section.

Access Token and Impersonation Examples

You can see how impersonation and access tokens work using the **Run As** feature in Windows Explorer. For this example, you need to create two new user accounts on your system. Call one Manager and the other Employee. Make sure you set their passwords to something you'll remember. Then create a folder named `Managers Only` somewhere on your hard drive. Right-click on the folder and click **Properties** from the context menu to bring up the **Folder Properties** dialog box. Locate the **Security** tab on the dialog box.

Note If you don't have a Security tab, then you may not be using NTFS or you may have Simple File Sharing enabled. To disable Simple File Sharing, select **Tools ➤ Folder Options** from the **Explorer** menu. This brings up the **Folder Options** dialog box. Click on the **View** tab and scroll through the options. Disable the **Use simple file sharing** option at the end of the list.

Add the Manager account to the **Group or user names** listing. Make sure all options in the **Permissions for Manager** listing are set to **Allow**. Add the Employee account to the **Group or user names** listing. Make sure all options in the **Permissions for Employee** are set to **Deny** (see Figure 12-4).

Allow access to the Manager role

Deny access to the Employee role

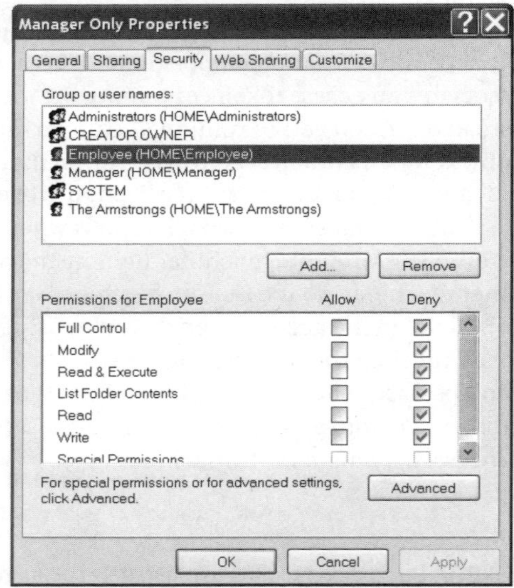

Figure 12-4. *Setting permissions on the* `Managers Only` *folder*

Create a text file in the `Managers Only` folder and enter some text into it. Now, log in using the Employee account, launch Notepad, and try to open the text file in the `Managers Only` folder. An Access Denied message appears informing that the Employee account is denied access to the file because the files inherit permission settings from the folder, and Notepad is running under the Employee security context.

■Note If you don't grant a user access to a folder (for example, `c:\secure\`), but grant the user access to a file in that folder (for example, `c:\secure\filename.txt`), the user can still access that file. It may be difficult, however, as the user *cannot* browse through the folder to locate the file because the user hasn't been given permission to access the folder.

Navigate to `C:\Windows\`. Locate `cmd.exe` and right-click it to display the context menu. Select the **Run As** option from the context menu. This displays the **Run As** dialog box, which allows you to impersonate a different account without having to log in as someone else (see Figure 12-5).

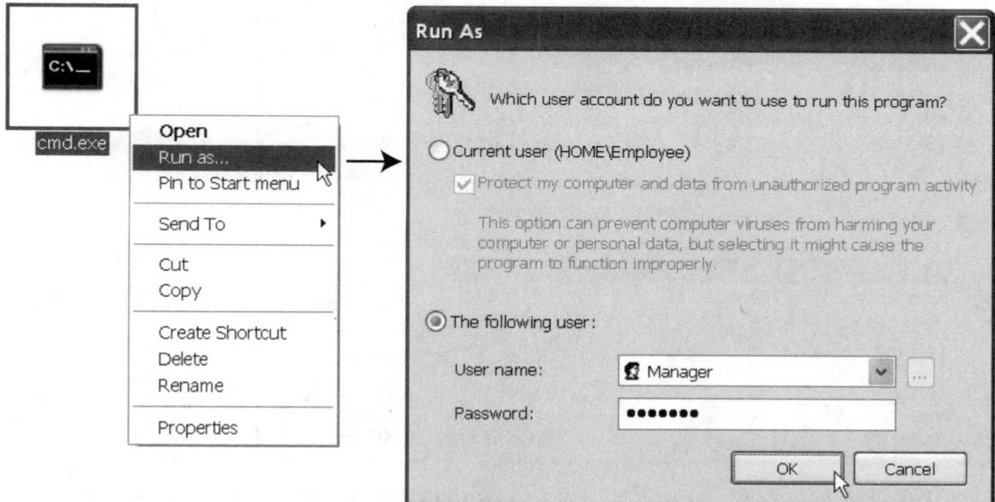

Figure 12-5. *Running an application under a different account*

Select the **The following user** option button and enter **Manager** and the password you set up for the Manager account in the appropriate text boxes. Then click okay. You'll see the command prompt displayed, but the `CMD.EXE` process has the Manager access token associated with it instead of the Employee access token. You can confirm this by running Windows Task Manager (by right-clicking on the taskbar and selecting the **Task Manager** option) and looking at the **Processes** tab. Notice that the username associated with `CMD.EXE` is Manager, not Employee.

Next, type **Notepad.exe** into the command prompt and press Enter. This launches Notepad. Open the Task Manager again and look at the username associated with the `Notepad.exe` process (see Figure 12-6).

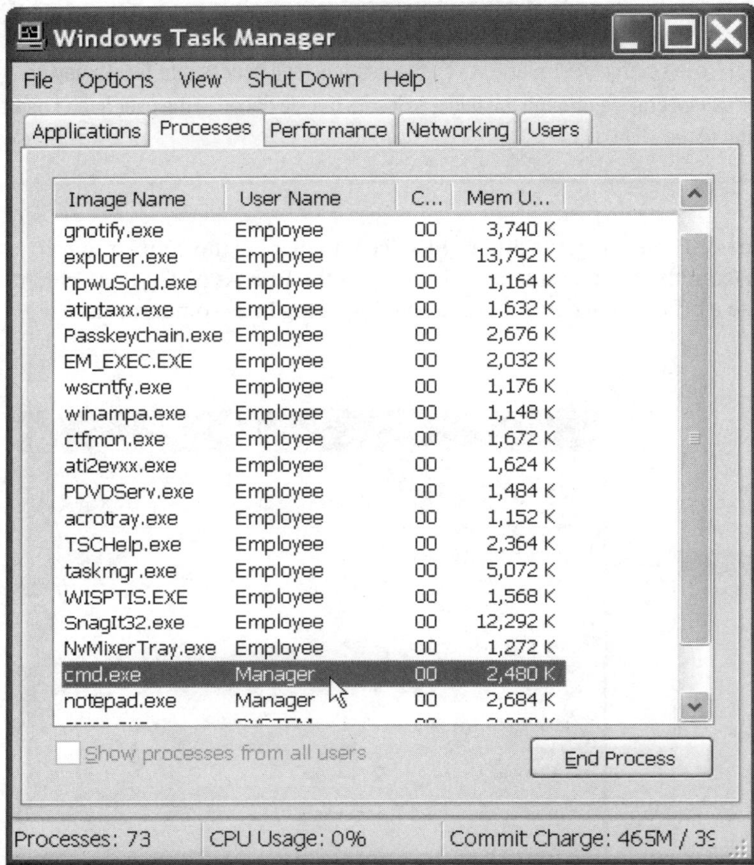

Figure 12-6. *Notice that* `cmd.exe` *and* `notepad.exe` *are running under the Manager account, whereas the other processes are running under the Employee account*

Since you launched the `Notepad.exe` process from the `CMD.EXE` process, and the `CMD.EXE` process has a Manager access token, the `Notepad.exe` process also has a Manager access token. Use Notepad to open up the text file in the `Managers Only` folder. Now you can access the folder and file because Notepad is running under the appropriate security context.

ASP.NET Security Architecture Overview

Determining an appropriate security strategy for your application requires a basic understanding of how the different components associated with ASP.NET work together and communicate security information to one another. This section provides you with an overview of the security touch points between the browser, IIS, ASP.NET, and various system resources such as the file system, databases, and enterprise services. It also describes various internal security mechanisms in ASP.NET.

Because this discussion focuses on security interaction between various components, it may help you to have a visual roadmap of those components. Figure 12-7 shows the items involved in processing an ASP.NET request and the sequence in which the request passes through those components.

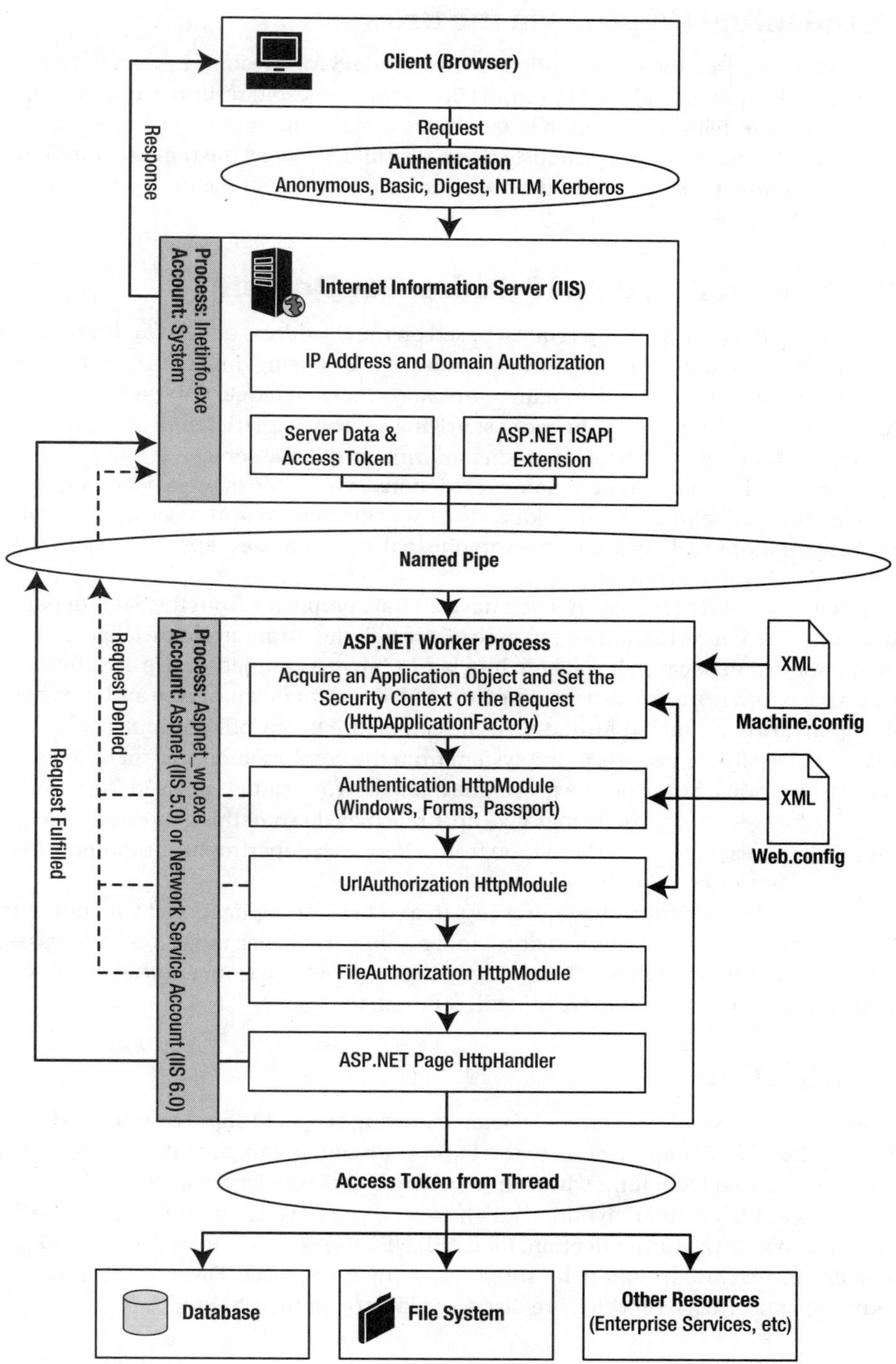

Figure 12-7. *Security between the browser, IIS, ASP.NET, and various system resources*

Sending the Initial Request via the Browser

Browsers kick off the entire process by sending a request to IIS for a resource managed by ASP.NET. Initially, the request only contains the URL of the requested resource and various HTTP headers. No identifying information is sent in the initial request because browsers attempt to connect to resources anonymously when possible. Because the request comes in via a TCP/IP connection, IIS knows certain network information about the browser, such as the IP address.

IIS Authorization Based on IP Address or Domain

IIS has the capability to allow or deny a request based on the IP address or domain from which the request originated. Remember, the browser sends a request using the TCP/IP protocol, so IIS inherently has access to the IP and domain information for each request. IIS generates a 403 Access Denied HTTP error whenever the request originates from a restricted IP address or domain, effectively keeping users from accessing information on the server.

You can use IP address and domain name restrictions in a couple of ways. First, let's say that you have an internal application developed for a specific department or group. You can use IP address restrictions to deny access to everyone in the company except the subset of IP's for the individuals who actually need access.

What does this do? Well, let's say that you have an irate employee from the Sales department who wants to steal information stored in the Research department's knowledge management application because it will help him land a job at a competitor. He acquires a username and password from an unsuspecting Research department employee and runs back to his desk to pull down as much information as he can before taking off. Without any IP restrictions, he can easily gain access to the system from the comfort and safety of his own office. With IP restrictions, however, the username and password cannot be used from the computer in his office. At that point he may give up, or he may do something more likely to get himself caught like access research information from a Research department computer, where he is more likely to be noticed.

You can also use IP restrictions to deny access to a website or application if you notice an unusually large amount of suspicious activity coming from a particular range of IP addresses. Of course, they can always get around this by accessing your website from another location, but anything you can do to make it more difficult for them the better.

IIS Authentication

ASP.NET may require a user to authenticate before allowing access to some resources. If you have configured the ASP.NET application to use Forms Authentication, then the user is simply redirected to a web-based login form where they can enter their credentials; ASP.NET disregards IIS authentication information entirely. If, however, you have configured the ASP.NET application to use Windows Authentication, then ASP.NET uses the IIS authentication information to determine user information. IIS supports Anonymous, Basic, Digest, NTLM, and Kerberos authentication, each of which are discussed later on in this chapter.

Note IIS authentication settings are independent of your ASP.NET configuration. In other words, configuring ASP.NET to use Windows Authentication does *not* mean IIS automatically uses Windows Authentication. Nor does using Forms Authentication mean IIS automatically uses Anonymous Authentication. You must configure the ASP.NET application (via `Web.config`) and the IIS application (via the IIS console) to use appropriate authentication types.

IIS forces users to authenticate by denying anonymous requests with a 401 Unauthorized HTTP error. Response headers returned with the error identify the type of authentication mechanism the browser should use when communicating with IIS. The supported authentication mechanisms may change from resource to resource depending on how you have configured individual applications in IIS. Upon receiving a 401 Unauthorized HTTP error, browsers know to prompt the user for credentials and to retry the request with the appropriate authentication data. Assuming the browser supports one of the authentication types specified, it resends the request with the appropriate authentication data. If not, the browser should inform the user that the authentication method is not supported.

Authentication data is normally acquired when the browser displays a username and password dialog box, and the user enters the credentials. Internet Explorer, however, supports an authentication mechanism called Integrated Windows Authentication (which ultimately uses NTLM or Kerberos Authentication). Integrated Windows Authentication uses Internet Explorer's access token to provide IIS with authentication data. Assuming IIS can authenticate that browser's access token, which usually requires the user's computer and the server to be in the same internal network, this provides a dialogless login process for Internet Explorer users that most people tend to appreciate. Otherwise, IIS rejects the credentials and Internet Explorer prompts the user to enter a different username and password.

Note Firefox supports Integrated Windows Authentication, but it displays a dialog box to the user.

After IIS receives the request with the appropriate authentication data, it verifies that authentication data either against a local data store or Active Directory and either rejects or accepts the authentication. If authentication fails, IIS generates another 401 Unauthorized HTTP error and allows the browser to attempt authentication again. If authentication succeeds, IIS creates an access token for the user.

Note IIS always generates an access token for each request it passes to ASP.NET. If the user has not explicitly authenticated with IIS (for example, Anonymous or Forms Authentication is in use), then IIS generates an access token using the anonymous account (normally `IUSR_<machinename>`) configured in the IIS virtual directory settings.

IIS then passes that access token and server information about the request to the ASP.NET ISAPI extension (`ASPNET_ISAPI.DLL`, for reference), which in turns hands the request to the ASP.NET worker process that actually fulfills the request.

The ASP.NET ISAPI Extension and the ASP.NET Worker Process

IIS is a web server geared toward serving static files, so it doesn't inherently have the capability to process dynamic ASP, ASP.NET, JSP, or PHP files. It does, however, support an extensible framework called the Internet Server Application Programming Interface (ISAPI) that allows for plug-ins that can handle dynamic files. IIS hosts various ISAPI extensions in its own memory space and allows you to map certain file types to certain extensions. If a request for an ASP 3.0 page comes through, IIS knows to send it to the ASP 3.0 ISAPI extension. If a request for an ASP.NET page (or related resource) comes through, IIS knows to send it to the ASP.NET ISAPI extension (see Figure 12-8).

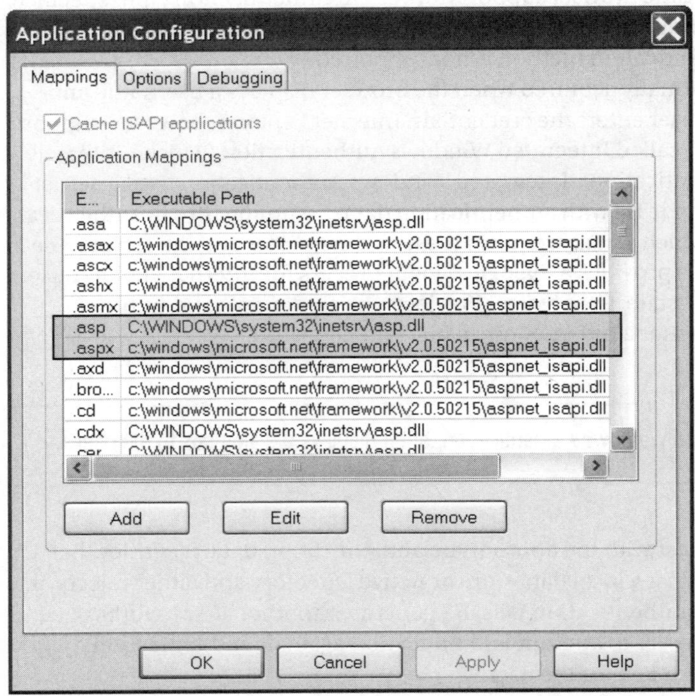

Figure 12-8. *ISAPI application mappings. Notice that* `.asp` *pages are sent to the* `asp.dll` *for processing and* `.aspx` *pages are sent to the* `aspnet_isapi.dll` *for processing.*

Most ISAPI extensions process their dynamic files directly from the ISAPI extension hosted in the IIS process. This means that an exception in the ISAPI extension could extend into the IIS process causing the entire process to crash, and ultimately cut off all access to the web server until IIS can restart. This is bad. Microsoft designed ASP.NET to avoid crashing the IIS process by running the core ASP.NET compilation and execution functionality in an entirely different process outside of IIS and the ASP.NET ISAPI extension. The external process that actually does all the processing work for an ASP.NET request is aptly named the ASP.NET worker process.

The ASP.NET ISAPI extension is responsible for starting and monitoring the ASP.NET worker process. At any given point in time, you can only have as many worker processes running as you have processors on the system. If you have one processor, then you can only have one worker process. If you have four processors, then you can have up to four worker processes. If the worker process crashes, hangs, or hits predefined performance limits, then the ASP.NET ISAPI extension simply kills the process and starts a new worker process in its place.

■ **Note** Technically, you could have more than one worker process running per processor because the ISAPI extension attempts to allow the worker process to finish any remaining requests before it terminates the process.

This allows IIS to continue running in the event an ASP.NET application has a serious error. When the ASP.NET worker process starts up, the ASP.NET ISAPI extension uses configuration settings from `Machine.config` to authenticate an account and give the worker process an appropriate access token to define the security context under which it may run. By default, ASP.NET runs under the least privileged ASPNET/Network Service account.

Notice that the ASP.NET ISAPI extension passes the request, server data, and the access token IIS created for the request to the worker process using a named pipe. The server data contain important information used to set up the `Server`, `Request`, and `Response` objects in ASP.NET, and the access token defines the account IIS authenticated. The named pipe is used because IIS and the ASP.NET worker process run in two separate processes. Processes can't directly communicate with one another because they are isolated by the operating system. The isolation is what allows ASP.NET to crash without affecting IIS. Thus, communication between the two processes must occur over a named pipe. Named pipes are operating system mechanisms that allow two processes to pass information back and forth while still maintaining their isolation.

At this point, the request resides in the ASP.NET worker process, and IIS waits for a response from the worker process so it can fulfill the request. Now let's take a look at how the worker process handles a request.

Application Objects and the Security Context of the Request

After the ASP.NET worker process receives the request, it routes the request through a series of objects known as the HTTP pipeline. All the objects in the HTTP pipeline are associated with an `HttpApplication` object, so the first responsibility of the HTTP pipeline is to find an appropriate `HttpApplication` object to handle the request.

The first object in the HTTP pipeline is the Application Factory, represented by an `Http➥ApplicationFactory` object. This object creates and maintains pools of `HttpApplication` objects. When a request passes through the `HttpApplicationFactory`, the factory determines which application the request is targeting and acquires an appropriate `HttpApplication` object for the request. The HttpApplication object may come from a pool, or the HttpApplication➥Factory may need to create a new HttpApplication object if one isn't already available.

After acquiring the appropriate HttpApplication object, ASP.NET can assign the thread processing the request an appropriate security context. By default, the thread inherits the same security context as the process in which it runs, meaning that the thread normally runs using the same security context as the ASP.NET worker process. If you have impersonation enabled, then the worker process assigns the thread a security context based on your configuration settings in Web.config. If you're using applicationwide impersonation, then ASP.NET assigns the thread the security context of the account you have configured for the application. If you're using user-based impersonation, then ASP.NET assigns the thread a security context using the access token it received from IIS.

Next, ASP.NET runs through all the modules for the HttpApplication object acquired from the Application Factory. An HTTP module is a class that implements the IHttpModule interface. In the next sections, you'll learn about the Authentication, UrlAuthorization, and File➥Authorization HTTP modules.

ASP.NET Authentication Modules

The ASP.NET authentication modules handle authentication details (if necessary) and load user information into the context of the request. The context is a set of information that follows the request through the HttpPipeline (you can access the context via the Context object in ASP.NET). Each authentication type in ASP.NET uses a different mechanism to determine if a user is authenticated. Regardless of the authentication mechanism used, however, the user information must make its way into the User property of the Context object. There are three authentication modules: the WindowsAuthentication module, FormsAuthentication module, and the PassportAuthentication module (not covered).

First, we'll look at the WindowsAuthentication module. Any time IIS hands off a request to the ASP.NET worker process, it passes the worker process a token that identifies the user. If the user connects anonymously, then IIS passes ASP.NET the anonymous user token, which gives the user the permissions associated with the anonymous user account. If the user authenticates against IIS, then IIS passes ASP.NET a token identifying the user and the user's individual permissions. Although ASP.NET can use this token for impersonation, it only does so if it has been configured for user-level impersonation. Also understand that the ASP.NET worker process associates the user token with the thread that handles the request before it sends the requests through the HttpPipeline. When the request reaches the WindowsAuthentication module, the module does not need to re-authenticate the user because it already has access to the user token, meaning the user has already been authenticated. As such, the Windows➥Authentication module just copies the user information from the token into the User property of the Context object (more on the details of that in a second).

The FormsAuthentication module has a bit more work to do because it disregards the token it receives from IIS (ASP.NET always receives a token from IIS). Forms Authentication bases a user's authentication status on the presence of a valid authentication ticket contained within a cookie or URL. So the FormsAuthentication module checks for the authentication ticket in the authentication cookie (normally, ASPXAUTH) and the URL. If no ticket is found, or the ticket is found but is invalid or expired, then the module loads anonymous user information (blank username) into the User property of the Context object and denotes that the user isn't authenticated. If the ticket is found, then the module loads the appropriate user information into the User property.

Each authentication module is responsible for creating an IPrincipal object representing the authenticated account and placing it in the User property of the Context object. The Context object provides contextual information for a request, including user information, session data, request specifics, and so on. An IPrincipal object is an interface for defining principal objects in the .NET Framework. Various principal objects have varying degrees of functionality. Windows Authentication, for example, results in a System.Security.➥Principal.WindowsPrincipal object that exposes basic functionality for identifying an authenticated account and checking role information. Forms Authentication results in a System.Web.Security.RolePrincipal object capable of account identification, role checking, and additional functions geared toward storing authentication data in a cookie or URL.

ASP.NET allows you to uses the IPrincipal object in the HttpContext for identity and role checking in ASP.NET, but access to outside resources is still dictated by the security context defined by the access token attached to the thread. In other words, ASP.NET authentication has no effect on the security context of the thread. The resulting IPrincipal object from ASP.NET authentication is, however, used in URL authorization.

URL Authorization Module

URL authorization gives you the ability to allow or deny access to certain directories for individual users or roles. ASP.NET uses the IPrincipal object in the HttpContext to run identity and role checks for URL authorization, so you can define access permissions based on Windows accounts if you're using Windows Authentication or non-Windows accounts if you're using Forms Authentication.

If an incoming request does not pass URL authorization, and the application is using Windows Authentication, then ASP.NET generates a 401 Unauthorized HTTP error and returns it to the client. If the application is configured for Forms Authentication, then ASP.NET redirects the user to the login page specified in Web.config.

File Authorization Module

Configuring your ASP.NET application to use Windows Authentication (via Web.config) enables the file authorization module. The file authorization module checks the NTFS file permissions to determine whether or not the authenticated user has access to the requested resource.

NTFS permission checks are normally performed using the access token of the thread requesting the file. When impersonation is disabled, however, the thread processing the request runs under the security context of the ASPNET/Network Service account for every single user, making it impossible to enforce user-level permissions on requested files. The file authorization module alleviates this issue by using the access token generated by IIS to check NTFS file permissions on the requested file. The IIS token is always representative of the authenticated user, even when impersonation is disabled, making it possible to enforce user-level file permissions.

Why not just enable impersonation? There may be performance issues with database connection pooling that arise when using integrated SQL Server security and user-level impersonation. Thus, the file authorization module allows you the benefit of user-level NTFS permission checking without the performance issues associated with user-level impersonation.

Processing the Actual Request

Finally, after passing through all the modules in the HTTP pipeline, ASP.NET actually executes the requested page. During execution, the page may access various resources, such as files, a database, or enterprise services. Code execution runs under the security context of the thread, so any external resource requests are made using the thread's security context.

This can make for some interesting situations when using Windows Authentication. Remember, the file authorization module uses the access token from IIS to check NTFS permissions on the requested resource and only the requested resource. If the requested resource is an ASP.NET page, that page may attempt to access other resources. At that point, access to files is governed by the access token associated with the thread, not the access token from IIS.

Here's a situation in which this could be an issue. Let's say that your application is configured to use Windows Authentication without impersonation, and a user access an ASP.NET page in that application, logging in as Joe Bloggs. The file authorization module checks the NTFS permissions on the requested resource using the Joe Bloggs security context and allows access to the file. ASP.NET then begins executing the page code. Code inside the page then attempts to read from a file to which the Joe Bloggs security context is denied access according to NTFS permissions. But the file is accessed using the ASPNET/Network Service security context and this allows the file to be read. The contents of the file are then displayed to Joe Bloggs even though Joe Bloggs is explicitly denied access to the file.

Of course, you can also use this behavior to your benefit. If, for instance, you wanted to deny users the ability to view files over the network, but you wanted to grant them the ability to view those files in a web application, then this behavior is great. You just need to be aware of the various behaviors, how they work, and whether or not they will work for your particular situation.

■ **Note** Access to some resources, such as databases, may be governed by security that has nothing to do with the access token associated with the thread. For instance, you may access a database using a connection string with embedded credentials, in which case, the access token has nothing to do with connecting to the resource.

Now that you understand the overall security architecture of ASP.NET, let's look at configuration examples.

Security Configuration

Your application's first line of defense is a proper security configuration. IIS, ASP.NET, and system resources all expose configuration options allowing you to tweak security settings to suit your needs, you just need to know how and when to use them. This section guides you through those decisions, showing you practical configuration settings and the scenarios in which you should use them.

IIS Security Configuration

IIS allows you to configure authentication, IP and domain restrictions, application mappings, and secure communications on an application-by-application basis. This gives you a great deal of flexibility when deploying multiple applications because you can custom-tailor the server security for each individual application.

Most of the security settings in IIS are available from the **Directory Security** tab in the application properties dialog box. You can view the application properties by clicking on the **Internet Information Services** icon in the `Administrative Tools` folder in the **Control Panel**. Expand the navigation tree until you locate the folder that contains the application whose properties you want to view. Right-click on the folder and select the **Properties** option from the context menu. This opens the properties window. Select the **Directory Security** tab from the tabs shown at the top of the window. Figure 12-9 shows the IIS window, expanded folders listing, and the properties window for the Chapter 12 application.

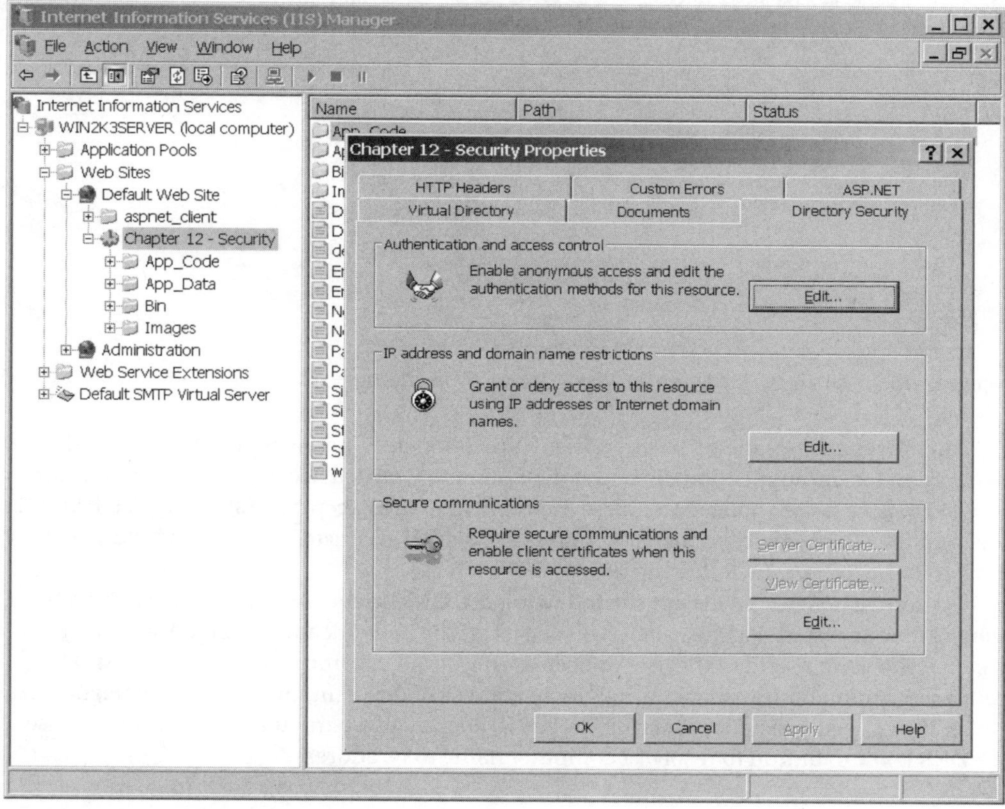

Figure 12-9. *IIS management console and the Chapter 12 Security Application Properties (Directory Security tab shown)*

IP and Domain Restrictions

You can choose to allow or deny access to an application based on the network address of the requestor. To do so, click on the **Edit** button in the **IP address and domain name restrictions** section of the **Directory Security** tab (visible in Figure 12-9). This displays the **IP Address and Domain Name Restriction** dialog box shown in Figure 12-10.

■ **Note** Only Windows NT and Windows Server 2003 allow you to specify IP and Domain Restrictions. You can't set up restrictions on Windows XP. If you view the **Directory Security** tab in Windows XP, the **Edit** button for the IP and domain restrictions is disabled.

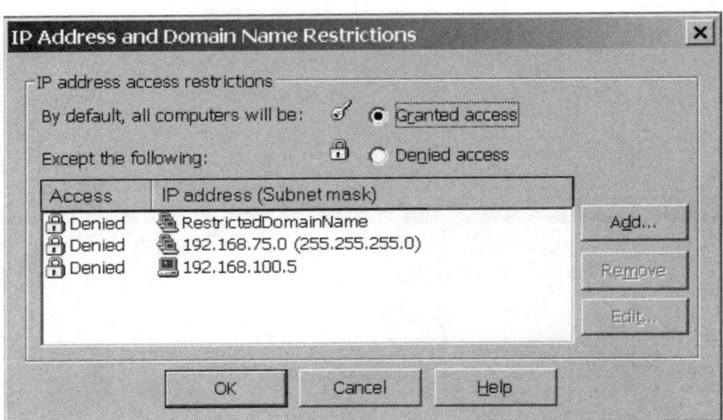

Figure 12-10. *IP Address and Domain Name Restrictions dialog box*

On the restrictions dialog box, you'll see two option buttons allowing you to set the default permission for the application. If you set the option to **Granted access**, then computers are allowed to access the application unless they appear in the **Except the following** list. If you set the option to **Denied access**, then computers are denied access to the application unless they appear in the **Except the following** list.

To add an item to the **Except the following** list, click on the **Add** button. This displays the **Deny/Allow access** dialog box where you can enter the network address of the system or systems you want to add to the list. You can specify a single computer by using the **Single computer** option button and entering the IP address of the computer as shown in Figure 12-11. If you need assistance determining the IP address of a particular system, you can use the **DNS Lookup** button to resolve a computer name to its address.

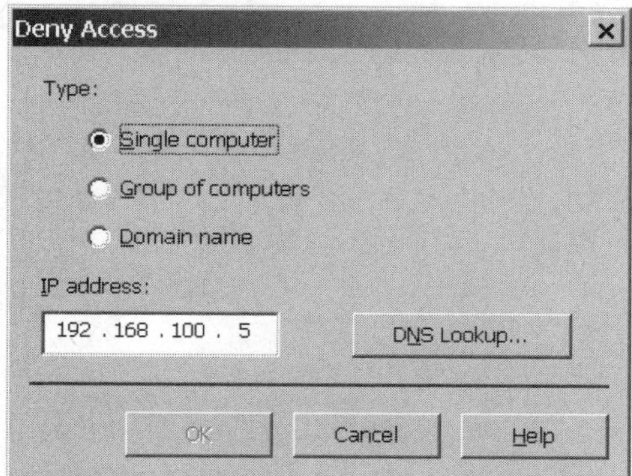

Figure 12-11. *Denying a single computer by IP address*

You can specify a range of computers by selecting the **Group of computers** option button and entering an IP address and a subnet mask as shown in Figure 12-12 (for example, 192.168.75.0 as the IP address and 255.255.255.0 as the subnet mask will include all machines that have an IP address in the range 192.168.75.0 to 192.168.75.255).

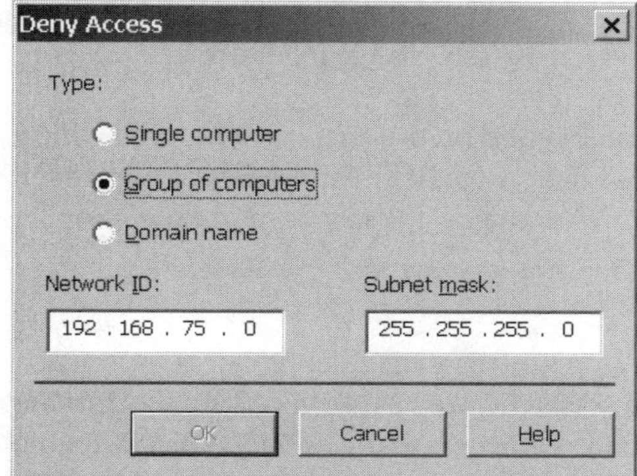

Figure 12-12. *Denying a group of computer by entering an IP address and subnet mask*

Or you can specify a domain name as shown in Figure 12-13.

■ **Caution** Specifying a domain name instead of an IP address or masked IP address requires IIS to do a reverse DNS lookup on the incoming IP address to determine whether it is part of a restricted domain. This takes time to process and may adversely affect performance.

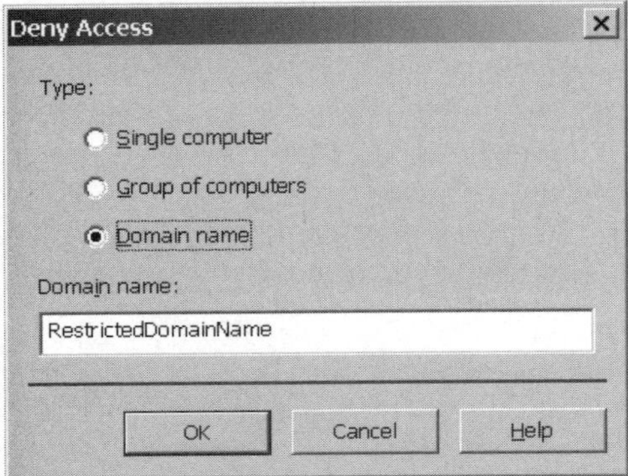

Figure 12-13. *Denying a group of computer by entering domain name*

Authentication

As mentioned before, IIS supports Anonymous, Basic, Digest, and Integrated Windows Authentication. Windows Authentication chooses between NTLM and Kerberos based on availability (IIS uses Kerberos when available but reverts to NTLM if necessary). You can configure the authentication settings for a particular application in IIS via the **Authentication Methods** property window, which is accessible by clicking on the **Edit** button in the **Authentication and access control** section of the **Directory Security** tab (visible in Figure 12-9). Figure 12-14 shows the **Authentication Methods** property window.

You should choose an authentication mechanism based on the needs of your application and the ASP.NET authentication type you plan to use. Below you'll find more information each authentication type and the situations in which you should use it (Passport authentication is beyond the scope of this book).

Anonymous Authentication

At the top of the **Authentication Methods** dialog box (see Figure 12-14), you'll see the **Enable anonymous access** check box, which enables anonymous access to the application. Under the check box, there are two text boxes where you may specify a username and password for the anonymous user account. Remember, IIS always processes requests using the security context of a Windows account. Whenever an anonymous user request a resource, IIS uses the security context of the anonymous user account instead of making the user authenticate. By default, the anonymous user account is called `IUSR_<MACHINE>` (where `<MACHINE>` is the name of your system), and IIS manages the password for the anonymous account. You can opt to change the account or manage the password manually, which is useful if you need to allow the anonymous account for delegation.

You should always enable anonymous access when you use Forms Authentication. The whole point of Forms Authentication is that IIS allows requests to pass through anonymously and lets ASP.NET authenticate those incoming requests using tickets. You should also enable anonymous access when your application is configured using the None authentication option.

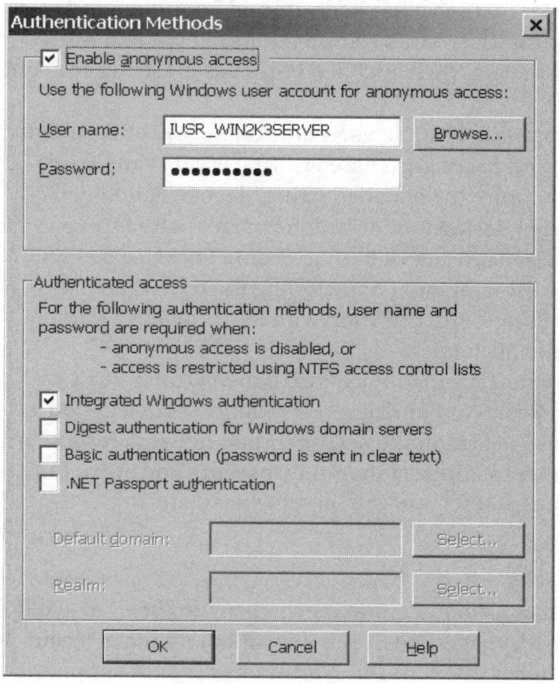

Figure 12-14. *Authentication Methods property window*

If your application uses Windows Authentication, you can still enable anonymous access, but you may have to do a bit more work specifying NTFS file permissions for anonymous users. Windows Authentication causes the file authorization module to become active, so you need to create NTFS permission entries to allow read access for the anonymous user account. If your application is using Windows Authentication and you're not planning to allow anonymous users to access the application, then you should disable anonymous access.

Anonymous access isn't really a type of authentication as much as it is a lack of authentication. Thus, all browsers should support anonymous access so you should never have compatibility issues between browsers when using it.

Basic Authentication

You can enable Basic Authentication in IIS by selecting the **Basic authentication** check box in the **Authenticated access** section of the **Authentication Methods** dialog box (refer to Figure 12-14). You can also specify a default domain and a realm for basic authentication. By default, IIS authenticates credentials against the domain to which the server belongs. If you want IIS to authenticate users against a different domain, specify the domain in the **Default domain** text box. The **Realm** text box allows you to specify text to display to the user when the browser requests credentials; it is informational in nature and does not change the authentication behavior in any way.

Basic Authentication was defined in HTML 1.0, so it has been around for a while and is the most widely supported form of authentication. Users are prompted for their credentials (a username and password), and those credentials are then encoded into a base64 string and sent back to IIS where they can be authenticated.

The biggest issue with Basic Authentication is that the username and password are sent over what amounts to clear text. Encoding and decoding a base64 string is very simple, so anyone with a network scanner can easily capture the encoded string, decode it, and determine someone's username and password. So, Basic Authentication isn't a secure form of authentication in and of itself. There is, of course, a caveat to that. Secure Sockets Layer (SSL) can encrypt all communications between a browser and IIS, including the base64 encoded string used in Basic Authentication. Using Basic Authentication with SSL provides a very secure and widely supported authentication mechanism.

Basic Authentication is a good option when compatibility is an issue because most browsers do support Basic Authentication. Basic Authentication also supports delegation, so it's useful in scenarios where you need to use delegation to access certain network resources. You should always be aware that Basic Authentication is inherently insecure and strive to secure the communication line between the browser and the server when using it.

Digest Authentication

Digest Authentication is a challenge/response authentication mechanism designed to avoid the obvious problems with sending a clear-text password over a network. It's a more recent authentication mechanism than Basic Authentication, so some browsers may not support it. You can enable Digest Authentication in IIS by selecting the **Digest authentication for Windows domain servers** check box in the **Authenticated access** section of the **Authentication Methods** dialog box (refer to Figure 12-14). Digest Authentication is only available if you're running Active Directory.

In Digest Authentication, IIS creates a challenge string and sends it to the browser. The browser then displays a dialog box where the user may enter the credentials, but it does not send those credentials back to IIS unencrypted. Instead, it concatenates the password to the end of the challenge string and hashes the concatenated string. This results in a set of characters known as a digest, which is sent back to IIS along with the username. IIS receives the digest and the username from the client and retrieves the password for the username from Active Directory. It then concatenates the password on the end of the challenge it sent the browser and uses the same algorithm as the browser to create a digest of its own. If the digest sent back from the browser and the digest created by IIS match, then the user is authenticated because IIS can reasonably assume that the user entered the appropriate password.

This is more secure than Basic Authentication because the password isn't sent over the network; however, it comes with its own security risks. Hackers can use replay attacks to overcome Digest Authentication. In a replay attack, hackers use a network scanner to capture a challenge string and the resulting digest. They can then "replay" the captured response, and IIS authenticates them. It takes a little more time and effort than stealing the password outright, but it's still effective.

Digest Authentication isn't as widely supported as Basic Authentication, but is more widely supported than Integrated Windows Authentication. It does not support delegation and requires Active Directory to store account passwords using reversible encryption because IIS needs the original unaltered password to validate the digest. One-way encryption is a more secure password storage format, so you may find some network administrators resistant to the idea of using reversible encryption. You should use Digest Authentication when you don't need to use delegation, and when compatibility is a concern but Basic Authentication is too much of a security risk (for example, you can't secure it with SSL).

Integrated Windows Authentication

Integrated Windows Authentication is a very secure challenge/response style authentication mechanism that offers Internet Explorer users a seamless login experience. Instead of prompting the user for credentials, Internet Explorer uses the logged-in user's credentials to attempt authentication. If authentication succeeds, the user never sees a login screen. If authentication fails, Internet Explorer prompts the user for a different set of credentials. For authentication to be seamless, both the client and server must have access to the same Active Directory or have identical accounts defined on both machines (that is, accounts with the same username and same password). You can enable Integrated Windows Authentication in IIS by selecting the **Integrated Windows authentication** check box at the bottom of the **Authentication methods** dialog box.

The biggest problem with Integrated Windows Authentication is that it is a Microsoft-specific authentication mechanism designed to work in Internet Explorer, making browser compatibility questionable. Firefox supports Integrated Windows Authentication, but it displays a dialog box to the user instead of attempting automatic authentication. Other browsers, such as Opera, simply display a message stating that the authentication type isn't supported. You should not use this authentication method if you need to support a variety of browsers.

Integrated Windows Authentication is actually made up of two different authentication mechanisms, Kerberos and NT LAN Manager (NTLM). By default, Windows 2000 and 2003 servers attempt to use Kerberos Authentication, but fall back on NTLM if the accounts involved are not properly configured. IIS on Windows XP uses NTLM because Kerberos is dependent on Active Directory. Kerberos Authentication may be delegated, but NTLM cannot be delegated, so delegation is highly dependent on configuration. Unfortunately, configuring accounts to use Kerberos Authentication in Active Directory domain controllers is beyond the scope of this book.

Another notable issue is that Integrated Windows Authentication may not work through a firewall when used over a proxy unless sent over a Virtual Private Network (VPN) using Microsoft's Point-to-Point Tunneling Protocol (PPTP).

Integrated Windows Authentication is the preferred authentication type for internal intranet applications where client and servers have access to the same Active Directory, and it can be reasonably assumed that everyone accessing the system uses Internet Explorer. It isn't intended for public-facing websites.

Mixing Authentication Methods

You're not limited to using a single authentication or access method. You can enable anonymous access and support Basic, Digest, and Integrated Windows Authentication all at once. In this type of situation, IIS first attempts to allow the request to occur anonymously. If the anonymous request fails because authentication is required, IIS sends back a request for the browser to authenticate using Integrated Windows, Digest, or Basic Authentication. The browser looks as the authentication options and chooses the most secure one that it supports.

Opera, for instance, does not support Integrated Windows Authentication, so it falls back on Digest Authentication because it's more secure than Basic Authentication.

Application Mappings

As mentioned before, IIS supports an extensible framework to support the processing of dynamic files. Part of that framework is the concept of application mappings. Application mappings contain information that tells IIS which ISAPI extension to use to process certain types of files. This is how IIS knows to process requests for `.aspx` pages using the ASP.NET ISAPI extension.

Application mappings play a big role in ASP.NET security because ASP.NET can only manage security for files mapped to the ASP.NET ISAPI extension. Otherwise, IIS handles the entire request and never passes it off to ASP.NET for processing. If you're using Integrated Windows Authentication in IIS and Windows Authentication in ASP.NET, then you won't notice any problems due to application mappings. Both IIS and ASP.NET use the same account and group information to make authentication and authorization decisions. If, however, you're using Anonymous Authentication in IIS and Forms Authentication in ASP.NET, then you may experience some odd behavior for file extensions not mapped to ASP.NET.

Here's a scenario that will help outline the problem. Let's say that you have a web application to help people track expenses. Employees can enter expenses into the system and managers can see expense tracking reports generated from those entries. Your application writes Excel files with the tracking information to a reports folder. An ASP.NET page in that folder called `ViewReports.aspx` allows managers to easily search for reports. To ensure that only managers can access the Excel reports in that folder, you create a `Web.config` file with an `<authorization>` section allowing the Manager role to access the directory but denying access to the Employee role. Unfortunately, Excel files are not mapped to the ASP.NET ISAPI extension. Now let's see how this affects access to those files.

A user with manager-level access logs in to the application. ASP.NET authenticates the user and creates a ticket identifying the user as a member of the Manager role. The user then requests the `ViewReport.aspx` page. The ASP.NET authorization module knows that only users in the Manager role may request files in the Reports folder, so it checks the role information associated with the user. Because the user is in the Manager role, ASP.NET authorizes the request and displays a list of reports to the user. The user clicks on a report to open it. The request for the Excel file goes to IIS, but it isn't routed to ASP.NET. Because IIS is using anonymous access, IIS checks the NTFS permissions on the file to determine if the anonymous user account has access to the file. It does not. The user is denied access to the file even though the user is logged in as a Manager in the ASP.NET application. A worse scenario occurs if the anonymous user account has access to the files because IIS always serves the file, even to users who should not have access.

You can avoid this issue by creating application mappings for file types you want managed by ASP.NET security. This forces ASP.NET to process the requests and enforce security constraints on the requested file. However, allowing ASP.NET to handle files will hinder performance because of the extra steps involved in passing the request off to ASP.NET.

To create a new application mapping, open your application's properties window. Click on the **Directory** tab (this will be Home Directory, Virtual Directory, or simply Directory depending upon what tpe of directory it is). Click on the **Configuration** button in the bottom-right section of the window (shown in Figure 12-15).

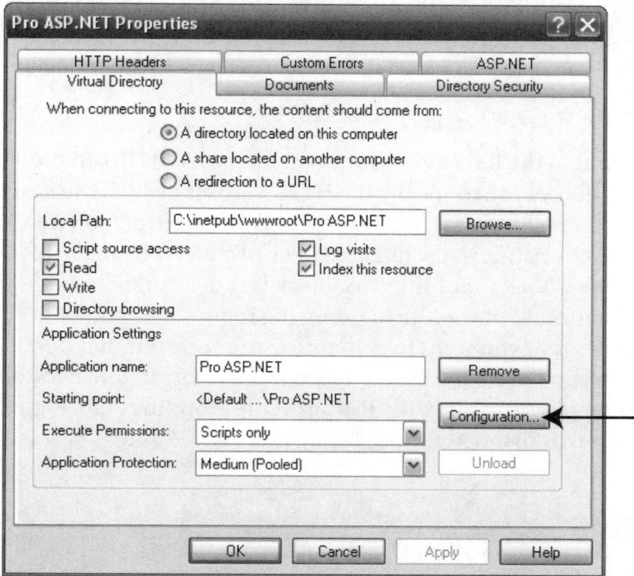

Figure 12-15. *Properties window showing the* ***Configuration*** *button*

This displays the **Application Configuration** dialog box. Select the **Mappings** tab if it isn't already selected. You can see a listing of extensions, their respective ISAPI extension mappings in this tab, and buttons allowing you to add, edit, or delete mappings (shown in Figure 12-16).

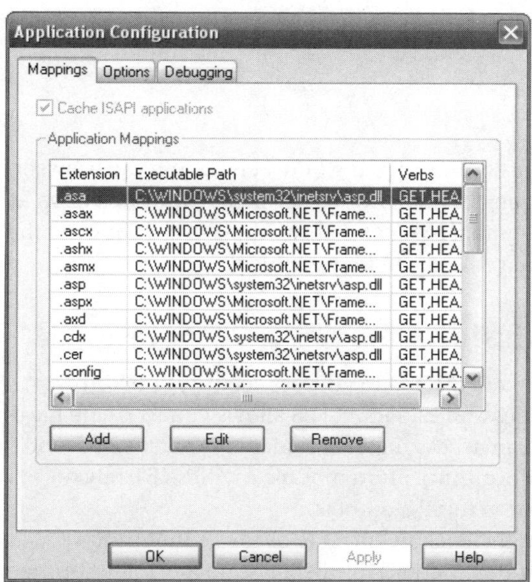

Figure 12-16. ***Mapping*** *tab displaying all the file extension mappings in the application*

Click the **Add** button to display the **Add/Edit Application Extension Mapping** dialog box (shown in Figure 12-17). To add a mapping to ASP.NET, click the **Browse** button and locate `aspnet_isapi.dll`. It is usually located in

```
C:\Windows\Microsoft.NET\Framework\<version>\aspnet_isapi.dll
```

You may then specify the extension of the file type you want to map to ASP.NET in the **Extension** text box. The **Verbs** section allows you to specify the HTTP verbs for which the ISAPI mapping is valid. Unless you have a compelling reason to do otherwise, use the default **All Verbs** option. Leave the **Script engine** check box in its default, checked state. It deals with execution permissions for the `.DLL`. The **Check that file exists** check box determines whether IIS will check the file system for the requested file before handing the request off to the ISAPI extension. This is helpful for virtual files that you want to generate using code but that don't actually exist on the file system. When you have entered the appropriate information, click on the **OK** button. You'll see your new mapping appear in the listing on the **Mappings** tab. Figure 12-17 shows the **Add/Edit Application Extension Mapping** dialog box.

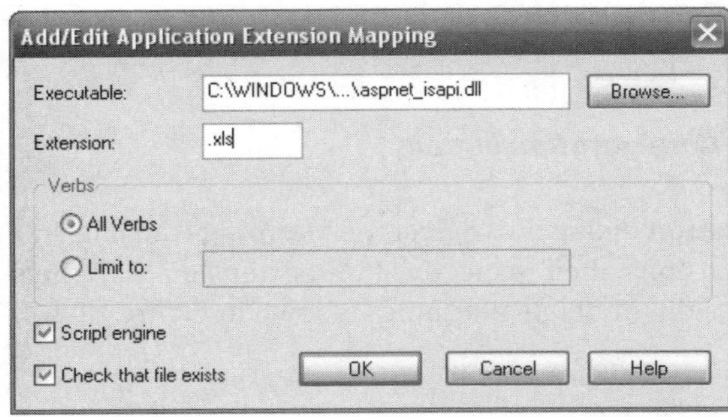

Figure 12-17. *Adding a new extension mapping*

Securing Communications

IIS supports the HTTPS protocol for encrypting communicating between IIS and the browser. It requires a valid server certificate, which can be obtained from a certificate authority such as VeriSign. A complete discussion of certificate management and network security is beyond the scope of this book, but know that this is the area where you may enable it.

Securing Files with NTFS Permissions

Microsoft created the New Technology File System (NTFS) to address security concerns regarding users, groups, and access rights to files and folders. NTFS allows you to create file- and folder-level permissions that define who can access files, list folder contents, and even execute applications. Security in IIS and the file authorization module in ASP.NET rely on NTFS permissions to determine whether or not to fulfill a request.

You can configure NTFS permissions by right-clicking on a file or folder in Windows Explorer and selecting **Properties** from the context menu. This displays the file/folder properties dialog box. Select the **Security** tab to view the NTFS permissions, which are shown in Figure 12-18.

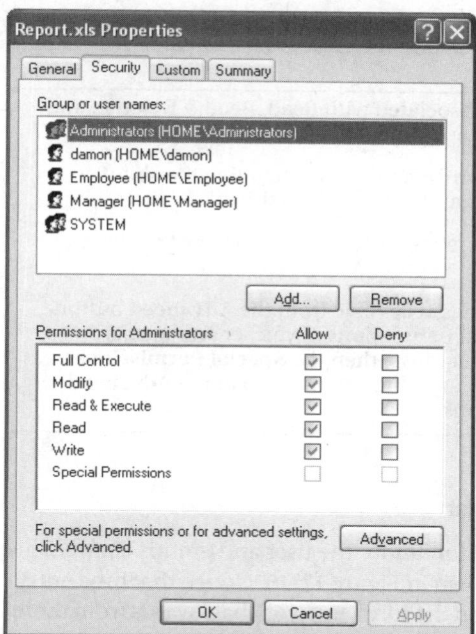

Figure 12-18. *NTFS permissions in the* ***Security*** *tab of the file/folder properties dialog box*

On the **Security** tab, you'll see two distinct areas. The top area displays a list of users and groups for which permissions are defined. You can select an individual user or group by clicking on the name of the item. When an item is selected, the security permissions for that user or group appear below the user and group listing, showing whether the particular permissions is allowed or denied. Permissions explicitly defined for the file/folder are shown as normal check boxes, whereas any inherited permissions are shown as checked but grayed out check boxes. You can use the permission check boxes to either allow or deny a user or group the ability to perform certain actions, but you can't change the inherited permissions. Table 12-2 lists the various permissions and what it allows the user or group to do in regards to the file or folder.

Table 12-2. *General NTFS Security Permissions*

Permissions	Description
Read	Allows user or group to read the file, file attributes, extended attributes, and NTFS permissions.
Read & Execute	Allows the user or group all privileges associated with the Read permissions and the ability to execute the file if it is an executable (`WinWord.exe`, `Notepad.exe`, `CMD.exe`, and so on).
Write	Write permission on a folder allows the user to create files and subfolders in the folder and write attributes/extended attributes for folders. Write permission on a file allows the user to append or overwrite data in the file and write attributes/extended attributes for the file.

Table 12-2. *General NTFS Security Permissions (Continued)*

Permissions	Description
Modify	Allows the user or group all privileges associated with Read, Read & Execute, and Write, as well as the ability to delete a file or folder.
Full Control	Allows the user or group complete control over the file, including the ability to change permissions for users or groups and to take ownership of the file.
List Folder Contents	This is a folder specific permission that gives the user rights to view the files and folders inside of a folder.
Special Permissions	There are a total of 13 permission settings accessible from the **Advanced** button that allow for a more granular control of permissions. If you set any special permissions using these more detailed settings, then the **Special Permissions** check boxes may be checked. This indicates that you must go to the **Advanced** settings to view all the actual permissions.

Adding Accounts or Groups to the Permissions List

You can add an account by clicking on the **Add** button under the user and groups listing. This displays the **Select Users or Groups** dialog box shown in Figure 12-19. Notice the three entry fields on the form. I'll start with the last entry field on the form and work backwards from there.

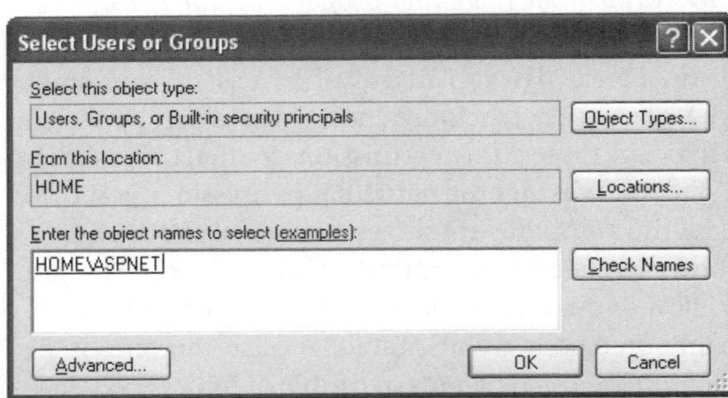

Figure 12-19. *Select Users or Groups dialog box*

Near the bottom of the **Select Users or Groups** add dialog box, you'll see a text entry area. This area allows you to enter a single principal (user or group) or a semicolon delimited list of principals. You can fully qualify the principal name, that is, **domain\principal**, or you can enter a nonqualified principal, that is, **principal**, and the add process will qualify the principal using the default location (which is defined in the second entry field). After you've entered all the items you want to add, click on the **Check Names** button to verify the names you have entered or click the **OK** button (which checks the names and submits changes). The **Select Users or Groups** dialog then attempts to verify the principal names you have entered. If all the names are located successfully, they appear in the text area with an underline. If not, you'll see a **Name Not Found** dialog box that allows you to correct the error or search for the appropriate principal. You can also use the **Advanced** button to bring up a more fully featured search mechanism by which to locate principal names.

In the middle of the **Select Users or Groups** dialog box, you'll see a **From this location** entry field. This defines the default location against which unqualified names are checked. Valid locations include your local machine's account and groups and any domain servers to which you have access. If you're connected to a domain, then the location defaults to that domain. Thus, you'll need to fully qualify or change the location to your local machine when creating permissions for local accounts (such as the ASPNET account).

At the top of the dialog box, you'll see an entry area allowing you to specify the object types you want to add. By default, you can add any type of object—users, groups or built-in security principals. You can narrow this down to a specific type of object if you so desire. This may help reduce the name verification process if you have a large number of users and groups through which to search. It could also help if you make a mental mistake and enter a group name instead of a user account name. Normally, however, you'll just leave it at its default settings.

After you click the **Add** button, the verified principal names are added to the **Group or user names** list on the **Security** tab of the file/folder properties dialog box.

Allowing, Implicitly Denying, and Explicitly Denying Permissions

Although there are check boxes for allowing and denying permissions, there are actually three settings for NTFS permissions. You can explicitly allow a permission by checking the **Allow** check box. You can explicitly deny a permission by checking the **Deny** box. Or you can implicitly deny a permission by not checking anything. When NTFS checks permissions, it does so by first checking whether or not the permission is explicitly denied, then whether or not the permission is explicitly allowed. If it is neither denied nor allowed, then it is implicitly denied because it was not allowed.

Explicit denial has serious ramifications because account permissions are an aggregate of the account permissions and any group permissions with which the account is associated. If an account is explicitly allowed permission to access a certain file, but is part of a group that is explicitly denied access to the file, then the user will be denied access to that file. This is why Microsoft recommends that you use implicit denial instead of explicit denial unless you have a compelling reason to do otherwise.

Permission Inheritance and Behavior

By default, files and folders inherit permissions from their parent folder. A folder that is 5 or 10 levels deep in the file system may be inheriting permissions from a root-level folder or drive. If you don't want a folder inheriting permissions from its parent, then you can disable inheritance. You can do this via the **Advanced Security Settings** dialog box shown in Figure 12-20, which you can bring up by clicking on the **Advanced** button in the **Security** tab of the file/folder properties dialog box (refer to Figure 12-18).

The **Inherit from parent...** check box near the bottom of the **Permissions** tab allows you to turn off inheritance. You'll then be asked whether you want to Copy or Remove the inherited permissions. Copying the permissions means that all the inherited permissions will now be explicitly defined for the file or folder. Removing the inherited permissions simply clears any inherited permissions on the file or folder.

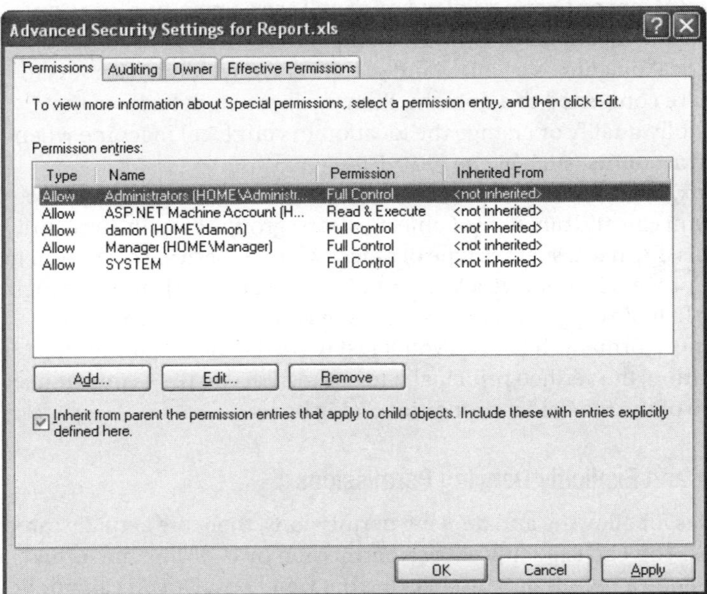

Figure 12-20. *Advanced Security Settings* *dialog box. Notice the* ***Inherit from parent...*** *check box near the bottom of the screen.*

■ **Tip** Another useful feature of the **Advanced Security Settings** dialog box is the **Effective Permissions** tab. This allows you to specify an account and see a permission listing for that account that includes permissions from groups with which the account is associated. This can be helpful when trying to determine why a particular account can't access a specific resource.

Files and folders can have both inherited and explicitly defined permissions. So, you can inherit a base set of permissions from a parent folder and then add additional permissions to specific files and folders as you so choose.

Another interesting aspect of NTFS permissions is that you don't need access to a parent folder to have access to child folders or files. For example, let's say you want to access a file named `C:\FolderA\FolderB\FolderC\Report.xls`. Let's say you've been denied read and write access to `FolderA`, `FolderB`, and `FolderC`, but have been allowed read and write access to `Report.xls`. You can actually open `Report.xls` as long as you know the full path to the file. You can't browse for the file because you'll get an Access Denied error trying to browser through any of the folders.

Now that you've seen both IIS and NTFS configuration settings, lets take a look at the various ways you can configure ASP.NET.

ASP.NET Security Configuration Settings

In the beginning of this chapter, you learned that ASP.NET has its own security mechanisms for handling authentication and authorization. You also looked at impersonation and how the security context of a process or thread dictates the security rights of an application. In this section, you'll learn how to configure authentication, authorization, and impersonation for an ASP.NET application.

Unless otherwise noted, you should assume that configuration setting discussed in the following sections should be placed in `Web.config` located in the application's root folder.

Configuring ASP.NET Authentication

As you know, ASP.NET supports Windows, Forms, Passport, and Anonymous (None) Authentication. You learned about the benefits and drawbacks to each earlier on in this chapter, so I'll focus solely on configuration here. (I'll not discuss Passport Authentication because it isn't something most developers will encounter.)

Anonymous Authentication

Anonymous Authentication is the easiest authentication mechanism to configure because it requires very little ASP.NET configuration and no NTFS configuration. Listing 12-1 shows how it looks in `Web.config`.

Listing 12-1. *Configuring Anonymous Authentication in* `Web.config`

```
<configuration>
    <system.web>
        <authentication mode="None" />
    </system.web>
</configuration>
```

You should configure IIS to allow anonymous access when using Anonymous Authentication in ASP.NET if you truly want the access to be anonymous. Otherwise, IIS will force the user to authenticate before handing the request off to ASP.NET for processing, and the user still shows up as anonymous in ASP.NET because none of the authentication modules which load the user information into the context are enabled when the mode is set to `None`.

Windows Authentication

Windows Authentication also has a fairly simple ASP.NET configuration, but requires more work configuring NTFS file permissions (see Listing 12-2). Remember, configuring your application to use Windows Authentication also enables the file authorization module, discussed earlier in this chapter, which enforces NTFS file permissions for the authenticated user. ASP.NET uses Windows Authentication by default if no mode is specified in `Web.config`.

Listing 12-2. *Configuring Windows Authentication in* `Web.config`

```
<configuration>
    <system.web>
        <authentication mode="Windows" />
    </system.web>
</configuration>
```

You must configure IIS to authenticate the user when your application uses Windows Authentication. Although it's called Windows Authentication in ASP.NET, you're not limited to Integrated Windows Authentication in IIS. You can use Basic and/or Digest Authentication as well.

Forms Authentication

Forms Authentication has more configuration settings than Anonymous or Windows Authentication, but most of them are seldom used or can be automatically configured with the Web Site Administration Tool. Listing 12-3 shows a basic Forms Authentication configuration in `Web.config`.

Listing 12-3. *Configuring Forms Authentication in* `Web.config`

```
<configuration>
    <system.web>
      <authentication mode="Forms">
        <forms loginUrl="Login.aspx" defaultUrl="default.aspx" timeout="60"/>
      </authentication>
    </system.web>
</configuration>
```

You specify settings specific to Forms Authentication in the `<forms>` element, which is a child of the `<authentication>` element. The `<forms>` element has a number of parameters, all of which are optional, allowing you to custom-tailor Forms Authentication for your particular application's needs. Table 12-3 lists the various parameters, their purpose, and their default values when left unspecified.

Table 12-3. `<forms>` *Element Attribute Descriptions*

Attribute Name	Default Value	Description
`loginUrl`	`login.aspx`	Defines the location relative to `Web.config` to which unauthorized users are redirected when they attempt to access a protected resource. When they are sent to this page, the redirection includes a query string value indicating the page they were attempting to access so they can be redirected there after logging in.
`defaultUrl`	`default.aspx`	Defines the default location to which users are redirected after successfully logging in. If the user was directed to the login page while trying to access a protected resource, then the user is returned to the protected resource, not to the location defined by this attribute.
`cookieless`	`UseDeviceProfile`	Forms Authentication can store a user's authentication data in a cookie or as a query string value. The query string is widely supported, but often results in authentication data being lost during navigation. Cookies are more reliable, but security-conscious users may disable cookie support. The cookieless attribute has four settings that allow you to configure how Forms Authentication should store authentication data as listed next.

cookieless Values	Description
`UseCookies`	Forms Authentication always uses cookies. If the browser does not support cookies, or cookies have been disabled, the user isn't allowed to access the application.
`UseUri`	Forms Authentication always stores authentication data in the query string and does not attempt to use cookies. This is good if your target users normally have cookies disabled or are using older browsers that don't support cookies.

cookieless Values	Description
AutoDetect	Browsers send information identifying the type and version of the browser, and ASP.NET maintains a repository of browser types, versions, and the features they support. If ASP.NET knows, based on that repository, that the browser supports cookies, then ASP.NET probes the browser to determine if cookies are enabled. If cookies are enabled, then ASP.NET writes authentication data to the cookie. Otherwise, ASP.NET writes data to the query string.
UseDeviceProfile	This works similarly to the AutoDetect, but the decision to use cookies is solely based on ASP.NET's browser feature repository. ASP.NET does not probe to check whether cookies are enabled. If the browser is known to support cookies, but the user has disabled cookies, the user is unable to access the application.

Attribute Name	Default Value	Description
name	.ASPXAUTH	Defines the name of the cookie that contains the user's Forms Authentication data. If you're running multiple applications on a single server and each one requires its own authentication cookie, then you'll need to change the name of this cookie for each individual application to avoid issues with overwriting authentication data.
timeout	30	Defines the length of time a cookie is valid (in minutes). Users who are idle for more than this time period must log in to the application again. The cookie timeout does not apply to permanent cookies.
sliding➥Expiration	False	Conventional logic dictates that cookie timeouts should be reset on every request. Using the default 30-minute timeout as a guide, this means that if a user accesses a page at 12:00 and then again at 12:10, the timeout won't occur until 12:40. Such isn't the case because ASP.NET is optimized to reduce cookie setting to lessen network traffic and to avoid accosting users who have cookie alerts enabled. By default, ASP.NET only resets the timeout when more than half of the timeout time has passed. So, a user accessing a page at 12:00 and then again at 12:10, is still subject to a timeout at 12:30. You can force ASP.NET to reset the timeout on each request by setting the slidingExpiration attribute to True.
domain		Defines the domain for which the cookie is valid. Before the browser requests a page, it checks to see if any cookies match the domain and path of the request. If so, it sends that cookie along with the request.
path	/	Defines the path in your application past which authentication cookies should be sent. For example, if you specify /Protected/ as the path, then cookies are only sent to your application if the user requests something in the /Protected/ folder or a subfolder of the /Protected/ folder. Be wary of using this setting because case-sensitivity issues may result in a browser not sending the cookie.
protection	All	Defines the protection placed on Forms Authentication cookies as listed next.

Protection Values	Description
None	Cookies are not validated or encrypted. This has a slight performance benefit, but it means that malicious users could read and or alter cookie information. Only consider using this option if your application requires SSL (HTTPS) because cookies are encrypted along with all other communications over SSL connections.
Validation	Creates a MAC by hashing the cookie data using a validation key. The resulting MAC hash is then appended to the cookie data. When ASP.NET receives the cookie on a subsequent request, it hashes the cookie data using the same validation key and checks the result against the MAC hash in the cookie. If both items match, then the data in the cookie has not been altered and the cookie is considered valid.
Encryption	Cookie data is encrypted using DES or Triple DES encryption and stored in the cookie. On subsequent requests, ASP.NET decrypts the cookie data. Validation isn't used in this scenario, so the cookie may be susceptible to attacks. You specify the encryption algorithm in the `<machineKey>` element in `Machine.config` or `Web.config`.
All	Applies both `Validation` and `Encryption` to the cookie. `All` is the most secure option and is therefore both the recommended and default option as well.

Attribute Name	Default Value	Description
requireSSL	False	Defines whether an SSL connection is required to send the authentication cookie. When set to `True`, ASP.NET informs the browser that the cookie should only be sent over a secure connection.

Forms Authentication also supports a `<credentials>` section that allows you to hard-code users and passwords directly in `Web.config`. This was a quick and dirty way for developers to create users for a Forms application without having to use a database. It was seldom used in ASP.NET 1.1, and its use will continue to decline because of the built-in membership and role providers in ASP.NET 2.0 (see Chapter 5). For the sake of completeness, however, Listing 12-4 shows an example of how to use the `<credentials>` element.

Listing 12-4. *Configuringing Forms-Based Users with the* `<credentials>` *Element*

```
<configuration>
  <system.web>
    <authentication mode="Forms">
      <forms>
        <credentials passwordFormat="Clear">
          <user name="UserA" password="PasswordA"/>
          <user name="UserB" password="PasswordB"/>
          <user name="UserC" password="PasswordC"/>
        </credentials>
      </forms>
```

```
    </authentication>
  </system.web>
</configuration>
```

You can store a user's password in clear text format or as an MD5 or SHA1 hash. You can specify the password format in the passwordFormat attribute of the <credentials> section (Clear, MD5, or SHA1).

Configuring ASP.NET Authorization

Authorization in ASP.NET applications relies on the User property of the HttpContext associated with the request. You'll remember from earlier in the chapter that each authentication module in ASP.NET is responsible for populating the User property with an appropriate IPrincipal object containing the identity and role information for the user. This allows ASP.NET to run authorization-based account and group information from any location.

You define authorization settings in the <authorization> section of Web.config by creating allow and deny entries for specific users, roles, or wildcards. Listing 12-5 is an example <authorization> section showing you a number of different entries.

Listing 12-5. <authorization> *Section Example*

```
<configuration>
  <system.web>
    <authorization>
      <deny  users="?"/>
      <deny  users="Rob, Matt"/>
      <allow users="Kirk"/>
      <deny  roles="NoReports"/>
      <allow roles="Manager, ReportViewer"/>
      <deny  users="*"/>
    </authorization>
  </system.web>
</configuration>
```

ASP.NET runs through the authorization entries sequentially until it locates one applicable to the requesting user, and then applies it, which means the order of the entries is very important. Let's take a look at how ASP.NET will interpret the preceding entries. Let's assume users are attempting to access a report page in a directory protected by this authorization configuration.

The first entry contains the "?" wildcard, which represents anonymous users. This entry forces ASP.NET to reject all anonymous requests for the report and redirects the users to the loginUrl specified in the <forms> element so they can authenticate. The second entry is a comma-separated list of usernames. If Rob or Matt attempts to access the report, then the request is rejected. Kirk, however, is allowed access because of the third entry. Next, you see a deny entry for the NoReports role. Users who are part of the No Reports role are denied access to reports because of this entry. The next entry allows users who are part of the Manager or RepoertViewer role to view the report. Understand, however, that if a user is a member of both the No Reports role (from the last entry) and the Manager role (from this entry), then the user will be denied authorization because of the last entry. Remember, order is very important.

Finally, all other users are denied access. You'll want to put a catchall deny entry like this at the bottom of your authorization section because, by default, users are granted access to resources. Therefore, a user named Joe who is in an Employee role would have access to reports if the catchall was not in place, unless of course Joe or the Employee role were specifically denied, but such isn't the case in this example.

ASP.NET uses the authorization settings from Web.config file of the folder where the requested resource exists to determine whether or not to authorize the request. If ASP.NET can't find a Web.config in the folder, it checks the parent folder. It continues checking parent folders until it reaches the application root. This means that you can create authorization settings on a folder-by-folder basis or let folders inherit authorization settings from a parent folder.

■ **Tip** You can also specify authorization rules for subfolders in the root Web.config using the <location> element.

For example, let's say that you have an application structure with three protected folders and one public folder. You want to disable anonymous access to the protected folders, enable access to the public folder, and do as little configuration as possible. To do this, you would create a Web.config in the application's root folder and a Web.config in the public folder. Figure 12-21 shows how it would appear.

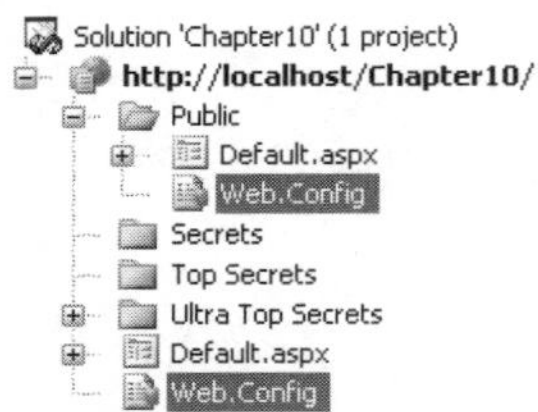

Figure12-21. *Multiple authorization settings in multiple* Web.config *files*

You would then place the following <authorization> section in Web.config file of the application's root directory (see Listing 12-6).

Listing 12-6. *Applicationwide Authorization Settings*

```
<configuration>
  <system.web>
    <authorization>
      <deny users="?"/>
    </authorization>
  </system.web>
</configuration>
```

And you would place the following `<authorization>` section in `Web.config` file of the public folder (see Listing 12-7).

Listing 12-7. *Public Folder Authorization Settings*

```
<configuration>
  <system.web>
    <authorization>
      <allow users="?"/>
    </authorization>
  </system.web>
</configuration>
```

If an anonymous user attempts to access a protected folder, ASP.NET ultimately uses authorization settings from `Web.config` in the application's root directory and denies the request. If an anonymous user attempts to access the public folder, ASP.NET uses the authorization settings from `Web.config` in the public folder and allows the request.

■ **Tip** You can use the Web Site Administration Tool to configure authorization. The tool automatically creates `Web.config` files and their authorization settings from a web-based interface so you don't have to manually code the configuration files yourself.

Configuring Application-Level Impersonation

Application-level impersonation forces all threads that process requests for your application to run using a specific security context. You configure application-level by enabling impersonation and specifying account credentials in the `<identity>` element as shown in Listing 12-8.

Listing 12-8. *Application-Level Impersonation*

```
<configuration>
  <system.web>
    <identity impersonate="true" userName="domain\username" password="Password"/>
  </system.web>
</configuration>
```

You must set the `impersonate` attribute to `True` to enable impersonation. Specifying a `userName` and `password` without setting the `impersonate` attribute has no effect on the security context of the application. In the `userName` attribute, you can specify a local account by specifying the username (such as `"username"`) or a domain account by specifying the domain and username (such as `"domain\username"`).

Configuring User-Level Impersonation

User-level impersonation forces the thread processing the request to run under the security context of the authenticated user from IIS. User-level impersonation resembles application-level impersonation, but you don't need to specify account credentials because IIS provides the account information for user-level impersonation (see Listing 12-9).

Listing 12-9. *User-Level Impersonation*

```
<configuration>
  <system.web>
    <identity impersonate="true" />
  </system.web>
</configuration>
```

Remember, user-level impersonation may cause database performance issues because it can have an adverse effect on connection pooling.

Configuring Accounts for Delegation

Delegation involves impersonation on a local computer and authentication of the impersonated account on a remote computer. Delegation requires two things: an authentication mechanism that supports delegation and credentials that are valid on both the local and remote computer. If you have an account that is valid on both computers, but was authenticated using a nondelegable authentication mechanism, then delegation fails. If you have an account that isn't valid on both computers, then it won't matter that the authentication mechanism supports delegation.

Basic- and Kerberos Authentication both support delegation. Delegation is also supported when you enter credentials in a configuration file, as you do with application-level impersonation. Digest- and NTLM Authentication don't support delegation. If you need to use delegation, you should use application-level impersonation or user-level impersonation with IIS configured to use Basic- or Integrated Windows Authentication. Integrated Windows Authentication attempts to use Kerberos Authentication when possible, but falls back on NTLM if Kerberos isn't supported. Kerberos Authentication must have the appropriate Active Directory entries to allow delegation, but those configuration settings are beyond the scope of this book.

You can create accounts that both the local and remote machine can understand in one of two ways. The first method is to create identical local accounts. Identical local accounts are two accounts on two separate machines, but both accounts have the same username and password. This allows both machines to independently verify the credentials and authenticate the user. The second option is to use an Active Directory account and allow both the local and remote computer to authenticate against the Active Directory. Because both machines are authenticating the same credentials against the same source, authentication succeeds. Figure 12-22 shows how to and how not to configure accounts to support delegation.

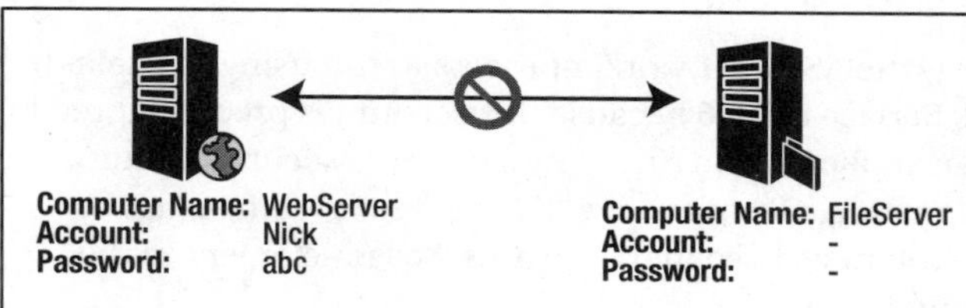

Non-Matching User

In this scenario, WebServer attempts to delegate Nick's credentials to FileServer. FileServer does not have a user named Nick defined locally. Authentication fails.

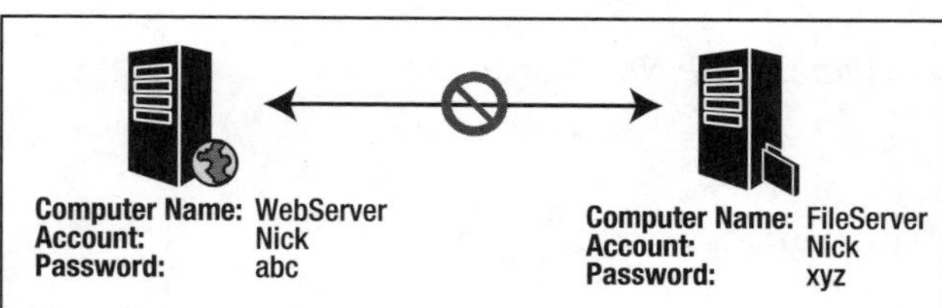

Non-Matching Password

In this scenario, WebServer attempts to delegate Nick's credentials to FileServer. FileServer has a user named Nick, but the incoming password for Nick does not match the local password for Nick. Authentication fails.

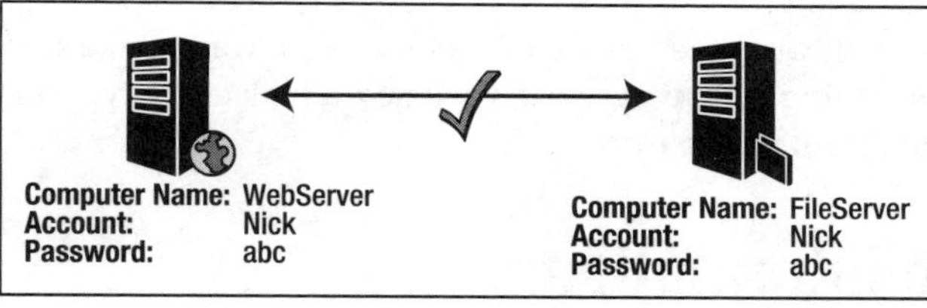

Identical Local Accounts

In this scenario, WebServer attempts to delegate Nick's credentials to FileServer. FileServer has a user named Nick, and the incoming password for Nick matches the local password for Nick. Authentication succeeds.

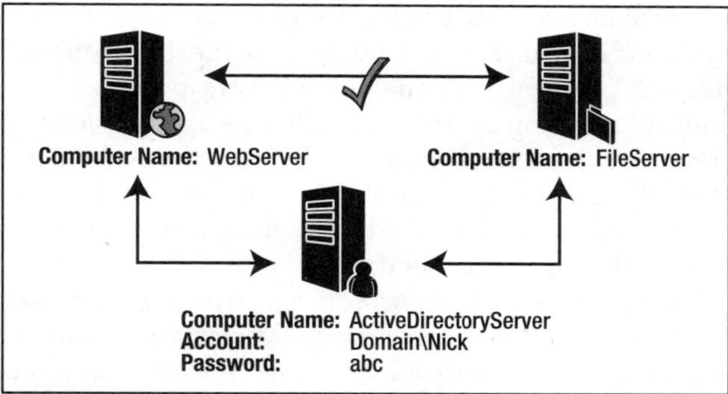

Domain Account

In this scenario, WebServer and FileServer both use the same Active Directory Server to authenticate Nick's credentials. Since the credentials are the same, and the authentication source is the same, authentication succeeds.

All of these scenarios assume you are using an authentication method that supports delegation. Remember, NTLM and Digest do NOT support delegation even if you are using identical local accounts or a domain account.

Figure 12-22. *Configuring accounts for delegation*

Configuring the ASP.NET Worker Process Account

Microsoft recommends that you allow the ASP.NET worker process to run using the default ASPNET account in IIS 5 or Network Service in IIS 6 because this account is preconfigured for least-privileged access. If you need an application to run using a different security context, you should use application-level impersonation. Of course, if you have a compelling reason to change the worker process account, you may do so in the `<processModel>` element in the `Machine.config` file as shown in Listing 12-10.

Listing 12-10. *Configuring an Account to Run the ASP.NET Worker Process*

```
<configuration>
  <system.web>
    <processModel userName="user" password="pwd" />
  </system.web>
</configuration>
```

Once again, don't make changes to the `Machine.config` file lightly, and always make sure you back up your changes in case something goes awry. Next, we'll take a look at encryption and how to protect secure information from prying eyes.

Encrypting Sensitive Information

Authentication and authorization are absolute necessities because they keeps people from casually accessing data to which they should have no access. However, they are by no means a complete solution. Determined individuals can steal credentials or find ways to attack a system and bypass authentication and authorization controls. Actually, one of the easiest and least risky ways to steal data is to approach a disgruntled employee and offer to pay them in exchange for a copy of any data to which they have access. You should take a layered approach to application security to ensure data isn't compromised when one security layer is breached. Encryption is simply another layer that can help protect your data.

Encryption allows you to make information unusable even if someone does happen to gain access to it. For example, let's say hackers attack your retail site so they can steal your customer records and credit card numbers. They successfully access your system and pull down a copy of your customer database, but they find out that it contains encrypted data. Even with the most powerful computers on the planet, encryption is still very difficult and time consuming to break. So, even though your data is in unauthorized hands, it does not do them much good.

Cryptography, which is the science of encrypting and decrypting messages, involves a lot of complex mathematical principles and algorithms. Fortunately, ASP.NET abstracts you from most of the complexities and offers an object-oriented model for protecting your data. In the sections that follow, you'll learn how to encrypt configuration settings to the Registry and look at one way and two way encryption.

Securing Configuration Settings

Microsoft encourages you to store configuration settings and connection strings in the `Web.config` file because it creates a central location for settings and helps you avoid hard-coded references in your application. However, that opens up a huge security concern because usernames and passwords for various systems are often stored as plain text in the configuration file. Malicious users know exactly where to look for sensitive information and anyone with read access on the file can open it up and look at its contents.

ASP.NET 2.0 allows you to encrypt sections in `Web.config` to protect sensitive data from being read as plain text. More importantly, the configuration architecture has built-in support for decrypting that configuration data. As long as you're working with a configuration section that has a valid configuration section handler (see Chapter 2), ASP.NET automatically decrypts the data before sending it to your configuration handler. This means that you don't have do to any extra coding to work with a configuration section that has been encrypted.

Using the aspnet_regiis.exe Command-Line Utility

The easiest way to encrypt a configuration section is to use the `aspnet_regiis.exe` command-line utility located in the ASP.NET `Framework` folder for your version of the framework (normally `C:\Windows\Microsoft.NET\Framework\<Framework Version>\aspnet_regiis.exe`). It creates all the necessary `Web.config` entries to configure encryption on a particular configuration section, and it encrypts any data already present in that section.

The `aspnet_regiis.exe` utility configures a number of items related to IIS, so you have to run the utility with specific parameters to tell it to encrypt a configuration section. Here is the general syntax to encrypt a configuration section:

```
aspnet_regiis.exe -pe "sectionName" [-app "/application"] [-prov "provider"]
```

You'll find an explanation of these command line parameters in Table 12-4.

Table 12-4. *Command-Line Parameters for* `aspnet_regiis.exe`

Parameter	Description
`-pe`	Informing the utility that it needs to encrypt a configuration section
`"sectionName"`	Section name that should be encrypted (for example, `connectionStrings`, `appSettings`, and so on). You must enter the section name exactly as it appears in the configuration file as this item is case sensitive. You don't need to include surrounding `< >` brackets. To encrypt a section that is nested within another section, use the `/` to separate sections. For example, to encrypt the `webServices` element, you should use `system.web/webServices`.
`-app`	Informs the utility that it should encrypt the configuration file for a specific application in IIS.
`"/application"`	Identifies the application whose configuration section should be encrypted. This must include the leading slash (`/`).
`-prov`	Informs the utility that it should encrypt the configuration section using a specific encryption provider.
`"provider"`	Identifies the provider to be used. ASP.NET ships with two encryption providers: the `RsaProtectedConfigurationProvider`, which is the default, and the `DpapiProtectionConfigurationProvider`. Unless you have a compelling reason to do otherwise, stick with the default provider.

If, for instance, you want to encrypt the `<connectionStrings>` section in `Web.config` for an application residing at `http://localhost/MyApplication`, using the default encryption provider, then you would type the following in the command line:

```
aspnet_regiis.exe -pe "connectionStrings" -app "/MyApplication"
```

You can also decrypt a configuration section using the utility by specifying the `-pd` switch instead of the `-pe` switch. To decrypt the section you just encrypted, you would simply specify the following in the command line:

```
aspnet_regiis.exe -pd "connectionStrings" -app "/MyApplication"
```

This returns the configuration section back to its original plain-text state so you can make changes to the configuration section using a standard text editor. After you finish updating the file, however, remember to encrypt it again.

■ Note You can only encrypt configuration files for applications hosted by IIS using the `aspnet_regiis.exe` utility.

Giving ASP.NET Access to the Default RSA Encryption Container

By default, ASP.NET uses the `RSAProtectedConfigurationProvider` to encrypt and decrypt configuration sections. The RSA provider maintains a set of keys that it uses in its encryption algorithms, and users must have access to these keys before they can encrypt and decrypt configuration sections. This keeps unauthorized users from decrypting a configuration section using the same utility you used to encrypt it. Of course, it also means the security context running the ASP.NET worker process must be given access to the key container or else ASP.NET will error out trying to read the encrypted data.

You can give users access to the RSA provider keys using a different command-line parameter for the `aspnet_regiis.exe` utility. Here's the syntax:

```
aspnet_regiis -pa "NetFrameworkConfigurationKey" "domain\user"
```

This gives the `"domain\user"` account access to the `"NetFrameworkConfigurationKey"` container, which is the default RSA encryption container. If you're setting up a local account, you don't need to include the domain for the user.

If you're using IIS 5, you need to give the ASPNET account access to the container key, using the following command:

```
aspnet_regiis -pa "NetFrameworkConfigurationKey" "ASPNET"
```

And if you're using IIS 6, you need to give the Network Service account access:

```
aspnet_regiis -pa "NetFrameworkConfigurationKey" "Network Service"
```

■ **Caution** You must give the account running the ASP.NET worker process access to the `NetFramework➥ConfigurationKey` container for ASP.NET to properly read encrypted configuration sections. If your application is configured for user-level impersonation, this means that each individual user must be given access to the key container. With that access, however, each user could run the `aspnet_regiis.exe` utility to decrypt the section and read the data in plain text.

You can create additional key containers, export and import key containers, and configure the encryption provider to use specific key containers, but that is beyond the scope of this book. You may need more in-depth key management in a server farm or a hosting environment where you have a number of different applications and clients, but the default encryption scheme should provide you with adequate protection in most circumstances.

Encrypted Configuration Sections in Web.config

After encrypting a configuration section, you'll see a couple of changes to your configuration file. The biggest change is, obviously, the encrypted configuration section that once contained plain-text data. But there are a few other changes you should be aware of so you can still manage the configuration file.

Let's take a look at a configuration file as it appears before being encrypted, and then again after running the `aspnet_regiis.exe` utility on it. For this example, we'll say that you have a `Web.config` file with a `<connectionStrings>` and an `<appSettings>` section. Listing 12-11 shows what it looks like in plain text.

Listing 12-11. *Unencrypted* `Web.config`

```
<configuration xmlns="http://schemas.microsoft.com/.NetConfiguration/v2.0">

  <connectionStrings>
    <add name="Database" connectionString="username=Usr;password=db_pwd;" />
  </connectionStrings>

  <appSettings>
    <add key="smtpServer" value="127.0.0.1"/>
    <add key="fileServerName" value="fileShareBox"/>
  </appSettings>

</configuration>
```

You want to encrypt the `<connectionStrings>` section because it contains database usernames and passwords, but you want to leave the `<appSettings>` section alone because it does not have any sensitive information. After running the `aspnet_regiis.exe` utility on the `<connectionString>` section, your `Web.config` looks like Listing 12-12.

Listing 12-12. *Unencrypted* `Web.config`

```
<configuration xmlns="http://schemas.microsoft.com/.NetConfiguration/v2.0">

  <protectedData>
    <protectedDataSections>
      <add name="connectionStrings" provider="RsaProtectedConfigurationProvider"
           inheritedByChildren="false" />
    </protectedDataSections>
  </protectedData>

  <connectionStrings>
    <EncryptedData Type="http://www.w3.org/2001/04/xmlenc#Element"
                   xmlns="http://www.w3.org/2001/04/xmlenc#">
      <EncryptionMethod
          Algorithm="http://www.w3.org/2001/04/xmlenc#tripledes-cbc"/>
      <KeyInfo xmlns="http://www.w3.org/2000/09/xmldsig#">
        <EncryptedKey Recipient="" xmlns="http://www.w3.org/2001/04/xmlenc#">
         <EncryptionMethod Algorithm="http://www.w3.org/2001/04/xmlenc#rsa-1_5"/>
          <KeyInfo xmlns="http://www.w3.org/2000/09/xmldsig#">
            <KeyName>Rsa Key</KeyName>
          </KeyInfo>
          <CipherData>
            <CipherValue>
              uYfTKol/aAdtizclKuVIOb85Gzd4IefKZE9WH4SMpasslJOzJrTINVec/1VuxbFUF1o
              Qkku4OGT+HDUOvaObBWhtZrAun3FEr5f3jH/VlmzD21X+quDApFXFYtA9zV9AiEIxvE
              dL5XuERwnk8vtHdDD7WCo/6fp8+jKiJGTr4nw=
            </CipherValue>
          </CipherData>
        </EncryptedKey>
      </KeyInfo>
      <CipherData>
        <CipherValue>
          dA+kmSeqkyJZhmp5ed9FCg6BlLT7VA5GStpPyb2FziuGWvi5QyTSOoQNYpfCmSg9bXtDOezx
          g4KnyLsqAaqJ5n2352qoVU5cIZ9aRSsTe6LjKpgGb5Z/qKAp3b23X+IE3SbvAjWpOFbOJjif
          NDvnf+9a/43z9Gh+JIKOL3YxRoI=
        </CipherValue>
      </CipherData>
    </EncryptedData>
  </connectionStrings>

  <appSettings>
    <add key="mailPassword" value="mail_pwd"/>
    <add key="networkPassword" value="net_pwd"/>
  </appSettings>

</configuration>
```

Notice at the top of the modified `Web.config` file, a new section named `<protectedData>`. This section identifies which sections in the configuration file are encrypted and what encryption provider encrypted the data. ASP.NET uses this information to determine which sections require encryption and decryption when reading and writing configuration values. You can see that there is still a `<connectionStrings>` section, but it has been encrypted and can't be read by the naked eye. Also notice that the `<appSettings>` section still appears as plain text and has not been altered in any way.

After you have encrypted a section, don't try to modify the encrypted data in that section. You'll also want to avoid changing the security provider or removing the encrypted section from the `<protectedData>` section. Otherwise, you'll experience errors trying to access configuration data.

Modifying Encrypted Configuration Settings

In their plain-text format, configuration files allow you to quickly make changes to application settings without too much effort. Encrypted configuration sections, however, can't be modified with such ease. They have to be decrypted, edited, and then encrypted again. You can always revert to the `aspnet_regiis.exe` utility to decrypt and encrypt files, but there are some shortcuts that can help you out.

All the Microsoft configuration tools support automatic encryption and decryption of configuration values. You can use the Web Site Administration Tool to add, edit, and delete encrypted application settings from the `<appSettings>` section just as easily as you can manage unencrypted settings. You can also use the configuration tools in IIS to manage the `<appSettings>`, `<connectionStrings>`, and another other configuration sections supported by the IIS tool without worrying about encryption (see Chapter 1 for more information on the new IIS configuration tools for ASP.NET 2.0). If you have a custom configuration section, however, you'll probably need to revert to decrypting it with the `aspnet_regiis.exe` utility.

Hashing Data with One-Way Encryption

Most people think of encryption as a two-way process. You encrypt data and you decrypt data. It goes two ways. Hashing is a form of encryption known as one-way encryption that creates an encrypted value, called a hash value, which can't be definitively decrypted. There is simply not enough information in the hashed value to restore the original encrypted message.

Hashing is useful for communicating that you know something without actually communicating what you know. For example, you and a friend both claim to know the capital of Peru. You think your friend is bluffing. Your friend thinks you're bluffing. Neither of you want to say the answer outright because it could give the answer away to your opponent. How can you both determine whether or not you both know the capital without actually divulging the answer? This is a situation where one-way encryption can help communicate that you know something without actually communicating what you know. You tell your friend to hash the value of the capital using a specific algorithm. You also hash the value of the capital using the same algorithm. If both hashed values match up, then you can both reasonably assume you know the answer.

Hashing is also used to encrypt passwords in databases. Users log in by entering their plain-text password. That password is then hashed and checked against the hashed password stored in the database. If the hashes match up, then the user is authenticated. This keeps hackers and rouge database administrators from stealing passwords out of the database. They can only steal the password hashes, and password hashes are worthless because they can't be decrypted. So hashing protects user credentials in the event of a database break-in.

Hashing Algorithms

You generate hash values using a hashing algorithm. Hashing algorithms are responsible for processing an input and producing a specific hash value for the input. In other words, if you hash a specific value twice, then you get back the same hash value both times. Hashed values are not unique, so you could receive the same hash value for two different inputs, although that's highly unlikely given today's hashing algorithms.

Let's take a look at a simple hashing algorithm so you can see how one works. Listing 12-13 shows a simple hashing algorithm that accepts a string and outputs an integer as the hash value.

Listing 12-13. `MyHashAlgorithm` *Example*

```
'***************************************************************************
Private Function MyHashAlgorithm(ByVal input As String) As Integer

    Dim charArray() As Char = input.ToCharArray()
    Dim hashValue As Integer = 0

    For Each c As Char In charArray
            hashValue += Asc(UCase(c))
        Next
    Return hashValue

End Function
```

`MyHashAlgorithm` accepts the string variable `input` as its only parameter. The function turns `input` into a character array and declares `hashValue` as an integer. It then iterates through each character in the string, uppercases it, and adds up the ASCII code value of each character in the `hashValue` variable. Finally, the function returns `hashValue`, which contains a summation of the character codes from the string.

Table 12-5 contains a list of input values and their corresponding hashed values as calculated by the `MyHashAlgorithm`.

Table 12-5. *Input Values and Hashed Values from the* `MyHashAlgorithm`

Input Value	Hashed Value	Calculation
A	65	65=65
B	66	66=66
AB	131	65+66=131
MITE	303	77+73+84+69=303
ITEM	303	73+84+69+77=303
FEAST	371	70+69+65+83+84=371

Input Value	Hashed Value	Calculation
GREAT	371	71+82+69+65+84=371
SOFTWARE	619	83+79+70+84+87+65+82+69

You can see from the hashed values that items don't have unique hashed values. ITEM and MITE both have hashed values of 303 because they both have the same letters, and thus have the same letter values. The letters just appear in different positions. FEAST and GREAT have the same hash even though they have different letters because their letter values both happen to sum to the same number. This also shows another important property of hash: you can't conclusively decrypt a hashed value because the hash value (371) could represent a variety of different character sequences (FEAST or GREAT).

Obviously, the MyHashAlgorithm is a weak hashing algorithm and you would not want to use it to encrypt data. Instead, you can use any one of the six hashing algorithms that ships with the .NET Framework: MD5, RIPEMD160, SHA1, SHA256, SHA384, SHA512. Each algorithm produces a different sized hash: 128, 160, 160, 256, 384, and 512 bits, respectively. Larger hashes are less likely to produce duplicate hash values and are therefore more secure, but take longer to process. The MD5 or SHA1 algorithms should be sufficient for most applications.

Creating a Reusable Hashing Class

Hashing normally involves hashing a string and returning the hash value for the string. Microsoft, however, designed the hashing algorithms so they could hash just about anything, even binary files. As such, the hashing code revolves around byte arrays, not strings or other data types, and requires a bit of code to implement. Instead of recoding hashing functionality every time you need it, you should encapsulate it into a reusable class.

Microsoft implemented each hashing algorithm in a separate class, but all hashing algorithms inherit from the HashAlgorithm base class in the System.Security.Cryptography namespace. This makes it easy to create a generic hashing class from which you can access all the hashing algorithms. Listing 12-14 shows the code for the Hashing class, which resides in the EcnryptionLibrary project of the sample application.

Listing 12-14. Hashing *Class*

```
Imports System.Security.Cryptography
Imports System.Text

'****************************************************************************
Public Class Hashing

    'Algorithm Enermations
    Public Enum HashAlgorithmTypes
        MD5
        SHA1
```

```
        SHA256
        SHA384
        SHA512
    End Enum

    '***************************************************************************
    Public Shared Function CreateHash(ByVal valueToHash As String, _
      ByVal algorithmType As HashAlgorithmTypes) As String

        'Set up variables
        Dim algorithm As System.Security.Cryptography.HashAlgorithm
        Dim encoder As ASCIIEncoding = New ASCIIEncoding()
        Dim valueByteArray As Byte() = encoder.GetBytes(valueToHash)
        Dim hashValue As String = ""
        Dim hashValueByteArray As Byte()

        'Acquire algorithm object
        Select Case algorithmType
            Case HashAlgorithmTypes.SHA1
                algorithm = New SHA1Managed()
            Case HashAlgorithmTypes.SHA256
                algorithm = New SHA256Managed()
            Case HashAlgorithmTypes.SHA384
                algorithm = New SHA384Managed()
            Case HashAlgorithmTypes.SHA512
                algorithm = New SHA512Managed()
            Case Else 'use MD5
                algorithm = New MD5CryptoServiceProvider
        End Select

        'Create binary hash
        hashValueByteArray = algorithm.ComputeHash(valueByteArray)

        'Convert binary hash to hex
        For Each b As Byte In hashValueByteArray
            hashValue &= String.Format("{0:x2}", b)
        Next

        Return hashValue

    End Function

End Class
```

At the top of the class, you'll see an enumeration named `HashAlgorithmType`, which outlines all the hash algorithms this class supports. This enumeration makes it easier to select which algorithm you want to use to hash a value because IntelliSense displays a listing of the various algorithms in the Visual Studio IDE when you use the CreateHash function. Notice that you can use the MD5, SHA1, SHA256, SHA384, or SHA512 hashing algorithms.

CreateHash is a Shared function that accepts two parameters: the string value to be hashed, and a HashAlgorithm enumeration value indicating which algorithm to use. CreateHash uses five different variables to create a hash value:

- algorithm is a HashAlgorithm variable that can store a reference to any of the five different algorithm classes.
- encoder is a an ASCIIEncoding object used to convert valueToHash into a byte-array.
- valueByteArray stores the byte-array representation of the valueToHash.
- hashValue is the temporary string value that stores the return value for the function.
- hashValueByteArray stores the byte-array representation of the hashValue string variable.

After defining its variables, CreateHash uses the algorithmType to determine which hash algorithm object to load into the algorithm variable. Because all hash algorithms derive from the HashAlgorithm class, the algorithm variable can store a reference to any hash algorithm and calls its hashing methods.

After a hash algorithm object has been acquired, the function calls the ComputeHash method of the algorithm object, passing in the valueByteArray. ComputeHash runs the complex hashing logic and returns a byte-array containing the hashed value. CreateHash then stores that value in the hashValueByteArray variable.

Next, the function iterates over each byte in the hashValueByteArray, converts it into a hexadecimal character, and then appends it to the hashValue string. And lastly, the function returns the hashValue variable containing the string representation of the hashed value.

Using the Hash Class in Code

The Hash class contains a single shared method, so you don't have to instantiate an object before you use it. You just pass in a value to hash and the algorithm to use, and it returns a hashed value as shown in Listing 12-15.

Listing 12-15. *Hashing Examples*

```
hashedValue1 = Hash.CreateHash("ASP.NET", MD5)
hashedValue2 = Hash.CreateHash("ASP.NET", SHA1)
hashedValue3 = Hash.CreateHash("ASP.NET", SHA256)
hashedValue4 = Hash.CreateHash("ASP.NET", SHA384)
hashedValue5 = Hash.CreateHash("ASP.NET", SHA512)
```

That's all there is to it. You can use this feature to encrypt passwords in your user database if you're not using the built-in user management features that ship with ASP.NET, or whenever you need to generate a hash value.

■ **Note** You can tell ASP.NET to automatically encrypt user passwords if you're using the built-in user-management features that ship with ASP.NET 2.0.

One-way encryption has a limited set of uses that mostly focuses around passwords and authentication. If you actually need to decrypt data, then you need to use two-way encryption, which is coming up next.

Encrypting and Decrypting Data with Two-Way Encryption

Most people are familiar with the concept of encryption and decryption. You take a value and encrypt it using a specific encryption algorithm and key. The encryption algorithm produces an encrypted value that can be stored in a database, file, or sent to a third party. Encrypted information is useless without the key, so you don't have to worry about the data being stolen. Only those individuals or systems with access to the key can decrypt the message. Protecting data therefore becomes a matter of keeping your encryption key safe.

Symmetric cryptography uses the same key to encrypt and decrypt a message. Asymmetric cryptography, also known as Public Key Encryption, uses one key to encrypt a message and another to decrypt the message. Asymmetric cryptography is outside of the scope of this book. In this section, you'll learn about the symmetric cryptography architecture in .NET and how to use it to create your own encryption library.

Cryptography Architecture in .NET

Cryptography support in the .NET Framework comes from two different types of objects: `SymmetricAlgorithm` objects and `ICryptoTransform` objects. Microsoft supports four different encryption routines: DES, RC2, Triple DES, and the Rijndael algorithm. Each algorithm is encapsulated in its own class, but all the classes ultimately derive from the `SymmetricAlgorithm` class. `SymmetricAlgorithm` classes are responsible for setting up the key, mode, and initialization vector (which may be required depending on the mode) for the algorithm. The class can then generate an `ICryptoTransform` object to encrypt or decrypt streams of data. Because the `ICryptoTransform` object deals with streams, you need to convert any data you want encrypted into a byte array for processing. Keys and initialization vectors are also stored as byte arrays.

As mentioned previously, Microsoft.NET supports four different encryption routines: DES, RC2, Triple DES, and the Rijndael algorithms. The algorithms use a 64-bit, 128-bit, 192-bit, and 256-bit key, respectively. Each algorithm also supports Cipher Block Chaining (CBC), in which one block of data is encrypted using data from the previous block of data. This ensures that identical blocks of data don't result in identical encrypted values. CBC requires an initialization vector to set up CBC to run on the first block of data. The initialization vectors is, in effect, a secondary key that makes your data that much more secure. DES, Triple DES, and the RC2 algorithms all use 64-bit initialization vectors, and the Rijndael algorithm uses a 128-bit initialization vector. If you don't want the extra protection of CBC, you can opt to use the Electronic Code Book (ECB) mode, which does not require an initialization vector.

Base64 Strings

Most applications store encryption keys and initialization vectors in text-based configuration files. Byte arrays are more binary in nature than textual, so storing a byte array directly in a text file is problematic. Base64 encoding, which is often used to transmit binary data via text-only mediums on the Internet, can be used to create a string-based representation of a byte array that can be easily stored in a configuration file. It does this by encoding 3 bytes of binary data as 4 bytes of printable ASCII text that only uses the letters a-z, A-Z, 0-9, +, /, and =. Base64 encoding also allows for the easy conversion of a base64 string back into a byte array.

You can convert a byte array to a base64 string and a base64 string back into a byte array using the static methods of the `Convert` class found in the `System` namespace. `Convert.ToBase64String()` accepts a `Byte` array and returns a base64 `String`. `Convert.➥ ToByteArray()` accepts a base64 `String` and returns a `Byte` array.

Creating an Encryption Library

You have to write a little bit of code to encrypt and decrypt information in .NET because the cryptography framework revolves around byte arrays and memory streams. Chances are that you don't want to have to rewrite encryption routines each time you need to encrypt something, so it makes sense to put it in a reusable encryption library.

Listing 12-16 shows the code for the `Encryption` class, which resides in the `Ecnryption➥ Library` project of the sample application in the Source Code area of the Apress website (http://www.apress.com). This class allows you to easily choose between encryption algorithms and encrypt and decrypt data in your application.

Listing 12-16. *Encryption Class of the* `EncryptionLibrary` *Project*

```
Imports System.Security.Cryptography
Imports System.Text
Imports System.IO

Public Class Encryption

    '************************************************************************
    Public Enum EncryptionAlgorithmType
        DES
        RC2
        Rijndael
        TripleDES
    End Enum

    '************************************************************************
    Public Enum CryptoDirection
        Encrypt
        Decrypt
    End Enum
```

```
'****************************************************************************
Public Shared Function GetAlgorithm( _
 ByVal type As EncryptionAlgorithmType) As SymmetricAlgorithm

    'Determine the type and return the approrpiate Symmetric Algorithm Class
    Select Case type
        Case EncryptionAlgorithmType.DES
            Return New DESCryptoServiceProvider
        Case EncryptionAlgorithmType.RC2
            Return New RC2CryptoServiceProvider
        Case EncryptionAlgorithmType.Rijndael
            Return New RijndaelManaged
        Case EncryptionAlgorithmType.TripleDES
            Return New TripleDESCryptoServiceProvider
        Case Else
            Throw New ArgumentException("Invalid Algorithm Type")
    End Select

End Function

'****************************************************************************
Public Shared Function GenerateKey( _
  ByVal type As EncryptionAlgorithmType) As Byte()

    Dim algorithm As SymmetricAlgorithm = GetAlgorithm(type)
    algorithm.GenerateKey()
    Return algorithm.Key()

End Function

'****************************************************************************
Public Shared Function GenerateIV( _
  ByVal type As EncryptionAlgorithmType) As Byte()

    Dim algorithm As SymmetricAlgorithm = GetAlgorithm(type)
    algorithm.GenerateIV()
    Return algorithm.IV()

End Function

'****************************************************************************
Private Shared Function GetCrytoTransfomer( _
  ByVal type As EncryptionAlgorithmType, _
  ByVal direction As CryptoDirection, ByRef key As Byte(), _
  ByRef IV As Byte()) As ICryptoTransform

    Dim algorithm As SymmetricAlgorithm = GetAlgorithm(type)
    algorithm.Mode = CipherMode.CBC
```

```
    'Give key to algorithm, or get auto-generated key from algorithm
    If key Is Nothing Then
        key = algorithm.Key      'Allow algorithm to generate key
    Else
        algorithm.Key = key      'Set key
    End If

    'Give IV to algorithm, or get auto-generated IV from algorithm
    If IV Is Nothing Then
        IV = algorithm.IV        'Allow algorithm to generate IV
    Else
        algorithm.IV = IV        'Set IV
    End If

    'Return the appropriate ICryptoTransformer for the Direction
    Select Case direction
        Case CryptoDirection.Decrypt
            Return algorithm.CreateDecryptor()
        Case CryptoDirection.Encrypt
            Return algorithm.CreateEncryptor()
        Case Else
            Throw New ArgumentException("Invalid Crypto Direction")
    End Select

End Function

'***************************************************************************
Public Shared Function EncryptString(ByVal valueToEncrypt As String, _
  ByVal type As EncryptionAlgorithmType, ByRef key As Byte(), _
  ByRef IV As Byte()) As String

    Dim encoder As New ASCIIEncoding
    Dim value = encoder.GetBytes(valueToEncrypt)
    Dim encrypted = EncryptByteArray(value, type, key, IV)
    Return Convert.ToBase64String(encrypted)

End Function

'***************************************************************************
Public Shared Function EncryptByteArray(ByVal byteArrayToEncrypt As Byte(), _
  ByVal type As EncryptionAlgorithmType, ByRef key As Byte(), _
  ByRef IV As Byte()) As Byte()

    Dim algorithm As ICryptoTransform
    algorithm = GetCrytoTransfomer(type, CryptoDirection.Encrypt, key, IV)
```

```
        Dim buffer As New MemoryStream
        Dim encStream As New CryptoStream(buffer, algorithm, CryptoStreamMode.Write)

        'Write data to encryption stream which stores it in the buffer
        Try
            encStream.Write(byteArrayToEncrypt, 0, byteArrayToEncrypt.Length)
            encStream.FlushFinalBlock()
        Catch ex As Exception
            Throw New IOException("Could not encrypt data", ex)
        Finally
            encStream.Close()
        End Try

        Return buffer.ToArray()

    End Function

    '**************************************************************************
    Public Shared Function DecryptString(ByVal valueToDecrypt As String, _
      ByVal type As EncryptionAlgorithmType, ByRef key As Byte(), _
      ByRef IV As Byte()) As String

        Dim encoder As New ASCIIEncoding
        Dim value = Convert.FromBase64String(valueToDecrypt)
        Dim decrypted = DecryptByteArray(value, type, key, IV)
        Return encoder.GetString(decrypted)

    End Function

    '**************************************************************************
    Public Shared Function DecryptByteArray(ByVal byteArrayToEncrypt As Byte(), _
      ByVal type As EncryptionAlgorithmType, ByRef key As Byte(), _
      ByRef IV As Byte()) As Byte()

        Dim algorithm As ICryptoTransform
        algorithm = GetCrytoTransfomer(type, CryptoDirection.Decrypt, key, IV)

        Dim buffer As New MemoryStream
        Dim decStream As New CryptoStream(buffer, algorithm, CryptoStreamMode.Write)

        'Write data to encryption stream which stores it in the buffer
        Try
            decStream.Write(byteArrayToEncrypt, 0, byteArrayToEncrypt.Length)
            decStream.FlushFinalBlock()
        Catch ex As Exception
            Throw New IOException("Could not decrypt data", ex)
        Finally
```

```
            decStream.Close()
        End Try

        Return buffer.ToArray()

    End Function

End Class
```

Imports and Enumerations

The Encryption class uses a number of classes from the System.Security.Cryptography namespace, the ASCIIEndoding object from the System.Text namespace, and the MemoryStream class from the System.IO namespace. All the namespaces are imported at the top of the file to keep the code succinct.

In the actual class itself, there are two enumerations. EncryptionAlgorithmType contains a listing of all supported encryption algorithms in the .NET Framework. This enumeration makes it easy to choose which algorithm you want to use to encrypt and decrypt information. The Visual Studio IDE pops up a listing of the enumerations when you use encrypt and decrypt functionality in the encryption library. CryptoDirection contains values that allow you to define whether you want to return an encrypting or decrypting ICryptoTransform object from the GetCrytoTransfomer method (discussed shortly).

Acquiring an Algorithm Object with the GetAlgorithm Function

Before you can encrypt or decrypt data, you need to have an object that exposes the encryption algorithm you want to use. GetAlgorithm allows you to pass in an EncryptionAlgorithmType enumeration named type identifying which algorithm you want to use. The function then uses a SELECT statement to determine which type you requested and returns the appropriate SymmetricAlgorithm object for that algorithm.

Generating Keys and Initialization Vectors with GenerateKey and GenerateIV

Each algorithm requires encryption keys and initialization vectors to be a certain size. The GenerateKey and GenerateIV functions may be used to create randomly generated keys and initialization vectors appropriately sized for the specified algorithm.

The function accepts an EncryptionAlgorithmType parameter named type identifying the algorithm for which you want to create a key or initialization vector. Each function acquires an appropriate algorithm object using the GetAlgorithm function, calls the GenerateKey or GenerateIV method of that algorithm object, and then returns the key or initialization vector that was generated.

You can use these functions to generate keys and initialization vectors for storage in your application's Web.config file. Simply create a trash page in your application and use the GenerateKey and GenerateIV functions to create a key and an initialization vector. Make sure to convert them to base64 strings using the Convert.ToBase64String function, and then store them in Web.config in your application. Delete the trash page from your application and encrypt the Web.config section containing the key and initialization vector. Any time you need the key or initialization vector, acquire it from Web.config, convert it from a base64 string to a byte array using Convert.FromBase64String, and use it in the encryption library routines.

Getting a Cryptographic Transformer with the GetCryptoTransformer Function

Before you can encrypt or decrypt data, you need to acquire an ICryptoTransform object. This object is responsible for encrypting or decrypting data as it is written to a memory stream. GetCryptoTransfomer is responsible for providing the appropriate encryption or decryption transformer from a specific algorithm and setting up default encryption keys and initialization vectors if none are provided.

GetCryptoTransformer accepts four parameters:

- type is an EncryptionAlgorithmType defining the algorithm from which the transformer should be acquired
- direction is a CryptoDirection defining whether to acquire an encryption or a decryption transformer
- key and IV are both byte arrays identifying the key and initialization vector the transformer should use during processing. Notice that the key and IV parameters are passed ByRef because they could be given randomly generated values if they are passed into the function without values (that is, Nothing).

The function begins by acquiring an appropriate algorithm object using the GetAlgorithm function. It then sets the algorithm mode to CipherMode.CBC. If you don't want to use an initialization vector, then you can set the mode to CipherMode.ECB. Or, if you're looking for even more flexibility, you can define the mode as a parameter. I always use CBC for the extra protection it provides. If you don't specify a value, the mode defaults to CBC.

After setting the mode, the function checks to see if an encryption key was provided. If not, it acquires a randomly generated key from the algorithm object. If so, it sets the Key property on the algorithm object to the provided key. You can also see that the function runs the same logic on the initialization vector. If the initialization vector isn't provided, GetCryptoTransformer sets it to a randomly generated one from the algorithm object. If it was provided, it sets the IV property on the object to the provided initialization vector.

Lastly, the function checks the direction parameter to determine which type of transformer to return. It returns the transformer object from the algorithm's CreateDecryptor method if the direction parameter is set to Decrypt, or the transformer object from CreateEncryptor if the direction parameter is set to Encrypt.

Encrypting a String with the EncryptString Function

Encryption in .NET centers on byte arrays, but encryption in your applications will likely center around strings. This function converts a string into a byte array, calls the EncryptByteArray function to encrypt the byte array, and returns the encrypted byte array as a base64 string.

EncryptString accepts four parameters: the value to encode, the algorithm type, the encryption key, and the initialization vector. The key and IV parameters are both passed by reference because they could be populated with data. EncryptString begins by creating an ASCIIEncoding object named encoder. It then uses encoder to convert the incoming string into a byte array and stores it in the value variable. EncryptString then passes values into the EncryptByteArray function, which returns an encrypted byte array and stores this in the encrypted variable. The function then converts the encrypted array into a base64 string and returns that string as the value of the function.

■ Note If you're working with Unicode strings instead of ASCII strings, then you'll want to use a UnicodeEncoding object instead of an ASCIIEncoding object in the encryption library.

Encrypting a Byte Array with EncryptByteArray

Most of the real encryption work is done in the EncryptByteArray function. This function is responsible for using a ICryptoTransform object to create an encrypted byte array.

EncryptByteArray accepts four parameters: the byte array to encode, the algorithm type, the encryption key, and the initialization vector. The key and IV parameters are both passed by reference because they could be populated with data. The function begins by acquiring a transformer object using the GetCryptoTransfomer function. Because the objective of the function is to encrypt a byte array, the direction parameter of the GetCryptoTransformer call is set to Encrypt. EncryptByteArray then creates a new memory stream named buffer. This memory stream stores the encrypted byte array as it is being written. The function also declares a CryptoStream named encStream under the buffer variable. Notice that encStream stream is passed to both the buffer and the transformer object. When you pass the data into the encStream, it uses the transformer object to encrypt the incoming data, and then stores the encrypted data in the underlying buffer. So the encrypted data ends up in the buffer byte array.

Inside of the Try..Catch block, EncryptByteArray calls encStream.Write and passes in the byte array that should be encrypted, the position at which writing should start, and the number of bytes to write (it always writes the entire array). Inside the Write function, the byte array to be encrypted passes through the transformer object. The transformer object uses the key and initialization vector to encrypt the incoming data, and writes it out to buffer. Flush➥FinalBlock() ensures that any remaining data in encStream is written to the buffer. EncryptByteArray then closes encStream and returns the encrypted byte array stored in the buffer variable.

Decrypting a String with the DecryptString Function

Decrypting a string is the reverse of encrypting a string. Instead of starting with a string and ending up with an encrypted base64 string, it takes an encrypted base64 string and ends up with a decrypted string. You can also see that it uses the DecryptByteArray function to do the heavy decryption work.

Decrypting a ByteArray with the DecryptByteArray Function

DecryptByteArray is identical to the EncryptByteArray function except for the CryptoDirection parameter of the GetCryptoTransformer function call. It passes in Decrypt as the direction instead of Encrypt. This acquires a decryption transformer instead of an encryption transformer. Inside the Write method of the encStream, the encrypted byte array passes through the decryption transformer, which writes the decrypted byte array to the buffer variable. The function then returns the decrypted byte array stored in buffer.

Using the Encryption Library

To use the encryption library, add a reference for the EncryptionLibrary assembly to your project. Place an imports statement for the EncryptionLIbrary at the top of the page in which you want to use the library, or include a global imports statement for the library in your project.

All the methods in the Encryption class are shared, so you don't need to instantiate an object to use them. Listing 12-17 shows an example of how to get a base64 key and initialization vector from Web.config, convert them into byte arrays, and use them to encrypt and decrypt a string.

Listing 12-17. *Encryption and Decryption Example*

```
Imports EncryptionLibrary
Imports System.Configuration.ConfigurationManager
...

'Acquire Base64 strings from Web.config
Dim keyBase64 As String = AppSettings("TripleDESKey")
Dim IVBase64 As String = AppSettings("TripleDESIV")

'Convert to byte arrays
Dim key As Byte() = Convert.FromBase64String(keyBase64)
Dim IV As Byte() = Convert.FromBase64String(IVBase64)

Dim TextToEncrypt As String = "Please encrypt this text"

Dim EncryptedText As String = Encryption.EncryptString(TextToEncrypt, _
                  Encryption.EncryptionAlgorithmType.TripleDES, key, IV)

Dim DecryptedText As String = Encryption.DecryptString(EncryptedText, _
                  Encryption.EncryptionAlgorithmType.TripleDES, key, IV)

If DecryptedText = TextToEncrypt Then Success = True
```

This is a fairly straightforward example. First, it acquires the base64 string version of the key and initialization vectors from Web.config and stores them in two variables. It then converts those base64 keys back into their native Byte array format and declares text to encrypt. Next, it encrypts the text using the TripleDES algorithm with the key and IV acquired from Web.config and stores the text in the EncryptedText variable. It then decrypts the EncryptedText variable using the same algorithm, key, and initialization vector. Lastly, it checks to make sure the `DecryptedText` and the original `TextToEncrypt` are the same to prove encryption and decryption succeeded.

So now you can encrypt just about anything you want, and it's in an easily reusable library that you can port from application to application.

Summary

Whether from external hackers trying to gain access to your data or a vengeful employee on the inside, your business data is under constant threat of theft or loss. Protecting your information is a constant battle, but with appropriately layered security, you can increase the changes of thwarting an attack. In this chapter, you learned a great deal about the ASP.NET security model, authentication, authorization, NTFS access permissions, and ways to protect information using one-way and two-way encryption.

Security, of course, does not end with the ability to configure accounts and implement encryption. You can also look into protecting your systems with firewalls, intrusion-detection systems, and appropriate user training to make sure people know the value of not giving out or writing down passwords. And never forget physical security, such as a lock on the sever room door. There's no point in spending thousands of dollars of encryption and network configuration security when someone can hijack your server the old-fashioned way.

CHAPTER 13

■ ■ ■

Using HTTP Handlers: Request Processing, Image Generation, and Content Management

Scheduling systems require extensive reporting capabilities because they help drive many other areas of business. Knowing how many people are going to be in which location at what time helps managers determine preparation requirements, staffing needs, and inventory control. As such, the scheduling project I was working on had its fair share of reports. Although each was unique in its own way, they all shared two common requirements: they had to expose an "export" feature allowing users to download the report data as an Excel file, and each Excel file had to follow a specific naming convention based on the report type and creation date.

Exporting data to Excel is a fairly simple process because you can output the data as a comma-separated value (CSV) file or as an HTML table. Excel can use both to create a spreadsheet. Getting file names to follow a standard naming convention, however, is another story. In theory, browsers support the `Content-Disposition` HTTP Header, which allows you to specify a file name using the following syntax:

```
Content-Disposition: attachment; filename="<filename.ext>"
```

In practice, however, not all browsers support the `Content-Disposition` header so the specified file name is often disregarded. Instead, the browser uses all or part of the page name from which the report was generated. So, if you create the report from a page named `GenerateReport.aspx`, then the browser tries to save the generated file as `GenerateReport.aspx` or even `<filename.ext>.aspx`. This was the crux of my problem.

Because the `Content-Disposition` header was failing, I had to find some other way of naming files that would work with all browsers. That's when I turned to an HTTP Handler to solve the issue. HTTP Handlers allow you to define how ASP.NET handles an HTTP request, and they open up some creative options. In my case, the application uses an HTTP Handler to "handle" requests for Excel reports that do not actually exist on the file system. Instead of trying to return an existing Excel file, the HTTP Handler generates the content for the Excel file during the request. Because the file doesn't really exist, the application can "name" the Excel file by specifying the file name in a URL (for example, a link to `/XlsReports/ReportA.➥2005.08.19.xls`). When a user clicks on the link to the report, the browser thinks it is requesting a static Excel file. Unbeknownst to the browser, the HTTP Handler intercepts the request (because it handles all requests for `.XLS` files), generates the Excel file content, and returns the content to the browser. The browser then prompts the user to save the Excel file using the only file name it has, the one from the link (for example, `ReportA.2005.08.19.xls`). And it works on all browsers.

HTTP Handlers are a powerful tool to add to your development arsenal that will allow you to create eloquent solutions in a number of complex scenarios. This chapter delves into the architecture behind HTTP Handlers, what they are, how they work, and covers some of the most common situations when HTTP Handlers are employed. Here's a breakdown of what you'll find inside:

- *HTTP Handler Overview:* Describes the basics of HTTP Handlers, including the `IHttpHandler` interface, ASP.NET's HTTP Pipeline, the concepts involved with building custom request handlers, and the `Web.config` settings needed to set them for specific file types.
- *Processing Virtual Files with URL Rewriting:* Discusses a number of URL rewriting topics as you implement the cross-browser file-naming solution discussed in the opening section of this chapter.
- *Thumbnail Image Generation with an HTTP Handler:* Explains how to use an HTTP Handler to manipulate graphics files to create thumbnails or other special effects.
- *Content Management Backend:* Demonstrates how to use URL rewriting and a design pattern called *front controller* to create the backend for a small-scale content-management system.

Let's examine HTTP Handlers and the ASP.NET architecture behind them before we get in too deep into the technicalities of their implementation.

HTTP Handler Overview

ASP.NET uses HTTP Handlers to process client requests for resources that are mapped to the ASP.NET ISAPI handler. When a request is passed to ASP.NET, it looks at the resource type being requested and instantiates an appropriate HTTP Handler for the given resource. The HTTP Handler then processes the request and returns any content required by the request. ASP.NET uses the `PageHandlerFactory` HTTP Handler to process `.aspx` files, the `Web➥ServiceHandlerFactory` HTTP Handler to process `.asmx` files, the `TraceHandler` HTTP Handler to process the `trace.axd` file, and the `HttpForbiddenHandler` to handle files that users should not be allowed to access, such as `.vb`, `.ascx`, `.vbproj`, `.master`, `.skin`, and so on (the handler generates a HTTP 403 Forbidden response code for these files). Microsoft designed the HTTP Handler architecture to be highly extensible, so you can create your own custom HTTP Handlers to process requests in any way you choose.

In this overview, you'll be looking at the architecture behind HTTP Handlers and the entire server-side programming model known as the HTTP Pipeline. You'll learn about how HTTP Handlers are being used in applications today, and then have a chance to implement and configure a simple HTTP Handler example.

IIS and the ASP.NET HTTP Pipeline Process Model

Although ASP.NET is commonly thought of in terms of page processing, it actually exposes an entire server-side programming model for processing requests that begins long before page processing ever occurs. The programming model is known as the HTTP Pipeline, and it's a highly extensible framework for building your own server-side processing components without having to face the complexities of creating an ISAPI component. The HTTP Pipeline is so powerful, in fact, that the core features of ASP.NET—such as page processing, web services, Forms Authentication, caching, and state management—are implemented as HTTP components.

You should have at least a design-level understanding of how an HTTP Request is handled and how the different components of the HTTP Pipeline fit into the overall server-side programming model. Figure 13-1 shows the pipeline components involved in request processing and where they fit in the overall model. In the sections that follow, you'll take a more detailed look at each component and the role each component plays after an HTTP Request is received from the client.

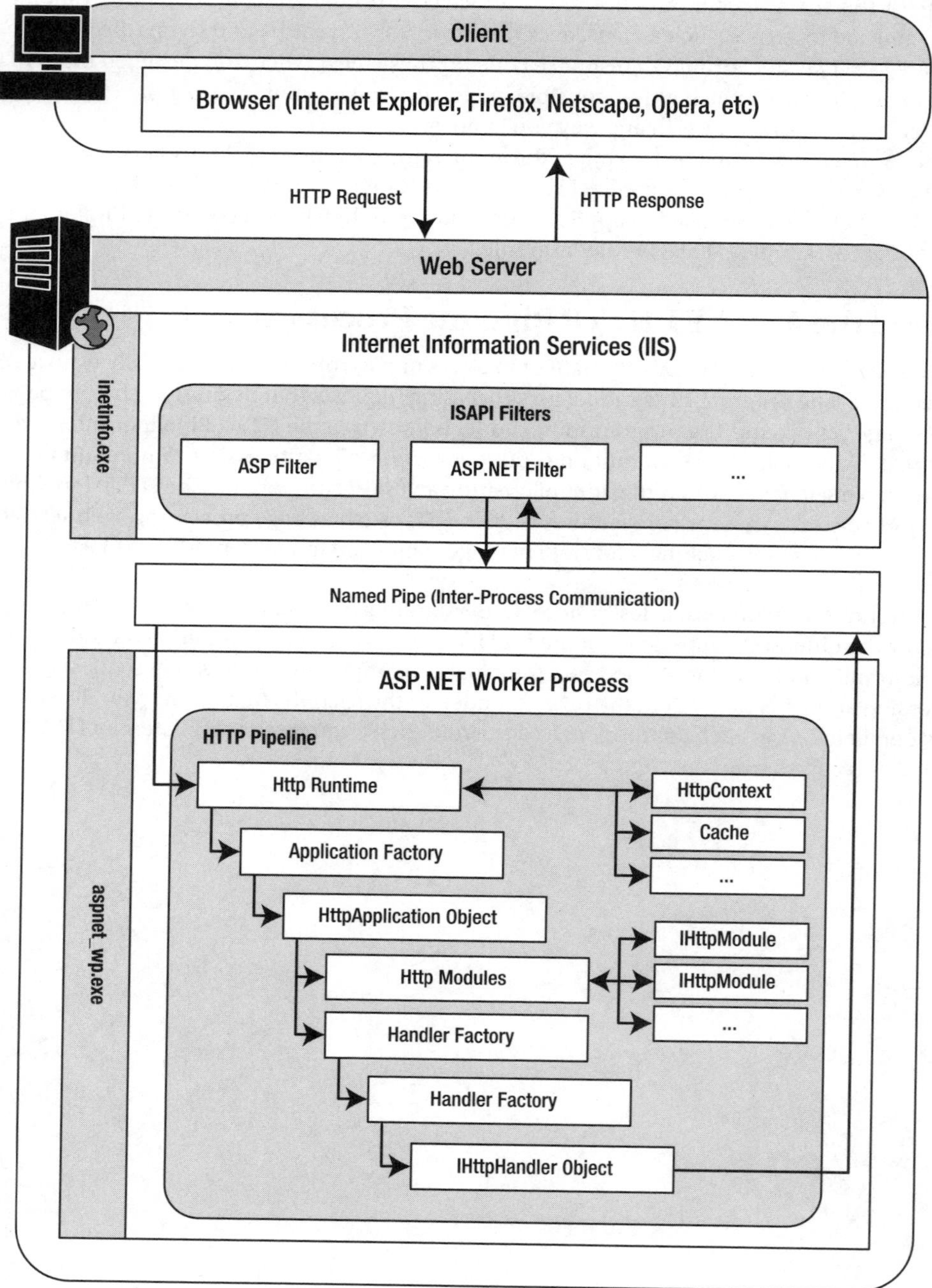

Figure 13-1. *HTTP Request processing diagram*

IIS and ISAPI Filters

IIS is a web server, and it natively supports the capability to fulfill requests for static items such as HTML pages, text-based documents, and image files. Requests for dynamic resources—such as ASPs, ASP.NET pages, or even Cold Fusion or Java Server Pages (JSP)—are handled by deferring the request to an ISAPI filter. The ISAPI filter then becomes responsible for filling the request and returning a static response to IIS. In turn, IIS then passes that response back to the client. Next you'll see what this process looks when a client requests an ASP.NET page.

ASP.NET ISAPI Filter

IIS uses the ASP.NET ISAPI filter to fulfill requests for ASP.NET resources, but the filter isn't actually responsible for executing any ASP.NET code. The filter is responsible for starting the ASP.NET Worker Process (if it's not already running), for passing requests to the Worker Process using a named pipe, for receiving output from the Worker Process from a named pipe, and for killing the Worker Process if it starts performing poorly or crashes.

Named Pipes

If you take a good look at Figure 13-1, you'll notice that IIS and the ASP.NET Worker Process run independently of one another in separate processes. Separating the processes means that the Worker Process can be cleanly killed if a major error occurs, without decimating IIS. One of the downsides of having separate processes is that they can't natively share data because they are in separate memory spaces.

One of the most effective methods for interprocess communication is through *named pipes,* which allow information from one process to be piped into another without having to use physical files. This is how the ASP.NET ISAPI filter and the ASP.NET Worker Process handle back-and-forth communication.

ASP.NET Worker Process and the HTTP Pipeline

As you know from the previous sections, the ASP.NET Worker Process is created by the ASP.NET ISAPI filter, runs in a separate process from IIS, and communicates with IIS via named pipes. After the ASP.NET Worker Process has been created, it remains in memory to continue processing requests. It isn't re-created on each request.

The ASP.NET Worker Process is responsible for hosting the CLR and for sending the incoming request into the HTTP Pipeline. The name HTTP Pipeline is just a term used to describe the series of steps that occur inside the Worker Process during the processing of an ASP.NET resource.

HTTP Runtime

When the Worker Process receives a request, its main task is to create an `HttpRuntime` object that is responsible for setting up a number of helper objects to fulfill the request. One of the most important is the `HttpContext` object, which contains request and response information used by almost every component in the HTTP Pipeline. After the helper objects have been created, the HTTP runtime needs an `HttpApplication` object to continue processing the request, so it uses the Application Factory to create the correct `HttpApplication` object for the application.

Application Factory

Every ASP.NET application has a distinct `HttpApplication` class, and the Application Factory uses the URL of the request to determine the specific class that needs to be handed back to the `HttpRuntime`. It also maintains a pool of previously instantiated `HttpApplication` objects to speed processing response times. After the appropriate `HttpApplication` class has been determined from the URL, the Application Factory checks to see if that type of `HttpApplication` object exists in the pool. If it does, the existing object is returned to the `HttpRuntime`. If not, an appropriate `HttpApplication` object is created and returned. The `HttpRuntime` then passes the processing of the request off to the `HttpApplication` object.

■ **Note** After a request is completed, the `HttpApplication` object isn't always discarded. It may be added back into the Application Factory pool to be reused for a subsequent request.

HTTP Application

The `HttpApplication` object exists to store application-level data, to store application event handlers, and to process HTTP Modules and HTTP Handlers. As a developer, you can define application-level variables and event handlers in `global.asax`, and you can configure additional HTTP Modules and HTTP Handlers in `Web.config`.

When processing a request, the `HttpApplication` object first executes any necessary HTTP Modules (covered in the next section). This allows the HTTP Modules to complete any required preprocessing for the request. The `HttpApplication` object then uses the Handler Factory to determine which HTTP Handler should be used to process the request. The Handler Factory returns the appropriate handler, and the `HttpApplication` object then lets the appropriate handler process the request. When the request has been completely processed, the `HttpApplication` object is returned to the Application Factory object pool.

HTTP Modules

Although this book does not specifically delve into HTTP Modules, they are an important part of the ASP.NET framework. HTTP Modules are executed each time a request is made, so they can be used to set up important information for use later during request processing, or they can be used to inspect or alter the request or response objects. You can also set up event handlers so HTTP Modules can respond to `Application` events. Windows Authentication, Forms Authentication, NTFS file authorization, URL authorization, caching, and state management are just a few examples of functionality in ASP.NET implemented as HTTP Modules.

Handler Factory

The Handler Factory uses the URL of the requested resource, along with HTTP Handler configuration data from `Machine.config` and `Web.config`, to determine which `HttpHandler` should be used to process the request. It maintains a pool of previously instantiated `HttpHandler` objects to speed up processing times. After the appropriate `HttpHandler` class has been determined from the URL, the Handler Factory checks to see if that type of `HttpHandler` object exists in the pool. If so, the existing object is returned to the HttpApplication. If not, an appropriate HttpHandler object is created and then returned. The HttpApplication then passes the processing of the request off to the HttpHandler object.

HTTP Handlers

Finally, we get to the component on which this chapter is based. HTTP Handlers are designed to process a request for a specific type of resource. The key difference between HTTP Handlers and HTTP Modules is that every HTTP Module will be called during a request, but only one HTTP Handler will be called. The primary purpose of an HTTP Handler is to generate a response to a request directly or defer the request to some other component that can generate a response, such as a web form.

After the request has been processed, the HttpHandler object that fulfilled the request is queried to determine the value of its IsReusable property. If the HttpHandler object is reusable, it is returned to the Handler Factory object pool. If not, it is destroyed. The response generated by the HttpHandler is passed from the ASP.NET Worker Process to the named pipe, then to the ISAPI filter, then to IIS, and finally out to the client. And with the request fulfilled, that ends the HTTP Pipeline.

Common Uses for HTTP Handlers

Now that you know the basic architecture behind HTTP Handlers, and the whole server-side processing model for that matter, it's time to take a look at some more uses of HttpHandlers out in the business world.

Transforming Existing Files

One prominent use of HTTP Handlers is in file transformation. As an ASP.NET developer, you actually deal with file transformations every time you run a web form. You place a request for a page, and that page is parsed, compiled, and executed, and the resulting content is returned to the client. You can use HTTP Handlers in a similar fashion to transform data from one format into another.

Processing Requests for Virtual Files

HTTP Handlers allow you to fulfill requests for files that do not exist (assuming the file type is handled by ASP.NET) by generating content for the request before a 404 error is generated. This is the mechanism employed to fix the file-naming issue described at the beginning of this chapter, and it can be leveraged in a number of other scenarios such as creating reports or pulling binary data out of a database.

You can easily see this type of HTTP Handler in action because ASP.NET uses one to fulfill requests for the application trace log. When you have tracing enabled in your web application, you can request the Trace.axd file from the root folder of your application. If you look at your root folder, you'll quickly notice the file does not exist, but when you request the file from the browser, you'll see an output of the trace log. When ASP.NET receives a request for the Trace.axd file, it uses the System.Web.Handlers.TraceHandler to process and output tracing information.

Generating Thumbnails

Another popular use of HTTP Handlers is for generating thumbnail images. This relies on many of the same principles as fulfilling requests for virtual files, but it represents a very specific task in which HTTP Handlers are routinely employed.

A thumbnail image is a smaller version of an image that allows you to decide whether or not you want to look at the full image. They take anywhere from 30 seconds to a couple of minutes to create depending on the imaging application being used, the size of the photo, and your skill level with the software. That may not seem like a lot of time if you're dealing with a relatively limited number of images, but if you're dealing with hundreds or thousands of images, then you're talking about days or hours of tedious, repetitive work.

HTTP Handlers can output binary data just as well as textual data, so they can be used to automatically convert large images into thumbnails using the graphical routines available in the .NET Framework. This can save a lot of time and energy that would otherwise be expended on image processing.

Managing Content

Information on Web sites constantly needs to be updated, and often the individuals responsible for updating content are not HTML savvy. There is a growing need for businesses in the area of content management to allow lay users to easily update information without having to bury themselves in the complexities of HTML.

HTTP Handlers can be used to implement basic content management using a design pattern known as the *front-controller pattern* and a technique known as *URL rewriting*. In this type of scenario, page definitions and content are stored in a database, not as physical files in the web folder. The HTTP Handler captures incoming page requests and analyzes their URLs to determine which page the client wants. The content for the requested page is then pulled out of the database, assembled, and then returned to the client. An administration tool allows business users to easily modify the content of the page without having to directly interact with the HTML.

Now that you know some of the most popular uses for HTTP Handlers, let's take a look at some of the more technical details.

Implementing the IHttpHandler Interface

All HTTP Handlers implement the `IHttpHandler` interface, which exposes one method and one property. The `ProcessRequest(ByVal context As HttpContext)` method of the `IHttpHandler` interface is called to process an incoming request. The request can either be processed entirely by the handler, or the handler can pass the request off to another component and allow that component to fulfill the request.

The `IsReusable()` property of the interface identifies whether or not the instantiated HTTP Handler can be placed in a pool and reused for another request. If you're creating a handler that will be used often in your application, or requires a significant amount of time for instantiation, then you'll likely want to make it reusable. On the other hand, if your handler will be used infrequently, then you may not want it taking up memory space in an object pool while it's lying dormant. If you do make it reusable, remember that the handler may still have lingering values from a previous request.

Listing 13-1 is the code for a very simple Hello World HTTP Handler. This handler is designed to output "Hello World" along with a short message about how it was created by an HTTP Handler. Make sure you place this code in a class file, not in a generic handler page (`.ashx` file).

Listing 13-1. *Basic HTTP Handler Example*

```
Imports System.Web

Public Class HelloWorldHandler
    Implements IHttpHandler, SessionState.IRequiresSessionState

    '*************************************************************************
    Public Sub ProcessRequest(ByVal context As HttpContext) _
      Implements IHttpHandler.ProcessRequest

        context.Response.Write("<HTML><BODY><H1>Hello World!</H1><HR>" & _
                               "This content was output by an HTTP Handler " & _
                               "for the .hello file type.<BODY></HTML>")
    End Sub


    '*************************************************************************
    Public ReadOnly Property IsReusable() As Boolean _
      Implements IHttpHandler.IsReusable
        Get
            Return True
        End Get
    End Property

End Class
```

Because the `HelloWorldHandler` class is an HTTP Handler, it should come as no surprise that it implements the `IHttpHandler` interface. But notice that it also implements the `SessionState.IRequiresSessionState` interface. `IRequiresSessionState` is a marker interface that does not require any methods or properties to be implemented. It just lets ASP.NET know that the HTTP Handler requires access to session-state information (that is, the `Session` object). If you attempt to access the `Session` object in the handler without specifying `IRequiresSessionState`, you'll receive a null reference exception.

Actually, this Hello World example does *not* require access to state information. This was simply a good time to introduce the `IRequireSessionState` interface.

■ Caution If you need to access the `Session` object in your HTTP Handler class, then your class should implement the `System.Web.SessionState.IRequiresSessionState` marker interface. Failure to do so could result in null reference exceptions when the `Session` object is accessed.

You'll see the first method in the class is the `ProcessRequest` method. This method has a single parameter, `context`, through which the method has access to the `Response`, `Request`, `Server`, `Session` (remember to implement `IRequiresSessionState` if you need the `Session` object), and other standard web objects. The `ProcessRequest` method processes the request by writing out an HTML message to the `Response` object. When a client sees the response in their browser, it will look like any other normal HTML page.

In the next section of the `HelloWorldHanlder` class, you'll see the `IsReusable` property. Remember that this property helps the Handler Factory determines whether or not to return the handler to its object pool. Because the `HelloWorldHandler` is fairly lightweight and won't take up much memory in the object pool, this property returns `True`.

At this point, you have a fully functional HTTP Handler. Now you have to configure IIS to map the request for the required extension (`.hello`) to ASP.NET and configure your application to use the HTTP Handler by adding it to `Web.config`.

Mapping File Extensions in IIS

IIS maintains a mapping of file types to different ISAPI filters so it can determine how to process those files. Because the `.hello` file isn't exactly a mainstream file type, IIS does not have a preconfigured mapping for it. So, you'll need to map the file manually to the ASP.NET ISAPI filter.

Open the IIS management console and locate the folder for your application. Right-click on the folder and select **Properties** from the context menu. You'll see the properties dialog box for your application. From the **Directory** tab (it may be **Home Directory**, **Virtual Directory**, or just **Directory**), click the **Configuration** button located near the lower section of the screen. This brings up the **Application Configuration** dialog box shown in Figure 13-2.

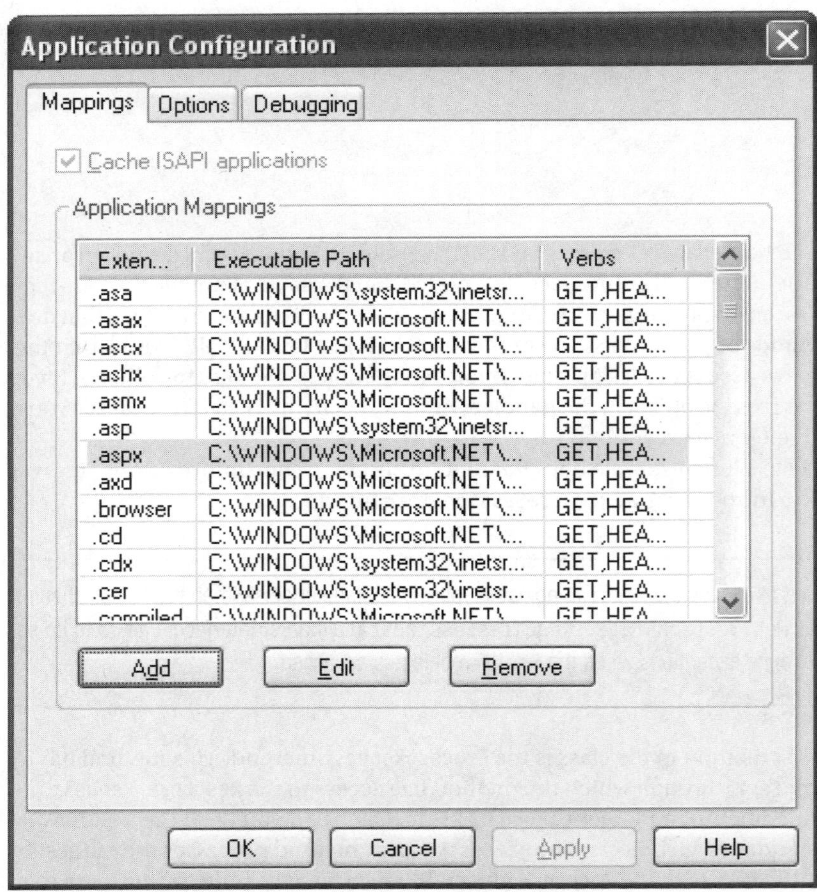

Figure 13-2. *IIS Application Configuration dialog box*

On the **Mappings** tab of the **Application Configuration** dialog box, you'll see a list of file extensions and their respective mappings. Notice that the files associated with ASP.NET are mapped to aspnet_isapi.dll. You want to map the .hello file extension to aspnet_isapi.dll as well so IIS will send requests for .hello files to ASP.NET. Click on the **Add** button to open the **Add/Edit Application Extension Mapping** dialog box shown in Figure 13-3.

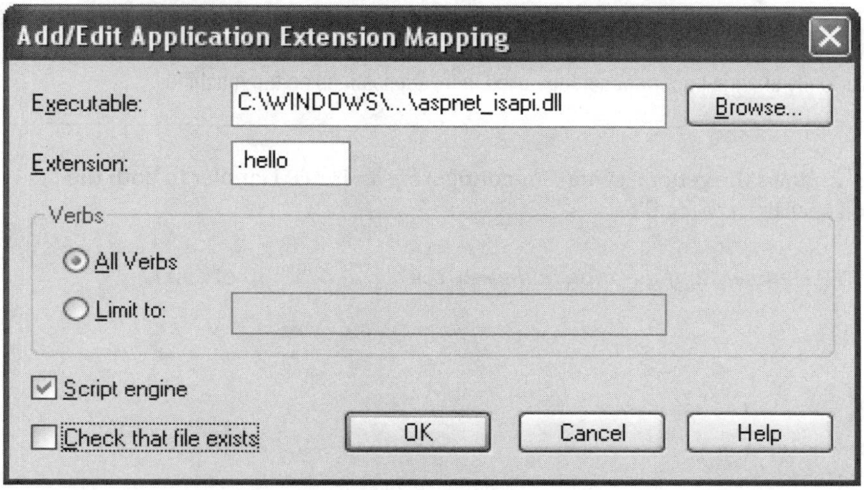

Figure 13-3. *IIS Add/Edit Application Extension Mapping dialog box*

The **Add/Edit Application Extension Mapping** dialog box allows you to enter the extension, the executable (ISAPI filter) that will handle the extension, HTTP verbs that help control when the filter should be used, and whether or not IIS should confirm the existence of the file before passing control over to the ISAPI filter.

To configure a new mapping, you first need to locate aspnet_isapi.dll. This file usually resides in the <Windows>\Microsoft.NET\Framework\<version>\ folder. Use the **Browse** button to locate and select the file. You can also determine the location of the .dll from one of the standard ASP.NET mappings, such as the .aspx entry, from the application mapping list if you prefer. Next, add the file extension .hello to the **Extension** field. You must specify the preceding "." for the file extension before you can add the mapping. Then you need to determine which verbs you want to allow for the mapping. You can either allow all verbs or limit the verbs to a specific subset. Normally, you should use the same verb subset as an .aspx page, so select the **Limit to** option and enter **GET**, **POST**, **HEAD**, **DEBUG** in the **Limit to** text box. Finally, make sure the **Script Engine** check box is checked and the **Check that file exists** check box is unchecked. Remember, the .hello file does not actually exist, so you don't want IIS checking for it before passing off the request to ASP.NET.

When you're finished, click on the **OK** button and the new mapping is added to the list on the **Mapping** tab of the **Application Configuration** dialog box. Click **OK** on all the dialog boxes until you're back at the IIS management console. At this point, your application is able to respond to .hello requests.

Configuring an HTTP Handler in ASP.NET

Application-level HTTP Handler settings are stored in `Web.config`, and machine-level HTTP Handler settings are stored in `Machine.config`. On rare occasions, you'll need to add an HTTP Handler to `Machine.config`, but for the most part. you'll be working with application-specific HTTP Handlers in `Web.config`.

■ **Caution** Do *not* go poking around `Machine.config` unless you know what you are getting yourself into. You could inadvertently change important settings used in all applications on the machine.

Listing 13-2 shows the general syntax for configuring an HTTP Handler in both the `Web.config` and `Machine.config` files.

Listing 13-2. *HTTP Handler Configuration in the* `Web.config` *and* `Machine.config`

```
<configuration>
    ...
    <system.web>
        ...
        <httpHandlers>
            <clear/>
            <remove verb="*,GET,POST,<etc>" path="<dir>/<file>.<ext>"
            <add verb="*,GET,POST,<etc>"    path="<dir>/<file>.<ext>"
                 type="<type>,<assembly>"  validate="True|False"/>
        </httpHandlers>
        ...
    <system.web>
</configuration>
```

HTTP Handler settings appear as `<add>`, `<remove>`, or `<clear>` elements nested in the `<httpHandlers>` element. By far, `<add>` is the most popular. It is used to add an HTTP Handler to your application so the handler can process requests. The `<add>` element has four important parameters as shown in Table 13.1.

Table 13-1. *Parameters of the* `<add>` *Element*

Parameter	Description
verb	Comma-separated list specifying the HTTP verbs to which the handler may respond. You can use the wildcard character * to indicate all verbs. This is commonly set to "GET, POST" or to "*". As a rule of thumb, use "*" unless you have a compelling reason to do otherwise.
path	Specifies a path that an incoming request must match before the handler may respond. You can use the wildcard character in the path string. This parameter allows you to specify a handler for a specific file extension (*.<ext>), specific a file extension for a specific folder <folder>/*.<ext>), a specific file (<directory>/<file>.<ext>), and countless other matching scenarios.
type	Identifies the type name and assembly where the type is located. You must specify both the type name and the assembly. Because you won't know the assembly name for the compiled web application, place your handler class in a separate class library whose name is known so it can be referenced appropriately in this parameter.
validate	Determines whether or not your HTTP Handler entry will be validated when the web application starts. Setting this to false can speed up start times, but it also allows invalid configuration information to go unchecked until it is actually required. By default, validate is True, but you can set it to False if you're confident of your configuration settings.

You probably won't need to use the <remove> or <clear> elements very often when working with HTTP Handlers, but they are included just in case. The <remove> element can be used to remove an existing HTTP Handler. It accepts two parameters, verb and path. The verb and path must exactly match the verb and path of an existing handler. If a match is found, the existing handler is removed. The <clear> element has no parameters and clears out all existing HTTP Handlers.

You may be thinking to yourself, why would you want to remove or clear a bunch of HTTP Handlers that you just defined? Actually, you wouldn't want to clear or remove ones that you just defined, but you may want to clear or remove ones that your application has inherited from Machine.config or a parent application.

If you think back to the HelloWorldHandler example, you'll remember that it was intended to handle files with the .hello extension. Listing 13-3 shows the Web.config settings necessary to configure that HelloWorldHandler example (we'll accept the default validate attribute setting of True).

Listing 13-3. *HTTP Handler Configuration for the* HelloWorldHandler

```
<configuration>
  <system.web>
    <httpHandlers>
      <add verb="*" path="*.hello" type="Handlers.HelloWorldHandler, Handlers" />
    </httpHandlers>
  </system.web>
</configuration>
```

You can see by the assembly name specified in the type parameter that the HelloWorld➥
Handler class is defined in a class library named Handlers. After you have specified these settings in Web.config, ASP.NET is completely setup and ready to use your HTTP Handler. If you're using Visual Studio 2005, you can run the application on the ASP.NET development server, request any .hello file, and see the handler in action. If you're using IIS, however, you need to configure the application mappings so IIS knows to pass requests for the .hello file off to ASP.NET.

■ **Note** All requests coming into the development web server that ships with Visual Studio .NET 2005 are handled by ASP.NET, so there's no need to configure application mappings when using the development web server.

Processing Virtual Files with URL Rewriting

You've already seen one basic example an HTTP Handler, but this example goes into a bit more detail and hands off request processing to another ASP.NET page, which is what URL rewriting is all about. This example also demonstrates how you can implement cross-browser file-naming conventions for generated reports, such as the solution mentioned in the opening of this chapter.

Here is the hypothetical story behind this example. There are three ASP.NET pages responsible for generating three different Excel files: ReportA.aspx, ReportB.aspx, and ReportC.aspx. Each report receives a date and other report specific information in the URL and outputs a report using that data. Each report also has a specific naming convention that must be followed to ensure the downloaded file can be easily referenced.

The solution for this situation is implemented as an HTTP Handler named XlsReport➥
Handler that accepts requests for virtual Excel files, but fulfills those requests using actual ASP.NET pages. The handler uses URL information to determine which reporting page should process the request, and then hands processing of the request over to that page. In effect, the XlsReportHandler "rewrites" the incoming request so it's handled by an actual page. The XlsReportHandler also loads report data from the URL into the Context object so it's readily available on the report page.

Because there are normal Excel files located in various areas of the application, the XlsReportHandler only responds to requests from inside the XlsReports folder. You can see a basic outline of the solution architecture in Figure 13-4.

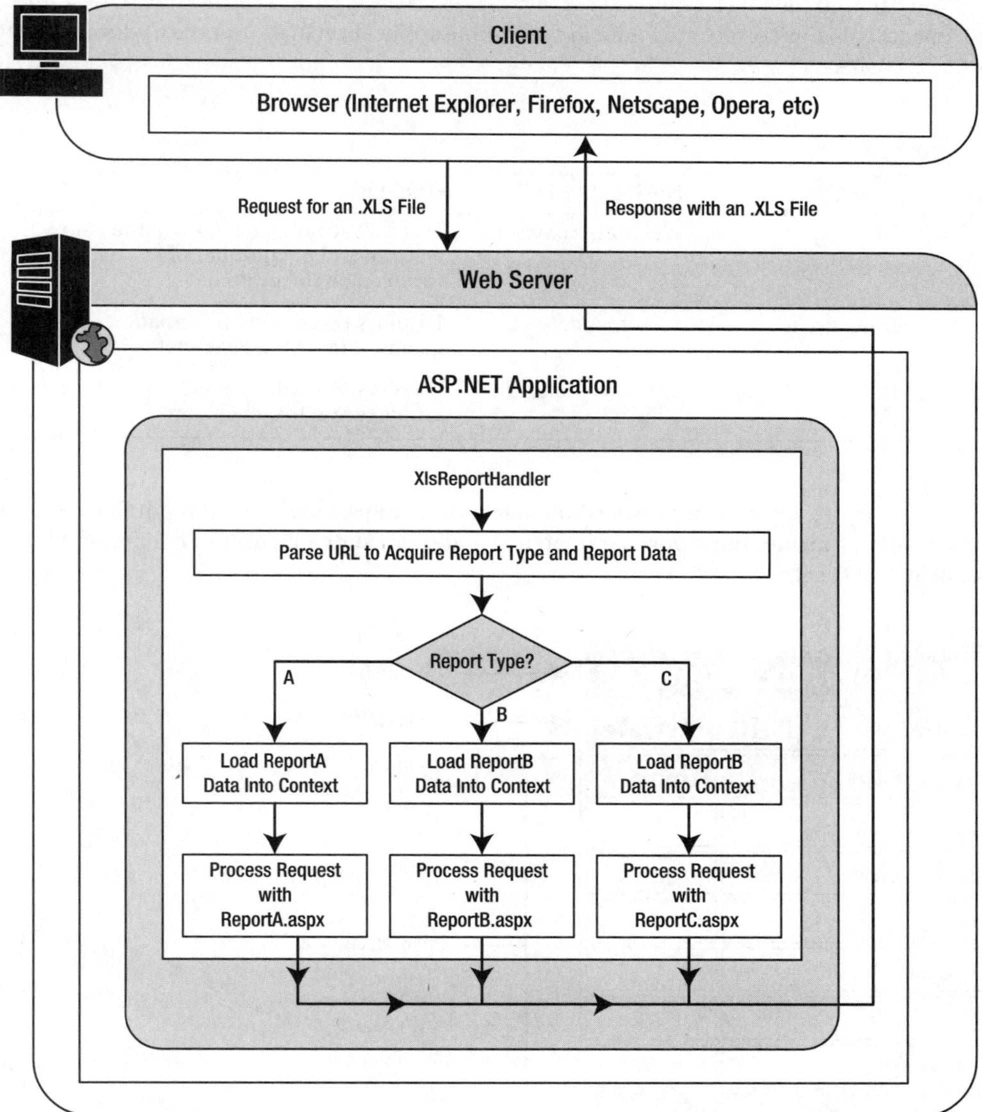

Figure 13-4. *Architectural overview of the Excel file example*

Creating the Report Pages

Request processing is ultimately handled by the individual reporting pages in this example application, so they need to return valid Excel data. The objective of this example is to demonstrate HTTP Handlers, not report generation, so we'll leverage Excel's capability to read HTML by placing hard-coded HTML tables with mock data in the design files of the report pages. This alleviates most of the coding needed to generate reports for this example. In the real world, however, you would need to generate useful information from these pages.

You can find the mock reports ReportA.aspx, ReportB.aspx, and ReportC.aspx, described in Table 13-2, in the XlsReports folder in the sample application in the Source Code area of the Apress website.

Table 13-2. *Example Reports*

Report Name	Parameters	File Naming Ex.	Description
Report A	Date	WebStats.<date>.xls	Displays a listing of pages on the company website and the number of hits each page received on the given date.
Report B	Date, Room	<room>.<date>.xls	Displays reservation information for the given room on the given date.
Report C	Date, Employee	<name>.<date>.xls	Displays a detailed timesheet for the given employee on the given date

These reports dynamically display titles and report dates, but the main report data will not change when you alter the report parameters. Figure 13-5 shows an example report in the Visual Studio Designer.

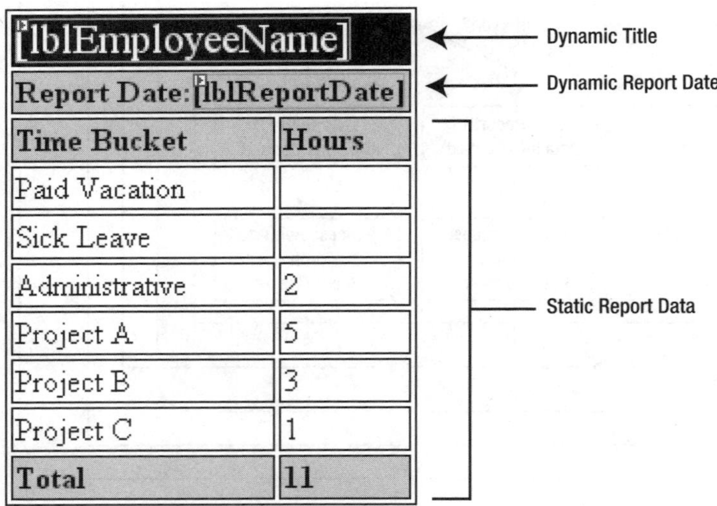

Figure 13-5. *Report C as seen in the Visual Studio Designer*

One important piece of code that exists in each of the mock reports is the line that sets the content-type for the output stream. By default, the content-type is set to text/html. Granted, you are in fact outputting HTML, but you need the browser to recognize the HTML as Excel data. Thus, you'll want to change the content-type of the output stream to application/vnd.ms-excel. Following is the code in ReportC.aspx.vb. In the Page_Load event handler, you'll see the line that changes the content-type of the output stream and sets up the dynamic title and report date in the markup (see Listing 13-4).

Listing 13-4. *Code Behind for the Example Excel report Generation Page*

```
Partial Class ReportC
    Inherits System.Web.UI.Page

    '***************************************************************************
    Private ReadOnly Property ReportDate() As Date
        Get
            If IsDate(Context.Items("Date")) Then
                Return CDate(Context.Items("Date"))
            Else
                Return Now()
            End If
        End Get
    End Property

    '***************************************************************************
    Private ReadOnly Property Employee() As String
        Get
            If CStr(Context.Items("Employee")) = String.Empty Then
                Return "Unknown Employee"
            Else
                Return CStr(Context.Items("Employee"))
            End If
        End Get
    End Property

    '***************************************************************************
    Protected Sub Page_Load(ByVal sender As Object, ByVal e As System.EventArgs) _
      Handles Me.Load
        Response.ContentType = "application/vnd.ms-excel"
        Me.lblReportDate.Text = Format(ReportDate, "MM/dd/yyyy")
        Me.lblEmployeeName.Text = Employee
    End Sub

End Class
```

Notice that the `ReportDate` and `Employee` properties acquire their values from the `Context` object. The `XlsReportHandler` places report data into the `Context` object because it has to parse the URL to determine which report the user requested. Because the report data is stored in the URL, the handler does everything at once to avoid re-parsing the URL on each report page.

Now that you have seen how reports are implemented, you can now focus on the HTTP Handler that processes requests for Excel files and routes the requests to the appropriate report.

Building the XlsReportHandler

Our HTTP Handler, `XlsReportHandler`, is responsible for determining which report needs to be executed and for passing the request off to the appropriate report. To do this, you need to set up some rules that govern how the XlsReportHandler determines the report type and report parameters.

In this example you'll see how to store report parameters directly in the URL instead of in the query string. Older browsers sometimes attempt to save files using everything to the right of the last slash in the URL. As such, a request that looks like

```
/XlsReports/MyReport.xls?Type=ReportA&Date=1/1/2005
```

the browser may attempt to save the file as

```
MyReport.xls?Type=ReportA&Date=1/1/2005
```

which is invalid because it contains the characters ? and /, which are not allowed in file names. Users are easily confused when the default file name is invalid, so you should avoid the situation by embedding parameters before the file name as part of the URL:

```
/XlsReport/<ReportType>/<Date>/<ReportName>.xls
/XlsReports/ReportA/1-1-2005/MyReport.xls
```

Notice that the URL contains the report parameters but they look like part of the folder structure. Browsers don't attempt to store incoming files using the folder structure, so the file name is preserved even on older browser versions. Table 13-3 outlines the various parameters passed to the various reports and the parameter positions in the URL.

Table 13-3. *Report Request Examples*

Report Type	Report Parameters and Example URL
Report A	/XlsReports/<ReportType>/<Date>/WebStats.<Date>.xls
Example	/XlsReports/ReportA/2005-08-20/WebStats.2005.08.31.xls
Report B	/XlsReports/<ReportType>/<Room>/<Date>/<Room>.<Date>.xls
Example	/XlsReports/ReportB/Room A19/2005-06-03/Room A19.2005.06.03.xls
Report C	/XlsReports/<ReportType>/<Employee>/<Date>/<Employee>.<Date>.xls
Example	/XlsReports/ReportC/Nick Reed/2005-12-24/Nick.Reed.2005.12.24.xls

XlsReportHandler Code Listing

After the guidelines for determine report types and parameters is defined, you can begin creating the actual HTTP Handler. Listing 13-5 shows the entire code listing for the XlsReportHandler class.

Listing 13-5. XlsReportHandler *class*

```
Imports System.Web
Imports System.Web.UI

Public Class XlsReportHandler
    Implements IHttpHandler
```

```
'***************************************************************************
Private ReadOnly Property IsReusable() As Boolean _
  Implements System.Web.IHttpHandler.IsReusable
    Get
        Return True
    End Get
End Property

'***************************************************************************
Private Function GetReportName(ByVal UrlParts As String()) As String
    For index As Integer = 0 To UrlParts.Length - 1
        If UCase(UrlParts(index)) = "XLSREPORTS" Then
            If index < UrlParts.Length - 1 Then
                Return UrlParts(index + 1)
            End If
        End If
    Next
    Return ""
End Function

'***************************************************************************
Private Sub ProcessRequest(ByVal context As System.Web.HttpContext) _
  Implements System.Web.IHttpHandler.ProcessRequest

    Dim ReportHandler As IHttpHandler = Nothing
    Dim UrlParts As String() = Split(context.Request.Path, "/")

    Select Case GetReportName(UrlParts)
        Case "ReportA"
            '================================================================
            Try
                context.Items("Date") = CDate(UrlParts(UrlParts.Length - 2))
                context.RewritePath("~/XlsReports/ReportA.aspx")
                ReportHandler = PageParser.GetCompiledPageInstance( _
                  "~/XlsReports/ReportA.aspx", Nothing, context)

            Catch ex As Exception
                ReportHandler = PageParser.GetCompiledPageInstance( _
                  "~/XlsReports/Invalid.aspx", Nothing, context)
            End Try

        Case "ReportB"
            '================================================================
            Try
                Dim Room As String = UrlParts(UrlParts.Length - 3)
                Dim ReportDate As Date = CDate(UrlParts(UrlParts.Length-2))
```

```
                context.Items("Room") = UrlParts(UrlParts.Length - 3)
                context.Items("Date") = CDate(UrlParts(UrlParts.Length - 2))
                context.RewritePath("~/XlsReports/ReportB.aspx")
                ReportHandler = PageParser.GetCompiledPageInstance( _
                  "~/XlsReports/ReportB.aspx", Nothing, context)

            Catch ex As Exception
                ReportHandler = PageParser.GetCompiledPageInstance( _
                  "~/XlsReports/Invalid.aspx", Nothing, context)
            End Try

        Case "ReportC"
            '==============================================================
            Try
                context.Items("Employee") = UrlParts(UrlParts.Length - 3)
                context.Items("Date") = CDate(UrlParts(UrlParts.Length - 2))
                context.RewritePath("~/XlsReports/ReportC.aspx")
                ReportHandler = PageParser.GetCompiledPageInstance( _
                  "~/XlsReports/ReportC.aspx", Nothing, context)

            Catch ex As Exception
                ReportHandler = PageParser.GetCompiledPageInstance( _
                  "~/XlsReports/Invalid.aspx", Nothing, context)
            End Try

        Case Else 'Invalid report requested
            '==============================================================
            ReportHandler = PageParser.GetCompiledPageInstance( _
              "~/XlsReports/Invalid.aspx", Nothing, context)

    End Select

    ReportHandler.ProcessRequest(context)

  End Sub

End Class
```

Nothing overly noteworthy occurs in the first part of the code listing. Naturally, the `XlsReportHandler` needs to implement the `IHttpHandler` interface just like every other HTTP Handler with which you'll work. Also, the `IsReusable` property returns true so this handler can be pooled by the Handler Factory.

GetReportName Function

After the `IsReusable` property, you'll see a function named `GetReportName`, which accepts an array of strings as input. This function is designed to return the report name embedded in the URL of the request. If you look back to Table 13-3, you'll notice each report request has a similar syntax:

```
/XlsReports/<Report Name>/<Param 1>/<Param 2>/.../<Param n>/<File Name>.xls
```

Thus, you can split the URL into an array of strings using / as the delimiter, and the string following the "XlsReports" string will be the report name.

The UrlParts function parameter contains the split version of the URL. GetReportName iterates through each item in that array looking for the "XlsReports" string. It forces everything into uppercase to avoid case-sensitive mismatches. When a match is found, it then checks to make sure it isn't at the end of the array, then returns the next item in the array. If no match is found, the function simply returns an empty string.

ProcessRequest

ProcessRequest is responsible for determining which report needs to be run and handing off the processing of the request to the appropriate report page. A large part of that responsibility is acquiring report parameters and ensuring that they are available to the report when it executes, so much of this discussion focuses on the report parameters and how they get to the report pages.

As you look at the ProcessRequest method, you'll notice it uses two variables named ReportHandler and UrlParts. ReportHandler holds a reference to another HTTP Handler that ultimately processes the report request, and UrlParts is the string array that holds each section of URL after it has been split. The URL is split on the same line on which UrlParts is declared using the / character as a delimiter.

ProcessRequest uses the GetReportName function in its main Select Case statement to determine which report is being requested. It then chooses the appropriate Case statement and executes the associated code. If no Case statement match is made, or an error occurs setting up a report for processing, then the function assigns the ReportHandler variable a reference to the compiled Invalid.aspx page instance (instead of a report page). Later on, when ReportHandler processes the request for the report, the Invalid.aspx page display an error message to the user instead creating a downloadable Excel report.

Each section of code in the three Case statements is fairly similar. First, the code sets up a Try Catch block to deal with any exceptions that arise. If an exception occurs, the Catch block sets up the ReportHandler to display the Invalid.aspx page. Inside the Try block, the method acquires the report parameters from the URL and places them into the Context object. To do this, it needs to know the location of the parameters in the URL, which requires a bit of explaining. Remember, the method split the URL into the UrlParts string array using the / character as a delimiter. So, the folders and file name from the URL exist inside the UrlParts array, minus the / characters because the delimiter is removed when you split a string. In the following code snippet, you'll find example URLs for Report A and Report B showing the UrlParts index of the various parts of the URL (parameters are shown in bold).

```
Report A:
 /<Application Dir>/XlsReports/ReportA/2005-8-21/WebStats.2005.08.21
0 1                  2          3       4        5

Report B:
 /<Application Dir>/XlsReports/ReportB/Room/2005-8-21/Room.2005.8.21.xls
0 1                  2          3       4    5         6
```

Notice that the URL starts off with a / character (the delimiter). Any time the Split function encounters a delimiter, it always places data from the left and right of the delimiter into the array. In this case, there is nothing to the left of the delimiter, so the Split function places an empty string into the array at position 0. If you split the string "///" you would end up with an array of four empty strings ("<empty>/<empty>/<empty>/<empty>").

So the method pulls parameters out of the `UrlParts` array and stores them as named items in the `context` object. Storing information in the `Context` object is very similar to the `Session` object, but data stored in the `Context` object exists only for the duration of the current request.

Also note that parameter positions are not absolute. For example, on Report A, you can't assume that `UrlParts(4)` is the report date. The application folder may actually be a nested virtual folder, which can throw off the indexing. That is, it could be something like `<Parent Web>/<Application Dir>`, which would make the report date `UrlParts(5)`. Thus, you have to work your way backwards and reference the report date for Report A as `UrlParts(UrlParts.Length - 2)`.

After the parameters have been loaded into the context, the code rewrites the internal path by calling `Context.RewritePath` and passing in the location of the item that is to be executed. Report A's rewrite looks like this:

```
Context.RewritePath("~/XlsReports/ReportA.aspx")
```

Understand that this method isn't transferring execution to `ReportA.aspx`, it just updates the properties on the `Request` object like the `Path`, `PhysicalPath`, and `QueryString` (if applicable). Remember, the request is ultimately handled by another page and that page may expect these properties to contain values indicative of the page processing the request and not of the resource the user requested. For example, say you had an error logger in `ReportA.aspx` and were passing the `Path` variable in as the location of the error. If you don't use `Context.RewritePath`, then the error location will contain something like

```
/XlsReports/ReportA/2005-08-20/WebStats.2005.08.31.xls
```

whereas if you use `Context.RewritePath`, then the error location will contain

```
/XlsReports/ReportA.aspx
```

Unless you have a compelling reason to do otherwise, it's a good practice to call `Context.RewritePath` before allowing another page to handle a request.

■ **Note** If you call RewritePath inside of an HTTP Module, then the path information will be changed before the HTTP Handler Factory checks it. This means that the Handler Factory will return the handler for the page specified in the new path. Thus, you can alter execution by changing `RewritePath` in an HTTP Module, whereas it has no direct effect on execution when called from inside an HTTP Handler.

Finally, the `Case` statement calls `PageParser.GetCompiledPageInstance` from the `System.Web.UI` namespace to acquire the HTTP Handler that ASP.NET would have used to process the request had the report page been called directly. It stores this handler in the `ReportHandler` variable so it can be called later.

After `ProcessRequest` exits the `Select Case`, it's ready to execute the handler for the report (or the `Invalid.aspx` page if an exception occurred). It does this by calling `ReportHandler.➥ProcessRequest` and passing the `context` object into the method. This passes processing of the request to the new handler, and all resulting output is sent to the client.

HTTP Handler Design Considerations

One thing that I have learned over the years is that the same thing can be accomplished in many different ways, and each of those different ways has its pros and cons. So, before taking a look at how to request files using the XlsReportHandler, let's take a second to discuss a few design elements that went into it and why they were chosen.

Context vs. the Querystring

As noted previously, the XlsReportHandler passes report parameters via the Context object. Another option is to pass those parameters in the query string. Most people are more familiar with the query string and therefore more comfortable with it, so the decision to place items in the Context object may be a bit confusing at first.

Here's the logic behind it. Query strings have to be parsed to be useful. You'll notice that we had to do our own parsing to pull out the report parameter in the first place, so putting it back into a format that would then need to be reparsed seems wasteful. Thus, it's a question of efficiency.

Of course, there are times when using the query string makes perfect sense. For example, if you have already built out your reporting page and it expects parameters to be passed in using the query string, then you may as well pass parameters to the page using the query string to avoid having to recode the page.

Passing Parameters Using the Query String

The Querystring property of the Request object is read-only, meaning that you can't add or modify query string items. If you want to pass items in along the query string, you'll need to create a new query string and attach it to the page path you pass into the RewritePath method. The RewritePath method removes any existing information from the Querystring property and reinitializes it with the new query string data.

Let's take a look at an example so you can see exactly how this is done. Report B accepts two different parameters, a room name and a report date. Listing 13-6 shows how to create a query string containing these two parameters and pass it into the RewritePath method.

Listing 13-6. *Passing Parameters via the Query String*

```
Dim Room As String = UrlParts(UrlParts.Length - 3)
Dim ReportDate As Date = CDate(UrlParts(UrlParts.Length - 2))
Dim QueryString As String = "?Date=" & _
  Server.UrlEncode(ReportDate.ToString() & "&Room=" & Room)
context.RewritePath("~/XlsReports/ReportB.aspx" & QueryString)
```

This allows the report page to acquire its parameters using the familiar syntax Request.Querystring("Date") or Request.Querystring("Room").

Avoiding Server.Transfer

Many developers are familiar with the Server.Transfer method, which allows you to handle a redirect on the server without having to make a round trip to the client. This method also leaves the Context and Request objects in tact during the transfer, so it may seem tempting to use it in an HTTP Handler such as XlsReportHandler. I didn't use it in this example as a matter of efficiency. `Server.Transfer` makes ASP.NET treat the transfer as an entirely new request. This means that all the components in the HTTP Pipeline get run twice. Using the technique used by the `XlsReportHandler`, ASP.NET does not have to reprocess the request. Of course, you may actually *want* to treat the transfer as a new request for reasons outlined in the next "Security Considerations" section.

Security Considerations

When you use the HTTP Handler returned by the `PageParser.GetCompiledPageInstance` method, you avoid having to rerun the entire HTTP Pipeline to execute the page. Of course, many of the core security features in ASP.NET such as authentication and authorization are implemented as part of the HTTP Pipeline, so there are some security considerations that you need to keep in mind when you're designing your application.

If you look at `Web.config` in the `XlsReports` folder of the sample application, you'll notice that access to all content is denied to all users. If you attempt to access any of the report-generation pages directly, you'll get an Access Denied error. But you can access the report without any problem when you request a file using a "fake" URL such as

```
/XlsReports/ReportA/2005-08-31/WebStats.2005.08.31.xls
```

When this request goes through the HTTP Pipeline, the authorization module runs under the assumption that you're actually requesting a "real" file when in reality the path does not exist. Because there are no authorization restrictions on the nonexistent path, the request passes authorization. When you acquire a page using `Pageparser.GetCompiledPageInstance`, you bypass the authorization module entirely. This means that you could accidentally display a page to a user who does not have the appropriate permissions to view the page. One way to avoid this issue is to use code-based authorization directly in the restricted page as shown in Listing 13-7.

Listing 13-7. *Ensuring Authorization Inside a Restricted Page*

```
If Not Context.User.IsInRole("Admin") Then
    FormsAuthentication.RedirectToLoginPage()
End If
```

The authorization code in the page runs even if the authorization module does not, so your page remain secures whenever it executes. Now it's time to look at how to use the `XlsReportHandler` to get reports.

Using the XlsReportHandler to Retrieve Reports

Receiving reports using the `XlsReportHandler` requires two things. The first is a properly configured `Web.config` file so the handler can catch requests for Excel files in the `XlsReport` folder. The second thing is a way to generate the appropriate file names for each report so the `XlsReportHandler` can determine which report is being requested and what parameters should be sent to the report.

■ **Note** Make sure you update the IIS application extension mappings to allow ASP.NET to process `.XLS` files. Otherwise, you'll receive a 404 error when you try to use the `XlsReportHandler`. See the "Mapping File Extensions in IIS" section earlier in this chapter for more information on these mappings.

Configuring the XlsReportHandler

You'll be placing the HTTP Handler configuration for the XlsReportHandler in a Web.config file in the XlsReport folder of your application. This will simplify the actual configuration settings because it requires a single entry (see Listing 13-8).

Listing 13-8. *Configuring the* XlsReportHandler

```
<configuration>
  ...
  <system.web>
    ...
    <httpHandlers>
      <clear />
      <add verb="*" path="*.xls" type="Handlers.XlsReportHandler,Handlers" />
      <add path="Invalid.aspx" verb="*" type="System.Web.UI.PageHandlerFactory" />
      <add path="*" verb="*" type="System.Web.HttpMethodNotAllowedHandler" />
    </httpHandlers>
  </system.web>
</configuration>
```

There are four items in the <httpHandlers> section of Web.config. The first, <clear />, ensures the folder does not inherit any unwanted handler settings. The next ensures that any requests for an Excel file in this folder, or any subfolder of this folder, pass through to the XlsReportHandler. The third allows the standard page handler to accept requests for the Invalid.aspx file. We need to explicitly allow the standard page handler to accept requests for Invalid.aspx because the final entry blocks all other request. This means people can't directly access ReportA.aspx, ReportB.aspx, ReportC.aspx, or Web.config.

Building File Names for the XlsReportHandler

After Web.config has been set up to route all Excel file request through the XlsReportHandler, you need a way to build out Excel file names that the XlsReportHandler can understand. You can refer back to Table 13-2 and Table 13-3 for file-naming conventions and examples for each report.

Following you'll find the code to build out the file names for each report type. These method can be found in the RequestReport.aspx code-behind in the sample application (see Listing 13-9).

Listing 13-9. *Methods to Help Build the Report URLs*

```
'**************************************************************************
Private Function GetReportAPath(ByVal ReportDate As Date) As String

    Return String.Format("XlsReports/ReportA/{0}/WebStats.{1}.xls", _
                         Format(ReportDate, "yyyy-MM-dd"), _
                         Format(ReportDate, "yyyy.MM.dd"))
End Function

'**************************************************************************
Private Function GetReportBPath(ByVal Room As String, _
                                ByVal ReportDate As Date) As String
```

```
    Return String.Format("XlsReports/ReportB/{0}/{1}/{0}.{2}.xls", _
                         Room, _
                         Format(ReportDate, "yyyy-MM-dd"), _
                         Format(ReportDate, "yyyy.MM.dd"))
End Function

'***************************************************************************
Private Function GetReportCPath(ByVal Employee As String, _
                                ByVal ReportDate As Date) As String

    Return String.Format("XlsReports/ReportB/{0}/{1}/{0}.{2}.xls", _
                         Employee, _
                         Format(ReportDate, "yyyy-MM-dd"), _
                         Format(ReportDate, "yyyy.MM.dd"))
End Function
```

Each function accepts a set of parameters that matches the parameters required by the report. Then they use the `String.Format` and `Format` methods to construct an appropriately named file before returning the file name as the result of the function.

Downloading the Reports

Now that you have built out the `GetReportAPath`, `GetReportBPath`, and `GetReportCPath` functions, you need to use those functions on a page to generate a link to a report. You can do this using a redirect from a button or you can set up a clickable hyperlink.

Creating a hyperlink is as easy as dropping a `Hyperlink` control on your form, setting its `ID` and `Text` properties, and then assigning one of the report path functions to the `NavigateUrl` property. Listing 13-10 provides an example.

Listing 13-10. *Linking to a Report Using a Hyperlink*

```
Me.hlnkReportA.NavigateUrl = GetReportAPath(Now())
Me.hlnkReportB.NavigateUrl = GetReportBPath("Conference Room", Now())
Me.hlnkReportC.NavigateUrl = GetReportCPath("Nick Reed", Now())
```

You can also use the get report path functions directly in redirect. Listing 13-11 provides the code for a button click event that will redirect the user to Report C.

Listing 13-11. *Linking to a Report Using a Form Button*

```
'***************************************************************************
Protected Sub btnGetReportC_Click(ByVal sender As Object, _
  ByVal e As System.EventArgs) Handles btnGetReportC.Click

    Response.Redirect(GetReportCPath(txtEmployee.Text, _
      CDate(txtReportCDate.Text)))

End Sub
```

You can see all this code in action by opening up the RequestReport.aspx page in the sample application in the Source Code area of the Apress website. It has data-entry forms for all three reports, so you can see all of them in action.

Thumbnail Generation with an HTTP Handler

As digital photo technology has become more and more advanced, image sizes have become larger and larger. My first digital camera took 640 x 400 pixel images when it was in high-resolution mode. I don't know if the camera I have right now can even take a picture that small. Digital images can easily take up 1 or 2 megabytes and I have seen many that exceed 5 or 10.

Businesses that offer their product over the web usually take product images to give customers some idea of what the item looks like. Of course, it's not easy to incorporate a large product image into the design of a product page, so a thumbnail image is used instead. Thumbnails are just a smaller version of a picture that gives the viewer a basic idea of what the image contains. If the user wants to see the whole image, they click on the thumbnail to download the larger version. The catch, of course, is that you have to make the thumbnail image before you can use it.

I saw the process of thumbnail creation while working with a client who sold crafts online. The client hired a college student to come in, photograph the products, save those images to a pictures folder, and then resize each image in Photoshop to create a thumbnail image which was stored in a thumbnails folder. Judging by his demeanor, it had become a tedious and mind-numbing process after the first couple of images.

Thumbnail generation using an HTTP Handler saves you the trouble of having to manually create thumbnails by generating them on-the-fly using an HTTP Handler.

Objectives and Solution Architecture

The main objectives of this example are to demonstrate how HTTP Handlers can be used to generate and return binary data and to show how you can cache that generated data by saving the data to disk and referencing it later. This example is *not* intended to be an exhaustive reference of graphical routines that you can apply to a thumbnail image. I'll only focus on resizing the image.

Here's how this solution works. All pictures files will be stored in the Pictures folder, or in subfolders located in the Pictures folder. This allows you to either have one folder full of pictures, or a series of subfolders to help organize the pictures. There will also be a Thumbnails folder in the Pictures folder.

When an image is requested from the Thumbnails folder, the request will be intercepted by an HTTP Handler named ThumbnailHandler. This handler checks to see if the requested thumbnail exists, the corresponding full-sized image file exists, and that the thumbnail isn't out of date. It checks to see if the thumbnail is out of date by comparing the thumbnail's last modified date to the full-sized image's last modified date. If the full-sized image has been updated more recently than the thumbnail image, then the thumbnail is considered to be out of date. If everything is in order, it will read the thumbnail file and send it back to the client. If not, it will create a new thumbnail from the full-sized image and save the thumbnail to the thumbnails folder so it can be used during a later request. This process is outlined in Figure 13-6.

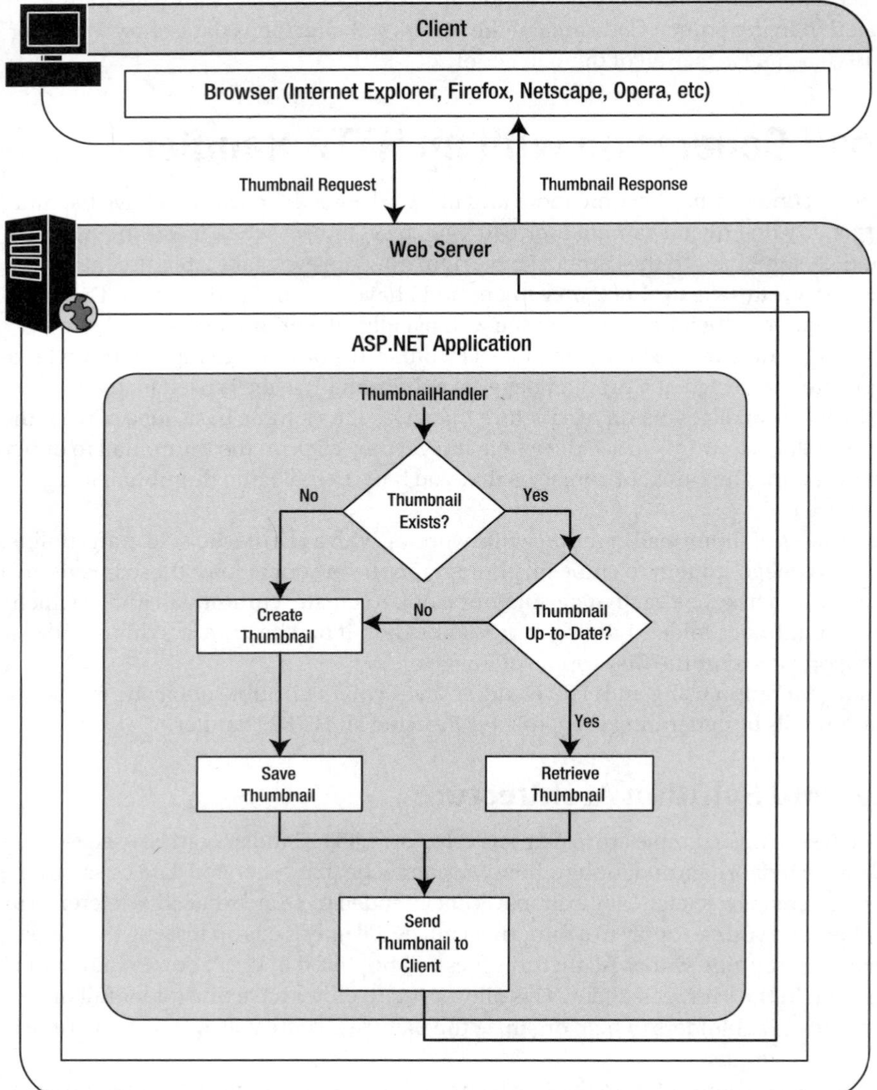

Figure 13-6. `ThumbnailHandler` *architecture*

Requests for thumbnail images must map to existing full-sized images in the `Pictures` folder. Table 13-4 shows some example thumbnail requests and the thumbnail's corresponding full-sized image.

Table 13-4. *Thumbnail Request Mappings*

Requested Thumbnail	Corresponding Full-Sized Image
`/Thumbnails/Image01.jpg`	`/Pictures/Image01.jpg`
`/Thumbnails/SubFolder/Image02.jpg`	`/Pictures/SubFolder/Image02.jpg`

Notice that the only difference between the thumbnail request and the actual file is that thumbnails are stored in the /Thumbnails folder and the full-sized images are stored in the /Pictures folder. This makes mapping the thumbnail request to the actual file fairly easy because you just have to replace /Thumbnails with /Pictures in the string. You'll see the code for this in the ProcessRequest method.

■ **Note** You are not required to place the Thumbnails subfolder inside the Picture folder. With some minor changes, you could place it in the root folder or in another folder in your application. In this example, it was placed in the Picture folder simply as a matter of preference.

Building the ThumbnailHandler

The code for the ThumbnailHandler class is a bit lengthier than the previous HTTP Handlers because it processes the entire request directly in the class. You'll find the entire code listing for ThumbnailHandler in Listing 13-12, and a discussion on its more important methods follows.

Listing 13-12. ThumbnailHandler *class*

```
Imports System.Drawing
Imports System.IO
Imports System.Web

Public Class ThumbnailHandler
    Implements IHttpHandler

    '***************************************************************************
    Public ReadOnly Property IsReusable() As Boolean _
      Implements System.Web.IHttpHandler.IsReusable
        Get
            Return True
        End Get
    End Property

    '***************************************************************************
    Public Sub ProcessRequest(ByVal context As System.Web.HttpContext) _
      Implements System.Web.IHttpHandler.ProcessRequest

        'File info objects used to determine file existence and modified dates
        Dim Thumbnail As New FileInfo(context.Server.MapPath(context.Request.Path))
        Dim FullSized As New FileInfo(context.Server.MapPath( _
                             context.Request.Path.Replace("/Thumbnails", "")))

        'Full-sized version of thumbnail should exit for thumbnail to be returned
        If Not FullSized.Exists Then
            If Thumbnail.Exists Then Thumbnail.Delete()
```

```
            Throw New Exception("Full sized image does not exist")
        End If

        'Determine whether or not to create or retrieve the thumbnail
        If Thumbnail.Exists Then
            If FullSized.LastWriteTime > Thumbnail.LastWriteTime Then
                Thumbnail.Delete()
                CreateThumbnail(context, Thumbnail, FullSized)
            Else
                RetrieveThumbnail(Thumbnail, context)
            End If
        Else
            CreateThumbnail(context, Thumbnail, FullSized)
        End If

    End Sub

    '*****************************************************************************
    Private Function GetContentType(ByVal FI As FileInfo) As String
        'Returns appropriate content type based on file extension

        Select Case UCase(FI.Extension)
            Case ".GIF"
                Return "image/gif"
            Case ".JPG", ".JPEG"
                Return "image/jpeg"
            Case Else
                Throw New Exception("Invalid image type")
        End Select

    End Function

    '*****************************************************************************
    Private Function GetImageFormat(ByVal FI As FileInfo) As Imaging.ImageFormat
        'Returns appropriate image format based on file extension

        Select Case UCase(FI.Extension)
            Case ".GIF"
                Return Imaging.ImageFormat.Gif
            Case ".JPG", ".JPEG"
                Return Imaging.ImageFormat.Jpeg
            Case Else
                Throw New Exception("Invalid image type")
        End Select

    End Function
```

```
'***************************************************************************
Private Sub RetrieveThumbnail(ByVal Thumbnail As FileInfo, _
                              ByVal context As System.Web.HttpContext)

    Dim img As Image = Image.FromFile(Thumbnail.FullName)
    context.Response.ContentType = GetContentType(Thumbnail)
    img.Save(context.Response.OutputStream, img.RawFormat)
    img.Dispose()

End Sub

'***************************************************************************
Public Function GetSizeMultiplier(ByVal img As Image) As Single
    'Gets size multiplier used to maintain image aspect ratio

    Const MaxWidth As Integer = 150
    Const MaxHeight As Integer = 150

    Dim HeightMultiplier As Single = MaxWidth / img.Width
    Dim WidthMultiplier As Single = MaxHeight / img.Height


    If HeightMultiplier > 1 Then HeightMultiplier = 1
    If WidthMultiplier > 1 Then WidthMultiplier = 1

    If HeightMultiplier < WidthMultiplier Then
        Return HeightMultiplier
    Else
        Return WidthMultiplier
    End If

End Function

'***************************************************************************
Private Sub CreateThumbnail(ByVal context As System.Web.HttpContext, _
                            ByVal Thumbnail As FileInfo, _
                            ByVal FullSized As FileInfo)

    Dim img As Image = Image.FromFile(FullSized.FullName)
    Dim imgFormat as Imaging.ImageFormat = GetImageFormat(FullSized)
    Dim SizeMultiplier = GetSizeMultiplier(img)

    img = img.GetThumbnailImage(CInt(img.Width * SizeMultiplier), _
            CInt(img.Height * SizeMultiplier), Nothing, Nothing)
    img.Save(context.Response.OutputStream, imgFormat)
    If Not Thumbnail.Directory.Exists Then Thumbnail.Directory.Create()
    img.Save(Thumbnail.FullName, imgFormat)
```

```
        img.Dispose()

    End Sub

End Class
```

ProcessRequest Method

The ProcessRequest method is responsible for determining whether or not a thumbnail image should be created or retrieved, and for returning the thumbnail image to the client.

It starts by creating two FileInfo objects named Thumbnail and FullSized. If you haven't worked with FileInfo objects before, then you need to know a couple of things about them. The FileInfo constructor requires a path to a file, but that file does not have to exist. It then uses that path information to provide you information about the file specified like whether or not the file actually exists, the file size, creation date, folder location, and other helpful file-specific pieces of information. The Thumbnail FileInfo object is created by passing in the following path:

```
Server.MapPath(context.Request.Path)
```

The context.Request.Path property contains the URL where the thumbnail image resides, or where it should reside after it has been created. Server.MapPath simply translates the URL contained in context.Request.Path into a physical file path that the FileInfo object can understand.

FullSized's path is created in much the same way as Thumbnail, but the /Thumbnail folder is replaced with an empty string. This effectively gives you the location of the full-sized image. Table 13-4 (shown previously) contains mapping examples that help show why this replacement correctly maps to the full-sized image:

```
context.Server.MapPath(context.Request.Path.Replace("/Thumbnails","/Pictures"))
```

After both FileInfo objects have been created, ProcessRequest checks to see if the full-sized image exists by calling FullSized.Exists. If the file does not exist, then ProcessRequest deletes the thumbnail image (if it exists) and throws an exception. It doesn't make sense to keep a thumbnail for an image that doesn't exist.

After ensuring the full-sized image exists, ProcessRequest then determines if the thumbnail image exists by calling Thumbnail.Exists. If the thumbnail does not exist, then ProcessRequest calls the CreateThumbnail method. If the thumbnail image exists, then the code compares the LastWriteTime property of the Thumbnail and FullSized FileInfo objects. If the full-sized image is newer than the thumbnail image, then ProcessRequest creates a new thumbnail. Otherwise, it calls RetrieveThumbnail to retrieve the existing image.

GetContentType and GetImageFormat Methods

The ThumbnailHandler is only designed to work with JPEG and GIF files. You can extend it to handle whatever files you so desire, but for the purposes of this example those are the two file types it accepts. GetContentType and GetImageFormat are both helper functions that return the specific content-type and ImageFormat settings required by the two different formats.

Both functions share a similar structure. Each accepts a FileInfo object as a parameter, and then uses the Extension property of that FileInfo object in a Select Case statement to determine whether the file is a GIF or a JPEG. The code throws an exception if any other extension is detected.

GetContentType returns a string containing either "image/gif" or "image/jpeg", depending on the file type. This content-type string is used to set the Response.ContentType property, which tells the browser which type of image data to expect.

GetImageFormat returns a System.Drawing.Imaging.ImageFormat object that tells the image-saving mechanism how to encode the image when it's saved to disk.

RetrieveThumbnail Method

This method accepts a FileInfo object named Thumbnail, and an HttpContext object named context as parameters. It's responsible for reading the existing thumbnail file specified in Thumbnail and sending it back to the client via the context object.

RetrieveThumbnail accomplishes its tasks by creating an Image object named img and initializing it using the Image.FromFile method. Image.Load accepts the path to an image file, reads the image file from disk, and creates an Image object containing the image data. The physical path to the thumbnail file is in the Thumbnail.FullName property.

After reading the image from disk, RetrieveThumbnail sets the ContentType property of the Response object using the GetContentType method. This helps the client know how to handle the incoming data.

Next, the code calls img.Save(context.Response.OutputStream, img.RawFormat). This causes the image data from the img object to be output to the Response.OutputStream, where it ultimately will be received by the client. The second parameter, img.RawFormat, simply tells the Save method to use the native image encoding for the file. This property is set up when the image is loaded from disk using Image.FromFile. After the data has been sent to the client, the method calls img.Dispose to ensure the data store in the img object is released immediately.

GetSizeMultiplier Function

When you create a thumbnail image, you'll want to maintain the original image's aspect ratio in the thumbnail. *Aspect ratio* refers to the height to width ratio. If you have an image that is 100 x 50 pixels and another that is 50 x 25 pixels, then they have the same aspect ratios (2:1) because both images are twice as wide as they are tall. If you fail to maintain the aspect ratio when reducing an image, the thumbnail may appear distorted. Figure 13-7 shows some extreme cases of this distortion.

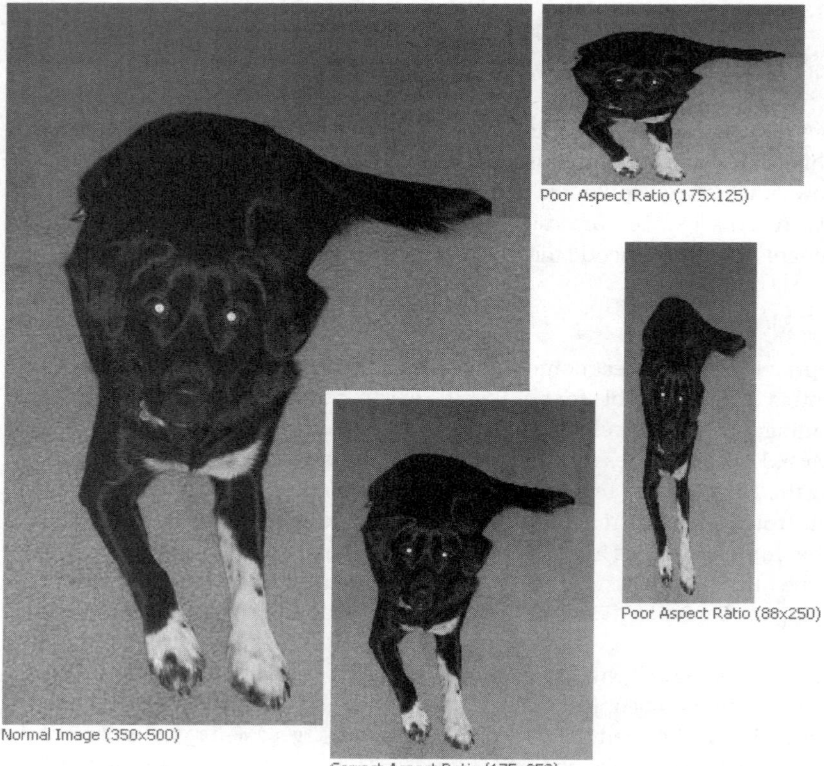

Figure 13-7. *Transforming a picture of Cloe, our dog, using various aspect ratios*

`GetSizeMultiplier` analyzes the height and width of an image, and determines a number that you can use to multiply both the height and width by to ensure the image will fit nicely within a predefined space while maintaining the image aspect ratio.

First, `GetSizeMultiplier` defines the `MaxWidth` and `MaxHeight` constants that define the maximum height and width for an image. In the real world, you would probably want these to be configurable, but constants will suffice for this example.

Then the function determines the appropriate value for the `HeightMultiplier` variable. The `HeightMultiplier` variable holds the number by which the image height needs to be multiplied to equal the `MaxWidth` constant. Thus, if the `MaxWidth` is 100, and the image size is 200, then the `HeightMultipler` will be 0.5 because 200 * 0.5 = 100. The function also determines the `WidthMultiplier` value using the same logic for the image width.

The possibility exists that an image's height or width may be smaller than the maximum height or width. If this is the case, then `HeightMultiplier` or the `WidthMultiplier` will be greater than one. You don't want a multiplier that is greater than one because it will stretch the image, so the code ensures that this will not happen.

Finally, the function determines which multiplier is smaller and returns it. You want to return the smaller multiplier because it guarantees that both the height and the width will be under the maximum size.

CreateThumbNail Method

This method accepts an HttpContext object named context, and two FileInfo objects named Thumbnail and FullSized. FullSized holds a reference to the full-sized image location, and Thumbnail holds a reference to the location where the thumbnail image should be saved. The CreateThumbNail method is responsible for reading the full-sized image file, creating a thumbnail out of that image, sending the image to the client via the context object, and saving the image to disk to avoid having to recreate it for future requests.

At the beginning of the method, CreateThumbNail creates a variable named img to store the full-sized image data. The code initializes the img object it by calling Image.FromFile(FullSized), which loads the full-sized image information from disk. Then the imgFormat variable is created and stores the ImageFormat object returned by GetImageFormat(FullSized). Finally the size multiplier is acquired by calling GetSizeMultiplier(img) and stored in the SizeMultiplier variable.

After the method variables are set up, the CreateThumbNail has everything it needs to create the thumbnail image. Conveniently enough, the Image class exposes a function called GetThumbnailImage which, as you may have guessed, is used to create a thumbnail for an image:

```
img = img.GetThumbnailImage(CInt(img.Width * SizeMultiplier), _
                    CInt(img.Height * SizeMultiplier), Nothing, Nothing)
```

GetThumbNailImage accepts four parameters: width, height, callback, and callback data. For this example, you should only be concerned with the width and height, which is why the last two parameters in the code are set to Nothing. To determine the width and height of the thumbnail image, you just multiply the existing width and height by the SizeMultiplier. The resulting thumbnail image information is then stored back into the img variable.

Next, the code sets up the appropriate content type for the response and outputs the image to the Response.OutputStream. Notice that you need to use the imgFormat as the second parameter of the Save method instead of the img.RawFormat property as shown in the RetrieveThumbnail code. When the image is loaded from a file, the RawFormat property is initialized to whatever format the file is in. When the thumbnail image was created, it lost the encoding information stored in img.RawFormat. So, the imgFormat variable that we populated earlier lets the Save method know how to encode the data (for example, as a JPEG or a GIF file). If you attempt to use the img.RawFormat property here, you'll get an error.

After the image information has been sent out to the client, the code will then save the thumbnail to disk. First it checks to make sure the folder in which the file is to be placed exists. If not, it creates the folder. It then saves the image using the Save method, the physical file path information stored in the Thumbnail FileInfo object, and the imgFormat variable. Then it disposes of the img object to clear up memory.

Configuring the ThumbnailHandler

The ThumbnailHandler needs to be configured so it only handles image requests for GIF and JPEG images located in the Pictures\Thumbnails folder. To do this, create a Web.config file in the Pictures\Thumbnails folder and add the configuration settings in Listing 13-13 to it.

Listing 13-13. *Configuring the* `Thumbnails` *Folder to Create Thumbnails for Specific File Types*

```
<configuration>
  <system.web>
    <httpHandlers>
      <add verb="*" path="*.GIF" type="Handlers.ThumbnailHandler,Handlers" />
      <add verb="*" path="*.JPG" type="Handlers.ThumbnailHandler,Handlers" />
      <add verb="*" path="*.JPEG" type="Handlers.ThumbnailHandler,Handlers" />
    </httpHandlers>
  </system.web>
</configuration>
```

The preceding configuration explicitly sets up the handler for each file type with which the handler can interact. Another option is just route all requests to the `ThumbnailHandler` and just assume that only JPEG and GIF files will be requested (see Listing 13-14).

Listing 13-14. *Configuring the* `Thumbnails` *Folder to Create Thumbnails for All File Types*

```
<configuration>
  <system.web>
    <httpHandlers>
      <add verb="*" path="*" type="Handlers.ThumbnailHandler,Handlers" />
    </httpHandlers>
  </system.web>
</configuration>
```

Either method is acceptable in this example because only JPEG and GIF files should be requested out of this folder. If, however, there were also web forms (.aspx pages) then you would need to use the first listing that explicitly defines each file extension. Remember that configuration will setup ASP.NET to use the `ThumbnailHandler`, but you'll need to map the `.GIF`, `.JPG`, and `.JPEG` file extensions to the `aspnet_isapi.dll` in IIS. Also make sure you do *not* check the **Check that file exists** option in the mapping setup.

■ **Caution** Mapping image extensions to your ASP.NET application means that ASP.NET handles *all* image requests, not just the image requests in the `Thumbnails` folder. When you request an image from ASP.NET running on IIS 5.0, it returns the image file as you would expect. When you request an image from ASP.NET on IIS 6.0, however, it gives you a 404 error. As a workaround, you can set up the `Thumbnails` folder as its own application in IIS 6.0, copy the `bin` folder from the application into the `Thumbnails` folder (so it has access to the handler assembly), and set up the mappings solely for the `Thumbnails` folder without affecting the other portions of the application.

Viewing Thumbnails

Now that you've seen how to make a thumbnail generator, it's time to see it in action. The `Thumbnails.aspx` page in the sample application contains code that looks for all the `.GIF`, `.JPG`, and .JPEG files in the Pictures folder. Then it creates a Hyperlink control for each image it finds, sets the Hyperlink control's NavigateUrl property to the location of the picture and the ImageUrl to the image's corresponding thumbnail. It then adds the Hyperlink control to a PlaceHolder control named phThumbnails and sets up some text to output the name of the picture as shown in Listing 13-15.

Listing 13-15. *Viewing Thumbnails for All Images in a Folder*

```
'***************************************************************************
Protected Sub Page_Load(ByVal sender As Object, ByVal e As System.EventArgs) _
  Handles Me.Load

    Dim Dir As New DirectoryInfo(Server.MapPath("Pictures"))
    Dim Files As FileInfo() = Dir.GetFiles()
    Dim img As HyperLink
    Dim lit As Literal

    For index As Integer = 0 To Files.Length - 1
        If IsSupportedExtension(Files(index)) Then
            img = New HyperLink()
            lit = New Literal()

            img.NavigateUrl = "~/Pictures/" & Files(index).Name
            img.ImageUrl = "~/Pictures/Thumbnails/" & Files(index).Name
            lit.Text = String.Format( _
                        "<BR><A HREF='Pictures/{0}'>{0}</A><BR><BR>", _
                        Files(index).Name)
            phThumbnails.Controls.Add(img)
            phThumbnails.Controls.Add(lit)
        End If
    Next

End Sub

'***************************************************************************
Private Function IsSupportedExtension(ByVal FI As FileInfo) As Boolean
    Select Case UCase(FI.Extension)
        Case ".GIF", ".JPG", ".JPEG" : Return True
        Case Else : Return False
    End Select
End Function
```

This is a relatively simple routine that uses a DirectoryInfo object to iterate through all the files in the Picture folder. It then determines whether or not the file is supported using the IsSupportedExtension function, which just checks to make sure the file extension is .JPG, .JPEG, or .GIF. Then it constructs the appropriate links and thumbnail image locations, builds text to display under the image, and adds the link and text information to the phThumbnails➥ PlaceHolder control.

When you run the page, you'll see a series of thumbnails displayed on the screen. Clicking on any of the thumbnails will link you directly to the full-sized image.

Content Management Backend

Keeping Internet and intranet content up to date is a considerable task, and that task often falls on the shoulders of people who are not really equipped to handle it. One of my first projects was working on a reporting module in a custom content-management project for an extremely large company, so I've seen the scenario play out a number of times.

Most often, it starts when a contractor or an employee with web experience builds a departmental intranet site. Everyone in the department begins to use it more and more extensively as they realize how easy it is to find information. People get hooked. Then the inevitable happens. The contractor or employee leaves. People still need to get information published to the web, so someone else has to be elevated to the status of web master. This is usually decided by looking at arbitrary technical skills that have nothing to do with web-based technologies. Therefore, the individual with the best Excel formula and chart-making skills becomes the departmental web master. Of course, his or her other responsibilities don't go away, so now the "web master" has to learn HTML, update people's web content, publish files to the departmental web server, and still do everything he or she was doing before.

Content-management systems store content information in a database, and programmatically assembly pages based on that database content. Many content-management systems offer a web-based tool for adding, updating, and removing content from the database, so anyone who knows how to use a web page can modify information in the content-management system. This allows the burden of updating a departmental website to be spread out over everyone in the department.

You may even find it convenient to use a miniature content-management system in your applications so you can easily change descriptions and instructions on web forms. There have been countless times when customers have called me to make minor changes that they could have done if properly equipped.

Objectives and Solution Architecture

Content management is an extensive subject involving a number of components such as user management, security, file sharing, caching, and complex user-interface tools for creating and updating content. Covering each of these areas could fill an entire book, so this example will focus only on a subset of content-management functionality. Specifically, it focuses on storing content in a database and creating a component to assemble that content into a page.

Architecturally, this solution implements the front-controller design pattern to accomplish its content-management tasks. A design pattern is just a well-documented solution for a specific type of problem. Without getting into the complexities of it, the front-controller pattern basically says that you can reduce code duplication by consolidating logic into a component and routing all requests though that component. The front-controller pattern is a match for this situation because all incoming requests need to be routed through a component that can pull content information from a database and assemble a page to send back to the client. You may find it helpful to refer to Figure 13-8 during the discussion of the solution.

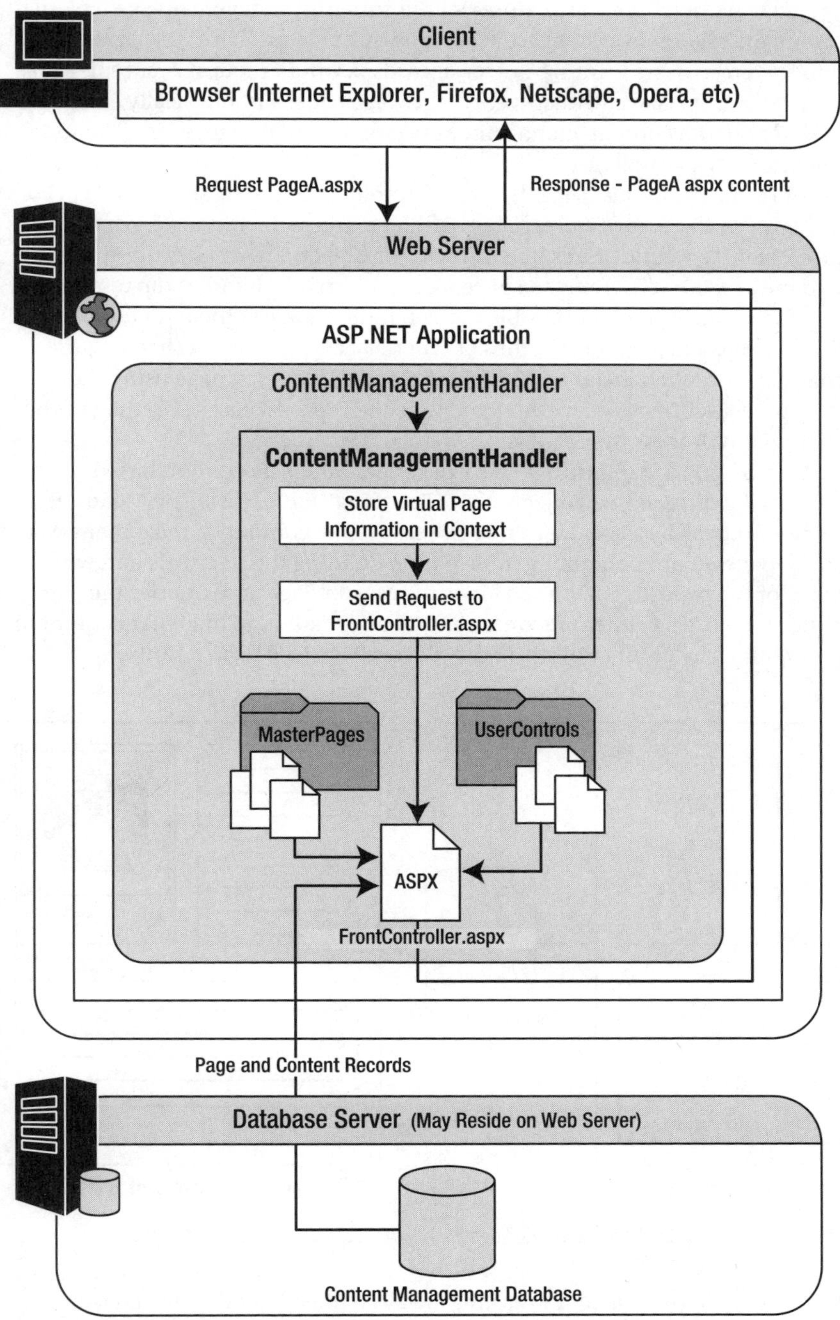

Figure 13-8. *Solution architecture*

Say there is a page named PageA.aspx stored in the content-management system. All the pages in the content-management system are accessible through the ContentManagement folder in the application folder, so users wanting to see PageA.aspx would request /Content➥ Management/PageA.aspx. But /ContentManagement/PageA.aspx does not physically exist in the folder because content in the content-management system is actually stored in a database. In other words, PageA.aspx is a virtual file.

All requests for resources in the ContentManagement folder are processed by an HTTP Handler named ContentManagementHandler. This handler extracts the requested virtual file name, in this case PageA.aspx, and stores it in the Context object. This makes the virtual file name available to the FrontController.aspx page, which ultimately handles the request. After storing the virtual file name in the Context object, the handler rewrites the path to point at the FrontController.aspx file which resides in the ContentManagement folder. It then acquires a standard page handler compiled instance of the FrontController.aspx page using the PageParser.GetCompiledPageInstance method and uses the ProcessRequest method of the standard page handler to process the request.

FrontController.aspx is a standard ASP.NET page that builds its content based on the virtual file name stored in the Context object. When FrontController.aspx first loads, it queries the database to check if a PageA.aspx record exists in the content-management system. If so, it retrieves the page record containing information defining the page title and which Master Page to use for the page layout. It then loads the Master Page, and queries the database for the page's content records. Content records contain information about what content to place in which ContentPlaceHolder controls of the Master Page (see Figure 13-9).

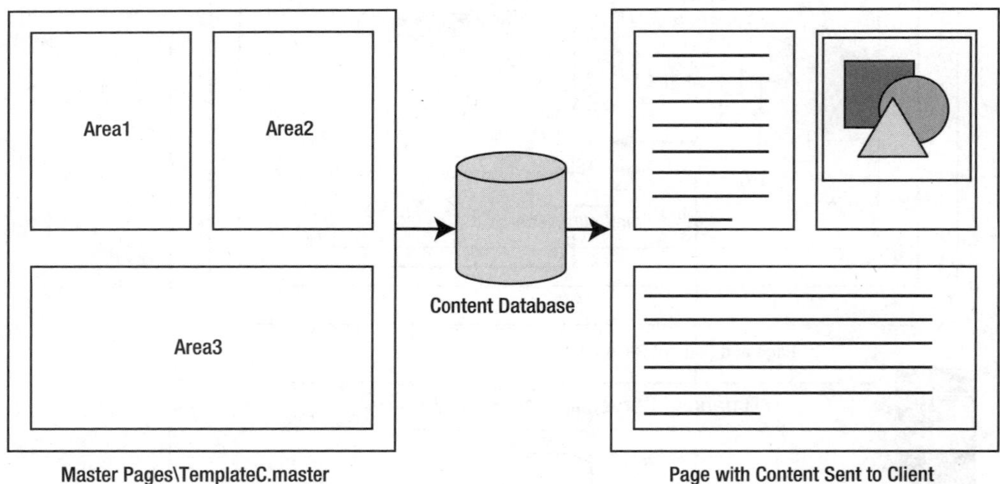

Figure 13-9. *Master Pages and* ContentPlaceHolder *controls (Area1, Area2, Area3)*

ContentPlaceHolders in the Master Pages area always named "Area" followed by a numeric index. Thus, the first ContentPlaceHolder on the Master Page is always named Area1, the second Area2, the third Area3, and so on. In this simple content-management example, there are six different types of content that can appear inside a content area: titles, paragraph text, hyperlinks, images, hyperlinked images, and user controls.

After placing the appropriate content in the appropriate ContentPlaceHolder controls, FrontController.aspx returns the PageA.aspx content to the user. From the user's perspective, it looks like PageA.aspx actually exists as a physical file on the server because the entire process is transparent.

Content Database Design

Page and content information is stored in a database. Because this is a simple content-management implementation, the database design is also fairly simple. In fact, there are only two tables. The Page table stores page information like the Master Page to use and the title, and the Content table stores content items that are ultimately output on the page.

Figure 13-10 shows a database diagram showing the columns and table relationships, and Table 13-5 gives you more detail about each column and its purpose.

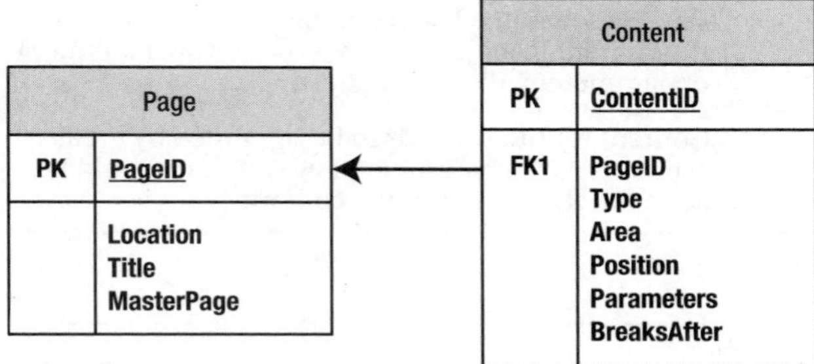

Figure 13-10. *Content-management database design and relationship*

Table 13-5. *Content-Management Database Fields*

Table	Field	Type	Description
Page	PageID	Integer	Auto-generated primary key used to identify a page record
Page	Location	VarChar(100)	File location of the requested page, relative to the ContentManagement folder.
Page	Title	VarChar(50)	Page title to be displayed in the client's browser.
Page	MasterPage	VarChar(50)	File location of the Master Page (for example, page template), relative to the ContentManagement\Master Pages folder.
Content	ContentID	Integer	Auto-generated primary key used to identify a content record.
Content	PageID	Integer	Foreign key identifying the page to which the content belongs.
Content	Type	VarChar(50)	English text which identifies the type of content to be output to the page. This example supports the following content types: Title, Paragraph, Image, Link, ImageLink, and UserControl.

Table 13-5. *Content-Management Database Fields (Continued)*

Table	Field	Type	Description
`Content`	`Area`	`Integer`	Index identifying the `ContentPlaceHolder` in the Master Page into which the content should be placed (1 = Area1, 2=Area2, and so on).
`Content`	`Position`	`Integer`	Index identifying the order in which content appears inside of a `ContentPlaceHolder`. You can place multiple content items inside a single `Content➥PlaceHolder` control, so you need a way to define which items appear in what order. When returning content records, the database sorts the records according to the `Position` field in ascending order, so a content record with a `Position` value of `1` appears before a content record with a `Position` value of `2`, and so on.
`Content`	`Parameters`	`Text`	Pipe (|) separated list of parameters used to set up the content. Each content type has its own unique set of parameters (discussed shortly).
`Content`	`BreaksAfter`	`Integer`	Content routinely needs to be separated by breaks. This specifies the number of breaks that should be added to the page after the content.

■ **Note** In a full implementation, the content types should be defined in a separate table and the type field in the content table should contain a link to the type instead of the name of the content type.

Creating the ContentManagementHandler

Compared with the HTTP Handlers you looked at in the last two examples, the `Content➥ManagementHandler` looks very simple. Listing 13-16 is the code for the class.

Listing 13-16. *Displaying Thumbnails for All Images in a Folder*

```
Imports System.Web
Imports System.Web.UI

Public Class ContentManagementHandler
    Implements IHttpHandler

    '*************************************************************************
    Public ReadOnly Property IsReusable() As Boolean _
      Implements System.Web.IHttpHandler.IsReusable
        Get
            Return True
        End Get
    End Property
```

```
    '***************************************************************************
    Private Function GetVirtualPage(ByVal context As HttpContext) As String
        Return context.Request.Path.Replace( _
                context.Request.ApplicationPath & "/ContentManagement/", "")
    End Function

    '***************************************************************************
    Public Sub ProcessRequest(ByVal context As System.Web.HttpContext) _
      Implements System.Web.IHttpHandler.ProcessRequest

        'Store the virtual page value in context
        context.Items("VirtualPage") = GetVirtualPage(context)

        'Acquire the Front Controller HTTP Handler
        Dim FrontController As IHttpHandler = _
          PageParser.GetCompiledPageInstance( _
          "~/ContentManagement/FrontController.aspx", Nothing, context)

        'Rewrite the path and allow the Front Controller to Process the Request
        context.RewritePath("ContentManagement/FrontController.aspx")
        FrontController.ProcessRequest(context)

    End Sub

End Class
```

GetVirtualPage Function

FrontController.aspx uses the virtual page path to locate the page record in the database, but the paths in the database are relative to the ContentManagement folder. The GetVirtualPage function is responsible for removing the extraneous application path and the /Content➥Management/ folder from the path, and returning just the virtual page as it should appear in the database.

ProcessRequest Method

There are really only four lines of code in the ProcessRequest method. The first line stores the virtual page value in the context object using the GetVirtualPage function. This allows the FrontController.aspx page to access the value later on when processing the request. Next, the method acquires a reference to the HTTP Handler for the FrontController.aspx page. After acquiring the handler, the method rewrites the URL path using context.RewritePath, and then allows the handler to process the request by passing the context into the FrontController.➥ProcessRequest method.

Configuring the ContentManagementHandler

Like all HTTP Handlers, the `ContentManagementHandler` needs to be configured so ASP.NET knows when and where to use it. Add it to `Web.config` in the `ContentManagement` folder so it only picks up requests for virtual pages under that folder. Listing 13-17 shows how that `Web.config` file should look.

Listing 13-17. *Configuring the* `ContentManagementHandler`

```
<configuration>
  <system.web>
    <httpHandlers>
      <add verb="*" path="*.*" type="Handlers.ContentManagementHandler,Handlers" />
    </httpHandlers>
  </system.web>
</configuration>
```

Notice that this will pick up *any* request that comes in for a page under the `Content➥Management` folder. Thus, you can specify pages with any extension you want: `.asp`, `.aspx`, `.html`, or even `.cfm` or `.jsp` if you really want to confuse people. Of course, you'll need to map nonstandard extension to ASP.NET in IIS or else you'll just get a 404 Not Found error.

Creating Content Templates using Master Pages

Master Pages define templates for ASP.NET web forms. Like any template, there are regions of the template that can be altered to display non-template content. In a Master Page, this region is called a `ContentPlaceHolder`. You can add ASP.NET controls to the `ContentPlaceHolder`, and those items appear in place of the `ContentPlaceHolder` when the page renders. The content-management code loads content from the content database, locates the appropriate `ContentPlaceHolder` on the Master Page, and then loads the content item into that `Content➥PlaceHolder`. Figure 13-10 from earlier in the chapter shows a basic diagram outlining this process.

The content-management code knows which content goes into what `ContentPlaceHolder` because of the `Area` column on each content record (Table 8-5). This field stores an integer representing the `ContentPlaceHolder` into which the content is loaded. The naming convention for a `ContentPlaceHolder` is Area<index>, where <index> is an integer greater than or equal to 1 (for example, Area1, Area2, Area3, and so on). If the `Area` value specified in the content record does not exist, then the content does not display

You'll find three example Master Pages in the example application. `TemplateA.master` has a single content area, `TemplateB.master` has two, and `TemplateC.master` has three. Listing 13-18 shows the markup for `TemplateA.master`.

Listing 13-18. *Markup for* `TemplateA.master`

```
<%@ Master Language="VB" CodeFile="TemplateA.master.vb" Inherits="TemplateA" %>
<%@ Register TagPrefix="cc" Namespace="Handlers" Assembly="Handlers" %>
<!DOCTYPE html PUBLIC "-//W3C//DTD XHTML 1.1//EN"
  "http://www.w3.org/TR/xhtml11/DTD/xhtml11.dtd">
```

```
<html xmlns="http://www.w3.org/1999/xhtml" >
<head runat="server">
    <title>Untitled Page</title>
    <style>
        body{font-family:arial;font-size:10pt;}
        .ContentAreaHeading{background-color: darkblue;color: white;
                            font-weight:bold;border-bottom: 1px solid black;}
    </style>
</head>
<body>
    <cc:ActionlessForm id="form1" runat="server">
        <strong>
          <span style="font-size: 16pt; text-decoration: underline">
            Content Management Template A
          </span>
        </strong><br /><br />
        <table cellpadding=3 cellspacing=0
          style="width:100%; border: 1px solid black;">
            <tr>
                <td class="ContentAreaHeading">
                    Content Area #1
                </td>
            </tr>
            <tr>
                <td>
                    <asp:ContentPlaceHolder id=Area1 runat=server />
                </td>
            </tr>
        </table>
    </cc:ActionlessForm>
</body>
</html>
```

Notice that the Master Page contains a custom control named `ActionlessForm`. This is an important item that we'll be discussing shortly. Refer to the sample application (in the Source Code area of the Apress website) for the `TemplateB.master` and `TemplateC.master` markup.

Building the FrontController.aspx Page

The `FrontController.aspx` page is a fairly simple page because it should only contain the Page directive and no other HTML or ASP.NET controls. Listing 13-19 shows the markup for the whole page.

Listing 13-19. *Markup for* `FrontController.aspx`

```
<%@ Page Language="VB" AutoEventWireup="false" CodeFile="FrontController.aspx.vb"
        Inherits="FrontController" %>
```

You want the page to be completely blank because this page dynamically loads a Master Page to define its layout and pulls its content from a database. You can't have ad-hoc HTML on a page that uses a Master Page; all content must go inside a `Content` control (which ends up in the `ContentPlaceHolder`). If there is any text on the page, ASP.NET throws an exception when the page executes. Also know that the Master Page is dynamically loaded at runtime based on the page information from the database, so there is no `MasterPageFile` attribute specified in the `Page` directive.

Building the FrontController.aspx.vb Code Behind

The code for the `FrontController.aspx` web form is fairly lengthy because it contains a number of database access routines' content-creation logic. It's not difficult, just lengthy. Listing 13-20 gives the entire code-behind listing for the page. All methods and functions are discussed after the code listing.

Listing 13-20. `FrontController.aspx.vb` *Code Behind*

```
Imports System
Imports System.Configuration.ConfigurationManager
Imports System.Data.SqlClient

Partial Class FrontController
    Inherits Web.UI.Page

    '********************************************************************************
    Private _PageID As Long
    Private _Title As String
    Private _MasterPage As String

    '********************************************************************************
    Private Function SqlString(ByVal text As String) As String
        Return text.Replace("'", "''")
    End Function

    '********************************************************************************
    Private Function AcquirePageInfo() As Boolean

        Dim DbConn As SqlConnection
        Dim SQL As String
        Dim DbCmd As SqlCommand
        Dim Dr As SqlDataReader

        DbConn = New SqlConnection(ConnectionStrings("Database").ConnectionString)

        'Create SQL command and setup parameters
        SQL = "SELECT * FROM [Pages] WHERE [Location]=@Location;"
        DbCmd = New SqlCommand(SQL, DbConn)
        DbCmd.Parameters.Add("@Location", Data.SqlDbType.VarChar).Value = _
          Context.Items("VirtualPage")
```

```
    DbConn.Open()
    Dr = DbCmd.ExecuteReader()
    If Dr.Read Then
        _PageID = CLng(Dr("PageID"))
        _Title = CStr(Dr("Title"))
        _MasterPage = CStr(Dr("MasterPage"))
        AcquirePageInfo = True
    Else
        AcquirePageInfo = False
    End If
    DbConn.Close()

End Function

'*****************************************************************************
Protected Sub Page_PreInit(ByVal sender As Object, ByVal e As EventArgs) _
  Handles Me.PreInit

    'Acquire the page info and setup the master page
    If AcquirePageInfo() Then
        Me.MasterPageFile = "~/ContentManagement/Master Pages/" & _MasterPage
        Me.Title = _Title
    Else
        'If the page is not found in the database, send a 404 error
        Response.StatusCode = 404
        Response.End()
    End If

End Sub

'*****************************************************************************
Protected Sub Page_PreLoad(ByVal sender As Object, ByVal e As EventArgs) _
  Handles Me.PreLoad
    LoadPageContent()
End Sub

'*****************************************************************************
Private Sub SetupBreakLiteral(ByVal lit As Literal, ByVal Count As Integer)
    For index As Integer = 1 To Count
        lit.Text &= "<br />"
    Next
End Sub

'*****************************************************************************
Public Sub LoadPageContent()

    Dim CPH As ContentPlaceHolder
    Dim DbConn As SqlConnection
```

```
Dim SQL As String
Dim DbCmd As SqlCommand
Dim Dr As SqlDataReader

'Create database connection
DbConn = New SqlConnection(ConnectionStrings("Database").ConnectionString)

'Create SQL command and setup parameters
SQL = "SELECT * FROM [Content] WHERE [PageID]=@PageID " & _
      "ORDER BY [Area],[Position];"
DbCmd = New SqlCommand(SQL, DbConn)
DbCmd.Parameters.Add("@PageID", Data.SqlDbType.Int).Value = _PageID

'Open database and execute command
DbConn.Open()
Dr = DbCmd.ExecuteReader()

While Dr.Read

    'Store data reader values in strongly typed variables
    Dim ContentType As String = CStr(Dr("Type"))
    Dim ContentArea As Integer = CInt(Dr("Area"))
    Dim ContentParams As String = CStr(Dr("Parameters"))
    Dim ContentBreaksAfter As Integer = CInt(Dr("BreaksAfter"))
    Dim Params As String() = Split(ContentParams, "|")

    'Locate the ContentPlaceHolder into which the content should be loaded
    CPH = CType(Master.FindControl("Area" & ContentArea), _
         ContentPlaceHolder)

    'Only load the content if the ContentPlaceHolder control is located
    If Not CPH Is Nothing Then

        Select Case UCase(ContentType)

            Case "TITLE"
                Dim lbl As New Label
                lbl.Font.Bold = True
                lbl.Font.Underline = True
                lbl.Font.Size = WebControls.FontUnit.Point(12)
                If Params.Length > 0 Then lbl.Text = Params(0)
                CPH.Controls.Add(lbl)
                If ContentBreaksAfter > 0 Then
                    Dim lit As New Literal
                    SetupBreakLiteral(lit, ContentBreaksAfter)
                    CPH.Controls.Add(lit)
                End If
```

```
Case "PARAGRAPH"
    Dim lbl As New Label()
    If Params.Length > 0 Then lbl.Text = Params(0)
    Dim lit As New Literal
    SetupBreakLiteral(lit, ContentBreaksAfter)
    CPH.Controls.Add(lit)

Case "HYPERLINK"
    Dim hlnk As New HyperLink()
    If Params.Length > 0 Then hlnk.Text = Params(0)
    If Params.Length > 1 Then hlnk.NavigateUrl = Params(1)
    CPH.Controls.Add(hlnk)
    If ContentBreaksAfter > 0 Then
        Dim lit As New Literal
        SetupBreakLiteral(lit, ContentBreaksAfter)
        CPH.Controls.Add(lit)
    End If

Case "IMAGE"
    Dim img As New Image()
    If Params.Length > 0 Then img.ImageUrl = Params(0)
    CPH.Controls.Add(img)
    If ContentBreaksAfter > 0 Then
        Dim lit As New Literal
        SetupBreakLiteral(lit, ContentBreaksAfter)
        CPH.Controls.Add(lit)
    End If

Case "LINKIMAGE"
    Dim hlnk As New HyperLink()
    If Params.Length > 0 Then hlnk.ImageUrl = Params(0)
    If Params.Length > 1 Then hlnk.NavigateUrl = Params(1)
    CPH.Controls.Add(hlnk)
    If ContentBreaksAfter > 0 Then
        Dim lit As New Literal
        SetupBreakLiteral(lit, ContentBreaksAfter)
        CPH.Controls.Add(lit)
    End If

Case "USERCONTROL"
    If Params.Length > 0 Then
        Dim ctrl As UserControl = CType(LoadControl( _
          "~/ContentManagement/UserControls/" & Params(0)), _
          UserControl)
        CPH.Controls.Add(ctrl)
```

```
                        If ContentBreaksAfter > 0 Then
                            Dim lit As New Literal
                            SetupBreakLiteral(lit, ContentBreaksAfter)
                            CPH.Controls.Add(lit)
                        End If
                    End If

                End Select

            End If

        End While

        Dr.Close()
        DbConn.Close()

    End Sub

End Class
```

Class Variables

This class has three variables–_PageID, _Title, and _MasterPage–that correspond to the PageID, Title, and MasterPage columns in the Page table of the content database. These variables are acquired in the AcquirePageInfo function.

AcquirePageInfo Function

This function serves two purposes. Remember the virtual page information that was stored in the context object in the ContentManagementHandler? AcquirePageInfo uses the virtual page information to look up the page record in the content database. The content database connection string is defined with the key "Database" in the <connectionStrings> section of Web.config.

If the record for the virtual page is found, then the function populates the _PageID, _Title, and _MasterPage variables with the data from the record. It also sets the return value for the function to True because the record was located. If the record isn't located, then the function will return False.

Page_PreInit Method

Another new feature in ASP.NET 2.0 is the Page.PreInit event. This event fires before the Master Page for the web form has been loaded, so you can specify or change a Master Page for a web form in this event. Master page information is loaded directly after this event method is executed, so any attempt to change the Master Page after the Page.PreInit event fires will result in an error.

Before the Master Page can be specified, however, the method needs to know which Master Page the requested virtual page wants to use. So, Page_PreInit calls AcquirePageInfo. If the page information is acquired successfully, then Page_PreInit will set the Title and

MasterPageFile properties for the page. If not, the user is redirected to a page indicating that they have requested an invalid page.

Page_PreLoad Method

After the Master Page has been loaded, the Page_PreLoad method executes. This method is new in ASP.NET 2.0 and is a great location for setting up content because it executes after the Master Page has been loaded, but before the Page.Load event has fired. Many UserControls need to respond to the Page.Load event, so they have the opportunity to do so if they are added in this method.

All the content logic is handled in the LoadPageContent method, so this method just calls LoadPageContent and allows it to process content for the virtual page.

SetupBreakLiteral Method

Before jumping into the LoadPageContent, let's discuss the SetupBreakLiteral method, which accepts a Literal control named lit and an Integer named Count as parameters. A Literal control is an ASP.NET control used to output raw HTML text.

This method is designed to add as many HTML line breaks (<BR/>) to the end of the Literal control as are specified in the Count parameter. This method is used in conjunction with the ContentBreaksAfter field in the Content table of the database (refer to Table 8-5) to add white space between content elements.

LoadPageContent Method

Now we come to the lengthy LoadPageContent method that contains the page rendering logic. It is responsible for retrieving page content records from the database, reading those content records, assembling the appropriate controls to display that content, and outputting the content to the appropriate ContentPlaceHolder on the Master Page. Let's see how it works.

LoadPageContent uses a number of different variables to help execute database queries, store database values, and maintain control references. Table 8-6 contains a listing of the variables found in the method and their purposes.

Table 8-6. *Variables in the* LoadPageContent *Method*

Name	Type	Description
CPH	ContentPlaceHolder	Holds a reference to the active Content➥ PlaceHolder in the Master Page
DbConn	SqlConnection	Connects to the content-management database
SQL	String	Stores parameterized SQL query
DbCmd	SqlCommand	Executes parameterized SQL query
Dr	SqlDataReader	Stores results of SQL query
ContentType	String	Stores the Type column from the content record
ContentArea	Integer	Stores the Area column from the content record

Table 8-6. *Variables in the* LoadPageContent *Method (Continued)*

Name	Type	Description
ContentParams	String	Stores the Params column from the content record
ContentBreaksAfter	Integer	Stores the BreaksAfter column from the content record
Params	String()	Stores the parameter list in a String array after ContentParams is split using the pipe (|) as the delimiter
lbl	Label	Holds a reference to a Label control when adding a Title or Paragraph content to the page
hlnk	Hyperlink	Holds a reference to a Hyperlink control when adding a Hyperlink or LinkImage content to the page
ctrl	UserControl	Holds a reference to a UserControl when adding UserControl content to the page

The LoadPageContent method starts out by establishing a connection to the content database and requesting all the content items that match the _PageID variable. Remember, _PageID was determined in the AcquirePageInfo function. LoadPageContent then iterates through each content item using a While loop. The first few lines of code inside the While loop store values from the data reader into the Content variables (for example, ContentType, ContentArea, and so on), which makes accessing the content data a bit faster and more manageable in the code.

Notice that the code splits the parameters from the ContentParams string into a string array and stores the results in Params. This allows individual parameter values to be accessed using Params(0), Params(1), and so forth. This method requires the parameter string in the database to be a bit ugly (for example, value1|value2|value3|, and so on), but it works for the sake of this example. If you so desire, you can implement your own key-value pair splitting routine if you want to make parameter declaration in the database a bit more user friendly.

After loading the content variables, LoadPageContent uses Master.FindControl to locate the ContentPlaceHolder into which the content should be placed. Notice that it builds the ContentPlaceHolder control name by concatenating "Area" and the ContentArea integer value. This produces names such as "Area1", "Area2", and so on, which match our naming convention for ContentPlaceHolders in the Master Page. If the FindControl method locates the ContentPlaceHolder, then it returns a reference to the control. Otherwise, the method returns Nothing. Either way, the FindControl result is stored in the CPH variable.

The next line in the method checks to see if the CPH variable is set to Nothing. If so, it means the ContentPlaceHolder for the content could not be located, and the method simply moves on to the next piece of content. If CPH points to a valid ContentPlaceHolder, then the method sets out to add the content to the control.

Finally, we get to the content creation section of the LoadPageContent method. This section determines which ContentType is being requested using a Select Case statement. The only valid values for the ContentType are Title, Paragraph, Hyperlink, Image, LinkImage and User➥ Control. Each content type requires a specific ASP.NET control to be instantiated, initialized, and added to the control referenced by the CPH variable.

Each piece of content uses a specific ASP.NET control to hold the content and has a specific set of parameters. Table 8-7 shows a list of content types, the ASP.NET controls used to create the content, descriptions of the content, and information on their parameters.

Table 8-7. *Content Types in the Content-Management System*

Name	Object	Parameters
`Title`	`Label`	`Param(0) - Title` text (may include HTML)
`Paragraph`	`Label`	`Param(0) - Paragraph` text (may include HTML)
`Hyperlink`	`Hyperlink`	`Param(0) - Link` text (may include HTML) `Param(1) - Link` location
`Image`	`Image`	`Param(0) - Image` URL
`LinkImage`	`Hyperlink`	`Param(0) - ImageURL` `Param(1) - Link` location
`Usercontrol`	`Usercontrol`	`Param(0) - Usercontrol` location relative to the `ContentManagement\UserControls` folder

All the content creation routines are fairly similar, so, for the sake of brevity, I'll only cover the creation of "Title" content. The first line of the title creation code instantiates a new `Label` object that will house the title content. It was arbitrarily determined that titles in this content-management system should be bold, underlined, and have a 12-point font size. You can see these properties are set for the label object right after it is created. Titles are only supposed to have one parameter, the text that appears in the title. The code checks to make sure that the one parameter exists by checking if `Params.Length` is greater than `0`, and then assigns `Params(0)` to the `Text` property of the `Label`. Then, the `Label` object is added to the `ActiveCPH` area using `ActiveCPH.Controls.Add(lbl)`.

After the title label has been added, the title-creation code checks to see if any line breaks should appear after the label. If so, the method creates a new `Literal` control, sends it to the `SetupBreakLiteral` method (which adds `<br>` tags to the `Literal`), and then adds the `Literal` to the `ActiveCPH` area, effectively adding breaks after the title.

Web User Controls and the NoActionForm

One feature of the content-management system is the ability to load user controls. This means that you can create server-side code for those user controls that responds to events. This means that you'll be dealing with postbacks that fire those events. And this means that you'll have a problem.

When the server-side form from an ASP.NET page is rendered, it includes an `action` attribute that identifies the page to which the form should be submitted. On normal pages this isn't an issue because the `action` attribute points to a page that really exists. In the content-management system, however, it is an issue because the `action` attribute will be set to the page that handled the request, not the page that was originally requested. Thus, all forms attempt to submit to `FrontConroller.aspx` because it handles all requests for virtual pages. When a post-back is submitted to `FrontController.aspx`, the `ContentManagementHandler` assumes a virtual page is being requested, so it tells FrontController.aspx to try to find a virtual page named FrontController.aspx, which does not exist. This causes the user to be redirected to the Invalid.aspx page.

This issue is relatively easy to get around. If a <form> tag does not contain an action attribute, then it submits to the same page the browser requested. Because the browser is requesting a virtual page, it submits back to that virtual page, which is the behavior you desire. Implementing this solution requires you to implement your own HTML Form control that outputs a <form> tag without the action attribute. Fortunately, ASP.NET already has an HTML form control from which you can inherit, so the process is painless (see Listing 13-21).

Listing 13-21. ActionlessForm *Control*

```
Imports System.Web.UI.HtmlControls

Public Class ActionlessForm
    Inherits HtmlForm

    '***************************************************************************
    Protected Overrides Sub RenderAttributes( _
      ByVal writer As System.Web.UI.HtmlTextWriter)
        writer.WriteAttribute("name", Me.Name)
        writer.WriteAttribute("method", Me.Method)
        Attributes.Render(writer)
    End Sub

End Class
```

Creating a <form> element without an action parameter only requires that you inherit from the HtmlForm control and override the RenderAttributes method. The HtmlForm control normally creates the action attribute inside of the RenderAttribute method, so overriding the method effectively omits the action attribute. There are, however, important attributes that need to be output, such as the name and method attributes. You can see that these are explicitly output in the overridden method. Attributes.Render(writer) will output any additional attributes that were defined by the user directly in the control declaration.

You need to use the ActionlessForm control on all the templates that you create. This requires that you add a reference to the control to the top of the page (or Web.config if you so choose) as shown in Listing 13-22.

Listing 13-22. *Registering and Using the* ActionlessForm *Control on a Page*

```
<%@ Register TagPrefix="cc" Namespace="Handlers" Assembly="Handlers" %>
```

Then replace the <form runat=server> and </form> tags with the following:

```
<cc:ActionlessForm id="form1" runat="server">
    <!-- ASP.NET controls go here -->
</cc:ActionlessForm>
```

With this in place, your pages can postback to the appropriate location.

Next Steps for the Content-Management Backend

At this point, you have the backend for a content-management system and a number of different options ahead of you. You can extend the functionality by implementing more content types. You can build out a frontend for the system and allow people to create entire sites using this framework. You can even use the content-management system in your applications to easily allow instructions or informative text to be changed and updated. There are a number of different ways you can leverage content management in your application and business, so be on the lookout for them.

Summary

It should be obvious at this point that HTTP Handlers can be used to accomplish a variety of different tasks. In this chapter alone, you have seen them used to ensure files download with the appropriate names, generate reports, create thumbnail images, and even implement a content-management system.

Keep HTTP Handlers in the back of your mind when you're analyzing business issues because they can be very powerful solutions in certain situations. You may also want to look into HTTP Modules and Handler Factories if you want a more in-depth understanding of the HTTP Pipeline and how you can use it to your advantage.

Index

Symbols

Numerics

A

B

C

M

U

X

Z